Great Horned Owls

MACMILLAN McGRAW-HILL
Science

Lucy H. Daniel
Jay Hackett
Richard H. Moyer
JoAnne Vasquez

About the Cover
Great horned owls are also known as hoot owls or cat owls. Although great horned owls are now found all over the United States and Canada, they were first observed in the Virginia colonies in the 1700s. They are large owls with a wingspan up to 60 inches. The females are larger than the males.

INQUIRY **What else would you like to know about great horned owls? Write your own question or questions to answer.**

McGraw Hill **Macmillan McGraw-Hill**

Program Authors

Dr. Lucy H. Daniel
Teacher, Consultant
Rutherford County Schools, North Carolina

Dr. Jay Hackett
Professor Emeritus of Earth Sciences
University of Northern Colorado

Dr. Richard H. Moyer
Professor of Science Education
University of Michigan-Dearborn

Dr. JoAnne Vasquez
Elementary Science Education Consultant
Mesa Public Schools, Arizona
NSTA Past President

Contributing Authors

Lucille Villegas Barrera, M.Ed.
Elementary Science Supervisor
Houston Independent School District
Houston, Texas

Mulugheta Teferi, M.A.
St. Louis Public Schools
St. Louis, Missouri

Dinah Zike, M.Ed.
Dinah Might Adventures LP
San Antonio, Texas

The features in this textbook entitled "Amazing Stories," as well as the unit openers, were developed in collaboration with the National Geographic Society's School Publishing Division.

Copyright © 2002 National Geographic Society. All rights reserved.

RFB&D 🎧
learning through listening

Students with print disabilities may be eligible to obtain an accessible, audio version of the pupil edition of this textbook. Please call Recording for the Blind & Dyslexic at 1-800-221-4792 for complete information.

The McGraw·Hill Companies

Macmillan McGraw-Hill

Published by Macmillan/McGraw-Hill, of McGraw-Hill Education, a division of The McGraw-Hill Companies, Inc., Two Penn Plaza, New York, New York 10121.

FOLDABLES is a trademark of The McGraw-Hill Companies, Inc.

Printed in the United States of America

ISBN 0-02-281216-4 /6

7 8 9 071/043 09 08 07 06

Teacher Reviewers

Life Science

Consultants

Dr. Carol Baskin
University of Kentucky
Lexington, KY

Dr. Joe W. Crim
University of Georgia
Athens, GA

Dr. Pradeep M. Dass
Appalachian State University
Boone, NC

Dr. Marie DiBerardino
Allegheny University of
Health Sciences
Philadelphia, PA

Dr. R. E. Duhrkopf
Baylor University
Waco, TX

Dr. Dennis L. Nelson
Montana State University
Bozeman, MT

Dr. Fred Sack
Ohio State University
Columbus, OH

Dr. Martin VanDyke
Denver, CO

Dr. E. Peter Volpe
Mercer University
Macon, GA

Earth Science

Consultants

Dr. Clarke Alexander
Skidaway Institute of
Oceanography
Savannah, GA

Dr. Suellen Cabe
Pembroke State University
Pembroke, NC

Dr. Thomas A. Davies
Texas A & M University
College Station, TX

Dr. Ed Geary
Geological Society of America
Boulder, CO

Dr. David C. Kopaska-Merkel
Geological Survey of Alabama
Tuscaloosa, AL

Physical Science

Consultants

Dr. Bonnie Buratti
Jet Propulsion Lab
Pasadena, CA

Dr. Shawn Carlson
Society of Amateur Scientists
San Diego, CA

Dr. Karen Kwitter
Williams College
Williamstown, MA

Dr. Steven Souza
Williamstown, MA

Dr. Joseph P. Straley
University of Kentucky
Lexington, KY

Dr. Thomas Troland
University of Kentucky
Lexington, KY

Dr. Josephine Davis Wallace
University of North Carolina
Charlotte, NC

Consultant for Primary Grades

Donna Harrell Lubcker
East Texas Baptist University
Marshall, TX

Teacher Reviewers (continued)

Beth Lewis
Wilmington, North Carolina

Cindy Hatchell
Wilmington, North Carolina

Cindy Kahler
Carrborro, North Carolina

Diane Leusky
Chapel Hill, North Carolina

Heather Sutton
Wilmington, North Carolina

Crystal Stephens
Valdese, North Carolina

Meg Millard
Chapel Hill, North Carolina

Patricia Underwood
Randleman, North Carolina

E. Joy Mermin
Chapel Hill, North Carolina

Yolanda Evans
Wilmington, North Carolina

Tim Gilbride
Pennsauken, New Jersey

Helene Reifowitz
Nesconsit, New York

Tina Craig
Tulsa, Oklahoma

Deborah Harwell
Lawton, Oklahoma

Kathleen Conn
West Chester, Pennsylvania

Heath Renninger Zerbe
Tremont, Pennsylvania

Patricia Armillei
Holland, Pennsylvania

Sue Workman
Cedar City, Utah

Peg Jensen
Hartford, Wisconsin

Letter from Sally Ride

When I put on my helmet and climbed into the space shuttle I knew I was in for the adventure of a lifetime. That trip into space was the fulfillment of a dream that began when I was in elementary school. And studying science made it possible!

I've always been interested in science. In the sixth grade I read every book about Mars that I could find. That year our teacher brought a TV set into the classroom so that we could all watch the first astronauts blast off into the unknown. I wanted to do that, too!

Neither of my parents were scientists, but that didn't matter. They encouraged me to read books and to explore the things that interested me. And they encouraged me to be curious, to ask questions, and to think about things for myself. All of these things helped me become a scientist and an astronaut.

Maybe some of you have dreams like mine. Maybe you dream of exploring Mars one day. Whatever you dream of doing, it will help you to have the skills of a scientist—ask questions and explore things for yourself! And always

Reach for the stars!

Sally K Ride

Be a Scientist! PAGE S1

v

UNIT A

Life Science

Organisms and Environments PAGE A1

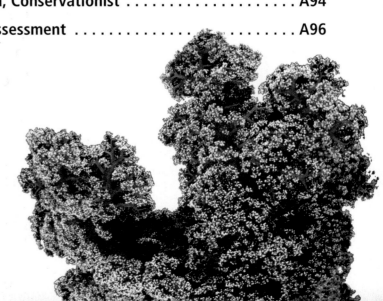

Organization of Living Things PAGE B1

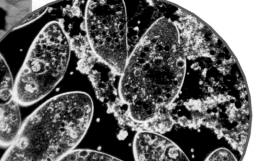

Earth Science

Observing the Sky PAGE C1

Interactions of Matter and Energy PAGE E1

UNIT F

Physical Science

Motion, Work, and Machines

PAGE F1

Activities

For Your Reference

FOLDABLES™

by Dinah Zike

Using Foldables for Data Collection

A Foldables organizer is a 3-D, interactive graphic organizer. It can be a valuable learning tool to help you organize, review, and remember information. You will find suggestions for using Foldables organizers to help you collect and record data in Quick Lab activities throughout this book.

Basic Shapes

The figures on this page illustrate the basic folds that are the building blocks for all Foldables organizers used in the Quick Labs. The basic folds have friendly names, such as "hot dog fold," so that you can easily visualize and remember what they look like. Step-by-step folding instructions for each type of Foldables organizer used in the Quick Labs are given on pages R41–R44.

on pages R41–R44.

Basic Shapes

Hot Dog Fold

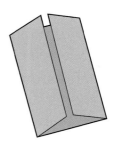

Shutter Fold

Hamburger Fold

Valley Fold

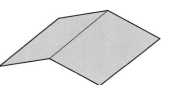

Mountain Fold

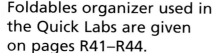

Science Safety Tips

In the Classroom

- Read all directions. Make sure you understand them. When you see **BE CAREFUL!**, be sure to follow the safety rule.
- Listen to your teacher for special safety directions. If you don't understand something, ask for help.
- Wash your hands with soap and water before an activity.
- Be careful around a hot plate. Know when it is on and when it is off. Remember that the plate stays hot for a few minutes after it's turned off.
- Wear a safety apron if you work with anything messy or anything that might spill.
- Wipe up a spill right away or ask your teacher for help.
- Tell your teacher if something breaks. If glass breaks, do not clean it up yourself.
- Keep your hair and clothes away from open flames. Tie back long hair, and roll up long sleeves.
- Keep your hands dry around electrical equipment.
- Don't eat or drink anything during an experiment.
- Put equipment back the way your teacher tells you.
- Dispose of things the way your teacher tells you.

- Wear safety goggles when your teacher tells you to wear them. Wear them when working with anything that can fly into your eyes or when working with liquids.
- Clean up your work area after an activity and wash your hands with soap and water.

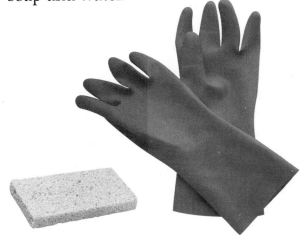

In the Field

- Go with a trusted adult—such as your teacher or a parent or guardian.
- Do not touch animals or plants without an adult's approval. The animal might bite. The plant might be poison ivy or another dangerous plant.

Responsibility

- Treat living things, the environment, and one another with respect.

Be a Scientist!

Where on Earth is this?

Mars!

Science is a way of understanding the world around us. The work of scientists often begins when scientists ask questions about something they observe. Asking and answering questions is the basis of inquiry.

In this section, you will see how scientists use inquiry skills, visual literacy, reading skills, technology and information literacy, math skills, and writing skills as they study the planet Mars.

The diagram on this page shows what is usually called the "scientific method." Scientists don't always follow all these steps in the same order, but they often start with an observation about the world around us.

   You, too, are constantly making observations every moment you are awake. You might look out the window to see if it is raining. You might listen for the sound of thunder to find out if a storm is coming.

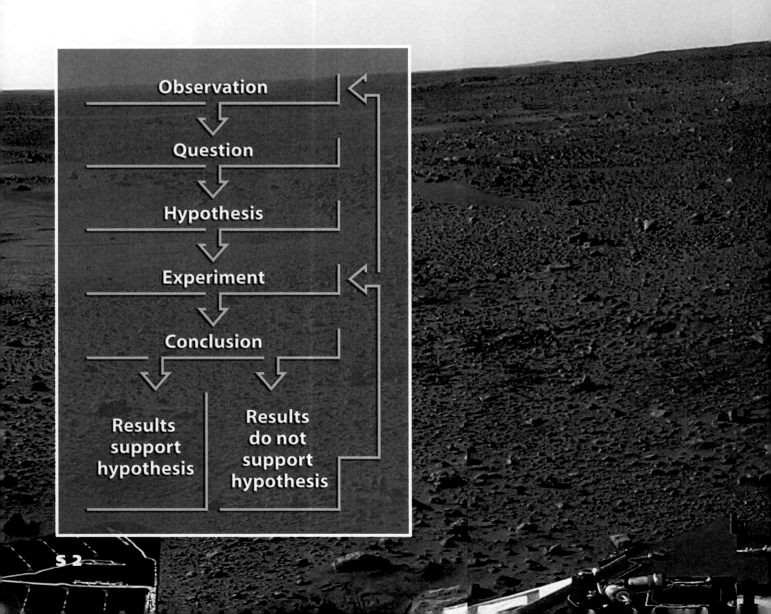

Observation

Question

Hypothesis

Experiment

Conclusion

Results support hypothesis

Results do not support hypothesis

Inquiry Skills

When you make observations, you use these skills.

Observe Use your senses to learn about an object or event.

Classify Place things that share properties together in groups.

Measure Find the size, distance, time, volume, area, mass, weight, or temperature of an object or an event.

Visual Literacy

More than half the information you get comes from pictures, or visuals. Pictures, maps, graphs, charts, and diagrams are tools. When you use them to improve your observation skills and to understand what you read, you are increasing your visual literacy.

Do you think this photograph was taken on Earth or on Mars? What clues in the photo can help you answer this question?

he work of scientists often starts with an unanswered question. If scientists cannot find an answer to a question, they go one step further. They propose a possible answer that can be tested experimentally. This is known as *forming a hypothesis*. A good hypothesis must

- be based on what you observe.
- be testable by performing an experiment.
- be useful in predicting new findings.

When scientists looked at this photo of the surface of Mars (inset), they wondered if the channel might have been formed by running water, similar to a stream on Earth. How do you think scientists might find the answer to this question?

Reading in Science

Before doing an experiment to answer a question, scientists often read to try to find the answer or to find out what others have learned from their experiments. You can use these reading strategies and skills to help you understand science. While you read, ask yourself these questions:

▶ **Compare and Contrast** How are two things alike? How are they different?

▶ **Main Idea and Supporting Details** What is the paragraph about? Which details add more information?

▶ **Predict** What do you think will happen next?

▶ **Cause and Effect** Why did something happen? (This is the cause.) What happened as a result? (This is the effect.)

▶ **Draw Conclusions** What do I know from the evidence?

▶ **Sequence of Events** What happened first, next, and last?

▶ **Summarize** What is this lesson or paragraph about?

Inquiry Skills

When you ask questions and form hypotheses, you use these skills.

Infer Form an idea from facts or observations.

Form a hypothesis Make a statement that can be tested to answer a question.

Define terms based on observations Put together a description that is based on observations and experiences.

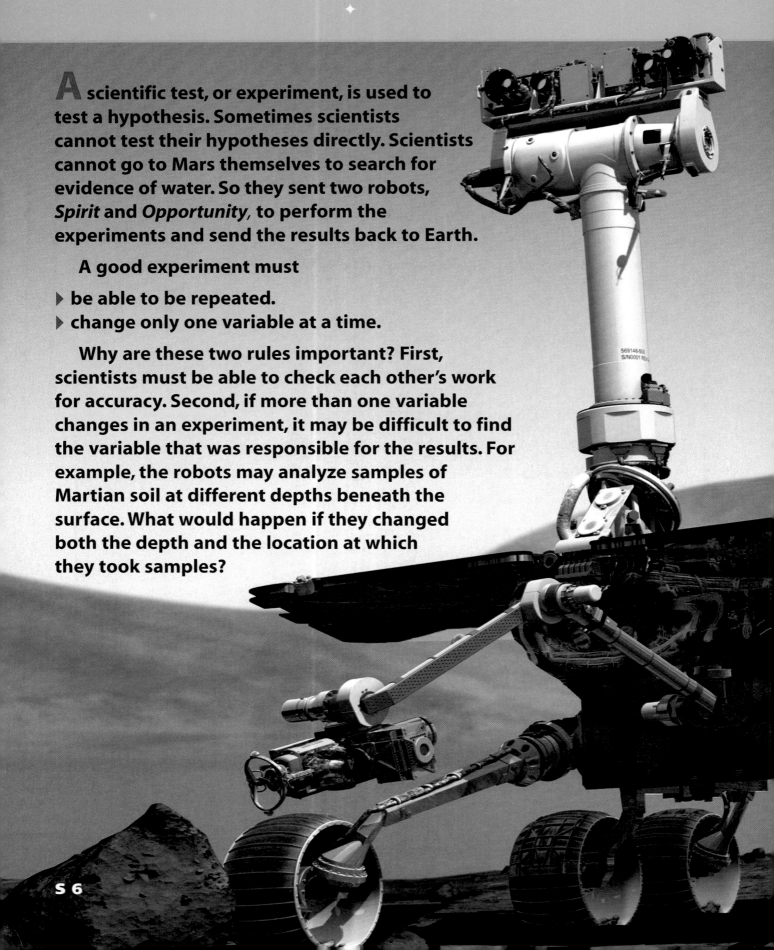

A scientific test, or experiment, is used to test a hypothesis. Sometimes scientists cannot test their hypotheses directly. Scientists cannot go to Mars themselves to search for evidence of water. So they sent two robots, *Spirit* and *Opportunity*, to perform the experiments and send the results back to Earth.

A good experiment must

▶ be able to be repeated.
▶ change only one variable at a time.

Why are these two rules important? First, scientists must be able to check each other's work for accuracy. Second, if more than one variable changes in an experiment, it may be difficult to find the variable that was responsible for the results. For example, the robots may analyze samples of Martian soil at different depths beneath the surface. What would happen if they changed both the depth and the location at which they took samples?

Inquiry Skills

When you experiment, you use these skills.

Experiment Perform a test to support or disprove a hypothesis.

Use variables Identify things in an experiment that can be changed or controlled.

Predict State possible results of an event or experiment.

Make a model Make something to represent an object or event.

Technology Literacy

In an experiment, scientists use tools to collect and analyze data. They may use simple tools, such as clocks and rulers. They also use more powerful tools, such as microscopes and computers.

Information Literacy

Information literacy begins with knowing how to search for and use books, magazines, newspapers, and other media. Today, information literacy also includes searching for information on CD-ROMs, DVDs, and the Internet.

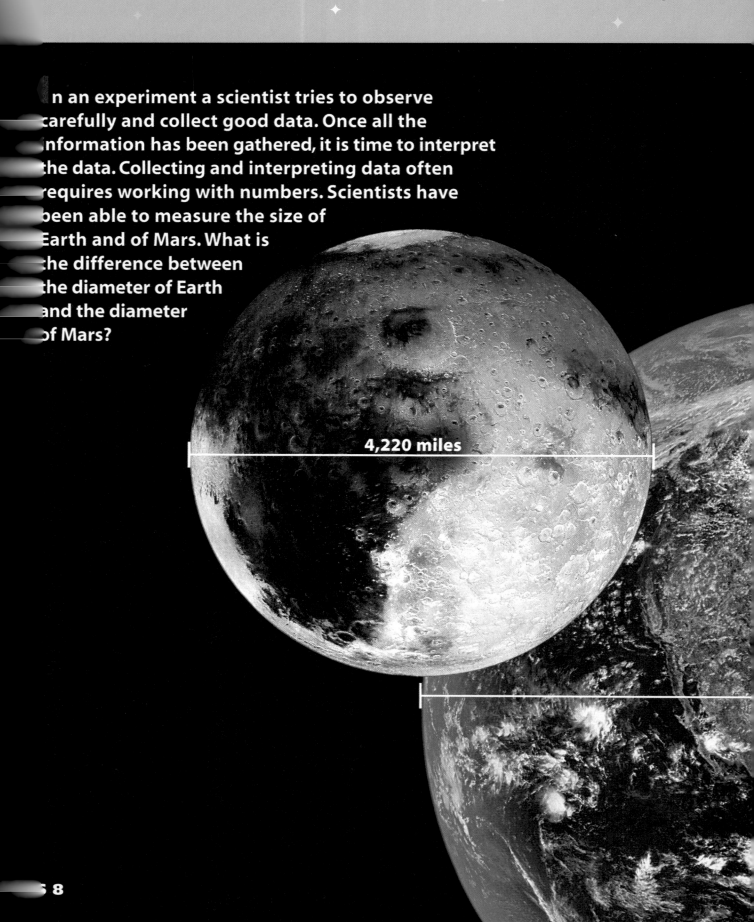

In an experiment a scientist tries to observe carefully and collect good data. Once all the information has been gathered, it is time to interpret the data. Collecting and interpreting data often requires working with numbers. Scientists have been able to measure the size of Earth and of Mars. What is the difference between the diameter of Earth and the diameter of Mars?

4,220 miles

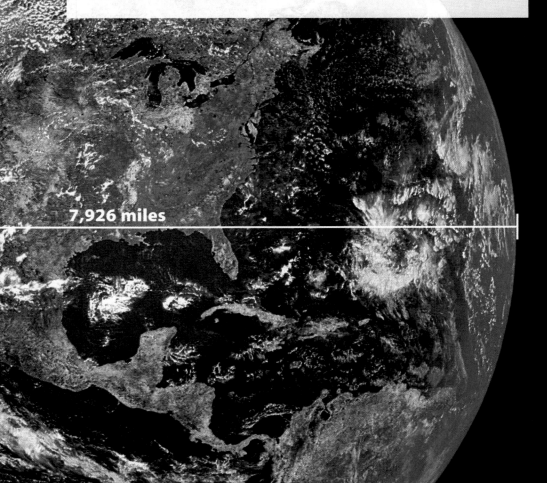

Math Literacy

Scientists often use math skills when they collect and interpret data as part of their experiments. A **Math Link** in each lesson of this book asks you to use several types of math skills, including:

▶ **Number Sense and Operations** This includes estimation, addition, subtraction, multiplication, and division.

▶ **Measurement** This includes using and converting standard and metric units of size, distance, time, volume, area, mass, weight, or temperature.

▶ **Data Analysis and Probability** This includes calculating the likelihood that an event will happen, and making and interpreting bar graphs and line graphs.

▶ **Problem Solving** This means using skills and strategies to solve problems.

Inquiry Skills

When you collect and interpret data, you use these skills.

Use numbers Order, count, add, subtract, multiply, and divide to explain data.

Measure Find the size, distance, time, volume, area, mass, weight, or temperature of an object or an event.

Interpret data Use the information that has been gathered to answer questions or solve a problem.

7,926 miles

fter interpreting the data, it is time to draw a conclusion. A conclusion is a statement about whether or not the hypothesis ia valid based on the data collected. Sometimes the data do not support the hypothesis. Perhaps different experiments and observations are needed. A new question may result.

Scientists also tell other scientists, as well as members of the public, about what they have discovered. Scientists at the Jet Propulsion Laboratory announced their preliminary findings at a televised press conference. Later, they will analyze the data sent by the robots on Mars and print their conclusions in scientific journals.

Inquiry Skills

When you draw conclusions and communicate results, you use this skill.

Communicate Share information.

Writing in Science

Writing is a tool you can use to communicate, or share information, about science. A **Writing Link** in each lesson of this book asks you to use one of these types of writing:

▶ A **Personal Narrative** tells about an event in your life.

▶ **Writing a Story** uses characters, setting, and a sequence of events.

▶ **Persuasive Writing** tries to get your readers to agree with your opinion.

▶ **Explanatory Writing** tells how to make or do something.

▶ **Writing That Compares** tells how two things are alike and different.

▶ **Expository Writing** presents facts and explains ideas.

Using Your Book

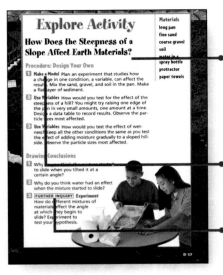

The **Explore Activity** is a hands-on way to learn about the lesson. The title is in the form of a question that you will answer in the activity.

The **inquiry skills** in the Explore Activity are the same skills that scientists use.

The last step of the activity provides an opportunity for **further inquiry**.

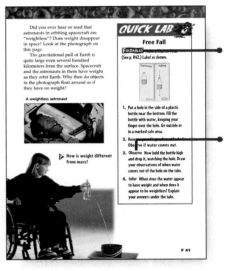

You can use different kinds of **Foldables™ organizers** to collect and record data in the Quick Lab.

Inquiry skills are also used in the Quick Lab.

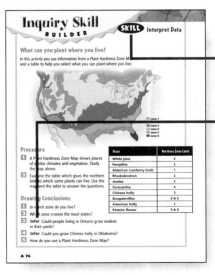

Each Inquiry Skill Builder focuses on a specific **inquiry skill**.

Other **inquiry skills** are also reinforced in the Inquiry Skill Builder.

Visuals include both **photographs** and **graphics**. This question will help you get information from the photograph at the beginning of each unit of this book.

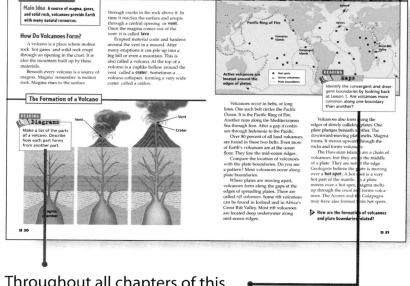

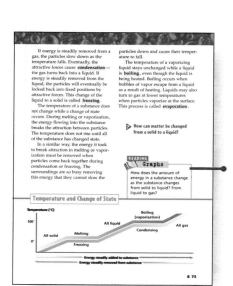

Throughout all chapters of this book you will get information by **reading graphics**. Graphics are pictures such as:
• diagrams
• charts
• maps
• graphs

This box contains the **Main Idea** of the lesson. Keep the main idea of the lesson in mind as you read.

Before Reading Read the large red question before you read the page. Try to answer this question from what you already know.

During Reading Look for new **Vocabulary** words highlighted in yellow. Look at the pictures. They will help you understand what you are reading.

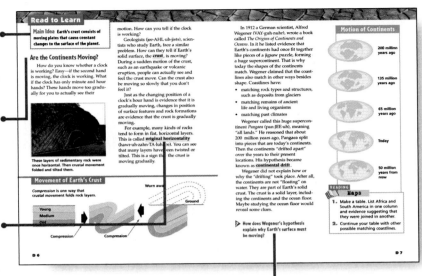

After Reading ▶ This arrow points to a question. It will help you check that you understand what you have read. Try to answer the question before you go to the next large red question.

On one page in each lesson, you will find a question that practices the **Chapter Reading Skill**. In any chapter, you will find one of these skills:
- compare and contrast
- main idea and supporting details
- predict
- cause and effect
- draw conclusions
- sequence of events
- summarize

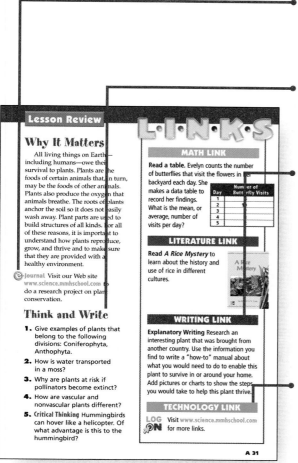

At the end of every lesson, you can log on to **e-Journal** for tips and suggestions about how to write a research report.

Think and Write questions at the end of every lesson give you an opportunity to write about what you learned in the lesson.

A **Writing Link** at the end of every lesson allows you to express yourself through several different types of writing:
• Personal Narrative
• Writing a Story
• Persuasive Writing
• Explanatory Writing
• Writing That Compares
• Expository Writing

A **Technology Link** at the end of every lesson gives you an opportunity to log on to our Web site www.science.mmhschool.com for additional links.

Write About It questions on selected Sally Ride Science, Time for Kids, and magazine-style features give you an opportunity to write about what you learned.

A **LogOn reference** on every Sally Ride Science, Time for Kids, and magazine-style feature allows you to learn more about each topic.

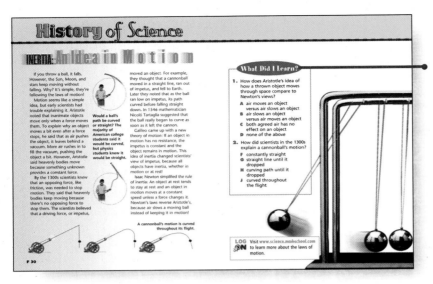

There are **What Did I Learn? questions** on selected Sally Ride Science, Time for Kids, and magazine-style features. Answering the questions gives you an opportunity to practice using a standardized test, multiple choice format.

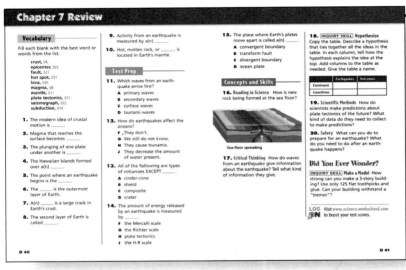

A two-page **review** at the end of each chapter allows you to show what you know using a variety of assessment formats:
- fill-in
- multiple choice
- short answer

Performance Assessment at the end of every unit provides an opportunity to demonstrate what you've learned through hands-on activities and projects.

UNIT A

Organisms and Environments

Organisms and Environments

LOOK!

A coral reef is home to many unusual animals, such as these brightly colored parrot fish. What makes up a coral reef?

CHAPTER

The Kingdoms of Life

Did You Ever Wonder?

How many kinds of different living organisms are there?
Scientists analyze the characteristics of living things to group
them into categories. The main categories are kingdoms. In this
photo you can see examples of two kingdoms, the plant kingdom
and the animal kingdom.

INQUIRY SKILL Classify Why aren't all organisms in this photo
grouped in the same kingdom? How would you classify them?

Classifying Living Things

Vocabulary

organism, A8

kingdom, A8

phylum, A8

species, A9

microbe, A14

Get Ready

A pond ecosystem is filled with a diverse group of organisms. The most easily recognized are plants and animals. Do you think all living things can fit into just these two groups? The photograph shows a great blue heron wading in the water. What other organisms do you think live in this pond? How would you classify them?

Inquiry Skill

You **experiment** when you perform a test to support or disprove a hypothesis.

Explore Activity

How Can Living Things Be Classified?

Materials

research books

microscope (optional)

coverslips, slides (optional)

living specimens (optional)

pond or aquarium water (optional)

Procedure

1. **Observe** Look at the organisms on the next two pages. Read the descriptions carefully. List some basic facts about each organism. Add to the facts from what you know or what you may look up in books.

2. Look at the organisms two at a time. How are they alike? How are they different? Record your findings.

3. **Classify** Find ways to group the organisms. For example, you might group them based on whether they are one celled or many celled, or whether they take in food or make their own food.

Drawing Conclusions

1. **Classify** Combine your findings so that you have from three to five groups. What are your final groupings? What do the members of each group have in common?

2. Can you find more than one way to classify an organism? If so, why did you decide on one way rather than another?

3. FURTHER INQUIRY **Experiment** Add other organisms to your classification system. Study living specimens around you. You might observe organisms in a drop of pond (or aquarium) water.

Takes in food	Makes its own food	Moves from place to place	Stays in one place

Main Idea Living things are classified based on their characteristics.

What Are the Characteristics of Some Living Things?

Which of these living things have you seen before? These pictures represent a wide variety of organisms from different environments on Earth. Scientists observe the characteristics of organisms and use these observations to classify them.

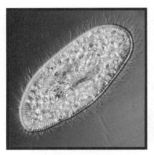

Paramecium is a one-celled organism that lives in fresh or stagnant water. It is covered with cilia, tiny hairs that beat, helping it move and take in food.

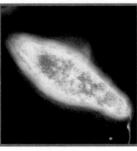

Euglena, a one-celled freshwater organism, makes its own food. It moves with flagella, long whiplike hairs.

A cloud of spores is released into the air by puffballs. They get their nutrition from organic material in soil, such as dead plants or fallen trees.

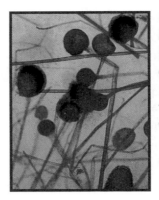

Bread molds grow on bread that has been left in a warm, damp, dark place. These molds have short, threadlike filaments that extend down into the bread and digest starches.

A mushroom grows when the cap breaks through the soil. A mushroom cannot make its own food. It takes in nutrients from its surroundings.

Mosses grow in large groups that spread out like mats. They have short stems that lift delicate leaves above the ground. The leaves are generally about one cell thick.

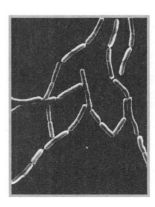

Most kinds of bacteria move about and take in food for energy and growth. Bacteria are found in three basic shapes—rodlike, spherical, and spiral.

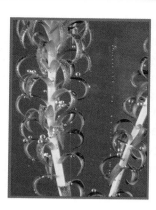

Elodea is often called waterweed. Its stems can reach lengths of up to 1.1 meters (3.5 feet). Its flowers are small, and its fruit ripen underwater.

Hinged lobes at the edge of each leaf of the Venus's-flytrap are lined with sensory hairs. When prey comes into contact with the hairs, the lobes fold together, trapping the prey.

Geraniums have colorful flowers with five overlapping petals. Their roots absorb moisture from the soil and anchor the plants.

A goldfish's color comes from structures below colorless scales. Goldfish take in oxygen through gills.

Hermit crabs live in and drag shells that have been cast off by other animals, such as sea snails.

▷ **What is a characteristic shared by two of these living things?**

Hamsters dig long burrows underground. Their cheek pouches are used for storing and carrying food.

Most snails move due to contractions along the bottom of a muscular foot. When disturbed the snail can withdraw into its spiral shell. Snails feed off dead and decaying matter.

How Are Organisms Classified?

Why do scientists classify living things? About 350 B.C., the Greek philosopher Aristotle classified **organisms** (AWR·guh·niz·uhmz), or living things, into two groups—plants and animals—based on their structure and function. He was trying to make order or sense out of the variety of living things that he studied.

The invention of the microscope in the 17th century gave scientists the opportunity to see organisms that did not fit into either category. As research improved, the two kingdoms of life were expanded to include new discoveries.

About 1735, Carolus Linnaeus, a Swedish scientist, developed a way of naming organisms. He gave each living thing a scientific name based on its classification. This way he could divide the **kingdom**, the largest group used to classify living things, into smaller groups. Each kingdom is divided into two or more **phyla** (FIGH·luh) (singular, *phylum*). All members of a phylum share at least one important structure or other characteristic. For example, elephants and earthworms all belong to the animal kingdom. However, elephants have a backbone and earthworms do not. All animals with backbones belong to the same phylum. This phylum includes seals, dogs, fishes, and humans. Earthworms are grouped in a phylum with leeches and sandworms.

Animal Kingdom

All animals with a backbone belong to one phylum.

Animals in all other phyla have no backbone.

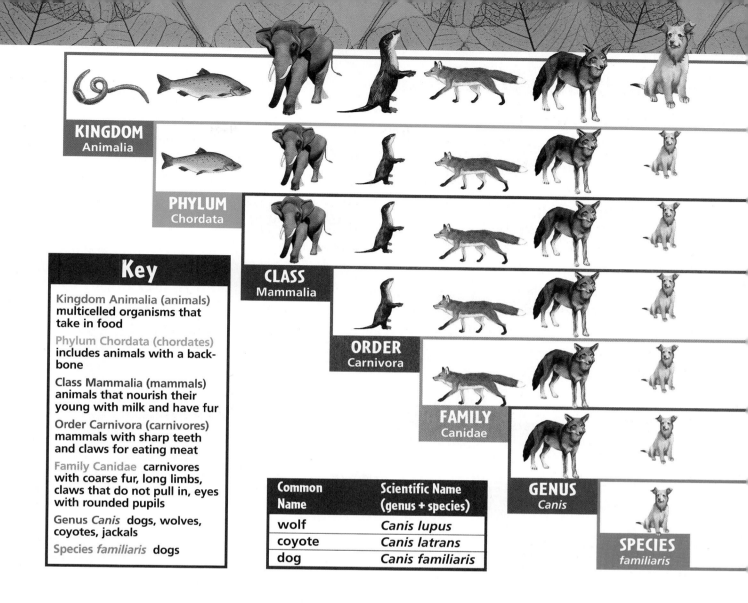

Key

Kingdom Animalia (animals) multicelled organisms that take in food

Phylum Chordata (chordates) includes animals with a back-bone

Class Mammalia (mammals) animals that nourish their young with milk and have fur

Order Carnivora (carnivores) mammals with sharp teeth and claws for eating meat

Family Canidae carnivores with coarse fur, long limbs, claws that do not pull in, eyes with rounded pupils

Genus *Canis* dogs, wolves, coyotes, jackals

Species *familiaris* dogs

KINGDOM Animalia

PHYLUM Chordata

CLASS Mammalia

ORDER Carnivora

FAMILY Canidae

GENUS Canis

SPECIES familiaris

Common Name	Scientific Name (genus + species)
wolf	*Canis lupus*
coyote	*Canis latrans*
dog	*Canis familiaris*

Because life on Earth is so diverse, each phylum has to be divided into smaller groups called *classes*. For example, the class Mammalia includes all animals that have fur or hair and produce milk for their young.

Members of a class that have the most in common are put into smaller groups called *orders*. The most similar members of an order are grouped into a *family*. The most similar family members are grouped into a *genus*.

The most similar members of a genus belong to a **species**. A species has the most similar members in a kingdom. That is why all members of a species can mate and reproduce more of their own kind.

Each living thing is given a scientific name based on its classification—that is, its genus and species. Many organisms in different parts of the world have different common names. Latin is used in scientific names to make them easier to understand.

▷ **What are the levels of the system used to classify living things?**

A 9

How Are Members of the Animal Kingdom Classified?

What characteristics help to classify an organism as an animal? Is the organism multicelled or one celled? Does it make food, take in (eat) food, or absorb food?

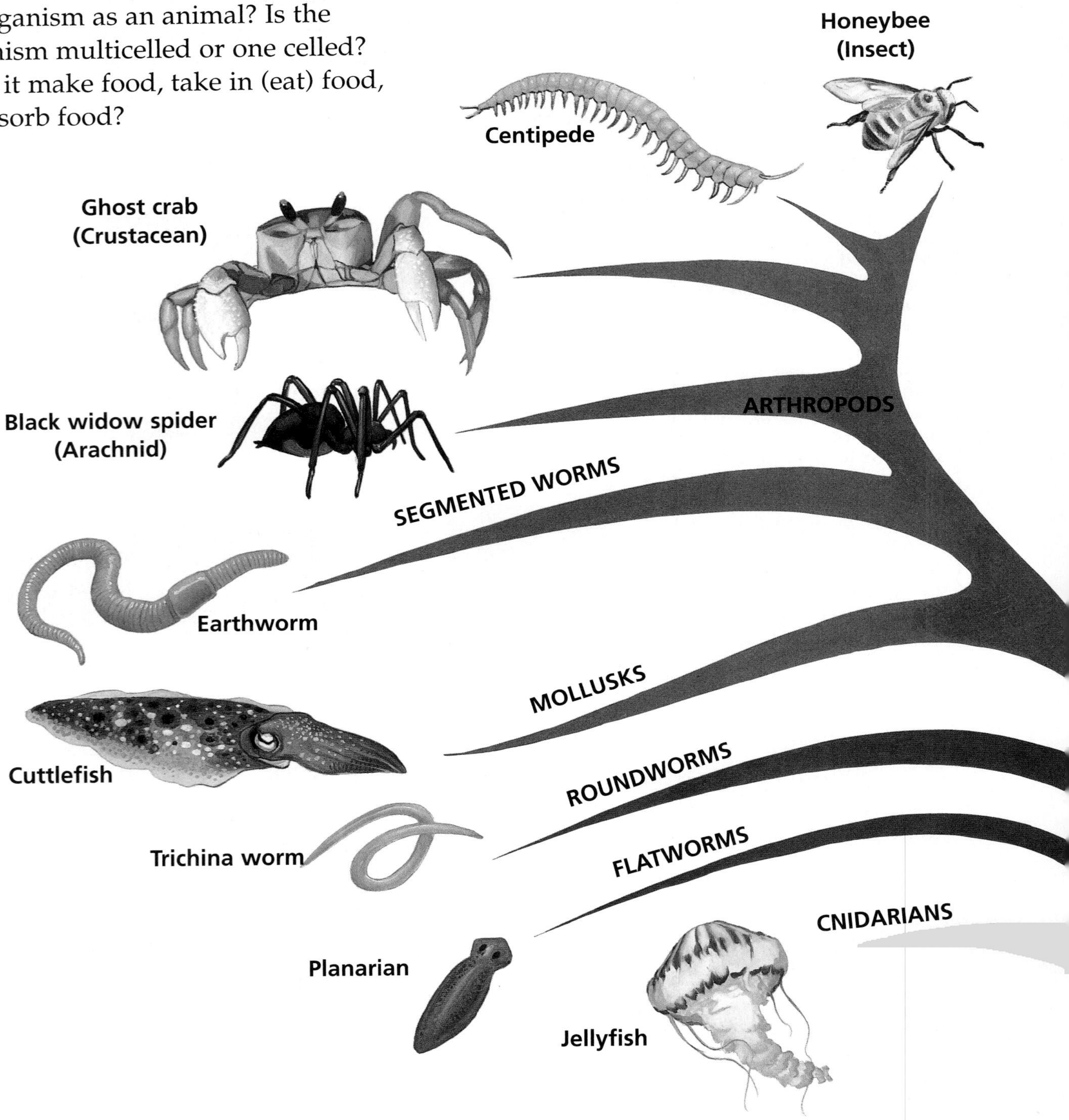

Honeybee (Insect)

Centipede

Ghost crab (Crustacean)

ARTHROPODS

Black widow spider (Arachnid)

SEGMENTED WORMS

Earthworm

MOLLUSKS

Cuttlefish

ROUNDWORMS

Trichina worm

FLATWORMS

CNIDARIANS

Planarian

Jellyfish

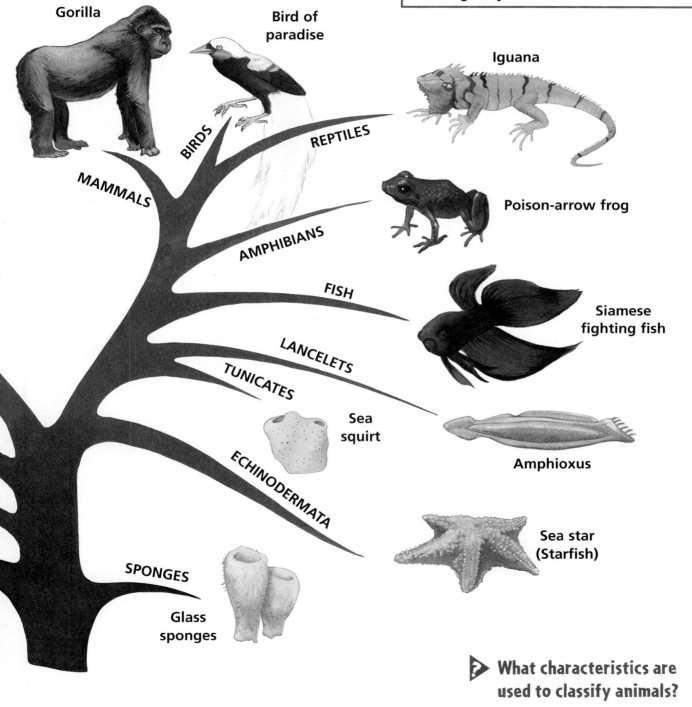

Characteristics of Animals

They are multicelled organisms.

They eat and digest other organisms.

Most can move from place to place.

They have tissues organized into organs and organ systems.

Gorilla

Bird of paradise

Iguana

BIRDS

REPTILES

MAMMALS

Poison-arrow frog

AMPHIBIANS

FISH

Siamese fighting fish

LANCELETS

TUNICATES

Sea squirt

Amphioxus

ECHINODERMATA

Sea star (Starfish)

SPONGES

Glass sponges

▶ **What characteristics are used to classify animals?**

How Is the Plant Kingdom Organized?

Plants are grouped into divisions, rather than phyla. Some divisions of the plant kingdom are shown here.

Flowering plants reproduce by seeds that develop inside a protective chamber called an ovary. Like ferns and cone-bearing plants, they have true roots, stems, and leaves.

Mosses were among the first plants to live on land. They have no special tissues for transporting water or nutrients. They do not reproduce by producing seeds.

Horsetails are usually found in moist, sandy places. They absorb silica, which makes them feel rough. They have tiny scalelike leaves that form rings around the stem.

Cone-bearing plants reproduce with seeds. They carry their seeds in cones, rather than in pods or fruit. Like ferns, they have true roots, stems, and leaves. Examples include redwoods, pines, firs, spruces, and hemlocks.

Ferns have special tissues to transport water and nutrients. This allows them to grow taller than mosses. Like mosses, ferns are seedless plants.

Club mosses, unlike true mosses, have true roots, stems, and leaves. Club mosses grow mainly in damp, shady areas. Some are found in deserts and on mountains.

READING Charts

1. Name a seedless plant.

2. What are the two main kinds of seed plants? Describe their differences in a paragraph.

▷ **What are some of the divisions of the plant kingdom?**

What Is in the Fungus Kingdom?

Fungi (FUN·jigh) (singular, *fungus*) are grouped into divisions, rather than phyla. This kingdom includes **microbes** (MIGH·krohbz), living things that are so small they can be seen only with microscopes. It also includes larger organisms.

Mold is an example of a fungus. When you think of mold, you might visualize the blue-black kind you see on bread. However, some molds are useful to humans. In 1928, Alexander Fleming discovered that the mold *Penicillium notatum* killed bacteria. This accidental discovery led to the development of the world's most widely used anti-biotic, penicillin.

▷ **What are the characteristics of fungi?**

Mushrooms are an important food crop. You should never eat wild mushrooms because many of them are poisonous.

Mold on bread is a microbe that is part of the fungus kingdom.

What Is in the Protist Kingdom?

Protists make up the most diverse of the kingdoms. This kingdom includes mostly microbes but also includes larger organisms.

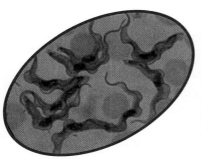

Animal-like protists, called protozoa, move by a variety of methods. Some have whiplike flagella.

About 40,000 species of amoeba-like protozoa move by extending pseudopodia, or false feet.

Other protozoa move by using tiny hairs that beat, called cilia.

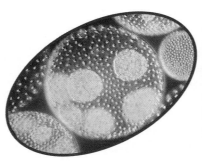

Algae, unlike many other protists, make their own food. They are classified according to the kind of pigment they contain.

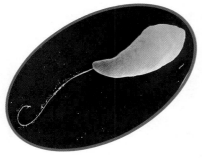

A *Euglena* has animal-like characteristics, such as moving by means of its whiplike flagellum, but it can also make food, as plants do.

Some types of algae are multi-celled. They range from small seaweeds to giant kelps. Like plants, they all produce their own food.

A *Paramecium* and several other animal-like protozoa move by using cilia. They move about, taking in food, such as bacteria.

▷ **What are the characteristics of protists?**

What Are the Two Kingdoms of Bacteria?

All bacteria are microbes. However, they are grouped into two kingdoms.

The eubacteria, or "true bacteria," kingdom includes bacteria that cause diseases and decay matter in soil.

The archaebacteria, or "ancient bacteria," kingdom includes bacteria suited to survive in conditions that were found on Earth long ago. They are usually found in salt marshes, sulfur springs, and volcanic vents at the ocean floor. This includes places with no oxygen at all!

Bacteria can be either spiral shaped, sphere shaped, or rod shaped.

Characteristics of Bacteria

Most are one-celled organisms.

They do not have a cell nucleus.

Most do not make their own food but break down or decompose other living or once-living things.

Some bacteria (cyanobacteria) make their own food.

The spiral-shaped bacterium shown is carried by several species of ticks. This bacterium, which causes lyme disease in humans, can be transferred through the bite of one of these ticks.

? **How are bacteria organized?**

Sphere-shaped bacteria may be found clumped together like a bunch of grapes, or they may grow in chains.

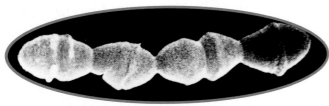

Rod-shaped bacteria often have whiplike structures that propel them along in tumbling motions.

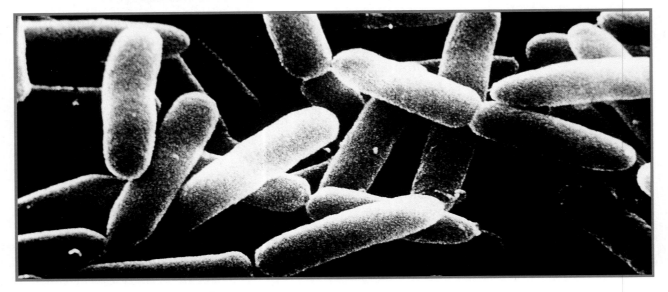

What Are Viruses?

Viruses are not found among the kingdoms of living things. Viruses are not made up of cells, a basic characteristic of living things. Viruses are much smaller than cells. A virus is basically made up of hereditary material. This material is surrounded by a protein coat. The protein coat can have many different shapes.

Unlike true organisms, viruses do not grow, eat, or respond to stimuli. They can reproduce only inside a living cell. Once inside a cell, a virus directs it to produce new virus particles. The new viruses are released from the cell and can infect other cells. That is how viruses can cause diseases.

Familiar diseases that are caused by viruses include measles, mumps, influenza (flu), and polio. Vaccines have been developed to help prevent these diseases. New diseases, such as West Nile virus and SARS (Severe Acute Respiratory Syndrome), are also caused by viruses. Scientists are working on new vaccines for these diseases.

▷ How do viruses reproduce?

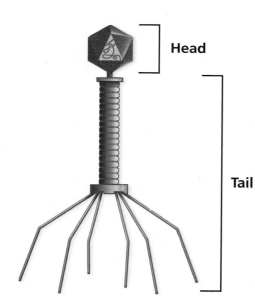

Head

Tail

The polio virus has many sides and looks like a crystal.

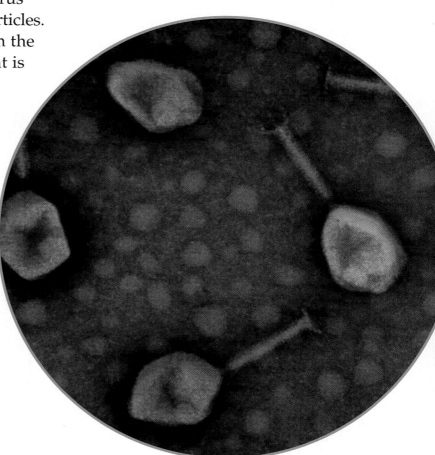

A bacteriophage is a virus that attacks and destroys bacteria.

Inquiry Skill
BUILDER

How Can You Group Organisms?

All kingdoms have one main characteristic in common. The members are made of living cells—or just one cell. By comparing other characteristics, you can classify organisms into kingdoms.

Materials
ruler (or computer with a "table" tool)

Procedure

1 Draw a table with seven columns, one for the characteristics and one for each kingdom.

2 **Classify** Add rows to the table. Label each row with a main characteristic—such as "Multicelled" and "One Celled." For each column in a row, write the word *yes* if the label fits the kingdom.

3 Add as many rows as you need to show how kingdoms are alike and yet very different.

4 **Classify** Draw a diagram like the one shown on this page. Based on your table, fill in each box of the diagram. Each box represents a kingdom.

Drawing Conclusions

1 Which kingdoms do you think are most alike? Most different? Support your answers with information from the table.

2 **Classify** How might you reorganize the kingdoms to fit into only two, three, or four groups?

3 Why do you think we need six kingdoms altogether?

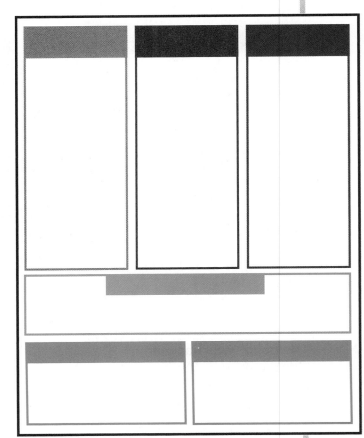

Why It Matters

When we learn new things about organisms classified in our kingdom, phyla, class, or order, we are also learning about ourselves.

The same thing applies to all living things and viruses. For example, being able to tell a bacterium from a virus is very important in treating diseases caused by these organisms because all bacteria and all viruses share basic characteristics.

 -Journal Visit our Web site **www.science.mmhschool.com** to do a research project on the differences between bacteria and viruses.

Think and Write

1. List the main characteristics used to classify animals.

2. How are the members of the plant and fungus kingdoms alike? Different?

3. How do the two bacteria kingdoms differ from the other kingdoms?

4. **INQUIRY SKILL** **Classify** How might you break apart any of the kingdoms into smaller kingdoms?

5. **Critical Thinking** Would you classify viruses as living things? Would you classify them as nonliving things? Explain.

L·I·N·K·S

WRITING LINK

Expository Writing The system of classifying living things is always changing. From the Greek philosopher Aristotle, in about 350 B.C., to the the present day, scientists have been trying for centuries to classify the millions of living things on Earth. Research classification systems. Is the current system the final system? Write a brief report on your findings. Use more than one reference source.

MATH LINK

Find the surface area. Use craft materials to make a model of a virus. Use triangles to make the head of the virus. Calculate the surface area of the head of your model.

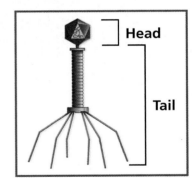

Head

Tail

TECHNOLOGY LINK

 Science Newsroom CD-ROM Choose *It's a Class Act* to visit a park or nature preserve to observe and classify different types of organisms.

LOG ON Visit **www.science.mmhschool.com** for more links.

The Plant Kingdom

Vocabulary

nonvascular, A24

vascular, A24

sexual reproduction, A25

asexual reproduction, A25

angiosperm, A28

gymnosperm, A28

seed dispersal, A29

pollinator, A30

Get Ready

How many different kinds of plants do you see in this photograph of a tropical rain forest?

Tropical rain forests have the greatest diversity of plants and animals of any place on Earth. They contain thousands of species of plants. How do scientists classify so many plants? How do these plants compare with plants that grow where you live?

Inquiry Skill

You infer when you form an idea from facts or observations.

Explore Activity

How Can You Classify Leaves?

Materials

research books
(optional)

living specimens
(optional)

Procedure

Observe Look at the photographs on this page or leaf specimens in your classroom. For each leaf, use the leaf key to write a name.

Drawing Conclusions

1 **Observe** Which leaves have the most in common? On what did you base your answer?

2 FURTHER INQUIRY **Infer** How can a classification key be useful? Test your inference by designing a classification key for 10 items. (You may use leaves, flowers, plants, seeds, or other items.) Report your results.

a
Lobes

b

c

Leaf Key	
1. Leaf blade deeply divided Leaf blade not deeply divided	Green ash Go to 2.
2. Leaf blade long and narrow Leaf blade not long and narrow	Willow Go to 3.
3. Leaf blade not cut into lobes Leaf blade cut into lobes	Go to 4. Go to 5.
4. Base flat, leaf heart-shaped Base uneven	Cottonwood American elm
5. Lobes rounded Lobes pointed	White oak Silver maple

d
Lobes

e

f

Main Idea Plants vary greatly in their structure and function.

What Are the Divisions of the Plant Kingdom?

Scientists have discovered more than 260,000 different kinds of plants. They can be separated into a dozen major groups. These groups are called *divisions*. Plants are divided first according to whether they have veins, roots, stems, and leaves. This is called *vascular tissue*. Many vascular plants reproduce by forming seeds. Some form seeds enclosed in cones, while others bear flowers and produce seeds in fruits. The photos show one way plants can be organized into divisions.

Lycophyta Club moss. About 1,000 species. Have veins, stems, roots, and leaves, but no seeds.

Psilophyta Whisk ferns. Only a few species. Simplest of all vascular plants, or plants that have veins. Do not have true roots, leaves, or seeds.

Sphenophyta Horsetails. Fifteen species. Have veins, stems, roots, and leaves, but no seeds.

Bryophyta Mosses, liverworts. About 15,000 species. Small plants. Do not have veins, true roots, leaves, or stems. Grow in moist areas.

Anthophyta
Roses, orchids, fruit trees, maple and oak trees, berry bushes, vegetable crops, grasses, palms. About 235,000 species. Bear flowers, and bear seeds in fruits.

Ginkgophyta Ginkgo. One species. Bears seeds. Fan-shaped leaves. Slow-growing tree, 30 meters (99 feet) or taller. Sheds leaves in autumn.

Gnetophyta Gnetum, ephedra, welwitschia. About 70 species. Bear seeds. Vines and shrubs.

▷ **Why are pine, spruce, and redwood trees grouped in the same division?**

Cycadophyta Sago palm (not a true palm). About 100 species. Bear seeds on cones. Many are shrubs, but some grow to 18 meters (59 feet).

Coniferophyta Pine, spruce, redwood trees. Evergreen shrubs. About 550 species. Bear seeds on cones. Most have needle-shaped leaves. Include Earth's tallest trees.

Mosses cannot grow as tall as trees because mosses cannot transport water and nutrients to great heights.

How Do Nonvascular Plants Get Nutrients?

The divisions of the plant kingdom can be divided into two categories. One category contains plants that do not have veins, **nonvascular** plants. The other category contains plants that do have veins, which are called **vascular** plants. The term *vascular* means "vessels," such as the blood vessels that carry blood throughout your body.

In your body, blood vessels carry nutrients to places where they are needed to help you grow and stay alive. Vascular plants also have such vessels, which are sometimes called veins or tubes. These vessels carry water and dissolved nutrients to all parts of the plant to help the plant grow and stay alive. The plants in the first division of the plant kingdom—

the liverworts, hornworts, and mosses—do not have veins. How are water and nutrients delivered to all parts of these plants?

The water and nutrients—which are dissolved in the water—pass directly from outside of the plants into their cells, and from one cell to the next. This process works well over short distances but does not work well over long distances. This is one reason why plants such as mosses are very short.

If mosses were taller, like trees, the force of gravity would prevent water from moving from cell to cell to the top of the plants. As you will soon discover, the vessels in tall plants allow them to overcome this problem.

▶ **How does the height of a moss affect how it gets its nutrients?**

How Do Mosses Reproduce?

Mosses reproduce in a life cycle that has two very different stages. In the two stages, mosses produce structures that enable them to reproduce in two different ways.

Sexual Reproduction

Mosses look like a leafy green carpet on a forest floor. The leafy plants produce two kinds of branches, male and female. They are often on the same plant, but sometimes on separate plants. These branches produce sex cells. The female branches produce eggs, which are female sex cells. The eggs are formed in a sac on the branch, where they remain. The male branches produce sperm, which are male sex cells. Sperm have structures that enable them to swim in water.

Sperm swim to the sac on the female branch. When a sperm reaches an egg in the sac, the two cells join into a single cell. This joining is called *fertilization*. This stage in the life cycle of the moss is called **sexual reproduction**. Sexual reproduction is reproduction that requires two parents.

Asexual Reproduction

In time the fertilized egg cell grows into a new moss plant. This is not a leafy plant, but a thin stalk with a capsule, or spore case, at the top. Inside this case, spores are produced. This stage of the moss life cycle is called **asexual reproduction**. Asexual reproduction is reproduction that requires only one parent—in this case, one kind of cell, the spores. In time the spores are released and grow into leafy moss plants. The cycle starts again.

▷ **What are the two main ways mosses reproduce?**

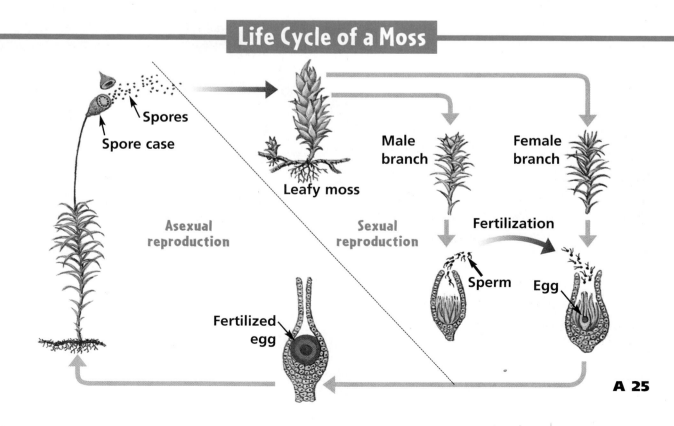

Life Cycle of a Moss

Spores

Spore case

Leafy moss

Male branch

Female branch

Asexual reproduction

Sexual reproduction

Fertilization

Sperm

Egg

Fertilized egg

What Is a Vascular Plant?

More than 90 percent of all the plants on Earth are classified as vascular plants. With the exception of liverworts, hornworts, and mosses, every plant you see in a field or forest is a vascular plant.

As you learned earlier, vascular plants share one major characteristic: they have a system of tubes, or veins, that carry water and dissolved nutrients to all parts of the plant. These tubes run through roots, stems, and leaves, which are other characteristics of vascular plants.

The roots of vascular plants absorb water and dissolved nutrients from the soil. The roots of a corn plant can absorb as much as 2 liters (2 quarts) of water a day. Because soil tends to hold water, vascular plants can grow in relatively dry climates, with their roots growing very long to reach water. The deepest root ever found ran 121 meters (397 feet) into the ground and belonged to a wild fig tree in South Africa.

The water and nutrients are piped from the roots into the stems and then to the leaves. Stems support the leaves

A wild fig tree like this one has roots about as deep as a soccer field is long.

The stem, or trunk, of some redwood trees is more than 100 m (328 ft) tall and 3 m (10 ft) in diameter.

and allow vascular plants to grow tall so their leaves can be bathed in sunlight. This is important because the leaves use the energy in sunlight, plus water from the soil and carbon dioxide gas from air, to manufacture the plant's food. This food can then travel through the plant's vascular system to all parts of the plant. In some plants, such as the potato plant, the food is stored in an underground stem. That is the part of the potato plant you eat.

▷ **How are vascular plants different from nonvascular plants?**

Leaves of the raffia palm can reach lengths of 20 m (66 ft).

QUICK LAB

Vascular Plants

FOLDABLES™ Make a Three-Pocket Book. (See p. R42.) Label the tabs as shown.

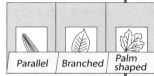

| Parallel | Branched | Palm shaped |

BE CAREFUL! Do not touch leaves. Some of them can be harmful.

1. Vascular plants have structures that carry soil water from the roots through the stem into the leaves. The structures in the leaves are veins. Look at the veins on the leaves you see in this lesson.

2. **Observe** With an adult, carefully observe leaves on plants in your schoolyard or in neighborhood parks. Study leaves of trees as well as bushes and shrubs.

3. **Observe** Look closely with a hand lens. Observe the shape of the leaf itself as well as any pattern through the veins across the leaf.

4. Make a sketch of each kind of leaf and its veins.

5. **Classify** Into how many vein patterns can you group your sketches? Use your Three-Pocket Book to sort the leaves. Explain.

What Kinds of Plants Have Seeds?

Vascular plants can be divided into two categories: those that bear seeds and those that do not bear seeds. Whisk ferns, club mosses, horsetails, and ferns are vascular plants that do not bear seeds.

Plants that do bear seeds are divided into two groups, the gymnosperms and the angiosperms. **Angiosperms** have seeds that are contained in fruits. Apple trees, pea plants, rosebushes, coconut palms, wheat plants, strawberry bushes, grasses, walnut trees, and cacti are all angiosperms. Here is another way to identify an angiosperm: If it has flowers, it is an angiosperm. As a matter of fact, angiosperms are called "flowering plants."

A vascular plant that bears seeds but does not have fruits or flowers is a **gymnosperm**. The word *gymnosperm* means "naked seed." In other words, these seeds are not found inside of structures such as fruits. Most

Angiosperms, such as apple trees, bear seeds inside of fruits and have flowers.

gymnosperms are conifers, or plants whose seeds are carried on cones. Examples of conifers are pines, spruces, firs, redwoods, junipers, yews, and cypress trees.

Gymnosperms also include plants that do not have cones; that is, they are not conifers. These include cycads, ginkgos, and gnetophytes.

▷ **What is the difference between the two types of seed plants?**

Conifers, such as pine trees, are examples of gymnosperms that bear seeds on the surface of cones.

How Do Seeds Get from One Place to Another?

Plants need space to grow and develop in a normal way. Young seedlings that sprout too close to their parents may not be able to get enough nutrients and water from the soil or enough sunlight from the sky. The bigger plants close by may get the largest share of both, leaving little for the seedlings.

Seed plants have many strategies to overcome such drawbacks. One of the most important involves **seed dispersal**, or the spreading around of seeds.

Here are some ways that seeds can be dispersed far from their parents, perhaps to places where conditions are better suited for the survival of the seedlings.

Wind The feathery seed-filled dandelion fruits shown here are blown long distances by the wind.

Animals Many seed-holding fruits, like those of a burdock plant, have bristly spines that stick to animal fur.

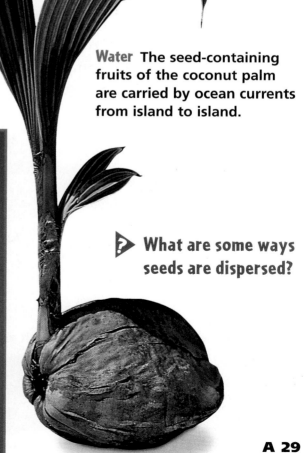

Water The seed-containing fruits of the coconut palm are carried by ocean currents from island to island.

▶ **What are some ways seeds are dispersed?**

How Do Flowers Help Plants to Reproduce?

Unlike animals, plants can't move from place to place. How do flowering plants find mates and produce offspring? The answer to this riddle is hidden in the flowers of such plants.

The flowers hold female and male sex cells. The diagram on this page will help you understand the life cycle of flowering plants. The pollen produced in the anther contains male sex cells. Female sex cells are in the ovary of the pistil. Once the pollen grains are transferred to the stigma of a flower, a tube grows from the pollen grain down the style, and into the ovary. At the ovary, the sperm cell fertilizes an egg cell. The fertilized egg cell becomes a seed that develops into a plant.

Millions of years ago, flowering plants relied on the wind to bring their sex cells together. As you can guess, this was not a very efficient process.

Then, one day, a curious beetle might have been attracted to a flower by its aroma or the sweet nectar it produced. The beetle entered the flower, fed itself, and left in search of another flower. Unknown to the beetle, tiny grains of pollen, which contain male sex cells, had rubbed off the flower onto the body of the beetle. When the beetle later visited a female flower, some of the pollen fell off.

In the same way, many other animals move pollen from one flower to another. Animals that do this are called **pollinators**. These animals visit flowers because of their attractive scent, sweet nectar, or bright colors. Many flowering plants could not survive without these visits, and some plants rely on only one kind of animal to help them reproduce. If that animal should become extinct, so would the plant.

READING **Draw Conclusions**
Why are flowers important to a plant?

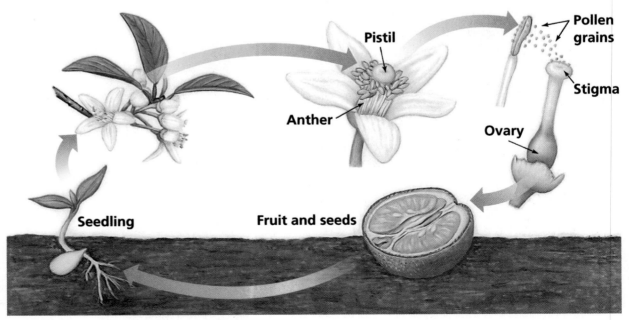

Pistil

Pollen grains

Stigma

Anther

Ovary

Seedling

Fruit and seeds

Why It Matters

All living things on Earth—including humans—owe their survival to plants. Plants are the foods of certain animals that, in turn, may be the foods of other animals. Plants also produce the oxygen that animals breathe. The roots of plants anchor the soil so it does not easily wash away. Plant parts are used to build structures of all kinds. For all of these reasons, it is important to understand how plants reproduce, grow, and thrive and to make sure that they are provided with a healthy environment.

ⓔ-Journal Visit our Web site **www.science.mmhschool.com** to do a research project on plant conservation.

Think and Write

1. Give examples of plants that belong to the following divisions: Coniferophyta, Anthophyta.

2. How is water transported in a moss?

3. Why are plants at risk if pollinators become extinct?

4. How are vascular and nonvascular plants different?

5. Critical Thinking Hummingbirds can hover like a helicopter. Of what advantage is this to the hummingbird?

L·I·N·K·S

MATH LINK

Read a table. Evelyn counts the number of butterflies that visit the flowers in her backyard each day. She makes a data table to record her findings. What is the mean, or average, number of visits per day?

Day	Number of Butterfly Visits
1	8
2	10
3	7
4	3
5	2

LITERATURE LINK

Read *A Rice Mystery* to learn about the history and use of rice in different cultures.

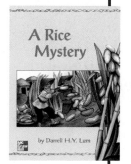

A Rice Mystery

by Darrell H.Y. Lum

WRITING LINK

Explanatory Writing Research an interesting plant that was brought from another country. Use the information you find to write a "how-to" manual about what you would need to do to enable this plant to survive in or around your home. Add pictures or charts to show the steps you would take to help this plant thrive.

TECHNOLOGY LINK

 LOG ON Visit **www.science.mmhschool.com** for more links.

Botanizing

Utricularia

Would you like to make a scientific discovery and have it named after you? Your best chance of doing this probably involves plants. Botanists, or plant scientists, estimate that there are about 300,000 flowering plants on Earth. About 50,000 of these plants are waiting to be officially discovered.

You don't have to be an expert to join the search. Amateur botanists around the world put on their walking shoes and go botanizing. Botanizing involves finding and studying plants in the wild. Many amateurs have found previously unknown species of plants.

Most undiscovered plants probably live in tropical regions. However, some experts estimate there are at least 1,800 undiscovered plants in the United States. Most of these plants are angiosperms—complex seed plants that produce both flowers and fruit. One amateur botanist in Nevada has found 19 new flowering plants in the last 20 years!

Some of the new plants are amazing. For example, botanists hiking in a wildlife station in central Florida discovered a new

species of the utricularia flower. The new species is a meat-eating plant that grows underground without direct sunlight. Only a tiny yellow flower appears above ground in spring. Its leaves, stem, and roots are all under the sandy soil. The plant can sense underground insects. When an insect gets close enough, an opening on the plant's stem sucks it in. The plant can perform photosynthesis because it grows in loose, sandy soil that allows sunlight to pass through it.

Most newly discovered plants grow only in very specific habitats. Often the habitats are in remote, unexplored locations. Surprisingly, though, many new plants are found near cities and other developed places. As habitats around the world are destroyed or altered by people, new plants are at risk of extinction.

Botanists study plants growing in a greenhouse.

This is why botanizing is so important. Plants are vital to human survival. Many of our medicines come from plants. A still undiscovered flower might produce a cure for cancer. That flower could be growing in your own backyard!

Write ABOUT IT

1. What is botanizing? Why is it important?
2. Why is utricularia such an amazing plant?

 LOG ON Visit www.science.mmhschool.com for more amazing stories and facts about botanizing.

Utricularia flowers grow in central Florida.

The Animal Kingdom: Invertebrates

Vocabulary

invertebrate, A36

vertebrate, A36

exoskeleton, A42

Get Ready

The spider in the photo is a banded argiope spider. What do spiders have in common with other animals such as frogs and crabs? How are they different? They are all animals, but unlike the frog, the crab and spider do not have a backbone. They have a hard outer covering instead. What other animals do not have a backbone? How do they move, eat, or catch their prey?

Inquiry Skill

You infer when you form an idea from facts or observations.

Explore Activity

What Are the Differences Among Invertebrates?

Materials
jar lid

water

paintbrush

planarian culture

hand lens

aluminum pan

paper towels

earthworm

Procedure

BE CAREFUL! Handle live animals gently and carefully.

1. **Experiment** Fill the jar lid half full of water.

2. Use the paintbrush to transfer two planarians from the culture to the jar lid.

3. **Observe** Look at the planarian with the hand lens, and answer the questions in the Data Table. Record your observations in a table similar to the one shown.

4. Line an aluminum pan with a moist paper towel, and place an earthworm in the pan.

5. **Observe** Use the hand lens to observe the earthworm, and record your observations in your table.

Data Table
Can you find the head and tail? Are there any sense organs on the head?
How does it move?
Where is the mouth?
Does it have one or two openings in its digestive system?
Do you see any evidence of blood vessels or observe a pulse?
What do you think is the most likely habitat for this animal?

Drawing Conclusions

1. How is the earthworm's body different from the planarian's body?

2. How do their methods of movement differ?

3. How are the earthworm and planarian similar?

4. **FURTHER INQUIRY** **Infer** From your observations, infer which of these animals is more complex. Explain your answer.

Read to Learn

Main Idea Invertebrates are the large variety of animals without a backbone.

What Is an Invertebrate?

Planarians and earthworms are different and similar. You can see this by observing their external characteristics. You will find that these two kinds of animals are linked in a very large group by what is inside of them.

The animal kingdom is divided into two major groups. Planaria, earthworms, and a great many other kinds of animals belong to one group—the **invertebrates**. An invertebrate is an animal that does not have a backbone. All other animals belong to a group called **vertebrates**. All of these animals have a backbone.

Invertebrates live in water and on land. Some of those that live in water spend part of their lives stuck in one spot. Others swim through or on the water. Still others crawl or walk on the bottoms of oceans, streams, or lakes. Invertebrates that live on land can move on it, in it, or over it.

The variety of invertebrates is very great. There are more than one million different kinds of invertebrates. However, these millions can be divided into 12 phyla. Some of these phyla are shown here.

▷ **How do invertebrates differ from vertebrates?**

Cnidaria Hydras, jellyfish, sea anemones, corals. 10,000 species. Live in water; some kinds attached to rocks; have tentacles and stinging cells around mouth.

Platyhelminthes Flatworms. 20,000 species. Live in water, damp soil, or as parasites in other animals; have flat bodies.

Porifera Sponges. 9,000 species. Simplest of all animals; live in water; adults attached to rocks and cannot move.

Arthropoda (arthropods) Insects, spiders, scorpions, ticks, millipedes, centipedes, lobsters, crabs, and shrimp. 1,000,000 species. Live in water and on land; many can fly; have a hard outer body covering and jointed legs; bodies have one to three main sections.

Echinodermata (echinoderms) Sea stars (starfish), sea urchins. 7,000 species. Live in salt water; have spiny skins; move very slowly or are attached to rocks.

Annelida (segmented worms) Earthworms, leeches. 15,000 species. Live in water or damp soil; body is long, rounded, and divided into ringlike segments.

Nematoda Roundworms. 90,000 species. Live in water and moist soil, and as parasites in plants and animals; body is shaped like a cylinder.

Mollusca (mollusks) Clams, snails, squids, octopuses, oysters, scallops, and mussels. 150,000 species. Most live in salt water; some live in fresh water and on land; all have a foot, internal organs, and tissue called a mantle that covers the internal organs; many have shells.

What Are the Simplest Invertebrates Like?

The simplest invertebrates live in water. That is where animals first appeared. At first sight some of these simple invertebrates may not look like animals at all, but plants. This is especially true of sponges and some cnidarians (nigh·DAYR·ee·uhnz), such as sea anemones and corals.

Sponges and Cnidarians

Not only are these organisms often brightly colored, like plants, but the ones you would recognize in the sea do not move from place to place. Like plants, these organisms are *sessile* (SES·uhl), or unable to move. This may seem puzzling to you. One of the characteristics of an animal is the ability to move around. As it turns out, sponges, sea anemones, and corals do move around, but not as adults. They move around when they are very young. They then find a place to attach themselves, and they live the rest of their lives in that place.

How do these animals get their food? Sponges have pores in their bodies through which water flows. If there are particles of food in the water, a sponge will trap them as they pass through the pores.

Most cnidarians have armlike structures called *tentacles* around the mouth. Stinging cells on the tentacles capture prey. Although they do not have a brain, cnidarians do have muscles and nerves. These work together so that the tentacles can push the prey into the mouth.

When a fish bumps into a tentacle, the stinging cells of a sea anemone release a poison. The poison stuns the fish. The tentacles wrap around the fish and pull it into the mouth.

Flatworms and Roundworms

Unlike sponges and jellyfish, worms have a body plan made of two similar halves. If a worm is divided down the middle, one half looks much like the other.

Flatworms are the simplest worms. They have a head, a tail, and a flat body. Inside the body are organ systems. The digestive system has just one opening, a mouth.

Planarians are flatworms that live in fresh water. One feature you can see on a flatworm is its "eyespots." These spots help it sense light. They are part of the animal's nervous system. The system includes a simple brain.

Tapeworms are flatworms that live inside the body of another organism. They feed off digested food from the organism.

Roundworms have a tubelike body. The body comes to a point at each end. They have a digestive system with two openings—a mouth and an anus. Food enters the mouth. Undigested remains leave through the anus. Roundworms may live in soil, fresh water, or salt water. Many of them also live inside animals and plants.

> ▶ **How do sponges and cnidarians differ from flatworms and roundworms?**

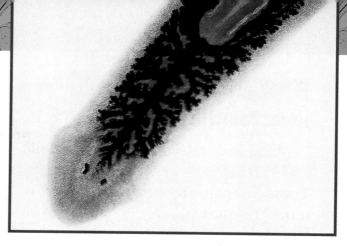

The head of a planarian has two eyespots. These are light-sensitive areas. When the eyespots detect light, messages are sent through a simple nervous system. Muscles are activated. The animal swims away from the light.

Ascarids are intestinal round-worms. They can grow up to 30 cm (12 in.) long.

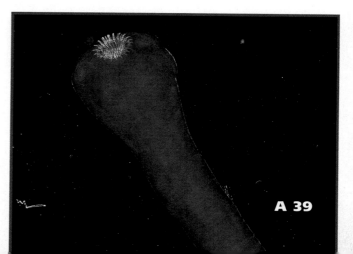

A tapeworm has hooks and suckers on its head. It uses these structures to attach itself to the intestine of an organism. Tapeworms can live inside dogs, cats, humans, and other animals.

What Are More Complex Invertebrates Like?

After it rains, you might see snails and earthworms in a yard or lawn. These animals are members of two more complex phlya.

Mollusks

Mollusks are found on land or in fresh or salt water. They are soft-bodied animals. The body is covered by a thin tissue called a *mantle*. In many mollusks this mantle produces a hard shell. The organ systems are underneath the mantle. Mollusks get food by moving about. They have a kind of "foot." You can tell different classes of mollusks by the foot and the shell.

Snails can move into their shell when the air is cool and dry.

Snails are "stomach footed." That is, they have a muscular foot along their bottom surface. They also have a large single shell. Slugs belong to the same class, but have no shells.

Clams belong to the "hatchet-footed" class. The muscular foot can reach into the sand or mud. Then the end spreads out into a hatchetlike shape. This shape helps the clam dig down into the sand or mud. A clam has a shell in two halves (or valves) joined by a hinge. This shell gives these animals the name "bivalves." The shell can open and shut. Oysters and scallops are also bivalves. Scallops move by a fast open-and-close motion of their shells.

Octopuses and squids belong to the most complex class of mollusks. They are "head footed." They have tentacles that extend from the head. They use the tentacles for capturing prey. Octopuses also use them to move on the sea floor. Octopuses have no shell. Squids have a shell on the inside.

A squid moves by forcing water out through an opening, called a jet, near its head. The water squirts out in one direction, and the squid moves in the opposite direction.

Early in life oysters attach their flat lower shell to a solid surface. They do not move about after that. If a sand grain enters the shell, the oyster covers it with layers of a chemical. This process can form a pearl.

Segmented Worms

Earthworms and leeches are segmented worms. Their bodies are made up of segments, or rings. You can see the segments clearly as an earthworm crawls past you. Through the inside of the body is a tube-shaped digestive system with two openings. The worm has a circulatory system with hearts and blood vessels. Nerves in each segment are connected to a main nerve cord. Bristles on the body help the worm burrow into the soil. These structures enable the animal to respond to light, temperature, and moisture.

Echinoderms

Have you ever felt the spiny skin of a starfish or sea urchin? These animals belong to the phylum of echinoderms. They are very different from mollusks and earthworms, or in fact, from any other invertebrates. One main difference is a kind of water-pumping system. Water-filled vessels extend from the mouth into the arms of the animal. The water is pumped to the *tube feet*, structures that help the animal grasp and move.

Earthworms live in the soil and help recycle soil nutrients.

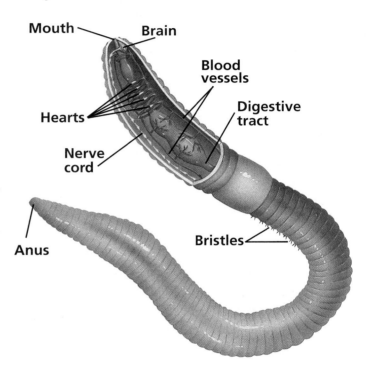

Mouth — Brain
Blood vessels
Hearts
Digestive tract
Nerve cord
Anus
Bristles

Find the five hearts that pump blood connected to two vessels. Find the nerve cord connected to the brain.

The tube feet on the underside of the starfish's arms allow it to pry open the shell of a clam.

▷ **How are starfish different from mollusks and earthworms?**

What Are the Most Complex Invertebrates Like?

Two-thirds of the species on Earth are arthropods. Scientists estimate that there are many trillions of individual arthropods. Members of this phylum live in almost every part of Earth—in deserts, jungles, and grasslands. They live high in the mountains, in cities, and in fresh and salt water. One group of arthropods, the insects, holds more different species than all the other species of living things combined.

What do arthropods have in common? They have jointed limbs, including legs for walking and jumping. Some have jointed wings, flippers, or claws. Their bodies are in sections. They have an outer skeleton, or **exoskeleton** . Here are some major classes of the arthropods.

Arachnids include this scorpion as well as spiders, ticks, and mites. They all have eight legs and one or two body sections. Many are poisonous.

Insects, such as this grasshopper, have three sections to their bodies and three pairs of legs. Most, but not all, insects also have two pairs of wings. Ants, flies, bees, beetles, termites, mosquitoes, fleas, and body lice are other examples of insects.

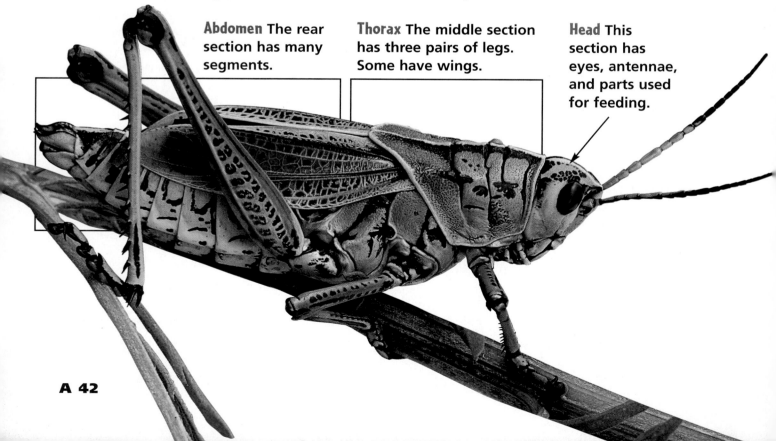

Abdomen The rear section has many segments.

Thorax The middle section has three pairs of legs. Some have wings.

Head This section has eyes, antennae, and parts used for feeding.

Lobsters, shrimp, crayfish, and crabs are all *crustaceans*. These animals, like the lobster in the photo, can have two or three body sections. They have three or more pairs of limbs that may be used for walking, grasping, and eating.

READING Summarize
How can you identify an arthropod?

Centipedes and millipedes have long bodies and many legs. Each segment of a millipede has two pairs of legs. Each segment of a centipede has only one pair of legs.

QUICK LAB

Fruit Flies

FOLDABLES Make a Two-Tab Book. (See p. R42.) Label the tabs as shown.

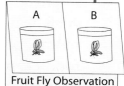

Fruit Fly Observation

1. **Label** two containers of fruit flies, one A and one B.

2. **Predict** What do you think the fruit flies' reaction will be if you place the container on ice?

3. **Observe** Place A on ice. Observe what the fruit flies do. Sketch what you observe on tab A of your Two-Tab Book and record your observations under the tab. Take the container off the ice.

4. **Predict** Cover one half of container B with black paper. Leave it for an hour. What do you think the fruit flies will do?

5. **Observe** Count the number of fruit flies that are not covered by the black paper. Sketch what you observe on tab B of your Two-Tab Book, and record your observations under the tab. Compare the location of the fruit flies in both containers.

6. **Interpret Data** Why did the conditions noted above have an effect on the fruit flies?

A 43

How Do Invertebrates Affect People?

Invertebrates affect people in many important ways. Some invertebrates, such as bees, butterflies, wasps, and moths, pollinate plants that produce food crops, such as peach, apple, and pear trees.

Other invertebrates, such as insect pests, attack and destroy the same crops. Scientists estimate that there are more than 2,000 species of insect pests.

Still other invertebrates, such as mosquitoes, ticks, flies, lice, flatworms, and roundworms, cause or transmit diseases of humans. Malaria, a disease that affects millions of people around the world, is transmitted by mosquitoes.

Animals are also the victims of diseases transmitted by invertebrates. Many of these animals provide people with meat, milk, and the raw materials of clothing—such as sheep's wool. Some invertebrates, such as termites and carpenter ants, can even destroy people's homes if the homes are made of wood.

The corn borer is an insect pest that attacks corn plants.

However, many invertebrates also support the lives of people directly. For example, if you love seafood, you'll find many tasty invertebrates on a restaurant's dinner menu, including lobsters, shrimp, clams, mussels, crabs, and oysters. As far as breakfast is concerned, the product of bees—honey—can go a long way to making pancakes a sweet delight.

You can even wear the products of invertebrates. For example, in the caterpillar stage of its life, a moth called *Bombyx mori* produces the fine threads that are woven into silk fabrics. The common name of this caterpillar is the silkworm, although it is not a worm at all.

▷ **What can invertebrates do for us?**

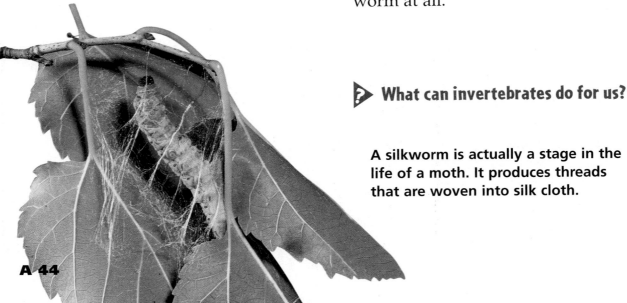

A silkworm is actually a stage in the life of a moth. It produces threads that are woven into silk cloth.

Why It Matters

Invertebrates include helpful and harmful animals. For example, European red mites can destroy apple trees. Red mites are arthropods. Bees, which are also arthropods, help apple trees to produce apples. Since both of these kinds of arthropods live in the same places, controlling the red mites while preserving the bees can be a problem.

e-Journal Visit our Web site **www.science.mmhschool.com** to do a research project on the ways invertebrates affect people.

Think and Write

1. What is the major difference between an invertebrate and a vertebrate?

2. Where do the simplest invertebrates live?

3. Name three kinds of mollusks that people eat.

4. By counting legs, how can you tell whether an arthropod is an insect or an arachnid?

5. **Critical Thinking** The giant African snail is not a problem in its home environment in Africa. Its population does not change much there. Why might its numbers increase rapidly if it were released in the United States?

WRITING LINK

Persuasive Writing Research the Great Barrier Reef. What can people do to ensure its survival? Write an editorial for your school or local newspaper about why it is important to save the Great Barrier Reef. Use persuasive language and strong reasons to get your readers to agree with your opinion.

MATH LINK

Solve this problem. Ten insect pests invade an apple orchard. If left alone, these pests will increase their population 100 times every 20 days. How many of these insects will there be in the orchard after 60 days? What is this amount in words?

ART LINK

Draw spider webs. You can find them both inside and outside of your home. Draw the design of several webs. How are they alike? Different? Read about spiders and their webs in different research books. What determines the characteristics of the webs you observed?

TECHNOLOGY LINK

 LOG ON Visit **www.science.mmhschool.com** for more links.

The Animal Kingdom: Vertebrates

Vocabulary

chordate, A48

endoskeleton, A48

cartilage, A51

tetrapod, A52

cold-blooded, A53

warm-blooded, A54

mammary gland, A55

Get Ready

"You've got to have more backbone." Some people say this to suggest that someone should stand up for his or her rights. When people say those words, they usually don't think of science, but there is a lot of science behind those words. Think of your backbone. Could you stand up without it? What other animals have backbones? Do we share any other traits with these animals?

Inquiry Skill

you predict when you state possible results of an event or experiment.

Explore Activity

What Are the Characteristics of Vertebrates?

Procedure

1 **Observe** Look at each animal photograph carefully. Note the sizes of the animals in the photographs by reading the scale provided for each.

2 Compare and contrast the animals. Make a data table showing your comparisons.

4.5 cm

Drawing Conclusions

1 What characteristics did you use in your comparison? Why?

2 Based on your observations, what characteristics do all vertebrates have in common?

3 **FURTHER INQUIRY** **Predict** Use research books to find photos of other animals. Do they belong in the vertebrate grouping? Why or why not?

1.4 cm

1 cm

4.4 cm

A 47

Main Idea Vertebrates make up the division of animals with a backbone.

What Do Vertebrates Have in Common?

Vertebrates, animals that have backbones, can be found in almost any surroundings. Observing such animals from the outside can tell you a lot about their characteristics. Now you will get a chance to peer inside these animals.

Before you take a journey inside of vertebrates, you ought to know how they are grouped. First of all, all vertebrates belong to the phylum *Chordata*, or the **chordates** (KAWR·dayts). A chordate is any animal that at some time in its life has a large nerve cord running down its back.

The simplest chordates, such as the tiny fishlike lancelets, do not have backbones surrounding their nerve cords. The more complex chordates, such as humans, dogs, and elephants, do have backbones surrounding their nerve cords. These animals are vertebrates.

In addition to having a backbone, vertebrates share other characteristics. They have an internal skeleton that supports their bodies. An internal skeleton is called an **endoskeleton**. Most vertebrates also have two sets of paired limbs, such as fins, arms, or legs.

Vertebrates are grouped in seven classes. Look at the photos on the next page to explore these classes.

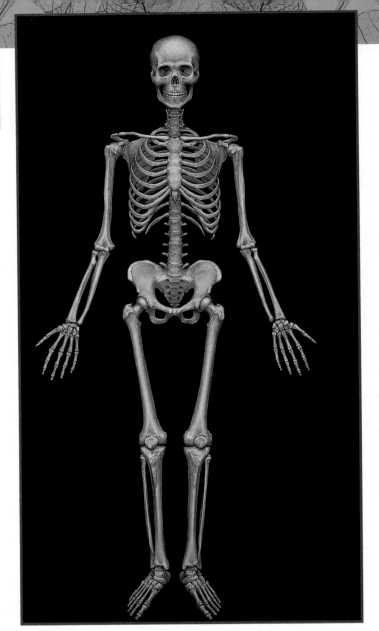

All vertebrates, such as humans and fish, have a backbone and an internal skeleton.

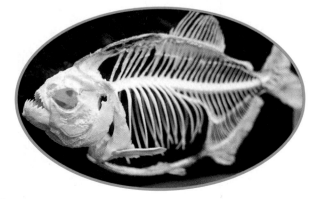

▶ **What are some characteristics that vertebrates have in common?**

Classes of Vertebrates

Jawless fish Hagfish and lampreys. Live in water; do not have jaws; soft skeleton; breathe through gills.

Birds Eagles, sparrows, robins. 8,600 species. Live on land; hard, bony skeleton; have jaws; have feathers; most can fly; breathe through lungs.

Cartilaginous, soft-boned fish Sharks, rays, skates. 750 species. Live in water; have jaws; soft skeleton; breathe through gills.

Mammals Humans, cats, dogs, whales, bats. 4,500 species. Live on land and in water; hard, bony skeleton; have jaws; have hair or fur; feed young mother's milk; breathe through lungs.

Bony fish Trout, salmon, tuna, goldfish. 30,000 species. Live in water; have jaws; hard, bony skeleton; have scales; breathe through gills.

Amphibians Frogs, toads, salamanders. 4,000 species. Most live in water when young and on land as adults; hard, bony skeleton; have jaws; smooth skin; breathe through gills when young and through lungs as adults.

Reptiles Snakes, turtles, alligators, lizards, dinosaurs (extinct). 7,000 living species. Live in water and on land; hard, bony skeleton; have jaws; have scales; breathe through lungs.

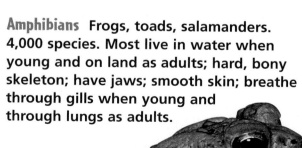

A 49

A hagfish's mouth has tentacles it uses to catch food.

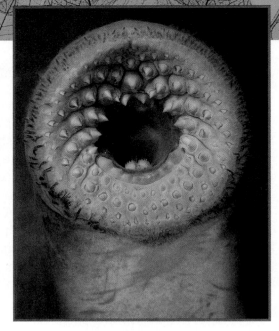

The mouth of a lamprey uses suction to attach to its prey.

What Are Jawless Fish Like?

The first vertebrates appeared about 540 million years ago. They were fish that did not have jaws. Heavy armored plates protected their bodies. These were the ancestors of modern fish.

About 440 million years ago, these animals evolved into two different kinds of fish. One group had jaws and teeth. The other group did not have jaws or teeth. This group gave rise to hagfish and lampreys.

The body of a hagfish or lamprey is long and slender, like a garden hose. Unlike other vertebrates, hagfish and lampreys do not have two sets of paired limbs. Although hagfish and lampreys share these characteristics, they are different in other ways.

You might be wondering: If hagfish and lampreys do not have jaws or teeth, how do they eat? The way these fish eat reveals some differences between them.

The mouth of a lamprey is round and might remind you of a plunger you use at home to clear a clogged drain. It fastens onto objects like the suction cup of a plunger fastens onto the area around a drain. However, the object is not a drain opening. It is the body of another fish.

Once the lamprey's mouth has a good grip on a fish, the lamprey uses its tongue—which has sharp edges on it like a file—to make a hole in the fish. The lamprey then feeds on the blood of the fish.

Hagfish do not have the same kinds of mouth parts as lampreys, so they cannot attack other fish. Instead, hagfish simply wander through the water in search of bits of a dead fish or a careless sea worm. Short tentacles in their mouths help hagfish grab their meals.

▶ **What is the main difference between hagfish and lampreys?**

How Do Cartilaginous and Bony Fish Compare?

If you were in the water and you saw a shark approaching, you would not care much about what is inside it—as long as it is not you. However, biologists have used this information to place sharks and their relatives in a different class from most other fish.

The skeletons of sharks, rays, and skates are made of a tissue called **cartilage**. Cartilage is a body tissue that is not as hard as bone or as soft as flesh. The tip of your nose and the flaps of your ears are shaped by cartilage beneath your skin.

The skeletons of bony fish are, of course, made of a harder substance— bone. Curiously, the skeletons of all vertebrates—including humans—start off as being made of cartilage. In most other vertebrates, the cartilage is gradually replaced by bone. For some unknown reason, this replacement process does not happen in sharks, rays, or skates.

Bony fish differ from cartilaginous fish in another important way. Bony fish have an organ called a swim bladder that sharks and their relatives do not have. The swim bladder is like an air sac. Air enters the bladder from the fish's blood or leaves the bladder and goes into the fish's blood.

When air enters the bladder, the fish becomes less dense and tends to rise in the water. When air leaves the bladder, the fish becomes more dense and tends to sink. This lets bony fish save energy if they want to stay at a constant depth. Their bodies automatically adjust the amount of air in the swim bladder so they neither rise nor sink. A bony fish can stay at any depth without using up energy. They simply hover motionless. On the other hand, sharks and their relatives must remain in motion to stay at the same depth. Staying in motion uses up energy.

READING **Summarize**

What are the differences between cartilaginous fish and bony fish?

Hammerhead sharks are cartilaginous fish.

Tuna and other bony fish have a swim bladder that fills with and releases air so that the fish can hover motionless at any depth and save energy.

What Are the Characteristics of Amphibians?

About 365 million years ago, an unusual vertebrate struggled out of the water and did something no vertebrate had done before. It walked on the land!

The vertebrate was an amphibian, and it walked on four feet. Hundreds of millions of years later, a scientist would describe these amphibians as the first **tetrapods**. The word *tetrapod* comes from two Greek words: *tetra*, which means "four," and *podos*, which means "foot." Tetrapods are four-footed vertebrates.

As it turns out, not all amphibians have four feet. One group of amphibians, the apodans (the *a* means "without"), have no legs and look like worms. All other amphibians, such as frogs, toads, and salamanders, do have four legs and four feet. How do salamanders and frogs differ? For one thing, salamanders have tails. Adult frogs do not have tails.

The name *amphibian* gives you a clue about the lifestyle of these

Salamander

vertebrates. The name also comes from Greek. It means "both lives." Put another way, many amphibians lead two lives. The first is a life in water. The second is a life on land.

Frogs begin their lives as legless tadpoles that have tails and breathe through structures called gills. However, over a period of days, the tadpoles sprout legs, lose their tails, and develop lungs. Soon—as adult frogs—they fill the night air with croaks and hop from place to place on land in search of insects to eat.

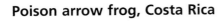

Poison arrow frog, Costa Rica

> ❓ **What characteristic of amphibians gives them their name?**

Although most amphibians move from water to land, some do not. For example, some frogs spend their whole lives in water, while others spend their whole lives on land. The same is true of salamanders.

What Are the Characteristics of Reptiles?

Reptiles first appeared on Earth about 300 million years ago. For more than 200 million years after that, more reptiles—and more different kinds of reptiles—roamed Earth than any other vertebrates. This period is now called the "age of reptiles."

Most of these ancient reptiles—including the dinosaurs—became extinct. Today there are only four major groups of reptiles on Earth. They are the snakes, the turtles, the lizards, and the crocodilians, which include crocodiles and alligators.

All reptiles have lungs and breathe air. All have hard scales that are waterproof. Most lay eggs on land, although some give birth to live offspring. The eggs have shells that tend to be soft and leathery. The eggs of amphibians and fish do not have shells.

An eggshell keeps the egg from drying out on land. Since fish and amphibians lay their eggs either in water or in moist places on land, an eggshell would be of little advantage to them. It is of great advantage, however, to reptiles.

All reptiles are **cold-blooded**. This means that a reptile cannot

Giant tortoise (and passenger)

automatically keep its body temperature steady. Fish and amphibians also are cold-blooded. The blood of a cold-blooded animal can be cold or warm, depending on its surroundings. Put another way, the body temperature of a reptile is almost always at—or close to—the temperature of its surroundings. For example, on a hot day in the desert, the body temperature of a rattlesnake is high. On a cold day in a forest, its body temperature is low.

Dinosaurs are reptiles that became extinct about 65 million years ago.

▷ **What distinguishes reptiles from other animals?**

Nile crocodile, Masai Mara National Park, Kenya

What Are the Characteristics of Birds?

You might find it puzzling to learn that some scientists think birds are living dinosaurs. That's because birds and reptiles share some characteristics, such as skin covered with hard scales and eggs covered with a shell.

Today's birds have feathers. They do not have teeth in their mouths as dinosaurs did. They do not have claws on their front legs—their wings—as some dinosaurs did. How can scientists claim that birds may be living dinosaurs?

Many years ago scientists discovered the remains of a 150-million-year-old animal that had feathers. Since having feathers is a key characteristic of a bird, the scientists had reason to believe that the remains were those of an ancient bird—perhaps the first bird. Scientists named this bird *Archaeopteryx* (ahr·kee·AHP·tuhr·iks), which means "ancient wing."

When the scientists examined the remains carefully, they made three startling observations: the "bird" had toes and claws on its wings, teeth in its mouth, and a long tail with bones in it like those of a dinosaur. The animal seemed to be part reptile and part bird.

Classifying *Archaeopteryx* may be a difficult task. Classifying modern birds is much easier. They all have feathers. They all have wings. They have very lightweight bones, which makes it easier for them to lift off the ground and stay in flight for a long time. They do not have teeth, but they do have beaks. As you know from experience, the eggs of birds are covered with a hard shell. Finally, birds are **warm-blooded** .

In this case, *warm-blooded* really does mean having warm blood. Birds, along with mammals, are the only vertebrates that automatically keep their body temperature constant—and warm, which is what *warm-blooded* means. Although modern reptiles are cold-blooded, some scientists have uncovered evidence that at least some dinosaurs may have been warm-blooded.

 **What do birds have in common?**

The 150-million-year-old *Archaeopteryx* shown here may have been the first bird, and therefore an ancestor of the hawk above.

What Are the Characteristics of Mammals?

The first mammals—but not humans—lived among the dinosaurs 220 million years ago. These mammals were no bigger than your hand, probably hunted at night, and ate insects.

For millions of years, the dinosaurs dominated Earth. Then, about 65 million years ago, the dinosaurs became extinct. Mammals began to take their place as the dominant animals on Earth. Mammals were successful because of certain characteristics that only they have.

- Mammal mothers feed their young a balanced diet loaded with a mixture of all the food groups— proteins, fats, sugars, minerals, and vitamins. The diet is made up of a single substance—mother's milk. The milk is made in organs called **mammary glands** .

- Mammals are covered with hair or fur, which helps keep them warm in cold weather.

- Mammals have sweat glands, which help them keep cool in hot weather.

- The part of a mammal's brain responsible for intelligence is more developed than that of other vertebrates.

Mammals live everywhere on Earth. Some mammals, such as whales

Placentals, such as the orangutan, give birth to fully developed offspring.

and dolphins, live in the ocean. Others, such as lions and humans, live on land. Some, such as bats, can even fly.

Mammals also come in all sizes. The largest mammal, and the largest animal ever to live on Earth, is the blue whale. Blue whales can be as long as an 11-story building is tall! They can weigh as much as about 200 medium-sized cars.

The smallest mammal is the bumblebee bat of Thailand. Its body is no longer than your pinkie finger, and it weighs less than a teaspoon of water.

▷ **What characteristics do mammals share?**

Marsupials, such as the kangaroo, give birth to partly developed offspring that finish their development in the mother's pouch.

Mountain gorillas live in central Africa's forests, which are being destroyed to make room for farms.

Why Are Species Endangered?

Earth loses species of living things every day, some of which have never even been discovered. If a species becomes extinct the last one of its kind dies. When this happens, the species is gone forever.

Species can become extinct naturally. Over the billions of years of Earth's history, most of the species that developed have become extinct. In many cases they became extinct when they could not survive natural changes in their environment, such as changes in climate. However, scientistis estimate that only 1 to 10 species become extinct naturally per year. Human activities cause extinctions to be 100 to 1,000 times higher.

All living things have *adaptations* suited to a particular environment. If that environment is threatened, so are the living things in it. Different activities of people can threaten the life of a species indirectly by threatening its environment. Some activities of people, like overhunting can threaten a species directly.

Habitat Loss

Habitat loss is a major cause of species becoming endangered. This means animals losing their homes. For example, as native prairie habitat in the United States was lost, prairie animals, such as the bison, declined in number.

The giant pandas of China face extinction because their main source of food, bamboo, is being cut down to provide land for new communities.

Snow leopards of central Asia are threatened with extinction because they are hunted for their fur.

Peregrine Falcon

Overhunting

Sometimes animals are hunted in larger numbers than their populations can withstand. This is called over-hunting. Public education and laws limiting the hunting of animals have stopped most overhunting.

Pollution

Pollution—harmful substances added to our air, water, and soil—is dangerous to all living things. Peregrine falcons became endangered because of pesticides, but they are now being saved.

Exotic Species

Exotic species, or species that are introduced to an area, often do not have natural predators or diseases in the new area. This allows them to overcome native species quite easily. Exotic species may harm native species. Exotics may also spread disease to native species.

▷ **What are some things that endanger a species?**

QUICK LAB

Zoo Hunt

FOLDABLES™ Make a Trifold Book. (See p. R 42.) Label the columns as shown.

Species	Threatened / Endangered	Cause

1. **Do research to locate a local zoo or aquarium that has some rare species.**

2. **List the name of each species in the first column of your Foldables Trifold Book.**

3. **Classify** Identify the species as threatened or endangered in the second column.

4. **Find out why each species became threatened or endangered. List the cause in the third column.**

5. **Communicate** What can you do to help save threatened and endangered species? Write your ideas on the back of your Foldables Trifold Book.

What Can People Do to Save Species?

Since the activities of people can threaten to make a species extinct, they can also be important in making sure a species is safe. There are many things people can do to save threatened species. However, time is running out for some of the species. Here are some things that can be done to make sure a species is safe.

- Build parks and reserves where endangered animals can live in safety.
- Support and pass laws that keep people from destroying the habitats of endangered species.
- Restore destroyed land to what it once was so that members of an endangered species can find a new home.
- Breed and raise endangered species in places such as zoos and aquariums.
- Outlaw, or limit, the hunting of endangered species for any purpose.
- Outlaw, or limit, the use of pesticides that poison useful or harmless species.

People and their governments can and have done all of these things, but it is not easy. For one thing, conserving species may mean giving up some things, such as land for farms or houses, fur for clothing, and even meat for food. The problem is to find ways of satisfying such needs without sacrificing the living things with which we share our planet.

▷ **How can you help to save endangered species?**

In Africa some countries have set aside huge areas of land where animals of all kinds can live in safety.

Why It Matters

Many vertebrates have been domesticated and are very important to people. Wild vertebrates are also important to people because they help maintain the equilibrium of the environment.

As people become more aware of the importance of saving animals from extinction, we devise various ways of protecting fragile animal populations.

e-Journal Visit our Web site **www.science.mmhschool.com** to do a research project on your state's game commission.

Think and Write

1. How are hagfish and lampreys different from all other vertebrates?

2. Why can you say a frog has two lives?

3. What can a cold-blooded vertebrate not do that a warm-blooded vertebrate can?

4. Infer If you found an animal that lays eggs and spends most of its life in water, why couldn't you be sure it was a fish, amphibian, reptile, or bird?

5. Critical Thinking What facts would you have to consider before voting on a law that bans the catching of a certain species of fish?

L·I·N·K·S

WRITING LINK

Expository Writing Research the Endangered Species Act. Write an essay about this law. Why was this law passed? How does it protect endangered species? Write about your findings. Begin each of your paragraphs with a main idea. Support each main idea with facts and details.

MATH LINK

Solve this problem. Scientists estimate about 117 bird species have become extinct in the last 400 years. What percentage of bird species is this if there were 9,000 bird species 400 years ago? Show your work.

SOCIAL STUDIES LINK

Learn about protected areas. Do a research project on the nearest protected area to your home.  Who is responsible for it? What plants and animals does it protect? Write an article on your findings.

TECHNOLOGY LINK

LOG ON Visit **www.science.mmhschool.com** for more links.

Amazing Stories

Endangered Primates

Of all the animal groups that make up the class of mammals, none consists of more intelligent animals than the primates. Primates belong to a level of classification called an order, which is just below a class. It is to this order that humans, apes, monkeys, and other "smart" animals belong.

In spite of their intelligence, at least 25 species of primates are on the verge of extinction. They are simply no match for the damage that humans have done to their territories.

These threatened primates live in Africa, South America, and Asia. Let's get to know a few of them.

GOLDEN LION TAMARIN

Leaping from branch to branch in the shrinking forests of eastern Brazil, the population of this lively little animal has fallen to about 900. Its body, about the length of your hand, trails a foot-long tail. Its golden hair flashes in the sunlight. Why is its middle name "lion"? The silky hair on its head falls on its shoulders like a lion's mane. Scientists are trying to save it by breeding it in captivity.

MOUNTAIN GORILLA

Standing up to six feet tall and weighing in at 450 pounds, a male mountain gorilla is the largest primate on Earth. If you came upon one in the mountains of central Africa, your heart might pound with fright. Surprisingly, the gorilla might feel the same way. Mountain gorillas are gentle and intelligent animals. There are only about 600 mountain gorillas in the wild.

GOLDEN-CROWNED SIFAKA

This big-eyed, golden-crowned sifaka almost became extinct before it was discovered by western scientists in 1974. This animal belongs to the primate family of leaping lemurs. A family is a classification just below an order. Sifakas live on the island of Madagascar, off the east coast of Africa. Traveling through the forest in groups of 3–10, they hunt for fruits, leaves, and buds. They usually feed twice a day, in the morning and in the afternoon. In between they lie around sunning themselves. Unfortunately for this rare primate, whose population is about 5,000, their forest home is being rapidly destroyed. Unless something is done to stop the forest destruction, the golden-crowned sifaka population will also be destroyed.

What Did I Learn?

1. Golden-Crowned sifaka are endangered because
   A people hunt them for their body parts.
   B people hunt them for the belief that they are magical.
   C their home is being destroyed.
   D they are dangerous.

2. Apes, monkeys, and humans all belong to the same
   F order.
   G species.
   H family.
   J genus.

 LOG ON Visit www.science.mmhschool.com to learn more about endangered animals.

Chapter 1 Review

Vocabulary

Fill each blank with the best word or words from the list.

> **angiosperms,** A28
> **exoskeleton,** A42
> **kingdom,** A8
> **mammary gland,** A55
> **microbes,** A14
> **nonvascular,** A24
> **organism,** A8
> **phylum,** A8
> **sexual reproduction,** A25
> **species,** A9

1. The _____ of a mammal is what allows it to produce milk for its young.

2. The most detailed level of classification is _____.

3. In the process of _____, a sperm cell joins with an egg cell.

4. The hard covering of an insect is called a(n) _____.

5. All plants belong to a(n) _____.

6. A bacterium is a one-celled _____.

7. Molds are examples of _____.

8. Plants whose seeds are protected by an outer flesh, or fruit are _____.

9. All animals with backbones belong in the same _____.

10. Mosses and liverworts are _____ because they do not have a system of transportation for their nutrients.

Test Prep

11. What two kingdoms contain bacteria?

  A Eubacteria and Archaebacteria

  B Eubacteria and plant

  C Eubacteria and protist

  D Archaebacteria and fungus

12. All of the following are mollusks EXCEPT _____.

  F clams

  G spiders

  H mussels

  J octopuses

13. How is a fungus different from a plant?

  A It makes its own food.

  B It has chlorophyll.

  C It does not make its own food.

  D It is green.

14. All of the following are NOT reptiles EXCEPT

   F sharks.

   G salamanders.

   H turtles.

   J frogs.

15. The two physical characteristics that are shared by mammals and no other vertebrates are _____ and _____.

   A hair, mammary glands

   B hair, backbones

   C backbones, fur

   D mammary glands, backbones

Concepts and Skills

16. Product Ads What if you were planning to open a store? Classify your products into groups to help your customers find what they need.

17. Critical Thinking Explain why mosses cannot live in a dry climate even if there is water in the soil.

18. Reading in Science What is the relationship between people and many endangered animal species?

19. INQUIRY SKILL **Classify** How would you complete this table to account for all the kingdoms of life?

Kingdom	Number of Cells	Makes Its own Food
		yes
	multicelled	

20. Scientific Methods You come upon the very ancient remains of an animal that looks like this. Why would you have difficulty classifying it?

Did You Ever Wonder?

INQUIRY SKILL **Classify** Refer to the classification sheet you completed at the beginning of the chapter. Classify each of the organisms in as much detail as you can with the information given in the chapter.

LOG ON Visit www.science.mmhschool.com to boost your test scores.

Ecosystems

Did You Ever Wonder?

All living things are part of an ecosystem. The Mexican poppies, lupines, and organ pipe cactus in the picture belong to an ecosystem. The soil that provides these plants with nutrients and the animals that help them reproduce belong to this ecosystem too. An ecosystem may be smaller than a puddle or as large as Earth itself.

INQUIRY SKILL **Define** What are the characteristics of an ecosystem?

Comparing Earth's Biomes

Vocabulary

abiotic factors, A68

climate, A68

biotic factors, A68

biome, A69

Get Ready

This is a swamp in Alabama's Mobile River Delta area. A swamp is a wetland. In a wetland the water level is at or above ground most of the year. Why is water so abundant in some ecosystems and so scarce in others? Why are some parts of Earth warmer than others?

Inquiry Skill

You measure when you find the size, volume, area, mass, weight, or temperature of an object , or how long an event occurs.

Explore Activity

Materials

red pencil

blue pencil

What Are Biomes?

What determines where plants, animals, and other organisms live? Many regions of the world have similar soils and climates and as a result they have similar types of living things.

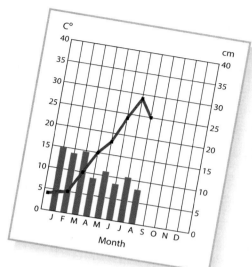

Procedure

1 **Measure** The tables in the Activity Workbook contain sample precipitation and temperature for the six land biomes for one year. Use the data in the table to make a graph for each biome with the red and blue pencils. Use the sample graph on this page as an example of how to complete your graphs.

Drawing Conclusions

1 Describe the climate in each biome.

2 Which of these regions is most like the area where you live? Why? Which organisms are common to your area?

3 What does plotting the temperature and precipitation of an area tell you about the area?

4 What other nonliving factors other than temperature and precipitation make up an environment?

5 **FURTHER INQUIRY** **Communicate** What are biomes?

Read to Learn

Main Idea Nonliving factors are different at different places on Earth.

What Are Biomes?

Living things are called **biotic factors**. All biotic factors need certain nonliving things in order to survive. These nonliving things are called **abiotic** (ay·bigh·AHT·ik) **factors**. They include water, minerals, sunlight, air, and soil.

Abiotic factors differ at different places. The amount of rainfall throughout the year differs from place to place. Temperatures differ also. For example, Fairbanks, Alaska, tends to have long, cold winters and short, warm summers. The precipitation is low all year. Places near the equator are hot year round and rainfall is plentiful.

The pattern of precipitation and temperatures throughout a year is called the **climate** (KLIGH·mit) of a region. Climates differ at different parts of Earth. Why? Areas closer to the equator receive more direct sunlight year round. Farther north and south, sunlight is received at differing angles during the year.

Climates also differ because places differ in how close they are to bodies of water, like oceans. Climates are affected by wind patterns and ocean currents. Places differ in how high

READING
Diagrams

How do seasons change as you go north from the equator?

Earth's Climate Zones

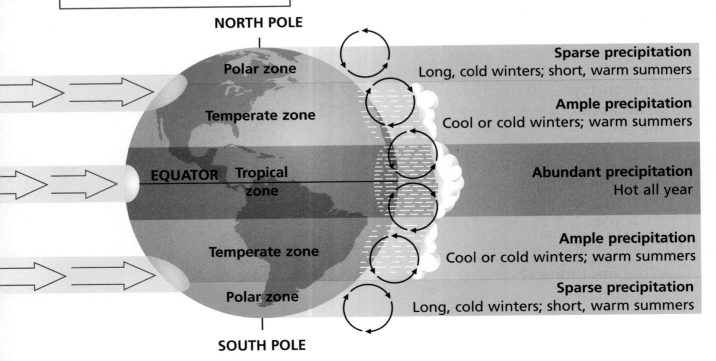

NORTH POLE

Polar zone

Temperate zone

EQUATOR Tropical zone

Temperate zone

Polar zone

SOUTH POLE

Sparse precipitation
Long, cold winters; short, warm summers

Ample precipitation
Cool or cold winters; warm summers

Abundant precipitation
Hot all year

Ample precipitation
Cool or cold winters; warm summers

Sparse precipitation
Long, cold winters; short, warm summers

above sea level they are. The higher the place is, the cooler the climate.

Land barriers, such as mountains, can result in differences in climate. Winds may push moist air from an ocean up one side of a mountain. The air loses its moisture and descends as dry air on the other side. The result is different climates on either side.

Winds, distance from a coast, mountains, distance from the equator—all these factors produce different climates around the world. Large land regions with given climates are called **biomes** (BIGH·ohmz). Each type of biome is characterized by a main kind of plant life. Each kind of plant requires its own conditions for growth, such as amount of sunlight, precipitation, and temperature. Each biome contains a number of ecosystems that are supported by these plants.

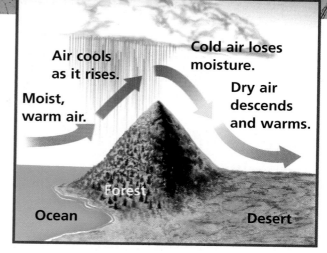

Mountain barriers produce different climates.

▷ **Why are there different biomes around the world?**

Earth's Biomes

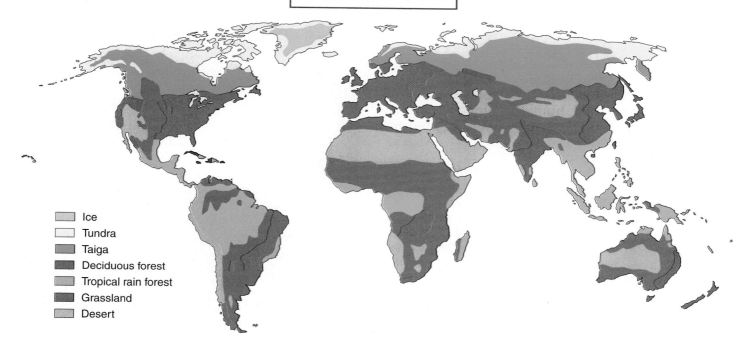

Ice
Tundra
Taiga
Deciduous forest
Tropical rain forest
Grassland
Desert

Tropical Rain Forest

Location: Near the equator
Climate: Hot all year round; 200–460 cm (80–180 in.) of rain a year; no change in seasons
Soil: Nutrient poor
Plants: Greatest diversity of any biome: vines, orchids, ferns, and a wide variety of trees
Animals: More species of insects, reptiles, and amphibians than any other biome; monkeys, other small and large mammals, birds, snakes, lizards, and insects
Typical adaptations: Many animals live in trees for food and protection. Different species are adapted to the forest canopy and the shaded forest floor.

Deciduous Forest

Location: Mid latitudes
Climate: Four distinct seasons a year, relatively mild, humid summers and cold winters; 76–127 cm (30–50 in.) of precipitation per year
Soil: Rich topsoil over clay
Plants: Hardwoods, such as oaks, beeches, hickories, and maples
Animals: Wolves, deer, bears, foxes, beavers, and a variety of other mammals, birds, amphibians, reptiles, and insects
Typical adaptations: Deciduous trees lose leaves, reducing winter water loss; some animals hibernate or migrate during winter.

Desert

Location: Mid-latitudes

Climate: Generally very hot days, cool nights; precipitation less than 25 cm (10 in.) per year

Soil: Poor in animal and plant decay products, but often rich in minerals

Plants: Sparse plant life, including cacti, yuccas, bunch grasses, shrubs, and a few trees

Animals: Rodents, snakes, lizards, tortoises, insects, and some birds. The Sahara in Africa is home to camels, gazelles, antelopes, small foxes, snakes, lizards, and gerbils.

Typical adaptations: Plants can store water in their stems; many animals are active at night; many avoid heat and water loss by burrowing in the ground during the day.

Grassland

Location: Mid-latitudes, interiors of continents

Climate: Cool in winter, hot in summer; 25–75 cm (10–30 in.) of precipitation per year

Soil: Rich topsoil; decay of grasses by bacteria forms a thick fertile soil.

Plants: Mostly grasses and small shrubs; some trees near sources of water

Animals: American grasslands include prairie dogs, gophers, jackrabbits, foxes, small mammals, snakes, insects, and various birds (wading birds); also grazers, such as bison and elk. African grasslands include elephants, lions, zebras, and giraffes.

Typical adaptations: Grazers have teeth for grinding grasses.

A 71

Taiga

Location: Mid-to-high-latitudes
Climate: Very cold, snowy winters; cool summers; about 50 cm (20 in.) of precipitation per year
Soil: Acidic, mineral poor, decayed pine and spruce needles on surface
Plants: Mostly conifers (spruces, pines, firs)
Animals: Rodents, snowshoe hares, lynx, sables, ermines, caribou, bears, wolves; birds in summer
Typical adaptations: Hoofed mammals have long legs for wading through deep snow; some animals have thick coats; evergreen leaves have a waxy coating to prevent water loss.

Tundra

Location: High-northern-latitudes
Climate: Very cold, harsh, and long winters; short and cool summers; 10–25 cm (4–10 in.) of precipitation per year
Soil: Nutrient poor, permafrost layer (permanently frozen soil) a few centimeters down; snow and ice cover the ground in winter.
Plants: Grasses, wildflowers, mosses, small shrubs; (Permafrost prevents large plants with deep roots from developing.)
Animals: Musk oxen, migrating caribou, arctic foxes, weasels, snowshoe hares, owls, hawks, various rodents, occasional polar bears
Typical adaptations: Caribou migrate here in winter; some animals are camouflaged with white fur or feathers.

What Biomes Can You Find on Mountains?

At the base of a mountain range, you might be in a desert or grassland. However, on the mountaintops, you can see snow and ice. Why? Remember, the higher a place is above sea level, the cooler its climate is. Moist air rising up one side of a mountain cools and drops off the moisture along the way. At the top it is frozen.

In some areas you may find tropical plants growing at the base of a mountain. Halfway up you may find pine forests. The trees end abruptly at the *timberline*. The timberline is a height above which it is too cold and dry for trees to grow. At the peaks you will find permanent ice and snow. Mountaintops have climates called

The plants of the chaparral grow no more than about 3 m (10 ft) high. They form dense thickets that people cannot easily walk through.

alpine tundra. Plant life here is close to the ground, an adaptation to survive the cold winds.

Chaparral

In the foothills of California's southern mountain ranges, you will find a special kind of ecosystem. It's a dry scrubland, called *chaparral.* The name *chaparral* refers to a thick growth of brush and small trees. Chaparral also exists in some other western states and in Mexico.

Animals here include deer, foxes, and rabbits. The plants here are mostly evergreen shrubs and small trees that can survive heat, very little water, and fire. In the fall the chaparral is tinder dry. Hundreds of acres can burn in a short time. These fires clear out dead plant matter. Nutrient-rich ash is added to the soil.

READING **Compare and Contrast**
How do biomes change as height increases along a mountainside?

Biomes change with height above sea level.

Snow and ice

Tundra

Coniferous forest

Deciduous forest

Desert or grassland

Tropical forest

What Can People Plant in Different Biomes?

Through most of human history people foraged for edible plants. At some point, either by reasoning or luck, they discovered that if they planted seeds plants would grow. Plants were domesticated and controlled to benefit people. This marked the beginning of **agriculture**. Agriculture is the science and art of cultivating soil, producing crops, and raising livestock.

You have learned that the main influences on the types of plants in an area are temperature and the availability of water. If plants were not near a source of water, people soon learned to use technology to bring water to the plants. Around 3100 B.C. the Sumerians (modern Iraqis) dug ditches and canals to bring water from the Tigris and Euphrates rivers to the land so people could grow crops. Today, farmers use Global Positioning Systems to pinpoint locations and data they can use to adjust levels of seeding, fertilization, and irrigation.

Tanzania shade-grown coffee plantation.

Tropical Rain Forest

The tropical rain forests near the equator yield crops such as sugarcane, bananas and plantains, oranges, mangoes, cacao, coffee, and rubber.

Deciduous Forest

Fruits and nuts, such as apples, pears, cherries, grapes, and walnuts, are the major crops of deciduous forests.

Because the soil is so fertile, it makes excellent farmland. However, once the trees have been cleared the soil is very vulnerable to erosion. In many areas, land that was once clear has been allowed to recover.

Desert

If you have eaten a date, you have had one of the desert's few crop plants.

Grasslands

The two types of grasslands are tropical grasslands and temperate grasslands. Together they make up about a quarter of the land on Earth. Tropical grasslands produce maize, rice, sorghum, cassava, and sweet potatoes.

Sometimes referred to as "the bread-basket of America," the American temperate grassland produces about $150 billion in crops annually. Seventy percent of the harvested crops are classified as grasses, such as wheat, corn, rice, barley, millet, sorghum, and sugar cane.

Agricultural Pests

The word *pest* is practically synonymous with "troublesome". But many animals become pests as a result of agricultural practices. When farmers raise only one plant species in a very large area, they give a tremendous advantage to the animals that feed on that plant species. This is usually accompanied by the elimination of predators. For example, insects flourish if there are no birds, and rodents prosper without carnivores. Since their food supply is increased, and their predators disappear, they become a problem to agriculture.

Monoculture, or the raising of one plant species, is also risky. If a farmer raises only one species that is susceptible to a particular pest, the entire crop can be wiped out. If the farmer had another species that was not susceptible to the same pest, the entire crop would not be destroyed.

For many years farmers relied on poisons, such as DDT, to eliminate plant-eating pests. Fortunately, we have learned how dangerous these chemicals are to the environment. Since then farmers, working with biologists and ecologists, have developed alternatives.

Lubber grasshopper from Florida.

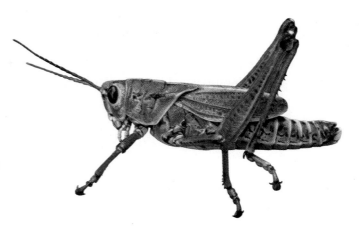

The most widely supported approach is Integrated Pest Management. This approach offers ways to manage pests and minimize environmental, health, and economic risks. It may involve using natural means for pest control and reserving pesticides for emergency situations only.

Plant diversity again plays an important role here. Different crops attract different insects or predators that feed on agricultural pests. An interesting example of this is seen in coffee-growing countries. Coffee growers who leave much of the natural forest to shade their plants are habitat havens for migratory songbirds, which feed on insects.

▷ **What can be planted in the area where you live?**

Inquiry Skill
BUILDER

What can you plant where you live?

In this activity you use information from a Plant Hardiness Zone Map and a table to help you select what you can plant where you live.

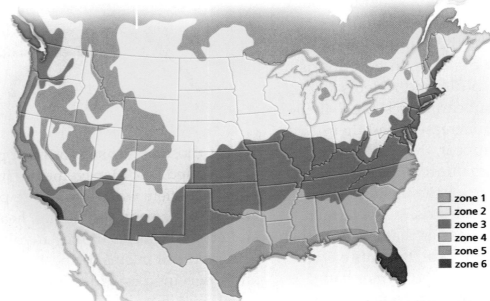

▨	zone 1
☐	zone 2
▨	zone 3
▨	zone 4
▨	zone 5
▨	zone 6

Procedure

1 A Plant Hardiness Zone Map shows places of similar climates and vegetation. Study the map above.

2 Examine the table which gives the northern limit to which some plants can live. Use the map and the table to answer the questions.

Drawing Conclusions

1 In which zone do you live?

2 Which zone crosses the most states?

3 **Infer** Could people living in Ontario grow azaleas in their yards?

4 **Infer** Could you grow Chinese holly in Oklahoma?

5 How do you use a Plant Hardiness Zone Map?

Plant	Northern Zone Limit
White pine	2
Forsythia	2
American cranberry bush	1
Rhododendron	2
Azalea	3
Pyracantha	4
Chinese holly	3
Bougainvillea	5 & 6
American holly	2
Passion flower	5 & 6

L·I·N·K·S

Why It Matters

Biomes around the world differ in the amount of sunlight and precipitation they receive and in their temperatures.

The biome where you are determines the plants, animals, and other living organisms that can survive in that place. It also determines the kinds of crops that people can plant, and the kinds of animals that people can raise.

Just as plants and animals have adapted to different biomes, people have adapted their lifestyles to the biome where they live.

e-Journal Visit our Web site www.science.mmhschool.com to do a research project on the biome where you live.

Think and Write

1. Why do climates differ around the world?

2. What biomes can you find in Africa?

3. Pick any two biomes. Describe how they differ.

4. What can people plant in the desert biome?

5. **Critical Thinking** Why does the tropical rain forest support the greatest diversity of life found in the six biomes?

WRITING LINK

Writing a Story What kind of biome would you use to create a strong plot for a story? For example, you could use the desert or the tundra to build a plot that focuses on how a character struggles against this biome in order to survive. In your story use information about this particular biome, including its location, climate, soil, plants, and animals.

MATH LINK

Make a bar graph. Compare the amount of rainfall in the six different biomes. Use data from pages A70–A72. Use two bars if needed to show greatest and least amounts. What does your graph help you understand?

LITERATURE LINK

Read *Tropical Rain Forests* to learn about what kids are doing to save the forest. Make your own plan to save the rain forests, and put it into action.

TECHNOLOGY LINK

LOG ON Visit www.science.mmhschool.com for more links.

Straddling Worlds

Imagine living in a place where waves continually pound you, a place that is dry one minute and submerged the next. That's what it's like for the creatures of the tidal zone. Within each distinct area, animals and plants are able to adapt and survive.

THE LOW-TIDE ZONE
Sea urchins dig holes in the rocks to assure that even at low tide, water will fill their homes. Sea urchins graze on algae. They scrape algae off surfaces with teeth around their mouth.

THE MIDTIDE ZONE
The spiny starfish, or sea star, uses its suction-cup feet to stay put even when the waves are rough. To eat, this animal sticks its feet to either side of a mussel shell, pries it open, inserts its own stomach, and digests the mussel!

THE HIGH-TIDE ZONE
The barnacle has a hard shell to bear the crushing weight of pounding surf. It also has a gluey substance on its head. It sticks to rocks so it won't wash away. To eat, a barnacle kicks its featherlike feet into the water and moves plankton into its shell.

THE SPLASH ZONE
Animals in the splash zone don't get as much moisture as animals in other zones. Periwinkle snails scrape algae off splash-zone rocks with their sharp tongues. However, a dogwinkle snail can drill through a periwinkle's shell and eat the animal inside!

Write ABOUT IT

What makes survival difficult for animals and plants in the tidal zone?

How have animals adapted to life in the tidal zone?

LOG ON Visit www.science.mmhschool.com to learn more about tidal zones.

LESSON

6

Ecosystems and Interactions

Vocabulary

ecosystem, p. A82

niche, p. A82

population, p. A82

community, p. A82

biodiversity, p. A84

Get Ready

Sea otters live in "forests" of giant seaweed, called kelp, in the Pacific Ocean off the coast of California. This sea otter is eating one of its favorite foods— abalone. What kind of ecosystem is this? Do the same kinds of plants and animals live in your area? Why or why not?

Inquiry Skill

You **measure** when you find the size, volume, area, mass, weight, or temperature of an object, or how long an event occurs.

A 80

Explore Activity

How Can You Measure an Ecosystem?

Materials
trowel or spade
meterstick
4 wooden pegs
string
thermometer

Procedure

1 As a class with your teacher, select an area on or near school grounds to study. Mark off a 2 m-by-2 m square plot with pegs and string.

2 **Measure** Collect data about your area. Measure the air temperature at ground level. Measure it also at 1 m above ground level.

3 **Measure** Dig a narrow hole about 30 cm deep. Measure the soil temperature of loosened soil at the bottom.

4 Find the depth at which the soil becomes moist.

5 **Observe** Note any living things in and around your plot.

6 Repeat your measurements each day for at least two weeks. You can continue through the year.

Draw Conclusions

1 **Communicate** Graph your temperatures and soil moisture information. Describe how the measurements change over time.

2 **FURTHER INQUIRY** **Infer** How do these conditions make it possible for living things to survive in this ecosystem?

How Are Organisms Organized?

You've learned what biotic and abiotic factors are. Biotic and abiotic factors, together with their interactions, make up an **ecosystem**.

Each kind of living thing, each species, has a role in the ecosystem. This role is called a **niche** (NICH). The niche includes what an organism eats, where it lives, and the way it raises its young. It includes whether a species is active in daytime or at night.

All the organisms of the same kind living in a particular place make up a **population**. The size of the population and its location may be large or small. A group of billions of bacterial cells found in a single puddle and hundreds of giraffes roaming an African grassland are both populations. All the populations living together in the same place make up a **community**.

Within a community, populations interact in different ways.

Competition Populations can share the same habitat, or home, but they cannot share the same niche for very long. This is why populations compete. Those populations with adaptations that make them better at a job will survive, reproduce, and eventually crowd out populations that are not as well suited.

Mutualism All living things behave in ways that increase their chances for survival. When a behavior is helpful to two populations, it is called mutualism. For example, many plants can grow only with the help of fungi that form on their roots. In turn, the fungi benefit from the products of photosynthesis. Both the plant and the fungi benefit in this mutualistic relationship.

Parasitism Parasitism is a relationship in which only one organism benefits while the other is harmed.

No two kinds of animals in the picture meet their needs in exactly the same way.

The Nitrogen Cycle

Air is made up of about 79 percent nitrogen gas.

Denitrifying bacteria turn nitrites in dead plants and animals into nitrogen gas.

Nitrogen-fixing bacteria turn nitrogen into substances plants can use.

Animals use nitrogen in plants to make proteins.

All living things use abiotic factors to survive. Abiotic factors include soil, water, and air. If every living thing uses these factors, how is it that we never run out? Many of the abiotic factors are constantly cycled through nature.

The Water Cycle Earth has a limited supply of water. This water is constantly cycled from the surface of Earth, through the atmosphere, and back through the main processes of precipitation, evaporation, and condensation.

The Oxygen-Carbon Dioxide Cycle Breathe in, breathe out—now you're part of the oxygen-carbon dioxide cycle! Oxygen and carbon dioxide are cycled through the environment by the processes of respiration and photosynthesis. Animals use oxygen and give off carbon dioxide during respiration. During photosynthesis, plants take in carbon dioxide and give off oxygen.

The Nitrogen Cycle All life requires nitrogen to make proteins. Although air is about 79 percent nitrogen, it is not in a form usable by plants and animals. The nitrogen must be "fixed," or made into usable nitrogen compounds. Nitrogen-fixing bacteria can do this. Living things then use these nitrogen compounds. When they die, bacteria break down the compounds and nitrogen gas is returned to the air.

The biotic and abiotic factors in an ecosystem determine the size of each population. If a drought reduces the vegetation in an area, then the deer population will decrease due to a lack of food. What do you think will happen to the coyote population in that area?

▶ **How do organisms interact with other things in their environment?**

How Do Organisms Interact?

The classification of life is continually changing as we find or learn about more species through greater research. Scientists estimate that there are between 5 million and 50 million species on Earth. However, fewer than 2 million species have been identified and named so far. This wide variety of life on Earth is **biodiversity**.

You have learned how the diversity of life is tied together through a system of classification. Each species has its own characteristics—its structures and behaviors for carrying out its daily activities.

Each species plays a part in all the kingdoms of life on Earth as a whole. Green plants convert a part of the Sun's energy into a form that is usable by other living organisms. They are Earth's primary producers. Animals that eat plants are primary consumers. Secondary consumers eat the plant-eaters. Each time something is eaten, food energy passes from one living thing to another. However, at each level some of the energy is lost.

An easy way to visualize this is with an energy pyramid. It shows you that the greatest amount of energy is found at the bottom of the pyramid, or among the primary producers. At each successive level, energy is lost and there is less food.

Some organisms get their food by breaking down dead organisms into nutrients. They are called decomposers. The energy is passed from the dead organism to the organism breaking it down.

READING **Draw Conclusions**
Why is the interaction of species important?

This energy pyramid shows the energy available at each level.

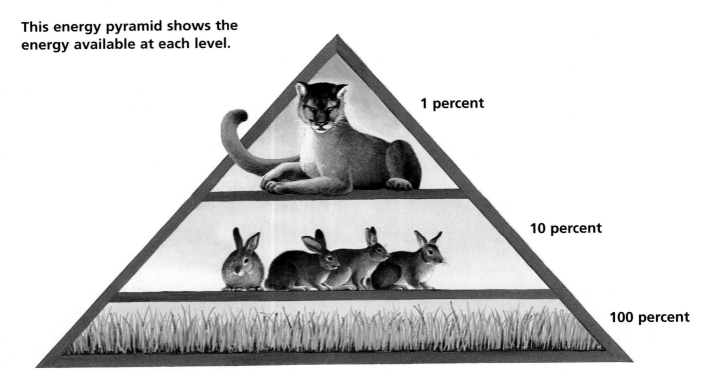

1 percent

10 percent

100 percent

What Is a Food Chain?

In every ecosystem there is a feeding relationship between the organisms. A food chain is a model of how the energy in food is passed from organism to organism in an ecosystem. Each organism is like a link in a *food chain*.

Plants are usually the producers in a food chain. A producer, or its seeds, is always at the beginning of a food chain. This means that energy flows through an ecosystem in one direction from the sun, through the primary producers, consumers, and decomposers.

As you move up the food chain you begin to see examples of predator/prey relationships. Primary consumers are plant-eaters, or herbivores. After that, consumers may be predator or prey depending on where they are in a particular food chain.

Decomposers are organisms that get their food by breaking down dead organisms into nutrients. The energy is passed from the dead organism to the organism breaking it down.

These feeding relationships are what help keep nature in balance. The biotic and abiotic factors in an ecosystem determine the size of each population. If a drought reduces the vegetation in an area, then the deer population will decrease due to a lack of food. What do you think will happen to the coyote population in that area?

▶ **How do organisms interact in a food chain?**

READING
Diagrams

What is the path of energy in this forest food chain?

Forest Food Chain

Third level consumer (eats animals)

Energy

Second level consumer (eats animals)

First level consumer (eats plants)

Decomposers

A 85

What Is a Food Web?

Nature is never quite so simple as a straight food chain. Most food chains are interconnected. Just as you don't eat the same thing every day, most animals have a varied diet. A predator one day can make a great meal for a variety of other animals the next.

Overlapping food chains combine into food webs. In a food web you see that a particular kind of animal can be a source of food for many other animals. Energy flow in a food web still begins with primary producers and moves through the various levels of consumers, just as it does in a food chain.

How do you think humans fit into a food web? As early hunter-gatherers we pretty much fit right in with other organisms as primary consumers of green plants. Humans were also predators and, at times, prey for larger animals.

When humans shifted from hunting and gathering to farming they became the first and only species to control their own food supply. While these practices have been beneficial, they do have consequences. Chemical insecticides and fertilizers flow through the ecosystem. Plants and animals grown in closed areas are more vulnerable to the spread of disease. Antibiotics used to control diseases become part of our food chain. As you can see, it is important for humans to consider the risks and benefits of their actions and seek safer alternatives.

▷ **How are food chains interconnected?**

What Lives in Salt Water?

Oceans contain nutrients that support a wide variety of life. Life forms differ from the shore, where the tide comes in and goes out, to deeper waters. In the shallow waters along the continental shelf (neritic zone) to the open ocean zone, life forms differ at greater depths, where there is less and less sunlight. Sunlight does not reach beyond 200 m (600 ft). Animals there feed on each other and materials that sink down from the lighted waters.

▷ **What factors affect life in the oceans?**

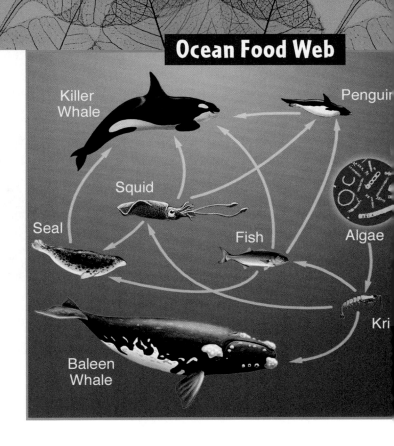

Ocean Food Web

Killer Whale
Penguin
Squid
Seal
Fish
Algae
Krill
Baleen Whale

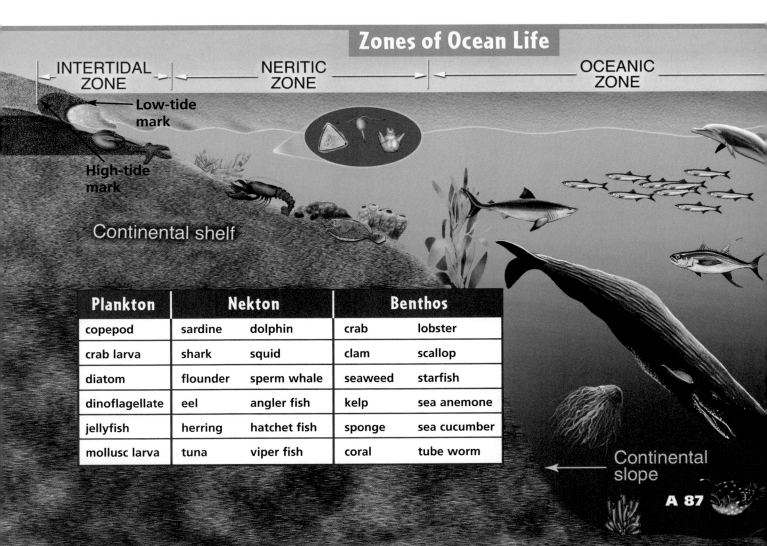

Zones of Ocean Life

INTERTIDAL ZONE — NERITIC ZONE — OCEANIC ZONE

Low-tide mark
High-tide mark
Continental shelf
Continental slope

Plankton	Nekton		Benthos	
copepod	sardine	dolphin	crab	lobster
crab larva	shark	squid	clam	scallop
diatom	flounder	sperm whale	seaweed	starfish
dinoflagellate	eel	angler fish	kelp	sea anemone
jellyfish	herring	hatchet fish	sponge	sea cucumber
mollusc larva	tuna	viper fish	coral	tube worm

Plants and microscopic algae make up the producers of food webs in water ecosystems.

What Are Freshwater Ecosystems Like?

On land ecosystems differ in their temperature, soil, the amount of light, and the amount of available oxygen and food. Soil is not a factor in water ecosystems. However, the other conditions still apply. They help determine the kinds of living things that can survive in a particular body of water.

Another factor in water ecosystems is salt. Oceans and seas have salt water. Lakes, streams, rivers, ponds, and certain marshes, swamps, and bogs tend to have little salt in them. They are freshwater ecosystems.

In fresh or salt water, living things are of three general groups. *Plankton* (PLANGK·tuhn) are organisms that float on water. These include microscopic algae and protozoa. *Nekton* (NEK·tahn) are animals that swim through water. *Benthos* (BEN·thahs) are bottom dwellers.

Ponds, Lakes, Rivers

Food chains and food webs in ponds, lakes, and streams are made of members of all three groups. Close to the shore, you will find many plants. Wading, you might get your feet caught in cattails, bur reeds, or arrowheads. You may spot some frogs, turtles, crayfish. Farther out you will find plankton as well as large trout or other game fish. At the bottom aquatic worms may be burrowing in the mud.

Along with the shore plants, many of the plankton are producers for food webs. They are eaten by small fish, insects, and other small animals. They, in turn, are eaten by larger fish, as well as birds and animals that visit the shore.

Wetlands

Wetlands are a mix of land and water ecosystems in one area. The water level is often at or above ground. Types of wetlands include marshes, swamps, bogs, and fens. These areas support a tremendous diversity of organisms, which are vital parts of the food web. Wetlands are also important for flood control, storm protection, water quality, as well as recreation and tourism.

Estuaries

Along coasts, where rivers flow into seas, water ecosystems are a blend of salt and fresh water. These ecosystems are estuaries. Rivers bring fresh water into estuaries. However, tides can bring in salt water from the sea. The wide variety of plants and animals that live here have adaptations to survive these changes in saltiness. Oysters, for example, close their shells during harmful changes in saltiness until conditions improve.

▶ **What factors affect life in water ecosystems?**

Chesapeake Bay is an estuary with a wide variety of plankton producers. Consumers include fish, shellfish, and shrimplike copepods.

QUICK LAB

Freshwater Food Chains

FOLDABLES™ Make a Folded Table. (See p. R44.) Label the table as shown.

Fresh water	Observation Sketch	Inferences
Sample #1		
Sample #2		
Sample #3		

1. **Obtain** samples of fresh water from a pond, lake, or stream. You can also use water from a freshwater aquarium or terrarium. Do not wade into fresh water on your own to collect samples. Have an adult do this.

2. **Observe** Place a drop of your sample on a microscope slide. Carefully drop a coverslip over it. Examine the slide under low power. Use high power with your teacher's help.

3. **Communicate** Draw the organisms that you see on your Folded Table. Use colored pencils to show differences.

4. **Infer** Can you tell which organisms are producers? Explain on your Folded Table.

5. **Infer** Can you identify any consumers? Explain on your Folded Table.

What Happens When Ecosystems Change?

In 10,000 B.C., around the time that agriculture began, the human population was 5-10 million. During the Industrial Revolution, which began in 1750, the population reached 1 billion. With the Industrial Revolution came advancements, which increased life expectancy. In a few hundred years our population grew to over 6 billion people!

Breakthroughs in science and technology occur at such phenomenal rates today that we no longer find them amazing, just routine. Life spans lengthen and the population grows. World population is expected to double in the next 49 years.

Numbers really mean nothing compared to the impact that humans have on their environment. Industrialized nations, such as the United States, consume far greater resources than developing countries. Americans make up only 5 percent of the world's population but account for 26 percent of global energy consumption.

Earth has the capabilities to recover from natural disasters, such as fire, flood, volcanic eruption, or drought. Indeed, these events often replenish soils with rich nutrients and new communities emerge.

However, as humans demand more space and resources it leaves less for the other species that make our survival possible. Numerous plants and animals become extinct every year due to loss of habitat.

We depend on the diversity of plant and animal species for many things—food, medicine, and shelter. The cycles in nature that provide clean water, breathable air, and the nutrients we need are interconnected with a variety of species. To preserve these things we all need to exercise the 3 Rs of conservation: reduce, reuse, and recycle.

▷ **Why did the Industrial Revolution cause the population to increase?**

Patches of clear cut mountain.

Startling Statistics in the United States over the last 200 years:	
71%	of our topsoil has been lost
50%	of our wetlands have been lost
99%	of our tall grass prairies have been lost
40%	of our surface waters are unfit for fishing or swimming

Why It Matters

Balance is critical to the survival of Earth's ecosystems. Throughout the ages Earth and its inhabitants have managed to interact and sustain the balance necessary for life. However, it seems that the more humans advance, the greater the impact on nature. Now we must use our intelligence for our greatest achievement ever, protecting our planet.

 e-Journal Visit our Web site www.science.mmhschool.com to do a research project on the effects of the industrial revolution on water ecosystems.

Think and Write

1. How are living and nonliving things alike? How are they different?

2. What is one effect of deforestation?

3. How are you part of the oxygen-carbon dioxide cycle?

4. Give some examples of a population.

5. **Critical Thinking** How would a decrease in a meadow's mouse population affect the hawk population?

L·I·N·K·S

WRITING LINK

Persuasive Writing Research an issue that is affecting Earth's ecosystems. Then write and record a public-service announcement to state your position on the issue. Include information about the issue, its impact on the environment, and what people can do to solve the problem. Use strong reasons to persuade your audience to agree with your argument.

LITERATURE LINK

Read *Jacques Cousteau: A Modern Hero.*
Explore the life of the world famous undersea explorer and crusader for saving our seas. Try the activities at the end of the book.

MATH LINK

Make a bar graph. Research population growth and make a graph of your data. Plot the years on the x-axis and the number of people on the y-axis.

TECHNOLOGY LINK

LOG ON Visit www.science.mmhschool.com for more links.

Chapter 2 Review

Vocabulary

Fill each blank with the best word or words from the list.

> **abiotic factors,** A68
> **biodiversity,** A84
> **biome,** A69
> **biomes,** A69
> **biotic factors,** A68
> **climate,** A68
> **community,** A82
> **ecosystem,** A83
> **niche,** A82
> **population,** A82

1. A _____ is made up of all the organisms of the same kind living in a particular place.

2. A tundra is an example of a(n) _____.

3. Living things are also called _____.

4. A(n) _____ is made of the interactions of biotic and abiotic factors in their environment.

5. The wide variety of life on Earth is _____.

6. Nonliving things, such as water and air, are types of _____.

7. The role of each species in the ecosystem is its _____.

8. Large land regions with given climates are called _____.

9. The pattern of precipitation and temperatures throughout a year is the _____.

10. All the populations together make up a(n) _____.

Test Prep

11. A relation between populations that is helpful to organisms of the two populations is called

A mutualism.

B competition.

C parasitism.

D reproduction.

12. What is the order of organization in an ecosystem from simple to complex?

F population, community, ecosystem

G ecosystem, community, population

H community, population, ecosystem

J ecosystem, population, community

13. The higher a place is above the sea level, _____.

A the warmer the climate is

B the higher the vegetation is

C the cooler the climate is

D the lower the precipitation is

14. Which of the following is NOT a reason why climates differ around the world?

   F wind

   G animals

   H land barriers

   J distance from the equator

15. What is the role of bacteria in the nitrogen cycle?

   A Making oxygen from nitrogen.

   B Adding nitrogen to the atmosphere.

   C Making excess nitrogen from oxygen.

   D Fixing nitrogen into compounds living things can use.

Concepts and Skills

16. **Reading in Science** How does energy move up an energy pyramid? Explain the role of the different organisms you include.

17. **Critical Thinking** Fertilizers that contain nitrogen are often added to plants to help them grow. What step in the nitrogen cycle is being bypassed by adding fertilizers?

18. **INQUIRY SKILL** **Define** What does the word *cycle* mean and how is it related to water, carbon, and nitrogen?

19. **Decision Making** Imagine you live near a river. You want to build a raft using the branches of trees in which birds are nesting. What would you do? How does you decision affect other organisms in the environment?

20. **Scientific Methods** Ecologists count and tag members of a population of organisms, such as giraffes, to learn how populations grow and change. What does the health of one population tell you about the health of other populations and the ecosystem in general?

Did You Ever Wonder?

INQUIRY SKILL **Make a Model** Choose an ecosystem and draw or cut at least 20 pictures of different organisms that belong in that ecosystem. Make sure you include organisms from the plant, animal, fungi, protist, and bacteria kingdoms. Make cards with the drawings or pictures and organize the cards to show a food web.

LOG ON Visit www.science.mmhschool.com to boost your test scores.

Sharon Matola

Conservationist

"From the time I can remember, I always had some creature I had made friends with. I always felt we could communicate with animals," Sharon Matola says.

Today, Matola spends a lot of time communicating with animals. She started up the Belize Zoo. Belize is a country in Central America, and the zoo is one of its most important conservation groups. The zoo houses 125 animals native to Belize, including many endangered species, such as jaguars, crocodiles, and scarlet macaws.

While growing up near Baltimore, Maryland, Matola wanted to be a veterinarian. In college, she began to be concerned about threats to natural environments. Instead of caring for animals as a vet, she wanted to find a way to care for them in their natural habitats.

LOG ON Visit **www.science.mmhschool.com** to learn more about conservationists.

The zoo began almost by accident. In 1983, Matola worked on a TV documentary about the wild animals of Belize. When the filming was over, Matola stayed in Belize, where she decided to build a zoo in her backyard. Today the modern zoo is located on 29 acres in the Belize rain forest.

As at most zoos, much of the work of the Belize Zoo helps protect endangered species and their habitat. Matola's pet project: breeding and releasing endangered harpy eagles. At the zoo, eaglets are hatched. When they are ready to be on their own, they are released into the wild. Matola says this will help bring the eagles back from the brink of extinction.

Matola hopes that there are children who want to help animals. "If you feel that attachment to animals in your bones, there's a job out there for someone like you."

Matola observes a harpy eagle in Belize.

TOP 5 Animals Native to Belize

As a conservationist, Sharon Matola gets to work with many animals that live in Belize. Here are some of them.

1. Jaguar

2. Ocelot

3. Tapir

4. Coatimundi

5. Margay

Write About It

1. Why did Sharon Matola decide to become a conservationist instead of a vet?

2. If you were a conservationist, what animal would you like to help save? Why?

KINGDOMS OF Life

Your goal is to make a chart that shows kingdoms of living things.

What to Do

1. Create a chart that shows how living things are organized. Use three columns and six rows.

2. In the boxes in the Kingdom column, list the six kingdoms of living things.

3. In the Description column, describe the characteristics that members of each kingdom have.

4. Provide two or more examples of each kingdom in the Examples column. Draw or glue magazine pictures of your examples in the boxes next to the organisms.

Analyze Your Results

1. The kingdom is the broadest level of classification. What are the other levels of organization used to classify living things?

2. What are two main classifications of plants? Give an example of a plant of each type.

Ecosystem Invention

Your goal is to make a model of an ecosystem.

What to Do

1. Invent the parts of an ecosystem. Use clay and other art supplies your teacher has provided. Make sure your model includes biotic and abiotic factors. Think about the relationships among them.

Analyze Your Results

1. What is the definition of an ecosystem? Does your model fit the definition? Explain.

2. Look at the following list. What part of your model represents each element of the ecosystem?

- Producers
- Competition
- Consumers
- Decomposers
- Energy
- Habitat
- Mutualism
- Parasitism

UNIT B

Organization of Living Things

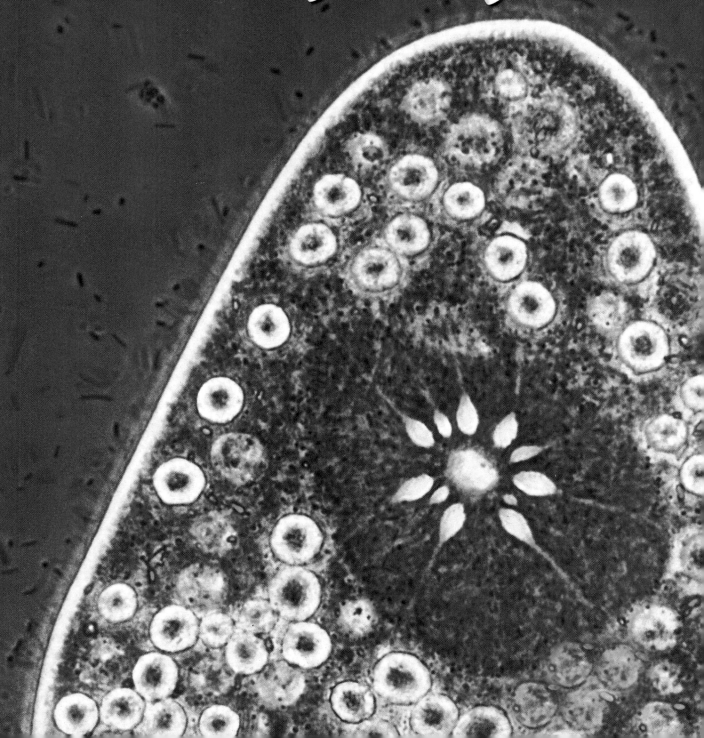

LOOK!

Millions of one-celled animals live in a freshwater lake. What life activities do they perform to survive?

Organization of Living Things

From Cells to Organisms

Did You Ever Wonder?

Where do frogs come from? Like all animals, every frog starts life as a single cell—an egg. In this photo, you can see tiny rain frogs inside the clear eggs. Where did these frogs come from?

INQUIRY SKILL **Hypothesize** How can a single egg cell develop into a full-grown animal with millions of body cells?

B 3

Structure of Living Things

Vocabulary

cell, B7

tissue, B10

organ, B11

organ system, B12

organism, B12

Get Ready

How can you tell a living thing from a nonliving thing? What do all living things have in common? What do they all do?

Do all living things move, for example? Compare a jet and a bird. How can you tell which is living and which is not? Can you tell whether something is or was alive by looking at it under a microscope? Is there some special characteristic that allows you to tell?

Inquiry Skill

You **classify** when you place materials that share properties together in groups.

Explore Activity

What Makes Up a Living Thing?

Procedure: Design Your Own

1 **Observe** Look at samples under a microscope. For example, try placing a few grains of salt on a microscope slide. Do not add a coverslip. Observe under low power. Draw what you see.

2 Design your own data table for recording the details of what you observe.

3 **Experiment** Repeat steps 1–2 with sand.

4 **Observe** Select your own samples. Repeat steps 1–2 using low power, and draw what you see. Use such samples as a wet-mount slide of a small piece of tomato skin, an *Elodea* leaf, a drop of yeast on a clean microscope slide with a coverslip over it, a prepared slide of human blood, and a wet-mount slide of a thin piece of cork.

Drawing Conclusions

1 **Observe** Describe the appearance of each of the specimens you observed.

2 **Classify** Classify the specimens you observed into two groups.

3 **Interpret Data** What is the greatest difference between these two groups?

4 **FURTHER INQUIRY** **Classify** Find at least two more examples that fit into each group. Why do these specimens fit into the groups that you have chosen?

Materials

microscope

6 microscope slides

microscope coverslip

dropper

water

toothpick

salt

sand

tomato skin

Elodea leaf

yeast

prepared slide of human blood

thin piece of cork

Main Idea Living things are made up of cells organized into tissues, which work together as organs.

What Do All Living Things Do?

Why do all living things need food? They need raw materials and energy to live and grow. They need the right temperatures in their surroundings. They meet their needs by carrying out certain activities.

Activities of Living Things

- **Nutrition** This is the intake and use of food by living things. All living things need food. Food provides the raw materials and energy for growth, repair, and other activities of living things.

- **Respiration** After food is digested, it combines with oxygen, and energy is released. Respiration is the process by which energy is released from food. This process produces wastes. When you exhale, you give off two waste products—water and carbon dioxide.

- **Excretion** Wastes from respiration and other activities can build up in your body. Some wastes are poisons. Fortunately, living things can remove such wastes. The removal of wastes produced by living things is called excretion.

- **Response and Movement** Living things respond, or react, to changes in their surroundings. For example, when you are cold, your body responds by shivering, which helps to warm you. Another type of response is movement. If you are outside and it starts to rain, you may run inside. Animal responses to stimuli are the animal's behavior. Plants also respond to their surroundings by moving. They slowly bend toward the sunlight.

- **Growth** All living things grow. To grow means to either increase in size or increase in the amount of material contained.

- **Reproduction** The process by which living things produce offspring is called reproduction. Reproduction allows each kind of living thing to exist on Earth for a long period of time.

 **What activities are common to all living things?**

When you eat, you take in raw materials and energy needed to live and grow.

What Are Cells?

Are living things made of elements just as nonliving things are? Living things are made of elements such as carbon, hydrogen, and oxygen. In addition, living things are organized into units or parts that make up the living things.

Life activities are carried out in the smallest part of a living thing. This basic unit of life is called a **cell** . All living things are made up of cells. Some living things are made up of only one cell. As you might guess, you'd need a microscope to see them. Many-celled living things, such as complex plants and animals, are made up of different kinds of cells, each with its own special function.

Plants and animals have cells that to a great extent have the same parts. However, there are important differences between them. Plant cells have a stiff outer covering, whereas animal cells do not. This covering helps a plant to stand upright. Many plant cells also contain a green substance that traps the energy of sunlight and enables the cells to produce their own food.

READING **Compare and Contrast**
How do cells differ?

Animals are many-celled living things. This is a cell from an animal.

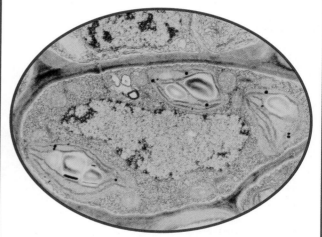

Plants are many-celled living things. This is a cell from a plant.

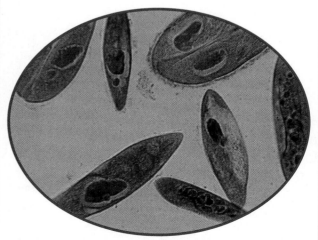

Bacteria, paramecia, and euglena carry out all of life's functions in a single cell.

How Were Cells Discovered?

Who was the first person to see cells? The first cells were seen in 1665 by Robert Hooke, an English scientist. He looked at cork under a microscope and saw little "boxes" that looked like the "cells" of a honeycomb. The invention of the microscope in the early 17th century enabled scientists such as Hooke to begin their exploration of the microscopic world. Although the cork cells that Hooke observed were not living, techniques were later developed to view live cells.

Since Hooke's first observation of cells, improved microscopes have allowed us to make cells appear to be hundreds or thousands of times their actual size. This allows us to examine and study the cells. It was not until the work of Anton van Leeuwenhoek (LAY·vuhn·hook), beginning in 1673, that a new world of one-celled living things was opened up. Leeuwenhoek was the first to observe one-celled living things such as bacteria and paramecia.

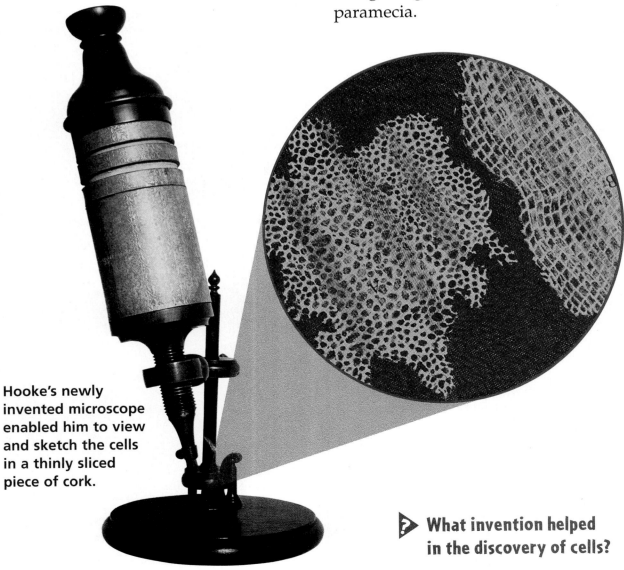

Hooke's newly invented microscope enabled him to view and sketch the cells in a thinly sliced piece of cork.

▷ **What invention helped in the discovery of cells?**

What Types of Cells Are You Made Up Of?

If you looked at cells under a microscope, would the size and shape tell you anything about the size of the living things from which they came? Although a human is much larger than a tomato or *Elodea* plant, the cells are about the same size.

Shapes of cells may give us a clue about the function of a particular cell. A human red blood cell is about one-tenth the size of the dot on this *i*. Its small size and flexibility allow it to pass through tiny blood vessels. A nerve cell in your leg may be up to a meter in length. Its long shape enables it to send messages through your body.

▷ **How do the size and shape of the different types of cells determine their function?**

Body Cells

There are about ten trillion cells in the human body.

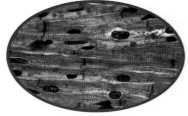

Cells in the wall of the human heart relay impulses to keep it pumping.

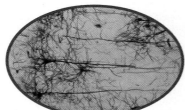

Human nerve cells

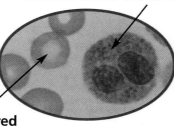

Human skin cells are flat and wide to protect the cells beneath them.

Human white blood cell

Human red blood cell

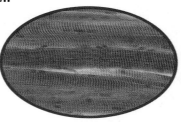

Human muscle cells work together to let you move.

READING
Charts

1. How many cells are in the human body?
2. What do skin cells look like?

What Are Tissues?

What discoveries were made because of improvements in microscopes in the 18th and 19th centuries? Scientists were further able to observe the structure and organization of cells. One-celled living things were found to carry out all of life's functions. In the 1820s a French biologist named René Dutrochet examined parts of animals and plants and concluded that the various parts of living things are made up of groups of cells.

In many-celled living things, cells do not work alone. They work in groups called **tissues**. A tissue is a group of similar cells working together performing the same function. Human tissues are composed of four main groups:

- *Epithelial tissue*, such as the cells that line your cheek, protects, lines, and absorbs.

- Cells in *nerve tissue* transport messages through the body.

- *Muscle tissue* is made up of cells that contract, moving bones and moving substances through the body.

- Bone, cartilage, tendons, fat, and even blood are all *connective tissue*, which supports the body.

Plants, too, have many different kinds of cells in their stems, roots, and leaves. The tissues in any part work together to transport food and water throughout the plant.

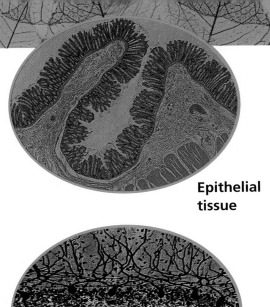

Epithelial tissue

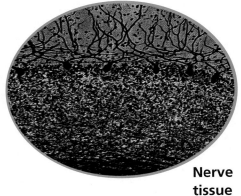

Nerve tissue

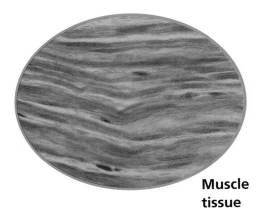

Muscle tissue

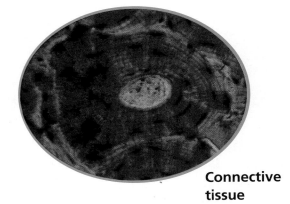

Connective tissue

The four types of plant tissues are:

- *Dermal* tissue covers the plant body much like animal epithelial tissue.

- *Vascular* tissue transports water, food, and other substances throughout the plant.

- *Ground* tissue is in charge of photosynthesis and storage.

- *Meristematic* tissue is where the new plants' cells are made.

Groups of different tissues called **organs** work together to carry out certain activities. Your heart, which is made up of muscle and nerve tissue, is an example of an organ. Other examples of animal organs are the eyes, the brain, and the lungs. These organs are all made to carry out a particular function.

The main plant organs are stems, leaves, and roots. The stems give the plant support and transport substances to and from the leaves and the roots. The leaves are the organs where photosynthesis takes place. The roots absorb nutrients and anchor the plant to the soil.

▶ **What are the four main types of tissues in plants and animals?**

QUICK LAB

A Model of Organization

FOLDABLES™
Make a Folded Table. (See p. R 44.) Label it as shown.

Does Show	Does Not Show

1. **Make a Model** Pile ten red, ten black, ten white, and ten blue buttons next to a sheet of paper. Let each button of the same color represent one kind of cell.

2. **How would you represent a tissue? How would you model an organ with three tissues?**

3. **How would you represent an organ system made of four organs, with each organ containing three tissues?**

4. **What are some things your model does not show? What does it show? Record your answers on your Folded Table.**

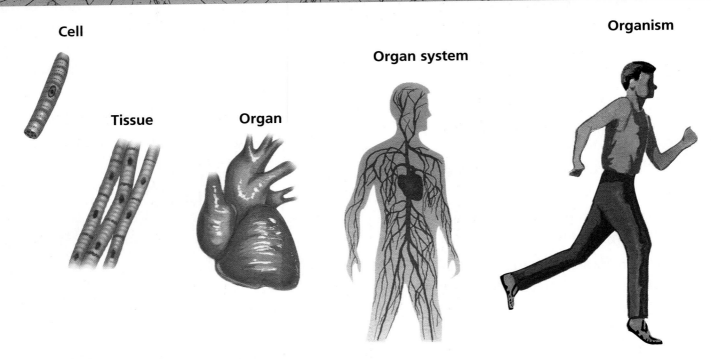

Cell

Tissue

Organ

Organ system

Organism

What Do Organ Systems Form?

Different organs are arranged into **organ systems** . These systems have specific functions and interact with each other in a variety of ways.

For example, your circulatory system delivers blood cells to and from the different parts of your body. As blood cells pass through the tissues of the lungs, a part of your respiratory system, exchange of oxygen and other gases takes place. Once the oxygen is transported to the cells of the body, it is used for growth and repair.

An example of a plant system is the shoot system. The shoot system is made of the stem, leaves, and flowers in angiosperms or cones in gymnosperms. This system is in charge of support, photosynthesis, reproduction, and transport of water to the leaves and sugars to the root.

All the organ systems together make up an **organism** . An organism is any living thing that can carry out its life activities on its own. Many-celled organisms are organized as cells, tissues, organs, and organ systems. But one-celled living things, such as paramecia and bacteria, are organisms, too. They carry out all their life activities in just one cell.

Shoot system

Root system

▷ **What is the organization of a many-celled organism's tissues?**

Why It Matters

Living things are organized internally from cells to tissues to organs to organ systems. Organ systems depend on each other to carry out life activities. For example, the circulatory system depends on the nutrients supplied by the digestive system to function.

Understanding the levels of organization of living things has helped people treat medical ailments.

e-Journal Visit our Web site **www.science.mmhschool.com** to do a research project on levels of organization in living organisms.

Think and Write

1. How are living and nonliving things alike? How are they different?

2. Why do cells in a many-celled organism differ?

3. How are living things put together?

4. Give some examples of the kinds of cells that make up your body.

5. **Critical Thinking** What if divers find a rock-like object on the sea floor? How would they decide if it is a living thing?

L·I·N·K·S

MATH LINK

Write a fraction as a decimal and as a percent. Animal cells can be as small as $\frac{1}{1000}$ of a millimeter. Write this number as a decimal and as a percent.

WRITING LINK

Expository Writing
The heart is an important organ in the human body. In an essay, explain the function of the heart. Include how the heart interacts with other organs. Use more than one source for your research. Develop your main idea with facts and details.

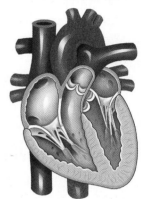

HEALTH LINK

Research the function of an organ system. Use encyclopedias, the Internet, and other resources to learn about the function of an organ system in your body. What happens if this organ system does not work properly?

TECHNOLOGY LINK

 LOG ON Visit **www.science.mmhschool.com** for more links.

History of Science

Small Steps, Giant Leaps

For thousands of years, scientists didn't know about the existence of a whole world of living things. Then along came the microscope, and it changed scientists' outlook on life!

Dutch scientist Anton van Leeuwenhoek improves lens technology. He describes cells in greater detail.

German scientists Matthias Schleiden and Theodor Schwann both recognize and state that all living things are made of cells.

| **1665** | **1670s** | **1831** | **1838–1839** |

English scientist Robert Hooke studies slices of cork through an early microscope. The cork seems to be made of little boxes, so he calls them cells.

Scottish scientist Robert Brown discovers the nucleus in plant cells.

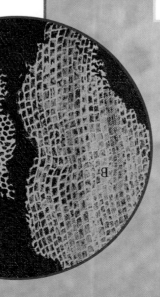

Scientists develop ways of staining and fixing tissues to make them easier to see and study.

German scientist Rudolf Virchow concludes that cells divide to form new cells. Scientists had thought cells formed from air or nothing!

We know the modern cell theory:
- All living things are made of one or more cells.
- Cells are the basic units of living things.
- All cells come from other cells.

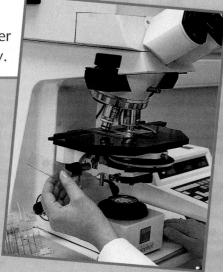

| 1858 | 1860s–1890s | 1940s | Today |

Electron microscopes, 200 times more powerful than light microscopes, help scientists better understand what happens in cells.

Write
ABOUT IT

1. Why did scientists think that cells formed from air or nothing?

2. Why did it take so long from the discovery of cells to knowing they are part of all living things?

LOG ON Visit www.science.mmhschool.com to learn more about cells.

Parts of a Cell

Vocabulary

cell membrane, B18

nucleus, B18

chromosome, B19

cytoplasm, B19

mitochondrion, B19

vacuole, B19

chloroplast, B19

cell wall, B19

transport system, B19

Get Ready

What makes a water lily different from a purple gallinule? You might say they are different because one is a plant and the other is an animal. What makes all plants and animals different? What makes them the same? One thing plants and animals have in common is that they are all made up of cells. Do you think they have the same kinds of cells?

Inquiry Skill

You **experiment** when you perform a test to support or disprove a hypothesis.

Explore Activity

What Are the Parts of Cells?

Materials

microscope

microscope slide

coverslip

forceps

dropper

Elodea leaf

prepared slide of human cheek cells

onion skin (optional)

Procedure

1 **Observe** Make a wet-mount slide of a leaf from the tip of an *Elodea* plant. Use the dropper to place a drop of water on the slide. Holding the leaf tip with forceps, drop it onto the water that is on the slide. Holding the cover slip by the edges, lower it onto the top of the leaf. Observe the leaf on low power, focusing on the top layer of cells. Focus on one cell. Describe what you see.

2 **Communicate** Look at the center of a cell on high power. Draw the *Elodea* cell, labeling the different structures that you can see. Return the microscope to low power. Remove and clean the slide and coverslip.

3 Get a prepared slide of cheek cells from your teacher. Locate the cells on low power. Repeat step 2.

Human cheek cells

Drawing Conclusions

1 Describe the similarities and differences in your observations of the *Elodea* cell and the human cheek cell.

2 **FURTHER INQUIRY** **Experiment** From your observations, make a hypothesis as to what the differences are between plant and animal cells. Test your hypothesis and report your results.

Elodea cells

Elodea plant

Main Idea Cells are made up of many parts, each with a special function, that help conduct all life processes.

What Are the Parts of Cells?

If you were to compare a lion with a rosebush, you would find many differences. However, when the individual cells of these organisms are compared, they have many characteristics in common. Cells are the basic units of structure and function for plants, animals, and all living organisms. All these cells have the same type of structures.

Cell Parts

The earliest microscopes clearly showed the outer edge of a cell. As microscopes improved, they showed that cells have small parts. Each part has a special function.

- All cells have an outer covering, called a **cell membrane**, that gives the cell shape and helps control materials that move in and out of the cell.

- The largest, most visible part of the cell, the **nucleus** (NEW·klee·uhs) (plural, *nuclei*), is separated from the cytoplasm by its own membrane. The nucleus is the control center of the cell. It directs the cell's activities.

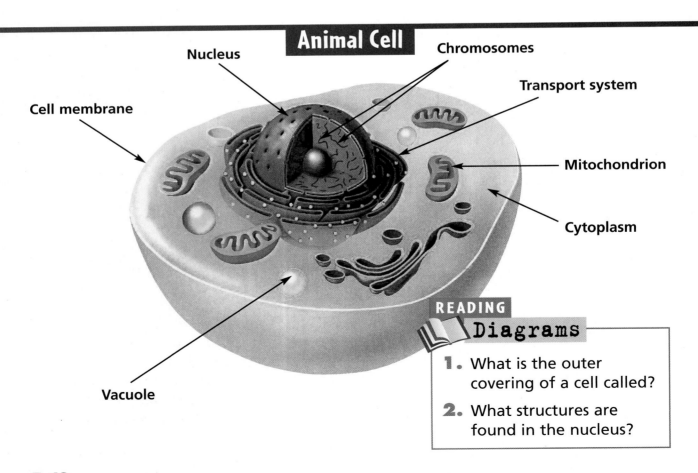

Animal Cell

Nucleus

Cell membrane

Vacuole

Chromosomes

Transport system

Mitochondrion

Cytoplasm

READING Diagrams

1. What is the outer covering of a cell called?

2. What structures are found in the nucleus?

- Long strands called **chromosomes** (KROH·muh·sohmz) can be found in the nucleus. They are like blueprints of the cell. They store directions for cell activities. They transfer the directions to the next generation of cells.

- **Cytoplasm** (SIGH·tuh·plaz·uhm), the gel-like substance inside the cell membrane, contains a large amount of water. Most of the cell's life processes take place within the cytoplasm. It also contains chemicals and other cell structures that carry out special jobs for the cell. Different structures have different functions.

- Rod-shaped structures, called **mitochondria** (migh·tuh·KAHN·dree·uh) (singular, *mitochondrion*), are often referred to as the "powerhouses" of the cell. They package and secrete materials containing energy, which can be used by the cell.

- **Vacuoles** (VAK·yew·ohlz) are sac-like storage spaces in cells. They store anything, from wastes (prior to removal) to food. Animal cells have smaller vacuoles than plant cells.

- **Transport system** The cell's transport system extends from the nucleus to the cell membrane.

READING **Compare and Contrast Which parts of the plant cell are not in animal cells?**

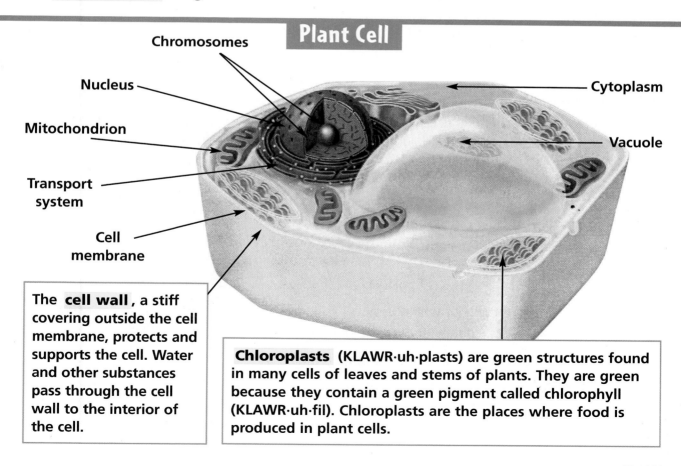

Plant Cell

Chromosomes

Nucleus

Mitochondrion

Transport system

Cell membrane

Cytoplasm

Vacuole

The **cell wall**, a stiff covering outside the cell membrane, protects and supports the cell. Water and other substances pass through the cell wall to the interior of the cell.

Chloroplasts (KLAWR·uh·plasts) are green structures found in many cells of leaves and stems of plants. They are green because they contain a green pigment called chlorophyll (KLAWR·uh·fil). Chloroplasts are the places where food is produced in plant cells.

How Are Cells Organized?

Many scientists use laboratory materials to develop physical representations so they can explain an idea, an object, or an event. The representations allow a person to get a "picture" of an object when that object is not available to touch. In this activity you will work in a group to make a model of a plant cell or an animal cell.

Materials

art materials such as clay, string, yarn, cotton, marbles, tape, beads

Procedure

1 Choose a cell that your group will represent—a plant cell or an animal cell. What cell parts will be included in your model? Record your choices. Choose from the list below.

- cell membrane
- nucleus
- cell wall
- vacuoles
- mitochondria
- cytoplasm
- chromosomes
- chloroplast
- transport structures

2 **Make a Model** Brainstorm with your group the types of materials you will need to construct your model. Gather the materials, and build your model.

Drawing Conclusions

1 **Interpret Data** How did your model compare with others of the same kind of cell? With the other kind of cell?

2 Is your model effective in representing a plant or animal cell? Explain why or why not. What improvements, if any, could you make in your model?

3 How would you change your model to build a model of a bacterium?

What Are Elements?

Tiny particles of carbon, sulfur, and other substances make up the parts of your cells. In fact, tiny particles called *atoms* make up all matter—not just your body but all solids, liquids, and gases. There are many kinds of atoms.

For example, a chunk of carbon is made up of billions of carbon atoms together. Oxygen in the air we breathe is made up of oxygen atoms. Substances such as carbon or oxygen are called elements. Elements are made up of just one kind of atom.

This chart lists some of the elements that make up the cells of your body. They are not in chunks but are the size of atoms, far too small to be seen with a microscope.

READING Charts

1. What element is most abundant in the human body? Least abundant?

2. How much of your body do carbon, hydrogen, and oxygen make up?

Elements That Make Up the Human Body

Symbol	Element	Percent
O	Oxygen	65.0
C	Carbon	18.5
H	Hydrogen	9.5
N	Nitrogen	3.3
Ca	Calcium	1.5
P	Phosphorus	1.0
K	Potassium	0.4
S	Sulfur	0.3
Na	Sodium	0.2
Cl	Chlorine	0.2
Mg	Magnesium	0.1

▶ What are the tiny particles that make up elements called?

What Are Compounds?

Elements don't exist by themselves in your body. They exist joined together in substances called *compounds*. For example, water is not an element. It is a compound made up of two elements, oxygen and hydrogen, joined together.

Carbon dioxide is a compound that your cells produce. It is part of what your body releases every time you exhale. Carbon dioxide is made up of atoms of two elements joined together—carbon and oxygen.

▷ **What are the parts of a compound?**

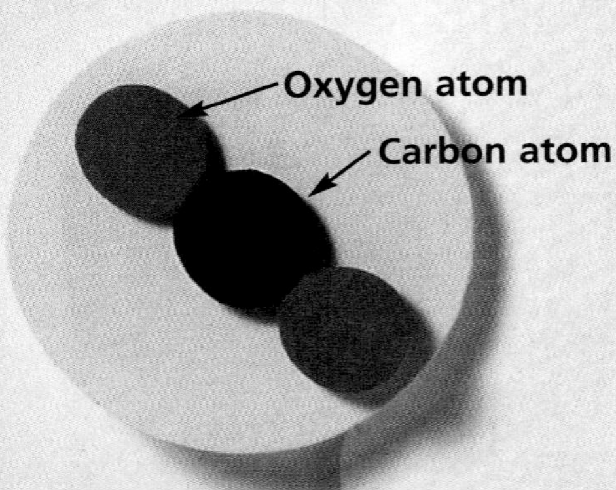

Oxygen atom

Carbon atom

The smallest amount of carbon dioxide you exhale is a carbon dioxide molecule. Each carbon dioxide molecule is made up of one carbon atom and two oxygen atoms.

The smallest amount of water that can exist is a water molecule. A glass of water contains billions of water molecules. Each water molecule is made up of two hydrogen atoms and one oxygen atom.

Oxygen atom

Hydrogen atom

What Compounds Make Up Your Cells?

Carbon is combined with other elements in the form of compounds that make up cell parts.

One group of carbon compounds is called *carbohydrates*. Carbohydrates supply energy for cell activities. Carbohydrates include sugars and starches. You get carbohydrates from foods such as honey, fruits, bread, spaghetti, and potatoes.

Lipids, or fats, are carbon compounds that store and release energy in even larger amounts than carbohydrates. Foods such as cream, butter, oils, and nuts provide these substances.

Proteins are carbon compounds needed for cell growth and repair. Your cells build their own proteins. Protein sources such as milk, eggs, fish, meats, and beans provide the materials for your cells to build proteins.

Another group of carbon compounds in cells is the *nucleic acids*. They contain a code that allows your cells to build proteins. Nucleic acids are found in chromosomes in the nucleus as well as in structures throughout the cytoplasm.

Each one of these compounds is vital to the survival of the organism. This is why a balanced diet is important.

▷ What carbon compounds are found in your cells?

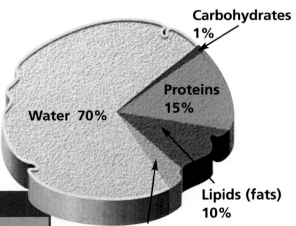

Contents of a Human Cell

Carbohydrates 1%

Proteins 15%

Water 70%

Lipids (fats) 10%

Nucleic acids 4%

Body Composition		
Carbon Compounds	**Components**	**Location**
Carbohydrates	carbon, hydrogen, oxygen	cell membranes
Lipids	mostly carbon, hydrogen, oxygen	cell membranes
Proteins	carbon, hydrogen, oxygen, nitrogen	cell membranes; cytoplasm
Nucleic acids	carbon, hydrogen, oxygen, nitrogen, phosphorus	chromosomes in the nucleus; cytoplasm

READING Graphs

1. What percent of your body is made up of carbon compounds?
2. What percent of your body is not made of water?

What Are One-Celled Organisms?

Animals and plants are made up of many cells. As you learned in Lesson 1, the cells are organized into tissues, organs, and organ systems. Do all living things have many cells? If you look at a drop of pond water under a microscope, you may find organisms made up of only one cell. Many kinds of *one-celled organisms* can be found not only in water but in the soil and on particles of dust in the air.

One-celled organisms have parts that you can find in cells of animals and plants. For example, an amoeba has a nucleus and cytoplasm. What other parts do you see?

Bacteria (singular, *bacterium*) are one-celled organisms, too. The Dutch scientist Anton van Leeuwenhoek first observed bacteria in the 1670s when looking at scrapings from his teeth and the insides of animals. Modern microscopes reveal that bacteria have a cell membrane and a cell wall, something like plant cells. However, unlike other kinds of cells, bacteria do not have a clearly defined nucleus with chromosomes inside. Instead these cells have their hereditary material located throughout the cytoplasm.

▷ **What are the parts of a one-celled organism?**

An amoeba

Bacteria

Amoebas and bacteria are one-celled organisms that may be found in water, soil, or air.

Why It Matters

Have you ever heard the phrase "You are what you eat"? This is somewhat true. The substances that form the cells and tissues in your body are made from similar substances in the foods you eat.

The cells of your body are made up of a number of elements, including carbon, hydrogen, and oxygen. You can use what you know about the composition of your body to help you plan nutritious meals.

e-Journal Visit our Web site www.science.mmhschool.com to do a research project on the cells of your body.

Think and Write

1. How are animal and plant cells alike? Different?

2. What are the major elements found in your body?

3. What are some kinds of carbon compounds found in your body?

4. INQUIRY SKILL Make a Model How would a model of bacteria cells be different from plant or animal cells?

5. Critical Thinking What if a robot was built that could do almost everything a living thing could do? Would the robot then be a living thing?

L·I·N·K·S

MATH LINK

Make a graph. Use the chart on page B21 to make a circle graph illustrating the proportions of each element present in the human body.

WRITING LINK

Personal Narrative Look at a food label on a can or package. The label shows how many carbohydrates and proteins are in the food, based on how much you need to take in each day. Keep a diary of the amount of each carbon compound that you take in based on these values. Use the notes in your diary to write a humorous true story about how the food you ate in one day affected you.

HEALTH LINK

Research calories. Many people try to limit the amount of calories from fat in the foods they eat. Why is this important? Are "fat calories" different from other calories? Use health books or the Internet to do research. Present your findings to the class.

TECHNOLOGY LINK

LOG ON Visit www.science.mmhschool.com for more links.

Movement and Nutrition in Cells

Vocabulary

diffusion, B28

passive transport, B29

osmosis, B30

active transport, B31

photosynthesis, B32

respiration, B33

fermentation, B33

Get Ready

Is this diver in any danger from the shark that looms outside the cage? Could smaller fish get into the cage? How are a cage and diver like a cell? The diver is surrounded by a cage. A cell is surrounded by a cell membrane. What might the cell membrane let in or keep out of a cell? Does the size of a particle affect what can pass through a membrane?

Inquiry Skill

You use variables when you identify and separate things in an experiment that can be changed or controlled.

Explore Activity

What Is Diffusion?

Materials

small jar with a lid

tea bag

warm water

sand

clock or timer

scissors

paper towel

plastic teaspoon

Procedure

BE CAREFUL! Handle scissors carefully.

1. Fill a jar with warm water. Place the tea bag in the water, and add 1 tsp. of sand.

2. **Observe** Shake the jar, then leave it undisturbed for 15 minutes. Record your observations. Be sure to look for the sand.

3. Remove the tea bag from the jar, and place it on the paper towel. Cut the tea bag open with scissors. Record what you observe.

Drawing Conclusions

1. **Observe** What color was the water in the container after 15 minutes? Was the color evenly distributed?

2. What entered the tea bag? What moved out of the tea bag?

3. **Infer** What do you think determines which particles move into or out of a tea bag?

4. **FURTHER INQUIRY** **Use Variables** Predict what would happen if you used food coloring instead of sand. Test your hypothesis and report your results.

Main Idea Cells conduct many processes, including transport, respiration, and waste removal.

What Is Diffusion?

Substances are flowing in and out of cells through the cell membrane all the time. Cells use substances to grow and get energy. How does it work? The clue is that cells are in a moist environment. The process works something like food coloring and water.

What would happen if you placed a drop of food coloring in a bowl of water? You would probably observe the water slowly turn color. *Molecules*, a group of tightly bonded atoms, are in constant motion. As they move about, they often collide and bounce off one another.

This movement causes the food-coloring molecules to spread farther apart until they are evenly spaced throughout the water. This process, called **diffusion** (di·FYEW·zhuhn), occurs when molecules of a substance move from an area of higher concentration to an area of lower concentration. That is, the molecules move from where they are crowded to where they are less crowded.

Diffusion also occurs in gases. If you open a bottle of perfume or bake cookies, the aroma will gradually spread throughout your home. Once the molecules that make up the aroma are in about the same concentration everywhere, they continue to collide and bounce off one another.

▶ **How does diffusion allow molecules to move in and out of a cell?**

Diffusion

Food-coloring molecules spread evenly throughout a beaker of water.

① ② ③

What Is Passive Transport?

The cell membrane is a kind of barrier. Cells get food, oxygen, and other substances from the environment. They also release wastes, such as the gas carbon dioxide. Substances move in and out of the cell through the cell membrane. Some kinds of molecules are able to pass through a cell membrane by diffusion. That is, they move from areas of high concentration to low concentration.

Molecules of sugar, water, oxygen, and carbon dioxide do not require energy to move from high to low concentration. Such movement through cell membranes without the use of energy is called **passive transport**.

Other molecules, such as proteins and bacteria, are so large they can only enter the cell with the help of special processes that take place in the cell membrane.

▷ **Why do you think that diffusion is called "passive" transport?**

Passive Transport

READING
Diagrams

1. Do oxygen molecules go into or out of the cell?

2. Do carbon dioxide molecules go into or out of the cell?

Oxygen In

BEFORE

Oxygen molecule

Cell membrane

AFTER

Carbon Dioxide Out

BEFORE

Cell membrane

AFTER

Carbon dioxide molecule

What Is Osmosis?

Do you realize that water makes up about 70 to 95 percent of a living cell, depending on the kind of cell it is? The movement of water in and out of a cell is important in keeping the cell alive. The diffusion of water through a cell membrane is **osmosis** (ahz·MOH·sis). Water molecules tend to move from an area of greater concentration to an area of lesser concentration. When the concentration of water molecules is the same on each side of a cell membrane, a state of *equilibrium*, or balance, is reached.

Look at the two photographs. The plant in the second photo is the same as the one in the first photo after it has been watered. How can you explain the wilting of the leaves in the first photograph?

Most likely there is less water in the soil around the roots. Cells in the leaves and stems of the plant are not supplied with adequate water from the roots. The loss of water from the cell membranes causes them to shrink away from the cell. As a result, the plant wilts. What other examples of osmosis can you think of?

Equilibrium is reached when water leaves the cells and enters the cells at the same rate.

▷ **How does osmosis work in a plant?**

Wilting occurs when more water leaves the cells than enters the cells.

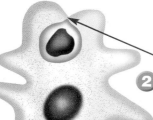

1 The cell membrane forms a sphere around the particle.

2 The sphere pinches off.

3 The resulting vacuole, with its contents, goes into the cell.

What Is Active Transport?

When materials require energy to move through the cell membrane, it is called **active transport**. In active transport molecules move from an area of lesser concentration to an area of higher concentration.

In some cases substances are too large to pass through the cell membrane by either active or passive transport. Materials such as large proteins and bacteria enter the cell by becoming enclosed in a part of the cell membrane. Some one-celled organisms, such as the amoeba, take in food this way.

READING Compare and Contrast
How is active transport different from passive transport?

QUICK LAB

Osmosis

FOLDABLES Make a Two-Tab Book. (See p. R 41.) Label the tabs as shown.

With Salt	Without Salt

Observations

BE CAREFUL! Wear goggles.

1. Fill two plastic cups about three-fourths full of water. Add 15 g of salt to one cup, and stir. Label it *Salt*.

2. **Predict** Place two slices of raw potato in each of the cups. What will happen to the slices?

3. **Observe** After 20 minutes remove the slices. Record your observations in your Two-Tab Book.

4. Do your observations support your hypothesis?

5. **Experiment** Design an experiment that tests whether temperature affects diffusion. Put a tea bag in each of three glasses that contain ice water, cool water, and warm water.

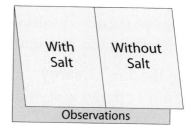

What Is Photosynthesis?

Cells need energy to carry on life processes like growing and active transport. Would you believe that cells get their energy from the Sun? Plant cells store the energy of the Sun. Other organisms get this energy from eating plants—in particular, molecules of carbohydrates, such as sugars.

Trapping the Sun's Energy

The Sun's energy is stored in food in the food-making process. This activity goes on in cells that have chloroplasts—for example, the cells of a green leaf of a plant. Chloroplasts contain a substance called chlorophyll. When a leaf is exposed to sunlight, the chlorophyll "traps" energy from the Sun.

Producers

The trapped energy is used for **photosynthesis** . This is a food-making process that uses sunlight to produce sugar. It occurs in cells of green plants and other kinds of *producers*, such as a one-celled euglena. The producers take in water from the soil and carbon dioxide from the air as raw materials and change them into two products. The products are sugar (the food) and oxygen. Green plants store food in storage organs such as potatoes and onions. Potatoes are part of the root system of a plant. Onions are part of the shoot system.

▷ **How does photosynthesis allow plants to make food?**

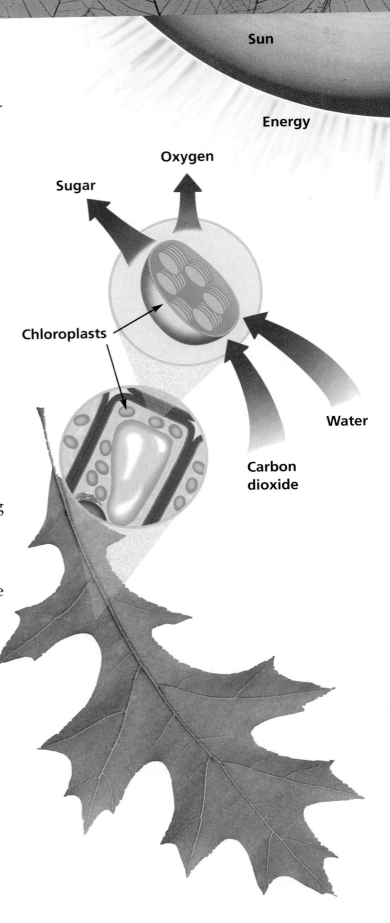

Sun

Energy

Oxygen

Sugar

Chloroplasts

Water

Carbon dioxide

What Are Fermentation and Respiration?

Energy for a cell's activities is locked within molecules of sugar. Plants store up the sugar for their own use. Animals get this energy by eating plants or other animals that have eaten plants. To use the energy, cells of an organism "unlock" the energy from sugar.

The energy in a sugar molecule is "unlocked" or released by a process called **respiration**. Respiration takes place in cells in the mitochondria. Think of respiration as a process of burning a fuel, such as wood or coal. Sugar is the fuel. Usually the process requires oxygen, which living things take in from air or water. The sugar molecules are broken down, and energy and wastes are released. The wastes are water and carbon dioxide.

Some cells carry on respiration without oxygen, a process called **fermentation**. For example, oxygen may not reach all your muscle cells when you exercise. In this case, fermentation releases the energy. It also releases a waste called lactic acid.

One-celled organisms called yeasts carry on fermentation by feeding on sugars. They break the sugars down and produce carbon dioxide and a kind of alcohol called ethanol.

Ethanol has many uses, from antifreeze to manufacturing. Ethanol is also being mixed with other chemicals to produce a fuel that can power motor vehicles. Scientists are working with plant products that can be fermented—wood chippings and corn, for example—to produce ethanol.

▷ **How do the processes of fermentation and respiration differ?**

Respiration

Oxygen

Sugar

Water

Carbon dioxide

Mitochondrion

READING Diagrams

1. What enters a mitochondrion?
2. What leaves a mitochondrion?

How Do Cells Remove Wastes?

Living cells make wastes as a result of respiration. In the cytoplasm, structures called *lysosomes* have the job of removing these wastes. Lysosomes are the cell's garbage disposal system.

Lysosomes are spherical structures surrounded by a membrane. Inside are chemicals that digest wastes and worn-out cell parts. The membrane keeps the chemicals inside from breaking down the cell.

Lysosomes are also responsible for digesting, or breaking down, the food that the cell takes in. Recall that when a cell takes in a food particle, the cell membrane forms a sphere around the particle. The sphere pinches off and forms a vacuole. Wastes are also stored in vacuoles. Lysosomes attach to either food or waste vacuoles and release their chemicals. These chemicals break down the food into compounds the cell can use.

Another important function of vacuoles is to destroy viruses or bacteria that could damage the cell. Finally, when a cell dies, the chemicals in the lysosomes quickly break down the cell and release the cell's compounds.

▷ **What is the job of lysosomes in a cell?**

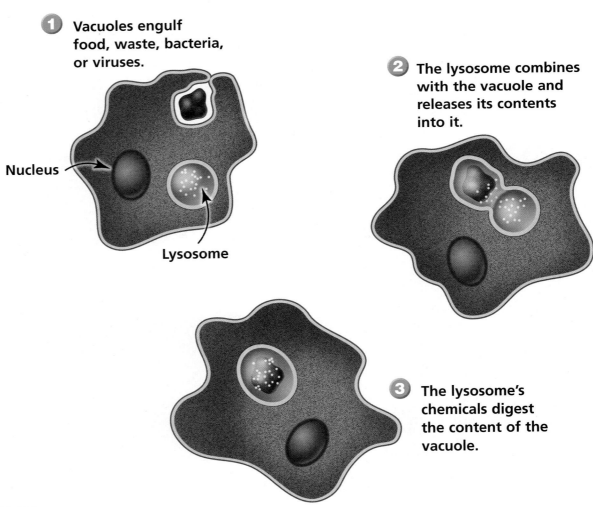

1 Vacuoles engulf food, waste, bacteria, or viruses.

Nucleus

Lysosome

2 The lysosome combines with the vacuole and releases its contents into it.

3 The lysosome's chemicals digest the content of the vacuole.

Why It Matters

The movement of particles into and out of the cell is very important for the cell to be able to get nutrients and energy.

Oxygen produced in photosynthesis is needed for respiration and carbon dioxide produced in respiration is needed for photosynthesis.

Yeasts are tiny organisms that produce carbon dioxide and alcohol during fermentation. When yeast is added to dough, the carbon dioxide that forms makes the dough rise.

e-Journal Visit our Web site www.science.mmhschool.com to do a research project on one of the cell processes discussed in this lesson.

Think and Write

1. Describe the process that allows you to smell an open bottle of perfume.

2. What is the role of the cell membrane in moving substances in and out of the cell?

3. Distinguish between passive transport and active transport.

4. How do cells get the energy they need to live?

5. **Critical Thinking** What does an organ like a potato tell you about the plant on which it grows?

L·I·N·K·S

WRITING LINK

Writing a Story. Why is photosynthesis important to human beings? Write a science fiction story about what life would be like without photosynthesis. Could people survive without it? Think about how your characters would live. What would the setting of your story be like?

MATH LINK

Add fractions and mixed numbers. Suppose your neighbor has a vegetable garden. He plants potatoes, carrots, and onions. He gives you $6\frac{3}{4}$ pounds of potatoes, $4\frac{1}{2}$ pounds of carrots, and $3\frac{1}{4}$ pounds of onions in a basket that weighs $\frac{1}{4}$ pound. How much do the basket and the vegetables weigh in total?

TECHNOLOGY LINK

LOG ON Visit www.science.mmhschool.com for more links.

Reproduction and Growth

Vocabulary

life cycle, B38

reproduction, B38

metamorphosis, B39

cell cycle, B41

mitosis, B41

external fertilization, B44

internal fertilization, B44

fertilization, B45

meiosis, B46

life span, B48

life expectancy, B48

Inquiry Skill

You interpret data when you use information that has been gathered to answer questions or solve a problem.

Get Ready

Did you ever wonder how a caterpillar turns into a butterfly? How is this similar to the way that you are becoming an adult?

All animals experience different stages of their life. A caterpillar's larva, or baby, stage looks much different from its adult stage. A human, though, looks similar throughout all the stages of development. Why are growth and development so important?

Explore Activity

What Is a Life Cycle?

Materials

butterfly larvae
(optional)

hand lens

Procedure

BE CAREFUL! If you are using live larvae, treat them with care.

1 **Observe** Look at the photo of the larva or the live larvae, if they are available. Record your observations about their color, size, shape, and texture.

2 Observe the live larvae daily as they change form, or look at each step of a larva's development in the photos. Draw what you think a larva looks like within a cocoon.

3 **Communicate** When the cocoon opens up, draw what emerges. Note its color and characteristics.

Drawing Conclusions

1 What emerged from the cocoon? How did its new form compare with what it was before it formed the cocoon?

2 What stages did the larva go through in its development? How long did it take to develop?

3 [FURTHER INQUIRY] **Interpret Data** What other animals go through similar changes while they are growing or developing? Draw a chart of the development of another animal. How does it compare with the butterfly?

Egg

Larva

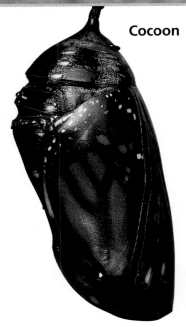

Cocoon

Read to Learn

Main Idea Living things reproduce and grow as part of a life cycle.

What Is a Life Cycle?

All living things go through stages in their lives. One stage is the birth of an organism. Another stage is that organism's death. In between there may be many or few changes, if any at all. Then the process happens all over again in the next generation.

This process goes around and around, generation after generation—like a bicycle wheel turning in a continuous circle. This is called a **life cycle**. A life cycle describes all the stages in a living thing's development from one generation to the next.

A cycle has no beginning and no end. However, the stages for any individual living thing always include birth and, later, may include **reproduction**. Reproduction is the process that a living thing uses to produce more of its own kind.

Exactly what happens between birth and reproduction varies from one living thing to another. This allows scientists to use life cycles to classify living things. Different kinds of living things have different life cycles.

Birth

Think of the human life cycle. You can compare and contrast it with the cycles of other animals. For example, humans, bears, and lions are all born looking like small adults. Many kinds of animals hatch from eggs. Young birds, reptiles (such as snakes and turtles), and fish hatch from eggs looking much like small forms of their parents too.

Growth and Development

After birth, humans go through infancy and then childhood. Childhood is followed by adolescence and, eventually, adulthood. All the while humans look like adults, becoming more adult in appearance as they develop. As we grow older, our body structures and functions change. Other kinds of animals develop into completely different forms as they grow.

▷ **What are some of the stages in a life cycle?**

The life cycle of a dog includes birth, and sometimes, parenthood.

What Is Metamorphosis?

When animals change from one form to a completely different form during their life cycle, it is called metamorphosis. Butterflies, lady bugs, grasshoppers, and frogs are examples of animals that undergo **metamorphosis** .

Some insects, such as grasshoppers, go through an *incomplete metamorphosis*, with only three stages. Butterflies, mosquitos, and amphibians, such as frogs, go through *complete metamorphosis*. This means they go through abrupt changes to reach their adult stage.

① **Egg**

② **Nymph** Resembles the adult, but has no wings. It will molt five times as it grows.

③ **Adult grasshopper**

▷ **What are the stages in the life cycle of a grasshopper?**

Grasshopper Life Cycle

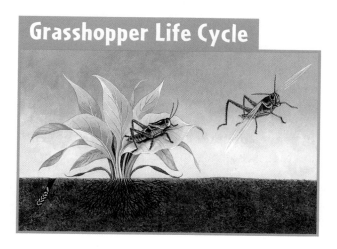

Frog Life Cycle

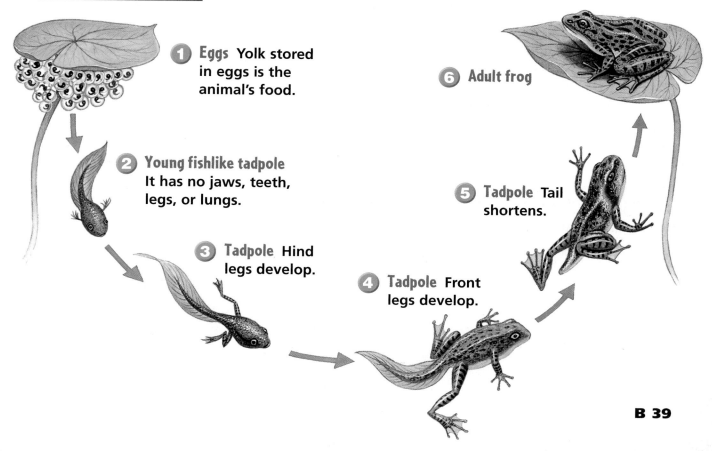

① **Eggs** Yolk stored in eggs is the animal's food.

② **Young fishlike tadpole** It has no jaws, teeth, legs, or lungs.

③ **Tadpole** Hind legs develop.

④ **Tadpole** Front legs develop.

⑤ **Tadpole** Tail shortens.

⑥ **Adult frog**

How Do Organisms Grow?

Cells in your body are growing all the time. How does this happen? Food molecules enter a cell through its membrane. A cell uses these substances to form new cell material. As a result, it grows. Eventually it divides.

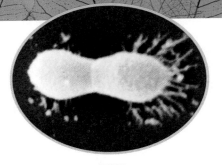

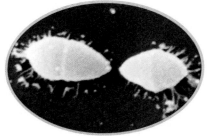

After a cell divides, substances that enter or leave the new cells have a greater cell surface area for moving in and out.

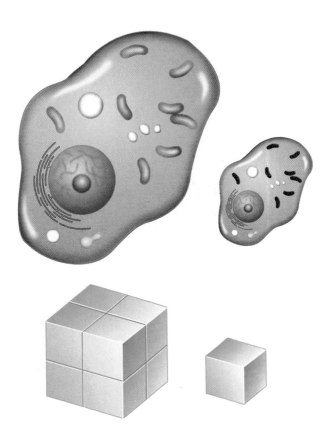

The volume of the first cell is eight times larger than that of the second cell, just as the bigger cube has a volume eight times that of the small cube. Is the surface area of the bigger cell or cube eight times larger than that of the small cell or cube? Less than eight times larger? How does the surface area compare with the volume?

As a cell grows, the space it takes up—or volume—increases much faster than its outer surface, the cell membrane. Cells cannot grow so large that their outer surface is too small to allow in enough needed materials and to allow wastes to be removed quickly enough. After reaching a certain size, the cell divides into two smaller cells.

While many cells in your body are growing and dividing, some are wearing out and dying. Worn-out cells on the surface of your skin peel off, such as cells on the palm of your hand. They are replaced by new cells from below.

All organisms go through stages, or a life cycle. For example, animals are born, they grow and develop, and they die. While you are growing, the cells of your body are growing and dividing at a greater rate than cells are wearing out. Your cells are increasing in number.

The Cell Cycle

INTERPHASE

GROWTH

Preparation
for division

CELL DIVISION (MITOSIS)

No matter how large an organism grows, its cells remain the same size throughout its life. Your body cells are about the same size they were when you were a baby.

Eventually you will be fully grown. Even then cells will still be growing and dividing—but more and more, they will be replacing worn-out cells. The number of cells in your body will not increase.

Every living cell is going through a cycle. The **cell cycle** is made up of a time of growth and a time of dividing. Most of a cell's cycle is spent growing and developing. This time is called *interphase*. During this time the cell prepares to divide.

Cell division is a continuous process—it does not stop and start. First, the nucleus of a cell divides into two identical nuclei. The division of a nucleus into two during the process of cell division is called **mitosis**. Then gradually the cytoplasm divides, and the cell division is complete.

What Causes Cancer?

Some researchers think that a "mistake" in the cell cycle is what causes cancer. Cancer is any of a group of diseases in which cells divide faster and more often than normal cells. These cells may spread throughout the body.

When cells divide rapidly, they may form growths or tumors. Some tumors are benign. They cause no harm to other cells. A malignant tumor, on the other hand, may spread through the body and damage healthy organs.

What causes cancer? Researchers identify certain chemicals as triggers of cancers. Chemicals in cigarette smoke, for example, can produce cancer in the lung, throat, windpipe, or stomach. Ultraviolet light from the Sun is also linked to skin cancer.

READING **Compare and Contrast**
How does a cell's life cycle compare to a human's life cycle?

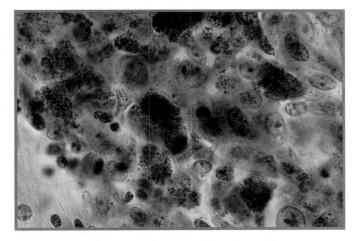

Skin cancer is very slow to develop. The sunburn you receive this week may take 20 years or more to cause skin cancer.

What Happens During Mitosis?

Mitosis takes place whenever your body cells divide. Body cells include skin cells, bone cells, blood cells, and muscle cells. Who first observed cells in various stages of division? It was Walther Fleming, a German scientist. In 1879 he observed cells in various stages, or phases, of cell division by using a dye and drawing what he saw.

While a body cell is dividing into two identical cells, the nucleus divides by a process called mitosis. Mitosis is a gradual, continuous process. During mitosis a second set of chromosomes is formed inside the cell. When the cell splits and produces two new cells, each set of chromosomes goes to a new cell. Each new body cell now has a full set of chromosomes and is identical to the original cell.

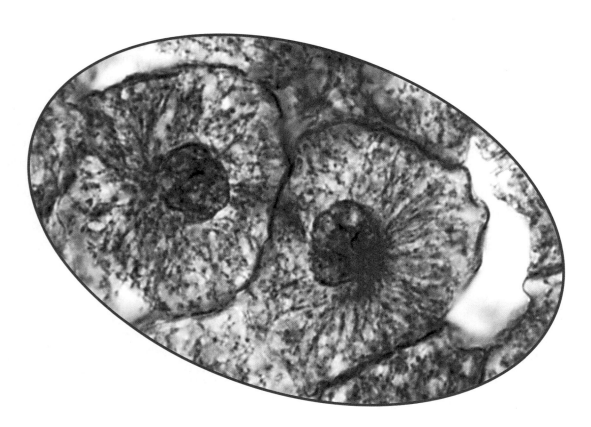

The cytoplasm divides. Two new cells are formed, identical to the original cell. Each new cell is in the growth stage of the cell cycle.

Phases of Mitosis

- **Interphase** The nucleus can be clearly seen. Chromosomes make copies of themselves.

- **Prophase** Chromosomes become visible. The membrane around the nucleus begins to disappear.

- **Metaphase** Chromosome pairs line up along the middle of the cell.

- **Anaphase** Chromosome pairs split apart and begin to move to opposite sides of the cell.

- **Telophase** A nuclear membrane forms around each set of chromosomes. Each new nucleus has the same number of chromosomes as the original cell. The cytoplasm divides. Two new cells are formed. Each new cell is in the growth stage of the cell cycle.

▶ **What are the stages of mitosis?**

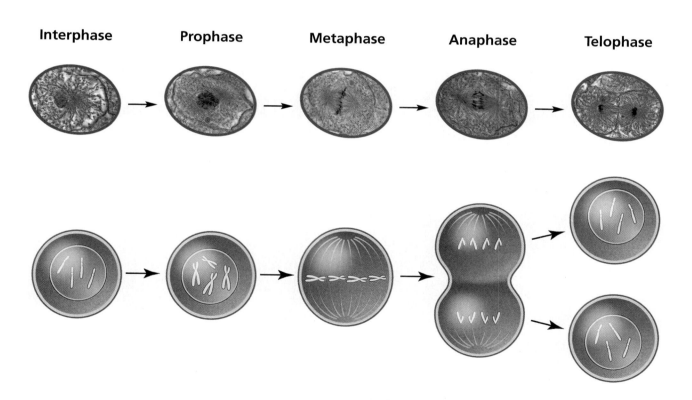

Interphase   Prophase   Metaphase   Anaphase   Telophase

READING

Charts

1. What happens after the chromosomes first become visible?

2. What happens after the chromosomes line up?

How Do Animals Reproduce?

All animals in the wild reproduce, otherwise their kind would vanish. However, not all animals reproduce in the same way. Animals reproduce in two basic ways—asexually and sexually.

Sexual reproduction occurs when a sperm cell from a male and an egg cell from a female join to make a fertilized egg. All vertebrates reproduce sexually, but they do so in two different ways.

Sperm cells and egg cells can come together outside of a female's body. This is called **external fertilization** and is the way most fish and some amphibians reproduce. Sperm and egg cells can also come together inside the female's body. This is called **internal fertilization**, which is the way that some fish, some amphibians, and all reptiles, birds, and mammals reproduce.

Asexual reproduction is a much simpler process since it does not require a sperm cell and an egg cell to find each other. In asexual reproduction, all inherited traits come from a single parent. Many invertebrates use asexual reproduction to produce offspring. Sponges reproduce this way. If a piece of a sponge falls off, it can grow into a new adult sponge. This kind of asexual reproduction is called *regeneration*.

Some invertebrates, like sea anemones, practice asexual reproduction by simply splitting in half. Hydras, which are cnidarians, form a bud that falls off to become a new hydra.

In asexual reproduction, offspring are produced by mitosis.

READING **Summarize** What are the different ways animals can reproduce?

Budding A hydra reproduces asexually by growing buds that break off to form new hydras.

Splitting A sea anemone reproduces asexually simply by splitting in half.

What Is Fertilization?

In sexual reproduction, an egg and a sperm cell join. Just before they join, a human sperm and an egg each have only 23 chromosomes. When they join, they become one cell with 46 chromosomes. The cell has received half the number of chromosomes from each parent cell. Since traits are inherited from both parents, offspring are never identical to either parent. The joining of an egg and a sperm is called **fertilization**. The cell that forms is called a fertilized egg, or *zygote*.

The zygote begins to divide by mitosis. Each new cell continues to have 46 chromosomes. The zygote develops and grows into a new organism.

Humans have 46 chromosomes in each of their body cells. Other animals and plants have different chromosome numbers. However, fertilization and cell growth work much the same way no matter how many chromosomes there are in a cell. Fertilization makes sure that each cell of the new organisms has the same number of chromosomes as in each parent. Half the number of chromosomes comes from each parent.

▶ **How does fertilization affect the number of chromosomes in each parent cell?**

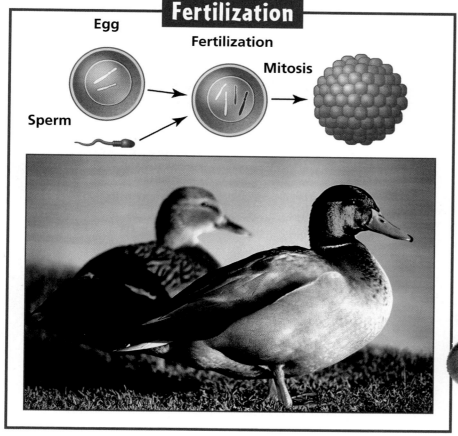

Fertilization

Egg

Fertilization

Sperm

Mitosis

The duck's eggs and the drake's (male duck) sperm combine in fertilization. The zygote divides by mitosis to grow into a duckling.

What Is Meiosis?

As you learned, most many-celled organisms reproduce from two parents through sexual reproduction. How does sexual reproduction work? Each parent produces a sex cell. During sexual reproduction these two cells join into one cell.

Humans have 46 chromosomes in each body cell. If a sperm and an egg each had 46 chromosomes, what would happen when they joined? The resulting cell would have 46 x 2, or 92 chromosomes, twice as many chromosomes as it should.

This does not happen, because sex cells are developed through a special kind of cell division. In a process called **meiosis**, the nucleus of a sex cell divides twice. As a result, the final, or *mature,* sex cells have only half as many chromosomes as the other cells of an organism—in this case, 23.

Phases of Meiosis

- **Interphase** The cell replicates its chromosomes.
- **Prophase I** Chromosomes become visible. The membrane around the nucleus begins to disappear.
- **Metaphase I** Pairs of chromosomes line up.
- **Anaphase I** Pairs of chromosomes separate.
- **Telophase I** Cell divides.
- **Meiosis II** The second division of meiosis is simply a mitosis of the products of the first division of meiosis.

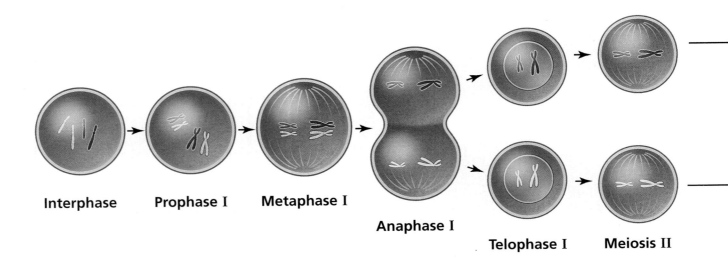

Interphase Prophase I Metaphase I Anaphase I Telophase I Meiosis II

Meiosis is a crucial process because it makes sexual reproduction possible. As you have learned, sexual reproduction is important because it results in different organisms having different traits. When organisms in a species have different traits it means the species has *variation*. Variation allows organisms to adapt to changes, and being able to adapt to changes is key to survival.

▶ **What is the difference in the number of chromosomes at the beginning and at the end of meiosis?**

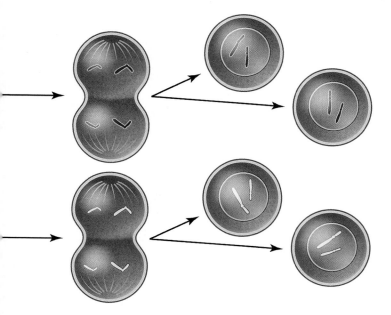

Anaphase II   **Telophase II**

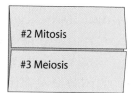

What Is Life Span?

An animal's life cycle may include birth, youth, old age, and death. The time it takes for this to happen is called an animal's **life span**. It is the length of time an animal can live under the best conditions. The life span of an animal is part of its characteristics, just like the shape of its body.

Do not confuse life span with **life expectancy**. Life expectancy is the average amount of time an individual animal might live according to the conditions around it. Life expectancy is affected by conditions in the environment, such as the amount of food or water nearby. Life span is not affected by these things.

For example, the life span of the average human living on Earth is more than 100 years, while the life expectancy of a human in the United States is a little over 76 years. In the country of Malawi in Africa, where enough food and clean drinking water are often not available, the life expectancy is less than 37 years. Life expectancy will never be greater than life span because life span is a prediction based on the best possible conditions.

The life span of animals varies from days to many years. The table shows the longest recorded life spans of different animals.

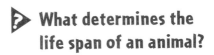 **What determines the life span of an animal?**

Frenchwoman Jeanne Louise Calment broke all records for the recorded life span of a human. She lived to the age of 122.

Longest Recorded Life Spans	
Animal	**Life Span**
Fruit fly	46 days
Housefly	76 days
Marine sponge	90 days
Blue crab	3 years
Honeybee queen	5 years
Golden hamster	10 years
Rabbit	18 years
Dog	29 years
House cat	34 years
Lobster	50 years
Ostrich	62 years
Freshwater oyster	80 years
Fin whale	115 years
Human	122 years
Marion's tortoise	150+ years

Why It Matters

Whether a species will survive or become extinct depends on a number of things. Among these things is its success at reproducing more of its own kind.

For this reason, scientists and other people interested in preserving Earth's animal species need to understand how different animals reproduce. Scientists also need to know what factors affect the life expectancies and life spans of animals.

 e-Journal Visit our Web site www.science.mmhschool.com to do a research project on life expectancies and life spans.

Think and Write

1. What are the four stages of a butterfly's life cycle?

2. Compare complete and incomplete metamorphosis, and give an example of each.

3. How do an organism's cells divide during asexual reproduction?

4. How do mitosis and meiosis differ?

5. **Critical Thinking** How might a knowledge of insect metamorphosis help in controlling insect pests?

L·I·N·K·S

LITERATURE LINK

Read *Flight of the Monarch* to learn about the monarch butterfly. Write a story about how the patterns of your life are similar to the butterfly's. Try the activities at the end of the book.

Flight of the Monarch

WRITING LINK

Writing That Compares Why do you think life expectancy depends on where you live? In an essay, compare the life expectancies in two countries. Use your research to compare and contrast other facts as well, such as the countries' major crop or climate. In your conclusion, explain what you think determines the life expectancy in a country.

MATH LINK

Multiply by 2-digit numbers. About 25,000,000 cells are produced per second in the human body through the process of mitosis. About how many cells are produced in one minute?

TECHNOLOGY LINK

LOG ON Visit www.science.mmhschool.com for more links.

Cycles

All living things go through cycles. Cells go through the cell cycle. The reproductive cycle allows living things to reproduce. Organisms go through the life cycle.

Paramecia and other one-celled organisms use the cell cycle to reproduce. The cell grows. The DNA in the cell's nucleus is copied. Then, as in a game of tug-of-war, proteins tug one set of DNA into each new cell. The cell divides. Now there are two paramecia—and they are exactly alike! In a short time, the cycle will start again.

Plants and animals with many cells use the cell cycle to grow and develop. Cells work well when they're small. So larger forms of life—people and trees—don't have bigger cells, they have more cells. It's hard to believe, but you started out as a single cell—a fertilized egg. It divided in two, then two divided into four, and so on. Your body is now over 50 trillion cells strong!

Whether a paramecium or a person, the whole organism goes through the life cycle. It is born, it grows, sometimes it reproduces, and it dies. The reproductive cycle is a big part of most plant and animal life cycles. It produces eggs and sperm with only half the number of chromosomes. But half of the instructions to build anything aren't enough! So an egg and a sperm must come together during fertilization. This gives the organism a

An oak tree goes through the life cycle. It is made of trillions of cells. It uses the cell cycle to grow and to replace damaged or worn-out cells, and the reproductive cycle to produce more trees.

full set of chromosomes. For example, a new cycle of life begins in plants when pollen lands on a flower of the same species. A pollen tube grows down the style into the ovary. When the sperm cell (from the pollen) and the egg cell (from the ovary) combine, a new plant is born.

What Did I Learn?

1. Compare and contrast the cell cycle, the reproductive cycle, and the life cycle.

2. What do plants and animals use the cell cycle for?

A paramecium uses the cell cycle to reproduce.

LOG ON Visit **www.science.mmhschool.com** to learn more about cycles.

Vocabulary

Fill each blank with the best word or words from the list.

cell wall, B38
chloroplast, B38
chromosome, B19
fertilization, B45
meiosis, B46
mitosis, B41
organism, B12
osmosis, B30
photosynthesis, B32
tissue, B10

1. The diffusion of water through a cell membrane is _____.

2. The nucleus of a cell divides twice in _____.

3. The division of a nucleus when the chromosome number ends up unchanged is _____.

4. Food making in plants is _____.

5. An egg and sperm join during _____.

6. Organ systems work together to form a(n) _____.

7. The _____, found in the nucleus, contains the cell's blueprints.

8. A(n) _____ is a green structure found in plant cells.

9. The stiff outer covering of a plant cell is its _____.

10. A group of similar cells working together at the same job is a(n) _____.

Test Prep

11. What is the order of organization in a plant or animal from simple to complex?

A tissue, cell, organ, organ system, organism

B organism, organ system, organ, tissue, cell

C cell, tissue, organ, organ system, organism

D cell, tissue, organ, organism, organ system

12. What are the stages of mitosis?

F Interphase, Prophase, Metaphase, Anaphase, Telophase

G Telophase, Interphase, Anaphase, Prophase, Metaphase

H Interphase, Metaphase, Anaphase, Prophase, Telophase

J Prophase, Metaphase, Anaphase, Telophase, Interphase

13. Which of the following is NOT a plant tissue?

   A dermal

   B nerve

   C vascular

   D ground

14. All of the following are found in an animal cell EXCEPT a _____.

   F cell membrane

   G vacuole

   H nucleus

   J cell wall

15. After meiosis, how does the resulting cell's chromosome number compare with the original number?

   A the same

   B half

   C double

   D depends on the type of cell

Concepts and Skills

16. Reading in Science How does the nucleus change as a cell divides?

17. Critical Thinking When a cell divides, the chromosome number is divided in half. Is this statement always true, sometimes true, or never true? Explain.

18. [INQUIRY SKILL] **Make a Model** What cell activity do the data in this table relate to? How would you complete this table to show the process? Explain why.

Number of Cubes Used	Volume	Surface Area
1	1	6
8		

19. Decision Making Suppose you work for an insurance company. Would you consider life span or would you consider life expectancy when selling life insurance?

20. Scientific Methods Which do you think will show diffusion—oil and water, warm water and cold water, ink and oil, ink and water? How would you test your answers?

Did You Ever Wonder?

[INQUIRY SKILL] **Hypothesize** Put two fresh stalks of celery in a glass of water and place in a refrigerator. Lay two other fresh stalks next to the glass. Hypothesize what will happen. Record your observations every two days for one week.

LOG ON Visit www.science.mmhschool.com to boost your test scores.

Inheriting Traits

Did You Ever Wonder?

Why do these cheetahs in Masai Mara, Kenya, look so much
alike? All cheetahs are closely related genetically. That means
that they share many of the same characteristics. How are these
characteristics passed from one generation of cheetahs to
the next?

INQUIRY SKILL **Predict** Why is sharing too many of the same
characteristics a problem for the cheetah population?

The History of Genetics

Vocabulary

Get Ready

What are some characteristics that plants or animals might pass along to their offspring? Not all of the puppies in this litter look exactly like their mother. Do the characteristics of both parents always show up in offspring? Can an offspring's characteristics always be predicted?

Inquiry Skill

You infer when you form an idea from facts or observations.

Explore Activity

What Are Inherited Traits?

Materials

purple-and-yellow ear of corn (as in C)

calculator

Each corn kernel is a separate seed, able to grow into a corn plant. The two ears of corn in A represent the parents of the corn in B. The two purple-eared corn plants (B) are the parents of offspring of two colors, as shown in C.

Procedure

1 **Observe** Count the number of purple kernels on your ear of corn. Record this number.

2 **Observe** Repeat step 1 for any yellow kernels.

3 **Use Numbers** Write a ratio of purple kernels to yellow kernels in your group's ear of corn.

$$\text{Ratio} = \frac{\text{purple kernels}}{\text{yellow kernels}}$$

4 **Use Numbers** Add up the class totals for purple kernels and yellow kernels. Find the average number of each color. Calculate the ratio of purple kernels to yellow kernels for the class averages. Use a calculator to help. Record this ratio.

Drawing Conclusions

1 How did the ratio for your ear of corn compare with the ratio for the class total?

2 [FURTHER INQUIRY] **Hypothesize** Form a hypothesis that explains your findings.

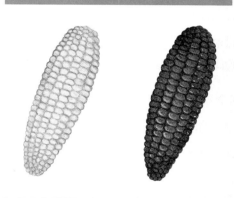

A. The "Parents"

B. Generation 1

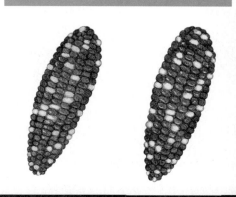

C. Generation 2

What Are Inherited Traits?

Have you ever heard of purple corn? Corn kernels can be purple as well as yellow. Color is a characteristic that is passed from the parent corn plants to the offspring. It is passed on through the seeds. The offspring grow from seeds produced by the parent plant.

The most common corn we eat is all yellow. Farmers can produce corn that has all yellow kernels. They make sure that the seeds form from parent plants that will pass on yellow color to their offspring.

Some purple ears of corn can produce plants with purple-and-yellow ears. By counting and comparing, you can find a ratio of purple to yellow kernels in the two-colored ears of corn.

A characteristic that is passed from parent to offspring is called an **inherited trait** . In corn, inherited traits include kernel color, ear size, and plant height.

Heredity is the passing of these traits from one *generation* to the next. The word *generation* refers to parents and offspring. Parents are one generation. Their offspring are another.

Heredity applies to all organisms, including plants, animals, and even bacteria. Fur color is an inherited trait passed from dogs to their puppies. Humans have inherited traits, too. Hair color, eye color, and dimples are examples of human inherited traits.

Just which traits are inherited and which are not? Scientists are still trying to find out. For example, you may inherit a body type, such as tall and slender, from your family. However, whether you develop fully into that type depends a lot on how much physical activity you do, your diet, the rest you get, and other health habits.

Do humans inherit ability to do math? Play a piano? Scientists are still trying to find out just what traits are inherited. They are still exploring how heredity is affected by the environment and health habits.

Physical features are just some of the traits children inherit from their parents. Inherited traits also include blood type, right- or left-handedness, color blindness, and even the ability to taste certain flavors.

Gregor Mendel (1822–1884) was the first person to count the numbers and types of offspring of pea plants to measure the inheritance of specific traits.

History of Genetics

People have always noticed that offspring inherit many traits from their parents, but the way heredity works was not very well understood until about 100 years ago. The scientific study of heredity began in the 19th century, when an Austrian monk named Gregor Mendel carried out experiments with different varieties of garden peas.

Mendel grew up on his family's farm. As he learned how to care for plants and animals, he became curious about how traits are passed from one generation to the next. He wondered why all brothers and sisters don't look alike.

After studying science and math in school and at a university, he became both a priest and a science teacher. In 1857 Mendel was put in charge of the gardens at the monastery where he lived.

He began conducting carefully controlled experiments to trace how certain traits were passed from parent pea plants to their offspring. Mendel studied the same kind of peas you've probably eaten. Pea plants have distinct traits, which are easy to trace from one generation to another. Peas' offspring grow and mature quickly, so Mendel was able to conduct many experiments and gather large amounts of scientific data. Mendel used scientific methods, kept detailed records, and analyzed his data mathematically. After eight years he presented his findings to the National Science Society in Austria.

Mendel wrote descriptions of his research in a scientific paper that was published in 1866. Scientists of that time did not pay much attention to Mendel's results. Years later, around the year 1900, three other scientists who had reached conclusions very similar to Mendel's rediscovered his published papers. These scientists recognized the value of Mendel's work. In 1909 the study of how heredity works became known as **genetics**. Since then Gregor Mendel has been called the father of genetics.

READING Main Idea
How do inherited traits affect how a person looks?

How Can Inherited Traits Be Studied?

Why did Mendel study pea plants? Garden peas were a good choice for Mendel's experiments. They are fast-growing plants, so Mendel was able to observe hundreds of generations. Large numbers of offspring are needed to obtain accurate results in genetic experiments.

Peas also have traits that are easy to observe. Several of these traits appear in only two forms. For example, the pea plants Mendel studied were either tall or short, their seeds were either yellow or green, and their flowers were either white or purple.

Pollination

The structure of pea plants made it easy to work with them. Mendel's goal was to study **pollination** (pahl·uh·NAY·shuhn) taking place. Pollination is the transfer of pollen grains from the male part of a flower to the female part of a flower. Pollen grains contain the male sex cells. The female part of the plant contains the female sex cells.

As a result of pollination, the male sex cells are able to travel to the female sex cells. When a male sex cell reaches a female sex cell (the egg cell), they join into one cell. The joining of the male sex cell and female sex cell is called *fertilization*. The cell that is formed when the two cells join eventually develops into a seed. The seed can grow into an offspring plant, the next generation.

The male and female parts of pea flowers are covered by the flower's

Pollination

Flowers are reproductive organs. Seeds develop in them. In a pea plant flower, you can see the parts very clearly.

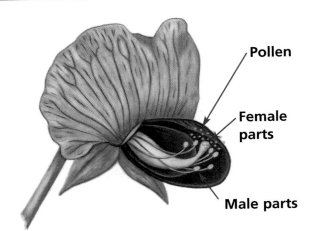

Pollen

Female parts

Male parts

Pea flowers are normally self-pollinated. Pollen grains formed in the male parts of the flower simply fall onto the female parts.

petals. The tightly closed petals prevent pollen from traveling from one flower to another. As a result, pollen formed in the male parts of a pea flower pollinates the female parts of the same flower. This is called *self-pollination.*

Cross-pollination takes place when pollen from one flower is transported to a different flower. Many kinds of flowers are cross-pollinated with the help of wind, birds, or insects. In an experiment, cross-pollination of peas requires removing the pollen-producing parts from a flower so it cannot self-pollinate. Then the egg cells in the flower are fertilized with pollen from a different pea flower. Mendel used cross-pollination whenever he *crossed* two pea plants. Before the pollen ripens, the male parts of the first flower are removed. Then pollen is taken from a second flower and

Pollen sticks to the body of a honeybee as it gathers nectar from a flower. When the bee visits another flower of the same type, some of the pollen rubs off onto the female parts of the second flower.

brushed onto the female parts of the first flower. The fertilized flower is then covered with a cloth bag to prevent more pollen from entering.

> **How did Mendel control pollination in order to study inherited traits?**

READING
Diagrams

1. How is self-pollination different from cross-pollination?

2. How are the two processes alike?

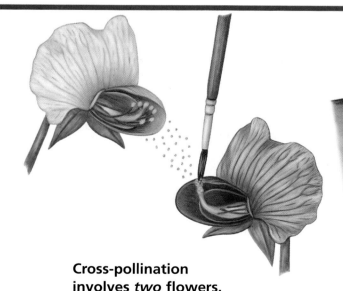

Cross-pollination involves *two* flowers.

Seed in soil

Growing seed

New pea plant

After pollination happens, seeds form in the female part of a flower. The seeds, when planted, can develop into offspring.

What Did Mendel's Experiments Show?

Mendel began his experiments by first selecting pea plants that were *purebred* for a particular trait. An organism is purebred for a trait if, when self-pollinated, the same form of that trait is shown in all of its offspring for several generations of self-pollination. For example, a pea plant purebred for tallness produces only tall offspring by self-pollination. A plant purebred for shortness produces only short offspring by self-pollination.

In one of his first experiments, Mendel cross-pollinated purebred tall peas with purebred short peas. All of the offspring resulting from this cross were tall. The offspring were **hybrids**. A hybrid is an organism produced by crossing parents that have two different forms of the same trait. In this case one parent was tall, the other short.

Why do you think all the hybrids were tall? When Mendel saw the results of this cross, he asked the same question. What happened to the short trait? Mendel hypothesized that the trait for shortness must have been present but was somehow hidden.

He did a second experiment to test his hypothesis. He allowed the tall hybrids from the first offspring generation to self-pollinate. This resulted in a second generation of offspring with both tall and short plants. The trait for shortness was indeed hidden in the first generation tall hybrids.

Mendel's Experiments

Because peas are self-pollinating, it was not difficult for Mendel to obtain purebred plants. To make certain that these two plants were purebred for tallness, all Mendel had to do was cross-pollinate them and check to see that all of their offspring were tall.

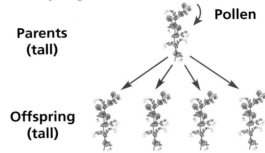

Parents (tall)

Pollen

Offspring (tall)

In Mendel's experiments he crossed purebred tall and short pea plants.

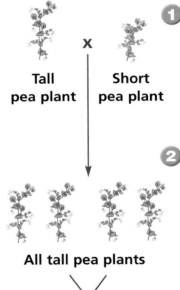

Tall pea plant   X   Short pea plant

All tall pea plants

3 tall, 1 short pea plants

1. The purebred parent plants are called the parent generation.

2. The tall hybrid plants that resulted from this cross are called the first offspring generation.

3. When the tall hybrids were allowed to self-pollinate, they produced a second offspring generation with a ratio of three tall plants to every short plant.

Mendel concluded that each tall hybrid in the first offspring generation carried both tall and short traits. He called tallness the **dominant trait**. A dominant trait is the form of the trait that appears in the hybrid generation, that is, after purebred parents with different forms of a trait are crossed. He called shortness the **recessive trait**. A recessive trait is the form of a trait hidden, or masked, in the hybrid generation.

Every time Mendel crossed two hybrids, he got the same result. For every three offspring that showed the dominant trait, one showed the recessive trait. There was always a ratio of three dominant to one recessive, or 3:1. A *ratio* is a mathematical term that describes the relationship between two quantities. You can also write the ratio 3:1 as "3 to 1" or as $\frac{3}{1}$.

▶ **How did Mendel's experiments show how traits are inherited?**

QUICK LAB

Using Mendel's Ideas

FOLDABLES Make a Folded Table. (See p. R 44.) Label as shown.

Cross 1	
Cross 2	
Cross 3	

1. **Predict** Use the description of each cross to predict what the offspring will look like. Write your predictions. The dominant traits in watermelons include round shape, solid green outer color, and red inside-flesh color.

Cross 1	A round watermelon is crossed with a long watermelon.
Cross 2	A solid-green watermelon is crossed with a striped watermelon.
Cross 3	A red-fleshed watermelon is crossed with a yellow-fleshed watermelon.

2. **Infer** Did cross 1 result in all long offspring, all round offspring, or some long and some round offspring? Explain in your Folded Table.

3. **Infer** Did cross 2 result in all striped, all green, or some striped and some green offspring? Explain.

4. **Infer** How do you think cross 3 turned out? Explain.

What Did Mendel Conclude?

What do you think it takes to be successful in what you do? Mendel was successful in his studies of heredity. Why?

For one thing, he kept his experiments simple. He studied only one or two traits at a time. This made it easier to analyze his results. He kept detailed records of the results of thousands of plants. This meant he had large amounts of data to analyze.

Mendel identified dominant traits and recessive traits very carefully. How? He purebred the plants for different forms of a trait. For example,

to study the trait of seed color, he developed purebred plants with yellow seeds and purebred plants with green seeds. When he crossed them, the hybrid generation all had yellow seeds. Yellow, therefore, is dominant. The trait that is masked, green, is recessive. It appears when two hybrids are crossed. Here are the dominant and recessive traits Mendel identified.

READING
Charts

If a pea plant has wrinkled seeds, is the trait expressed the dominant form or recessive form?

Traits in Garden Pea Plants Studied by Mendel

	Seed shape	Seed color	Plant height	Flower color	Flower position	Pod color	Pod shape
Dominant form	Round	Yellow	Tall	Purple	Sides of branches	Green	Full
Recessive form	Wrinkled	Green	Short	White	Tips of branches	Yellow	Flat

Mendel's Hypothesis

By comparing the traits of parents and their offspring, Mendel discovered that offspring show some traits of one parent and some traits of the other parent. However, offspring do not show all the traits of both parents. Mendel used this information to form a hypothesis to explain how traits are inherited.

Mendel hypothesized that

- inherited traits are passed on from parents to offspring during reproduction.

- traits are passed from parent to offspring. Offspring inherit a pair of "factors" for each trait—one factor from each parent. Offspring "express" one form of each trait.

- the factors in a pair may be the same or different. If they are different, the factor for the dominant form of the trait is shown, or expressed, in the offspring. It is the *dominant factor*. The factor for the recessive form of the trait is "masked" by the dominant factor. The masked factor is the *recessive factor*.

- in some hybrids dominant factors mask recessive factors. Recessive factors show up in offspring only when no dominant factor is inherited.

In the case of pea plants, each factor is responsible for either the dominant or the recessive form of the trait. The diagram above shows a way of representing dominant and recessive traits.

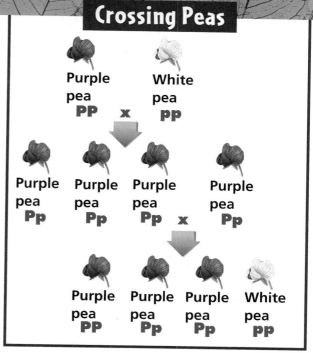

Crossing Peas

Mendel's "factors" for each trait can be represented by letters. A capital letter represents the dominant factor. A lower-case letter represents the recessive factor. In peas the factor for purple flower color is dominant (P). The factor for white flower color is recessive (p).

Mendel's research is important because the principles he discovered apply to all organisms, not just garden peas. *Geneticists* (juh·NET·uh·sists), scientists who study how heredity works, experimenting with fruit flies, corn, and other plants and animals, have shown that dominant and recessive factors pass from parent to offspring by the same patterns Mendel described.

Mendel did not know what his "factors" were. He did not know about all the parts of cells. Today we know that the factors are parts of cells, as you will find out later in this chapter.

▷ **What did Mendel conclude after his experiments?**

What Is Probability?

If you toss a coin, how many possible outcomes, or results, can you get? Try it.

There are two possible outcomes—heads or tails. There is a 50 percent **probability** that the coin will land heads up. *Probability* means "how likely it is that something will happen." The probability that something will happen can be calculated using mathematics.

Since there is an equal chance of getting heads or tails when you toss a coin, you would predict that several tosses will yield an equal number of heads and tails. The ratio of this predicted outcome is one head for every tail, or 1:1.

If you tossed the coin four times, you would predict an outcome of two heads and two tails. However, if you actually try it, your results might be different. You might get three heads and one tail, or no heads and four tails.

What if you toss the coin 100 times? The outcome will likely be much closer to the predicted 1:1 ratio, which would be 50 heads and 50 tails. The greater the number of observations, or trials, the closer the outcome will be to the prediction.

The coin landing heads up on one toss has no effect on what will happen during the next toss. If the coin lands heads up four times in a row, it is not more likely to land either heads up or tails up on the fifth toss.

Probabilities can be written as ratios. They can also be written as percentages or as fractions. The chance that a tossed coin will land heads up is $\frac{1}{2}$, $\frac{50}{100}$, or 50 percent.

Predicting Outcomes

When two parents have a child, there is about a 50 percent chance the child will be female. However, almost everyone knows a family with more girls than boys, or more boys than girls.

If you count the ratio of males to females in a large group, however, such as all the students in your school district, you will find that about half are female and half are male.

Using Probability to Predict Genetic Outcomes

You know how to predict the probable outcome of tossing a single coin. What if you tossed two coins at once? Each coin has two sides, so there are four possible outcomes. Each outcome has a 25 percent chance of being the result of a single toss. If coin 1 and coin 2 are tossed at the same time, there is one chance in four that both coins will land heads up. The probability that both coins will land tails up is also one chance in four, or 25 percent.

Notice that there are two ways in which the toss could result in a combination of heads and tails—coin 1 heads and coin 2 tails, or coin 1 tails and coin 2 heads. The probability of each heads-tails outcome is one chance in four, or 25 percent. Since there are two heads-tails combinations, the probability of getting heads-tails is 50 percent. The ratio of all four possible outcomes is 25 percent heads-heads, 50 percent heads-tails, and 25 percent tails-tails, or 1:2:1.

The possible outcomes of a two-coin toss are very similar to those of a genetic cross. Geneticists use the laws of probability to predict the results of genetic crosses. Why?

There are two possible factors for a trait. Each parent, like a coin, has two factors for a trait. Like tossing two coins, two parents give one factor each for a trait to the offspring. The offspring, like the result of a two-coin toss, gets two factors, one from each parent.

READING Main Idea
Why is probability important in genetics?

Coin-Toss Results			
After Toss		**Number of Combinations**	**Percent**
Coin 1	Coin 2		
(H)	(H)	1	$\frac{1}{4}$ = 25%
(H)	(T)	2	$\frac{2}{4}$ = 50%
(T)	(H)		
(T)	(T)	1	$\frac{1}{4}$ = 25%
Total number of combinations		4	

Try tossing two coins at the same time. Mark one coin "1" on both sides. Mark the other "2" on both sides. Record your results of 1 to 100 tosses.

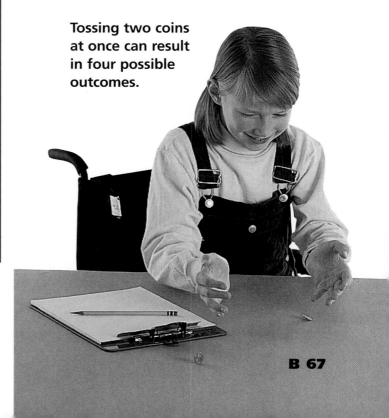

Tossing two coins at once can result in four possible outcomes.

This Punnett square predicts the outcome of a cross between two purebred bean plants. The male parent is purebred for red bean color, and the female is purebred for white.

This Punnett square predicts the outcome of a cross between two hybrid bean plants. There are three possible outcomes.

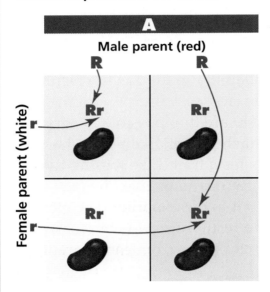

A

Male parent (red)

R   R

Female parent (white)

r → Rr   Rr

r → Rr   Rr

B

Male parent (red)

R   r

Female parent (red)

R   25% RR   25% Rr

r   25% Rr   25% rr

RR : Rr : rr

1 : 2 : 1

What Is a Punnett Square?

Have you ever used a multiplication table? How did it work?

In genetics you can use a kind of table to help predict inherited traits. The table is a **Punnett square**. A Punnett square is a table used to predict the outcome of crossing different forms of a trait, such as in Mendel's experiments.

In a Punnett square, letters are used to represent Mendel's factors for each trait.

- A capital letter stands for the dominant factor, and a lowercase letter stands for the recessive factor.

- To make a Punnett square, draw a large square and divide it into four smaller squares. Write the parents' factors for the trait outside the square.

- Fill in each square with the letter above it and the letter to the left of it. The squares show all the possible combinations of traits in the offspring.

A Punnett square shows the different combinations of factors offspring can inherit from their parents. A red-seeded bean plant could have inherited two dominant factors, RR, or one dominant

This Punnett square predicts the traits of offspring from a cross between a purebred parent and a hybrid parent.

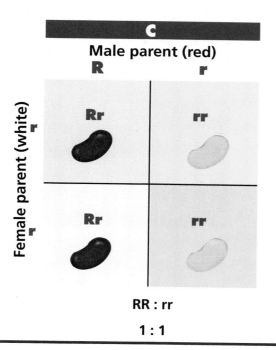

C

Male parent (red)

R   r

Female parent (white)

r   Rr   rr

r   Rr   rr

RR : rr

1 : 1

READING Diagrams

1. In which cross (A, B, or C) is there a 25 percent chance of getting white beans as offspring?

2. In which cross (A, B, or C) do all the offspring beans look alike and have the same factors for color?

The ratio of inherited factors is 1 RR (pure red, both dominant) to 2 Rr (hybrid red) to 1 rr (white, both recessive)—that is, 1:2:1.

Since both RR and Rr yield plants with red seeds, the ratio of red-seeded to white-seeded offspring would be 3:1. You would predict that, out of 100 offspring, 75 will have red seeds and 25 will have white seeds.

It is important to remember that the factors inherited by the first offspring of a cross have no effect at all on other offspring of that cross. For example, there is a 25 percent probability that offspring of a cross between two hybrid bean plants will inherit the factors RR. If one offspring inherits RR, there is still a 25 percent probability that the next offspring will also inherit RR.

▶ **How are Punnett squares used to predict traits?**

and one recessive factor, Rr. Only bean plants that inherited two recessive factors, rr, have white seeds.

The combination of factors inherited by offspring is not exactly the same thing as the physical appearance of the offspring. You cannot tell, based on appearance alone, whether a red-seeded bean plant is purebred or a hybrid.

However, you can use the probability ratios obtained from a Punnett square to predict how many offspring will have red seeds and how many will have white seeds. What if cross B shown on page B68 resulted in 100 offspring?

Inquiry Skill
BUILDER

How Can You Find Probability Using a Punnett Square?

Eyelashes can be long or short. Long eyelashes are the dominant trait. Short eyelashes are the recessive trait. To represent these traits, you can use the letters

- L (the factor for long eyelashes, dominant)

- l (the factor for short eyelashes, recessive)

A person with long eyelashes may have either two of the same factors (LL) or two different factors (Ll). A person with short eyelashes has two of the same factors (ll).

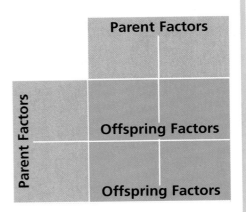

Procedure

1 **Make a Model** Two parents both have long eyelashes. Each parent has two different factors for eyelash length. Draw a Punnett square to show what factors for eyelash length a child might inherit from the parents.

2 How many different Punnett squares can you draw to show one parent with long eyelashes and one with short?

Drawing Conclusions

1 **Use Numbers** In your cross for step 1, what is the probability that the child will have short eyelashes? To tell, count the number of boxes in your Punnett square that show the two factors that give short eyelashes (ll). Compare this number of boxes with the total number of boxes.

2 For each Punnett square you drew in step 2, what is the probability of a child having short eyelashes?

What Is Incomplete Dominance?

Do all patterns of heredity follow Mendel's basic ideas? Some inherited traits do not. Mendel studied how recessive and dominant factors are passed from parent to child. However, there are some dominant factors that do not completely mask factors for the other form of the trait.

In four-o'clock flowers, for example, the dominant factor for color results in a red flower only if the plant has inherited two dominant factors for red color. Plants with one dominant factor for red color and one dominant factor for white color may have pink flowers—a combination of red and white.

This pattern of inheritance is called **incomplete dominance** . Incomplete dominance results when neither of the two forms of a trait completely masks the other. Red does not mask white. White does not mask red. Instead a third form of the trait appears—pink.

In this flower the factors for white color and red color are showing incomplete dominance. A plant with two factors for red color, RR, has red flowers. A plant with two factors for white color, WW, has white flowers. If these two flowers are crossed, neither factor masks the other.

In Mendel's experiments traits came in two forms—tall

▷ **How are traits expressed in incomplete dominance?**

or short plants, round or wrinkled seeds, and so on. However, traits don't always come in just two forms. There may be more. Human eye color is an example. Eyes can be brown, blue, hazel, gray, or green. These colors are controlled by more than just two factors.

Height and weight are traits controlled by more than just a pair of factors. So are body build, the shape of the eyes, and the shape of the lips. Skin color is controlled by three to six factors.

Four factors control fur color in rabbits, but each rabbit inherits only two factors, one from each parent. The C factor is dominant over all the others, so any rabbit with at least one C factor has a gray coat. Other colors result from different combinations of the other three factors.

READING

Diagrams

What is the result of crossing a red four-o'clock and a white four-o'clock?

Incomplete Dominance

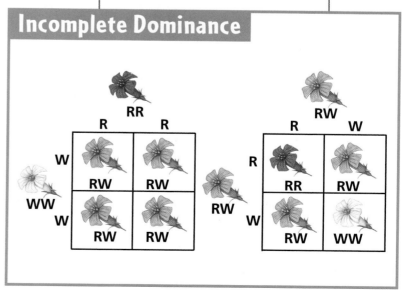

What Is a Pedigree?

Do you know what a pedigreed dog or cat is? It is an animal that has a family line that is recorded so that a given trait can be traced from parents back to grandparents and great-grandparents.

A **pedigree** (PED·i·gree) is a chart used to trace the history of traits in a family. A pedigree shows which members of the family have a particular trait, such as curly hair, long eyelashes, or attached earlobes. Symbols are used to make a pedigree.

- Shaded shapes stand for individuals who show a form of a particular trait, either dominant or recessive.

- Unshaded shapes stand for individuals who do not have that form of the trait.

- Circles are females, and squares are males.

- A square and circle connected by a horizontal line stands for male and female parents.

- A vertical line connects parents to their offspring.

- All the children in the family are also connected by a horizontal line. The oldest child is always at the left, and the youngest at the right.

In a pedigree some individuals are called **carriers**. A carrier is an individual who has inherited the factor for a particular trait but who does not show that trait. For example, the pedigree here shows that the mother has curly hair. The father does, too. Of their four children, three have curly hair and one has straight hair.

If you know that the inherited factor for straight hair is recessive, the pedigree tells you that both parents must be carriers of the straight hair factor.

READING
Diagrams

1. What trait is shown here? What are the two forms of that trait?

2. What is the ratio of each form of the trait among the children?

Pedigree for Curly Hair

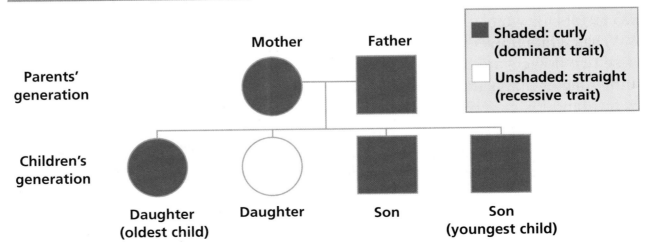

Mother   Father

Parents' generation

Shaded: curly (dominant trait)

Unshaded: straight (recessive trait)

Children's generation

Daughter (oldest child)   Daughter   Son   Son (youngest child)

Pedigree for Short Eyelashes

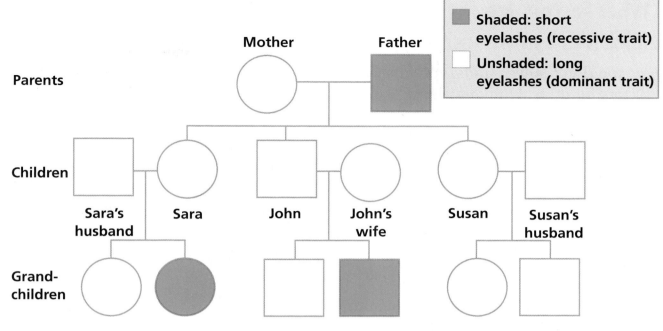

Parents

Mother   Father

Shaded: short eyelashes (recessive trait)

Unshaded: long eyelashes (dominant trait)

Children

Sara's husband   Sara   John   John's wife   Susan   Susan's husband

Grand-children

The pedigree above traces short eyelashes in three generations of a family. By analyzing the chart, you can tell which family members might be carriers of the recessive factor for short eyelashes. First, look at the parents' generation. Since the father has short eyelashes, he must have two recessive factors for eyelash length (ll). The father must have passed on one recessive factor to each child. Since the mother has long eyelashes, the pedigree cannot tell us whether she carries two dominant factors for eyelash length (LL) or one dominant and one recessive factor (Ll).

Second, look at the children's generation. No child has short eyelashes. However, since each child received one recessive factor from the father, all three children in this family must be carriers of the recessive factor for short eyelashes (Ll).

READING
Diagrams

If one or both of Susan's children had short eyelashes, what factors might the father have?

Third, look at the grandchildren's generation. One of Sara's children has short eyelashes. One of John's does, too. This tells us that both Sara and John, and their spouses, must be carriers of the recessive factor. Since neither of Susan's children has short eyelashes, the pedigree cannot tell us whether or not their father is a carrier.

▶ **How can a pedigree show how a trait is passed from generation to generation?**

What Factors Are Inherited by Humans?

You don't inherit traits, you inherit factors for traits. Humans inherit thousands of factors for traits from their parents. The color of your hair and skin, the color of your eyes, the thickness of your eyebrows, and even your height were determined by factors you inherited from your parents. Humans inherit one factor for each trait from each parent. That results in a total of two factors for each trait in the child.

One of the traits people inherit from their parents is earlobe shape. Some people have earlobes that are completely attached, while others have earlobes that are unattached. The factor for free earlobes is dominant—let E stand for free earlobes. The factor for attached earlobes is recessive—let e stand for attached earlobes.

Any person who has attached earlobes most likely has two recessive factors for the trait, or ee. There are two possibilities for anyone who has free earlobes. That person could have inherited two dominant factors from his or her parents, EE, or one dominant and one recessive, Ee.

> ▷ **What factors must be inherited in order for a person to show a recessive trait?**

Earlobe Shape

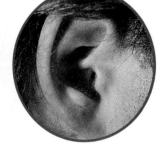

Free earlobe

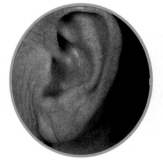

Attached earlobe

Hairline

Widow's peak

Straight hairline

Presence of Dimples

Dimples

No dimples

Why It Matters

The principles of heredity that Mendel discovered apply to all living organisms.

Understanding genetics has a lot to do with ratios and probabilities. How does probability work in your life? How can you increase the probability of getting to school on time so that you can be more sure of your result? You might get up earlier or pack your books the night before.

 e-Journal Visit our Web site www.science.mmhschool.com to do a research project on inherited and non-inherited traits.

Think and Write

1. What is a Punnett square used to show?

2. What does *heredity* mean? Give some examples.

3. What would a dog's pedigree tell you about the traits it expresses?

4. INQUIRY SKILL Use Numbers Explain how it is possible for two parents, each with a dominant factor for dimples, to have a child without dimples. Draw a Punnett square to explain your answer.

5. **Critical Thinking** How can you tell if an ear of purple corn was bred for the purple trait?

L·I·N·K·S

MATH LINK

Calculate probability. What is the probability of your school team winning an upcoming event? How else is probability a part of your life? Use Punnett squares to find the probability of different outcomes of events in your life.

WRITING LINK

Expository Writing Which physical traits are noticeable in families? Use reference books or the Internet to find photographs of famous historical families, such as the British royal family or the Kennedy family. Which common traits can you identify? Write an essay to share your observations. Use some descriptive details.

TECHNOLOGY LINK

 Science Newsroom CD-ROM Choose *Pass It Along* to learn more about Mendel's principles.

LOG ON Visit www.science.mmhschool.com for more links.

Vocabulary

gene, B78

DNA, B78

How DNA Controls Traits

Get Ready

What is a code? Braille is a code that stands for letters or words. The three-letter code on baggage tags tells airport workers where to send your bags. The bar code on each tag can be scanned by computers to help keep track of your bag when you travel.

Another type of code is found in every cell of your body. It controls traits that develop in every offspring. How do you think it works?

Inquiry Skill

You **predict** when you state possible results of an event or experiment.

Explore Activity

How Does a Four-Part Code Work?

Materials

genetic puzzle pieces (or 4 of each shown)

Procedure

1. **Make a Model** Assemble the pieces so that all of them fit together. Draw a copy of your assembled puzzle.

2. **Predict** How can you assemble the pieces in a different way? How many different models can you make?

3. **Communicate** How are your models like those of other students? Are any the same? If they are different, how?

Drawing Conclusions

1. Which parts fit together? Which parts do not? Explain why they do or do not fit.

2. **Experiment** Develop a simple way of showing the arrangement of the pieces without actually drawing the assembled pieces. How does your method work?

3. What is the main difference between the many ways you assembled the puzzle?

4. How might the different ways of assembling the puzzle be used as a code?

5. FURTHER INQUIRY **Predict** Create a fifth puzzle piece. Label it U. How would you have to shape the piece to make it fit into the puzzle? Will all of the pieces fit together—or will one have to be left out?

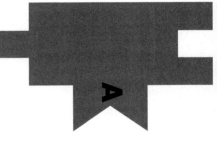

Main Idea DNA is a code found in every cell of your body that determines what traits you express.

What Is DNA?

Gregor Mendel realized that all organisms get two copies of each factor—one factor from each parent. Today scientists call these factors **genes** (JEENZ). A gene is the portion of a cell's chromosome that controls a particular trait. Genes contain the information needed for cells to function. Genes are arranged along the length of a chromosome.

Organisms have two copies of each gene for a given trait. They get one copy from each parent. For example, the length of your eyelashes was determined by one "eyelash" gene you got from your mother and one "eyelash" gene you got from your father. Both genes are located in the same place on each chromosome.

How the Code Works

Genes are portions of a long, complex molecule called deoxyribonucleic (dee·AHK·si·righ·boh·noo·klee·ik) acid, or **DNA**. DNA contains the codes that tell each cell how to operate. Each gene on a chromosome is a short section of the long DNA molecule that makes up the chromosome. The genetic characteristics of every living organism are contained in that organism's DNA. The DNA in each cell of a given organism is the same. The DNA of every organism is different from that of every other

Genes and DNA

A Pair of Chromosomes

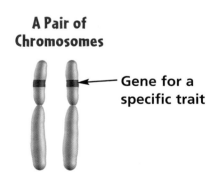

← Gene for a specific trait

A Cell

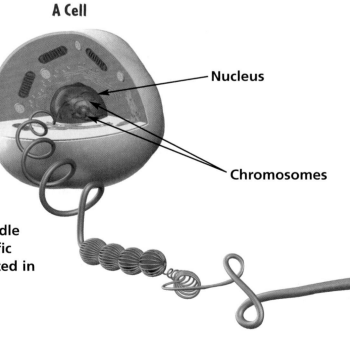

Nucleus

Chromosomes

Two copies of the same gene occur on each chromosome in a normal two-bundle set. The two genes that control a specific trait—such as eyelash length—are located in the same place on each chromosome.

organism, just as you are different from your classmates.

The codes that the DNA molecule contains are related to the molecule's shape and structure. The shape looks like a spiral staircase. The steps of the staircase are made of chemical compounds, called bases, that fit together like the pieces in a puzzle.

The four DNA bases are cytosine (C), guanine (G), thymine (T), and adenine (A). Each step of the DNA staircase is made up of two bases, either A and T, or G and C. The order in which the base pairs appear on the DNA helix is the code that tells the cell how to operate. There might be an A—T above a T—A, a G—C, a C—G, or another A—T. The order allows for a huge number of combinations.

There are many possible combinations of DNA base pairs.

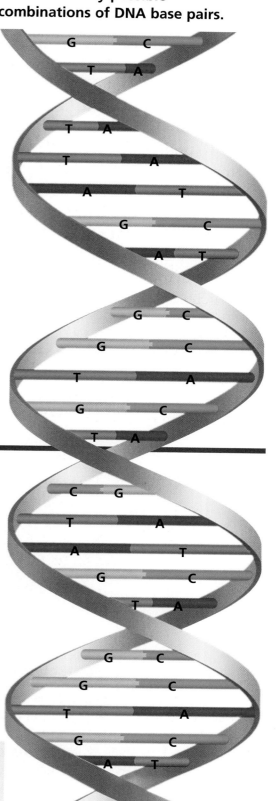

READING Main Idea

How are genes and DNA related?

Genes are strung along the length of each chromosome. DNA is the genetic material that makes up genes and chromosomes. The shape of the DNA molecule looks something like a spiral staircase or a twisted ladder. This shape is called a double helix.

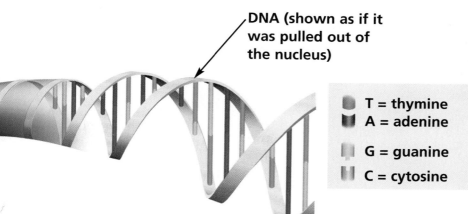

DNA (shown as if it was pulled out of the nucleus)

T = thymine
A = adenine

G = guanine
C = cytosine

Where Is DNA Located?

When Mendel conducted his experiments, he knew very little about cells or what cells contain. However, today we know that Mendel's factors, the genes, are inside the cell.

To understand how DNA works, it is important to find out where it is. It is a molecule found in the nucleus of a cell.

Every cell is surrounded by a cell membrane. Inside the cell membrane is a fluid called cytoplasm. In the center of the cytoplasm is the cell nucleus, which contains chromosomes. Chromosomes are made up of DNA.

Most of the time, the chromosomes form a tangled mass of thin threads inside the nucleus. The individual threads become visible under a microscope when a cell is preparing to divide in two. That's when you can actually count the chromosomes.

▶ **What part of the cell contains DNA?**

READING
Diagrams

In what part of the cell are chromosomes found?

The Cell

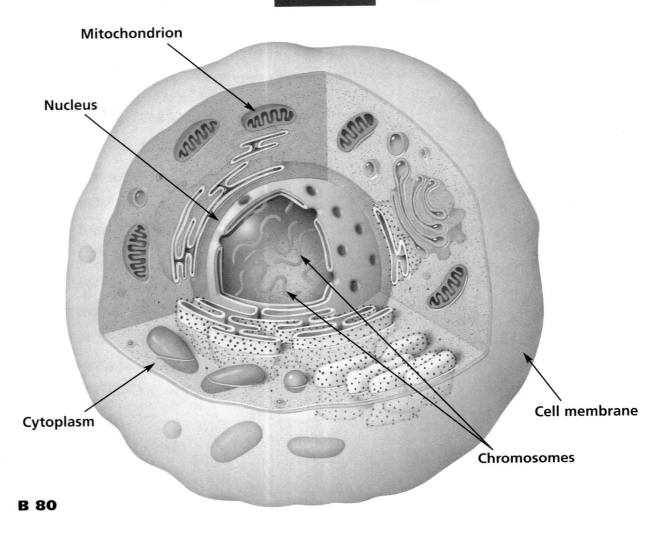

Mitochondrion

Nucleus

Cytoplasm

Cell membrane

Chromosomes

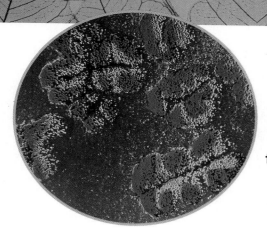

Chromosomes are made of the hereditary material (DNA) that controls the passing of traits from parent to offspring.

How Do Body Cells and Sex Cells Differ?

Many-celled organisms are made of two types of cells, body cells and sex cells. Your skin, bones, tissues, and organs are composed of body cells. The cells of a carrot root are body cells. So are the cells of a tree leaf. Most of the cells in any organism are body cells. All body cells contain a full set of chromosomes. A human body cell contains 46 chromosomes. A rabbit body cell contains 44 chromosomes. Every organism has its own number of chromosomes in its body cells.

Sex cells are produced inside the sex organs of an adult organism. When a sex cell from a female parent and a sex cell from a male parent join together, the single cell that forms can eventually develop into the offspring. Each sex cell contains only one-half the number of chromosomes in body cells. A human sex cell contains 23 chromosomes, for example. When two human sex cells join, the resulting cell has 46 chromosomes.

As you learned earlier, body cells form by mitosis, sex cells form by meiosis, and sex cells combine in fertilization to form a new organism.

▷ **What is the difference between body cells and sex cells?**

Chromosomes in Body Cells

Human
46

Rabbit
44

Carrot
18

Grasshopper
24

Copying DNA

FOLDABLES Make a Shutter Fold.
(See p. R 42.)

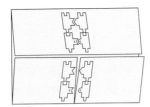

1. **Make a Model** Trace and cut out as many puzzle pieces from page B 77 as you need to model the way DNA duplicates. Build a model of one section of a two-stranded DNA molecule. Then "unzip it." Draw each step on your Shutter Fold.

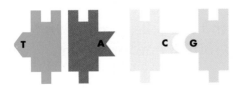

2. **Make a Model** Show the sequence of how each unzipped strand can become two complete DNA molecules.

3. **Communicate** Describe in detail how your model can be duplicated by someone else in your Shutter Fold. Give step-by-step directions. Then give your directions to another person to duplicate your model.

4. How good were your directions? How might you improve them?

How Is DNA Copied?

During mitosis the cell produces a second set of chromosomes. To copy each chromosome, the cell must make a second DNA molecule with exactly the same order of base pairs as the original.

DNA duplicates itself by splitting down the middle to separate the partners in each base pair. Bases floating in the cytoplasm of the cell move in to replace the missing partners, and a new sugar-and-phosphate chain is completed. The result is two new DNA molecules that are identical to the original.

▶ **What happens when DNA is copied?**

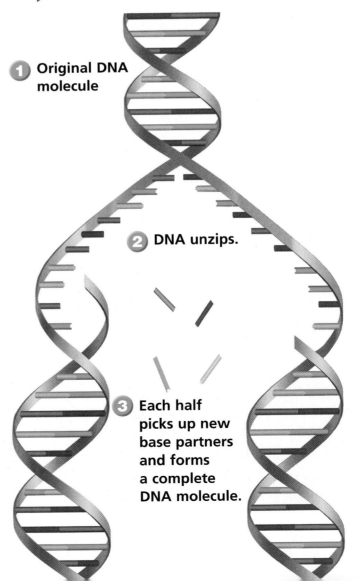

1 **Original DNA molecule**

2 **DNA unzips.**

3 **Each half picks up new base partners and forms a complete DNA molecule.**

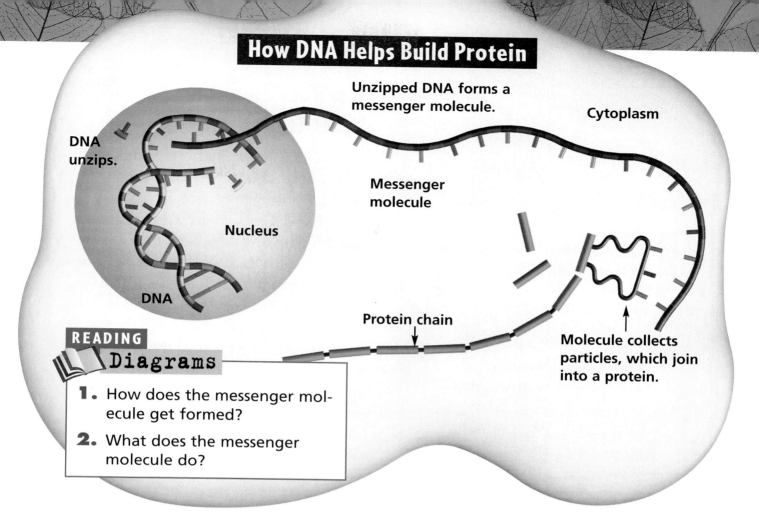

How DNA Helps Build Protein

Unzipped DNA forms a messenger molecule.

Cytoplasm

DNA unzips.

DNA

Nucleus

Messenger molecule

DNA

Protein chain

Molecule collects particles, which join into a protein.

READING Diagrams

1. How does the messenger molecule get formed?

2. What does the messenger molecule do?

How Does the DNA Code Instruct the Cell?

Each gene on a chromosome is made up of a particular number of base pairs on a DNA molecule. The number of base pairs varies from gene to gene. You've seen how the order of the base pairs in the DNA molecule can be copied. How does DNA tell the cell how to operate?

The portion of a DNA molecule that equals one gene can split open while the rest of the molecule can remain closed. When a gene splits open, the gene's bases are separated from their partners. Then other chemicals from the cytoplasm attach to each exposed base.

As the chemicals are attracted to the exposed bases, a messenger molecule is made. This new messenger molecule leaves the gene and goes off into the cell with the instructions for making proteins the cell needs. When the new molecule moves away, the original base pairs reattach, and the gene closes again.

The messenger molecule carries instructions for making a protein that the cell needs to perform particular tasks. In a plant the protein might be needed to make chlorophyll for photosynthesis. In an animal the protein might be needed to help digest food.

▶ **What does DNA use to instruct the cell to make proteins?**

When a hydrangea is grown in acid soil, the flowers are blue. If the soil is more basic, the flowers are pink.

On the left is a tree growing in a forest. On the right is a tree growing on a mountainside.

If the air temperature is fairly cool when certain types of fruit flies mate, the offspring will have larger wings. If the temperature is very high during mating, the offspring will have smaller wings.

How Does Environment Affect Traits?

You've learned that offspring inherit half their genes from each parent. Those genes contain instructions that determine how an organism will develop and function. However, genes are only part of the picture. The environment in which an organism lives and grows also has an effect. The environment can change how the information contained in the genes is expressed. The environment can even prevent a gene from being expressed.

Soil condition is one of the environmental factors that can influence the expression of genetic traits in plants. Flower color in hydrangeas is influenced by soil conditions. The height and shape of a tree is influenced by soil conditions, temperature, and the availability of water. A tree growing in deep, rich forest soil may grow hundreds of feet tall. However, the same tree growing in the rocky soil and harsh conditions of a mountainside may grow only 10 or 20 feet tall. Temperature can affect the trait for wing length in fruit flies.

▷ **What ways can the environment affect the expression of a trait?**

LINKS

Why It Matters

Are you just a bunch of genes? No. The traits that you have came from much more than just inherited genes. Genes are a starting point for inherited traits. In many cases, there are other factors than just genes involved. Your environment and health habits are factors.

The discovery of DNA and the genetic code was one of the most important scientific advances of the twentieth century. Since the genetic code of all living organisms is made from the same chemicals, scientists can use the code to expand our understanding of life.

e-Journal Visit our Web site **www.science.mmhschool.com** to do a research project on DNA.

Think and Write

1. How do body cells and sex cells differ in chromosome number?

2. Classify the following as cells or cell parts—gene, chromosome, DNA, egg, nucleus, sperm.

3. What is important about the order of the "pieces" of a DNA molecule?

4. How does the environment affect heredity?

5. **Critical Thinking** Is the DNA in a brain cell the same as the DNA in a skin cell? Explain your answer.

LITERATURE LINK

Read *The Code of Life.* Use newspapers or use the Internet to find more about how traits are controlled by DNA. Try the activities at the end of the book.

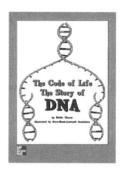

WRITING LINK

Explanatory Writing How does DNA make up chromosomes? Write an essay to explain the steps in the process. Think about your audience as you plan your writing. How much do your readers know about your topic? How much do they need to know?

MATH LINK

Make a bar graph. Compare the number of chromosomes in the body cells with the number of chromosomes in the sex cells of humans, rabbits, carrots, and grasshoppers using the information from page B81. Include other examples that you can find in research books and on the Internet.

TECHNOLOGY LINK

Science Newsroom CD-ROM Choose *A Common Thread* to learn more about DNA.

LOG ON Visit **www.science.mmhschool.com** for more links.

Genetics in Our Lives

Get Ready

What are some inherited traits that show a parent and child resemble each other? Does a daughter have her father's chin? Does she have her mother's eyes?

Some traits, such as curly red hair, may appear only once or twice in several generations. Other traits, such as dimples, may appear in every generation. Why do some traits skip generations and appear in others?

Inquiry Skill

You **communicate** when you share information with others.

Explore Activity

What Are Common Inherited Traits?

Procedure

1 **Observe** Have a partner check you for each of the traits listed in the table below. Record whether you have the dominant or recessive trait.

2 **Observe** Reverse roles and repeat.

3 Tally your results in a classroom chart on a chalkboard that lists all the traits.

Drawing Conclusions

1 **Classify** How many dominant traits do you have? How many recessive traits do you have?

2 **Communicate** Plot the data for the classroom chart on a bar graph.

3 **Infer** Are dominant traits always more common? Explain your answer.

4 **Experiment** How do your classroom results compare with a larger group? Plan an experiment that would answer this question.

5 **FURTHER INQUIRY**
Communicate Find the percent of each trait in the class. The percent is a way of telling the frequency of a trait— how often the trait appears. Do dominant traits have a high frequency?

Look For	Dominant Trait	Recessive Trait
Skin color	dark	light
Freckles	freckles	no freckles
Tongue rolling	can roll edges	cannot roll edges
Shape of hairline	pointed in middle	not pointed
Chin shape	indented in middle	not indented
Thumb	hitchhiker's thumb	straight thumb
Eyelash length	long	short
Eye shape	almond	round
Earlobes	free	attached

Main Idea Many traits follow the common patterns of inheritance, but some patterns are more complicated.

What Are Some Inherited Traits?

Do you have any dominant traits? Freckles, long eyelashes, and free earlobes are dominant traits. Their opposite forms—no freckles, short eyelashes, and attached earlobes—are recessive.

Some inherited traits in people are not as simple as dominant or recessive.

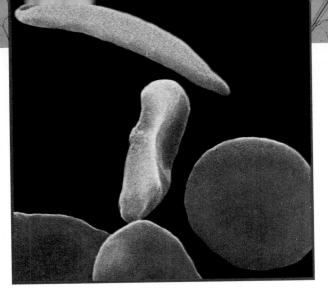

Sickle-shaped cells get their name because they are shaped like sickles. Sickles are curved cutting tools used in farming.

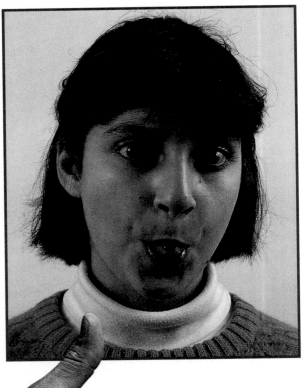

Two dominant traits are the ability to roll up the edges of the tongue and hitchhiker's thumb.

One example is the shape of red blood cells. Red blood cells carry oxygen and nutrients to all parts of the body. Normal red blood cells have a round shape. Sometimes red blood cells are curved like the blade of a sickle. Sickle-shaped cells cannot carry as much oxygen as round cells.

Let R stand for the gene for round red blood cells. R° stands for the gene for sickle-shaped cells.

- Most people have the gene pair RR. That is, they have only round red blood cells.

- People with R°R° genes have only sickle-shaped cells.

- However, people may also inherit one R gene and one R° gene. They have both round and sickle-shaped cells. The genes for round cells do not hide the appearance of the genes for sickle-shaped cells.

Human Blood Types

Blood Type	Inherited Genes	Can Receive	Can Donate To
Type A	$I^A I^A$ or $I^A i$	O, A	A, AB
Type B	$I^B I^B$ or $I^B i$	O, B	B, AB
Type AB	$I^A I^B$	O, A, B, AB	AB
Type O	ii	O	A, B, AB, O

Sickle-shaped cells cannot carry as much oxygen as normal cells. People who have two R° genes have the disease known as sickle cell anemia. Their body tissues and organs become damaged because the sickle-shaped cells cannot supply enough oxygen to keep them healthy. People with this disease can be treated with drugs to increase the amount of oxygen carried by their red blood cells. They may also be given transfusions of blood with normal red cells.

People who have inherited one R° gene and one R gene have the sickle cell trait. They have both normal and sickle-shaped blood cells. They are carriers of the disease but do not have the disease itself.

Blood Type

Blood type is another human trait that is not simply dominant or recessive. Three different genes control blood type. They are labeled I^A, I^B, and i. I^A and I^B are both dominant, masking i. Blood type genes A and B are not dominant for each other. The table shows how different combinations of these genes result in four blood types in humans.

Each person has only one of the four types of blood—A, B, AB, or O. Your blood type is based on a kind of protein found on the surface of red blood cells. There are two such proteins, A and B. Type A blood has only the A protein. Type B has only the B protein. Type AB has both proteins. Type O does not have either of the two proteins.

If unmatching blood types are mixed, the blood can clump. In some cases clumping can be fatal. A person may receive blood from another person with the same protein or with no protein.

Type O blood can be donated to anyone. A person with type O blood is called a "universal donor."

Type AB blood can be given only to a person with type AB blood. However, a person with type AB blood can receive all of the four types. That person is a "universal recipient."

▶ **How are the traits of sickle cell anemia and blood type inherited?**

What Determines the Sex of a Child?

Human chromosomes carry genes that control a variety of traits. Humans have 23 pairs of chromosomes. One of those pairs determines the sex of a person. They are the sex chromosomes. There are two kinds of sex chromosomes, the **X chromosome** and the **Y chromosome**.

- Females inherit two X chromosomes, one from each parent.

- Males inherit one X chromosome from one parent and one Y chromosome from the other. Only males have a Y chromosome.

The sex of a child is determined by the chromosomes received from the father. There is always a 50 percent probability a child will be male and a 50 percent probability that a child will be female.

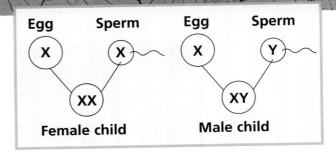

| | Egg | Sperm | Egg | Sperm |

Female child | Male child

These are the 23 pairs of chromosomes in a body cell of a human male. Notice the XY chromosomes.

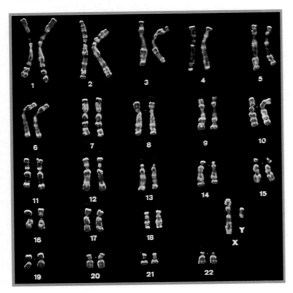

	Father	
	X	Y
X	XX	XY
X	XX	XY

(Mother)

XX: $\frac{2 \text{ boxes}}{4 \text{ boxes}} = 50\%$

XY: $\frac{2 \text{ boxes}}{4 \text{ boxes}} = 50\%$

Sex-Linked Traits

Like all chromosomes, the sex chromosomes carry genes for many traits. Some of the genes carried on the X chromosome are not found on the smaller Y chromosome. These are **sex-linked genes**. Traits determined by sex-linked genes in humans include color blindness and hemophilia. These are called *sex-linked traits*.

▶ **How is the sex of a child determined?**

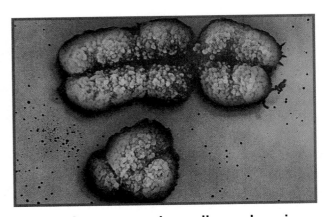

The Y chromosome is smaller and carries fewer genes than the X chromosome.

How Are Sex-Linked Traits Inherited?

Color blindness is the inability to recognize certain colors. A person who has red-green color blindness cannot tell the difference between red and green. The trait for color blindness is recessive, and only the X chromosome carries the gene for this trait.

We can show the X chromosome carrying the recessive gene for color blindness as X^C.

If a male child inherits the recessive gene from his mother, he will be color blind (X^CY). A female child will be color blind only if she inherits the gene from both her mother and father (X^CX^C). If she inherits only one recessive gene, she is a carrier (X^CX). She carries the gene but does not have color blindness. As a result, color blindness is more common in males than in females.

People with normal vision see the number 15 formed by dots. People with red-green color blindness see just dots.

READING Main Idea
How are some traits dependent on a person's sex?

QUICK LAB

Color Blindness

FOLDABLES Make a Two-Tab Book. (See p. R 41.) Label the tabs as shown.

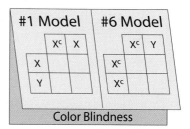

#1 Model			#6 Model		
	X^C	X		X^C	Y
X			X^C		
Y			X^C		

Color Blindness

1. **Make a Model** Set up a Punnett square on your Two-Tab Book to show a carrier mother (X^CX) and a father who is not color blind (XY).

2. **Use Numbers** Fill in the boxes. Tally the number of boxes that show a color-blind male child (X^CY), a male child with normal sight (XY), a color-blind female child (X^CX^C), a female carrier child (X^CX), and a female non-carrier (XX).

3. **Determine** the percentage of each.

4. **Infer** Will all male children be color blind? Explain in your Two-Tab Book.

5. **Infer** Will all female children be carriers? Explain in your Two-Tab Book.

6. **Make a Model** Repeat to show results if both parents are color blind.

Queen Victoria, who ruled England from 1837 to 1901, carried the gene for hemophilia. She did not have the disease but passed the gene on to some of her children. They passed it on as they married into Europe's royal families.

What Kinds of Disorders Are Inherited?

Sickle cell anemia is not a disease you can "catch" from someone else, like a cold or sore throat. It is a genetic disorder, because it is caused by the combination of genes an individual inherited from his or her parents.

Hemophilia (hee·muh·FIL·ee·uh) is an inherited disease. People who have hemophilia have blood that does not clot properly. Small cuts can cause severe bleeding. Hemophiliacs can also suffer from internal bleeding. Like color blindness, hemophilia is a recessive, sex-linked trait. As a result, the disease is more common in males.

Sickle cell anemia, dyslexia, cystic fibrosis, Down syndrome, and PKU are genetic disorders that are not sex linked.

- Dyslexia (dis·LEK·see·uh) is a genetic disorder that is sometimes called word blindness. People who have dyslexia may have trouble reading and writing because they see some letters and words backward. Special teaching methods help these people overcome the problems presented by dyslexia.

- Cystic fibrosis (SIS·tik figh·BROH·sis) is a genetic disorder that causes the buildup of too much thick, sticky mucus in the lungs and other organs. Children with cystic fibrosis have difficulty breathing, which means they may have trouble participating in sports and many other forms of exercise. These children also have trouble digesting food, so they are often kept on special diets. Children with cystic fibrosis do special breathing exercises and receive other kinds of treatment, including physical therapy.

- Down syndrome is a genetic disorder that occurs when a child inherits an extra copy of a specific chromosome. Scientists are studying the genes carried by chromosome number 21 to find out why having an extra copy causes Down syndrome. People

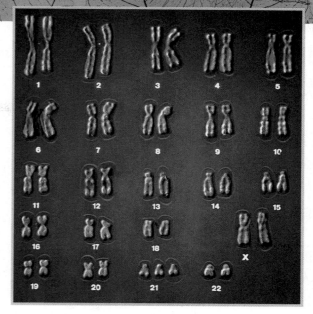

A person's chromosomes were removed from a cell sample and photographed under a microscope. When the chromosomes are paired up, you can see that there is an extra copy of pair number 21. The extra chromosome causes Down syndrome.

with Down syndrome may have severe mental retardation. They may also have problems with their heart, eyes, or intestines. However, many people with Down syndrome may lead active, productive lives.

- PKU is another inherited disease. This is short for phenylketonuria (fen·uhl·kee·tuh·NOOR·ee·uh). This disease affects the nervous system. The body cannot break down a certain substance. The substance builds up and can cause brain damage. This disease can be treated if the treatment starts soon after a child is born. There is a test for PKU for newborns.

Daily physical therapy treatments help to loosen the thick coating of mucus in the lungs of a child who has cystic fibrosis. Cystic fibrosis is the most common genetic disorder in Caucasians.

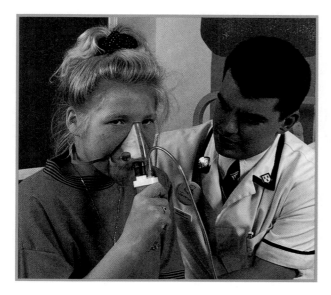

▶ **How is Down syndrome an inherited disorder?**

How Is Genetics Helping People Today?

Scientists are applying the techniques of genetic engineering to many aspects of human life. Insulin is now routinely made using gene-splicing.

Growth Hormone

Human growth hormone is also being produced by gene-splicing. People make their own growth hormone. It is a substance that regulates growth. However, some people do not produce enough. Thanks to gene-splicing, this substance can be produced in amounts that can help people who do not make enough of their own.

Foods

Supermarkets are popular destinations for genetically engineered products. Tomatoes have been genetically engineered to have a squarer shape—which makes them easier and cheaper to harvest and package. Tomatoes and other kinds of produce have been genetically engineered to stay fresh longer and to taste better. Some fresh fruits and vegetables are more nutritious because genes that make the plant retain more vitamins and minerals have been "spliced" into the plant's genes.

Some people question the safety of genetically engineered foods. Bovine growth hormone (BGH) causes dairy cows to give more milk. This increases dairy farmers' profits. Some consumers question BGH's safety, especially for growing children who drink lots of milk.

Genetic Counseling

Couples who are considering having children often want to know whether they are carriers of genes for a genetic disorder. This is especially true if there is a history of inherited disease in either family. Such couples may consult a genetic counselor. A genetic counselor provides the couple with information about the possibility of their passing on the genes for an inherited disease to their offspring.

▷ **How is genetics being used today?**

Why It Matters

Scientists have recently identified the genes that cause certain inherited disorders, including cystic fibrosis. Using genetic engineering, medical scientists hope to find a way to cure this disease by replacing or altering the gene that causes it. As we learn more about DNA, genes, and chromosomes, we may also be able to uncover the causes—and cures—of many other diseases, including some forms of diabetes and cancer.

e-Journal Visit our Web site www.science.mmhschool.com to do a research project on genetic disorders.

Think and Write

1. What are some disorders that can be inherited?

2. What are some examples of dominant traits?

3. Which parent determines the sex of the child? Why?

4. Tay-Sachs is a disease that is transferred to offspring on parents' genes. How does Tay-Sachs disease differ from an infectious disease such as pneumonia?

5. **Critical Thinking** Why are males more often affected by sex-linked traits?

L·I·N·K·S

WRITING LINK

Writing that Compares Write an essay to compare the way sickle cell anemia is inherited with the way blood type is inherited. What are the similarities? What are the differences? Organize your facts. One way to organize your essay is to give all the details about sickle cell anemia in one paragraph and all the details about blood type in another paragraph. Use your last paragraph to summarize your findings.

MATH LINK

Make a graph. Use the data in the table to make a pie graph of the distribution of blood types across the U.S. population.

Blood Type	Percent of U.S. Population
A	40%
B	11%
AB	5%
O	44%

HEALTH LINK

Research diabetes. Use encyclopedias and other resources to research diabetes and its treatment. Explain why genetically engineered human insulin represented an enormous breakthrough in the treatment of the diseases.

TECHNOLOGY LINK

 LOG ON Visit www.science.mmhschool.com for more links.

Science, Technology,

Lifesaving Genetics

Infectious diseases are caused by viruses, bacteria, fungi, and other microscopic parasites. Doctors need to know what causes a disease before they can treat it. Luckily every germ has its own pattern of genes, or DNA. Just as police track criminals by their unique fingerprints, doctors track harmful germs by their unique DNA! Here are ways they are using genetics to save lives.

Degenerative diseases, such as certain types of heart disease, are caused by a breakdown of a specific function. Often a donated organ can be substituted for a diseased one, but a recipient's body may reject it. This is less likely to happen if the DNAs of donor and recipient are compatible.

Cancer occurs when damage to genes makes cells grow out of control. Although many people may be exposed to the same environmental stress, such as secondhand smoke, some develop cancer and some don't. Why? Some people's genes break easier than others, or a person may have a gene that makes getting cancer more likely. These "at risk" people should get frequent checkups. Even if cancer starts, it can often be stopped.

Hereditary diseases are passed on from parents to offspring. A gene or combination of genes from the parents fails to create a key protein in

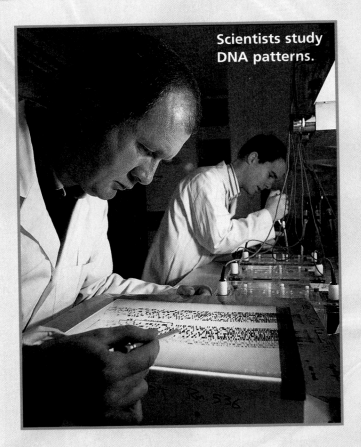
Scientists study DNA patterns.

the child or produces a protein that functions badly. Some proteins can be replaced, but in many diseases the precise amount of protein needed can't be sent to the right place in the body.

Some couples choose not to become parents if their child's inherited genetic makeup may result in disease. People who think they may carry risky genes can be tested. Their kids can be tested, too. After all, knowing a parents' genes provides only a probability of what an offspring's genes will be!

and Society

ADA is a rare genetic disease that doesn't let this boy's body fight infection. He had to live in a "bubble." Today such defective genes can be replaced so kids with ADA can live normal lives.

Write ABOUT IT

1. When people need organ transplants, members of their families often have their genes "fingerprinted." Why?

2. If work, such as mining coal, is known to cause stress to genes, should job applicants have their genes tested? Should they be hired even if their genes might produce cancer?

LOG ON Visit www.science.mmhschool.com to learn more about genetics and disease.

Using Genetics

Get Ready

An association between cats and people has existed for as long as 3500 years. Cats have only recently been bred selectively to show specific traits. Currently about 40 breeds of cats are recognized. The smallest cat breeds weigh about 2 to 3 kg (5 to 7 lb) when full grown and the largest weigh about 7 to 9 kg (about 15 to 20 lb). How are different breeds produced?

Inquiry Skill

You predict when you state possible results of an event or experiment.

Explore Activity

What is Selective Breeding?

Many domestic cat breeds, including the Maine coon, Manx, Russian blue, and Siamese, began as a naturally occurring variety of domestic cat native to a geographic area. Others, such as the Himalayan, are artificial breeds, the result of careful breeding for a desired look. Different breeds vary primarily in color, in length and texture of fur, and in temperament.

Maine coon

Procedure

1 **Observe** Look at the photos of the cats shown on this page. List the specific traits of each one.

Drawing Conclusions

1 What are the unique traits of each cat?

2 What traits do the cats have in common?

3 How are new breeds of cats produced?

4 **Define** What is selective breeding?

5 FURTHER INQUIRY **Predict** Choose two breeds to cross and predict what the results would be.

Persian

Manx　　　　**Abyssinian**　　　　**Siamese**

Main Idea People use selective breeding to produce desired traits in plants and animals.

What Is Selective Breeding?

What if you are a gardener who likes big, showy daffodils? You could produce the kind of flower you like by crossing two of the largest daffodils in your garden, then crossing two of the largest offspring from that cross. If you did this over and over again, after several generations you might find you've developed the largest daffodils anyone has ever seen.

The process of crossing plants or animals to produce offspring with certain desirable traits is called **selective breeding**. People have used selective breeding for centuries to produce better food crops, hardier domestic animals, and prettier flowers.

Growers have used selective breeding to develop many different color and shape variations in flowers.

Sheepdogs, like the one in this photo, were bred to herd sheep.

Farmers use selective breeding to produce drought-resistant wheat, sweeter corn, or crops that are resistant to damage from insects. Cattle are bred to produce more milk or leaner meat.

Most of the dog breeds we know today were developed by selective breeding, including sheepdogs. Beagles, terriers, and other small hunting dogs were bred for tracking small game, such as rabbits and foxes. These dogs have an excellent sense of smell, and their small size enables them to follow a hunted animal into its burrow. Siberian huskies are large dogs bred for pulling sleds across the snow. Huskies have thick fur that helps keep them warm and strong muscles for pulling heavy loads.

▷ **What are some examples of selective breeding?**

What Is Genetic Engineering?

People have used selective breeding for a long time. Scientists have recently developed a new method of controlling inherited traits in offspring. **Genetic engineering** is a way of changing the DNA sequence that makes up a gene so that the gene will produce a particular trait.

One type of genetic engineering involves moving a gene from one organism to another. A single gene in barley plants controls several traits, including strength, height, resistance to drought, and time to maturity. When this gene is inserted into wheat, rice, and soybeans, it produces shorter, stronger, drought-resistant plants.

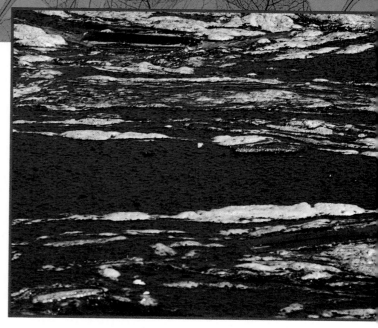

The foam in this photo of the ocean was made by bacteria. The bacteria help clean up oil spills. Genetic engineers have changed some of the DNA in normal soil bacteria to create bacteria that can break down oil particles.

Genetic engineering methods were used to insert the gene that produces light in fireflies into the cells of this plant.

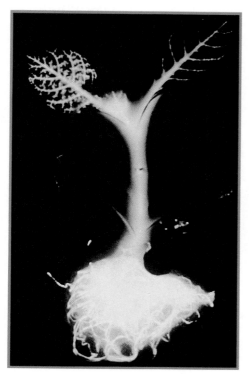

Bacteria that live in the soil have been genetically engineered to help clean up toxic wastes in the environment. Oil spills present a sticky problem. In the past the only way to get rid of the oil was to dig up the rocks and soil and take them to a toxic waste disposal site. Genetic engineering has been used to insert into the bacteria genes for producing substances that break down oil particles. If enough of these engineered bacteria are present, they will rid the area of spilled oil by breaking it down into harmless substances.

▶ **How is genetic engineering useful?**

What Is Gene-Splicing?

Today's researchers have made it possible to "splice" genes. **Gene-splicing** is a process in which scientists can take the genes from one organism and attach them to—or splice them to—the genes in another organism. Gene-splicing is used to produce substances people can use, such as insulin.

People with a form of the disease called diabetes do not produce enough of a substance called insulin. They can get insulin, however, produced in bacteria as a result of gene-splicing.

Biologists use plasmids, tiny circular genetic structures in bacteria. They also use enzymes or other chemicals as "knives" to cut out the part of the human gene that causes insulin production. Then the plasmid is also chemically "cut." Other enzymes or chemicals are used to attach the human DNA sequence into the DNA string of the plasmid.

The bacteria reproduce with the gene for making insulin. These bacteria become insulin-producing machines.

READING Diagrams

What part of the human cell is spliced into the bacterial chromosome?

Gene-Splicing

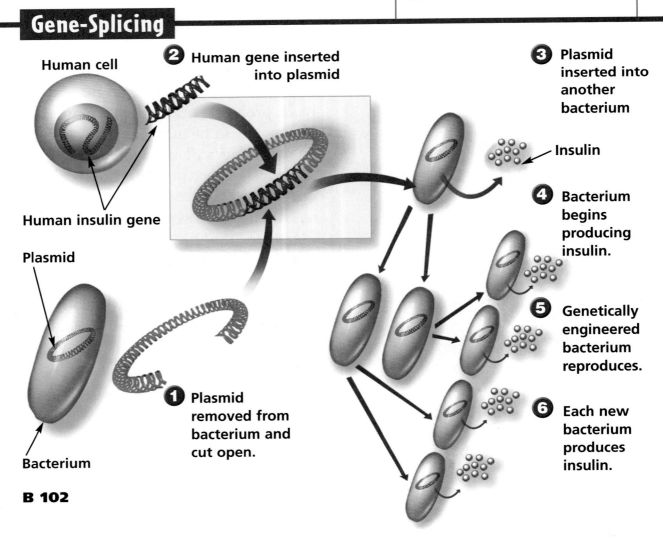

Human cell

Human insulin gene

Plasmid

Bacterium

2 Human gene inserted into plasmid

1 Plasmid removed from bacterium and cut open.

3 Plasmid inserted into another bacterium

Insulin

4 Bacterium begins producing insulin.

5 Genetically engineered bacterium reproduces.

6 Each new bacterium produces insulin.

B 102

On February 22, 1997, people around the world turned on their television sets and saw a lamb named Dolly. Dolly was a *clone*. A clone is a living thing that receives all of its DNA from just one parent.

Dolly's DNA came from a body cell of an adult female sheep. It did not come from sex cells. In nature a sperm cell from a male sheep joins with an egg cell from a female sheep. Each sex cell contains 27 chromosomes, one-half the number of chromosomes in a sheep's body cells. When a sperm and an egg are joined, they form a new cell with a full set of 54 chromosomes. That cell can divide into more cells. Then those cells divide, in time becoming cells of the parts of a baby sheep's body. Each body cell contains all 54 chromosomes.

It was the DNA from an adult female sheep that the Scottish scientist Dr. Ian Wilmut used to produce Dolly. First, he and others in his laboratory grew the body cell in a dish. Next, they stopped it from making a copy of its chromosomes.

Then, they took an egg cell from a different adult sheep. They removed the egg cell's nucleus, which contained its DNA. Finally, they brought the two cells together and applied a small amount of electricity. The electricity made the insides of the body cell, including all 54 chromosomes, go into the egg cell. The egg cell started to divide as if it had joined with a sperm cell. Six days later the egg cell had divided into a ball of cells. The ball of

Dolly

cells was placed inside a female sheep, which gave birth to Dolly. When Dolly was born, the scientists compared Dolly's DNA with the DNA from the sheep whose body cell was used. The two were identical.

No one knows what the future of cloning will be. One day, will clones of sheep or other mammals produce large amounts of medicines people need? This successful cloning of sheep has led scientists to question what could and should be done with this ability.

▷ **How is gene-splicing important in cloning?**

What Are Some Genetically Engineered Crops?

World population is now over 6 billion people. Our population is predicted to double in the next 50 years. Pause for a moment and think about this. As the number of people increases, what happens to the amount of land available for farming? What could happen if crop productivity and nutrient content could be doubled? Genetic engineering could allow us to grow more food in the same amount of space, saving forests from destruction.

For example, what if you could transfer the gene for cold temperature tolerance from a Pacific salmon to a tomato plant? Does it sound like science fiction? Already, special genes are inserted into tomato plants enabling them to produce tomatoes that have a longer shelf life.

Another purpose of genetic engineering is to make crops healthier. Genetic engineers have made some crops resistant to pests. To do this, the scientists inject a gene into the cells of crops, such as corn and potatoes. The gene makes a protein that kills certain insects. The result is a crop that makes its own pesticide. With fewer pests, the crops grow stronger and produce higher yields. In addition, many genetically engineered plants can fight off certain viral diseases.

Genetic engineering can also increase the nutritional content of foods. Scientists have succeeded in developing rice grains with increased levels of vitamin A and iron. In countries where rice is the mainstay of people's diets this helps solve the problem of iron deficiency anemia and vitamin A deficiencies.

As is the case with many new technologies, there is controversy about the use of genetically modified crops. People are concerned about introducing foreign genes into organisms and the possible side effects and risks. One such risk may involve allergic reactions to the new traits.

Scientists are also working on improving the techniques to reduce these risks. One new method is to reduce or enhance the performance of genes already present in an organism.

Terrace paddy fields in Bali, an island in Indonesia. Rice is the main food in three of the four most populated nations: China, Indonesia, and India.

Scientists can target specific genes, such as those responsible for the production of a vitamin, and alter them to increase that production. With this method they are not introducing foreign genes and therefore reduce any unintended side effects.

Genetically engineered plants pose several potential risks to the environment. Perhaps the biggest concern for now is increased weediness. Weeds are defined as all plants in places where humans do not want them. As a result of genetic engineering, crops may be able to thrive in environments where they would be considered weeds. For example, if a plant was engineered to be salt-tolerant and it invaded marine estuaries it could be disastrous for the organisms living there. Altered genes can also transfer to other plants through pollination. The new traits would then be passed on to wild or weedy relatives of the altered crop plants enabling them to thrive in places where they are not wanted.

▷ **How does genetic engineering increase the nutritional content of foods?**

What Did Carver and Burbank Do?

Since Mendel's time many plant breeders have experimented with crossbreeding to develop improved food crops. One of the most famous is George Washington Carver. Carver was an African American born just a year or so before slavery ended in the United States.

For most of his life, Carver was a professor and agricultural scientist at the Tuskegee Institute in Alabama. Carver conducted plant-breeding experiments to develop new varieties of cotton that yielded more than twice as much cotton per acre and grew well without very much fertilizer.

Carver is also well known for his work with peanuts. When a boll weevil infestation destroyed much of the Tuskegee area's cotton crops, he convinced the farmers to plant peanuts, as well as sweet potatoes and other crops. The peanut crop was very successful. During his life Carver discovered more than 300 uses for peanuts, using them to make margarine, cooking oil, shoe polish, cheese, dyes, soil conditioners, and even face creams and shaving lotion.

Luther Burbank was another famous plant breeder. Born in Massachusetts in 1849, Burbank decided early in life to make plant breeding his career. His first success was the development of a larger, whiter potato, known today as the

George Washington Carver lived from the early 1860s to 1945. He was a researcher and instructor.

Burbank potato. By crossing different kinds of fruits and vegetables, Burbank developed hundreds of unusual new varieties of plums, peaches, berries, prunes, tomatoes, nuts, and flowers.

He bred a white blackberry and a spineless cactus. Burbank also developed a method for attaching one type of fruit tree onto another to produce faster-growing varieties.

▷ **How did George Washington Carver and Luther Burbank continue the study of genetics?**

Why It Matters

Genetically engineered crops and animals are resistant to known diseases. These products can also be enhanced to last longer and to provide nutrients their natural counterparts lack.

The risks people fear from genetically engineered products are related to health and the environment.

It is important to understand what is involved in these food manipulations so that you can decide for yourself which products to consume.

e-Journal Visit our Web site www.science.mmhschool.com to do a research project on the risks and benefits of genetically engineered foods.

Think and Write

1. Is selective breeding a new breeding technique? Explain your answer.

2. How is genetic engineering used to clean the environment?

3. What is gene-splicing? Why is it used?

4. How did George Washington Carver improve cotton yields?

5. **Critical Thinking** What do you think are the pros and cons of cloning?

WRITING LINK

Expository Writing Write a research report about the history of the classification system. Use the Internet or library reference sources, such as an encyclopedia, to do your research. Include facts to explain how cross-breeding helped scientists identify new species of organisms. Draw a conclusion based on the information you find.

MATH LINK

Check for Reasonableness Of 3,218 pumpkins grown on a farm, all but 819 are genetically engineered to last longer. Ana guesses $\frac{3}{4}$ of the pumpkins are genetically engineered to last longer. Is this reasonable?

SOCIAL STUDIES LINK

Learn how genetics has been used in your state. Do a research project on how genetics has been used to enhance the crops and animals that are grown in your state.

TECHNOLOGY LINK

LOG ON Visit www.science.mmhschool.com for more links.

Vocabulary

Fill each blank with the best word or words from the list.

DNA, B78
gene, B78
gene-splicing, B102
genetics, B59
heredity, B58
hybrid, B62
pedigree, B72
pollination, B60
probability, B66
Punnett square, B68

1. A word for how likely it is that something will happen is

_____.

2. The passing on of traits from parents to offspring is _____.

3. The result of crossing parents who have two different forms of the same trait is a(n) _____.

4. A table used to predict the outcome of a cross is a(n)

_____.

5. The study of heredity is called

_____.

6. A(n) _____ is a portion of a chromosome that controls a particular trait.

7. _____ has been used to make bacteria that produce human insulin.

8. A(n) _____ shows which members of a family have a given trait.

9. The transfer of pollen from the male to the female part of a flower is _____.

10. _____ contains the codes that tell each cell how to operate.

Test Prep

11. What is the process of crossing plants or animals to produce offspring with certain traits?
   A genetics
   B selective breeding
   C genetic engineering
   D crossbreeding

12. When pollen from one flower is transported to a different flower, it is known as _____.
   F cross-pollination
   G crossbreeding
   H self-pollination
   J selective breeding

13. All of the following are part of the genetic code EXCEPT _____.
   A adenine
   B thymine
   C cytosine
   D adenosine

14. Traits controlled by genes of the X chromosome are ———.

   F dominant

   G recessive

   H sex-linked

   J incompletely dominant

15. A purebred white dog and a purebred black dog produce off-spring with black and white fur. How are these traits inherited?

   A Black fur is dominant.

   B White fur is dominant.

   C Both are recessive.

   D Both are incompletely dominant.

Concepts and Skills

16. Reading in Science Describe how DNA is copied when a cell is ready to divide in two.

17. Critical Thinking How does a cell with four chromosomes divide to form four sex cells?

18. INQUIRY SKILL **Use Numbers** Draw a Punnett square to show the probable outcome of a cross between a woman who carries one sex-linked gene for hemophilia (X^hY) and a man who has no gene for hemophilia.

19. Scientific Methods What if the gene that causes sickle cell anemia has a slightly different arrangement of DNA base pairs than the gene for normal red blood cells? How might scientists go about developing a cure?

20. Product Ads What measures do scientists need to take before they introduce a genetically engineered food product on the market?

Did You Ever Wonder?

INQUIRY SKILL **Communicate** Prince Alexis, born in Russia in 1904, was heir to the Russian throne. He was born with a blood disorder called hemophilia. His disorder can be traced back to Queen Victoria of England. How was this possible?

LOG ON Visit **www.science.mmhschool.com** to boost your test scores.

George Langford
Cell Biologist

George Langford has a lot of nerve. Actually, he has lots of squid nerves. That's because he does research using nerve cells taken from squids.

A biologist at Dartmouth College in New Hampshire, Langford is investigating the way nerve cells send signals throughout the body. Human nerve cells are very thin, about 0.001 millimeter (mm). However, squids have nerve cells that are much larger, about 0.1 mm. This makes it easier for scientists to study them. Langford hopes to pave the way for a better understanding of how nerves help the brain create and store memories.

Langford is trying to find out how neurotransmitters—special chemicals—move within a nerve cell. The chemicals have to get from the center of the cell, where they are made, to the cell ending, where they are used.

Langford grew up on his parents' North Carolina farm where they grew peanuts and corn. "We used to have baby chicks, too," he remembers. "I was always interested in how things grew and developed."

"In college I got interested in biology by using an electron microscope. I liked the challenge of interpreting what I saw. I could imagine a whole structure from the

Caribbean Reef Squid

thin slice you can view with the microscope."

Langford spends summers at the Marine Biological Laboratory in Woods Hole, Massachusetts. There he works with other scientists from around the world. Winters he's back at Dartmouth studying frozen squid samples he collected at Woods Hole.

"What I like about science is that you get to explore new frontiers," he says. "It gives you the ability to discover new and exciting things."

Squid neurons are much larger than human neurons.

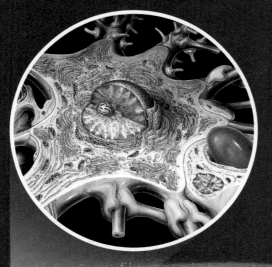

TOP 5 Squid Facts

Squids live in oceans around the world. Here are some amazing facts about them.

1. Squids have ten tentacles.
2. Squids and octopi have the biggest brains of any invertebrates.
3. Squids are mollusks, as are snails and clams.
4. The giant squid can grow to be 20 meters (65 feet) long.
5. Squids have a beak made out of shell-like material.

Write About It

1. What does Langford like about science?
2. Why is Langford studying squid nerves instead of human nerves?

LOG ON Visit www.science.mmhschool.com to learn more about the work of cell biologists.

Animal or Vegetable?

Your goal is to identify animal cell and plant cell parts.

What to Do

1. Make a large drawing of an animal cell and a plant cell. Use diagrams within the chapter to help you.

2. Label the following parts of your cell drawings: cell membrane, chloroplasts, cell wall, nucleus, nuclear membrane, and cytoplasm.

3. Place the two drawings side by side on a large sheet of poster paper.

4. Connect, with arrows or yarn of different colors, the common parts in both drawings. Label connecting lines.

5. Now show two major parts found only in plant cells.

Analyze Your Results

1. How do the cells differ?

2. How are they similar?

Hands UP

Your goal is to explain whether specific traits are inherited from parents.

What to Do

1. As a class, fold your hands. How many people put the left thumb on top? How many people put the right thumb on top? Record the results.

2. Make a family diagram including as many close relatives as you can.

3. Use this diagram to decide whether or not this trait is inherited.

Analyze Your Results

1. If you think the way we fold our hands is inherited, explain why. Then try to decide if one thumb position is dominant over the other.

2. Compare the conclusions that you have made from your family diagrams with those of other students.

UNIT C

Observing the Sky

Observing the Sky

LOOK!

The Hubble Space Telescope
circles high above Earth.
How do telescopes help us
learn about comets and
other objects in space?

The Earth-Moon System

Did You Ever Wonder?

How did the Moon form? Many scientists believe the Moon formed from material ejected into space after a giant object hit Earth billions of years ago. What effect does the Moon have on Earth today?

INQUIRY SKILL **Observe** For 28 days, record how the Moon looks each night. Ask an adult to help. The Moon may not be visible every night.

C 3

The Tools of Astronomers

Vocabulary

universe, C6

telescope, C7

refraction, C8

reflection, C8

wavelength, C9

frequency, C9

electromagnetic spectrum, C9

Get Ready

How do you observe something that's very far away? Maybe you use binoculars. How do they help you? We use many different tools to learn about the planets. This photo shows the surface of Mars with the Sojourner rover. Astronomers sent the rover to Mars to study the planet's features. What other tools can we use to get information from outer space?

Inquiry Skill

You experiment when you perform a test to support or disprove a hypothesis.

Explore Activity

How Do We Learn About the Planets?

Materials

newspaper-covered shoe box

sheet of thin, colored, transparent plastic

Procedure

1. **Make a Model** Use a newspaper-covered shoe box as a "mystery planet." Place it as far away as possible.

2. **Observe** View the mystery planet through a sheet of thin, colored, transparent plastic. This simulates looking at it from Earth, through Earth's atmosphere, using an Earth-based telescope. Describe the planet, and draw its picture.

3. **Use Variables** View the mystery planet without the plastic. This simulates looking at it from space, with no atmosphere, using a telescope that is in space. Describe what you see, and draw a picture.

4. **Use Variables** Have someone in your group walk near the mystery planet to observe it and report back observations. This simulates a space probe making a "flyby" of the planet.

Drawing Conclusions

1. Describe the differences between viewing the planet from an Earth-based telescope and from a telescope that is in space. Explain what causes the differences.

2. What new information were you able to get from the flyby? Explain some of the limitations.

3. **FURTHER INQUIRY** **Experiment** Suppose a "planetary probe" landed on the surface of the model. What additional information might the probe provide? Explain.

Read to Learn

Main Idea Scientists use many tools to observe and study the universe.

What Is Astronomy?

Look up in the sky on a clear night. What do you think is up there? What would you like to know about it?

The branch of science that deals with "what's up there" is astronomy. Astronomy is the study of the **universe** . The universe is everything that exists—Earth and all the things in space. The contents of space include the planets, stars, and galaxies.

An astronomer is someone who observes the universe and tries to explain what is observed. The universe is a huge place and has many different parts. This means that no one astronomer can study everything. Different astronomers study different parts of the universe.

- What are the planets made of?
- How fast do planets move?
- Why do stars shine?
- How hot are stars?
- How many stars are there?
- Did the universe always look as it looks now?

We will learn which of these questions can be answered with some certainty and which cannot.

Astronomers

What does it take to be an astronomer? Can you be an astronomer? Some people are professional astronomers. That is, they have made astronomy their careers. Other people are amateur astronomers. They buy telescopes and observe the stars and planets just for their own enjoyment. Professional or not, they all make observations that might lead to some new understanding.

Much of what astronomers discover has no practical benefits. Why then do they study astronomy? The reason is curiosity. Humans have a need to explore and understand the universe. Not only are the stars beautiful to look at; they also make people ask where they come from. Astronomers try to answer these kinds of questions. However, there are some practical benefits to studying astronomy. For example, navigators use their knowledge of star position to tell direction.

An amateur astronomer observes the stars through a telescope.

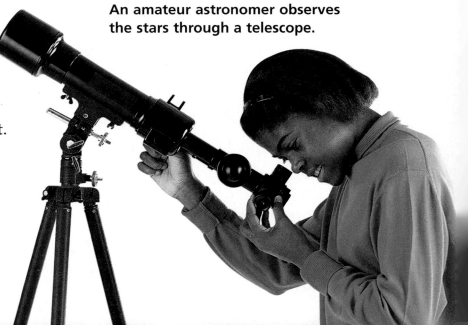

Observing the Universe

All sciences, including astronomy, are based on observation. There are several ways in which astronomers observe the universe. Which method is used depends on what astronomers wish to observe.

One method is to use the eyes. This is good for observing such things as day and night, the position of the Sun and Moon in the sky, and the location of some planets and stars. Of course, you should never look at the Sun directly because the light can harm your eyes.

A second method is to use a **telescope** (TEL·uh·skohp). A telescope is a device that collects light. It makes distant objects appear closer and larger. Most of our knowledge of the stars and planets comes from using telescopes.

Another way of observing objects such as the Moon is to send robots or humans there. Both robots and humans have traveled to the Moon. Only robots have been sent to study the other planets.

Models, Theories, Hypotheses

Once observations have been made, we try to understand and explain what we have observed. Scientists use models, hypotheses, and theories to help them understand observations.

Models are a way of simplifying the world so that we can understand it better. For example, Earth is not exactly a sphere. However, we often

Johannes Kepler (1571–1630), discusses planetary motion with Emperor Rudolph II, sitting. Kepler's work helped change people's view of their place in the universe.

use a sphere to represent Earth. That simple model helps us understand many observations.

A theory is a well-tested scientific explanation supported by evidence. It allows us to make a prediction about a scientific event or idea. For example, the theory of gravity explains the past motion of the planets. It also allows us to predict their future motion.

A hypothesis is a scientific explanation that has not yet been fully tested. As more and more evidence is gathered through observation, our certainty increases. However, we can never prove a theory with complete certainty. Science can only tell us what is likely, not what is certain. Sometimes new evidence does not support a theory's predictions. In that case, the theory must be changed.

▶ **What are two things astronomers do?**

What Is Light?

How can people learn about the universe? Most of our knowledge comes from light. Light is also called electromagnetic radiation, or electromagnetic waves, because light is related to electricity and magnetism. Light not only means light that we can see. It also means radio waves, infrared waves, ultraviolet waves, X rays, and gamma rays.

When light travels through empty space, it always travels at the speed of 300,000 kilometers per second (186,000 miles per second). This is the universe's speed limit. No matter or energy can travel faster.

When you turn on the light switch in your classroom, it seems like it takes no time for the light to reach your eyes. However, the Sun is so far away that it takes about eight minutes for light to travel from the Sun to Earth. Other stars are so far away that it takes years for their light to reach Earth.

Light as a Wave

It will help you understand light if you think of light as a wave. A wave carries energy from one place to another. Some waves need a medium to carry the wave. For example, water waves travel through water. Sound waves can travel through solids, liquids, or gases. Light waves are different because they do not need a medium. They can travel through empty space, which contains no solid, liquid, or gas.

Materials can be defined by the way they interact with light. *Opaque* (oh·PAYK) materials do not allow any light to pass through them. Your desk is opaque, since you cannot see your feet underneath it. Both *translucent* and *transparent* objects allow light to pass through them. The difference is that the image behind a translucent object is not clear, while it is clear behind a transparent object.

One property of waves is called **refraction** (ri·FRAK·shuhn). *Refraction* means "the bending of waves as they go from one substance to another." Refraction of light through a prism produces the different colors of the spectrum. It is also the basis of eyeglasses and some telescopes.

Another property of light is **reflection** (ri·FLEK·shuhn). *Reflection* means "the bouncing of waves off a surface." Mirrors and some telescopes use this property of light.

A model to help you visualize how a light wave travels is to shake a string. If you shake the end of a string continuously back and forth, a wave

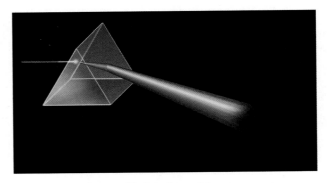

A prism refracts light, breaking up a beam of white light into all the colors of the rainbow.

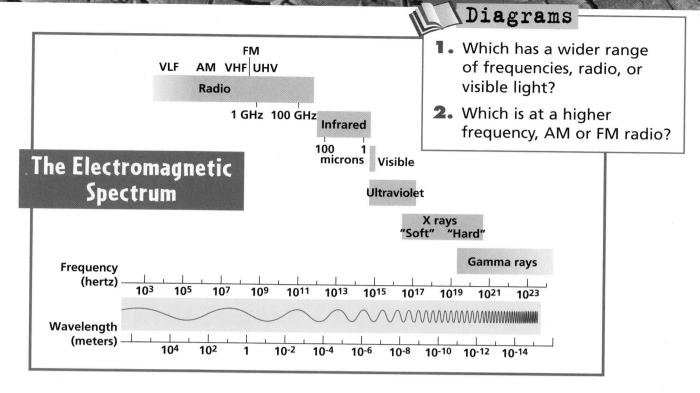

The Electromagnetic Spectrum

1. Which has a wider range of frequencies, radio, or visible light?

2. Which is at a higher frequency, AM or FM radio?

travels through the string, away from your hand. If we take a snapshot of the string, the string has a shape that repeats itself.

- The distance from one peak to the next on the wave is called a **wavelength** . Wavelength is measured in meters.

- If you tie a flag to the string at any point, that flag will vibrate as the wave passes through. The number of waves that pass through any point in a second is called the wave's **frequency** . Frequency is measured in cycles per second, or hertz.

In general, the longer the wavelength of a wave, the lower the frequency. Each light wave has a wavelength and a frequency, just as a wave on a string does.

The Electromagnetic Spectrum

Many objects in the universe, such as stars, give off light at many wavelengths and frequencies. These waves vary from very long wavelengths (low frequencies) to short wavelengths (high frequencies).

This diagram shows waves of light in order of their wavelengths (and frequencies). It is called the **electromagnetic spectrum** (i·lek·troh·mag·NET·ik SPEK·truhm). Different ranges of wavelengths have special names and properties.

In order of long to short wavelength, wavelengths are radio, infrared, visible, ultraviolet, X ray, and gamma ray.

▶ **What are two properties of light?**

How Do Telescopes Work?

The image of Mars on page C4 was taken by a *space probe*. A space probe is a vehicle sent beyond Earth to study planets and other objects within our solar system. This probe landed on Mars and sent the image to Earth.

This image was made by visible light. Remember, visible light is light that you can see. What are some other detectors of visible light? When you watch a movie, your eyes are detectors of visible light. So is the video camcorder you use at a soccer game.

You cannot use binoculars to see details of Mars. It's too far away. However, you can use a telescope. Two kinds of telescopes are used to gather visible light and magnify images.

- A reflecting telescope uses a mirror and a lens to form and magnify an image of a faraway object. Look at the diagram of a reflecting telescope. Describe the path that visible light follows as it travels from Mars to your eye. How is the image different from the object?

- A refracting telescope uses lenses to form and magnify an image of a faraway object. Look at the diagram of a refracting telescope. The refracting lens of this telescope bends the light passing through it.

▷ **How are reflecting and refracting telescopes alike and different?**

Two Types of Telescopes

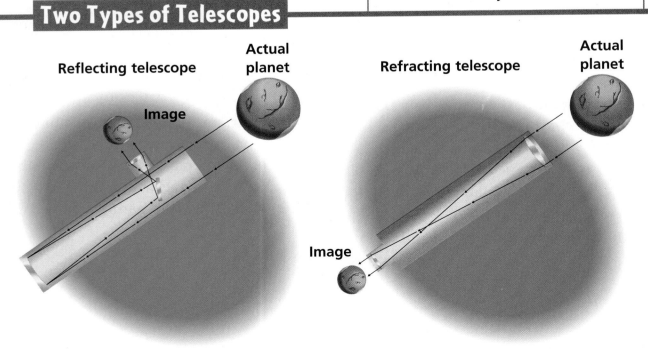

Reflecting telescope   Actual planet   Image

Refracting telescope   Actual planet   Image

What Instruments Detect Invisible Light?

You learned that the electromagnetic spectrum includes waves from low-frequency radio waves to high-frequency gamma rays. Different parts of this spectrum can be detected by different instruments. Our eyes are instruments that can detect visible light. In fact, it is called visible because our eyes can detect it.

However, our eyes cannot detect most of the electromagnetic spectrum. Humans need special detectors, such as special telescopes, to detect the whole spectrum. Astronomers learn a lot from the invisible part of the spectrum. For example, by detecting microwaves in space, they learn about the history of the universe. You will learn about this in Lesson 7.

Telescopes have been made to detect almost every kind of invisible light—radio, radar, infrared, ultraviolet, X ray, and even gamma ray. Each kind of telescope gives people information not possible with only visible light.

Astronomers observe the universe using different parts of the spectrum. The part chosen depends on what information they wish to know.

Look at the three pictures on this page. Each shows the Milky Way, a huge group of stars that includes the Sun (and Earth). Each was taken with energy from a different part of the electromagnetic spectrum. In each case different information was obtained. However, the partial information given by each picture gives a more complete picture of the Milky Way.

▷ **Why is it important to view space with different instruments?**

The photos above show the Milky Way as detected by a visible-light telescope, a radio telescope, and an infrared telescope.

Saturn, as viewed from Earth

Saturn, as viewed from *Voyager 2*

How Do We Get Information from Space?

What would happen to your view if you were looking through a cloud of dust? When you see objects through a telescope, you are looking through Earth's atmosphere. The atmosphere blurs what you see.

What if you took a photograph of a hurricane from the ground? This photograph would show the destruction the hurricane might have caused. However, it might not be able to provide other types of useful data. For this reason, scientists send *artificial satellites* into orbit high above Earth's atmosphere. The satellites transmit, or send back, data. These data reveal more detail of the clouds and the storm's center. However, they might not give much information about the destruction on the ground.

Look at these two pictures of Saturn. One of them was taken from Earth. The other was taken from *Voyager 2*, a space probe. Space probes travel away from Earth. They take photographs and perform experiments. They send the data back to Earth. Scientists put the data together, make observations, and draw conclusions.

Satellites and space probes do not carry crew members. They get their instructions from the ground. Space probes such as *Voyager 2* have been launched to fly by and photograph distant planets. Others, such as *Mars Pathfinder*, actually land on other planets.

Earth-orbiting satellites serve many different functions. Weather satellites track hurricanes and other large storms. Communications satellites allow us to see television pictures from around the world.

Satellites are sometimes sent up in a space shuttle. A space shuttle is a reusable spacecraft. It also carries astronauts. They do activities and experiments that could not be done by robots. After the tasks and observations are completed, the shuttle lands and may be reused in the future.

Space shuttle astronauts launched a special telescope called the Hubble Space Telescope. This telescope orbits above most of Earth's atmosphere. Pictures taken from Hubble are much sharper than those taken from the ground.

READING **Cause and Effect**
How does better technology improve our knowledge of space?

Space shuttle lifting off

What Would Life on a Space Flight Be Like?

What do you need to survive on Earth? What if you were an astronaut preparing to go to the Moon? What would you need to survive?

You need oxygen, water, and food to survive in space, as you do on Earth. Each day the average astronaut consumes about 0.9 kg (2 lb) of oxygen, 3.2 kg (7 lb) of water, and 1.4 kg (3 lb) of food. How are you going to store all this material? Scientists have come up with some solutions, but they are always trying to improve on them.

Astronauts inside a spacecraft

Oxygen

When you breathe, you inhale oxygen and exhale carbon dioxide. On the *Apollo* and *Skylab* spacecraft, exhaled gases were sent through canisters. These canisters removed the carbon dioxide. They also purified the oxygen in the spacecraft.

Water

In spacecraft water is also recycled. The water in the air is collected and then condensed into a liquid. It is then purified for reuse.

Food

As an astronaut you most likely would eat freeze-dried food cubes or powders to which you add water. Why do you think you would not be able to have hot meals and fresh fruit in a spacecraft?

A Martian Colony

You are on the replacement team of the first colonists on Mars. You are wearing a spacesuit with a supply of oxygen. The colony itself is enclosed in a dome. Why are these precautions necessary?

• The Martian atmosphere is mostly carbon dioxide, not breathable for humans.

• It is also very thin. Thin Martian atmosphere means the atmospheric pressure is very low. With a thin atmosphere and no magnetic field, there is very little to stop harmful radiation from outer space and the Sun from hitting the surface. Without protection you would not survive for long.

How does all the equipment in this picture help you and the colonists? What are some other reasons why the colony might look like this?

QUICK LAB

Needs in Space

FOLDABLES Make a Two-Tab Book. (See p. R41.) Label the tabs as shown. Use it to argue for and against sending humans to the Moon.

1. Write what you need to live on Earth. How do conditions on the Moon differ from those on Earth? How would what you need differ?

2. **Infer** Decide what you would have to do to be sure you could survive. What would you need if you were stranded on the Moon?

3. What are the arguments for and against sending humans to the Moon? Consider cost and risks. Also consider what might be gained.

▷ What are three necessities for life on Earth, as well as in space?

What Have We Done in Space So Far?

Some of the spacecraft sent into space contained crews. Some, such as the Hubble Space Telescope, did not. Look at the table below to learn about past space missions.

 **What was the first artificial satellite?**

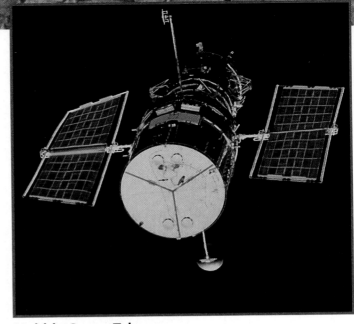

Hubble Space Telescope

Past Space Missions				
Year	Country	Spacecraft	Crew	Mission/Achievement
1957	U.S.S.R.	*Sputnik-1*	None	First artificial satellite
1958	U.S.A.	*Explorer III*	None	Discovered Earth's radiation belt
1969	U.S.A.	*Apollo 11*	Armstrong, Aldrin, Collins	First landing by humans on the Moon
1972	U.S.A.	*Pioneer 10*	None	Jupiter flyby: took over 500 pictures; collected magnetic data; crossed orbit of Pluto on June 13,1983, and left solar system.
1977	U.S.A.	*Voyager 1 and Voyager 2*	None	Spectacular photos of Jupiter, Saturn, (*Voyager 1 & 2*) Uranus, and Neptune (*Voyager 2*) between 1977 and 1989.
1989	U.S.A.	*Galileo*	None	Arrived at Jupiter 1995; circled planet 35 times, returning thousands of pictures. Discovered subsurface oceans on three of Jupiter's moons
1990	U.S.A. and Europe	Hubble Space Telescope	None	High resolution pictures of celestial objects
1996	U.S.A.	*Mars Global Surveyor*	None	First in a long-term program of Mars exploration known as the Mars Surveyor Program
1997	U.S.A. and Europe	*Cassini/Huygens*	None	Entered orbit of Saturn 2004 Designed to orbit Saturn 74 times, fly by Titan 44 times, and fly by many of Saturn's other moons.

Why It Matters

There are two reasons for scientists to learn about space. First of all, they do it for their own curiosity. Many of them just love to learn about what can be seen in the night sky. Fortunately for us, much of what they learn helps improve life on Earth. Experiments that are done on the space shuttle help us learn such things as better methods of farming and keeping healthy. In the future, outer space may also become as good a place as Earth to live.

e-Journal Visit our Web site **www.science.mmhschool.com** to do a research project on space exploration.

Think and Write

1. Why do you think people become astronomers?

2. What is meant by *light*? Is all light visible? Explain.

3. Describe two properties of light waves.

4. Describe some past space missions. What did we find out? What other questions did they bring up for scientists?

5. **Critical Thinking** What are the advantages of space travel over using telescopes to explore the universe? What are some disadvantages?

L·I·N·K·S

LITERATURE LINK

Read *Galileo's Secret* to learn about what it would be like to be such an amazing inventor. Try the activities at the end of the book.

WRITING LINK

Persuasive Writing Satellites have many different functions. However, non-working satellites and used launch vehicles often stay in orbit for long periods of time, creating space junk. Research the topic. Write a persuasive letter stating your opinion on the problem of space junk vs. the importance of satellites.

MATH LINK

From launch to impact, the *Galileo* spacecraft traveled $4,631 \times 10^6$ km ($2,878 \times 10^6$ miles) on 925 kg of fuel (246 gallons). How many km did it get per kg of fuel?

TECHNOLOGY LINK

Science Newsroom CD-ROM Choose *3-2-1 Blast Off!* to learn more about satellites.

LOG ON Visit **www.science.mmhschool.com** for more links.

LESSON 2

Vocabulary

rotation, C20

standard time zone, C22

International Date Line, C23

revolution, C24

Earth and the Sun

Get Ready

Does the Sun's position in the sky change? Can you tell where the Sun is located with respect to the structures in the photograph?

Shadows give us clues about the relative location of the Sun. How can we use shadows to learn about Earth and the Sun?

Inquiry Skill

You predict when you state possible results of

Explore Activity

What Do We Learn from Shadows?

Materials

sheet of paper

ruler

clay

transparent tape

string

protractor

Procedure

BE CAREFUL! Do not look directly at the Sun at any time.

1 Draw two lines on a sheet of paper (top to bottom and left to right) to make four quarters. Label map directions on the paper: *N* at the top center, *S* at the bottom center, *W* at the center of the left side, and *E* at the center of the right side.

2 **Make a Model** Stand a pencil upright in a blob of clay. Place the clay in the center of your paper.

3 Place the paper on a flat surface where the Sun will shine on it all day. Place it so the *N* points north.

4 **Observe** At 10 A.M. carefully trace the pencil's shadow. Put a heavy dot on the tip of the shadow tracing. Repeat at 11 A.M., 12 noon, 1 P.M., 2 P.M., and 3 P.M., and record your work.

Drawing Conclusions

1 **Interpret Data** What is the relationship between the shadow and the Sun's location?

2 **Observe** When was the shadow longest? Shortest?

3 **Infer** When was the Sun highest? Lowest? How could you tell?

4 **FURTHER INQUIRY** **Predict** What will be the direction and length of the shadow at 9 A.M.? At 4 P.M? Record your prediction and then test it.

Main Idea Earth's rotation on its axis and revolution around the Sun cause the cycle of day and night, and the four seasons.

How Do We Know Earth Is Rotating?

Does the Sun move across the sky? The Sun only seems to move because Earth is *rotating*, or spinning. It rotates on its axis, like a spinning top. The axis is an imaginary line through Earth from the North Pole to the South Pole.

One **rotation** is a complete spin on the axis. It takes just about 24 hours for Earth to make one rotation. What happens as a result of this motion? Any location on Earth experiences a cycle of day and night.

How do we know that Earth is spinning? One way is from data from satellites. Satellites can observe the rotation of Earth from space. An early piece of evidence was discovered by a French scientist named Foucault (few·KOH).

One day on Earth is the time needed for one rotation— 24 hours.

A heavy ball was hung by a long string. It was made to swing back and forth in one direction. Pegs were arranged in a circle around the ball. As the ball swung back and forth, it should have knocked down only two pegs. However, during the course of the day, many pegs were knocked down! It seemed the direction of the ball's swing changed. The ball's swing did not change. Instead, Earth rotated under the ball.

The shape of Earth is also evidence that Earth is rotating. Earth is not exactly a sphere. Earth is slightly flattened at the North and South Poles. It also bulges slightly at the equator. This is what happens to a flexible ball when it spins. It is similar to what happens in a washing machine. As the clothes spin around, they get thrown to the edge. As Earth spins, Earth's matter also gets thrown to the "edge." This creates a slightly bulging equator.

In 1851 the Foucault pendulum showed that Earth rotated.

You have learned that the Sun's position in the sky changes during the day. You also know that the cycle of day and night repeats every 24 hours. Why does all of this happen?

Earth's motion is similar to that of a spinning top. It, too, rotates on its axis, making one rotation every 24 hours. It does this 365 times each year. Any location on Earth receives a certain amount of sunlight and a certain amount of darkness each day.

As a day progresses, what does the Sun appear to do? As the diagram shows, the Sun rises in the east. It seems to travel west, rising higher in the sky as the day passes. At midday the Sun reaches its highest point in the sky. After midday it appears to get lower in the sky, until it sets in the west.

READING Diagrams

How can you tell the time of day by the position of the Sun in the sky? Write a description.

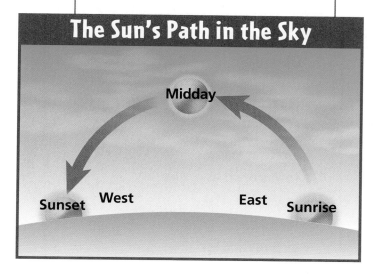

The Sun's Path in the Sky

Midday

Sunset West   East Sunrise

▷ **How does Earth's rotation cause day and night?**

These photos show the same covered wagon in the morning and in the afternoon. Notice the change in the position of the shadow.

QUICK LAB

What Time Is It?

FOLDABLES™ Make a Three-Column Table. (See p. R44.) Label columns and rows as shown.

1. **Observe** Use a map of the United States to locate as many towns or cities as you like. Make the Foldables table pictured and list the names.

Town/City	Zone	5 P.M. in Charlotte

2. **Classify** Use the time zone map on this page to give the time zone of each town or city you named.

3. **Infer** Which town or city on your list has the earliest time at any moment? The latest time?

4. **Infer** If it is 5 P.M. in Charlotte, NC, what time is it in each town or city on your list?

What Are Standard Time Zones?

When and where is it midday? When the Sun is at its highest over your town, it is midday there. However, it is not midday everywhere in the world. What time is it in other places of the world?

You can use the rotation of Earth to measure the passage of time. Earth spins toward the east. It rotates 360° (one complete turn) in 24 hours. In one hour Earth turns $\frac{360°}{24}$, or 15°. This angle defines a time zone. A **standard time zone** is a belt, 15° wide in longitude, in which all places have

Some U.S. Standard Time Zones

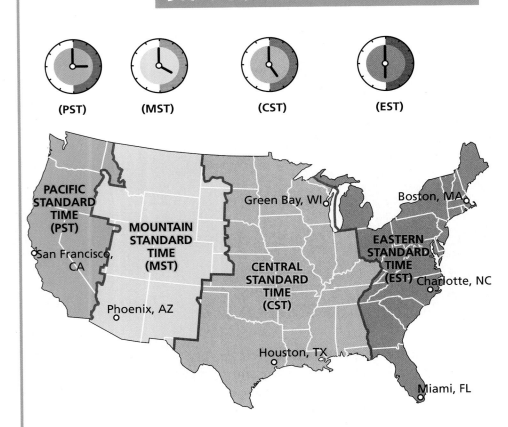

(PST)   (MST)   (CST)   (EST)

PACIFIC STANDARD TIME (PST)

MOUNTAIN STANDARD TIME (MST)

CENTRAL STANDARD TIME (CST)

EASTERN STANDARD TIME (EST)

San Francisco, CA

Phoenix, AZ

Green Bay, WI

Houston, TX

Boston, MA

Charlotte, NC

Miami, FL

the same time. There is a one-hour difference between time zones that are next to each other.

When you cross time zones, you have to change your clock's time. If you travel west, you must turn your clock back (subtract) one hour for each time zone you cross. If you travel east, you must set your clock ahead (add) an hour for each time zone you cross.

What if you are traveling west in a jet? You set your watch back one hour each time zone you cross. After 24 hours you are back home. However, the date on your watch is the same! What happened?

The **International Date Line** was created as the location where a new day begins. It is universally recognized. The International Date Line is the 180° line of longitude. If you cross the date line going west, you add a day.

▷ **Is it the same time everywhere on Earth?**

READING

Maps

Put your finger on any time zone. What is the time difference in zones to the east or west?

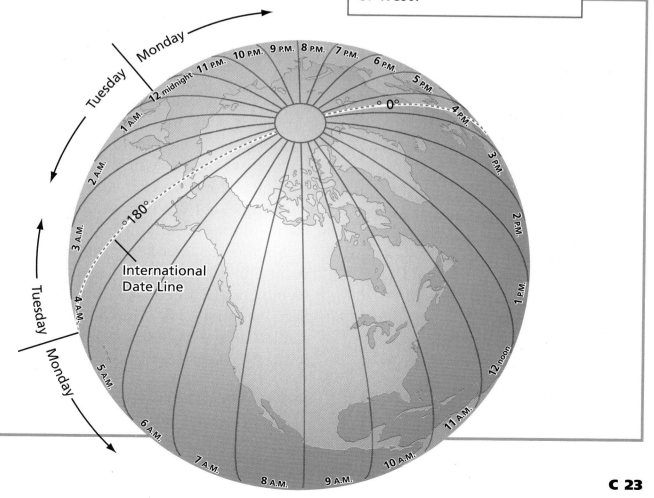

International Date Line

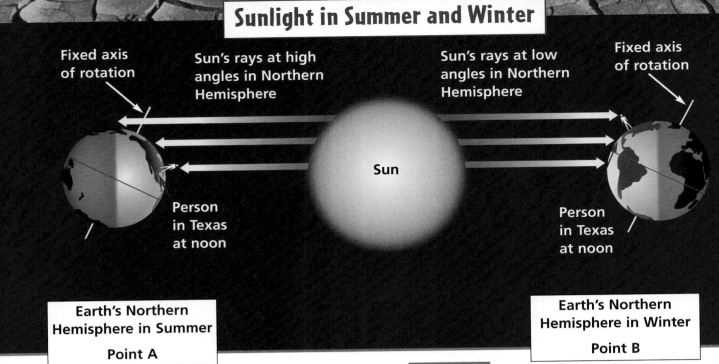

Fixed axis of rotation

Sun's rays at high angles in Northern Hemisphere

Sun's rays at low angles in Northern Hemisphere

Fixed axis of rotation

Sun

Person in Texas at noon

Person in Texas at noon

Earth's Northern Hemisphere in Summer
Point A

Earth's Northern Hemisphere in Winter
Point B

Why Are There Seasons?

As a year progresses, you observe the seasons change. You most easily notice this seasonal change as the average temperature rises and falls. This change is not caused by the change in distance between Earth and the Sun through the year. What then causes this change?

Earth takes $365\frac{1}{4}$ days to revolve, or travel in its orbit, once around the Sun. One complete trip around the Sun is called a **revolution** (rev·uh·LEW·shuhn). Remember that while it is revolving, Earth is also rotating on its axis. However, the axis is not vertical. It is tilted at an angle of $23\frac{1}{2}°$ and always points in the same direction. What happens as a result of this tilt?

The revolution of the tilted Earth around the Sun causes the seasons.

READING Diagrams

What season is it in the Southern Hemisphere when it is summer in the Northern Hemisphere? Explain your answer with examples.

As the diagram shows, when Earth is at point A in its orbit, the Northern Hemisphere is tilted toward the Sun. This causes the Sun's incoming rays to strike the Northern Hemisphere at high angles. At this time the Northern Hemisphere has summer.

Six months later Earth is now at point B in its orbit. Now the Northern Hemisphere is tilted away from the Sun. Incoming rays from the Sun are slanted at low angles. It is now winter in the Northern Hemisphere.

▶ **How would the seasons be affected if Earth was not tilted on its axis?**

Where Is the Sun in Summer and in Winter?

We learned that in the summer, incoming rays from the Sun hit Earth at higher angles. In the winter the Sun's rays are slanted at low angles. In spring and fall, the angles of the rays are somewhere in between.

From the diagram you can see that the steeper the angle of the Sun's rays, the higher in the sky the Sun will appear. This means that the Sun is higher at midday in the summer than it is in the winter.

During the day you are on the side of Earth facing the Sun. At the same time, Earth's opposite side is facing away from the Sun, experiencing night. You would be able to tell time by observing the Sun's position in the sky at any given point in the day. For example, at midday the Sun is at its highest point in the sky. After midday the Sun appears to get lower as it sets in the west.

▷ **Why do the Sun's summer and winter paths differ?**

READING Diagrams

1. Does the Sun rise in the same direction in summer and winter? Explain.

2. How can you tell the season by the Sun's path? Write a description.

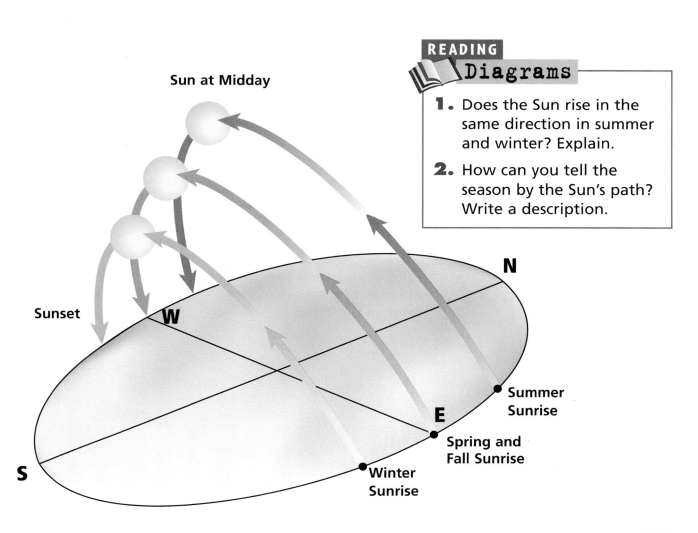

Sun at Midday

Sunset

W

N

S

E

Summer Sunrise

Spring and Fall Sunrise

Winter Sunrise

How Is the Sun an Important Energy Source?

The Sun is the energy source for life on Earth. Light from the Sun is necessary for the growth of most organisms. Plants, an example of Earth's producers, trap the Sun's energy and use it in their food-making process. Food made by producers is necessary to pass energy on to all other living things.

Fossil fuels that we use today—coal, oil, and natural gas—were formed over time from the decay of ancient living things. It is a chain of energy from the past to today. The Sun's energy became trapped in ancient producers, which became food for other living things. The energy was stored in the fuels that formed over time.

The Sun also provides energy for events involving nonliving things. The Sun is the source of energy for the water cycle. The Sun's energy causes ocean water to evaporate. As evaporated water rises, it forms clouds. High, wispy cirrus clouds are made of ice crystals. Puffy cumulus clouds and blanket-like stratus clouds may bring rain or snow. This water may fall into oceans, rivers, and lakes. It may also fall on land. Uneven heating of Earth's surface causes winds and contributes to surface ocean currents.

READING **Cause and Effect**
What would happen to the water cycle without the Sun?

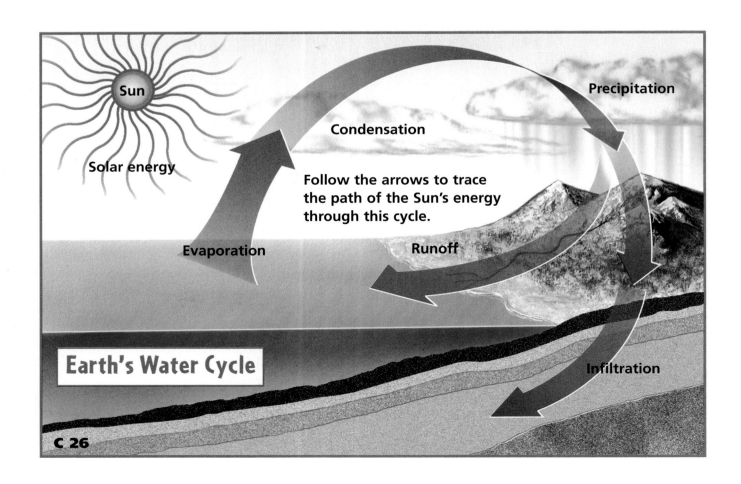

Sun

Solar energy

Precipitation

Condensation

Follow the arrows to trace the path of the Sun's energy through this cycle.

Evaporation

Runoff

Earth's Water Cycle

Infiltration

Why It Matters

Sunlight has a great effect on Earth. You learned that the length of the day depends on the season and on the latitude where you live. Near the North Pole, the Sun does not set from the first day of spring to the first day of autumn.

e-Journal Visit our Web site www.science.mmhschool.com to do a research project on life at the Arctic Circle.

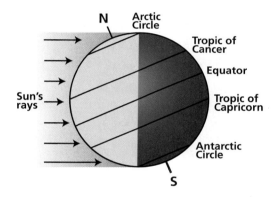

Think and Write

1. What causes day and night?

2. How are the time zones organized to help us know times around Earth?

3. How can you tell the difference between summer and winter by the Sun?

4. How is the Sun a source of energy for Earth?

5. **Critical Thinking** How does having time zones help people live their daily lives?

L·I·N·K·S

MATH LINK

Calculate distances to the Sun. Earth travels in an elliptical orbit. It is actually closer to the Sun in January than it is in July. Research the distances and calculate how much closer Earth is to the Sun in January than it is in July.

WRITING LINK

Expository Writing Fresh water is necessary for life. It is also used a great deal in industry. However, fresh water resources are limited, and world supply is unevenly distributed. Write an expository essay to describe what life would be like if the fresh water supply became extremely low or polluted. Introduce your main idea in a topic sentence and support it with facts.

ART LINK

Observe and record how the landscape changes with the seasons. Make a poster to illustrate your observational data.

TECHNOLOGY LINK

 LOG ON Visit www.science.mmhschool.com for more links.

Be Your Own Weather Forecaster

"What's the temperature going to be today?" That's the question we most often ask about the weather.

THERMOMETER

Air temperature is measured by a thermometer. The glass tube contains mercury or colored alcohol that expands (rises) or contracts (falls) with temperature changes.

BAROMETER

This simple barometer measures air pressure—the force on a given area by the weight of air. In this type of barometer, colored water is placed in a glass container. Changes in air pressure cause the water to rise and fall. A falling barometer can mean that a storm is coming.

ANEMOMETER

Winds are described by the direction from which they blow—a north wind comes from the north. Weather vanes show wind direction. An anemometer measures wind speed by counting the revolutions of the cups in a given amount of time.

°F 120 100 80 60 40 FREEZE 20 0 20 40 60

°C 50 40 30 20 10 0 10 20 30 40 50 60

Rising air cools and forms a low-pressure center, or low, which usually means cloudy skies and rain. Sinking air warms and forms a high-pressure center, or high, which usually means clear skies.

HYGROMETER

A hygrometer measures humidity, or the amount of water vapor in the air. This sling, or whirled, psychrometer is a type of hygrometer that consists of two thermometers, one dry and one covered by a wet sack. The instrument is whirled in the air, and the wet thermometer records a lower temperature. Meteorologists use a chart to convert the difference in temperatures to relative humidity.

RAIN GAUGE

A rain gauge measures how much rain falls. This instrument is simply a container that collects water. It has one or more scales for measuring the amount of rain.

Centi-
meters Inches
        5.0
12   4.5
11   4.0
10   3.5
9
8   3.0
7   2.5
6   2.0
5
4   1.5
3   1.0
2
1   .05

Write ABOUT IT

1. Collect data from weather instruments you have at home, or listen to weather reports on TV for five days. What patterns do you see? Can you use this information to track storms?

2. Research ways weather prediction can help people protect themselves from dangerous weather. Write a report.

LOG ON Visit www.science.mmhschool.com to learn more about weather forecasting.

The Moon in Motion

Get Ready

How do you think the Moon would look from its surface? What kind of shape does it have?

Looking from Earth, the shape of the Moon seems to change from day to day. What causes these changes in the Moon's appearance?

Inquiry Skill

You **infer** when you form an idea from facts or observations.

Explore Activity

What Causes the Moon to Change Appearance?

Materials
3 balls
black tape
crayon or felt-tipped pen

Procedure

1 **Make a Model** The Sun, Earth, and the Moon are each represented by a ball. The half-dark/half-light ball represents the Moon. The light side always faces the Sun. The dark side always faces away from it.

2 **Make a Model** Arrange your model of Earth, the Sun, and the Moon so that someone on Earth would see the lighted portion of the Moon as a circle. Remember to keep the lighted side of the ball facing the Sun.

3 Draw a diagram to show the location of Earth, the Sun, and the Moon in your model. Show where Earth's shadow falls.

4 **Experiment** Move the Moon around Earth in the model system so that different parts are lighted.

Drawing Conclusions

1 **Observe** How are Earth, the Sun, and the Moon arranged in order to see different parts of the Moon lighted?

2 Do you think the monthly cycle of light and dark on the Moon is caused by Earth's shadow on the Moon? Explain your answer.

3 FURTHER INQUIRY **Infer** In which direction must the Moon move around Earth to produce the shapes in proper order? Explain using a model.

Main Idea The Moon revolves around Earth, causing different Moon phases to appear in the night sky and the ocean tides to change.

Why Does the Moon Change Its Appearance?

How can we summarize the motion of Earth and the Moon? The Moon revolves around Earth, and Earth revolves around the Sun. You also know that the Moon changes its appearance in monthly cycles. The amount of the bright part of the Moon changes shape. The **phase** of the Moon is the shape of the lighted part of the Moon that we see at any given time. What causes these shapes?

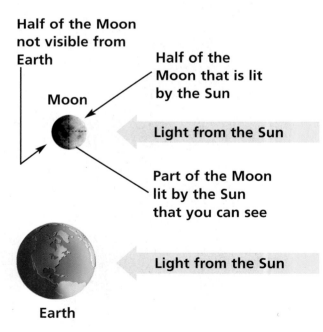

Half of the Moon not visible from Earth

Moon

Half of the Moon that is lit by the Sun

Light from the Sun

Part of the Moon lit by the Sun that you can see

Light from the Sun

Earth

Note the positions of the Sun, the Moon, and Earth during the waxing crescent phase.

Half of the Moon is always lighted by the Sun. However, you can't always see all of that half. Sometimes you can see only small amounts of this portion of the Moon. Sometimes you can see a lot. Sometimes you can't see any of the lighted half of the Moon at all!

The phase, or shape, of the Moon that you see depends on the position of the Sun, the Moon, and Earth with respect to each other.

- **New Moon Phase:** At new Moon the Moon is between Earth and the Sun. The half of the Moon lit by the Sun is opposite the half that faces Earth. As a result, you cannot see any of the Moon's sunlit half.

- **Waxing Phases:** After the new Moon phase, more of its sunlit half becomes visible each night. When half of the sunlit side is visible, the Moon is at *first quarter phase*. As you see it, the right half of the Moon is visible. When all of its sunlit half becomes visible, the Moon has reached the phase called the *full Moon.*

  When the phase that you see is more than new Moon but less than first quarter, the phase is called a *waxing crescent. Waxing* means "growing larger." When the phase visible is more than first quarter but less than full Moon, the phase is a *waxing gibbous* Moon.

- **Waning Phases:** After full Moon the part of the sunlit half of the Moon you can see gets smaller. The phases you see are the same as from new to full, only in reverse.

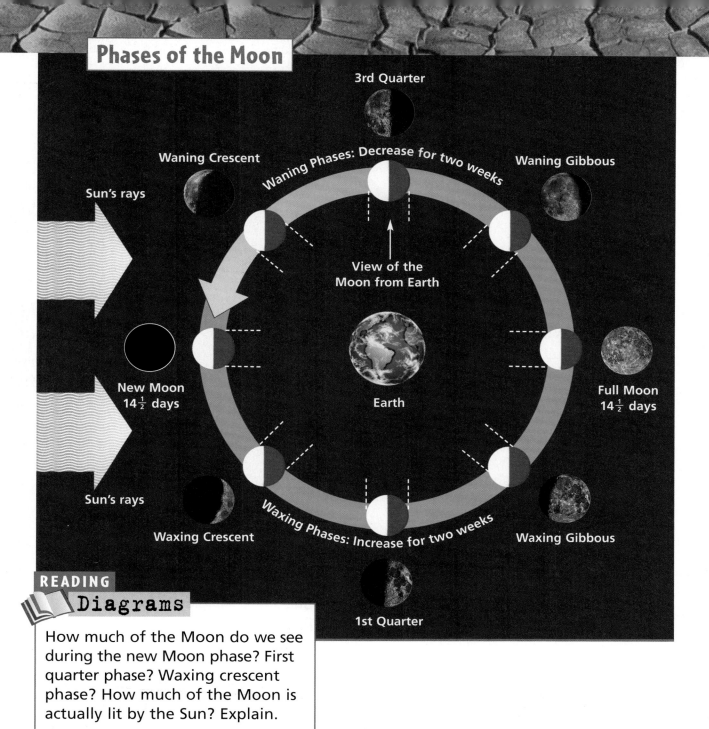

Phases of the Moon

3rd Quarter

Waning Crescent

Waning Phases: Decrease for two weeks

Waning Gibbous

Sun's rays

View of the
Moon from Earth

New Moon
$14\frac{1}{2}$ days

Earth

Full Moon
$14\frac{1}{2}$ days

Sun's rays

Waxing Phases: Increase for two weeks

Waxing Crescent

Waxing Gibbous

1st Quarter

READING
Diagrams

How much of the Moon do we see during the new Moon phase? First quarter phase? Waxing crescent phase? How much of the Moon is actually lit by the Sun? Explain.

When the left half of the Moon is visible, the phase of the Moon is the *third quarter*, or *last quarter*. The phase of the Moon that is less than full Moon phase but more than third quarter is called a *waning gibbous* Moon. *Waning* means "growing smaller." When the phase you see is less than third quarter but more than new Moon, the phase is called a *waning crescent*.

READING Cause and Effect
Why does the Moon appear to change shape throughout a month?

What Are Eclipses?

Recall that the Moon revolves around Earth. Recall also that at the same time, Earth revolves around the Sun.

The path of the Moon's orbit is tilted to the path of Earth's orbit around the Sun. As a result, the Moon is usually above or below Earth's orbit. Twice a month the Moon crosses the path of Earth's orbit. When this takes place at full Moon, the Moon might pass through Earth's shadow. When this happens, very little sunlight falls on the Moon. The Moon becomes dark for a time until it moves out of Earth's shadow. This is called a **lunar eclipse**.

Partial lunar eclipse

READING
Diagrams

Why is our view of the Moon blocked during a lunar eclipse?

The umbra is the dark part of the shadow where the Sun is completely blocked. The penumbra is the lighter part of the shadow where the Sun is only partially blocked.

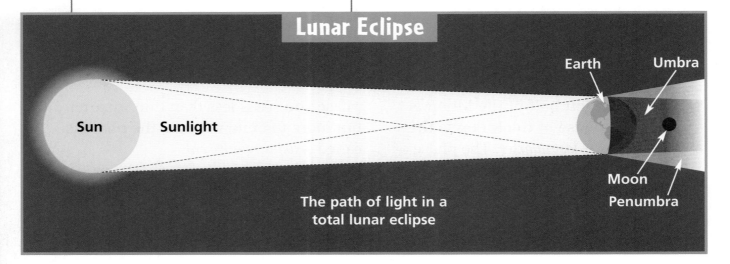

Lunar Eclipse

Sun

Sunlight

Earth

Umbra

Moon

Penumbra

The path of light in a total lunar eclipse

Total solar eclipse

Always follow safety procedures when observing the Sun. Never look at the Sun directly. Use special "eclipse" glasses.

READING
Diagrams

Where must the Moon be in order for a solar eclipse to occur?

Solar Eclipse

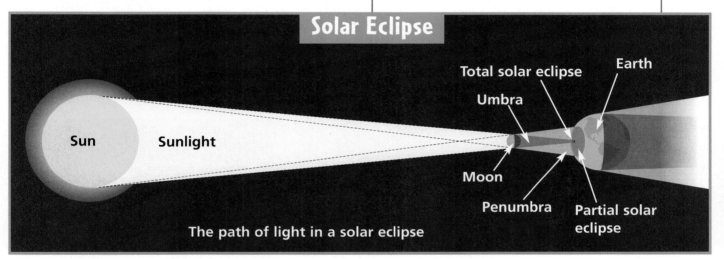

Sun

Sunlight

Total solar eclipse

Umbra

Earth

Moon

Penumbra

Partial solar eclipse

The path of light in a solar eclipse

When Earth passes through the Moon's shadow, a **solar eclipse** occurs. At what phase must a solar eclipse occur?

For a solar eclipse to occur, the Moon must be in a straight line between the Sun and Earth. This arrangement happens at new Moon phase. A solar eclipse can occur when the Moon crosses the plane of Earth's orbit at new Moon phase.

Have you ever seen a total solar eclipse? It is a fascinating sight. At the greatest part of the eclipse, the Moon completely hides the Sun. All you can see is the gases in the outer atmosphere surrounding the Sun.

▶ **What is the difference between a lunar eclipse and a solar eclipse?**

What Are Tides?

Have you ever been at the seashore and watched the ocean waves? If you have, you may have noticed that as time passed, the waves came higher up on the shore. You were looking at the **tide** coming in. Tides are the regular rise and fall of the water level along a shore.

The tides are caused mainly by the pull between Earth and the Moon. This mutual pull of gravity is stronger on the side of Earth that is facing the Moon. This causes the water to bulge on this side of Earth. A bulge also forms on the side facing away from the Moon.

This photo shows the Oregon coastline at low tide. Notice the high-tide water marks on the rocks.

At certain times of the year, the alignment of the Sun, the Moon, and Earth causes what are called *spring tides* and *neap tides*.

 How are tides affected by the Moon?

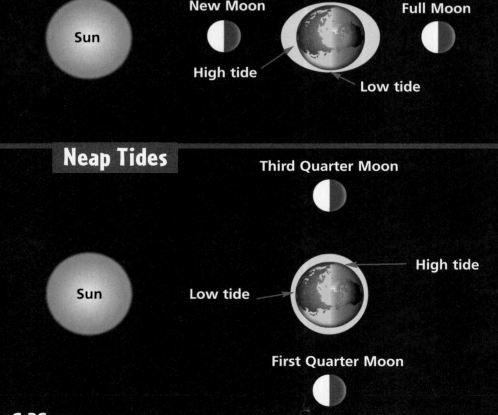

Spring Tides

Sun

New Moon

High tide

Full Moon

Low tide

High tides are higher than usual. Low tides are lower than usual. This happens twice a month at the phases shown.

Neap Tides

Third Quarter Moon

Sun

Low tide

High tide

First Quarter Moon

High tides are lower than usual. Low tides are higher than usual. This happens twice a month at the phases shown.

Inquiry Skill
BUILDER

SKILL Observe

Observing the Tides

Procedure

1 **Make a Model** How are you going to arrange the materials to model a spring tide? A neap tide? How are you going to model the pull on Earth due to the Moon and the Sun? Talk with your partner. Record your ideas.

2 **Experiment** Test your model. Repeat your test, switching roles with your partner.

3 **Communicate** Sketch your model. Write or draw the results of your test.

Drawing Conclusions

1 **Observe** How did you model the pull of the Moon and the Sun on Earth? What results did you obtain?

2 **Interpret Data** How well did your model work? What went right with your model? What things did you have difficulty with in your model?

3 **Communicate** Share your model and your results with your classmates. Did other teams have similar successes or difficulties? How would you change your model to make it work better?

Materials

large ball
(the Sun)

balloon, not
fully inflated
(Earth)

small ball
(the Moon)

What Does the Moon's Surface Look Like?

When you look at the Moon through a telescope, it shows several interesting features. When the *Apollo* astronauts visited the Moon in the 1960s and 1970s, they took close-up pictures of many of these same features. Some of the features looked the same way they looked from Earth. Some of them looked very different.

- **Craters** were formed by the impact of objects from space. Some have peaks in the center. Some craters also seem to have rings that make them look like bull's-eye targets. When the meteorites hit the surface, the impact sent out waves, just like when you throw a rock into a pond. The waves formed rings, or rims, around the craters. Even though the Moon and Earth are hit by space objects at about the same rate, there are more craters on the Moon. This is because erosion on Earth wears away Earth craters.

- **Maria** (singular, *mare*) are large, dark, flat areas. They were the "seas" seen by the people of long ago. You can still see them if you look now. However, the maria are not really seas. They were formed by huge lava flows that covered low-lying areas, including the craters, billions of years ago.

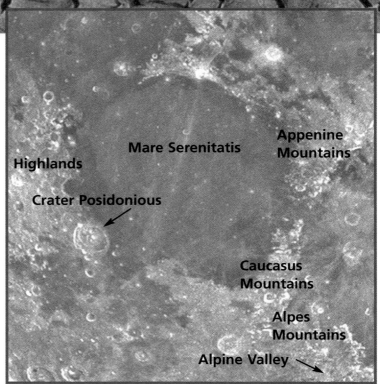

Various features of the Moon's surface as observed from Ringgold, Georgia.

- **Highlands** are light-colored, heavily cratered regions at higher elevations than maria.

- **Mountains** are scattered throughout the highlands. They are named after mountain ranges on Earth. The highest mountain peaks on the Moon are nearly as tall as Mount Everest on Earth.

- **Valleys** are cigar-shaped depressions. The most famous is the Alpine Valley. It is located in the mountain range known as the Alpes. The Alpine Valley is on the northwestern edge of Mare Imbrium.

▷ **What are the different features of the Moon's surface?**

Why It Matters

The *Apollo* missions changed our ideas about the Moon. These missions provided a great deal of data, as have telescopes and probes sent to the Moon. We know that the Moon has no magnetic field today, though it may have had one in the past. Seismometers show that the Moon is still being hit by meteors. Moon rock samples have even given us clues about Earth's early history. The *Clementine* and *Lunar Prospector* missions found evidence of water on the Moon.

e-Journal Visit our Web site www.science.mmhschool.com to do a research project on missions to the Moon.

Think and Write

1. Why do we see the phases of the Moon?
2. How is a lunar eclipse different from a solar eclipse?
3. How does the Moon's surface compare with Earth's?
4. | INQUIRY SKILL | **Observe** Where are the Sun, Moon, and Earth during a neap tide? A spring tide?
5. **Critical Thinking** During a total lunar eclipse, how does the Moon look from Earth? What do you think Earth looks like from the Moon?

L·I·N·K·S

MATH LINK

Calculate Earth's rotation. As water moves to and from the tidal bulges, the friction of the water against the solid Earth slows Earth's rotation by 0.00000002 second per day. How much slower does Earth rotate each year?

WRITING LINK

Writing a Poem Write a poem based on daily observations of the Moon. Start with a new Moon phase. Observe just after sunset from new Moon to full Moon. Then observe the Moon at sunrise. Where does the Moon rise in relation to the Sun? How does its position in the sky change? Use descriptive language.

SOCIAL STUDIES LINK

Learn about cultural beliefs. Research ancient beliefs about eclipses. How did they affect those who believed in them? Do people still believe them today?

TECHNOLOGY LINK

Science Newsroom CD-ROM Choose *It's Just a Phase* to learn more about the Moon.

LOG ON Visit www.science.mmhschool.com for more links.

Amazing Stargazing

Astronomer Sandy Faber uses the Hubble Space Telescope to study the most distant galaxies.

Have you ever gazed up at the night sky and wondered about Earth's place in space? You are not alone. The universe is magnificent and mysterious. Humans have been trying to understand it for thousands of years.

Some of the earliest stargazers were shepherds and farmers in Africa and Asia. They saw that the Sun, Moon, and stars followed certain patterns each season. Early astronomers built on these observations. They came up with theories that weren't always popular. Polish scientist Nicolaus Copernicus upset many people when he said that the Sun, not Earth, was the center of our solar system. But his theory was correct! It changed our view of the universe forever.

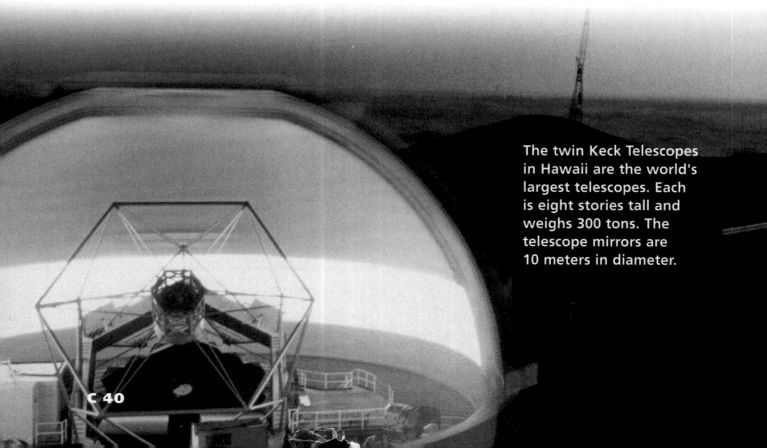

The twin Keck Telescopes in Hawaii are the world's largest telescopes. Each is eight stories tall and weighs 300 tons. The telescope mirrors are 10 meters in diameter.

Sally Ride Science

Astronomers learned much more after the telescope was invented in the seventeenth century. Scientists discovered three planets—Uranus, Neptune, and Pluto—that had never been seen before. They also discovered moons circling other planets. And they learned that our Sun is a star—one of billions of stars in our galaxy.

Scientists have learned a lot since the days of Copernicus. But there are still many fascinating questions that today's astronomers are working hard to answer. Their instruments are high-tech telescopes, satellites, and spacecraft.

Sandy Faber is one astronomer eager to learn more. She uses the powerful Hubble Space Telescope and giant telescopes on Earth to look deep into space and far back in time.

Sandy Faber's knowledge of telescopes helped to fix the Hubble Space Telescope.

What Did I Learn?

1. What we know about astronomy today took centuries to learn. Why?

2. Copernicus waited until he was on his deathbed to publish his controversial ideas. Should scientists worry about how their ideas will be accepted? Why or why not?

This hand-held telescope allowed the Italian astronomer Galileo to discover the Moon's craters and four of Jupiter's moons.

LOG ON Visit www.science.mmhschool.com to learn more about the solar system.

Chapter 5 Review

Vocabulary

Fill each blank with the best word or words from the list.

**electromagnetic
  spectrum,** C9
frequency, C9
lunar eclipse, C34
reflection, C8
refraction, C8
revolution, C24
rotation, C20
solar eclipse, C35
tide, C36
wavelength, C9

1. When the Moon blocks our view of the Sun, it is called a(n) _____.

2. The regular rise and fall of the water level along a shore is called the _____.

3. During a(n) _____, the Moon passes into Earth's shadow.

4. Earth makes one _____ around the Sun each year.

5. One _____ of Earth takes about 24 hours.

6. Light waves that bounce back are a(n) _____.

7. Light waves that bend in a substance are a(n) _____.

8. Light waves are measured from peak to peak, or by _____.

9. The number of waves that pass through a point in a second is called the wave's _____.

10. Light waves are part of the _____.

Test Prep

11. How do the wavelengths of radio waves compare to those of visible light?
  A They are longer.
  B They are shorter.
  C They are higher.
  D They are lower.

12. Telescopes can be designed based on what two properties of light?
  F wavelength and frequency
  G refraction and reflection
  H refraction and frequency
  J wavelength and reflection

13. Astronomers do all of the following EXCEPT _____.

   A study the universe

   B try to find how objects are formed

   C look for relationships between objects and events

   D study the ocean bottom

14. The flattening of Earth at the poles and the bulging at the equator is evidence of _____.

   F Earth's rotation

   G Earth's revolution

   H the Moon's rotation

   J the Moon's revolution

15. The Moon looks completely dark as seen from Earth during _____.

   A Full Moon phase

   B First Quarter phase

   C New Moon phase

   D Third Quarter phase

Concepts and Skills

16. Reading in Science How do astronomers find out about the universe if they cannot leave Earth?

17. Critical Thinking How is the cycle of seasons due to the tilt of Earth's axis?

18. INQUIRY SKILL **Observe** How does the arrangement of Earth, the Sun, and the Moon affect the tides on Earth?

19. Safety Why is looking at an eclipse without protective eyewear dangerous?

20. Scientific Methods The force of gravity depends on your distance from Earth's center. How would you test this hypothesis?

Did You Ever Wonder?

INQUIRY SKILL **Predict** Start with a full moon. Make a calendar showing one month of Moon phases.

LOG ON Visit www.science.mmhschool.com to boost your test scores.

The Solar System and Beyond

Did You Ever Wonder?

What kinds of strange objects might you see in outer space? The photo shows a huge cloud of gas and dust called the *Horsehead Nebula* against a background of stars. How do you think it got its name?

INQUIRY SKILL **Infer** *Pioneer 10,* the first spacecraft to leave the solar system, carries a map showing which planet it came from. Why do you think this was put on the probe?

The Inner Solar System

Vocabulary

planet, C48

solar system, C48

asteroid, C54

Get Ready

This photo shows a comet and the stars as streaks of light because it was taken over a period of several hours. On clear nights, away from city lights, stars appear to be points of light. However, some of these points of light are not stars. Some are planets, such as Jupiter and Venus. How can you tell them from stars?

Inquiry Skill

You define based on observations when you put together a description that is based on observations and experience.

Explore Activity

Why Do Planets Seem to Move?

Materials

4 marbles

4 lumps of clay

Procedure

1 **Experiment** Work with a copy of this drawing. Use clay to fix a marble in each of the three star locations. Fix a marble on Planet X for the March observation. Look at Planet X from Earth's March position. Note its position with respect to the stars. Write a 1 to mark where Planet X appears between the stars.

2 **Experiment** Repeat step 1 for May, June, July, and September. Write a 2, 3, 4, or 5 in the field of stars for these monthly observations.

3 **Observe** Study the pattern of numbers showing the changing position of Planet X.

Drawing Conclusions

1 **Measure** Compare the distances Earth and Planet X seem to move in one month. Which seems to be traveling faster?

2 In what direction does Planet X appear to move from March to May with respect to the stars? From May to July? From July to September?

3 **Communicate** Did the stars seem to move? If so, describe what you saw.

4 FURTHER INQUIRY **Define** How can you tell the stars from the planets in the night sky? Make observations to test your idea.

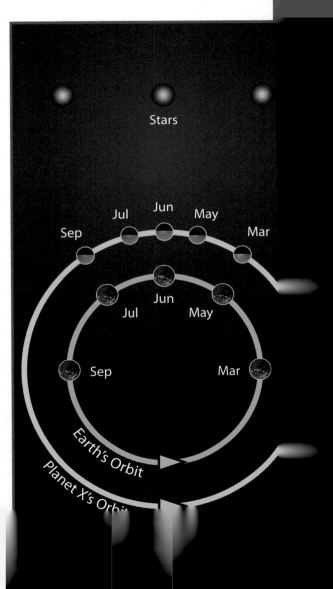

Main Idea Mercury, Venus, Earth, and Mars revolve around the Sun, composing the inner solar system.

How Can We Tell Planets from Stars?

Long ago, before telescopes, astronomers noticed stars (balls of glowing hot gas). They also noticed objects that changed position from night to night against the background of stars. These objects are the **planets**. Planets are large bodies orbiting a star. In this case the star is the Sun. The Sun's gravity keeps the planets in orbit.

The ancient astronomers did not know what the planets were. They tried to explain how these moving objects could change position. Early ideas of how objects in the universe were organized put Earth at the center of everything. It did not move. The Sun, the Moon, and the stars revolved around Earth.

However, this organization had some problems. What about the planets? (Planet comes from the Greek word meaning "wanderer.") The planets seemed to wander among the stars. This, in fact, was how ancient astronomers could recognize planets. Sometimes the planets seemed to be moving backward!

Some astronomers said the Sun was at the center. Earth and everything else revolved around it.

At the time it was introduced, this model was very unpopular. Many people did not like to know about things that would challenge their ideas about the order of things. However, this new model explained the motions of the planets. It explained them more simply than the Earth-centered idea.

Astronomers today are still interested in the motions of planets. They are also interested in their properties. The planets are part of the **solar system**. The solar system is the Sun and all of the planets, moons, and other bodies traveling around it.

▷ **How do planets and stars appear from Earth?**

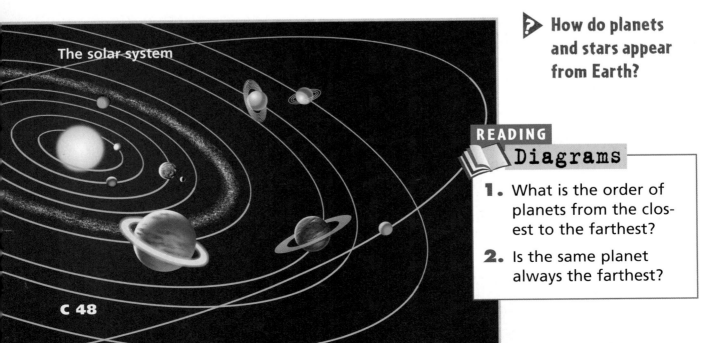

The solar system

READING
Diagrams

1. What is the order of planets from the closest to the farthest?

2. Is the same planet always the farthest?

Paths in Space

How do planets and other objects in the solar system move? Does the path depend on the speed of the object? Is the path affected by gravity? Write a hypothesis.

In this activity you are going to use observations of a model to test your hypothesis.

Materials

rubber ball

2 different-colored pencils

paper

Procedure

1 **Make a Model** Draw a large circle on your paper. This circle is Earth. Draw a dot about 10 cm above Earth's surface. The dot represents a ball.

2 **Experiment** Drop a ball from 1 m above the ground (Earth's surface). Observe its path, and draw it above the circle.

3 **Use Variables** Now hold the ball the same height as in step 2, but toss it sideways with just a little speed. Observe the ball's path. Draw the path.

4 **Use Variables** Repeat step 3 three more times. Each time throw the ball sideways a little faster.

Drawing Conclusions

1 **Observe** What did you observe about the path of the ball as you increased the sideways speed?

2 **Infer** What if a cannon can fire the ball faster and faster? Using the second colored pencil, draw the path you think the ball would take.

3 Is there a speed the cannon could fire the ball at so that it circles Earth but never lands again? If so, draw the path the ball would take.

4 Do you think there is a speed at which the ball would escape Earth, that is, never come back? If so, draw its path.

What Do We Know About Mercury and Venus?

Mercury

Mercury is the closest planet to the Sun and the second-smallest planet. The *Mariner 10* space probe sent back most of the data on Mercury. Here is some of the information collected by *Mariner 10*:

- Mercury has cliffs, craters, and lava flows.

- Mercury revolves around the Sun in 88 Earth days. It rotates once every 59 Earth days.

- Temperatures on Mercury range from −183°C (−297.4°F) to 467°C (872.6°F).

- Mercury has a very weak magnetic field.

- Mercury's density is about the same as Earth's density.

Mercury

- Deep inside craters at Mercury's poles, where the Sun's light never reaches, there may be water ice.

Venus

Venus has been visited by space probes. *Pioneer Venus* (U.S.A. 1978), the *Venera 15* and *16* probes (U.S.S.R. 1983–1984), and *Magellan* (U.S.A. 1990–1994) all visited the planet.

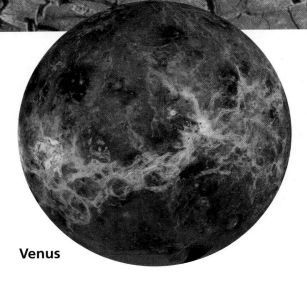

Venus

They sent back fascinating data:

- Venus has a surface covered with vast plains, lava flows, thousands of volcanoes, huge mountains, and craters.

- A day on Venus is longer than its year. Venus rotates once every 243 Earth days. It revolves around the Sun in 225 Earth days. Venus also rotates in a direction opposite that of Earth's rotation.

- Venus has a dense atmosphere of carbon dioxide and is covered by a thick layer of clouds. This may be producing a runaway greenhouse effect resulting in extremely high temperatures. Temperatures on Venus hover around 480°C (900°F).

- Pressure at the surface is about 90 times the atmospheric pressure at Earth's surface.

READING **Compare and Contrast How are Mercury and Venus alike and different?**

What Is Earth Like?

Earth is the third planet from the Sun. Its day is 23.9 hours long. Its year is 365.26 days long. Its diameter is only a few hundred kilometers larger than that of Venus. It is the only planet in the solar system known to support life.

- Earth has a strong magnetic field. This field is distorted into a teardrop shape by high-energy particles from the Sun (the solar wind).

- The first American satellite, *Explorer 1*, discovered what are now called the Van Allen radiation belts. These belts are areas around Earth where particles from the Sun are trapped, much as a bar magnet traps paper clips.

- Earth is an active planet, with earthquakes, volcanoes, and building up and wearing away of land masses.

- Temperatures on Earth average 15°C (59°F) on the surface.

- The atmosphere protects us only from small debris from space. It does not protect us from large objects. There might have been as many craters on Earth as on the Moon. However, erosion on Earth caused these craters to disappear.

Earth

▷ **What is unique about Earth compared with other inner planets?**

READING

Diagrams

How does the thickness of Earth's hydrosphere compare to that of its mantle?

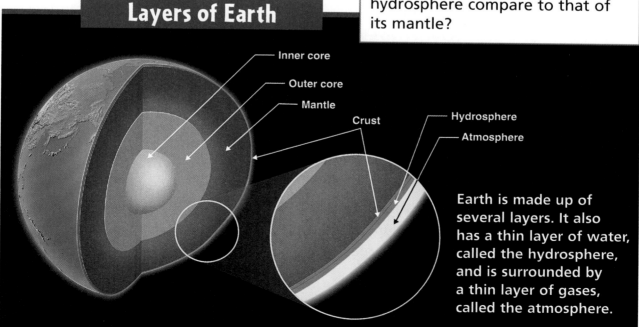

Layers of Earth

Inner core

Outer core

Mantle

Crust

Hydrosphere

Atmosphere

Earth is made up of several layers. It also has a thin layer of water, called the hydrosphere, and is surrounded by a thin layer of gases, called the atmosphere.

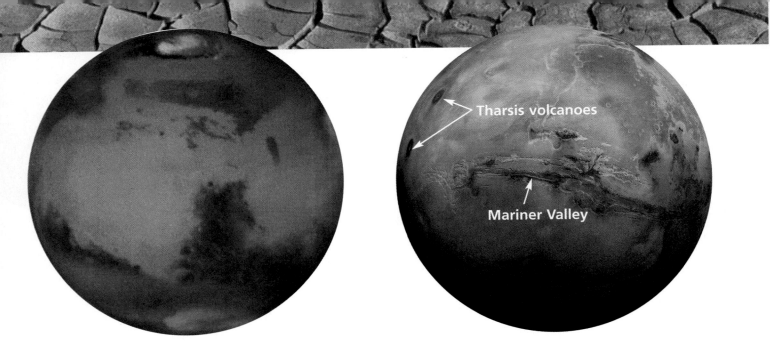

Mars from Hubble Space Telescope

Mars from *Mariner 9*

Tharsis volcanoes

Mariner Valley

What Is Mars Like?

Here are some facts about Mars:

- The planet Mars is 6,786 kilometers (4,218 miles) in diameter. At 228 million kilometers (142 million miles) from the Sun, it is the fourth planet. It has a rotation period of 24.6 hours, almost the same as Earth's. Its year is about twice as long as ours, and its axis is tilted 25°. This means Mars also has seasons.

- The *Mariner 4* space probe showed many craters on Mars, especially in the southern hemisphere. *Mariner 9* discovered huge volcanoes in the northern hemisphere. One of them, Olympus Mons, rises 27 kilometers (almost 17 miles) above the surrounding plain. That's about three times as high as Mount Everest!

Mountains can "build" higher on Mars because its gravity is less than Earth's.

- *Mariner 9* also photographed a vast canyon. It was named the Mariner Valley. If this canyon were on Earth, it would stretch from New York City to Los Angeles! Evidence indicates it may have been formed by running water.

- In 1997 the *Mars Pathfinder* landed on Mars. It sent out the six-wheeled rover Sojourner to study the area near the lander.

▷ **What feature of Mars makes its volcanoes so much higher than those on Earth?**

Why Is Earth's Atmosphere Special?

How do the atmospheres of the inner planets compare?

- Mercury has no true atmosphere, but hydrogen, helium, argon, oxygen, sodium, and potassium have been detected.

- Venus's atmosphere consists primarily of carbon dioxide (96%) and nitrogen (3%), with traces of sulfur dioxide and other gases.

- Mars has a very thin atmosphere. Its primary components include carbon dioxide (95%), nitrogen (2.7%), and argon (1.6%). The sky appears to be pink. This is because a lot of reddish dust is suspended in the atmosphere.

- Earth has an atmosphere made up of nitrogen (78%) and oxygen (21%). Why is Earth's atmosphere so different from that of its neighbors? Oxygen has been building up on Earth for billions of years. Green plants and other producers release oxygen into the atmosphere as part of photosynthesis, the food-making process.

Earth's atmosphere is very complex. It is divided into several layers. The troposphere is the part of the atmosphere nearest Earth's surface. All weather occurs in this layer. The stratosphere is the layer just above the troposphere. Ozone in the stratosphere helps absorb harmful ultraviolet radiation from the Sun. Above the stratosphere is the mesosphere, and above it, the thermosphere.

▷ **What is the composition of Earth's atmosphere?**

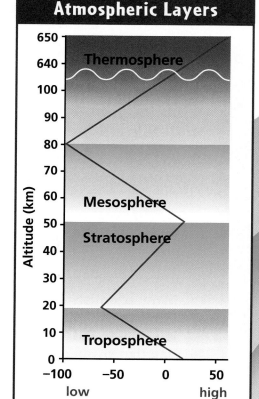

Atmospheric Layers

Thermosphere

Mesosphere

Stratosphere

Troposphere

Altitude (km)

Temperature (°C)
low   high

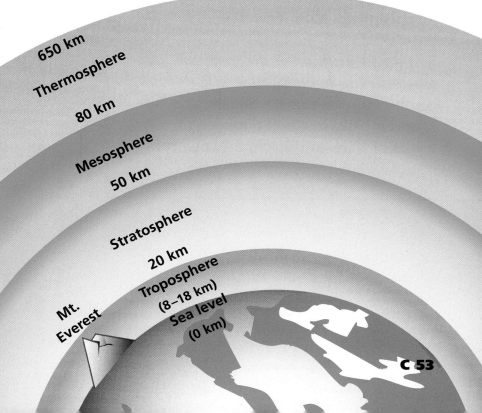

650 km
Thermosphere

80 km
Mesosphere

50 km
Stratosphere

20 km
Troposphere
(8–18 km)
Sea level
(0 km)

Mt. Everest

What Are Asteroids?

It is early morning 65 million years ago. The air is already hot. The *Tyrannosaurus rex* doesn't seem to mind. It's busy eating its food. Suddenly it stops eating. It sniffs the air. Then it hears something. At first it was just a hissing, but now it is a sizzling sound, very menacing. The dinosaur begins to run. Then there's a blinding flash, and it's blown away by terrific winds.

Is this science fiction, or is it real? Scientists explain events from the past using evidence. These explanations are called *theories*. The asteroid theory is a possible explanation for the extinction of the dinosaurs. Near Winslow, Arizona, there is a crater. It was caused by an **asteroid**. Asteroids are rocky or metallic objects that orbit the Sun. They are too small to be considered planets. That crater was formed by a small asteroid. If the asteroid had been large, who knows what might have happened?

Some astronomers suggest that asteroids are material that never combined to become a planet. They are found mostly in a belt between the orbits of Mars and Jupiter. They orbit the Sun just like planets. Some asteroids travel out as far as Saturn's orbit. Others have orbits that cross Earth's path.

Gaspra

Space probes have passed by asteroids and obtained much information. On June 27, 1997, the spacecraft *NEAR* encountered the asteroid Mathilde. This and other flybys by space probes are giving a good picture of the nature of these smaller members of the solar system. The spacecraft *Galileo* flew by the asteroids Gaspra in 1991 and Ida in 1993.

▷ **What is the possible origin of the asteroid belt?**

Meteor Crater, Arizona

Many scientists think an asteroid, larger than the one that crashed in Arizona, caused the dinosaurs to become extinct.

Why It Matters

Why is it important to study the inner planets? Looking at one of Earth's closest neighbors may provide an answer.

Venus has what is known as a runaway greenhouse effect. Infrared light given off by Venus cannot escape its atmosphere. This trapped infrared light causes the high temperature on Venus. By studying Venus, scientists hope to learn how to keep Earth's own greenhouse effect under control.

ⓔ-Journal Visit Our Web site www.science.mmhschool.com to do a research project on Venus.

Think and Write

1. How can we distinguish a planet from a star?

2. How are the inner planets alike? Different?

3. What is an asteroid?

4. INQUIRY SKILL Experiment How does the path of a thrown ball demonstrate the path of the planets around the Sun? How does changing how it is thrown demonstrate the effect of gravity?

5. Critical Thinking What would happen to the planets' orbits if gravity were suddenly shut off?

L·I·N·K·S

WRITING LINK

Persuasive Writing How does the greenhouse effect cause changes on Earth? What is being done to counteract this effect? Research the greenhouse effect. Write an editorial to state your opinion about the topic. Do you think more needs to be done by governments? By scientists? Support your opinion with facts. Save your strongest argument for last.

MATH LINK

Make a bar graph. Calculate the height of each layer of Earth's atmosphere using the diagram on page C53. Make a bar graph comparing the data.

SOCIAL STUDIES LINK

Research different solar system models. Investigate the solar system models of Ptolemy, Albatenius, Nicolaus Copernicus, Sir Isaac Newton, Galileo, Tycho Brahe, and Johannes Kepler. Make a poster to present your findings.

Copernicus

TECHNOLOGY LINK

LOG ON Visit www.science.mmhschool.com for more links.

El Niño

Torrential rain in San Diego? Snow in Miami? What kind of weather is this? It's El Niño!

El Niño is a weather pattern that happens every three to seven years. When El Niño develops in the Pacific Ocean, it can affect weather around the world. It can bring heavy rain or snow to some places and severe drought to others. And it can bring disaster.

El Niño begins in the western Pacific Ocean when temperatures in a huge pool of water start to rise. The pool of warm water grows, sometimes to twice the size of the United States. At the same time, winds that usually blow near the equator die down. The ocean currents reverse direction, and the warm water charges east! The result is bizarre weather around the world.

Here's why it happens. When you take a hot bath, the air in the bathroom gets warm and steamy. The same thing happens over that enormous "bathtub"

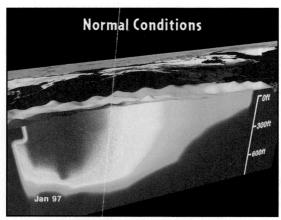

Normal Conditions

Jan 97

0ft
300ft
600ft

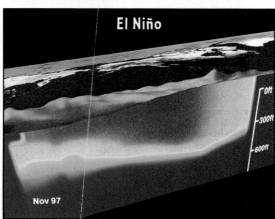

El Niño

Nov 97

0ft
300ft
600ft

During an El Niño, ocean currents at the equator change direction and warm water flows east. These disturbances in the ocean and atmosphere affect weather around the world.

Coral reefs are home to many types of plants and fish. The warmer ocean water during an El Niño destroys algae that protect coral. The coral then bleaches white and dies.

The ground is bone-dry and cracked. Severe droughts can occur in some parts of the world during an El Niño.

of water in the Pacific. The moist, hot air rises. When it reaches cooler air, the moisture condenses and forms rain clouds. But these aren't just any rain clouds, they're huge thunderstorms. They follow the warm water east toward North America and South America. They also pump warm, moist air high into the atmosphere—more than 50,000 feet high. This changes weather patterns around the planet.

The El Niño of the winter of 1983 caused massive mudslides, floods, and severe droughts.

Today, buoys in the ocean and satellites in space are on the lookout for signs of the next El Niño. They monitor the ocean temperature, currents, and winds. Weather forecasters around the world use this information to help all of us prepare for El Niño's extreme weather.

Write About It

1. Where does the El Niño weather pattern start?

2. How would you describe an El Niño pattern?

LOG ON Visit **www.science.mmhschool.com** to learn more about El Niño.

LESSON 5

The Outer Solar System

Vocabulary

comet, C64

meteoroid, C65

meteor, C65

meteorite, C65

Get Ready

How much do we know about the other planets in our solar system?

Scientists use observatories such as this one in Hawaii to study planets and other objects in space. Can tools such as this help us compare the planets? How do the distances between planets compare?

Inquiry Skill

You classify when you place things that share properties in groups.

C 58

Explore Activity

How Are the Planets Arranged?

Materials

cellophane tape

roll of waxed paper

meterstick

crayon (or modeling compound)

Procedure

1 **Make a Model** Set up a scale of the average distance of each planet from the Sun. To do so, divide by 10 the distance in millions of kilometers from the Sun to each planet. Record this data.

2 **Use Numbers** Change the units from kilometers to millimeters.

3 **Measure** Based on your scale of distances, use the meterstick to plot on the waxed paper each planet at the correct distance from the Sun.

Planet	Distance to the Sun (millions of kilometers)
Mercury	58
Venus	110
Earth	150
Mars	230
Jupiter	780
Saturn	1,400
Uranus	2,900
Neptune	4,500
Pluto	6,000

Drawing Conclusions

1 **Interpret Data** How does the spacing of the inner planets contrast with the spacing of the outer planets?

2 Between which two neighboring planets is there the greatest gap in space?

3 **FURTHER INQUIRY** **Classify** Use your results to classify the planets into at least two groups. Explain your reasoning. How did you set up your measuring scale?

Main Idea Beyond the asteroid belt, Jupiter, Saturn, Uranus, Neptune, and Pluto complete the solar system.

What Are the Outer Planets?

The planets Jupiter, Saturn, Uranus, Neptune, and Pluto are called the *outer planets*. Scientists distinguish these from the inner planets you learned about in Lesson 4 (Mercury, Venus, Earth, and Mars).

A gap—the asteroid belt— separates the inner planets from the outer planets. The four largest outer planets—Jupiter, Saturn, Uranus, and Neptune—share many properties. They are much larger than the *inner planets*. They also rotate very rapidly. Finally, their interior structure is different from the inner planets. With the exception of Pluto, the outer planets tend to have a small solid core, surrounded by a liquid, then a thick gaseous atmosphere.

Jupiter

Jupiter

Imagine a ball of gas so big that 1,000 Earths could fit inside it. Imagine a "storm" that has lasted for at least 300 years! Such a planet actually exists. It is called Jupiter.

Jupiter is the largest planet in the solar system. Its diameter is 143,000 kilometers (89,000 miles), 11 times Earth's diameter. At 778 million kilometers (480,000,000 miles) from the Sun, it is 5 times more distant from the Sun than Earth. It also has more mass than all the other planets combined.

- Ground-based observations of Jupiter have shown cloud belts. These cloud belts are made primarily of hydrogen and helium, with smaller amounts of methane, ammonia, and water vapor.

- Ground-based observations of Jupiter have also shown the Great Red Spot. This ranges from about one to three Earths in diameter. This feature has lasted for over 300 years. Some years it is more visible than others.

- Jupiter has more than 60 satellites, or moons. The four largest— Ganymede, Callisto, Io, and Europa —were first seen by Galileo in 1610.

Scientists have learned additional information about Jupiter from the *Voyager* flybys in 1979, the *Cassini* flyby in 2000, and the *Galileo* spacecraft exploration of the Jupiter system from 1995 to 2003.

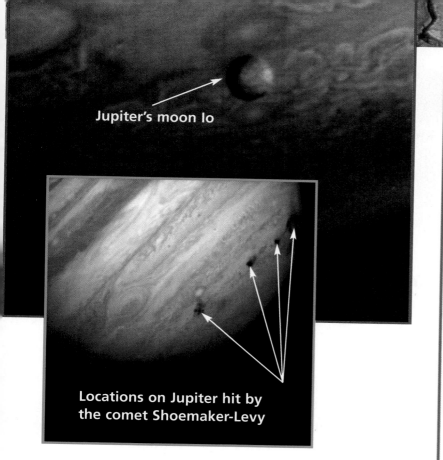

Jupiter's moon Io

Locations on Jupiter hit by the comet Shoemaker-Levy

In July 1994 people on Earth witnessed a very spectacular and very unusual event. A comet, Shoemaker-Levy, plunged into the atmosphere of Jupiter. The actual impact occurred when the collision site was on the part of Jupiter not yet facing Earth. Soon after the impact, the collision site rotated into Earth's view. The result was spectacular! The Hubble Space Telescope took pictures of the places that were hit. The picture above shows these places. There are several locations because the comet broke into about 20 pieces before it hit Jupiter.

READING **Compare and Contrast**
How are the inner and outer planets alike? Different?

QUICK LAB

A Planet Model

FOLDABLES Make a Four-Row Table. (See p. R44.) Label the sections as shown.

1. Use the data in the table below. Pick a scale to show the total depth of the planet (for example, 1 cm = 10,000 km) and make the table pictured to help you calculate each layer.

Layer	Jupiter	Saturn	Compare
hydrogen gas			
liquid hydrogen			
solid rocky core			

2. **Make a Model** Draw a large circle, using the scale you described in step 1. This circle will represent the planet.

3. **Use Numbers** Calculate how deep each layer of the planet's atmosphere will be in your model. Color each layer on your scale model. Be sure to include a color key.

4. Which layer is largest? Which is smallest?

Planet	Distance from Center of Planet	Chemical Composition
Jupiter	71,000–54,000 km 54,000–10,000 km 10,000–0 km	hydrogen gas liquid hydrogen solid rocky core
Saturn	60,000–28,000 km 28,000–16,000 km 16,000–0 km	hydrogen gas liquid hydrogen solid rocky core

Saturn

Uranus

How Do the Outermost Planets Compare?

Saturn

Saturn is the second-largest planet. It is about 1.4 billion kilometers from the Sun. It takes almost 29.5 years for Saturn to make one complete trip around the Sun. Much of what we know about Saturn is due to the *Voyager* flybys of 1980–1981.

- Saturn is noticeably flattened at the poles. This may be because of its very fast rotation (1 day = 10 hours 39 minutes).

- The atmosphere is composed mostly of hydrogen and helium. It has broad cloud belts similar to Jupiter's, but not as distinct. Saturn is also less dense than water.

- Winds on Saturn move at about 500 meters per second near the equator.

- There are seven major rings. Some of the rings are made of thinner rings. These are called ringlets. The rings are made of particles ranging from a few centimeters to a few meters in size and are up to 1 kilometer (3,200 feet) thick. One of the goals of the Cassini mission is to understand how and why the rings exist.

Uranus

Uranus is the seventh planet from the Sun. It lies at a mean distance of 2.9 billion kilometers from the Sun and orbits it once every 84 Earth years. Its diameter of about 51,100 kilometers makes it the third-largest planet.

- The atmosphere of Uranus is composed of 83% hydrogen, 15% helium, and 2% methane, with small amounts of acetylene and other hydrocarbons. The blue-green color of Uranus is due to methane in the planet's upper atmosphere.

- Winds in the Uranian atmosphere move between 40 and 160 meters per second.

- Like Saturn, Uranus has a ring system. Eleven rings have been discovered. The rings are much dimmer than Saturn's.

- Uranus is unusual because it looks as though it was knocked on its "side." Its axis of rotation is tilted about 98° to its orbit. Because of this, summer at the north pole of Uranus lasts for 21 years. The same is true at its south pole.

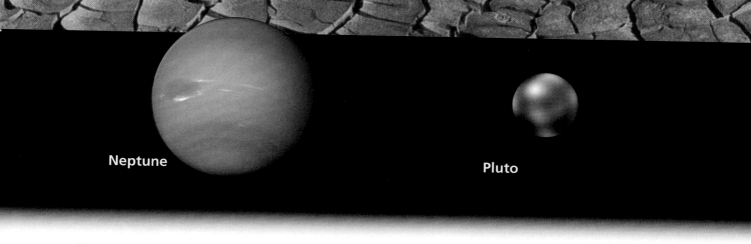

Neptune

Pluto

Neptune

Neptune is the last of the gas giants. Its radius is 24,764 kilometers. It lies at a mean distance of 4.5 billion kilometers from the Sun. Out here the light from the Sun is 900 times fainter than it is on Earth. Neptune's orbital period is 165 years. It has at least five rings, none of which are very bright.

- The atmosphere is composed of hydrogen, helium, methane, and water. Methane gives Neptune its blue color.

- Neptune has the strongest winds of any planet. In some spots the winds were measured by *Voyager* to blow at speeds up to 2,000 kilometers per hour.

- Many storms on Neptune have been detected by *Voyager*.

- Neptune has at least 13 moons. One moon, Triton, is larger than Pluto. Triton has similarities to Earth. It has geysers, and it also has seasons. This shows that in many ways Earth is not unique.

Pluto

The astronomer Percival Lowell predicted that a ninth planet must exist. It was named Pluto after a mythological Roman god, and also because the first two letters are Lowell's initials.

Pluto is the smallest planet. It is so different from the other planets that some scientists would not even classify it as a planet.

The orbits of Neptune and Pluto overlap. Pluto is usually farther from the Sun than Neptune.

- Astronomers discovered Pluto is covered with methane, nitrogen, and carbon dioxide ice. It has a thin methane and nitrogen atmosphere.

- Because Pluto is so far from the Sun, scientists think the atmosphere may freeze as the planet moves beyond Neptune's orbit.

- Pluto has one satellite, Charon. Charon is a little more than half the size of Pluto. The two revolve around each other about once every six days. Pluto and Charon always keep the same side facing each other.

▶ **How are Saturn, Uranus, Neptune, and Pluto alike and different?**

What Is a Comet?

On January 2, 2004, the Stardust spacecraft flew past Comet Wild 2 (pronounced Vilt-2) and collected samples of cometary material. Stardust is expected to return to Earth in January 2006, with comet material and interplanetary dust particles.

A **comet** is a ball of ice and rock that orbits the Sun. Comets come from the outer fringes of the solar system. One place where comets originate is a region stretching beyond Pluto's orbit. This region is called the *Kuiper* (KWIP·uhr) *Belt*. The Kuiper Belt probably contains about 40,000 to 70,000 objects with diameters of more than 100 kilometers. The asteroid belt, by comparison, has about 230 objects of this size.

How long do comets take to orbit the Sun? Some comets have orbits that take less than 200 years. The most famous of these comets is Halley's comet. Its orbit brings it past Earth every 76 years.

However, some comets have much larger orbits, which take more than 200 years. Comet Hyakutake (high·ah·kyew·TAH·kee) went past Earth in 1996. It will not return for 16,000 years! These comets come from a region called the *Oort* (AWRT) *Cloud*. This is a cloud that surrounds the solar system at about 15 trillion kilometers from the Sun.

What makes a comet visible? As the chunk of rock and ice approaches the Sun, sunlight begins to warm it.

READING
Diagrams

1. How would you describe the direction of the comet's tail as it travels around the Sun?

2. What happens to the size of the tail during the comet's orbit?

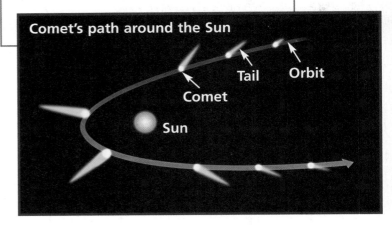

Comet's path around the Sun

Tail Orbit

Comet

Sun

The comet's ice begins to warm and forms a cloud surrounding the nucleus, or core, of the comet. As the comet gets closer to the Sun, the sunlight exerts pressure on the cloud. The pressure from the sunlight drives this cloud material away from the nucleus, forming the comet's tail. The tail always points away from the Sun.

Comet Hale-Bopp, seen in 1997, was first spotted when it was near Saturn's orbit. It was discovered to rotate like a lawn sprinkler, about once a week. The most interesting discovery concerned its tail. Comets usually have one or two tails. Hale-Bopp was the first comet to be found with three tails. It had a dust tail and an ion tail like most comets, and a third tail made of sodium atoms.

What makes a comet visible?

What Are Meteoroids?

In Lesson 4 you learned that the solar system has many asteroids. They are rocky, metallic objects in orbit around the Sun. Larger asteroids are in a belt between Mars and Jupiter. There are also small asteroids, which are often called **meteoroids** (MEE·tee·uh·roydz). Some travel to the edge of the solar system. Others spend their time within the orbits of the inner planets.

Some meteoroids come from material ejected by a passing comet. Other meteoroids are believed to have come from the asteroid belt. Sometimes a meteoroid collides with the atmosphere of a planet, such as Earth.

To get an idea of what happens, rub your hands together. The rubbing produces heat. When a meteoroid hits Earth's atmosphere, the rubbing, or friction, causes the meteoroid to burn. At this stage the meteoroid is sometimes called a **meteor**. We usually see the meteor as a bright streak of light.

Most times a meteor burns up completely. Any part of a meteoroid that reaches Earth's surface is called a **meteorite**.

Meteorites are usually classified into three types. Stony meteorites are made of rock. Metallic meteorites are made of metals (nickel and iron) or a mixture of metals and rock. Carbonaceous meteorites are rich in carbon.

Sometimes many meteoroids hit Earth's atmosphere at the same time. This often happens after a comet has recently traveled past Earth. The sudden occurrence of many meteors is called a *meteor shower*. Some meteor showers occur year after year.

The Perseid meteor shower is an example. Each year around August 11, if you look at the late night sky, you may see as many as 60 meteors an hour.

▷ **How do meteoroids, meteors, and meteorites differ?**

A meteor

Why Are Jupiter's Moons Special?

When Galileo discovered the four largest moons of Jupiter in 1610, he showed that other planets had moons. They were named the *Galilean* (gal·uh·LEE·uhn) *satellites* in his honor. Their names are Ganymede, Io, Europa, and Callisto. Over the centuries that followed, about 60 more moons have been found.

Ganymede Ganymede is the largest satellite in the solar system. At one time Saturn's moon Titan was thought to be largest. The *Voyager* flybys, however, showed that Ganymede is larger.

Voyager measurements showed that Ganymede has two kinds of land features. The surface has many craters on it. It also has curious features called grooves. They look like someone scraped parts of the surface with a rake! Scientists think these surface features mean that Ganymede's icy crust may be undergoing some kind of tectonic activity.

Io Io may be the most interesting of the Galilean satellites. When the *Voyagers* swept past Io, they discovered that Io had active volcanoes. The space probes detected nine eruptions. The *Galileo* spacecraft spotted hundeds more. The volcanoes are caused by a gravitational "tug-of-war" between Jupiter and the other Galilean satellites.

Europa Europa is a smooth world. *Voyager* showed it to have lots of cracks on its surface. They reminded scientists of how ice looks when it has

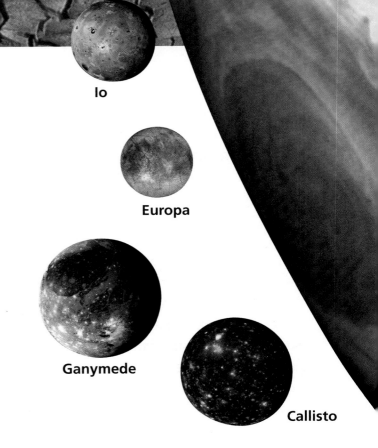

Io

Europa

Ganymede

Callisto

been broken and then refreezes. Below Europa's icy crust may be an ocean as deep as 50 kilometers.

Because Europa may have an ocean, scientists wonder if life may be present there. The *Galileo* spacecraft found evidence for oceans on Ganymede and Callisto as well as Europa.

Callisto The last of the Galilean satellites is Callisto. Callisto has a very old surface, with many craters. Long ago several large meteorites or other bodies must have hit the surface. Remnants of these impacts have been found.

▷ **What are the characteristics of Jupiter's four largest moons?**

Why It Matters

Scientists are very interested in Titan, the largest of Saturn's 31 satellites. Titan is the only satellite known to have a dense atmosphere. Titan's atmosphere is mostly nitrogen, but it also contains methane. Its atmosphere may be similar to Earth's atmosphere several billion years ago. By studying other planets and their satellites, scientists may learn more about Earth's history.

e-Journal Visit our Web site www.science.mmhschool.com to do a research project on Titan.

Think and Write

1. How far apart are the outer planets compared with the inner planets?

2. Describe the similarities and differences between the outer planets.

3. What are comets? How may they cause meteor showers?

4. Describe the moons of Jupiter.

5. **Critical Thinking** What if you had been a scientist directing the *Galileo* space probe around Europa? You want to know if life exists on Europa. What data would you have told the space probe to collect?

L·I·N·K·S

MATH LINK

Titan, a moon of Saturn.

Calculate Uranian wind speed. Winds on Uranus move between 40 and 160 meters per second. How fast do the fastest winds move in kilometers per hour?

WRITING LINK

Personal Narrative Which planet are you most curious about? What if you could travel to that planet? What observations would you make? What would you expect to see? Write a log entry about one adventure you had on your trip to that planet. Tell what happened and how you felt about it. Share the events in order.

LITERATURE LINK

Read *To Jupiter and Beyond* to discover how we learned about Jupiter. Think about what it would be like to travel there yourself. Try the activities at the end of the story.

TECHNOLOGY LINK

LOG ON Visit www.science.mmhschool.com for more links.

MOONSCAPES

Green cheese? No. But the moons in our solar system have certainly been full of surprises.

There are very few moons in the inner solar system. Mercury and Venus have none. Earth, of course, has one. Mars has only two very small moons. But the outer solar system is another matter! Each of the giant outer planets has lots and lots of moons. Some of the moons are smaller than a mountain on Earth. Others are larger than the planet Mercury!

Some moons formed billions of years ago with the planets that they circle. Some formed elsewhere in the solar system. But then they passed too close to a planet and were captured by its gravity. What's amazing is how different the moons are. Some are scarred with craters, evidence that they've been bombarded by meteorites. Some have mile-high mountains, others hide underground oceans. Io has so many erupting volcanoes that it is covered with molten lava. Europa is covered with a slick layer of ice. Oily lakes dot Saturn's largest moon, Titan. Icy geysers erupt on Neptune's largest moon, Triton.

Quite an assortment of moons!

Triton (above left) is Neptune's largest moon. Its frozen surface is 390 degrees below zero Fahrenheit (minus 148 degrees Celsius) – the coldest in the solar system. Part of its unusual landscape looks like the skin of a cantaloupe. Slushy lava oozes up through cracks in the ice, and icy geysers shoot nitrogen gas miles into Triton's thin air.

Charon (right) probably formed when a huge meteor hit Pluto and blasted part of the planet into space.

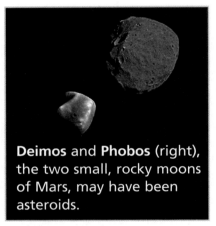

Deimos and **Phobos** (right), the two small, rocky moons of Mars, may have been asteroids.

Miranda is an odd-looking moon circling Uranus. It looks as though it's been broken apart and put back together again. Maybe it has! Part of it looks old and has lots of craters. Part of it has ice cliffs ten miles high and canyons ten miles deep.

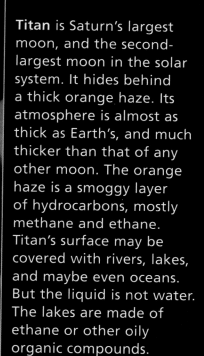

Titan is Saturn's largest moon, and the second-largest moon in the solar system. It hides behind a thick orange haze. Its atmosphere is almost as thick as Earth's, and much thicker than that of any other moon. The orange haze is a smoggy layer of hydrocarbons, mostly methane and ethane. Titan's surface may be covered with rivers, lakes, and maybe even oceans. But the liquid is not water. The lakes are made of ethane or other oily organic compounds.

Mimas is one of the small moons of Saturn. Something crashed into this moon and left a huge crater eighty miles wide—about one-third the diameter of the moon itself! The mountain at its center is higher than Mount Everest. The collision nearly broke Mimas apart.

Saturn (right), with two of its moons—**Tethys** (above) and **Dione**.

Write About It

1. Describe some characteristics of the many moons in the solar system.

2. Describe Saturn's moon Titan.

 LOG ON Visit **www.science.mmhschool.com** to learn more about the solar system.

Stars

Vocabulary

star, C72

constellation, C72

magnitude, C72

parallax, C73

light-year, C73

nebula, C76

supernova, C77

black hole, C77

Inquiry Skill

You predict when you state possible results of an event or an experiment.

Get Ready

In the past people saw stars arranged in groups. They traced heroes or other characters in the night sky. The ceiling of Grand Central Station in New York City shows some of these star pictures. In a star "picture," the stars appear to be side by side against a flat background. That would mean they are all the same distance from the observer.

Do stars really come in groups? Are they all the same distance away?

Explore Activity

Materials
3 tennis balls
meterstick

Are Stars at Different Distances from Earth?

Procedure

1. Using tennis balls to represent stars, work with a partner to design a model "star outline." Place three tennis balls 50 cm apart on a table.

2. **Observe** Have your partner arrange the model with all of the balls at one end of a long room. Stand at the opposite end, approximately 8 m away, and draw the pattern you see.

3. **Use Variables** Close your eyes. Have your partner move one ball forward 6 cm and one ball backward 6 cm. Open your eyes, and draw the outline as you see it.

4. Switch roles with your partner. Repeat steps 1–3.

Drawing Conclusions

1. **Interpret Data** Does the outline appear to change when the balls are not all the same distance away? Explain your answer.

2. **Observe** From your vantage point at the opposite end of the room, can you identify the balls that are farthest and nearest? What do you have to do to be sure?

3. FURTHER INQUIRY **Predict** How does a star's distance from Earth affect its brightness? Make your prediction. Design an experiment to test your prediction.

Main Idea Stars range in size, brightness, and distance from Earth.

How Can You Recognize a Star?

You may know what a **star** is, but how would you define it? A star is a large, hot ball of gas, which is held together by gravity and gives off its own light.

How can you find Rigel (RIGH·juhl) or other stars in the night sky? The easiest way to find a star is by looking for its **constellation** . A constellation is a number of stars that appear to form a pattern. For example, Rigel is a star in the constellation Orion, the hunter.

As Earth travels in its orbit around the Sun, its night side faces different directions. You see only the constellations that are in that direction. The constellation Orion, for example, is a winter constellation. We see it from the Northern Hemisphere in the winter months during our orbit around the Sun.

Some stars are brighter than others. Sirius (SIR·ee·uhs), in the constellation Canis Major, is the brightest star in the winter sky. It appears brighter than Rigel.

However, Rigel is actually a brighter star than Sirius. The reason Sirius appears brighter is that it is closer to us than Rigel. For example, if a very bright flashlight is side by side with a dimmer one, you can tell the difference. If the brighter flashlight is moved far behind the dimmer one, the brighter one seems to get dimmer and dimmer.

The word **magnitude** is used to describe the brightness of a star. The actual brightness of a star is the *absolute* magnitude. The brightness

Constellations

Orion
Pegasus
Vega
Lyra
Sirius
Rigel
Antares
Canis Major
Leo
Scorpius

of a star as you see it in the night sky is its *apparent* magnitude. That depends on how much light it gives off and how far away it is.

How do scientists know a star's distance? If the star is close, they view it from different points in Earth's orbit. The star appears to shift its location compared with other stars farther away. This apparent shift of an object's location when viewed from two positions is called **parallax** (PAR·uh·laks). The closer a star is, the greater the shift. By measuring the shift, scientists can estimate how far away the star is.

Astronomers use a unit called the **light-year** to describe distances in space. A light-year is the distance light travels in a year, or about 9 trillion kilometers. The star Alpha Centauri is 4.3 light-years from Earth. Light leaving that star now will reach Earth in 4.3 years.

READING **Compare and Contrast**
What is the difference between a star's absolute and apparent magnitude?

Parallax

	Pencil Shift	Star Shift	
Only left eye open		☆	January
Only right eye open		☆	July

Both pencil and star appear to shift because of parallax.

QUICK LAB

How Parallax Works

FOLDABLES Make a Seven-Row Chart. (See p. R44.) Label the rows as shown.

Parallax	
#1	
#2	
#3	
#4	
#5	
#6	

1. **Make a Model** Look at a distant object with your left eye. Hold your thumb about 10 cm in front of your face. Hide the object with your thumb. Look at the object with your left eye. Note the position of your thumb and use your organizer to record what you see.

2. **Use Variables** Close your left eye, and now look at the object with your right eye. What has changed? Write your observations.

3. **Use Variables** Now repeat the activity, holding the thumb farther away each time. Record your observations.

4. **Make a Model** What does your thumb represent in this model?

5. How does parallax work? Explain.

6. What happens as your thumb is farther and farther in front of your face?

| 3,000° | 4,000° | 6,000° | 10,000° | 20,000° or more |

What Properties Does a Star Have?

What color are stars? Sirius is blue-white. Antares (an-TAYR-eez), a bright summer star, is reddish.

A star's color is related to its surface temperature. Think of a coil of a toaster getting hotter. As the coil heats up, it turns bright red, then orange, and then orange-yellow. In stars this same relationship applies. The coolest stars are red and orange. Hotter stars are yellow, and the hottest are blue-white.

In the center of a star, nuclear reactions are occurring. These reactions make the star shine by releasing large amounts of energy. The light we see from a star is the energy released by the nuclear reactions. The high temperature produced tends to make the star expand. At the same time, gravity pulls in on the star's gases. Gravity tends to make the star contract. As long as these two forces balance, the star stays the way it is.

Surface temperature, size, and the distance from Earth are what determine the star's brightness. The higher the temperature is, the brighter the star. In general, the larger the star, the brighter it is. The closer a star is to Earth, the brighter it appears to be.

Two scientists, Ejnar Hertzsprung and Henry Norris Russell, tried to see if brightness and temperature were related. The *Hertzsprung-Russell (H-R) diagram* on page C75 shows the results of their work. An H-R diagram compares the temperatures and absolute magnitudes of stars.

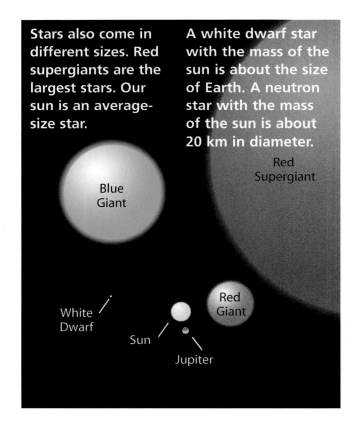

Stars also come in different sizes. Red supergiants are the largest stars. Our sun is an average-size star.

A white dwarf star with the mass of the sun is about the size of Earth. A neutron star with the mass of the sun is about 20 km in diameter.

Red Supergiant

Blue Giant

White Dwarf

Sun

Red Giant

Jupiter

To read the diagram, start at the bottom of the absolute magnitude scale. Move out to where the stars are plotted. Start at the bottom with the white dwarfs. White dwarfs are small, dim stars that are neither the hottest nor the coolest.

The coolest dim stars are the red stars at the end of the group called *main-sequence stars*. Most stars are found in the band called the main sequence. In the main sequence, the hotter a star is, the brighter it is.

Now move to the top of the absolute magnitude scale. Run your finger across to the supergiants. These are extremely large stars. Some are hotter than others. The remaining group, the giants, are large stars. They are just below the supergiants in the chart. That means they are dimmer than the supergiants.

▶ **What are three properties of a star?**

READING

Diagrams

1. List the stars in order from brightest to dimmest.

2. List the stars in order from coolest to hottest.

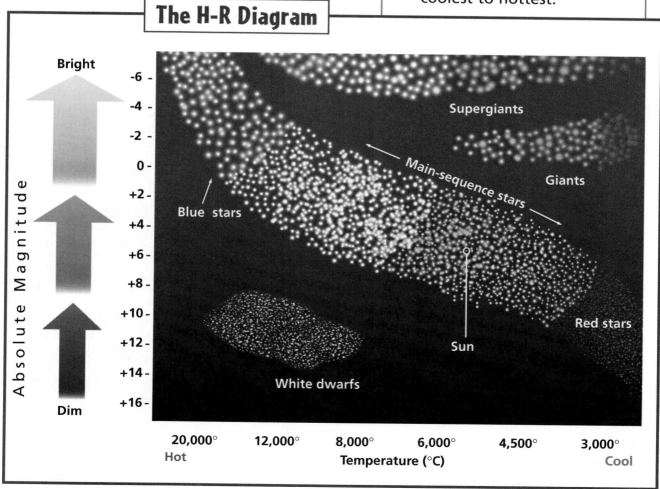

The H-R Diagram

Bright

Absolute Magnitude

Dim

-6
-4
-2
0
+2
+4
+6
+8
+10
+12
+14
+16

Supergiants

Main-sequence stars

Giants

Blue stars

Sun

Red stars

White dwarfs

20,000° 12,000° 8,000° 6,000° 4,500° 3,000°
Hot   **Temperature (°C)**   Cool

What Are the Life Stages of a Star?

What can we learn from an H-R diagram? The stars that are plotted on the H-R diagram are groups of stars classified by their temperature and brightness. They are also stars at different points or stages in the life cycle of stars. Stars go through different stages. They are born. They mature, grow old, and eventually die.

Beginning

A star begins its life as an enormous cloud of gas and dust in space, a **nebula** (NEB·yuh·luh) (plural, *nebulae*). As time goes by, gravity causes the nebula to contract. As the cloud shrinks, it heats up. The cloud has become a *protostar*. A protostar is a young star that glows as gravity makes it collapse.

Main-Sequence Stars

Eventually the center of the protostar reaches a temperature of several million degrees. At this point nuclear reactions occur. Four hydrogen atoms fuse and form one helium atom. Energy and electrons are released in this reaction. The energy moves outward, balancing against the force of gravity. The protostar is now a *main-sequence star*. A main-sequence star is a star that is fusing hydrogen into helium. A star spends most of its life on the main sequence.

Giants and Supergiants

As a star uses up the supply of hydrogen at its core, the star begins to expand. As it expands, the star's surface gets cooler. The star becomes a giant or supergiant star, depending on its mass.

Eagle Nebula

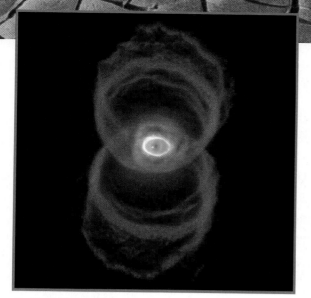

Colliding stellar winds in Helix Nebula

The remains of Supernova 1987A

Final Stage: Lower-Mass Stars

Stars up to about ten times the mass of the Sun become red giant stars. In a red giant's core, both hydrogen and helium are changed into heavier elements. Energy is also released. As a red giant, its gravity is not strong enough to hold on to its outer layer of gas. This expanding layer of gas, called a *planetary nebula*, slowly spreads out into space.

Meanwhile the star's core continues to shrink. Its surface heats up, becoming white hot. The star has become a white dwarf. Stars produce a wind of charged particles. Wind from a white dwarf often travels very fast. It catches up with the planetary nebula formed thousands of years earlier. As the wind hits the nebula, the wind makes the nebula shine. The wind also tears the nebula apart.

Final Stage: More Massive Stars

More massive stars, stars greater than ten times the mass of the Sun, become supergiants. These stars use up energy at a fantastic rate. As a result, the star becomes unstable. It may become a **supernova** (sew·puhr·NOH·vuh). A supernova is a star that explodes.

What happens next depends on the star's mass. Most supernova remnants become *neutron stars*, extremely dense stars made entirely of tightly packed neutrons. Neutron stars rotate very rapidly. Sometimes the neutron star seems to be blinking on and off like light from a lighthouse. When this happens, the star is called a *pulsar*.

When a star is very massive, something different occurs. It becomes a supernova. However, the remaining star does not become a neutron star. The star's core collapses. The star becomes a **black hole**. A black hole is an object whose gravity is so strong that even light cannot escape from it.

▶ **How does the protostar stage of a star's life cycle compare with the main-sequence stage?**

What Is a Supernova?

The place: China. The time: 1054. Some Chinese astronomers were observing the sky. Their focus was on the region known now as Taurus. Suddenly a new, bright star appeared. It was brighter than any other star in the sky. The astronomers called it a "guest star." They didn't know it, but the Chinese astronomers had just witnessed a supernova.

A supernova is an extremely powerful explosion in the universe. Some supernovas are so bright that they have been seen during the daytime, when the Sun was shining! What conditions are needed for a star to become a supernova?

Stars more massive than ten Suns become supergiants. These stars fuse heavier and heavier elements, releasing energy in the process. Finally they fuse iron. However, fusing iron doesn't produce energy, it uses it up. As iron fusion continues, more and more energy is used up. The star no longer produces energy to balance the pull of gravity. Suddenly the star collapses, exploding as a supernova. In the shock wave formed from the blast, heavier elements up through uranium are created. The core, or center, of a massive supernova will become a neutron star. An extremely massive supernova will become a black hole.

 How does a supernova form?

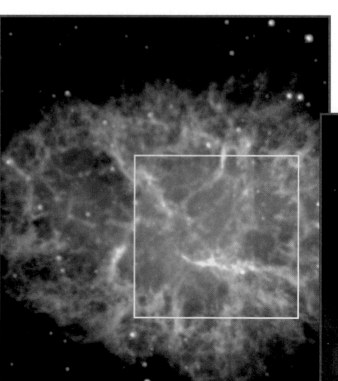

A supernova is a violent event. The photos show the remnants of the supernova that was seen in A.D. 1054. The photo at left is a view from Earth. The image at the right was taken by the Hubble Space Telescope.

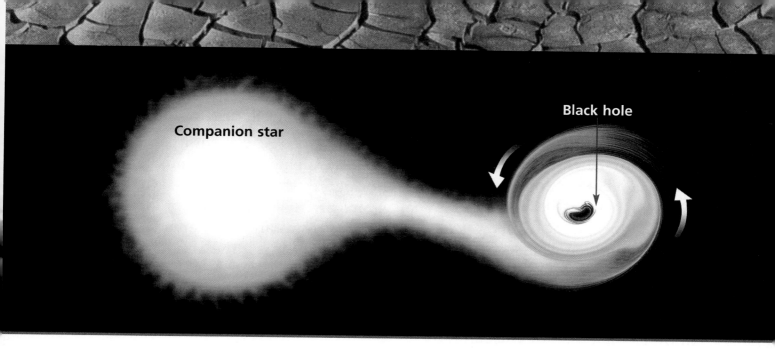

Companion star

Black hole

What Is a Black Hole?

After a supernova explosion, the leftover star collapses. Sometimes a star has too much mass to stop collapsing at the neutron-star stage. Its gravity is too strong. As a result, the star continues to collapse. Eventually it becomes so small that it warps, or bends, the space around it. The star's gravity becomes so powerful that not even light escapes it. The star has become a black hole.

Black holes don't give off light. They cannot be seen directly. The only way they can be seen is by observing their effects. Let's take a trip on an imaginary spacecraft to see what's happening around a black hole.

As you approach the black hole, you see that it has a companion star. (Many black holes may have companions, in fact.) Gas from the star is streaming toward the black hole. The gas spirals toward it in an orbit that keeps getting smaller. As the material spirals inward, it heats up. It gets

hotter as it gets closer to the black hole. Just before the gas enters the black hole, it emits X rays.

One example of a black hole is an X-ray source in the constellation Cygnus (SIG·nuhs), the Swan. It has a blue supergiant companion with the unusual-sounding name HDE226868. The X-ray source is called Cygnus X-1. It is 8,000 light-years from Earth.

▶ **When does a supernova become a black hole?**

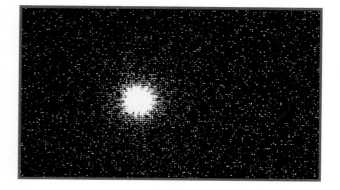

This is Cygnus X-1. Gas streaming off the blue supergiant is pulled into the black hole, giving off X rays.

What Kind of Star Is the Sun?

The Sun has 99.9 percent of all the mass in the solar system.

- The outermost part of the Sun, the *corona*, can be seen from Earth only during a total solar eclipse. Temperatures in the corona can reach 100 million degrees Celsius.

- The next layer in is the *chromosphere* (KROH·muh·sfeer). Like the corona, the chromosphere can be seen only during a total eclipse. The chromosphere appears pinkish.

- Beneath the chromosphere is the *photosphere* (FOH·tuh·sfeer). This is the part of the Sun that is visible. The photosphere is basically the "surface" of the Sun. The temperature of the photosphere is about 6,000°C. That makes the Sun a yellow star. It is placed in the middle of the H-R diagram, a middle-aged star. Never look at the Sun directly. Its brightness can harm your eyes.

- Past the photosphere is the interior of the Sun. Energy travels outward toward the Sun's surface by means of radiation and convection.

READING
Diagrams

Name the layers of the Sun in order, beginning at the interior and moving outward.

- The core, or center, of the Sun is the source of all the Sun's energy. The core is about the size of Jupiter.

The Sun is 92 percent hydrogen. It is slowly being changed into helium through nuclear reactions. Hydrogen atoms are fused together, producing helium atoms and light energy. Scientists estimate the Sun has enough hydrogen to last another five billion years!

The Sun has a diameter of 1,392,000 kilometers (865,000 miles). A million Earths would fit into the Sun! The distance from Earth to the Sun is 149,000,000 kilometers (92,960,000 miles). Like Earth, the Sun rotates on its axis. It takes 27 days to complete one rotation.

▷ **Where is the Sun in the H-R diagram?**

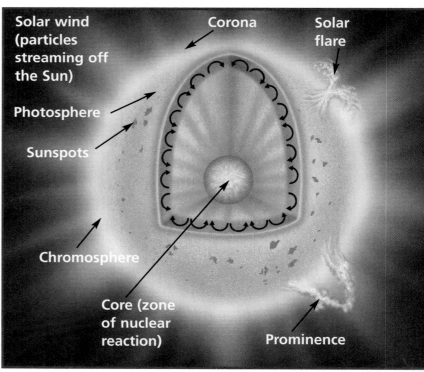

Solar wind (particles streaming off the Sun)

Corona

Solar flare

Photosphere

Sunspots

Chromosphere

Core (zone of nuclear reaction)

Prominence

Why It Matters

The Sun is a main-sequence star. Its life cycle will end in several billion years. In the meantime the Sun is an inexhaustible source of energy for Earth. Plants and other producers trap its energy by making food. In this way it makes possible the life cycles of all living things on Earth, including your own.

Plant matter decaying underground over millions of years produced today's limited fuel supplies of oil, natural gas, and coal. This fuel can be traced back to the Sun.

e-Journal Visit our Web site www.science.mmhschool.com to do a research project on stars.

Think and Write

1. How is the distance to a star determined?

2. How is the temperature of a star related to its brightness?

3. How are white dwarfs, neutron stars, and black holes alike? Different?

4. How are the parts of the Sun arranged from innermost to outermost?

5. **Critical Thinking** Why do you think the life cycle of a star depends on its mass?

L·I·N·K·S

ART LINK

Draw constellations. Try to observe the night sky in an area without lights. Draw different pictures that the stars make as you are viewing them. Use a local star map to check your drawings against those of familiar constellations.

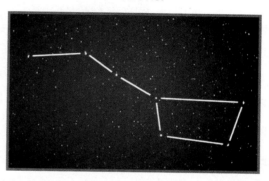

WRITING LINK

Expository Writing Use newspapers and other library resources to learn about the discovery of Supernova 1987A. How was it discovered? By whom? Present a report of your findings to the class.

MATH LINK

Solve this problem. The speed of light in space is 300,000 km/s. Earth's average distance from the Sun is 150,000,000 km. Calculate how long it takes light from the Sun to reach Earth.

TECHNOLOGY LINK

 LOG ON Visit www.science.mmhschool.com for more links.

LESSON 7

Galaxies and Beyond

Vocabulary

galaxy, C84

Milky Way, C85

spectrum, C86

expansion redshift, C86

big bang, C87

background radiation, C88

quasar, C90

Inquiry Skill

You classify when you place things that share properties in groups.

Get Ready

Galaxies are vast groups of stars in space. These groups have immense space in between them. The galaxy shown here, known as Messier 81, has the same shape as the Milky Way. The Milky Way is the galaxy in which our solar system is located.

Do all galaxies have the same shape? How do different galaxies in space compare?

Explore Activity

How Are Galaxies Classified?

Procedure: Design Your Own

1 **Observe** Study the galaxy pictures. Look for common shapes and properties. Make a list of shapes and properties.

2 **Classify** Sort the galaxy pictures into groups sharing the same shapes and properties.

Drawing Conclusions

1 How many groups did you make? Describe the common properties of galaxies in each group.

2 Decide on a name for each separate group. Let the shapes and properties guide your choices.

3 **Compare** How did your classification system compare to those of other student groups? Explain the similarities and differences.

4 **FURTHER INQUIRY** **Classify** Study galaxy photos from other sources such as the library or Internet. Study their shapes and properties. How would you group these galaxies using your classification system? Try it and share your results.

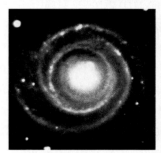

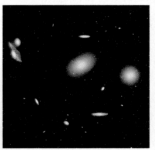

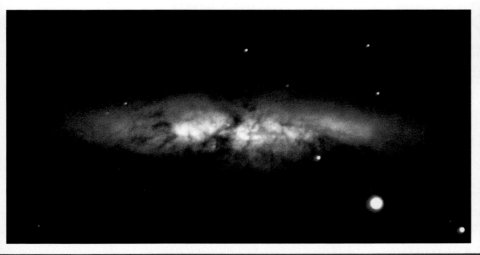

Main Idea The Milky Way is one of billions of galaxies that are moving away from each other in an expanding universe.

Spiral galaxy

What Are Galaxies?

Stars are grouped together throughout the universe in groups called **galaxies**. Galaxies are large groups of stars held together by gravity. These stars are also moving. They orbit the center of their galaxy.

A galaxy may contain around 200 billion stars. Scientists estimate that there are around 100 billion galaxies in the universe. Just as stars belong to a galaxy, galaxies are usually part of a larger group, or cluster.

You know that stars are different in size and structure. Galaxies also differ in size and structure. Astronomers classify galaxies into three main groups, based on the shapes galaxies can have.

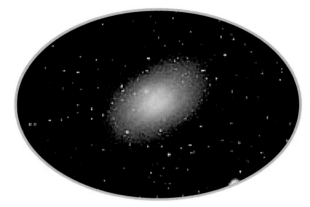

Elliptical galaxy

- A spiral galaxy is a whirlpool-like galaxy. Spiral galaxies can be tightly or loosely wound. They often have lots of dust in their spirals. Some spirals have a "bar" of stars, gas, and dust through the center, with the spirals going out from the bar.

- An elliptical galaxy is football or basketball shaped. It has no spirals and very little or no dust.

- An irregular galaxy does not have any recognizable shape. Many irregular galaxies have been involved in collisions with other galaxies.

Irregular galaxy

Without a telescope, galaxies look to us like points of light in the night sky, much like stars. Only with powerful telescopes can we look closer to see that the point of light is made up of many stars. The shape we observe also depends on the position from which the galaxy is viewed. Galaxies are three-dimensional, not flat. They look different if we see them head-on, at an angle, or edge-on.

The Milky Way Galaxy

You're out in the countryside, away from city lights. The Moon has set, and it is dark and cloudless. It's a beautiful summer night. You look at the sky overhead. What do you see? You might see a broad, patchy band of light stretching across the sky. You are looking at part of our home galaxy, the **Milky Way** .

As you can see from the diagrams below, the Milky Way is a spiral galaxy. It has some characteristic features.

- Stars are grouped in a kind of bulge in and around the center. All the stars in the Milky Way orbit its center. In general the closer a star is to the center, the faster it moves in its orbit.

- Several spiral arms, or narrow "lanes" of stars, extend out from the center. Getting farther and farther away from the center of the galaxy, stars become fewer in number.

- Surrounding the outer region of the Milky Way is a "halo." This halo is ball shaped and is made up of mostly faint stars.

Our solar system is located on one of the spiral arms. From our vantage point on an arm, we see a large grouping of stars when we look toward the center of our galaxy. As we look in other directions, stars appear less crowded.

To find the Milky Way's center, we look in the direction of the constellation Sagittarius. However, we cannot actually see the center because we are looking through the Sagittarius arm. The spiral arm contains lots of gas and dust. The spiral arm's dust hides the Milky Way's center from us.

READING **Compare and Contrast**
How is the Milky Way similar to other galaxies?

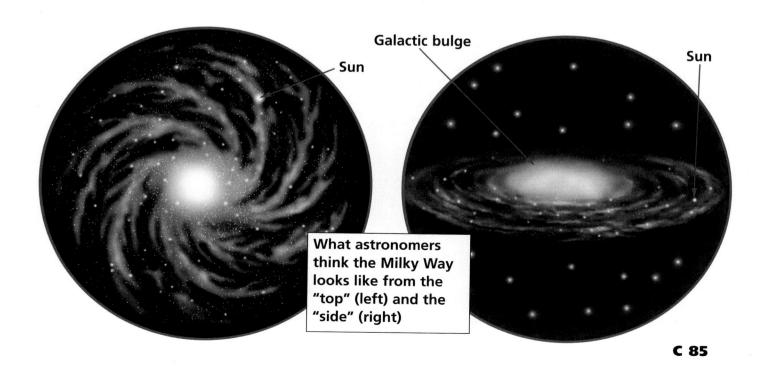

Sun

Galactic bulge

Sun

What astronomers think the Milky Way looks like from the "top" (left) and the "side" (right)

Are Galaxies Moving Away from Each Other?

Think of a rainbow. It is formed by drops of water. When a beam of light goes through a drop of water, the wavelengths become separated. We see a band of colors, from violet to red. This band is part of the electromagnetic spectrum, discussed in Lesson 1. A similar thing happens if you heat up a gas. The heated gases of stars produce waves of light. The light produces a **spectrum**. However, instead of just a band of colors, you also see a pattern of dark lines. When light from a star passes through the star's outer gases, some of the wavelengths of light are absorbed by these gases. The absorbed wavelengths "drop out" from the spectrum in the form of dark lines.

The dark lines help us identify a star or a galaxy. Each star or galaxy has its own pattern of lines.

When we look at spectra from the light from galaxies, the dark lines shift. Some shift to the blue end of the spectrum. On the average, however, the lines shift to the red end.

Galaxies move away from each other because the space between the galaxies is expanding. It is something like a piece of rubber expanding. As space expands, the wavelength of light traveling through space also expands. This increase in wavelength of light due to space expanding is called an **expansion redshift**. It is called a redshift because the light's spectrum has been shifted to longer (redder) wavelengths. If the light from a galaxy is shifted to the red end, then the distance between us and the galaxy is increasing.

READING Diagrams

What causes a redshift? A blueshift?

Wavelength Shift

1 No shift

2 Redshift

3 Blueshift

1 This is how a light wave between our galaxy and another galaxy would look if the galaxies were not moving.

2 If they are moving away from each other, the wavelength stretches out. It becomes longer.

3 If they are moving closer together, the wavelength is compressed. It gets shorter.

The Big Bang

Galaxies are moving away from each other. However, there is no "center" to the expansion. Observers in each galaxy could consider themselves to be at the center. This is because each observer would see the other galaxies moving away. It is useful to think of this as an expansion of space, not an explosion in space.

Looking "backward in time," astronomers say that in the past the galaxies must have been closer to each other. The early universe was very compressed. Because it was at a high pressure, its temperature was very high.

This beginning moment when the universe was very hot and dense is called the **big bang**. According to the big bang theory, the universe has expanded ever since the big bang. As the universe expanded, its density and temperature decreased.

According to recent data, many astronomers believe the universe will continue to expand forever. However, it may, instead, stop expanding and then start contracting.

▷ **How do we know that galaxies are moving away from each other?**

QUICK LAB

Expanding Dots

FOLDABLES Make a Three-Row Chart. (See p. R44.) Label the rows as shown.

| #2 Observe |
| #3 Observe |
| #6 Infer |

1. **Blow up a 9-inch, light-colored, round balloon just until it is about 5 cm in diameter.** Draw three dots on the surface of the balloon. Label the dots A, B, and C. Make the chart to record your data.

2. **Observe** Now blow up the balloon until it is about 20 cm in diameter. While you blow up the balloon, your partner should observe what is happening to the dots. Pause a couple of times to measure how far dots A and B are from dot C. Record your data.

3. **Observe** Slowly release the air from the balloon. Midway through, again record how far apart the dots are.

4. As the balloon was blown up, what happened to the dots on its surface?

5. What happened to the dots as you let air out of the balloon?

6. **Infer** If the balloon represents the universe, write about what the black dots represent.

How Did the Universe Form?

According to the big bang theory, long ago the universe was in the form of an extremely tiny, extremely dense "atom." It was also at a very high temperature. The high temperature and pressure resulted in a tremendous "explosion." This big bang sent matter in all directions. As matter expanded outward, the universe began to cool. Gravity caused the matter to collect into clumps. These clumps eventually became stars and galaxies. The galaxies continue to move outward.

The big bang helps explain why there is a different amount of each element in the universe. For example, it suggests that originally the universe was made of electrons and other tiny particles. As the temperature of the universe cooled down after the big bang, the small particles began to combine into hydrogen atoms. Most other elements were made inside the newly formed stars as hydrogen atoms were fused. The universe presently contains about 90 percent hydrogen.

Astronomers have discovered a form of electromagnetic waves coming from all directions in space. This radiation is left over from the beginning of the universe. It is called **background radiation**. Most of this energy is in the microwave part of the electromagnetic spectrum. The big bang theory predicted the existence of the background radiation in the 1940s. The background radiation was discovered in the 1960s.

▷ **What evidence supports the big bang theory of how the universe formed?**

Expanding Universe

Astronomers observe that the other galaxies are moving away from us. This supports the theory that the universe is expanding.

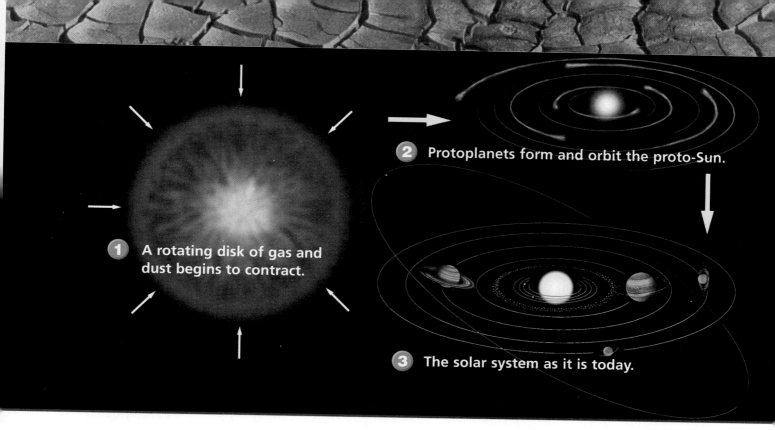

1 A rotating disk of gas and dust begins to contract.

2 Protoplanets form and orbit the proto-Sun.

3 The solar system as it is today.

How Did the Solar System Form?

One of the questions astronomers ask is "Where did the solar system come from?" Let's look at this question from the point of view of the big bang.

- Several billion years after the big bang, many galaxies have formed. Much dust and hydrogen gas remains. Some of it has gathered into nebulae. A few nebulae are massive enough to rotate slightly.

- Then perhaps a star passes nearby one of the nebulae. More likely the shock wave from a supernova hits the nebula. The wave makes small clumps of gas and dust form. Under the force of gravity, these clumps begin to contract. The supernova explosion carries with it heavier elements, such as oxygen, carbon, and iron. These elements make up most of the inner planets.

- As the cloud contracts, it begins to rotate faster. The gravity at the center of the cloud gets stronger. Most of the clumps drift into the center of the spinning cloud. The clumps that move to the center will gradually become the proto-Sun. The other clumps will eventually become the protoplanets. These protoplanets move in nearly circular orbits around the proto-Sun. As they move, they sweep up some of the gas and dust. They add it to their growing mass.

- The center of the cloud gets more massive. The temperature at the core of the proto-Sun climbs. Eventually, the temperature becomes high enough to start nuclear reactions. The star—the Sun—is now a full-fledged main-sequence star.

▷ **What is a theory for the formation of our solar system?**

Astronomers believe this image shows a collision between a quasar and a galaxy.

What Is a Quasar?

Why do some objects in the universe shine brighter than trillions of Suns? They have a size about equal to that of the solar system. They are **quasars** (KWAY·zahrz). A quasar is an extremely bright, extremely distant, high-energy source.

Since quasars are at a great distance, the light coming from them reaches Earth after traveling billions of years. That means quasars must be very, very old. In the time the light has been traveling, the space between the quasars and Earth has grown, because the universe is getting larger. Thus, the wavelength of light coming from them has lengthened. It has been shifted to the red end of the spectrum.

One interesting idea about quasars is that they might be galaxies in an infant stage. It has taken so long for the light from them to reach Earth that in the meantime they may have become galaxies. If so, we won't get light from these galaxies for billions of years to come!

Quasars might also be connected to black holes. In the past everything was closer together, and galaxies had a greater chance of colliding. Many astronomers hypothesize that when galaxies collide, they may feed material to supermassive black holes. These black holes would be able to gobble up entire stars. This would release tremendous amounts of energy as the stars spiraled into the black hole. This energy might be the energy we see as a quasar.

▶ **Why is the light we see from quasars very old?**

L·I·N·K·S

Why It Matters

When you look into the night sky, you look into the past. Light from stars and galaxies has been traveling for a long, long time.

Astronomers look into space to understand what has been going on in the universe for billions of years. By studying the stars, they are able to learn how the universe started, how it is changing, and what will happen to it in the future.

e-Journal Visit our Web site www.science.mmhschool.com to do a research project on galaxies.

Think and Write

1. Why are the spectra of galaxies shifted toward the red end?

2. What is a galaxy? List the characteristics of each of the three types of galaxies.

3. What kind of galaxy is the Milky Way? What is the approximate location of our solar system in the Milky Way?

4. What does "the big bang" mean? How does it explain the formation of galaxies?

5. **Critical Thinking** What might we learn by studying quasars?

LITERATURE LINK

Read *The Big Bang and the History of the Universe* to discover how scientists developed the Big Bang Theory. Try the activities at the end of the book.

WRITING LINK

Writing That Compares Compare two of NASA's Observatories astronomers have used to study the universe. Choose from the Hubble Space Telescope (HST), the Chandra X-Ray Observatory (CXO), and the Spitzer Space Telescope. How does each obtain images? Write about similarities and differences.

MATH LINK

Convert light-years to kilometers. The Andromeda galaxy is about 2.2 million light-years away. How many kilometers is that? You may wish to use scientific (powers of 10) notation.

TECHNOLOGY LINK

LOG ON Visit www.science.mmhschool.com for more links.

Chapter 6 Review

Vocabulary

Fill each blank with the best word or words from the list.

comet, C64
galaxy, C84
light-year, C73
nebula, C76
parallax, C73
planet, C48
quasar, C90
solar system, C48
star, C72
supernova, C77

1. The distance to close stars can be measured using _____.

2. A distant bright source of high energy is called a(n) _____.

3. One type of exploding star is called a(n) _____.

4. A group of stars held together by gravity is a(n) _____.

5. The Sun and all the objects in orbit around it is the _____.

6. The distance light travels in a year is a(n) _____.

7. An enormous cloud of gas and dust in space that is the beginning of a star is a(n) _____.

8. A _____ is a ball of ice and rock that orbits the Sun.

9. A _____ is a large, hot ball of gas that gives off its own light.

10. Nine _____ (s) are in orbit around the Sun.

Test Prep

11. What object's gravity is so strong that even light cannot escape it?
  A white dwarf
  B black hole
  C nebula
  D neutron star

12. What do astronomers call the patterns that we see in the stars?
  F galaxies
  G solar systems
  H constellations
  J H-R diagram

13. What do astronomers call a meteor that has landed on Earth?
  A meteorite
  B meteor
  C meteoroid
  D crater

14. All of the following are shapes of galaxies EXCEPT _____.

   F spiral

   G elliptical

   H irregular

   J round

15. The brightness of a star is its _____.

   A expansion

   B magnitude

   C temperature

   D redshift

Concepts and Skills

16. Reading in Science How is the speed of a planet related to its distance from the Sun?

17. Scientific Methods The universe is expanding. What evidence supports this theory?

18. **INQUIRY SKILL** **Experiment** What determines whether an object falls to Earth's surface or orbits Earth?

19. Critical Thinking What are the possible final states of a star? How can you tell the history of that star?

20. Decision Making The galaxies are moving away from each other. What force acts to oppose this expansion? Is this the same force that causes a ball to return to Earth after it is thrown upward?

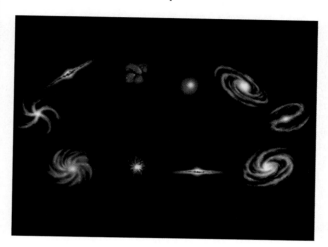

Did You Ever Wonder?

INQUIRY SKILL **Make a Model** Design a plaque to put on a spacecraft that will one day leave the solar system. What would you want to tell others about that spacecraft and the world it came from?

 LOG ON Visit science.mmhschool.com to boost your test scores.

Madhulika Guhathakurta

Astronomer

Madhulika Guhathakurta has come a long way from her childhood in India to her job at NASA headquarters in Washington, D.C. Lika, as she's known, runs a program called "Living With a Star." It's designed to find out everything that can be known about the Sun.

"We want to know how and why the Sun's energy varies. And we want to know how that affects people," she explains.

To do this, Lika's team is planning a mission to launch a solar observatory. Telescopes on the satellite will study different regions of the Sun, from deep in its core to its outer atmosphere. It's the Sun's outer atmosphere, or corona, that is of special interest to Lika.

"The Sun's core is between 5,000 and 6,000 degrees Centigrade [Celsius]. But the corona is 1 to 2 *million* degrees Centigrade.

Sometimes the solar wind can cause problems for radio and telephone transmissions. (That's Lika on the screen!)

What is making it so hot? That's a question we still haven't answered."

Lika hopes the information the observatory gathers will help people plan better for outbreaks of solar wind. Solar wind is made of particles that fly off the Sun's corona and speed through space. Sometimes the solar wind can cause problems with radio or telephone transmissions on Earth.

"We call it space weather," says Lika. "Everyone in the world is dependent on space weather." The solar observatory is one of a series of satellites NASA plans to launch to study the Sun. The information NASA scientists learn from these probes may help them better understand the workings of the Sun—before 2011. That's when scientists think the next big increase in solar activity will take place.

TOP 5 Future Solar Eclipses

Here's a list of some upcoming solar eclipses. Which ones might you be able to see?

1. **March 29, 2006**
   Africa, Europe, Asia
2. **August 1, 2010**
   North America, Europe, Asia
3. **November 13, 2012**
   Australia, South Pacific
4. **March 20, 2015**
   Iceland, Europe, North Africa
5. **March 9, 2016**
   Asia, Australia, South Pacific

Write About It

1. How do the Sun's corona and the solar wind affect people on Earth?
2. What question does Lika want to answer about the Sun's corona?

LOG ON Visit www.science.mmhschool.com to learn more about the Sun.

MOON WATCH

Your goal is to make a model that shows why the Moon has phases.

What to Do

1. Model the Earth-Moon-Sun system. Hold a ball at arm's length. Stand several feet away from a lighted lamp. Slowly turn in a complete circle, keeping the ball in front of you. Watch the changing light and shadow on the ball. Where is the ball when it is lit up like a full Moon?

2. Where is the ball when it looks like a new Moon? A quarter Moon? A crescent Moon?

Analyze Your Results

1. Draw a diagram of the Earth-Moon-Sun system for each phase modeled.

2. Are the phases of the Moon caused by Earth's shadow on the Moon?

Solar Model

Your goal is to make a model to compare distances within the solar system.

What to Do

1. Draw a picture of the Sun. Cut it out, and tape it to one end of a cardboard strip.

2. Model the solar system, using multi-colored pushpins. Let each pushpin represent a different planet. Use the table of planet distances shown here. Stick each "planet" into the cardboard strip at the right distance from the "Sun." Use a meterstick to make your measurements.

Analyze Your Results

On your model, 2.5 cm represents 1 astronomical unit or 148,730,560 km. Calculate and record how far away from the Sun each "planet" is. How is your model similar to and different from the real solar system?

Mercury, 1 cm	Mars, 4 cm	Uranus, 48 cm
Venus, 2 cm	Jupiter, 13 cm	Neptune, 75 cm
Earth, 2.5 cm	Saturn, 24 cm	Pluto, 98.5 cm

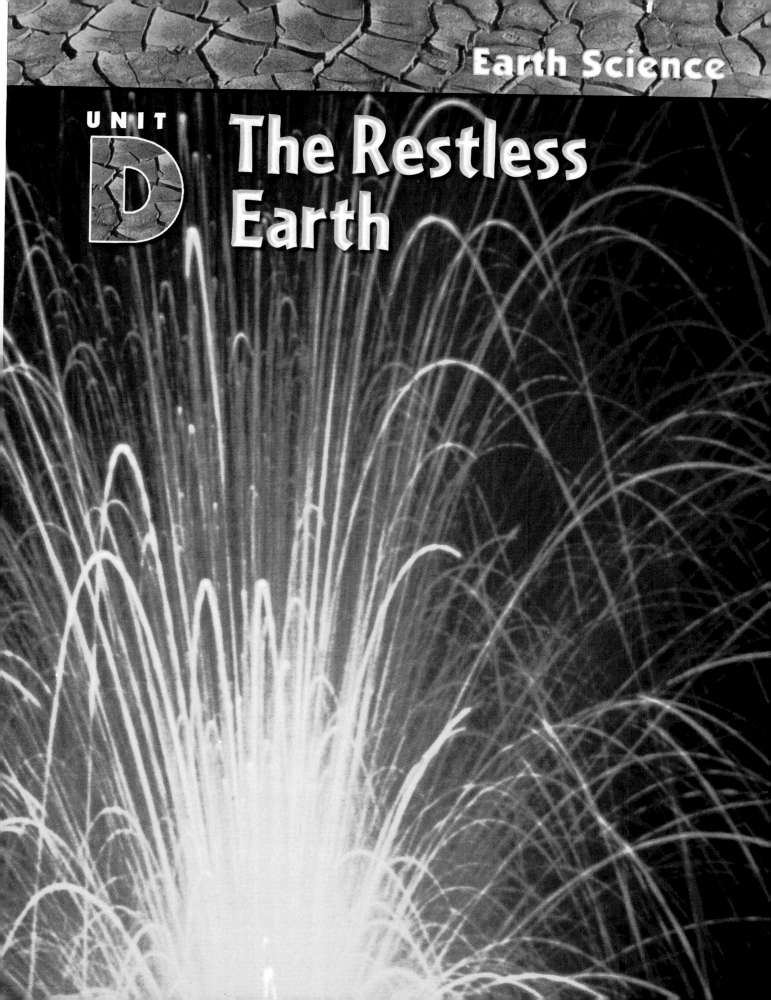

UNIT D

The Restless Earth

The Restless Earth

LOOK!

A volcano erupts with a
blast of hot, molten rock.
What forces inside Earth
cause volcanoes to erupt?

CHAPTER 7

Earth's Moving Crust

Did You Ever Wonder?

What causes earthquakes? Earthquakes are caused by movements in Earth's crust. These movements occur along fault lines, such as the San Andreas Fault in California. Many earthquakes have taken place along the San Andreas Fault. What do you think it would be like to live on or near a fault?

INQUIRY SKILL Communicate Research how you could stay safe in an earthquake. Make a poster showing what you would include in an earthquake survival kit.

D 3

Moving Plates

Vocabulary

crust, D6

original horizontality, D6

continental drift, D7

sea-floor spreading, D8

magma, D8

plate tectonics, D11

mantle, D11

subduction, D14

Get Ready

Have you ever put together a jigsaw puzzle? If so, how can you find the pieces that fit together? One way is to look for edges that meet and have opposite outlines.

Think of continents as huge pieces of a jigsaw puzzle. If they were huge, movable puzzle pieces, would any of the pieces fit together? Do all continents fit together?

Inquiry Skill

You infer when you form an idea from facts or observations.

Explore Activity

Are the Continents Moving?

Materials

map of the world

tracing paper

pencil

scissors

Procedure

BE CAREFUL! Be careful using scissors.

1. Place tracing paper over a map of the world. Trace the coastlines of North America, South America, Europe and Asia, Africa, and Australia.

2. Cut out the continents along their coastlines and label them.

3. Look at the coastlines of the continents for places they might fit together.

4. **Experiment** Using the continent cutouts like pieces of a jigsaw puzzle, find ways the continents fit together. Draw a sketch showing each way you can fit them together.

Drawing Conclusions

1. **Interpret Data** Which continents have coastlines that fit together most closely?

2. Which of your sketches shows the greatest number of continents fitting together? Do all of the coastlines in the sketch fit together equally well?

3. **FURTHER INQUIRY** **Infer** What if the pieces from your finished puzzle moved apart to the positions they are in today? If they keep moving, how might they be arranged in the distant future? Show how they might look.

Main Idea Earth's crust consists of moving plates that cause constant changes to the surface of the planet.

Are the Continents Moving?

How do you know whether a clock is working? Easy—if the second hand is moving, the clock is working. What if the clock has only minute and hour hands? These hands move too gradually for you to actually see their

These layers of sedimentary rock were once horizontal. Then crustal movement folded and tilted them.

motion. How can you tell if the clock is working?

Geologists (jee·AHL·uh·jists), scientists who study Earth, face a similar problem. How can they tell if Earth's solid surface, the **crust**, is moving? During a sudden motion of the crust, such as an earthquake or volcanic eruption, people can actually see and feel the crust move. Can the crust also be moving so slowly that you don't feel it?

Just as the changing position of a clock's hour hand is evidence that it is gradually moving, changes in position of surface features and rock formations are evidence that the crust is gradually moving.

For example, many kinds of rocks tend to form in flat, horizontal layers. This is called **original horizontality** (hawr·uh·zahn·TA·luh·tee). You can see that many layers have been twisted or tilted. This is a sign that the crust is moving gradually.

Movement of Earth's Crust

Compression is one way that crustal movement folds rock layers.

Young
Medium
Old

Worn away

Ground

Compression

Compression

In 1912 a German scientist, Alfred Wegener (VAY·guh·nuhr), wrote a book called *The Origins of Continents and Oceans*. In it he listed evidence that Earth's continents had once fit together like pieces of a jigsaw puzzle, forming a huge supercontinent. That is why today the shapes of the continents match. Wegener claimed that the coastlines also match in other ways besides shape. Coastlines have:

- matching rock types and structures, such as deposits from glaciers

- matching remains of ancient life and living organisms

- matching past climates

Wegener called this huge supercontinent *Pangaea* (pan·JEE·uh), meaning "all lands." He reasoned that about 200 million years ago, Pangaea split into pieces that are today's continents. Then the continents "drifted apart" over the years to their present locations. His hypothesis became known as **continental drift**.

Wegener did not explain how or why the "drifting" took place. After all, the continents are not "floating" on water. They are part of Earth's solid crust. The crust is a solid layer, including the continents and the ocean floor. Maybe studying the ocean floor would reveal some clues.

▶ **How does Wegener's hypothesis explain why Earth's surface must be moving?**

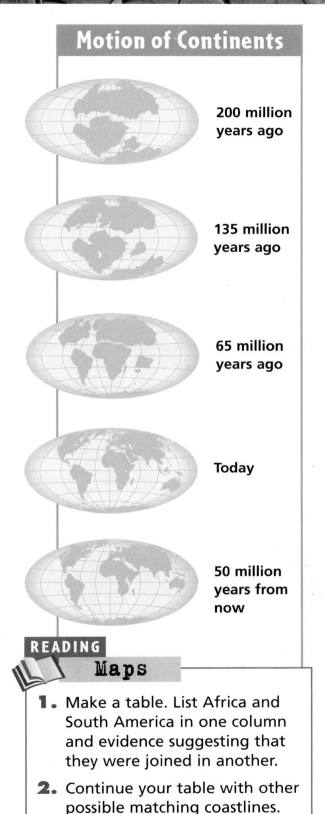

Motion of Continents

200 million years ago

135 million years ago

65 million years ago

Today

50 million years from now

READING Maps

1. Make a table. List Africa and South America in one column and evidence suggesting that they were joined in another.

2. Continue your table with other possible matching coastlines.

What Is Sea-Floor Spreading?

In 1947 the research ship *Atlantis* set out to map the floor of the Atlantic Ocean. Using depth sounders, the researchers discovered a series of mountains separated by huge valleys and canyons. They had discovered the Mid-Atlantic Ridge. They dredged up rock samples from the mountains. The rocks seemed to have been formed from volcanic activity.

By 1960 scientists found other oceans had mid-ocean ridges! Together these ridges form a chain of mountains winding through Earth's sea floors. Huge cracks split the tops of the ridges. Elsewhere, parts of the sea floor plunge downward in deep valleys, or *trenches*.

In the early 1960s, scientists suggested a model to explain these features. This model, called **sea-floor spreading**, states that new crustal material is forming at the ridges. As it forms, it spreads apart the old sea floor on both sides of the ridges.

How does it work? The mid-ocean ridges are pushed up by hot rock material from deep beneath the crust. The crust cracks where the sea floor is spreading apart. Just below the ridges of the sea floor, there is hot, melted rock called **magma**. Magma flows up through the cracks, cools, and hardens into new solid rock along the ridges. This process keeps making new rock material along the ridges and pushing older rock material farther away along the sea floor.

▷ **How does the sea floor show Earth's crust is moving?**

Sea-Floor Spreading

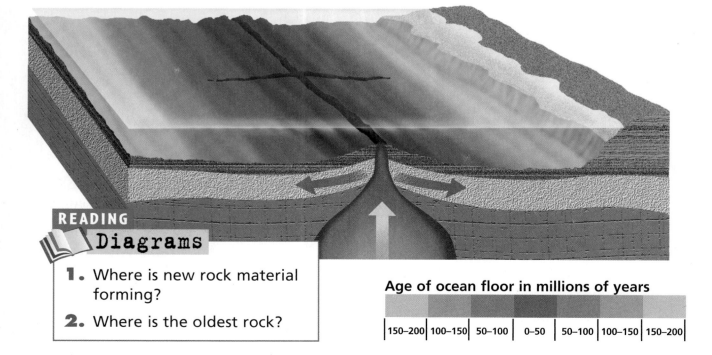

READING Diagrams

1. Where is new rock material forming?

2. Where is the oldest rock?

Age of ocean floor in millions of years

150–200	100–150	50–100	0–50	50–100	100–150	150–200

What Evidence Supports Sea-Floor Spreading?

Later in the 1960s, as scientists focused on the ocean floor, evidence came pouring in. Much of it was based on determining the age of rocks, a process you will explore in Lesson 7. The scientists found that

- rocks that make up the continents are much older than rocks of the ocean floor
- most ocean floor rocks are volcanic—that is, formed from cooling and hardening of magma
- the youngest ocean floor rocks are found at the mid-ocean ridges
- on either side of the ridge, the ocean floor rocks get older toward the continents

Some of the strongest evidence comes from the studies of Earth's magnetism. Earth has a magnetic field around it. A compass aligns with this field. The arrow points to the north pole of Earth's magnetic field.

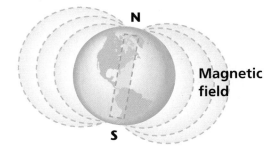

Magnetic field

In the past, however, Earth's magnetic field has reversed itself several times. The north and south poles switched back and forth. The rocks of the sea floor reveal a record of this reversal.

READING Diagrams

1. What is different about any two neighboring narrow strips?
2. How do the strips on both sides of the ridge compare?

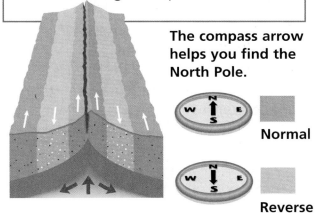

The compass arrow helps you find the North Pole.

Normal

Reverse

Magma contains magnetic particles, such as particles bearing iron. As the magma flows, the magnetic particles line up with Earth's magnetic field. As the magma cools and hardens, the magnetic particles are locked in place.

Scientists used magnetic detectors to study rocks along the sea floor. They found that the magnetism in the rocks alternates from one direction to the other. It is arranged in a simple pattern of narrow strips, and the pattern matches on either side of the mid-ocean ridges.

The simplest explanation is that rocks hardened along the ridge and then spread apart over time. Each time the rocks hardened in one of the strips, Earth's magnetic field was in a given direction. When the next strip formed, the magnetic field switched.

▷ **What have scientists learned about sea-floor spreading?**

Inquiry Skill
BUILDER

SKILL Hypothesize

What Makes the Crust Move?

Continental drift and sea-floor spreading explain observations. An explanation is called a hypothesis or a theory. Theories are more certain than hypotheses. As more and more evidence is gathered, an explanation may become more and more certain. Scientists are fairly certain that the theories of continental drift and sea-floor spreading are correct.

Procedure

1 **Communicate** List all the observations you have made involving movements of Earth's crust.

2 Make a two-column table, with "Continental Drift" and "Sea-Floor Spreading" as the column heads. In each column list observations that support each hypothesis.

3 **Hypothesize** Think of your own hypothesis to explain both continental drift and sea-floor spreading. To start, trace all the trenches and mid-ocean ridges on a world map. Then trace the world's mountain ranges. (Use a research book if you need to.) Look for patterns.

Drawing Conclusions

1 What are the strengths and weaknesses of your hypothesis? Which observations could you not explain?

2 Look at the theory on pages D11–D14. How is it like yours? Different from yours?

> **Materials**
>
> **world map**
>
> **research books/ Internet (optional)**
>
> **art materials**

What Is Plate Tectonics?

In the late 1960s, scientists built a new model to explain how continents and the sea floor move. This new model is **plate tectonics** (tek·TAHN·iks). It describes Earth's crust as broken into pieces, or plates. Each plate includes material from a layer below the crust, the **mantle**. Plates slide on the lower portion of the mantle.

The movement of the plates can explain movements of Earth's crust.

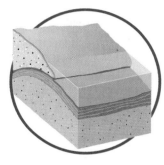

A plate is a piece of Earth's crust and upper mantle.

The plates can move away from each other, collide, or slide past each other.

For example, the Mid-Atlantic Ridge is located along a boundary where plates are moving away from each other. This explains sea-floor spreading. Each continent is a part of a plate. It moves with the plate. This movement explains continental drift. What causes the plates to move?

Hot melted rock from deep in the mantle rises upward and squeezes between the edges of two plates. This forces the two plates apart. The melted rock touching the plates cools, hardens, and becomes part of the plate. Melted rock continues to flow up, pushing the plates farther apart.

▷ **How does plate tectonics explain the movement of Earth's crust?**

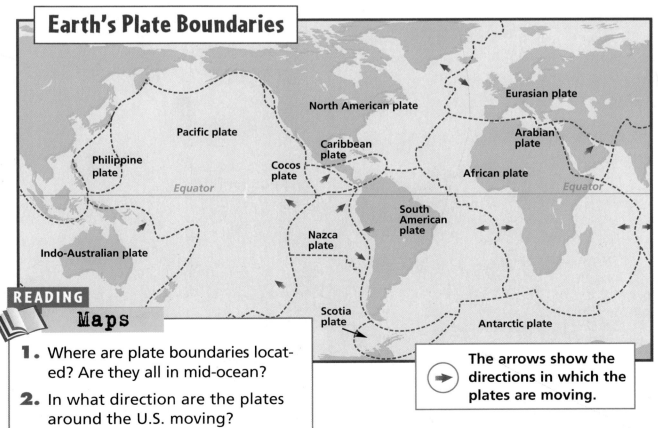

Earth's Plate Boundaries

North American plate

Eurasian plate

Pacific plate

Arabian plate

Philippine plate

Caribbean plate

Cocos plate

African plate

Equator

Equator

South American plate

Nazca plate

Indo-Australian plate

Scotia plate

Antarctic plate

READING

Maps

1. Where are plate boundaries located? Are they all in mid-ocean?

2. In what direction are the plates around the U.S. moving?

➡ The arrows show the directions in which the plates are moving.

What Happens at Plate Boundaries?

Places where plates move apart are called *divergent* (di·VUR·juhnt) *boundaries*. The Mid-Atlantic Ridge is located at a divergent boundary. This is where sea-floor spreading takes place. New rock material is formed when hot rock rises through cracks in the crust and hardens. The Great Rift Valley of Africa is at a divergent boundary. It is located at a place where a divergent boundary splits a part of a continent, rather than the sea floor.

Places where plates are colliding are called *convergent* (kuhn·VUR·juhnt) *boundaries*. When there is a continent on both of the colliding plates, the collision can cause rocks to crumple. This crumpling can build up mountains. For example, the Himalaya Mountains formed along a convergent boundary. This boundary is located where India meets the rest of Asia.

Some plates are carrying parts of the ocean floor. An "ocean" plate may collide with a plate carrying a continent. The ocean plate has the denser rock material of the two and slides

READING
Diagrams

Make a table. List the kinds of boundaries in one column. In another describe what happens at each boundary.

Types of Plate Boundaries

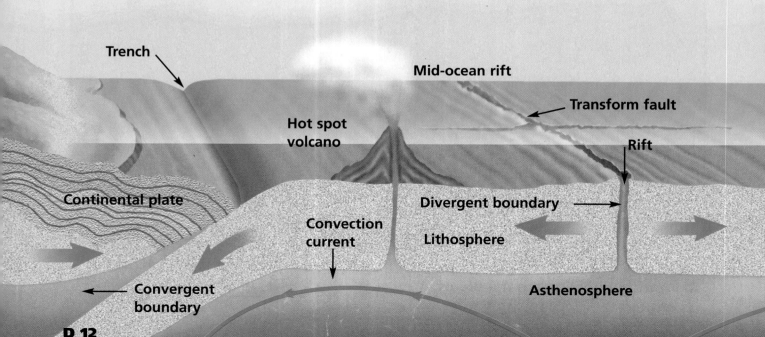

Trench

Mid-ocean rift

Transform fault

Hot spot volcano

Rift

Continental plate

Divergent boundary

Convection current

Lithosphere

Convergent boundary

Asthenosphere

beneath the continental plate. For example, off the coast of Chile, an ocean plate is sliding beneath the plate carrying South America.

Volcanoes are found at these boundaries. As one plate slides under another, hot rock material in the upper mantle is able to melt and become magma. It flows toward the surface, where it can erupt through cracks, producing volcanic mountains.

Two ocean plates may collide. The denser of the two slides beneath the other. The result can be undersea volcanoes or deep undersea valleys.

Sometimes plates just slide past each other. These boundaries are called *transform faults*. As the plates smash and grind past each other, there are many earthquakes. The rock along these margins gets broken and shattered. This shattered rock piles up in long, narrow ridges and valleys. The San Andreas Fault in California is along such a boundary.

READING **Cause and Effect**
What happens at divergent, convergent, and transform fault boundaries?

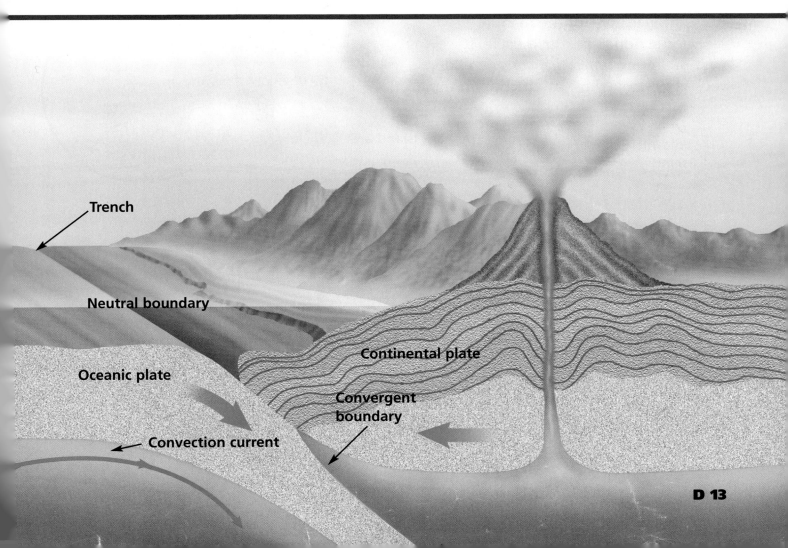

Trench

Neutral boundary

Oceanic plate

Continental plate

Convergent boundary

Convection current

D 13

How Is Earth's Crust Recycled?

Sea-floor spreading helped explain how continents move apart. It also posed a problem. New sea floor keeps being produced along the mid-ocean ridges. Why isn't Earth getting larger?

Plate tectonics offers an answer. While new crust is being formed in some places, older crust is being "disposed of" somewhere else.

Recall that when two plates collide, a denser ocean plate may slide under another plate. This is a process called **subduction** (suhb·DUHK·shuhn). The process continues as the plate sinks down into the mantle. The plate is carrying a part of the crust from the sea floor. This rock becomes part of the hot, softened rock of the mantle.

Subduction is part of a cycle. It is part of a huge *convection current*. Older rock is destroyed by subduction in the trenches. New rock is forming in the mid-ocean ridges.

This huge cycle has some interesting effects. As two ocean plates collide, a trench forms. Melted rock from beneath the sea floor can rise up to produce a string of volcanic mountains. They can rise up above the sea floor and result in a string of islands called an *island arc*. The islands of Japan are a volcanic island arc.

> ▷ **How is Earth's crust recycled through the mantle?**

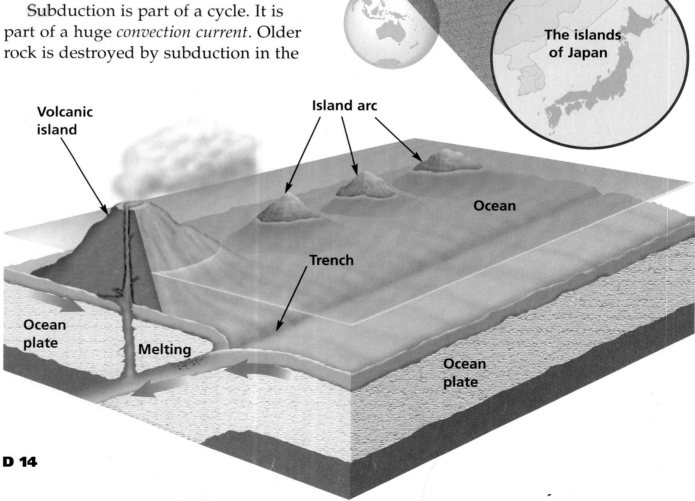

The islands of Japan

Volcanic island

Island arc

Ocean

Trench

Ocean plate

Melting

Ocean plate

Why It Matters

It is very important to learn about Earth and its crust. Many of the things you use every day come from Earth's crust. The fuel that keeps you warm comes from oil, gas, or coal. The concrete foundation on which your house sits is a mixture of rocks from the crust. Even your toothpaste may contain mild abrasives taken from the crust.

e-Journal Visit our Web site **www.science.mmhschool.com** to do a research project on plate tectonics.

Think and Write

1. How can two coastlines be separated by an ocean and have matching shapes?

2. What are mid-ocean ridges? What is happening to the crust at these places?

3. How can the continents and the sea floor move?

4. INQUIRY SKILL **Hypothesize** What do you think causes earthquakes? Make a hypothesis based on plate tectonics. What kinds of evidence would you need to support your hypothesis?

5. **Critical Thinking** Was Wegener's idea of continental drift wrong? Explain your answer.

L·I·N·K·S

SOCIAL STUDIES LINK

Research plate tectonics. Use newspapers and other library resources to learn about advances in technology for

mapping the sea floor. How does the improved technology relate to the advances in the field of plate tectonics?

MATH LINK

Calculate sea-floor spreading. Scientists estimate that the sea floor can spread at a rate of about 3 cm/year. Calculate how long it would take for 1 km of new sea floor to be added.

WRITING LINK

Writing a Story Write a story to describe what you would see if you could speed up time and watch the process of sea-floor spreading. Use descriptive language and scientific terms. Sequence the events.

TECHNOLOGY LINK

 LOG ON Visit **www.science.mmhschool.com** for more links.

Disaster Alerts

Scientists can often predict weather disasters, like tornadoes and hurricanes, thanks to modern technology. Can they also tell when there'll be a volcanic eruption or earthquake, and alert people to the danger?

Predicting Eruptions

In the past when a volcano erupted, there was often no time to plan an escape. Today almost all eruptions can be predicted early enough to warn people.

How do scientists know there might be an eruption? Magma moving inside a volcano causes swarms of small earthquakes that create a steady roar. Nearby seismographs record that magma is on the move. Scientists warn people to leave the area. When a giant volcano erupted in New Guinea in 1994, tens of thousands of people knew to leave the area. Many lives were saved.

Sometimes a volcano explodes through the side of its cone. Before it blows, a buildup of magma bulges the side. Lasers record ground swells around volcanoes to the nearest millimeter. Satellite radar detects even the tiniest ground motion. These clues can help predict which side of the cone will blow.

Volcanologists often risk their lives to study volcanoes.

In 1980 scientists predicted that Mount Saint Helens would erupt, but not exactly when.

Predicting Earthquakes

Earthquake prediction is still difficult, but one prediction was a big success. In the winter of 1974–1975, people in the Liaoning Province of China noticed bubbling, muddy water in their wells, odd behavior of domestic animals, and a series of small earthquakes. All this evidence predicted a great earthquake would hit Liaoning Province. People were warned to go outside. When the earthquake came, only a few hundred people were killed. The following year an estimated 655,000 Chinese were killed in an unpredicted earthquake in Tangshan.

In the contiguous United States, earthquakes have occurred from the Atlantic to the Pacific. Pins show places where earthquakes have happened.

What Did I Learn?

1. All of the following are ways scientists know a volcano might erupt EXCEPT

   A magma moving inside causes small earthquakes.
   B seismographs record magma movement.
   C a steady roar can be heard.
   D the volcano sinks slightly.

2. Earthquake prediction is important because

   F scientists can stop the earthquake.
   G some damage and death can be prevented.
   H all damage and death can be prevented.
   J nothing can be done.

LOG ON Visit www.science.mmhschool.com to learn more about volcanoes and earthquakes.

Earthquakes

Vocabulary

fault, D21

focus, D22

seismic wave, D22

epicenter, D22

aftershock, D22

seismograph, D22

magnitude, D25

Get Ready

Can earthquakes happen anywhere? Do they tend to happen in
just certain places?

In 1868, 1906, 1957, and 1989,
the city of San Francisco was
struck by an earthquake. That
makes four times in just over
100 years.

Why are certain areas
struck by earthquakes
over and over again? Is there
a pattern to locations where
earthquakes happen?

Inquiry Skill

**You predict when you state possible
results of an event or experiment.**

Explore Activity

Where Do Earthquakes Happen?

Materials

world map

bits of clay
(optional)

reference
books
(optional)

Procedure

1. Read the data table. It gives you the location of 16 different earthquakes. You may look up more in reference books.

2. **Communicate** On a world map, locate each earthquake by its latitude and longitude. Put a dab of clay on the map (or plot a point on a small outline map).

3. To locate by latitude, move north or south of the equator. For longitude move east or west of the prime meridian.

4. **Interpret Data** On an outline map, shade in areas where earthquakes are relatively near each other.

Drawing Conclusions

1. **Interpret Data** Were you able to identify a pattern to where earthquakes happen? Find a way to show frequency of earthquakes in any area. You may use the percent of earthquakes from the list.

2. **Infer** Why do you think earthquakes happen in the places you plotted on the map? What evidence supports your hypothesis?

3. FURTHER INQUIRY **Predict** Is there a relationship between earthquake locations and mountain ranges? How can you find out? Explain your results.

Year	Latitude	Longitude
1993	10°N	145°E
1989	37°N	123°W
1988	40°N	45°E
1987	34°N	118°W
1985	19°N	99°W
1982	49°N	129°W
1982	41°N	30°W
1982	37°N	72°E
1982	40°N	24°E
1981	33°S	73°W
1981	44°N	147°E
1981	49°S	164°E
1976	39°N	118°E
1964	61°N	148°W
1960	37°S	75°W
1923	36°N	140°E

Main Idea Earthquakes are caused by rocks moving along a fault that can send vibrations through the crust.

How Do Earthquakes Happen?

An earthquake is a sudden trembling of the ground. It is caused by something happening in the crust. Is there a pattern to where earthquakes happen? The dots on the map below show some of the places where earthquakes have happened. Compare this map with the map of Earth's plates from Lesson 1, on page D11.

Most dots on this map are at the boundaries of Earth's plates. Most earthquakes happen at the edges of plates, where plates meet. About 80 percent of all earthquakes happen along the edges of the Pacific plate.

Along their edges, plates may collide. They may slide past each other. They may pull apart. These motions can cause the rocks to bend and stretch until they break.

Earthquakes are less likely to happen at the centers of plates. Far from the edges, the centers of plates are more stable. Plate centers are places of relative quiet.

 Each red dot is a place where an earthquake has happened.

READING Maps

1. Along which ocean coastline are the dots most crowded? Where are dots crowded on land?

2. Do you see any patterns?

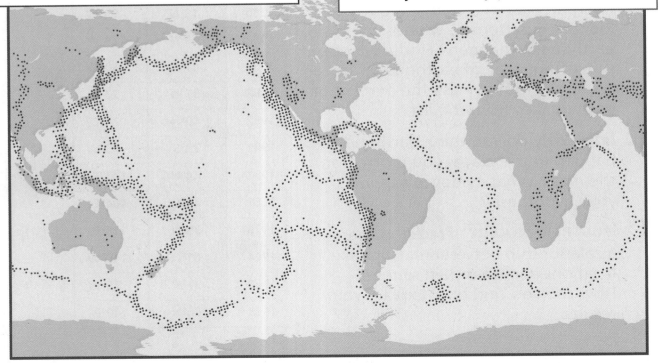

Three Kinds of Faults

Fault	Where Produced	How Produced	How Rocks Move	Example
Normal fault	Divergent boundaries	Plates pull apart.	Rocks above the fault surface move down.	Sierra Nevada in California
Reverse fault	Convergent boundaries	Plates push together.	Rocks above the fault move upward.	Himalayas in India
Strike-slip	Transform boundaries	Plates slide past each other without moving up or down.	Rocks slide past each other in different directions.	San Andreas Fault in California

READING Charts

1. Make a list of the ways the sides of a fault can move.

2. Describe the faults in a way that explains their differences.

When plates move, great forces are exerted on the rocks of the crust. At first the forces can make the rocks bend and stretch. Every material has a limit to how far it will bend before breaking. When the rocks in the crust reach their limit, they break. As a result, **faults** form at or below the surface of the crust. Faults are huge cracks in the crust.

Recall that there are three kinds of plate boundaries. At divergent boundaries plates pull apart. At convergent boundaries plates push together. Along transform boundaries plates move past each other. These different motions produce different faults.

The broken sides of a fault may scrape past each other. They can move gradually, centimeters a year. Sometimes they move all of a sudden. The energy released by this sudden action shakes the crust. It sets an earthquake in motion.

▷ **How do earthquakes start?**

How Do Earthquakes Make Waves?

An earthquake starts the moment rocks begin to scrape past each other along a fault. It may be a new fault that forms at just that moment or an old fault that has already formed.

The point where the earthquake starts, where the rocks begin to slide past each other, is the **focus**. It is usually below the surface. The sudden motion causes vibrations to spread out from the focus. These vibrations travel through the crust in the form of waves—**seismic waves**. They soon reach Earth's surface at a point directly above the focus. This point is the **epicenter**. It is at the epicenter that people can first feel the ground shaking.

This shaking is what causes most earthquake damage. Damage is usually greatest at the epicenter because it is so close to the focus. As the waves travel away from the focus, they get weaker.

After the first shaking, there may be relative quiet, followed by **aftershocks**. Aftershocks continue the damage of an earthquake. People have not recovered from the first shaking, and then there is additional shaking and destruction.

Earthquake Waves

How can seismic waves move through Earth's crust? A seismic wave starts with shaking caused by rocks scraping against each other. The shaking results in several kinds of seismic waves, which travel differently and at different speeds.

One kind of shaking is an accordion-like motion. Rock material squeezes together and spreads apart repeatedly. This motion produces seismic waves that move in the same direction that the rock is shaking. They are the fastest seismic waves—the first to reach any faraway location after an earthquake. They are *primary waves*, or *P waves*.

Another kind of shaking is like a ruler held off the edge of a desk and "twanged." This kind of motion in rocks produces seismic waves that move in a different direction from the vibration. These waves travel slower than primary waves. They are the second to arrive at any given faraway location. They are called *secondary waves*, or *S waves*.

Scientists study these waves using a **seismograph**. A seismograph shows patterns in the waves that arrive. By carefully studying the waves, a scientist can identify the P waves, S waves, and surface waves.

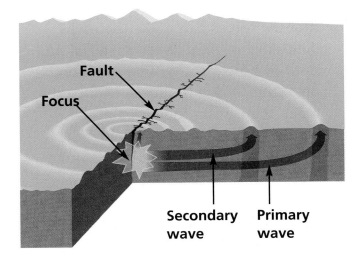

Seismic waves can move through Earth's crust in different directions.

A third kind of shaking causes Earth's surface to heave up and down like an ocean wave, or sway from side to side. The motion of these *surface waves* tears apart structures built on the surface.

Ocean Waves

If the focus of the earthquake is beneath the sea floor, the seismic waves can travel through the ocean. They can produce huge ocean waves called *tsunamis* (tsew·NAH·meez). When tsunamis reach a shoreline, they can rise to heights of more than 15 meters (50 feet). They can destroy everything in their path.

Tsunamis can race across the oceans at speeds up to 900 kilometers per hour (560 mph)—as fast as some jet planes! Produced by an earthquake, a tsunami about 46 meters (150 feet) high occurred off the coast of Chile in April 1971. It reached Japan, a distance of 15,600 kilometers (9,700 miles), in 24 hours.

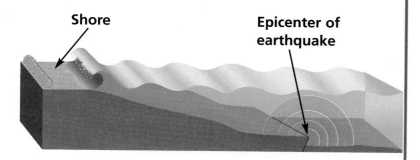

Shore

Epicenter of earthquake

READING Cause and Effect What kinds of waves are caused by earthquakes?

QUICK LAB

Seismographs

FOLDABLES Make a Three-column, Three-row Chart. (See p. R 44.) Label the columns and rows as shown.

1. Place a long sheet of paper on a table. Hold a felt-tip pen right over the paper to make a mark.

Amount of Force	Holding the Pen	Seismograph Model
Test 1: very forceful		
Test 2: less forceful		

2. Hold the pen securely so that it does not move. Have your partner pull the paper underneath the pen. Notice that your pen makes a line.

3. Tap the table with different amounts of force. Use the chart to record what happens.

4. **Make a Model** Design a way to position the pen over the paper so you don't have to hold it and so it records a zigzag line when the table shakes. Describe your method and test it.

5. **Interpret Data** How is your model like the seismograph pictured on page D24? How is it different? How do you think it would work if the ground trembled?

What Can We Learn from Seismic Waves?

You are at a seismograph station in Texas. Suddenly P waves begin to appear on your seismograph. Three minutes later you begin to see S waves. The time difference, or lag, between the arrival of the two waves is important. If you are very near an epicenter, the time lag will be short—just seconds. The farther away you are from the epicenter, the greater the time lag.

By knowing the time lag, you can tell how far away you are from the epicenter—but not in what direction. It can be anywhere along a circle around your station. The radius of that circle is the distance to the epicenter.

You call two other seismograph stations, in Virginia and Wisconsin. You learn the time lag noted at each station. Based on that information, you can tell how far the epicenter is from each place, but not the direction. You draw a circle around each place.

All three circles come together at one point. That point is the location of the epicenter.

> **How can seismograph readings be used to locate the epicenter?**

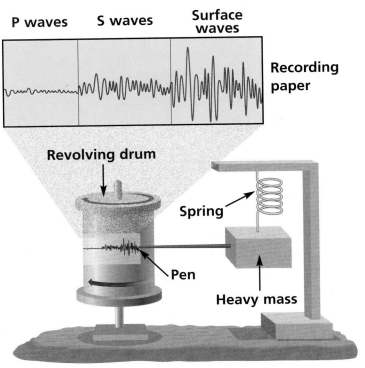

The motion of Earth during an earthquake causes the pen on this seismograph to move up and down, drawing lines on the recording paper. These lines indicate the strength of the waves.

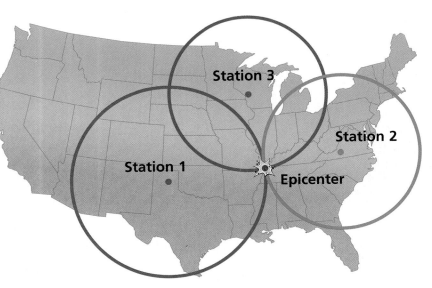

The point at which all three circles come together is the epicenter of the earthquake.

How Destructive Is an Earthquake?

The height of a wave on a seismograph is a measure of the **magnitude** of an earthquake. Magnitude is the amount of energy released by an earthquake. The more energy an earthquake releases, the more violent the shaking recorded.

Charles Richter, in 1935, devised a scale for comparing the energy of earthquakes. The Richter scale rates earthquakes from 1 to 10 according to magnitude. Each increase of 1 on the scale means an increase of about 30 times the energy released.

The Mercalli (mer·KAH·lee) scale is also used to describe earthquakes. The Mercalli scale is based on the amount of damage done at a given location.

The two scales actually measure different things. The Richter scale measures energy. The rating on that scale is the same no matter where it is measured. The Mercalli scale measures effects. The farther away from the epicenter a place is, the lower the rating will be. The effects are felt less at greater distances from the epicenter.

READING Tables

What are the differences between the two tables?

Summary of the Richter Scale

Magnitude	Estimated Number per Year	Effects at Epicenter
Less than 2.5	900,000	Not usually felt
2.5–5.4	30,000	Very minor damage
5.5–6.0	500	Some damage
6.1–6.9	100	Much damage; can be destructive in crowded areas
7.0–7.9	20	Severe damage
8.0 or greater	1 every 5 to 10 years	Total destruction

Summary of the Mercalli Scale

Mercalli Rating	Effects at Location Where Rating Is Taken
II	May be felt by a few persons at rest.
IV	Felt indoors by many, outdoors by few. Walls creak. Dishes shake. Parked cars rock.
VI	Felt by all. Heavy furniture moves. Books are knocked off shelves. Pictures fall. Chimneys may crack or crumble.
VIII	Monuments and walls may fall. Buildings may partially collapse, unless they were built to withstand damage.
X	Wooden and brick structures collapse. The ground cracks badly. Landslides may happen on steep slopes.
XII	Total or nearly total destruction. Objects are tossed upward. Waves are seen on the ground surface.

▶ How do the Richter and Mercalli scales measure the destruction of an earthquake?

How Can We Prepare for Earthquakes?

In 1964 a massive earthquake struck Alaska. The city of Anchorage suffered terrible damage. Valdez, on the other hand, suffered relatively little damage. Was Anchorage closer to the epicenter? No, Valdez was closer. Why did Valdez have less damage?

The answer lies beneath each location. Valdez is on top of solid rock—granite. Anchorage was built on top of a massive deposit of sediment.

We cannot change the rock underneath places where earthquakes are common. However, we can design buildings and highways to keep them from collapsing—to be *seismic safe*.

Many new building designs have huge shock absorbers built into their foundations. These absorb much of the wave motion of an earthquake. The building sways without collapsing— up to a magnitude of 8.3.

Highways can be made seismic safe by special supporting structures. They contain vertical rods wrapped with spiral steel rods. The wrapping helps hold the vertical rods together during an earthquake.

Older buildings were built with rigid materials, such as bricks and masonry, which crumble during an earthquake. Newer flexible materials have a better chance of bending without breaking. Using newer materials for water pipes and gas pipes will better assure they will survive an earthquake.

▷ **What can be done to prepare for an earthquake?**

Earthquake Safety Tips

Before an earthquake:

Take a first-aid and CPR course.

Put together an earthquake kit that includes such things as a flashlight, extra batteries, a portable radio, and a first-aid kit.

Make an emergency escape plan.

During an earthquake:

If you are in your house, go in the corner of the room away from windows, shelves, or mirrors.

If you are in school, get under your desk and follow the school emergency plan.

If you are outside, move into the open, away from buildings, street lights, and utility wires.

After an earthquake:

Know how and when to dial 911 and which radio station to tune to for emergency information.

Remind your parents to turn off natural gas, electricity, and water.

Check yourself for injuries.

Stay out of damaged buildings.

Why It Matters

Earthquakes are common along the West Coast, but can happen elsewhere, too. Knowing where and when earthquakes might occur can save lives. So can designing buildings and bridges to withstand severe earthquakes. Learn what to do in an earthquake. It might save your life.

Vertical rods wrapped with spiral steel rods help prevent damage to highways during earthquakes.

 e-Journal Visit our Web site **www.science.mmhschool.com** to do a research project on earthquakes.

Think and Write

1. Where are earthquakes more likely to happen? Explain.

2. "An earthquake starts at the epicenter." Is this statement true or false? Explain your answer. Include what causes earthquakes.

3. Why is it useful to record seismic waves with a seismograph?

4. How are the different scales used to measure earthquakes alike? How are they different?

5. **Critical Thinking** Why might waves from the same earthquake cause more damage in one area than another?

L·I·N·K·S

LITERATURE LINK

Read _Letter from San Francisco_ to learn about the San Francisco earthquake of 1906. Try the activities at the end of the book.

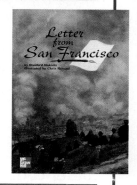

WRITING LINK

Persuasive Writing A new mayor has been elected in a town where few earthquake precautions have been taken. Write an essay to persuade the mayor to take appropriate action to make the town seismic safe.

MATH LINK

Calculate the difference. What would be the difference in the amount of energy released by the following earthquakes measured on the Richter scale: an 8.2 earthquake and a 7.5 earthquake? Show how you found your answer.

TECHNOLOGY LINK

 Science Newsroom CD-ROM Choose _Shake, Rattle, and Roll_ to learn how earthquakes affect structures.

LOG ON Visit **www.science.mmhschool.com** for more links.

Volcanoes

Vocabulary

vent, D30

lava, D30

crater, D30

hot spot, D31

cinder-cone
  volcano, D32

shield volcano, D32

composite
  volcano, D33

geothermal
  energy, D36

Get Ready

Italy has 13 active volcanoes. One of these has the longest record of eruptions in history. Since the first recorded eruption in 1500 B.C., Mount Etna has erupted 190 times! The most recent string of eruptions stretches back over decades. Recent eruptions have included fire fountains in early 1996.

Can volcanoes erupt at any time? Are some more likely to erupt than others? Are volcanoes more common in certain places rather than in others?

Inquiry Skill

You **hypothesize** when you make a statement that can be tested in answer to a question.

Explore Activity

Where Are Volcanoes Located?

Materials
large world map
modeling compound or small stick-on dots
small outline map
colored pencils

Procedure

1. Using bits of modeling compound or stick-on dots, plot the locations of active volcanoes on a world map. Use the data in the table to the right.

2. On a small outline map, shade in the areas where volcanoes are found.

3. **Interpret Data** Compare your finished map with other maps in this chapter, such as those in Lesson 1 and Lesson 2.

Drawing Conclusions

1. Are most volcanoes located near the edges or near the centers of continents?

2. **Interpret Data** Is there a pattern in the arrangement of volcanoes around the Pacific Ocean? Explain your answer.

3. Are Earth's active volcanoes grouped in certain areas? Explain your answer.

4. **FURTHER INQUIRY**
   Hypothesize What is the relationship between the locations of active volcanoes and the locations of earthquakes? Explain your answer using data from several resources.

Volcano	Latitude	Longitude
1	39°N	44°E
2	38°N	30°W
3	16°N	24°W
4	0.4°S	78°W
5	35°N	52°W
6	0.4°S	103°E
7	37°N	15°E
8	0.3°S	90°W
9	64°N	19°W
10	58°N	155°W
11	0.6°S	105°E
12	40°N	121°W
13	19°N	155°W
14	16°S	71°W
15	46°N	122°W
16	42°N	140°E
17	40°S	73°W
18	19°N	102°W
19	15°N	61°W
20	40°N	14°E

Main Idea A source of magma, gases, and solid rock, volcanoes provide Earth with many natural resources.

How Do Volcanoes Form?

A volcano is a place where molten rock, hot gases, and solid rock erupt through an opening in the crust. It is also the mountain built up by these materials.

Beneath every volcano is a source of magma. Magma, remember, is molten rock. Magma rises to the surface through cracks in the rock above it. In time it reaches the surface and erupts through a central opening, or **vent**. Once the magma comes out of the vent, it is called **lava**.

Erupted material cools and hardens around the vent in a mound. After many eruptions it can pile up into a big hill or even a mountain. This is also called a volcano. At the top of a volcano is a cuplike hollow around the vent, called a **crater**. Sometimes a volcano collapses, forming a very wide crater, called a *caldera*.

The Formation of a Volcano

READING
Diagrams

Make a list of the parts of a volcano. Describe how each part forms from another part.

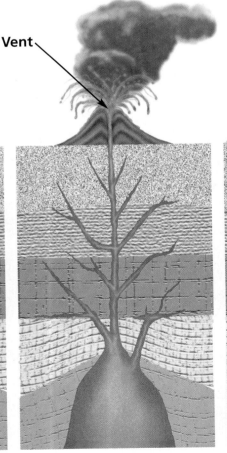

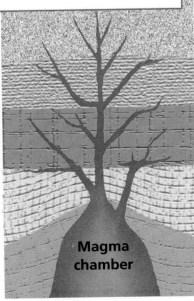

Vent

Vent

Crater

Magma chamber

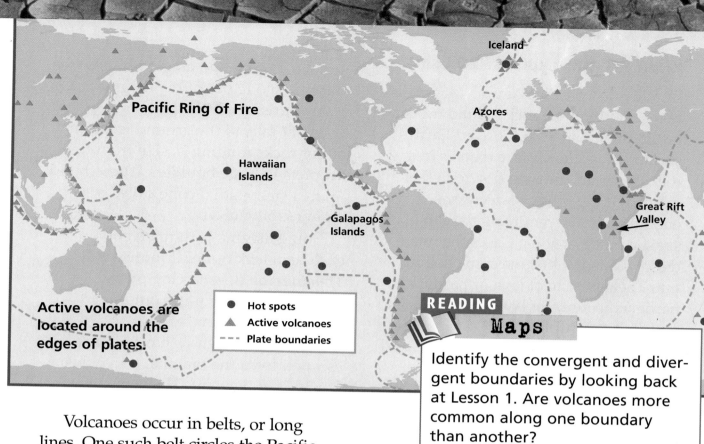

Pacific Ring of Fire

Iceland

Azores

Hawaiian
Islands

Galapagos
Islands

Great Rift
Valley

Active volcanoes are
located around the
edges of plates.

- ● Hot spots
- ▲ Active volcanoes
- --- Plate boundaries

READING

Maps

Identify the convergent and divergent boundaries by looking back at Lesson 1. Are volcanoes more common along one boundary than another?

Volcanoes occur in belts, or long lines. One such belt circles the Pacific Ocean. It is the Pacific Ring of Fire. Another runs along the Mediterranean Sea through Iran. After a gap it continues through Indonesia to the Pacific.

Over 80 percent of all land volcanoes are found in these two belts. Even more of Earth's volcanoes are at the ocean floor. They line the mid-ocean ridges.

Compare the location of volcanoes with the plate boundaries. Do you see a pattern? Most volcanoes occur along plate boundaries.

Where plates are moving apart, volcanoes form along the gaps at the edges of spreading plates. These are called *rift volcanoes*. Some rift volcanoes can be found in Iceland and in Africa's Great Rift Valley. Most rift volcanoes are located deep underwater along mid-ocean ridges.

Volcanoes also form along the edges of slowly colliding plates. One plate plunges beneath another. The downward-moving plate melts. Magma forms. It moves upward through the rocks and forms volcanoes.

The Hawaiian Islands are a chain of volcanoes, but they are in the middle of a plate. They are not at the edge. Geologists believe the plate is moving over a **hot spot**. A hot spot is a very hot part of the mantle. As a plate moves over a hot spot, magma melts up through the crust and forms volcanoes. The Azores and the Galapagos may have also formed from hot spots.

▷ **How are the formation of volcanoes and plate boundaries related?**

What Are the Types of Volcanoes?

Why do volcanoes erupt? Magma is less dense than the rock around it. As a result, magma rises up toward Earth's surface. Near the surface there is less rock overhead pressing down on the magma. If the pressure decreases enough, it is like removing the cap of a shaken bottle of soda. Gases that were dissolved in the magma come boiling out. The gases shoot lava or partly hardened chunks of lava out of the vent.

What an eruption is like depends on how much gas is in the magma and how thick the magma is.

Some magma is thick and has a lot of gas in it. Lumps of magma may get stuck as the magma rises to the surface. In time the magma bursts free. Gases explode out of the magma. Lava blasts outward. It hardens.

What falls to the ground is a rain of hot rocks ranging in size from tiny droplets to huge boulders. These build up in a steep-sided cone called a **cinder-cone volcano**.

Some magma is thinner, and gases can leak out of it more easily. This magma doesn't clog up as easily. Instead it squirts out as a fiery lava fountain.

If a lot of the gases have already escaped from the magma, it may just flow out of the vent. The lava spreads out and hardens into a wide, flat mound called a **shield volcano**.

Three Types of Volcanoes

Steep sides
Rock fragment layers
Magma

Italy's Stromboli is a cinder-cone volcano.

Magma

Hawaii's Mauna Loa is a shield volcano.

Sometimes an eruption "takes turns." An eruption may explode. It sends gas and lava high into the air and forms a rain of rocks of different sizes. Then the eruption may switch over to a quiet period. Lava may flow over the rocks from the explosive period. When this switching repeats over and over, it forms a **composite volcano**.

Shishaldin is a composite volcano in the Aleutian Islands. Composite volcanoes may have beautifully symmetrical shapes. That is, the shape on one side of the cone matches the shape on the opposite side.

▶ **How are the types of volcanoes alike and different?**

Layers of rock fragments and lava

Magma

Shishaldin, in the Aleutian Islands, is a composite volcano.

QUICK LAB

Volcanoes

FOLDABLES Make a Trifold Book. (See p. R 42.) Label the sections as shown.

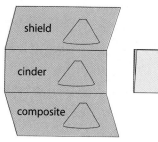

shield

cinder

composite

Volcanoes

1. **Make a Model** Build models of the three kinds of cones. Choose materials, such as sand, soil, or gravel, that show the differences. You can mix the particles with water to help hold them together.

2. Draw diagrams of your finished products on the book.

3. **Interpret Data** How well do the models show the differences?

4. How else could you show the differences among cones?

D 33

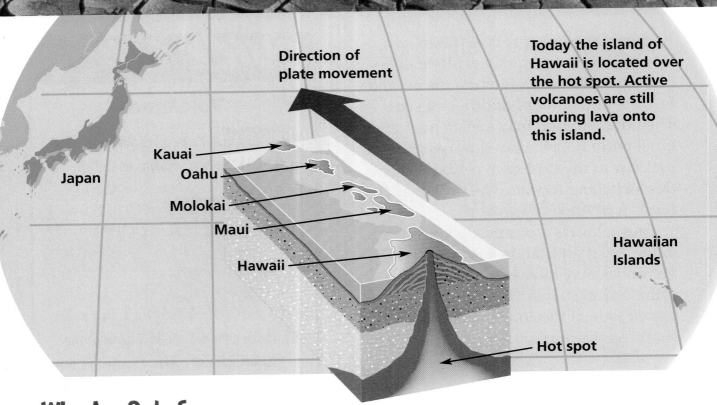

Direction of plate movement

Today the island of Hawaii is located over the hot spot. Active volcanoes are still pouring lava onto this island.

Japan

Kauai
Oahu
Molokai
Maui
Hawaii

Hawaiian Islands

Hot spot

Why Are Only Some Volcanoes Active?

Thousands of volcanoes are scattered over Earth's surface. However, very few of them are active. That is, very few are erupting now or have erupted recently. Many of Earth's active volcanoes are located in the Pacific Ring of Fire. For example, there are active volcanoes in Japan.

Japan is made up of volcanic islands. These islands were built up from the ocean floor along a convergent boundary. One plate is plunging down under another. Molten rock pushed through to the surface and formed a string, or arc, of volcanoes. The volcanoes grew in size over time, from undersea volcanoes to islands far above sea level.

In time, active volcanoes may stop erupting. They may become *dormant*.

Dormant is from a French word for "sleep." A dormant volcano has not been active for a long time but has erupted in recorded history.

Some volcanoes are considered *extinct*. An extinct volcano has not erupted in recorded history.

The Hawaiian Islands are volcanic islands. Many of these volcanoes are no longer active. The Hawaiian Islands, remember, were formed as the Pacific plate moved over a hot spot. The island of Kauai (KOW·igh) is the oldest island. It formed when it was located over the hot spot. As the plate moved, Kauai moved away from the hot spot and was no longer active. The plate continued to move, and other islands formed, one at a time.

▷ **What determines whether or not a volcano is active?**

How Does Magma Affect Land Features?

Sometimes underground magma cools and hardens before it reaches the surface. Magma can harden in many possible shapes and positions.

A *dike* is formed when magma hardens in vertical cracks. Dikes are vertical or nearly vertical structures. A *sill* is formed when magma hardens between horizontal layers of rock. A sill is flat. Dikes and sills vary in size from small to huge. When rocks around a large dike are worn away, the dike is exposed as a long ridge. Exposed sills take the shape of ridges or cliffs.

If the magma pushed into a sill is thick, it may not spread far horizontally. Instead it pushes upward, forming a *laccolith*. A laccolith is shaped like a dome.

When magma pushes upward, it may raise overlying rock layers into *dome mountains*. Dome mountains are broad, circular mountains formed from uplifted rock layers. Erosion then shapes the layers into mountains. The Henry Mountains of Utah were formed by laccoliths. Some dome mountains, like the Black Hills of South Dakota, were first uplifted layers. Then the overlaying rock layers were eroded away, leaving a mountain core of different rocks exposed.

The largest and deepest of all underground formations are *batholiths*. A batholith is huge and irregularly shaped. It reaches deep into the crust. Some batholiths have been uplifted to above sea level. As overlying rocks were worn away, the batholiths became exposed. They look like large, steep hills.

▷ **What are the different types of land features created by magma?**

Dikes, sills, laccoliths, and batholiths are formed by hardened magma beneath Earth's surface.

Dike · Laccolith · Sill · Batholith

READING
Diagrams

Compare and contrast the four features shown in the diagram.

How Can Magma Heat Underground Water?

Perhaps the most spectacular side effect of volcanism is a *geyser*. A geyser is an opening in the ground through which hot water and steam erupt periodically. The main vent of a geyser is filled with water. The water at the bottom of the column is heated and changed to steam. At first the steam is held down by the weight of the water above it. Pressure continues to build up as more water is changed to steam. It is like shaking a bottle of soda with the cap still on.

Finally, some steam pushes high enough to move the column of water. This action relieves some pressure. A jet of hot water and steam soon erupts from the geyser. After the geyser erupts, the vent fills with more water, and the cycle begins again.

Hot springs are also caused by underground heating. A hot spring is an opening in the ground where hot water and gases escape. The water is heated deep underground by magma. The heated water is forced up to an opening in the surface. The water may contain minerals. As the water cools, it may deposit a spectacular mineral load.

Sometimes the water evaporates quickly as it flows out. The remaining water may become thick with broken pieces of rock and minerals. The result is a hot, muddy pool, called a paint pot. The materials mixed in the water may make it look yellow, red, or black.

Can the heat from such hot springs and geysers be used? Today scientists are finding ways to use **geothermal energy**. Geothermal energy is heat from below Earth's surface.

In 1965 the first geothermal power plant in the United States was built in Healdsburg, California. Wells were dug to hot rock material below the surface. Steam was produced. It was used to run power plants that produced electricity.

READING Cause and Effect
What happens to heated underground water?

Geyser

Why It Matters

Did you know the United States ranks third (after Indonesia and Japan) for the highest number of historically active volcanoes? Volcanic eruptions have created many valuable natural resources. For example, volcanic ash falling around a volcano increases soil fertility. Forests and farm crops grow better because the ash adds nutrients and acts as a mulch.

Underground magma heats groundwater. The heated water can be used as a source of heat, or geothermal energy.

e-Journal Visit our Web site **www.science.mmhschool.com** to do a research project on volcanoes.

Think and Write

1. Are volcanoes distributed randomly or in a pattern? Explain your answer using examples.

2. Describe the parts of a volcano.

3. Why are there different kinds of volcanoes?

4. Describe different kinds of underground features caused by volcanoes.

5. **Critical Thinking** How do volcanoes support the theory of plate tectonics?

L·I·N·K·S

LITERATURE LINK

Read the book *Volcano Diary* to learn more about how it feels to be near an erupting volcano. If possible, visit a volcano monitoring center. Try the activities at the end of the book.

WRITING LINK

Expository Writing What effect do volcanic eruptions have on local and worldwide weather and climate? Write a research report to explain. Use print and online sources. Take notes. Begin your report with a strong topic sentence.

MATH LINK

Find the number of active volcanoes. Alaska has at least 40 active volcanoes. This is about eight percent of all the active volcanoes on Earth. Calculate about how many active volcanoes there are on Earth.

TECHNOLOGY LINK

LOG ON Visit **www.science.mmhschool.com** for more links.

NEW VIEWS OF AN OLD PLANET

It would be easier to make maps if Earth were flat! Ever since we've known Earth is round, mapmakers have had a problem. How do you show a round world on a flat piece of paper?

Mapmakers have to use math to translate the spherical Earth onto a rectangular map. This is called a projection. There are several types of projections, but each one distorts part of the world. To see this, look at Greenland on a globe, then look at it on a map. It looks much bigger on the flat map than it really is!

It's useful to have a map to get from one town to another. But how would you like to have a map that also tells you how many people live in each town? or how many restaurants are nearby? What about a map that tells you where the earthquake faults are? or what species of birds live in the area?

Thanks to Geographic Information Systems, or GIS for short, the old art of mapmaking has entered the twenty-first century. GIS are computer mapping programs that display all kinds of data layered on top of maps.

Today, satellites in space gather lots of information about our planet. Some measure the heights of mountains and the depths of canyons. From that, computers make 3D maps. Some satellites track storms. Others monitor changing conditions in rain forests around the world. Thanks to computers, you can display all these things on a digital map, and you can zoom in to get details. You can't do that with a paper map!

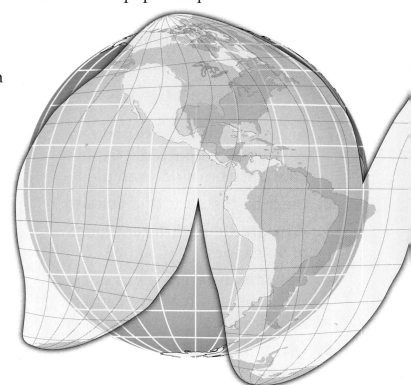

Imagine peeling the cover off a globe, then laying it out flat.

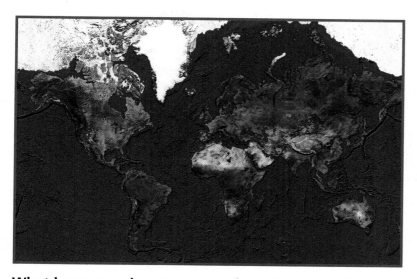

What happens when we try to show the round Earth on a flat map? Regions near the poles are stretched or distorted to fit a rectangular grid.

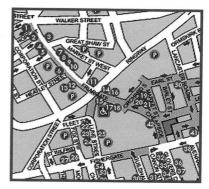

GIS maps can show all kinds of information. They can even show where schools, stories, movies, or restaurants are located.

GIS can help forecasters locate and track hurricanes long before they hit land.

Write About It

1. What are map projections?

2. How can a GIS program help during a hurricane?

 Visit **www.science.mmhschool.com** to learn more about maps.

Vocabulary

Fill each blank with the best word or words from the list.

crust, D6
focus, D22
fault, D21
hot spot, D31
lava, D30
magma, D8
mantle, D11
plate tectonics, D11
seismograph, D22
subduction, D14

1. The modern idea of crustal motion is _____.

2. Magma that reaches the surface becomes _____.

3. The plunging of one plate under another is _____.

4. The Hawaiian Islands formed over a(n) _____.

5. The point where an earthquake begins is the _____.

6. The _____ is the outermost layer of Earth.

7. A(n) _____ is a large crack in Earth's crust.

8. The second layer of Earth is called _____.

9. Activity from an earthquake is measured by a(n) _____.

10. Hot, molten rock, or _____, is located in Earth's mantle.

Test Prep

11. Which waves from an earthquake arrive first?
    A primary waves
    B secondary waves
    C surface waves
    D tsunami waves

12. How do earthquakes affect the oceans?
    F They don't.
    G We still do not know.
    H They cause tsunamis.
    J They decrease the amount of water present.

13. All of the following are types of volcanoes EXCEPT _____.
    A cinder-cone
    B shield
    C composite
    D crater

14. The amount of energy released by an earthquake is measured by _____.
    F the Mercalli scale
    G the Richter scale
    H plate tectonics
    J the H-R scale

15. The place where Earth's plates move apart is called a(n) _____.

    A convergent boundary

    B transform fault

    C divergent boundary

    D ocean plate

Concepts and Skills

16. Reading in Science How is new rock being formed at the sea floor?

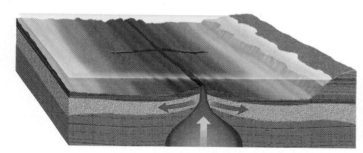

Sea-floor spreading

17. Critical Thinking How do waves from an earthquake give information about the earthquake? Tell what kind of information they give.

18. INQUIRY SKILL **Hypothesize** Copy the table. Describe a hypothesis that ties together all the ideas in the table. In each column, tell how the hypothesis explains the idea at the top. Add columns to the table as needed. Give the table a name.

	Earthquakes	Volcanoes
Continent		
Coastlines		

19. Scientific Methods How do scientists make predictions about plate tectonics of the future? What kind of data do they need to collect to make predictions?

20. Safety What can you do to prepare for an earthquake? What do you need to do after an earthquake happens?

Did You Ever Wonder?

INQUIRY SKILL **Make a Model** How strong can you make a 3-story building? Use only 125 flat toothpicks and glue. Can your building withstand a "tremor"?

LOG ON Visit www.science.mmhschool.com to boost your test scores.

How Earth Changes Over Time

Did You Ever Wonder?

What force carved out the Grand Canyon? The Grand Canyon was created by the rushing waters of the Colorado River. Each layer of the canyon represents a separate geologic period in Earth's past. As you go deeper into the canyon, you move farther back in time.

INQUIRY SKILL **Infer** How could studying rock layers help you learn how old the Grand Canyon is? How could it help you learn how Earth has changed over geologic time?

Making Mountains and Soil

Vocabulary

fold mountain, D46

fault-block mountain, D46

weathering, D47

erosion, D47

soil, D50

humus, D50

soil horizon, D51

groundwater, D52

Get Ready

Have you ever seen mountains from a distance? Up close? From a plane? In movies? What shapes do they have? Do they vary in size?

The photo shows a mountain chain. What formed these mountains? Are all mountains formed by the same process?

Inquiry Skill

You use variables when you identify and separate things in an experiment that can be changed or controlled.

Explore Activity

How Is a Mountain Made?

Materials

waxed paper

clay

2 sturdy wooden rulers

scissors

plastic knife (optional)

Procedure

BE CAREFUL! Be careful with sharp objects.

1. **Make a Model** Use the clay to make four thin (0.5-cm thick) square layers. They should be the same size (about 6–8 cm on a side).

2. Stack the four layers. Pinch them together along opposite sides. Place them on a sheet of waxed paper cut to fit the bottom of the layers. Draw a picture of the clay layers.

3. Place the waxed paper and clay on the table. You need to see the layers. Place the pinched-together sides of the clay against the two rulers.

4. Slowly move one ruler toward the other. Observe what happens. Draw a picture of the results.

Drawing Conclusions

1. **Observe** What happened to the clay as you moved the ruler?

2. What happens when bendable objects are squeezed?

3. **Infer** Can rocks bend? How do you know?

4. **FURTHER INQUIRY**
   Use Variables What would happen if a fault (crack) had been cut through the layers at an angle before they were squeezed? Make your prediction, then test it.

Main Idea Many types of landforms and soil are constantly restructured due to crustal movements, weathering, and erosion.

How Do Mountains and Plateaus Form?

As the crust moves, the rocks of the crust can change. They can change position. They can move up, down, or sideways. Rocks can also change their shape. They can be bent, squeezed, twisted, or broken.

These changes can cause different types of mountain features.

The most common type of mountain is a **fold mountain**. A fold mountain is a mountain made mostly of rock layers folded by being squeezed together.

A **fault-block mountain** is a mountain made by huge tilted blocks of rocks separated by a *fault*. A fault is a large crack in rocks along which there is movement. One block has moved up along the fault, and the other down.

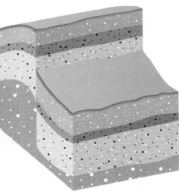

Cross section of a fault-block mountain

The Grand Tetons of Wyoming are fault-block mountains.

Cross section of a fold mountain

The Appalachian Mountains are fold mountains.

Another landform created by crustal movement is a *plateau* (pla·TOH). A plateau is a large area of flat land at a high elevation.

Plateaus are often found next to mountain ranges. They were probably raised by the same forces that formed the mountains. However, the rock plateaus were not folded and faulted as greatly as the rocks of mountains. Rock layers in a plateau are horizontal, but the surface of a plateau is often not level. Streams cut deep valleys and canyons into a plateau. The Grand Canyon was formed this way.

A plateau is different from a plain. A plain is a large area of flat land at a low elevation.

At the same time that these forces are building up the crust, other forces are breaking down the crust. The two main forces that are breaking down the crust are **weathering** and **erosion**. Weathering is the breaking down of rocks into smaller pieces by natural processes. Erosion is the picking up and removal of rock fragments and other particles.

These forces work as a kind of balancing act. As land is lifted up, it is being broken down. Land gets higher in elevation when it lifts up faster than it gets broken down.

Erosion can further break down a plateau into mesas and buttes.

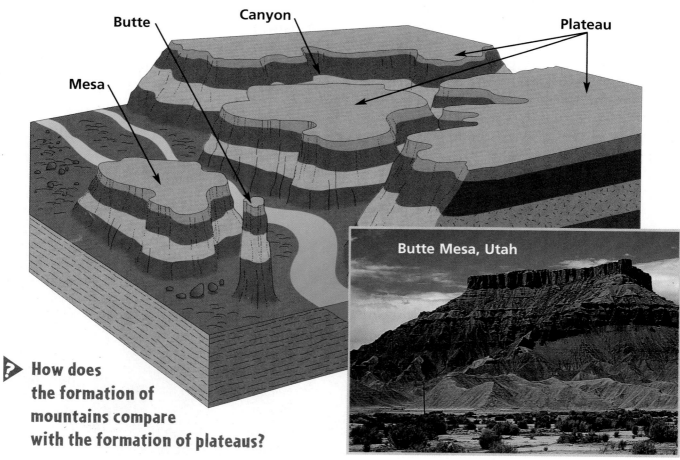

Butte

Canyon

Plateau

Mesa

Butte Mesa, Utah

▷ **How does the formation of mountains compare with the formation of plateaus?**

QUICK LAB

Freezing

FOLDABLES™ Make a Two-Column Chart. (See p. R 44.) Label the columns as shown.

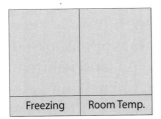

Freezing	Room Temp.

1. **Starting with 0 on the bottom, make marks at 1-cm intervals up the side of two identical plastic jars with screw tops.**

2. **Fill each jar with water exactly to the 10-cm mark. Cover each jar.**

3. **Use Variables** Put each jar in its own plastic bag. Leave one jar in a freezer overnight and the other on a counter.

4. **Compare** Make and use the chart shown to compare the appearance of the water and the water level in each jar. Sketch and write what you find.

5. **Calculate the percent change in the water levels. Use the formula.**

$$\frac{(\text{ice level} - \text{water level})}{\text{water level}}$$

Multiply the result by 100 to express as a percent.

What Is Mechanical Weathering?

Weathering is not one process, but many. Rocks are broken down by physical and chemical changes. *Mechanical weathering* is the breaking down of rock by physical changes. Frost action, abrasion in moving water, and the actions of plants and animals are some examples.

Frost action, or the repeated freezing and thawing of water, breaks rock apart. When water seeps into cracks in rock and then freezes, it expands. The expanding ice forces apart the cracks. Then the ice melts, and the water seeps in deeper. The next freeze widens the cracks even more.

The growth of plant roots in cracks in rock also breaks the rock apart. Burrowing animals such as ants, earthworms, and moles turn over the soil. This exposes fresh rock to weathering processes. Moving water transports pieces of broken rock. As the water churns through rapids or crashes against shores, pieces of rock collide and crumble into smaller pieces.

▷ **What are some examples of mechanical weathering?**

Tree roots can break apart rock.

What Is Chemical Weathering?

Chemical weathering breaks down rocks by changing their composition. Oxidation and the action of acids are important chemical-weathering processes.

Air contains oxygen. Rocks that are exposed to air can react with the oxygen in it. Many rocks contain iron. When oxygen combines with the iron in a rock, rust can form. This weakens the rock's structure, making it easier to break apart.

The air also contains water and carbon dioxide. When carbon dioxide combines with water, carbonic acid is formed. Carbonic acid reacts with some minerals. It can completely dissolve the mineral calcite, found in limestone, marble, and other rocks. Carbonic acid with water that seeps into the ground dissolves limestone. This can eventually form a large cavern. Water and carbon dioxide also dissolve rocks to create holes beneath streams.

READING **Sequence of Events**
How does chemical weathering create a cavern?

Cavern Formation

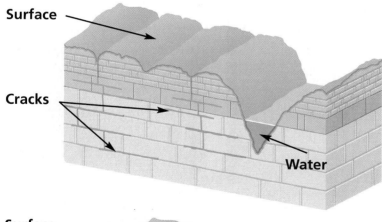

Cracks form in limestone.

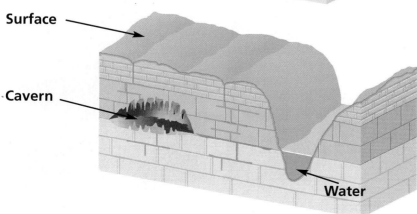

Carbonic acid and water dissolve limestone. A cavern forms. As the river deepens its channel, the water table falls, draining the cavern.

What Is Soil?

The end result of weathering is **soil**. Soil is loose, weathered rock that can support the growth of rooted plants. Soil is a mixture of weathered rock, humus, air, water, and living things. Bacteria, fungi, worms, and insects help in the formation of soil. **Humus** (HYEW·muhs) is material produced by breaking down plant and animal remains. Decayed plant and animal remains are the main source of nutrients for plant growth.

Soil takes thousands of years to form. The first step is the weathering of rock. The rock that a soil forms from is called its parent material. Then plants and animals grow in and on the soil. When they die, their remains enrich the soil. Over time the rock in soil breaks down into smaller and smaller pieces. Rainfall after rainfall seeps down through the soil.

READING Diagrams

How does soil form? Use the diagram to explain your answer.

Formation of Soil

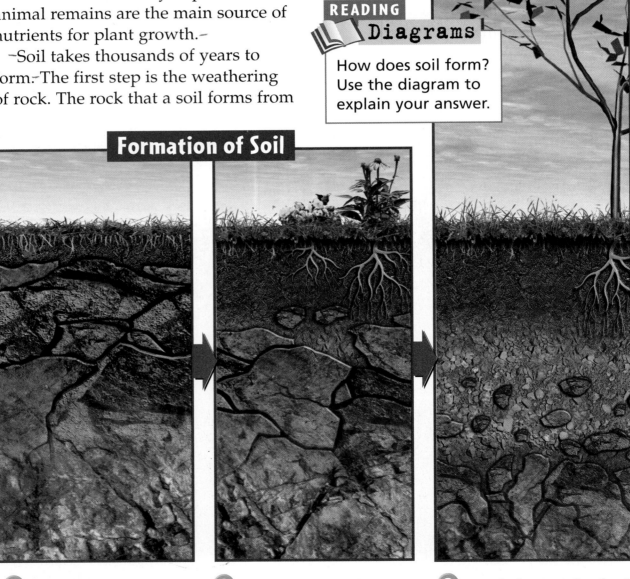

1. Soil begins as parent material.

2. The rocks break down into smaller and smaller rocks.

3. Dead plants and animals and rainwater enrich the soil.

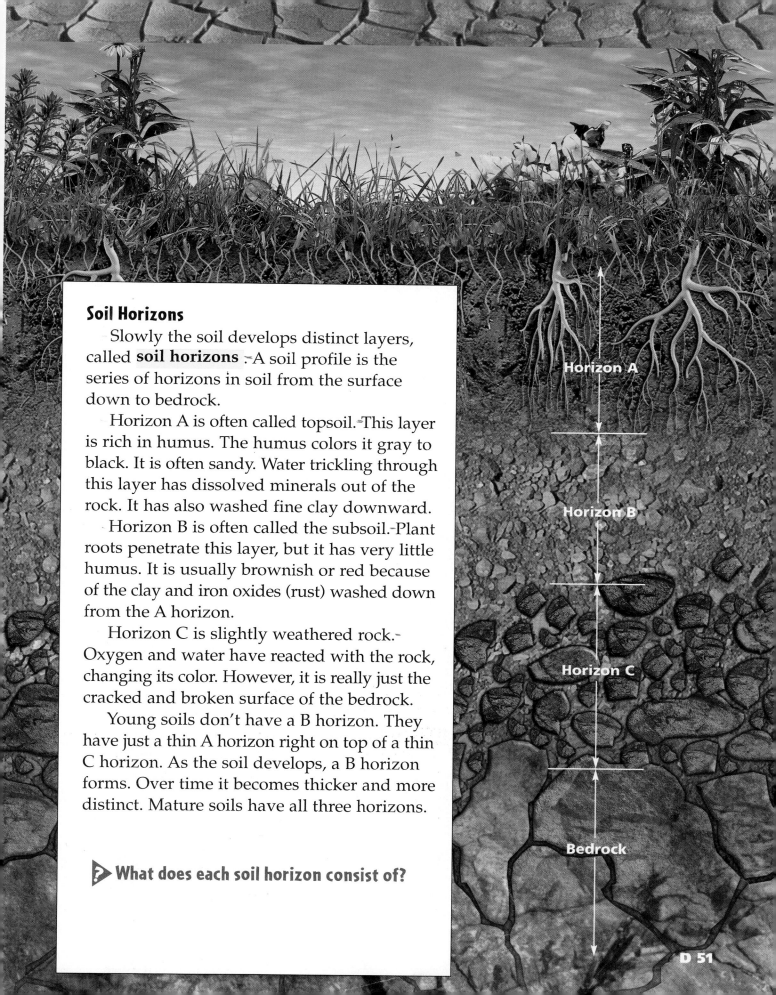

Soil Horizons

Slowly the soil develops distinct layers, called **soil horizons**. A soil profile is the series of horizons in soil from the surface down to bedrock.

Horizon A is often called topsoil. This layer is rich in humus. The humus colors it gray to black. It is often sandy. Water trickling through this layer has dissolved minerals out of the rock. It has also washed fine clay downward.

Horizon B is often called the subsoil. Plant roots penetrate this layer, but it has very little humus. It is usually brownish or red because of the clay and iron oxides (rust) washed down from the A horizon.

Horizon C is slightly weathered rock. Oxygen and water have reacted with the rock, changing its color. However, it is really just the cracked and broken surface of the bedrock.

Young soils don't have a B horizon. They have just a thin A horizon right on top of a thin C horizon. As the soil develops, a B horizon forms. Over time it becomes thicker and more distinct. Mature soils have all three horizons.

▶ **What does each soil horizon consist of?**

Horizon A

Horizon B

Horizon C

Bedrock

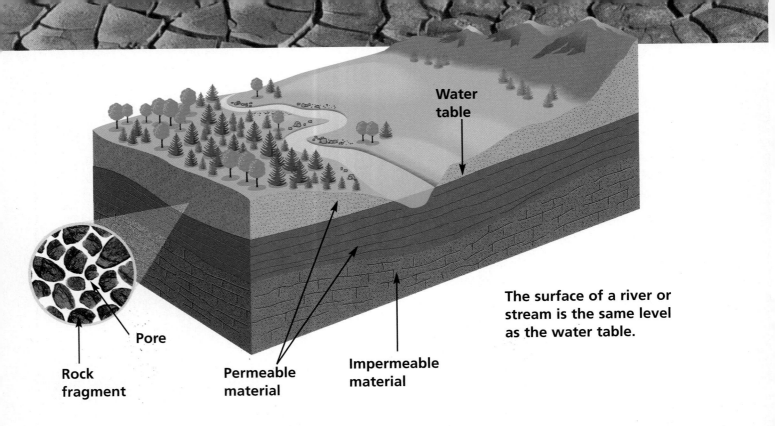

Water table

Pore

Rock fragment

Permeable material

Impermeable material

The surface of a river or stream is the same level as the water table.

How Is Soil Related to Groundwater?

Below the soil are weathered rock and solid rock layers. Soil and the layers below act like a sponge. Rainwater soaks into the spaces between rock fragments—the pores. It becomes part of **groundwater**.

A groundwater system is something like a river system. In a river system, many channels connect the water into a main river. The region that contributes water to a river or river system is called a *watershed*. If soil and rock are *permeable*, the pores connect, and water can pass through easily. Sandstone is a permeable rock.

Some soil and rock have few pores or none that interconnect. Fine particles of clay are an example. These are *impermeable*. Instead of passing through, water builds up on top of impermeable rocks.

How deep can water soak down into the ground? Groundwater goes down until it reaches an impermeable layer. The layers above it fill up with water. A rock layer that contains water and allows water to move though it is called an aquifer. The upper surface of the soil and rocks that are filled with water is called the *water table*. Where the water table rises above the surface, you will find a lake, a river, or some other form of surface water.

▷ **How does soil affect a groundwater system?**

L·I·N·K·S

Why It Matters

Why should we conserve soil? Almost everything you eat can be traced back to the soil. Fruits and vegetables come from plants grown in soil. Even the milk in ice cream comes from cows that ate plants growing in soil.

Humus can be added to soil to replace minerals lost through erosion or use. It helps soil absorb and hold water. This aids plant growth. Planting crops in different areas each year helps protect soil from mineral loss. Planting trees can stop soil from being blown away by the wind.

e-Journal Visit our Web site www.science.mmhschool.com to do a research project on soil.

Think and Write

1. How are mountains formed?

2. What types of forces make and shape landforms?

3. Describe the different kinds of weathering.

4. How is soil produced?

5. **Critical Thinking** Why is soil conservation important?

WRITING LINK

Expository Writing Think about how activities such as cutting down forests or intense farming have changed the environment's ability to support certain organisms. Research the topic and write a report. Use a variety of sources. List the sources at the end of your report.

MATH LINK

Calculate how far the river runs. The Colorado River runs for 2,333 km from the Rocky Mountains of Colorado to the Gulf of Mexico. About 19.1 percent of its length runs through the Grand Canyon. For about how many kilometers does the Colorado River run through the Grand Canyon?

TECHNOLOGY LINK

Science Newsroom CD-ROM Choose *Weathering the Storms* to learn more about chemical and physical weathering.

 LOG ON Visit www.science.mmhschool.com for more links.

The Plague of the Dead Lakes

In the 1960s, people in Sweden noticed something very wrong. There were no more fish in lakes that were once full of them! In fact there were no living organisms in the water at all! The lakes were "dead."

By the 1970s the dead-lake problem spread to mountain lakes and ponds of southeastern Canada. Even waters of the Adirondacks in the United States became abiotic, or without life.

Why did this happen? Scientists tested the water. It was very acid, sometimes as acid as vinegar! Small organisms couldn't live in it. Fish couldn't reproduce in it! Scientists concluded that the acid dropped from the sky, so they measured rainwater, snow, fog, and even windblown dust. Each showed high levels of sulfuric and nitric acids. Airborne acid that fell as precipitation was labeled "acid rain."

To learn how the acid got into the rain, scientists checked earlier studies. They found that in 1872 a Scottish researcher proved that lake water became acid because of coal smoke. Further research proved that smoke from modern coal-burning electric power plants contained sulfur dioxide. If it mixes with mist in the air, it produces sulfuric acid!

Not all acid rain was caused by burning coal. Truck and auto exhausts contain nitrogen oxide that, when mixed with moisture, creates nitric acid!

In 1990 the United States Congress passed clean air laws to gradually reduce acid rain. The goal was to cut sulfur dioxide production by 10 million tons and nitrogen oxides by 2 million tons. The Clean Air Act encouraged plants to reduce sulfur in smoke and required cars to use antipollution devices to control harmful gases in emissions.

From 1995 to 2000, over 400 coal-burning plants developed ways to reduce sulfur in their smoke.

Many stones dissolve in acid rain. Iron and paint wear away faster in acid conditions.

Forest fires, including those set to clear land, also put nitric acid in the air that mixes with rain.

What Did I Learn?

1. Acid rain is a term used to refer to

A precipitation that is acidic.
B any airborne acid.
C clouds that are acidic.
D lake water that is acidic.

2. The goals of the 1990 Clean Air Act include all of the following EXCEPT

F cut sulfur dioxide production
G cut nitrogen oxide production
H increase use of antipollution devices in cars
J decrease forest fires

"Scrubbers" in smoke-stacks remove particles before they get into the air. Retrieved parti-cles can be "mined" for valuable by-products.

LOG ON Visit www.science.mmhschool.com to learn more about acid rain.

Erosion and Deposition

Vocabulary

mass wasting, D58

deposition, D58

glacier, D62

till, D64

moraine, D64

Get Ready

What happened in the photo? Do you think this kind of change might have happened here before?

What might have caused this to happen? How does the steepness of a slope affect Earth materials?

Inquiry Skill

You experiment when you perform a test to support or disprove a hypothesis.

Explore Activity

How Does the Steepness of a Slope Affect Earth Materials?

Materials

long pan

fine sand

coarse gravel

soil

water in a spray bottle

protractor

paper towels

Procedure: Design Your Own

1. **Make a Model** Plan an experiment that studies how a change in one condition, a variable, can affect the results. Mix the sand, gravel, and soil in the pan. Make a flat layer of sediment.

2. **Use Variables** How would you test for the effect of the steepness of a hill? You might try raising one edge of the pan in very small amounts, one amount at a time. Design a data table to record results. Observe the particle sizes most affected.

3. **Use Variables** How would you test the effect of wetness? Keep all the other conditions the same as you test the effect of adding moisture gradually to a sloped hillside. Observe the particle sizes most affected.

Drawing Conclusions

1. Why do you think the mixture started to slide when you tilted it at a certain angle?

2. Why do you think water had an effect when the mixture started to slide?

3. FURTHER INQUIRY Experiment How do different mixtures of materials affect the angle at which they begin to slide? Experiment to test your hypothesis.

Read to Learn

Main Idea Water, wind, ice, and gravity are all factors that change the surface of Earth.

How Do Gravity and Wind Affect Earth's Material?

Along mountaintops and hillsides, weathering is breaking down rock into small pieces. These pieces can be fine bits of clay. They can be larger particles, such as sand or gravel. As this material forms, it is moved from place to place by erosion.

Most of Earth's surface is not perfectly flat. Some places are higher, and some places are lower. Gravity is always pulling things from high places down to low places. This downhill movement of Earth's material caused by gravity is called **mass wasting**.

Mass wasting depends largely on how steep a slope is. It can happen slowly, particle by particle, over years. It can happen suddenly when a buildup of loosened particles can no longer be supported by material beneath. It can happen after a heavy rain or an earthquake, or anytime.

The particles are dropped off at the bottom of the hill or at places where the hill becomes less steep. The dropping off of these particles is called **deposition** (dep·uh·ZISH·uhn). Deposited particles are known as *sediments*.

Erosion and deposition work together. Earth's materials are picked up from one place. Then they are dropped off somewhere else. As this happens, the shape of the land changes. Mountains wear down from steep pinnacles to low hills. Valleys widen, fill up with rock and soil, and become plains.

You've seen how gravity works. Wind is another way for erosion and deposition to work. You can see wind working on a beach, a desert, or a

The slope of sand dunes is steeper on one side than on the other. The lower side is where wind is picking up particles. The steeper side is where particles are dropped off.

plowed field. Wind easily picks up fine particles, like clay and sand. The faster the wind is, the larger the size of the particles it can carry. As the wind slows down, it drops the sediment off—in order. The biggest, densest particles are dropped first.

Wind can blow sediment against rocks. The windblown particles act like tiny sandblasters. They can dig into hillsides. They can polish stones.

As windblown sand is dropped off, the sand can build up into a dune. Wind blows sand particles over the tops of dunes. The dunes change shape and appear to drift forward in the direction of the wind.

There are many sand dunes found in the coastal areas of the United States. During storms these dunes help defend the inland from being destroyed by high winds and rain.

▷ **How do gravity and wind cause deposition?**

Soil Motion

FOLDABLES™ Make a Six-Row Chart. (See p. R 44.) Label the rows as shown.

Soil Motion
#1
#2
#3
#4
#5

1. **Dump dry soil into the center of a baking pan, forming a steep pile. Tap the side of the pan firmly. Observe and record the results on the chart.**

2. **Experiment** Start again with a steep pile. This time, stick toothpicks into the pile vertical with the level ground. Record what happens when you tap the pan.

3. **Use Variables** Set up step 2 again. Pour water slowly, drops at a time, onto the top of the pile. Record what happens.

4. **What did you observe?**

5. **How are your observations similar to mass wasting?**

How Does Flowing Water Affect Earth?

Flowing water makes a powerful force that changes the shape of Earth's surface. It can toss loose particles of rock around and carry them along as it flows downhill. The faster the water is moving, the bigger and denser are the particles it carries. In most streams large particles are carried along by rolling, sliding, or bouncing along the bottom. Smaller particles swirl along in the water or are even dissolved in the water.

The bits and pieces carried by moving water act like tiny drills. They slam into rocks and chip away at them. They chip away at the sides of a river, the banks. They "cut" down into the bottom of the river, the riverbed.

Whenever the water slows down, some of the particles are dropped off. What can cause a stream to slow down? An obstacle could block the flow of water. A steep river could flow onto a flat plain. The water could flow into a big standing body of water, like a lake or an ocean. In each case sediments are deposited when the water slows down. They form a mound or layer.

▷ **What can flowing water do to Earth's surface?**

Erosion and Deposition

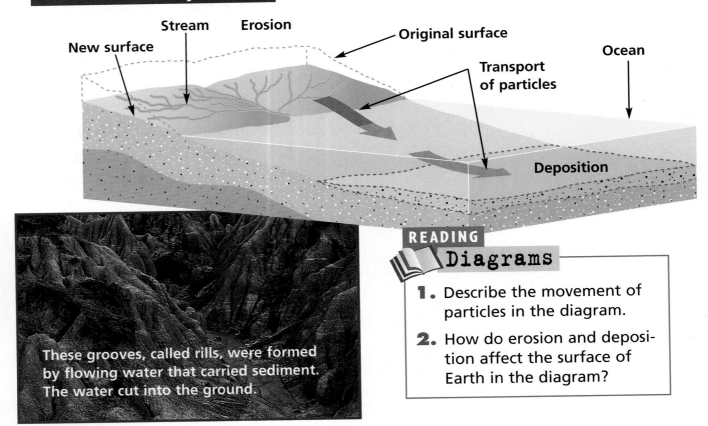

New surface · Stream · Erosion · Original surface · Ocean · Transport of particles · Deposition

These grooves, called rills, were formed by flowing water that carried sediment. The water cut into the ground.

READING Diagrams

1. Describe the movement of particles in the diagram.
2. How do erosion and deposition affect the surface of Earth in the diagram?

How Do Streams Change?

A river or stream carries particles downhill and deposits them elsewhere as sediment. As a result, the river or stream changes. Deep, fast streams become slower and shallower.

Curves develop. Water flows faster along the outside of a curve and eats away at it. On the inside of a curve, the water slows down and drops off sediment.

A river may have all these stages along its path. Some rivers are entirely one or two stages.

READING **Sequence of Events**
What happens to change the shape and flow of a stream?

Steeper River

The river flows along a steep path.

The path is straight.

The water is fast moving and carries much sediment.

The river cuts down into the bottom. It forms steep valleys with a V shape.

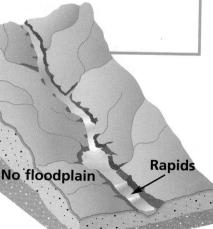

No floodplain   Rapids

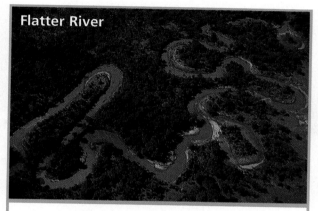

Flatter River

The path is flatter because the river has worn down the land.

Curves (called *meanders*) develop.

The river is slower and deposits much sediment.

The river is shallower and wider. Flat plains develop on the sides of the river.

Meandering stream

Floodplain

D 61

Valley glaciers form in high mountain valleys, where it is cold because of the elevation.

Continental glaciers form near the poles, where it is cold because of the latitude.

When a glacier reaches the edge of a continent, it breaks off into icebergs.

How Do Glaciers Shape the Land?

The huge sheets of ice you see here are like giant bulldozers. They are moving and can move rocks and sediment. These huge moving sheets of ice are **glaciers**. To know how glaciers move, you must know how they form.

Some glaciers form in valleys high up in the mountains. Others form near the poles. Glaciers form when more snow falls in the winter than melts in the summer. Over time the snow gets deeper and deeper.

Newly fallen snow is fluffy because it has air trapped inside. As snow piles up though, the weight of the snow on top squeezes the snow at the bottom into a solid mass of ice. When the ice gets to be about 100 meters (328 feet) thick, it can move. The weight above makes the ice at the bottom like a superthick syrup. The whole sheet of ice then moves downhill.

Glaciers Carry Rocks

Glaciers move like huge, slow bulldozers. They can push loose rocks and soil out of their path. They drag

What clues tell you that a glacier once moved through this valley?

Narrower glaciers dragged soil along. As they merged into one glacier, the soil became trapped in the middle, like a stream of soil.

sediment underneath. Loose rocks and soil get pushed up in piles along the front and sides of the glacier.

When a glacier moves over the ground, pieces of rock may freeze into the ice. If a rock freezes into the glacier, it can be "plucked" out of the ground as the glacier moves along. In this way huge chunks of rock may be picked up and carried great distances.

The rocks along the bottom and sides of a glacier can scrape against the land. They are like the blades of a huge plow. Any layers that a glacier passes over may be deeply scratched. Some exposed rock in a valley floor may become polished smooth.

As a glacier moves through a valley, it digs deep into the walls and floor. A once-narrow valley that had a V shape becomes wider. As a glacier moves through, the valley becomes U shaped.

▷ **What do glaciers do to land?**

What Happens When Glaciers Melt?

Glaciers eventually reach places where it is warm, and they melt. When the ice melts, the rocks that were frozen into it fall to the ground in a jumble. It is a jumble of many sizes of sediment, known as **till**.

A deposit of many sizes of sediment from a glacier that collects in front of or along the sides of the glacier is called a **moraine** (muh·RAYN). As the glacier melts away, the moraine is left behind as mounds or long ridges.

As a glacier melts, meltwater flows out from the edges of the glacier. This water carries particles from the glacier. The water may carry the particles for some distance before dropping them off. The result may be a wide, flat plain in front of a glacier, covered with layers of sediment.

Sometimes chunks of ice get buried in till. When the ice chunks finally melt, the till above them collapses, forming a bowl-like hole in the ground. These holes may fill up with water, forming ponds or lakes.

Glaciers also form lakes in other ways. Sometimes they scrape huge bowl shapes in the ground. The bowls fill up with meltwater when the glacier melts. Moraines may act as dams. They trap flowing meltwater into lakes.

Some piles of till get smoothed out if a glacier flows over them. These teardrop-shaped piles of till are called *drumlins*.

The Great Lakes (left) are five glacial lakes. They are the world's largest single source of fresh water. The drumlin below has a steeper side and a gentler side. How is this shape like a sand dune?

▷ **How do melting glaciers change the landscape?**

Why It Matters

Erosion and deposition are a part of your world. Glaciers may have carried valuable soil to your area in the past. If you live near a river, that river is a product of erosion and deposition.

Rivers provide easy transport routes. That is why so many cities are located on or near rivers.

 e-Journal Visit our Web site **www.science.mmhschool.com** to do a research project on erosion and deposition.

Think and Write

1. How can wind and gravity change Earth's surface?

2. How can flowing water cause erosion?

3. What can happen as a glacier moves through an area?

4. Why do glaciers form only in certain areas?

5. **Critical Thinking** How can a slow-moving river be made fast moving? Explain your answer.

L·I·N·K·S

MATH LINK

Calculate the difference. During the last Ice Age, glaciers covered 32 percent of Earth's land area. Today they cover about 10 percent. How much more land did glaciers cover during the last Ice Age than they do today?

SOCIAL STUDIES LINK

Learn about how cities grow. How are rivers important to a city's growth? How are they important to the city's economy? Pick a city. Research to learn how a river influenced its growth. Find out if the river influences its status today.

WRITING LINK

Explanatory Writing How do changes in glaciers affect Earth's sea levels? Write an explanatory essay to tell how growing and shrinking glaciers may cause sea levels to fall or rise. Present a logical series of steps. Use clear details to describe the process.

TECHNOLOGY LINK

LOG ON Visit **www.science.mmhschool.com** for more links.

Mapping Earth's Topography

What's topography? It's what's on Earth's surface! A topographical map shows the features of an area, such as mountains, bridges, buildings, and lakes. It also shows any changes in elevation—height above or below sea level. Contour lines connect places that have the same elevation. You can make a topographical map.

WHAT YOU NEED

▶ clear-plastic box with lid

▶ modeling clay

▶ marker

▶ ruler

▶ water

▶ pencil

WHAT YOU DO:

1. Mark elevations of 0 to 10 cm on the outside of the box.

2. Build a clay island inside the box.

3. Pour water up to the 1-cm mark.

4. Use a pencil to scratch a shoreline contour line around the island.

5. Fill the box with water, 1 cm at a time. Scratch contour lines each time you fill the box.

6. Pour the water out. Then place the lid on the box.

7. Trace the island's contour lines on the lid of the box to make your map.

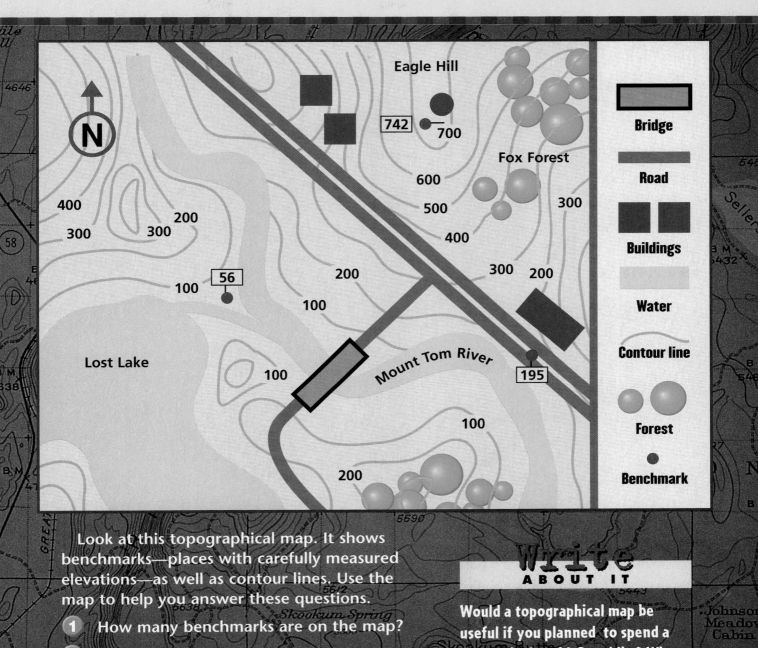

Look at this topographical map. It shows benchmarks—places with carefully measured elevations—as well as contour lines. Use the map to help you answer these questions.

1. How many benchmarks are on the map?

2. What's the highest elevation?

3. What's the contour interval, or difference in elevation between neighboring contour lines?

Write ABOUT IT

Would a topographical map be useful if you planned to spend a day at the beach? On a hike? Why or why not?

LOG ON Visit www.science.mmhschool.com to learn more about topography.

The Rock Cycle

Vocabulary

mineral, D70

igneous rock, D72

sedimentary rock, D74

metamorphic rock, D76

rock cycle, D78

Get Ready

Have you ever wondered where a rock came from? The red-hot material in the photo is molten rock that comes from below Earth's surface. At the surface it cools and hardens into solid rock.

Did all the rocks form in this way? Can you infer how a rock was made by carefully observing its physical properties?

Inquiry Skill

You **hypothesize** when you make a statement that can be tested to answer a question.

Explore Activity

What Are the Properties of Rocks?

Materials

rock samples

goggles

clear tape

marker

hand lens

plastic knife

index cards

sand in plastic cup (optional)

Procedure

BE CAREFUL! Wear goggles.

1 **Observe** Tag each rock sample with an ID number. Look carefully at each sample. Use a hand lens to observe details.

2 **Observe** How rough is the surface of each sample? Try scratching each rock gently with a plastic knife.

3 What characteristics can you use to tell your rocks apart? Color? Size of pieces that make up the rock? Roughness? Any other? Make a list.

4 **Communicate** Construct your own data table to record the characteristics of your samples.

Sandstone

Drawing Conclusions

1 Write a description of each sample on a card. Do not include the ID number. Ask a partner to match the cards and samples. The better your partner does, the better your descriptions are. How well did you do?

2 **Interpret Data** Which rocks shown here are similar to any of your samples? Explain your answer.

3 Do you think all your rocks have a similar history? Explain your answer based on your results.

4 **FURTHER INQUIRY** **Hypothesize** How could you turn a cup of sand into a rock? Share your ideas with others and your teacher before trying it.

Granite

Conglomerate

Marble

Main Idea Rocks continually change from one type of rock to another.

What Are the Properties of Rocks?

How would you know a rock when you saw one? You would need to know the properties of rocks. To begin with, rocks are solids. They make up Earth's crust. Look closely at many rocks and you see **minerals** in them. A mineral is a naturally occurring solid with a definite structure. Each mineral is made up of particular elements. It is not made of any matter that was once living, either plant or animal.

A rock can be one mineral or a mixture of minerals. You can tell minerals apart by their structure and properties. You can see a crystal structure in the minerals shown here—a geometric shape coming from the way atoms are arranged inside.

Properties include *hardness*, a measure of how easily a mineral can be scratched. Another property is *luster*, how a mineral reflects light. A mineral may shine like a metal or be dull, silky, or glassy. The *streak* of a mineral is its color when it is ground into a powder.

A rock is a mineral or mixture of minerals. Because most rocks are mixtures, they are not as

Talc, the softest mineral, has a silky luster.

Feldspar

Mica

Hornblende

Quartz

This rock, granite, is a mixture of minerals.

The Hardness Scale

Each object on the list can scratch items above it. The tools (nail, penny, file, and so on) are used to help tell the hardness of the minerals.

Minerals	Tool	Hardness
Talc		1.0
Gypsum		2.0
	Fingernail	2.5
Calcite		3.0
	Copper penny	3.5
Fluorite		4.0
	Iron nail	4.5
Apatite		5.0
Glass		5.5
Feldspar		6.0
	Steel file	6.5
Quartz	Porcelain Streak plate	7.0
Topaz		8.0
Corundum		9.0
Diamond		10.0

Diamond, the hardest mineral, has a glassy or brilliant luster.

easy to tell apart as individual minerals are. One way to identify a rock is by identifying the minerals it contains. Granite, for example, is made up of mica, quartz, feldspar, and hornblende.

Another way to tell rocks apart is by *texture*. Texture is based on the size and the shape of pieces of materials in the rock. A *coarse* rock is made of pieces large enough to see and feel. A *glassy* rock has no visible pieces and feels smooth.

Another way to tell rocks apart is by *structure*. The structure is the way the pieces of materials in the rock fit together. The structure may be crystalline (KRIS·tuh·lin). That is, the mineral crystals have grown together to make one interlocking mass. Otherwise the structure may appear to be made of chunks or fragments stuck together.

A rock gets its properties from the way it forms. Rocks form from several basic processes. They are classified into three main groups based on the way they form. As you learn about them, look for their textures and structures.

▷ **What three properties would you use to tell rocks apart?**

Texture and Structure of Rocks

Rock Textures	Rock Shapes	Rock Structures
Coarse — Gabbro	Angular — Breccia	Crystalline — Diorite
Fine — Marble	Rounded — Sandstone	Fragmental — Conglomerate
Glassy — Obsidian		

READING Charts

1. How are marble and gabbro different?

2. Which two of these rocks are most alike? Explain.

Forming Crystals

FOLDABLES Make a Two-Tab Book. (See p. R 41). Label the tabs as shown.

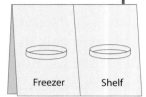

Freezer | Shelf

BE CAREFUL! Wear goggles.

1. **Measure** Pour 10 mL of Epsom salts solution from a jar of prepared solution using a graduated cylinder.

2. **Use Variables** Pour 5 mL of the solution into one petri dish, and place it in a freezer. Pour 5 mL of the solution into another petri dish, and place it on a ledge or shelf.

3. **Observe** Use a hand lens to examine the crystals that form in each of the two dishes. Use the book to sketch and write a description of the crystals. Write about each under its tab.

4. **Describe** how the shapes and sizes of the crystals are different and what affects crystal size.

What Are Igneous Rocks?

The rock forming from molten material on page D68 is an example of an **igneous** (IG·nee·uhs) **rock**. Igneous rocks form when hot liquid rock material cools and hardens into solid. There are many kinds of igneous rocks. Some have a much coarser, rougher texture than others. The difference depends largely on where the rocks form.

Some igneous rocks form from magma, below Earth's surface. Magma pushes its way up through cracks and may become trapped. Surrounded by solid rocks, the magma cools slowly. It may take centuries to harden. During this long time, the igneous rocks form with large crystals. Large crystals give the rocks a coarse texture.

Igneous rocks that form underground are called *intrusive* rocks. The *in-* in *intrusive* is for "inside" Earth's crust. Granite and gabbro are intrusive rocks.

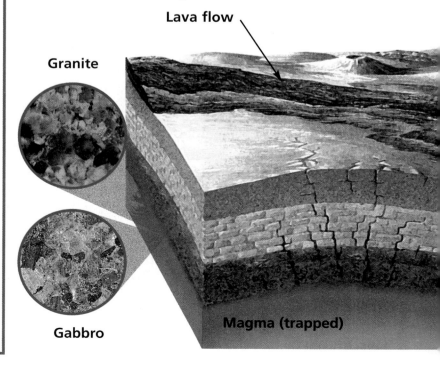

Lava flow

Granite

Gabbro

Magma (trapped)

Magma may reach all the way to Earth's surface before cooling and hardening. At Earth's surface the molten rock may flow from a volcano as *lava*. It may be hurled into the air when a volcano erupts suddenly.

At the surface lava is exposed to cooler temperatures. It cools and hardens quickly. There is not enough time for large crystals to form. These rocks have a fine texture. Some form so quickly, they look like solid glass.

READING **Sequence of Events**
How do igneous rocks form?

Classifying Igneous Rocks

Intrusive: formed below the surface		
Rock	**Texture**	**Color**
Granite	coarse	light
Gabbro	coarse	dark
Extrusive: formed above the surface		
Rock	**Texture**	**Color**
Rhyolite	fine	light
Basalt	fine	dark
Obsidian	glassy	dark
Pumice	fine	light

Igneous rocks that form above the ground are called *extrusive* rocks. The *ex-* in *extrusive* is for "outside" Earth's crust. Rhyolite and obsidian are extrusive rocks.

Rhyolite
(RIGH·uh·light)

Obsidian

Magma

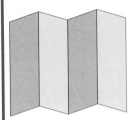

Sediment

FOLDABLES Make a Four-Column Chart. (See p. R 44). Label the tabs as shown.

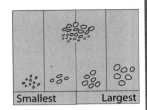

Smallest   Largest

BE CAREFUL! Wear goggles.

1. **Observe** Make the chart pictured. Spread unwashed sediment on the top half of the chart. Look at the sediment with a hand lens.

2. **Classify** Using tweezers, separate the sediment by size into the columns of your chart.

3. **Communicate** Tape examples of the sediment onto each section of your chart. Discard excess sediment. Describe each group you formed.

4. **Infer** How many different kinds of sedimentary rocks could form from your sediment? Explain.

READING Diagrams

Make a table listing these rocks in order of sediment size.

What Is Sedimentary Rock?

Did you know that a **sedimentary** (sed·uh·MEN·tuh·ree) **rock** is bits and pieces of rocks clumped together?

Remember that weathering breaks down rocks into bits and pieces. These particles, in turn, are carried away by wind, moving water, or other forces of erosion.

Eventually the sediment is dropped, or deposited, in a new location. Layers build up. The *pressure*, or weight over a given area, increases. The upper layers press sediment into a bottom layer. This can cause fine particles to squeeze together and harden into a layer of solid rock.

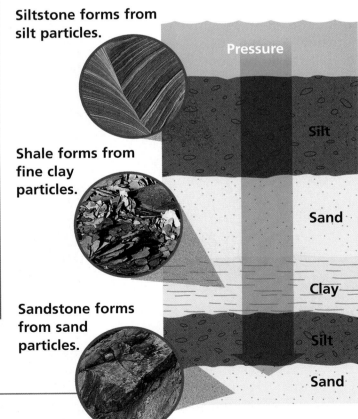

Siltstone forms from silt particles.

Shale forms from fine clay particles.

Sandstone forms from sand particles.

Pressure

Silt

Sand

Clay

Silt

Sand

Larger pieces of sediment become stuck, or cemented, together. Water helps in this process by dissolving minerals from the sediment. The dissolved minerals form a kind of glue that holds the sediment together.

Sedimentary rocks can form in other ways than just by squeezing and compacting bits of sediment. For example, the sediment in some sedimentary rocks is mineral crystals. These rocks form when water dissolves minerals from other rocks.

When the water dries up, the minerals are left behind as crystals.

Some sedimentary rocks are made of sediment that was once part of or made by living things. Many limestones are made of what were once parts of living ocean animals, such as shells. The fragments of shells piled up into layers that became solid rock.

> **What are different ways in which sedimentary rocks form?**

Sedimentary Rocks

Rock salt, or halite, is found in sedimentary layers. Halite crystals form on the surface of evaporating dry lakes, such as in Death Valley, California.

Many limestones formed from a chemical process. They formed in the past in layers under seas or oceans. Many of these areas today are dry land.

Conglomerate often consists of pebbles and boulders.

What Are Metamorphic Rocks?

As you have seen, rocks can have very complex histories. **Metamorphic** (met·uh·MAWR·fik) **rocks** may top the history list. The word *metamorphic* means "change." A metamorphic rock was another kind of rock that "changed." The rocks start out as igneous rocks, sedimentary rocks, or even other metamorphic rocks. Then great heat, great pressure, and even chemical reactions change them. They become rocks with different properties.

Metamorphic rocks often form deep underground. Temperatures are high, and the pressure is great from rocks above. In some parts of the crust, rocks over a large area are exposed to great heat and pressure. This can happen along boundaries of colliding plates of the crust. As plates collide, rocks are crumpled and thrust deep underground. The result is metamorphic rock.

Metamorphic rocks also form when rocks come in contact with hot magma or lava. As magma rises in the crust, layers of rock that it pushes through or against can change into metamorphic rock.

When a metamorphic rock forms, it does not melt. Melting would produce more magma. Instead, changes occur in the structure and texture of the rock.

Metamorphic Rock

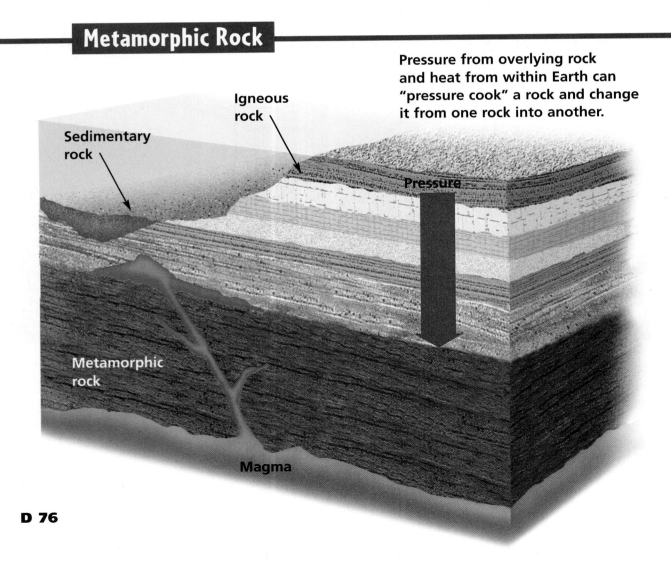

Pressure from overlying rock and heat from within Earth can "pressure cook" a rock and change it from one rock into another.

Igneous rock

Sedimentary rock

Pressure

Metamorphic rock

Magma

A metamorphic rock has undergone a tremendous change. Below are some examples of one rock changing into a metamorphic rock. Can you see a similarity from before and after?

One of the more visible effects of change is that you can often see layers form. Look at the layers in the gneiss, for instance. Sometimes, as in slate, you may not see the layers, but the rock breaks in layers. In other cases, such as marble or quartzite, no layers form at all.

▷ **What factors change rock into metamorphic rock?**

Examples of Rock Changes

Granite (igneous)
→
Gneiss (metamorphic)

Sandstone (sedimentary)
→
Quartzite (metamorphic)

Shale (sedimentary)
→
Slate (metamorphic)

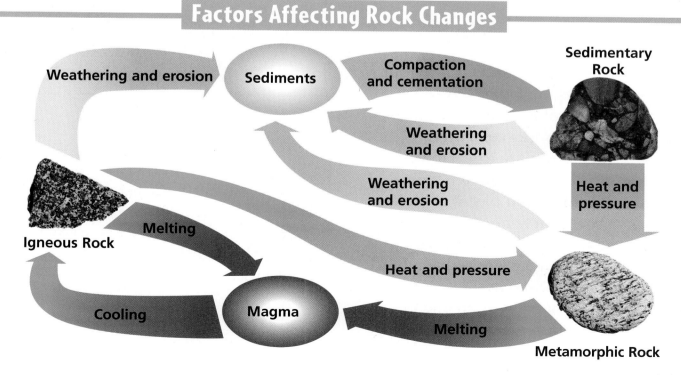

Factors Affecting Rock Changes

Weathering and erosion → Sediments

Sediments → Compaction and cementation → Sedimentary Rock

Weathering and erosion

Weathering and erosion

Igneous Rock

Melting → Magma

Cooling

Heat and pressure

Heat and pressure

Melting

Sedimentary Rock

Heat and pressure

Metamorphic Rock

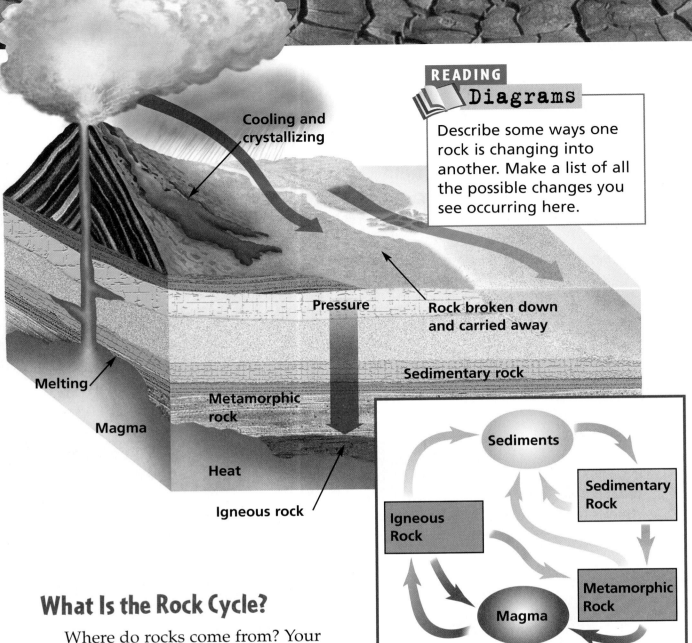

Cooling and crystallizing

Pressure

Rock broken down and carried away

Sedimentary rock

Metamorphic rock

Melting

Magma

Heat

Igneous rock

Sediments

Sedimentary Rock

Igneous Rock

Metamorphic Rock

Magma

READING
Diagrams

Describe some ways one rock is changing into another. Make a list of all the possible changes you see occurring here.

What Is the Rock Cycle?

Where do rocks come from? Your first thoughts might be: "Igneous rocks come from magma or lava." "Sedimentary rocks come from sediment." These are true. However, magma and lava are molten rock. Sediment is bits and pieces of broken rock. A rock had to already exist to be changed into metamorphic rock.

The simplest answer is that all rocks come from other rocks. Rocks are continually changing from one to another in a never-ending cycle called the **rock cycle**.

The rock cycle has no beginning and no end. However, rocks did have to begin somewhere. There is a lot of evidence that Earth started out totally molten. There was no solid rock, only magma. Perhaps the very first rocks to form and begin the rock cycle were igneous rocks.

▷ **How do rocks change throughout the rock cycle?**

Why It Matters

Rocks or minerals are always in demand. They are used to fertilize crops and insulate homes. They are used to sharpen tools, filter pools, and make chemicals, paints, and dyes. Concrete, a mixture of sand and other rock materials, is used to build roads and buildings. Clay, fine rock sediment, is used to make bricks, tile, fine china, and the glossy paper in books and magazines.

e-Journal Visit our Web site **www.science.mmhschool.com** to do a research project on rocks.

Think and Write

1. How are rocks and minerals alike? Different?

2. What causes differences in igneous rocks?

3. How can sediment change into sedimentary rock?

4. If igneous rocks and metamorphic rocks both form from heat, why are these two kinds of rocks different?

5. **Critical Thinking** Is a rock a permanent thing? Explain your answer.

SOCIAL STUDIES LINK

Consequences of Mining Research environmental problems mining can cause and ways to prevent or clean up such problems. Present a report to the class.

MATH LINK

Calculate Percentages Gold is a very soft mineral, so it is usually mixed with other metals. Gold purity is measured in karats (k). Pure gold is 24k. Gold jewelry is often 14k (14 parts gold and 10 parts other metals). Calculate the percentage of gold in a 14k object, and in an 18k object.

WRITING LINK

Expository Writing Choose a mineral that is rare, such as a gemstone, and one that is common. Research to see if there are substitutes for the rare mineral. Learn how both minerals are recycled. Write an expository essay to present your data. Discuss how recycling and the use of mineral substitutes can help reduce how fast mineral supplies are used up.

TECHNOLOGY LINK

 LOG ON Visit **www.science.mmhschool.com** for more links.

Geologic Time

Vocabulary

superposition, D82

relative age, D82

geologic column, D83

fossil, D84

index fossil, D85

half-life, D86

absolute age, D86

era, D86

Inquiry Skill

You make a model when you make something to represent an object or event.

Get Ready

This is Monument Valley in northeastern Arizona. How do you think this was built?

In the past, vast deposits of rock sediment built up one layer of rock over another. A mighty force of erosion dug through the area and left behind these unusual rock features along the valley floor.

In each rock feature, you can actually see individual layers of rocks. How can you tell which layer of rock formed first?

Explore Activity

Which Rock Is Older?

Materials

4 colors of modeling compound

plastic knife

toothpicks

tape

Procedure: Design Your Own

BE CAREFUL! Use caution when handling sharp objects.

1 **Make a Model** Make models to show rock layers in a hillside. They can be sedimentary rocks. There may be some granite. Label your model to show the order from oldest rock to youngest rock. For starters describe or draw your model.

2 **Make a Model** You might make a model of area A below. Choose a color of modeling compound to stand for each layer. Make numbered flags by taping scraps of numbered paper (1, 2, and so on) to toothpicks. Use the flags to number the ages of the layers (1 = oldest rock).

3 Now try area B. Flag the age of the fault as well.

Drawing Conclusions

1 Describe a history for areas A and B. That is, what happened first, second, and so on?

2 **Interpret Data** Do your models support your hypothesis? Explain.

3 **FURTHER INQUIRY**
Make a Model Make a model that has a complicated history. You might include faults and folds. Have others interpret your model.

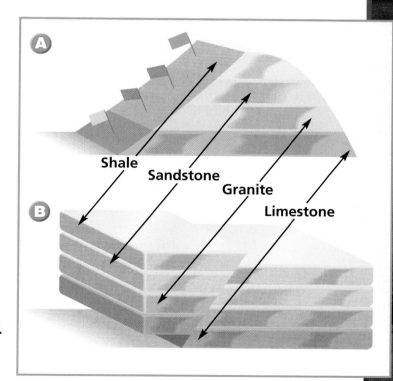

Shale

Sandstone

Granite

Limestone

Read to Learn

Main Idea Earth's history is divided into eras that were determined by studying the relative and absolute ages of rocks.

What Is a Rock's Relative Age?

Until the mid-1800s most people thought Earth was only a few thousand years old. Today there is much scientific evidence that some of Earth's rocks are several billion years old. How can people tell the age of a rock?

Finding the age of rocks is based on two ideas. One is original horizontality.

Recall from Lesson 1 that this idea explains that sedimentary rocks form in horizontal layers.

The other idea is **superposition** (sew·puhr·puh·ZISH·uhn). Simply put, in a series of rock layers, the bottom layer is the oldest, and the top layer is the youngest.

Using these two ideas, scientists try to determine the **relative age** of a rock. This is its age compared with another rock. In a hillside or canyon wall, for example, they can tell which layers are older than others.

Geologic Column

Limestone
Shale
Sandstone
Shale
Conglomerate

Plateau

Mountain

Exposed layers of a mountain

READING
Diagrams

1. Which layer is the oldest?

2. Which is the oldest layer of the geologic column? In which land-form is it visible?

READING
Diagrams

1. Which layer is oldest in the diagram below?

2. What do the wavy lines on top of the rock layer represent in the diagrams to the right?

Four layers of rock formed, one over the other. Then magma flowed up and hardened into solid granite. Then a fault formed near the surface.

① **Rocks form as horizontal layers.**

② **They tilt upward.**

③ **The tops erode away.**

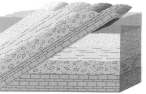

④ **Then they get buried under more layers.**

Scientists also compare the ages of rock layers in different areas. They may determine that the sandstone in a canyon might be the same layer of sandstone in a mountain miles away. By comparing rock layers from around Earth, scientists have put together a **geologic column**. This is a listing of Earth's rock layers in order from oldest to youngest. It is miles thick. We know how fast sediment builds up in layers today. Based on that rate, it would take millions of years to build up layers miles thick.

Telling the relative age of rock layers is not as simple as these two ideas seem to be. Sometimes forces within Earth tilt, fold, or overturn layers of rocks. Movements of the crust can cause older rock to be exposed at the surface.

When a rock layer is exposed at the surface, it becomes eroded at the top. Then the rock may become buried under other rock layers.

▷ **What affects a scientist's ability to tell relative age?**

What Are Fossils?

As people dig into rock layers, they often find **fossils**. Fossils are any remains, trace, or imprint of a living thing preserved in Earth's crust. Fossils tell us what kinds of creatures lived in the past. They are also clues to what the creatures' surroundings were like.

Many fossils formed when living things were covered, or buried, by mud or sand soon after they died. Otherwise the body quickly decays. This burial happens even today, most often in a body of water. There the constant "rain" of sediment settling to the bottom quickly covers any remains. The soft parts of the body still decay quickly, but the hard parts last long enough to be preserved. They may harden into rock. Hard body parts, such as teeth and bones, shells, seeds, pollen grains, and wooden stems of plants are often preserved as fossils.

READING **Sequence of Events**
How do fossils form?

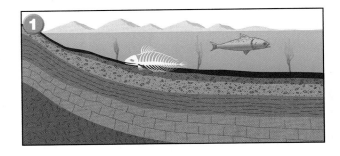

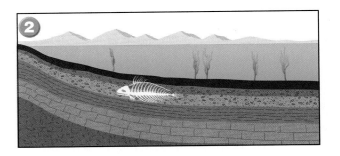

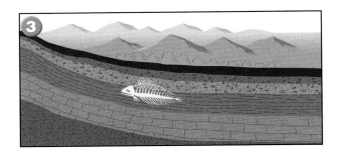

Fossils may be preserved in many different ways, each resulting in a different type of fossil. Recently deposited rock layers are more likely to contain fossils resembling existing species.

Trilobites lived in underwater environments.

Fern fossil

What Can We Learn from Fossils?

Fossils can provide clues to a rock's relative age. A number of fossils called **index fossils** are the remains of living things that were widespread but only lived for a short part of Earth's history. For example, for one long part of Earth's history, sea creatures called trilobites swarmed in the oceans of the world. Then, for some reason, trilobites all around the world died out—they became *extinct*. All rocks with trilobites in them probably date back to the same time in Earth's past, even if they are from different locations.

Fossils provide clues to ancient environments. Pennsylvania and West Virginia have big coal deposits. In the coal there are fossils of tropical ferns. Modern ferns of this type grow in warm, moist places, like tropical rain forests. What kind of environment do you think Pennsylvania and West Virginia had when the ferns in the coal were first buried?

Lots of other things give us clues to ancient environments, too. Rounded sand grains and shell fragments in a rock are like sand on modern beaches. Shell fragments in a rock layer in the mountains tell of an ancient ocean or sea. Lots of pollen from oak and birch trees tell of forests. Using many such clues, scientists have pieced together the geologic history of specific areas and of Earth as a whole.

▷ **How can fossils give us clues about ancient environments?**

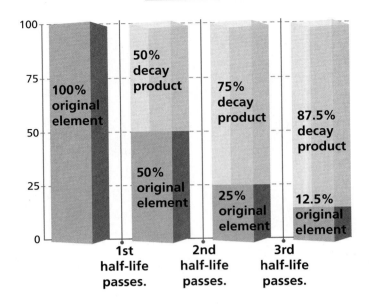

Half-Life

100

75

50

25

0

100% original element

50% decay product

50% original element

1st half-life passes.

75% decay product

25% original element

2nd half-life passes.

87.5% decay product

12.5% original element

3rd half-life passes.

READING

Graphs

1. After the 1st half-life, what has happened to the original element inside the rocks?

2. After the 4th half-life passes, how much of the original element would there be?

How Old Is a Rock?

The discovery of radioactivity gave scientists a way to tell how many years old a rock was. Certain radioactive elements in rocks break apart, or decay, into other elements. This happens at a constant rate, or pace, called **half-life**. Half-life is the time it takes for half the mass of an original element to change into a new product, the decay product.

By comparing the amount of original element to the amount of decay product, we can determine how long this process has been going on. That is how scientists tell the **absolute age** of a rock. The absolute age is the rock's age in years.

Scientists use these ages, as well as clues provided by fossils and evidence of crustal motion, to put together a history of Earth. They describe Earth's history in long stretches of time called **eras**. Each era is marked by the kinds of life on Earth, indicated by fossils from that time. A geologic time scale is drawn so that you can compare the lengths of the eras. The periods are shorter amounts of time within the eras. During each period major changes occurred on Earth's crust.

> **How can scientists tell how old a rock is?**

Geologic Time	
Era	**Period**
Cenozoic	Quaternary
	Tertiary
Mesozoic	Cretaceous
	Jurassic
	Triassic
Paleozoic	Permian
	Pennsylvanian
	Mississippian
	Devonian
	Silurian
	Ordovician
	Cambrian
Precambrian	

Inquiry Skill
B U I L D E R

What Is Half-Life?

We use models to learn about the parts of things and how they work. We also use them to collect and interpret data. You can use a penny-shake model to learn about half-life. You will collect data and interpret that data to look for patterns.

Materials

100 pennies (or 100 math counters–yellow and red sided)

shoe box or storage container with lid

Procedure

1 Place the pennies in the box. Cover the box, hold the lid on tight, and shake the box several times.

2 Open the box. Remove all the pennies showing heads.

3 **Communicate** Make a data table. Record the number of tails-up pennies still in the box and the total number of heads-up pennies.

4 Repeat steps 1–3 several times.

5 **Communicate** Make a bar graph to show your results.

Drawing Conclusions

1 Use the data in your table to describe how this model represents half-life.

2 **Interpret Data** How is your graph like or different from the graph on page D86? Use your data to explain your answers.

3 **Interpret Data** A box of 100 pennies is shaken every hour. A total of 87 heads-up pennies have been removed, and 13 tails-up pennies remain inside. How many times has the box been shaken? How many hours ago was it first shaken?

4 **Experiment** How might you repeat this activity with materials other than pennies? How might your results differ?

What Was Earth Like in Its Earliest Eras?

Earth's earliest era is called the Precambrian (pree·KAM·bree·uhn) era. It lasted about four billion years—about 80 percent of Earth's history. It began with Earth's formation. Few rocks from that time still remain.

The Paleozoic (pay·lee·uh·ZOH·ik) era began about 600 million years ago. Life flourished in seas and on land during that time.

Fossils of the first land life date back to the late Paleozoic. The first forests appeared. Coal beds formed from early forests. Insects, amphibians, and reptiles first appeared. Fossils of many types of invertebrates come from the shallow seas of the early Paleozoic. Over time many new life forms appeared. Fish became abundant.

During the early Paleozoic, the continents were close together. Sea level was high, and many continents were covered by shallow seas. During the late Paleozoic, continental plates collided. Mountains were lifted up, and shallow seas drained into oceans. The Appalachian Mountains were formed. Climates became drier and colder. Permian rocks show evidence of widespread glaciers.

Fossils are very rare because most living things were soft bodied. The oldest micro-fossils are more than three billion years old. Bacteria and algae developed during this era.

The Mesozoic (mez·uh·ZOH·ik) era, or "middle era," began about 245 million years ago. It lasted for 160 million years, a time of great change in Earth's living things.

Early in this era, continents began to break apart. As oceans filled in between the land masses, climates became milder. These conditions

PRECAMBRIAN	PALEOZOIC				
	CAMBRIAN	ORDOVICIAN	SILURIAN	DEVONIAN	MISSISSIPPIAN

Appalachian Mountains

The Rockies (above) are younger, more rugged, and taller than the Appalachian Mountains (left). The Appalachians are an ancient, worn-down range. They were once taller than the Himalayas.

formed a near-perfect environment for reptiles. The beginning of the Rocky Mountains and Andes dates to this era.

Fossils of the first mammals and birds date to this era. These life forms did not flourish in this era, but they survived. Dinosaurs flourished and became the dominant life form of the Jurassic period. By the end of the Mesozoic era, dinosaurs had died out—that is, become extinct.

Plants became better adapted to life on dry land. Fossils of the first flowering plants come from this era.

Triceratops

▷ **What were some of the characteristics of Earth during its earliest eras?**

		MESOZOIC			CENOZOIC	
PENNSYLVANIAN	PERMIAN	TRIASSIC	JURASSIC	CRETACEOUS	TERTIARY	QUATERNARY

The Grand Canyon

Woolly mammoth

What Has Happened During the Present Era?

The era we live in now, the Cenozoic (see·nuh·ZOH·ik), began about 70 million years ago. Several ice ages have occurred during this era, times when vast glaciers covered much of the land. The present time may be between ice ages.

Mammals are the dominant life form. The first mammals of this era were small in size. However, fossils show they became larger throughout the era. Fossils remain from many kinds of mammals, such as the early saber-toothed cat and the woolly mammoth, that have died out.

Many of today's mountain ranges were lifted up. The Alps and Himalayas formed. The Grand Canyon was formed. Earth has undergone a cooling and drying trend. General cooling has resulted in at least four ice ages.

In the future new collisions may occur, and new mountain ranges may rise up. A new ice age may begin. Then, as ice melts, seas may cover the land.

Whatever kind of change happens will take time. In your lifetime the Atlantic sea floor may spread the length of a car. The Pacific Ocean may shrink the length of a classroom. It may not seem a lot right now, but as the centuries pass—who knows?

▷ **What is the present era like?**

PALEOZOIC		MESOZOIC			CENOZOIC	
PENNSYLVANIAN	PERMIAN	TRIASSIC	JURASSIC	CRETACEOUS	TERTIARY	QUATERNARY

Why It Matters

Fossil fuels are the fuels—coal, oil, and natural gas—that heat your home and run cars. They formed from the gradual decay of ancient life forms. Fossil fuels take a very long time to form. Many of today's coal beds date back to the Paleozoic era.

It will take millions of years for new fossil fuels to form. We must conserve what we have. We must also search for other forms of energy that do not run out—such as energy directly from the Sun.

e-Journal Visit our Web site www.science.mmhschool.com to do a research project on fossils.

Think and Write

1. You look at exposed layers of rocks. How can you tell the relative ages of the rocks?

2. How can fossils help tell the age of a rock?

3. How is a rock's absolute age different from its relative age?

4. INQUIRY SKILL Interpret Data Give an explanation for this half-life model table. How would you complete it?

60 pennies	30 pennies	15 pennies
40 pennies	20 pennies	

5. Critical Thinking How are people able to decide on what happened during Earth's eras?

L·I·N·K·S

LITERATURE LINK

Read *History Under Their Feet* to learn how rocks near your home or school can reveal some of the history under your feet. Try the activities at the end of the book.

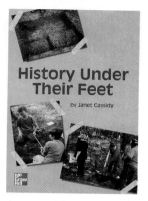

MATH LINK

Calculate half-life. What is the ratio of radioactive element to decay product after 12,000 years if the radioactive element had a half-life of 6,000 years?

WRITING LINK

Expository Writing Fossils give us clues to ancient environments. For example, fossil ferns are like ferns found in tropical rain forests today. Write an expository essay explaining how some fossils resemble existing life forms. Develop your main idea with strong facts and details.

TECHNOLOGY LINK

 LOG ON Visit www.science.mmhschool.com for more links.

Chapter 8 Review

Vocabulary

Fill each blank with the best word or words from the list.

erosion, D47
geologic column, D83
igneous rock, D72
metamorphic rock, D76
mineral, D70
moraine, D64
relative age, D82
rock cycle, D78
sedimentary rock, D74
soil, D50

1. The age of a rock compared with other rocks is _____.

2. A deposit found at the sides and end of a glacier is a(n) _____.

3. _____ is the picking up and removal of particles.

4. Putting rock layers in order by age results in a(n) _____.

5. _____ is loose, weathered rock that can support the growth of rooted plants.

6. Rocks are continually changing from one to another in the _____.

7. A rock contains one or more than one _____.

8. _____ forms from pieces of rock.

9. _____ forms from great heat or pressure.

10. Magma or lava hardens into a(n) _____.

Test Prep

11. All of the following are evidence of life in the past EXCEPT _____.
    A rocks
    B fossils
    C coal
    D grass

12. Two processes that work with erosion to change Earth's surface are _____.
    F chemical weathering and mechanical weathering
    G chemical weathering and water weathering
    H chemical weathering and fossilization
    J chemical weathering and the rock cycle

13. The act of breaking down rocks into smaller pieces is _____.
    A erosion
    B deposition
    C weathering
    D rock cycle

14. Two landforms created from forces that lift the crust are

_____.

    F mountains and plains

    G mountains and plateaus

    H mountains and oceans

    J plateaus and plains

15. The measure of a rock's age in years is its _____.

    A relative age

    B exact age

    C absolute age

    D half-life

Concepts and Skills

16. Reading in Science What is soil? How does it form differently in different places?

17. Critical Thinking How do glaciers and running water change Earth's surface?

18. INQUIRY SKILL **Interpret Data** Myra tosses a handful of two-sided chips. She puts in a cup all that land with one color up. She tosses what's left and repeats. What color is she putting in the cup? How many tosses will it take to have only three of the other color left?

	Red	Yellow
End of 1st toss	28	32
End of 2nd toss	15	

19. Product Ads Look at some of the labels on such products as toothpaste, cement, or facial cleansers. How many products can you find that are made from rock or rock materials?

20. Scientific Methods You are trying to find out what Earth processes have taken place where you live. What kinds of clues would you look for? Where would you look?

Did You Ever Wonder?

INQUIRY SKILL **Make a Model** Using a new bar of soap, a plastic knife, and warm water, how would you make a model to illustrate how water affects erosion?

 LOG ON Visit www.science.mmhschool.com to boost your test scores.

Meet a Scientist

Carol Hirozawa Reiss
Geologist

Carol Hirozawa Reiss is a geologist for the U.S. Geological Survey. Her specialty is coastal and marine geology. Sometimes her lab is on the ocean floor. "It's awesome to be on the sea floor and see things not even a camera can see," she says.

Reiss has been studying two oceanic plates in the North Pacific. The plates are enormous pieces of the ocean floor that are slowly moving apart. The spread is so slow that scientists usually estimate the change over thousands of years. But in this study, they are trying to measure the changes on a *daily* basis. To make their work possible, Reiss and others have traveled to the ocean floor in a submersible called *Alvin*.

In college, Reiss took some Earth science courses. She was amazed to find out how much people can learn about Earth's history from a rock. Rocks contain clues to how an area of Earth has changed over millions of years. They also help us better understand how Earth may change in the future.

Reiss is also studying the sediment on the ocean floor. She wants to find out about the dirt and sand's movements. That information will give clues to how pollution is spreading in the sea.

Diver explores the ocean floor.

TOP 5 Submersibles That Carry People

Submersibles are small vehicles that go deep below the ocean. Here are five submersibles and how deep they've gone.

1. *Shinkai* depth:
   6,500 meters (21,325 ft)
2. *Nautile* depth:
   6,000 meters (19,684 ft)
3. *MIR* depth:
   6,000 meters (19,684 ft)
4. *Alvin* depth:
   4,500 meters (14,764 ft)
5. *Johnson Sea Link* depth:
   914 meters (3,000 ft)

Write About It

1. What can geologists learn from studying rocks?
2. Why is Reiss studying the sedimentation on the ocean floor?

LOG ON Visit www.science.mmhschool.com to learn more about geologists.

PLATES in Ani-motion!

Your goal is to create an animation teaching the history of crustal movement.

What to Do

Using several sheets of paper draw a storyboard for each significant phase of crustal movement from Pangaea (250 million years ago) to the present. Staple the sheets together to make a flip book.

Analyze Your Results

Create a narration explaining each phase of crustal movement included in your book. Include supporting evidence for movement of Earth's land masses over time.

Mystery Model

Your goal is to make and identify a model of Earth's changing crust.

What to Do

1. Observe the model, which consists of layers of clay of different colors.

2. **BE CAREFUL!** Cut through the stacked layers with a knife.

3. Set the two blocks of clay side by side. Squeeze them together by slowly increasing the pressure. Observe what happens.

Analyze Your Results

1. In step 1, how was the stack of clay like Earth's crust? In step 2, what did the cut in the clay represent? In step 3, what process is being modeled?

2. Write a short essay about how mountains form.

UNIT E

Interactions of Matter and Energy

Interactions of Matter and Energy

LOOK!

A fierce forest fire burns
through a pine forest. How
does burning change matter?

CHAPTER

9

Properties and Changes of Matter

Did You Ever Wonder?

Why does an iceberg float? Unlike most substances, when water changes from a liquid to a solid, it becomes less dense. In fact, ice is only nine-tenths as dense as liquid water. This means that icebergs can float in the ocean, which can be dangerous for ships. All the objects you see around you have certain properties that you can use to describe them. What are some of these properties?

INQUIRY SKILL **Observe** Select an object in your classroom. List as many properties as you can. Try to use all your senses except taste.

E 3

Physical Properties of Matter

Vocabulary

matter, E6

mass, E6

volume, E6

density, E7

physical property, E8

physical change, E10

solution, E12

Get Ready

What happens when large quantities of oil spill into ocean water? This problem affects living things in the ocean.

Luckily, oil spills can be cleaned up. Do you know why? The answer is that oil floats on top of the water. It does not sink. Therefore, it can be cleaned off the surface of the water.

Why does oil float on water? Can the fact that a substance floats help you identify the substance?

Inquiry Skill

You predict when you state possible results of an event or experiment.

Explore Activity

What Things Float on Others?

Procedure

BE CAREFUL! Wear goggles.

1. **Measure** Use the 10-mL graduated cylinders to measure out 20 mL each of corn oil, baby oil, corn syrup, and water into separate cups. Add one drop of food coloring to the water. Stir. Pour the water into the 100-mL cylinder.

2. **Observe** Slowly pour the corn oil into the water as shown. Describe what happens. How do you think the other liquids will layer or not layer?

3. **Experiment** Continue the process in step 2 by adding 20 mL each of the baby oil and then the corn syrup.

Drawing Conclusions

1. **Interpret Data** What happened to the liquids as you added them to the cylinder?

2. **Communicate** In what order were the liquids arranged? Draw and label an illustration that shows which liquid appeared on top, in the middle, and on the bottom.

3. **Infer** Why do the liquids stack up as they do? How might using equal amounts of the liquids and a balance help you tell?

4. **FURTHER INQUIRY Predict** Will other objects float or sink in the water—a lump of clay, a birthday candle, a piece of cork? Test your predictions.

Materials

100-mL graduated cylinder

blue food coloring

20 mL each of corn oil, baby oil, corn syrup, and water, each in a plastic cup

spoon

four 10-mL graduated cylinders

small lump of clay

small piece of cork

small candle

balance and masses

goggles

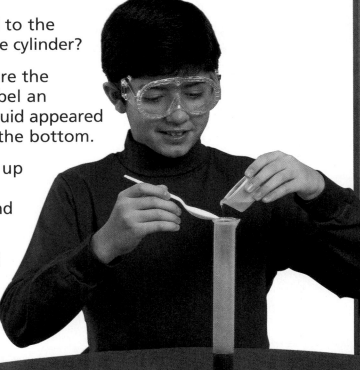

Main Idea Matter is anything that has mass and volume, and other physical properties.

What Is Matter?

Oil and water, like all other liquids, are kinds of **matter**. Matter includes solids, liquids, and gases. Mountains, footballs, lakes, clouds, and air are all examples of matter.

The amount of matter in an object is the object's **mass**. Scientists measure mass in units of grams (g) or kilograms (kg). A bowling ball has more mass than a volleyball, which has more mass than a table tennis ball.

The amount of the pull of gravity between an object and Earth is called the object's weight. Objects with more mass also have more weight. This relationship between weight and mass is used in making a balance. A balance measures an object's mass by allowing gravity to pull the object down.

The amount of space taken up by an object is called its **volume**. A basketball, for example, has a greater volume than a tennis ball. Scientists often measure volumes of solids in cubic centimeters, or cm^3. A cubic centimeter is the volume of a cube that measures 1 centimeter on each side. In a way, the volume of an object equals the number of cubes it takes to fill that object.

You can use a graduated cylinder to find the volume of a liquid. The unit of volume shown on a graduated cylinder is a milliliter (mL). One mL is one-thousandth of a liter, and it also equals 1 cm^3.

You can also use a graduated cylinder to find the volume of a solid. Drop a solid in water. The amount the water goes up equals the volume of the solid.

▷ **What are examples of matter?**

When the rock is placed in the water, the water rises and pours out of the spout.

Here enough water pours out to fill four cubes that are 1 centimeter on a side. This means the rock has a volume of 4 cm^3.

The bottom level of the curved surface of the water matches a mark on the cylinder. This curved surface is called a meniscus.

1 cm
1 cm

What Is Density?

Why does oil float on water? Does it have to do with measurements you can make? The photograph at the right shows two identical beakers sitting on a balance. One contains 50 mL of water, the other 50 mL of corn oil. Both samples take up the same amount of space. However, the water has more mass, because the balance tips down on its side. The amount of mass in a given amount of space is the **density** of an object.

You can find the density of an object by

- finding the mass,
- finding the volume,
- and dividing the mass by the volume.

$$\text{density (g/cm}^3) = \frac{\text{mass (g)}}{\text{volume (cm}^3)}$$

When an object is placed in a less dense liquid or gas, the object will sink toward the bottom. If the liquid or gas is more dense, the object will float toward the top. If the object has the same density as the liquid or gas, it will "hover" in place.

Some liquids float on others. Liquids will form layers themselves in order of density—the less dense liquid floats on the more dense—if the two liquids do not mix together.

When this student releases the table tennis ball she is holding, it will rise to the top, like the other one. Why does this happen?

Both beakers contain the same volume of liquid, but the masses of the liquids are different. Does the water or corn oil have the greater mass? Which has the greater density?

READING Summarize
How does the density of an object determine whether or not it floats?

What Are Physical Properties?

How would you describe the objects around you? You can describe objects by measuring them. You can also identify their *properties*. Properties are things you can observe with your senses.

For example, some properties of objects include odor, hardness, color, and shine. Look at the minerals on this page, and you will see many different properties. Talc is very soft, while diamond is one of the hardest substances known. All of the minerals have very different colors, shapes, and textures.

Properties such as color and odor are called **physical properties**. Physical properties can be observed without changing the identity of the substance. When you describe the color of a rock, the rock is not changing into something else—it stays the same.

The density of a substance is another example of a physical property. Rarely do two substances have the same density. Density can be used to tell substances apart.

Talc Talc is a white or gray mineral with a soft, soapy texture. It is used in powders and as paper coatings.

A material's ability to conduct electricity and its reaction to a magnet are also physical properties. For example, copper and iron are good conductors of electricity, while plastics are not. Also, copper and plastics are not attracted to a magnet, but iron is.

A substance's *state*, whether it is a solid, liquid, or gas, is another important physical property. Knowing what form a substance takes at different temperatures is another way of determining what that substance is. Water that is frozen is still water, but it is in a different state. You can describe its physical properties as cold, clear, and solid. Water at room temperature is no longer a cold solid but a clear, flowing liquid. These are important characteristics in describing a substance.

Diamond A diamond is a clear crystal. It is the hardest natural material known.

Pyrite Pyrite's bright yellow physical appearance gave it its nickname, "fool's gold."

Pick up a nearby solid object, like an apple, a book, or a pencil. Solids are easy to hold because they tend to keep the same size and shape. Holding a liquid is more difficult, however, because liquids change shape easily. As for gases, they change their size and shape. You need a closed container, like a balloon, to hold a gas.

How can you explain these properties of size and shape? The best way is to look at the tiny pieces, or particles, that make up solids, liquids, and gases. Take a look at the illustrations on this page.

> **What are some examples of physical properties?**

READING
Diagrams

1. Compare the shapes of solids, liquids, and gases.

2. Compare the movements of the particles in solids, liquids, and gases.

Like other solids, a pencil has a definite shape and volume. This is because the particles stay in a rigid arrangement and resist a change in position.

Solid

Liquid

Liquids fill the shape of their containers but keep the same volume. In liquids the particles are free to move around one another.

Gases change shape and volume to fill any container. Gas particles move quickly in all directions.

Gas

What Is a Physical Change?

When heat turns a solid into a liquid or a liquid into a gas, the identity of the substance is unchanged. For example, ice, liquid water, and water vapor are all forms of the same substance—water. Simply removing heat from water vapor (that is, cooling it off) turns it back into liquid water. Removing more heat turns the liquid water back into ice.

This is an example of a **physical change**. A physical change is a change in size, shape, or state without forming a new substance.

Physical Changes

Cutting, tearing and crushing are simple changes in size and shape. The wood keeps its identity when it is formed by the violin maker.

Gallium has a low melting point for a metal. Body temperature is enough to turn it into a liquid. The liquid and solid metals are both pure gallium.

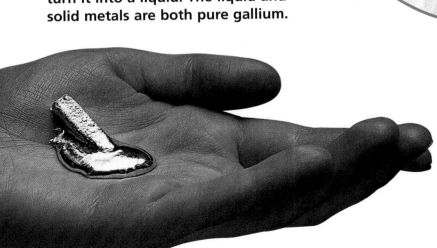

Mixing things together, like water and the powdered drink, is a type of physical change. Neither the water nor the powder is turned into a new substance when the drink is made.

Different substances are in different states at room temperature. The oxygen in the air is a gas, while water is a liquid, and steel is a solid. These substances also change state at different temperatures.

The temperature at which a substance changes from a solid to a liquid is called the *melting point*. This temperature is different from one substance to the next. In the same way, each substance has its own *boiling point*—the temperature at which it turns from a liquid to a gas. Like density, melting points and boiling points are physical properties that can help to tell substances apart.

When a substance is heated in a certain state, its particles tend to spread out as they move faster. As a result the substance expands. This is what makes the liquid in a thermometer rise when it is placed in a hot material. The rate at which different materials expand is a physical property.

▷ **What physical change occurs at a substance's melting point?**

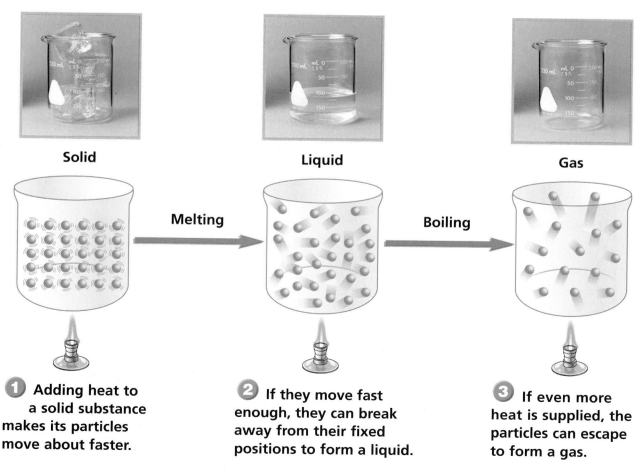

Solid   Melting   **Liquid**   Boiling   **Gas**

1 Adding heat to a solid substance makes its particles move about faster.

2 If they move fast enough, they can break away from their fixed positions to form a liquid.

3 If even more heat is supplied, the particles can escape to form a gas.

What Are Mixtures?

Any combination of two or more substances in which the substances keep their own properties is a *mixture*. For example, a tossed salad is a mixture.

Even though the substances in a mixture keep their own properties, you may not always recognize these properties. For example, perfumes are mixtures. If you separated the substances making up perfumes, you might find some of them have foul odors. However, when these substances are mixed together in perfumes, their odors blend to make a pleasing fragrance. If you were familiar with the odor of each substance, you could recognize it in the mixture. Perfume chemists can recognize odors of the individual substances in a mixture.

Suspensions

One type of mixture is called a *suspension*. A suspension is a mixture made of parts that separate upon standing. An example is a mixture of oil and water. Products marked "Shake well before using" are often suspensions. Solid particles separate from a suspension by settling to the bottom. Fine particles, however, often remain suspended a long time. You can separate them by using a strainer or filter.

Emulsions

Oil and water stay mixed only moments after shaking. For the

A magnet attracts iron but not sulfur. A magnet can be used to separate an iron-and-sulfur mixture.

short time that they are mixed together, however, they make up a kind of suspension called an *emulsion* (i·MUL·shuhn). An emulsion is a suspension of two liquids that usually do not mix together.

Colloids

Fog is a mixture of fine water droplets in air. The droplets do not settle out. Fog is not a suspension. Rather it is an example of a mixture called a *colloid* (KAHL·oyd). A colloid contains undissolved particles or droplets that stay mixed in another substance. Fog is a liquid-in-gas colloid. Smoke is a solid-in-gas colloid.

Solutions

Instant tea is a special kind of mixture called a **solution** . A solution is a mixture of one substance dissolved in another so that the properties are the same throughout. All parts of a solution have the same properties, such as color, odor, and taste.

The tea particles are *soluble* (SAHL·yuh·buhl) in water. *Soluble* means "can be dissolved." As the tea particles dissolve, they spread evenly throughout the water. The result is a mixture that looks the same throughout the pitcher. The tea particles are the *solute* (SAHL·yewt). The solute is the substance that becomes dissolved. The water is the *solvent* (SAHL·vuhnt). A solvent is the part of a solution that dissolves a substance. The solute (tea) is a solid, and the solvent (water) is a liquid. There are many other kinds of solutions. Solutions may contain any combination of solids, liquids, and gases.

Alloys

Most "metal" objects around you are actually solid solutions called *alloys*. Alloys are solutions of one or more metals and other solids. Alloys are made by heating, melting, and mixing the parts together. The solution then cools and hardens. The parts remain dissolved in each other in the solid phase.

Alloys are used to make all sorts of objects. Most gold jewelry is made from 14-carat gold, an alloy of gold, copper, and silver. Fancy silverware is made from sterling silver, an alloy of silver and copper. Pennies were once made of pure copper but now are made of an alloy of copper and zinc.

QUICK LAB

Separating Mixtures

FOLDABLES Make a Two-Tab Book. (See page R 41.) Label as shown.

Separating	Mixtures
• Black	• Green

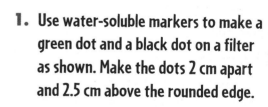

1. Use water-soluble markers to make a green dot and a black dot on a filter as shown. Make the dots 2 cm apart and 2.5 cm above the rounded edge.

2. Place the rounded edge of the cone in a saucer filled with water about 1.5 cm deep.

3. **Observe** Draw what happens to the ink on the front of the Two-Tab Book.

4. **Interpret Data** Explain what happened under the tabs.

 What are examples of mixtures?

Why Do Things Float?

Have you ever dived deep under the water while swimming? If so, you know that you feel more *pressure* on your ears as you go deeper. Pressure is the weight or force on a given area. The weight, in this case, comes from the air and water above you.

When any object is submerged in a fluid, the fluid "pushes" in on the object. The push is greater at the bottom than at the top, so the fluid actually pushes the object toward the surface. This push is called the *buoyant* (BOY·uhnt) *force*.

Any submerged object displaces fluid (moves fluid out of the way). The photograph shows how the water level rises when a lead mass is submerged in water. If you look at the weight readings on the spring scale, you will see that the reading is less when the lead mass is submerged—the buoyant force has made it seem lighter. It turns out that the amount of buoyant force equals the weight of the fluid displaced by the lead mass.

When an object first begins sinking into a fluid, little fluid is displaced. There is little buoyant force, and the object keeps sinking. However, some objects may displace a weight of fluid equal to their own weight before they sink all the way in. These objects float on the fluid. Other objects, though,

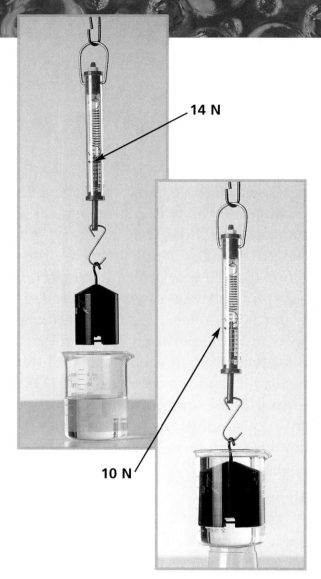

14 N

10 N

An object seems to lose weight when it is placed underwater. This is because the water pushes the object upward. The push is called the buoyant force. The unit of force is the newton (N).

cannot displace enough water to float. Even when fully submerged, these objects have more weight than buoyant force, and they sink to the bottom.

 **What is buoyant force?**

L·I·N·K·S

Why It Matters

Knowing about the different properties of substances allows us to produce better products, improve transportation, or clean up our environment. Alloys of metal have been used for thousands of years for both practical and decorative uses.

Submarines are the result of our knowledge of density. They can sink, rise, or just "hover" in the ocean. To make the sub sink, the crew pumps seawater into tanks onboard. This makes the sub have more weight than buoyant force, so it goes down.

e-Journal Visit our Web site **www.science.mmhschool.com** to do a research project on properties of matter.

Think and Write

1. Wood floats on water. Use this fact to compare the densities of wood and water.

2. State three physical properties of water.

3. What are the properties of solids, liquids, and gases?

4. What is the relationship between heat and the states of matter?

5. **Critical Thinking** When you run hot water over a metal lid that is stuck on a glass jar, it is easier to get off. Why?

MATH LINK

Solve this problem. Icebergs float because the density of ice is less than that of water. The density of ice is nine-tenths that of water. How much will 200 cm^3 of ice weigh if 200 cm^3 of water weigh 200 g? How much of the iceberg's volume will be above the water's surface?

WRITING LINK

Expository Writing How do life jackets or inflatable rafts keep you afloat? If steel sinks in water, how can it be used in boats? Research and write a report. Explain how density plays an important role in many nautical devices today.

SOCIAL STUDIES LINK

Visit an auto mechanic. Find out how the mechanic disposes of used motor oil. Learn about the laws that enforce this method of disposal.

TECHNOLOGY LINK

LOG ON Visit **www.science.mmhschool.com** for more links.

Elements and Atoms

Vocabulary

element, E18

atom, E18

nucleus, E20

proton, E20

neutron, E20

electron, E20

atomic number, E21

metal, E25

Get Ready

What holds this building together? What if you could see what kinds of pieces, or units, are within the walls? What would you see?

What do you think are the units that make up a diamond? Water? Helium in a balloon? How can you tell without seeing them?

Inquiry Skill

You **hypothesize** when you make a statement that can be tested to answer a question.

Explore Activity

What Is Inside the Mystery Fruit?

Procedure: Design Your Own

1. **Observe** Look at a piece of fruit that you have seen before. Make any measurements you think might help you describe it and its contents.

2. **Communicate** Describe the inside of the fruit from what you have learned from your own experiences.

3. Exchange your fruit with your partner's, and repeat steps 1 and 2.

Drawing Conclusions

1. **Experiment** Now observe a fruit that you have never seen before. Make a hypothesis about the inside contents or structure of the fruit. Does it have seeds? Is it fleshy? Does it have different parts? Draw what you think the inside of the fruit looks like.

2. How did you develop your hypothesis about the inside parts of your unknown fruit?

3. FURTHER INQUIRY **Hypothesize** What else can you do to try to determine the inside structures of unknown fruits? Test your hypothesis on other fruits you have never seen.

Main Idea Each element has its own special properties because each is made up of a particular type of atom.

What Are Elements and Atoms?

Mixtures of substances can be separated into pure substances by physical changes. Many pure substances can be broken down into simpler substances by chemical changes. However, there are at least 112 pure substances that cannot be broken down any further into anything simpler. These substances are called **elements**.

All matter in the world is made of elements. Elements can be solids, liquids, or gases. Sometimes elements are mixed together physically, like oxygen and nitrogen in the air. Other times elements are chemically combined to make compounds, such as salt and sugar. Salt is a chemical combination of the elements sodium (a solid) and chlorine (a gas). Salt has none of the properties of these elements. Sugar is a chemical combination of carbon, hydrogen, and oxygen. Few elements are found in their pure form.

What causes the differences among elements? We now know that elements are made of very tiny particles called **atoms**. Atoms are the smallest particles of an element that have the same chemical properties as the element. The atoms of one element are different from the atoms of any other element. Each element is made up of a particular type of atom and has its own special properties.

How big is an atom? Here's a way to think about an atom's size. What if you had one penny for every atom in the head of a pin? If you divided all these pennies among all of the people in the United States, each person would receive 20 billion dollars! How could the head of a pin contain that many atoms? Atoms must be very, very small!

A Pencil's Atoms

A pencil

What if you broke a pencil into smaller and smaller pieces? Eventually the pieces would be atoms of carbon and other elements.

Graphite—the "lead" in a lead pencil

How do you find out what is inside something without being able to "look" inside?

For centuries scientists have been trying to find out what is inside matter. They did not have the tools to just look inside. Instead they observed different elements. They compared how elements change physically and chemically. Based on these observations, they drew conclusions.

The idea that atoms are "inside" elements—that is, tiny particles make up matter—comes from an ancient Greek philosopher named Democritus. He believed that matter could not be cut into smaller and smaller pieces without limit. Sooner or later a particle would be reached that could not be divided any further.

Democritus's idea of atoms was not fully accepted by scientists until the 1800s. In 1803 an English school teacher, John Dalton, presented a simple atomic theory. He studied the way gases could be mixed together—such as oxygen and nitrogen. A liter of each could be mixed together and still fill up one liter, but with much higher pressure.

Dalton concluded that the gases were made up of solid particles (like very tiny marbles) with spaces between them. The spaces allowed the gases to be compressed—squeezed together under pressure.

Even by 1900 scientists still argued about the existence of atoms. After all, atoms are too small to be seen directly, even with powerful microscopes.

However, so many properties of matter could be explained by atoms that scientists accepted their existence soon after 1900. Today scientists are able to get images that reveal individual atoms on surfaces. Now that we can "see" single atoms, we have little doubt that atoms exist.

▷ **How are elements and atoms related?**

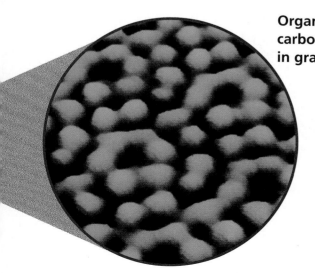

Organization of carbon atoms in graphite

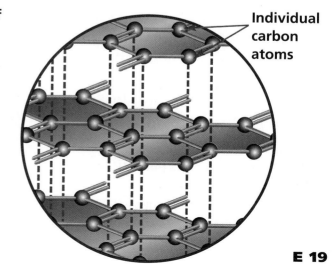

Individual carbon atoms

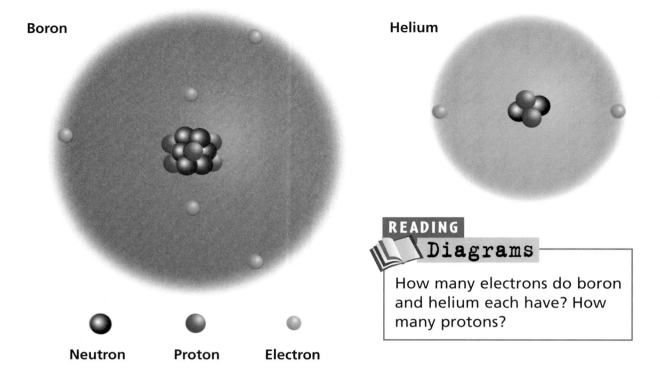

Boron

Helium

Neutron   Proton   Electron

READING
Diagrams

How many electrons do boron and helium each have? How many protons?

What Are Electrons, Protons, and Neutrons?

Atoms are too small to see inside them. Scientists had to use indirect evidence to find out how atoms are put together. In the early 1900s, Ernest Rutherford and his students fired particles from radioactive atoms through gold atoms. Most of the particles went straight through the gold atoms, while a few bounced back. This showed that atoms have a tiny body in the center, called the **nucleus**. The nucleus is the densest part of the atom, where most of its mass is. The rest of the atom is empty space.

Further studies by many researchers showed that the nucleus contains particles called **protons** and **neutrons**. Both of these particles have about the same mass, but the protons have a positive electric charge, while the neutrons have no charge. The *atomic mass* is the sum of an atom's protons and neutrons. It is measured in atomic mass units (amu) because it is too small to be measured in grams.

Earlier work had also showed that atoms contain even smaller particles called **electrons**. The electrons in atoms move around the nucleus and have a negative charge. Electrons are about 1,800 times less massive than protons. They are held near the nucleus by electrical attraction to the protons. An atom has equal numbers of protons and electrons, which makes the atom electrically neutral.

▷ **Where are the electrons, protons, and neutrons in relation to the nucleus?**

How Have Ideas About Atoms Changed?

In 1803 John Dalton proposed that atoms were solid, like tiny marbles that had no particles inside. By 1898 experiments by J. J. Thomson showed that atoms contained electrons. Thomson proposed that the electrons in atoms were sprinkled throughout a positive fluid, like raisins in a pudding.

By 1913 Ernest Rutherford and H. G. J. Moseley showed that the positive matter in atoms was packed into a tiny nucleus. The electrons were thought to orbit the nucleus. However, since 1926 scientists have thought of electrons as "clouds" surrounding the nucleus. They are not like planets traveling around the Sun.

The atoms of each element have a unique number of protons. This number is called the element's **atomic number** . Carbon atoms, for example, have 6 protons, while sodium atoms have 11 protons. The number of protons in an atom tells us what element it is.

Any element's atoms can occur naturally in different forms. The atoms of an element have the same number of protons but may have different numbers of neutrons. Atoms that have the same number of protons but different numbers of neutrons are called *isotopes*. Since the atoms of an element come in these different forms, we state an average atomic mass for each element.

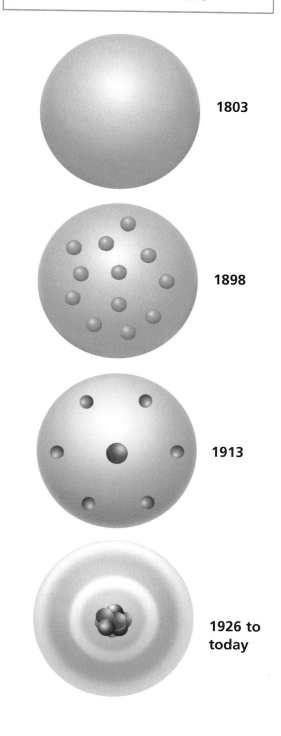

Models of Atoms over the Past 200 Years

1803

1898

1913

1926 to today

READING Summarize
What is the difference between today's model of the atom and the model of scientists in 1803?

How do Particles and Waves Compare?

Our universe contains waves of energy and tiny particles of matter—protons, neutrons, and electrons. Electrical attraction and other forces hold the tiny particles together as atoms. The same attraction can join atoms to form still larger particles that make up the many varieties of matter.

Small as they are, particles of matter have mass and volume and take up space. When gravity acts on them, they have weight.

Energy is not a substance. It has no mass or volume. In theory, a thimble could hold all the energy in the universe. You only know energy exists through its effect on matter. Energy can move matter, heat it, illuminate it, or make it do work.

Light is a form of electromagnetic energy. Scientists think of light as energy vibrations. These form waves that transmit energy as they move through space at enormous speed.

You can make waves in water by tossing a pebble into a pond. The disturbance sets the water molecules moving up and down. This creates a series of crests and troughs that radiate out horizontally as in the drawing. Spectators in stadiums use the same principle to make human waves.

 **How do the water molecules and ball move?**

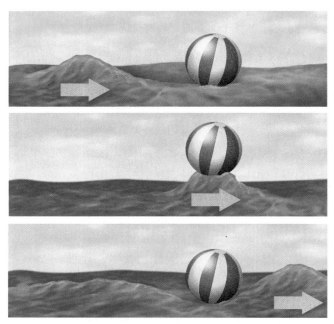

The waves move from left to right as the water molecules go up and down.

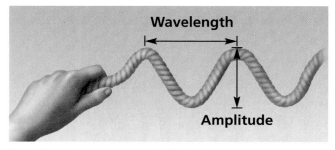

By vibrating one end of the jumprope up and down, you create waves that carry energy through space.

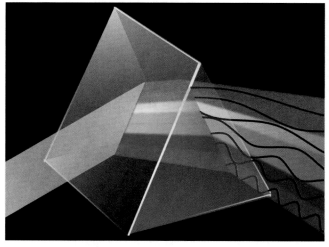

A prism separates the mixture of wavelengths in white light into colors.

Three features of a wave are its frequency, wavelength, and amplitude. *Frequency* is a measure of how many wave crests pass a point in a unit time. *Wavelength* is the distance between crests. Higher frequency waves have shorter wavelengths and greater energy. *Amplitude,* the height of the wave from trough to crest, is a measure of the wave's power.

White light is a mixture of waves of different frequencies and wavelengths. However, a mist of water can separate it into the colors of a rainbow, the visible part of the total electromagnetic spectrum (p. C9). Each color consists of similar frequencies and wavelengths. The invisible waves are used in radio, television, telephones, cooking, medicine, and science investigation.

Some substances are *transparent.* They transmit light, letting it pass through so you can see through them. Other substances are *translucent,* absorbing some of the energy and blurring the image. An *opaque* substance absorbs or reflects most of the waves so that you cannot see anything through it.

The smooth polished surface of a mirror can be flat (plane), curved inward (concave), or curved outward (convex). Each type of surface produces a different mirror image. Rough surfaces reflect light waves in many directions (scattering) and do not form mirror images.

Colored materials reflect or transmit only some visible light frequencies. These produce the colors you see. The materials absorb the wave energy of the other colors and you do not see them.

> **What causes the difference between red and blue light?**

Inside of spoon

Back of spoon

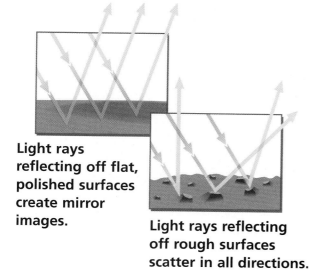

Light rays reflecting off flat, polished surfaces create mirror images.

Light rays reflecting off rough surfaces scatter in all directions.

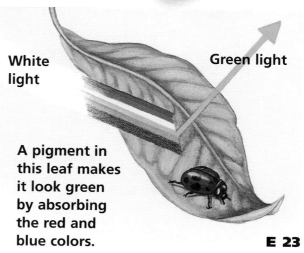

White light

Green light

A pigment in this leaf makes it look green by absorbing the red and blue colors.

E 23

What Is the Periodic Table?

By the 1800s scientists had noticed that many elements had very similar properties. Did these similarities have any meaning? Could there be a pattern to the elements?

In 1868 a Russian scientist named Dmitry Mendeleyev was experimenting with arranging the elements in different ways. When he arranged them according to atomic mass, he discovered a repetitive pattern to several properties, including density, metal character, and ability to react with other elements. Any repeating pattern is called periodic. Mendeleyev's discovery is called the periodic table of elements.

Mendeleyev's periodic table proved to be very successful. One reason was because he left blank spaces in the table when necessary to keep the periodic pattern. To explain the blank spaces, Mendeleyev boldly predicted that elements would be discovered to fill them! Sure enough, scientists soon discovered three elements—scandium, gallium, and germanium. Each had just the right properties to fill a blank space in Mendeleyev's table.

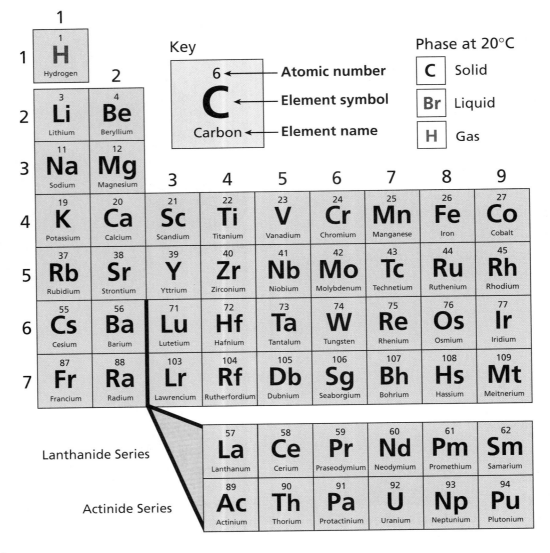

In Mendeleyev's day only 60 elements were known. Today at least 112 elements are known, some of them artificial. The modern form of the periodic table is shown below. The elements are arranged in order of increasing atomic number. The vertical columns contain elements that react with other substances in similar ways. They are chemically alike.

Each row of elements in the table is called a period. Notice that the periods become wider and wider as you move down the table. The first period has only two elements—hydrogen and helium.

The sixth and seventh periods, on the other hand, have 32 elements each.

According to their properties, elements can be placed in one of three groups—**metals**, *metalloids* (MET·uh·loydz), and *nonmetals*. Metals conduct heat and electricity, are shiny when polished, and bend rather than break. Nonmetals are just the opposite. Metalloids have only some properties of metals.

▷ **How is the periodic table divided?**

Metallic Properties

Li	Metal
B	Metalloid
C	Nonmetal

			13	14	15	16	17	18
								2 He Helium
			5 B Boron	6 C Carbon	7 N Nitrogen	8 O Oxygen	9 F Fluorine	10 Ne Neon
10	11	12	13 Al Aluminum	14 Si Silicon	15 P Phosphorus	16 S Sulfur	17 Cl Chlorine	18 Ar Argon
28 Ni Nickel	29 Cu Copper	30 Zn Zinc	31 Ga Gallium	32 Ge Germanium	33 As Arsenic	34 Se Selenium	35 Br Bromine	36 Kr Krypton
46 Pd Palladium	47 Ag Silver	48 Cd Cadmium	49 In Indium	50 Sn Tin	51 Sb Antimony	52 Te Tellurium	53 I Iodine	54 Xe Xenon
78 Pt Platinum	79 Au Gold	80 Hg Mercury	81 Tl Thallium	82 Pb Lead	83 Bi Bismuth	84 Po Polonium	85 At Astatine	86 Rn Radon
110	111	112		114		116		118

63 Eu Europium	64 Gd Gadolinium	65 Tb Terbium	66 Dy Dysprosium	67 Ho Holmium	68 Er Erbium	69 Tm Thulium	70 Yb Ytterbium
95 Am Americium	96 Cm Curium	97 Bk Berkelium	98 Cf Californium	99 Es Einsteinium	100 Fm Fermium	101 Md Mendelevium	102 No Nobelium

What Are the Properties of Elements?

Scientists have discovered over 100 different elements, but only about 50 of them are commonly found on Earth. That means that only 50 elements combine to form all the substances you see and use every day.

Elements have all sorts of different properties. Some are hard, shiny solids, like silver and aluminum. Others are clear gases that you can't see or taste, like oxygen and helium. Still others are liquids.

These photographs illustrate different elements. Notice that each square includes the element's atomic symbol.

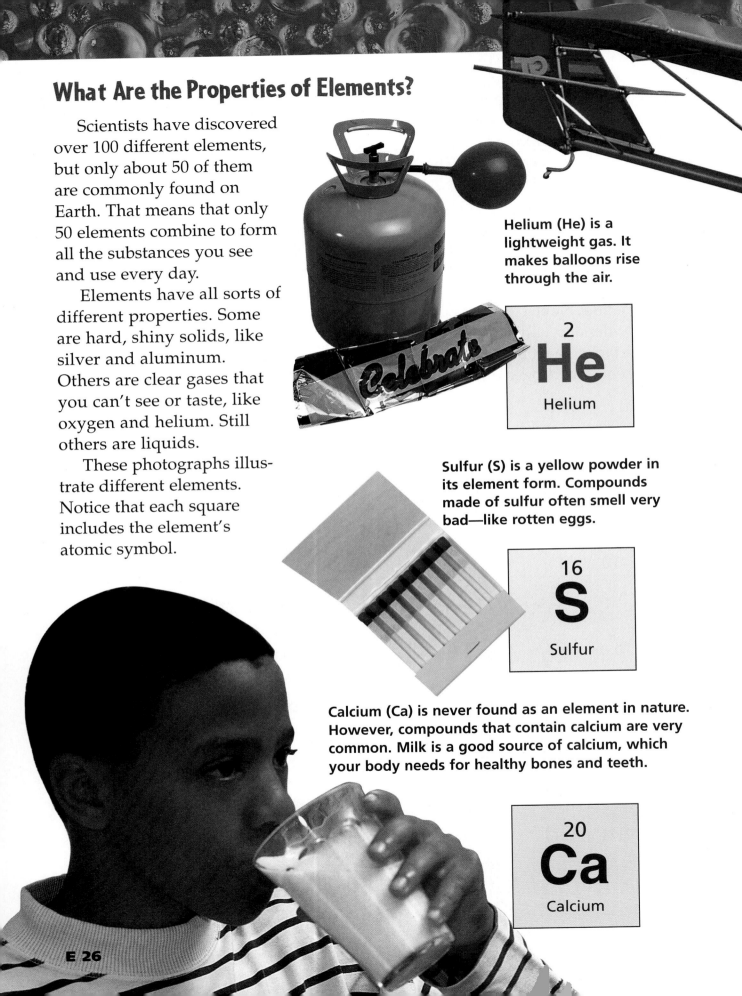

Helium (He) is a lightweight gas. It makes balloons rise through the air.

2
He
Helium

Sulfur (S) is a yellow powder in its element form. Compounds made of sulfur often smell very bad—like rotten eggs.

16
S
Sulfur

Calcium (Ca) is never found as an element in nature. However, compounds that contain calcium are very common. Milk is a good source of calcium, which your body needs for healthy bones and teeth.

20
Ca
Calcium

13
Al
Aluminum

Aluminum (Al) is light and strong. Aluminum is used for lots of products, including airplane parts and soft-drink cans.

29
Cu
Copper

Copper (Cu) conducts electricity very well, so it is used in electrical wiring.

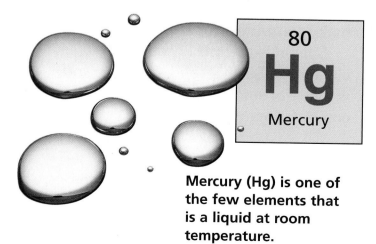

80
Hg
Mercury

Mercury (Hg) is one of the few elements that is a liquid at room temperature.

QUICK LAB

Element Lineup

FOLDABLES™ Make a Four-Tab Book. (See page R 44.) Label as shown.

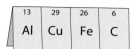

13	29	26	6
Al	Cu	Fe	C

1. **Observe** Look at samples of iron, copper, carbon, and aluminum.

2. **Classify** How would you classify these elements in groups? Compare, contrast, and record their characteristics under the tabs.

3. **Observe** Use a hand lens to look closely at each sample. Note any similarities and differences.

4. **Observe** Rub each sample with sandpaper. How does this help you classify the samples?

5. Which characteristics help you identify the most similar samples?

6. Which sample is most different from the others? How can you tell?

▶ **What are some properties of the elements on these two pages?**

What Are Metals, Nonmetals, and Metalloids?

About three-fourths of the elements are metals. As a group, metals conduct electricity. The metal copper is generally used for electric wires. The wires inside a cord for a lamp or a stereo are made of copper. To be safe, a rubber coating covers the wires in electrical appliances. Substances such as rubber and plastic are not good conductors of electricity.

Nonmetals tend to have the properties opposite to metals. Most nonmetals are poor conductors of heat and electricity. At room temperature most nonmetals are gases or solids. One, bromine,

Chlorine, a nonmetal, is very reactive and poisonous.

In this piece of computer circuitry, the peach-colored material is mostly silicon. The dark paths are silicon combined with boron or arsenic. The circuit works because the dark paths conduct electricity better than the surrounding silicon.

is a liquid. The solid nonmetals are brittle rather than bendable.

The elements boron, silicon, germanium, arsenic, antimony, tellurium, polonium, and astatine are metalloids. Their properties fall in between the properties of metals and nonmetals. An important use of metalloids is to make computer chips and circuits.

Silicon is the most abundant element in Earth's solid surface. Sand is made of silicon dioxide, a chemical combination of silicon and oxygen.

Sodium metal is so reactive that it has to be stored in oil.

To make silver more durable in jewelry and silverware, it is mixed with other metals.

▷ **What is the difference among metals, nonmetals, and metalloids?**

Why It Matters

You use elements in many ways. Copper and aluminum are used in pots for cooking. Light bulbs have a metal in them that conducts electricity.

The more we learn about elements, the more we will be able to make them work for us. It was only recently that silicon gained greater importance in technology. Along with boron and arsenic, it is essential in the circuits of computers.

e-Journal Visit our Web site **www.science.mmhschool.com** to do a research project on elements and atoms.

Think and Write

1. What do you think atoms are?

2. When electricity is passed through water, the water breaks down into two simpler gases. Could water be an element? Why or why not?

3. Why did scientists have to rely on indirect evidence to discover how atoms are put together?

4. The atomic number of chlorine is 17. What does this tell you about chlorine atoms?

5. **Critical Thinking** Of sulfur, argon, and sodium, which has chemical properties like oxygen? Why?

L·I·N·K·S

MATH LINK

Measure small objects. What units do scientists use to measure very small objects? Compare these units with the units you use to measure common objects.

WRITING LINK

Persuasive Writing Find out about a law that affects the use of metals in the environment. Then imagine that you are the editor of a newspaper. Write an editorial stating your opinion about this law. Use convincing reasons.

HEALTH LINK

Research salt. Salt is made of two elements— sodium and chlorine. Use library books or the Internet to learn how salt affects the human body. Write a report on your findings.

TECHNOLOGY LINK

Science Newsroom CD-ROM Choose *Piece by Piece* to learn more about atoms and elements.

 LOG ON Visit **www.science.mmhschool.com** for more links.

Chemical Changes

Vocabulary

chemical change, E32

compound, E32

chemical bond, E33

chemical formula, E33

ion, E35

chemical property, E38

molecule, E41

exothermic, E44

endothermic, E44

Get Ready

This was once a ship. When the ship was new, it looked very different. How has it changed? The ship is made of steel, an alloy of iron. Bicycles and automobiles are also made of steel.

What happens to things made of iron and steel as they age? Is there a way to find out what causes these changes? Can you prevent them from happening?

Inquiry Skill

You experiment when you perform a test to support or disprove a hypothesis.

Explore Activity

How Much Does It Rust?

Materials

clear-plastic cup

petri dish

modeling clay

steel wool

paper clips

water

vinegar

goggles

Procedure

BE CAREFUL! Wear goggles when you work with vinegar.

1. In this activity you will investigate what causes rust and how its formation may be prevented.

2. **Experiment** Design an experiment to see if rust will form on the steel wool and/or the paper clip. [HINT: Steel rusts more quickly in a moist air environment rather than when submerged in water.] What arrangement of petri dish and cup could produce a moist air environment? How can you expose the paper clip and steel wool to the same experimental conditions? Rinse the paper clip and steel wool in warm water and vinegar to remove any oil that may be present. Leave the set-up overnight, or longer, to see rust.

3. **Experiment** You may also experiment with the effect of temperature on rusting by placing your experimental set-up in a warm or cool location.

Drawing Conclusions

1. **Observe** What evidence can you observe that the steel has changed?

2. **Infer** What resulted in the most rust formation on the steel wool? The paper clip?

3. **FURTHER INQUIRY** **Experiment** Design a way to prevent the paper clip and/or the steel wool from rusting. Test your idea.

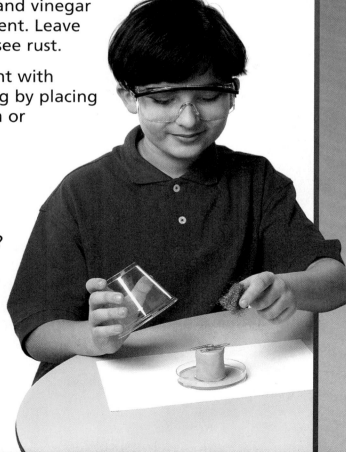

Main Idea Atoms can bond to form compounds with various properties.

What Is a Chemical Change?

If you leave your bike out in the rain, you may notice it has undergone a change. A reddish brown powder could have formed on parts that were once shiny silver. The powder forms because the iron metal on your bike has undergone a change. It has combined with oxygen in the air to form a new substance called rust. This is an example of a **chemical change**.

Chemical changes produce substances that have new and different properties. A change in color is one of the key signs of a chemical change. Other signs are when heat and light are given off, a gas is produced, or a powdery solid settles out of a liquid.

The mass of matter does not change during a chemical change. The total mass of all the starting substances equals the total mass of all new substances formed. This is known as the Law of Conservation of Mass.

Rust is an example of a **compound**. A compound is a chemical combination of two or more substances. Rust is iron oxide, a name that indicates that the elements iron and oxygen have combined. A compound has its own properties, different from the substances it is made of. Iron oxide is a crumbly brownish solid with no shine. Iron does not crumble and is gray in color.

Copper is a shiny orange-brown solid. You know a copper compound has formed when you see blackish or greenish spots on a copper pot or penny. Mixing cement and water chemically changes them into concrete, a new material with new properties.

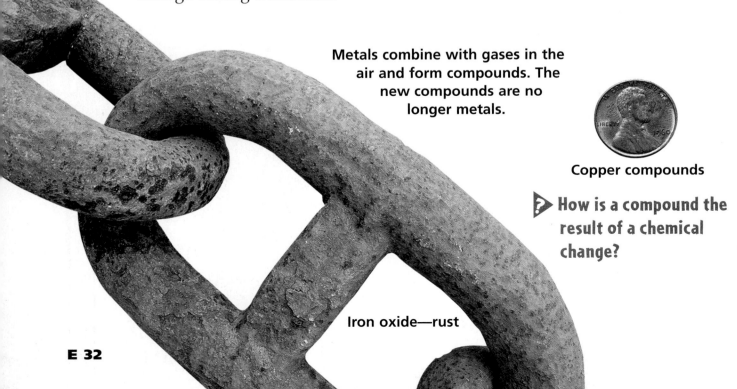

Metals combine with gases in the air and form compounds. The new compounds are no longer metals.

Copper compounds

▷ **How is a compound the result of a chemical change?**

Iron oxide—rust

What Are Chemical Bonds?

The compound carbon dioxide is made when carbon combines with oxygen. Carbon dioxide is a colorless gas, but carbon is a black solid. What makes carbon dioxide so different from pure carbon?

When chemical changes like the burning of carbon occur, atoms link together in new ways. The different linking patterns produce new substances that have their own unique properties. The links that atoms or electrically charged particles can form with one another are called **chemical bonds** . Chemical bonds result from electrical attraction between atoms. When the atoms of different elements bond together, compounds are formed.

When atoms form bonds, a certain number of one kind of atom always bonds to a certain number of another. The number can be in a ratio, like one carbon to two oxygens, or 1:2. The ratio in which atoms are bonded together in a compound is shown by a **chemical formula** . A chemical formula is a way of using letters and numbers to show how much of an element is in a substance. For example, the formula for carbon dioxide is CO_2 because carbon dioxide contains two oxygen atoms for every one carbon atom, as you can see in the diagram.

▶ **How does a chemical formula represent a chemical bond?**

The carbon in these charcoal briquettes is combining with oxygen from the air to make carbon dioxide gas. The flame is heat and light given off by the chemical change.

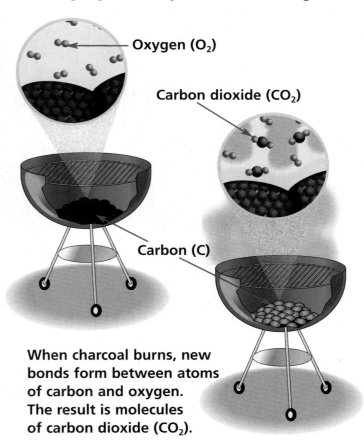

Oxygen (O_2)

Carbon dioxide (CO_2)

Carbon (C)

When charcoal burns, new bonds form between atoms of carbon and oxygen. The result is molecules of carbon dioxide (CO_2).

READING Diagrams

1. What molecules were in the air above the unlit grill?

2. What molecules were in the air above the lit grill? Why?

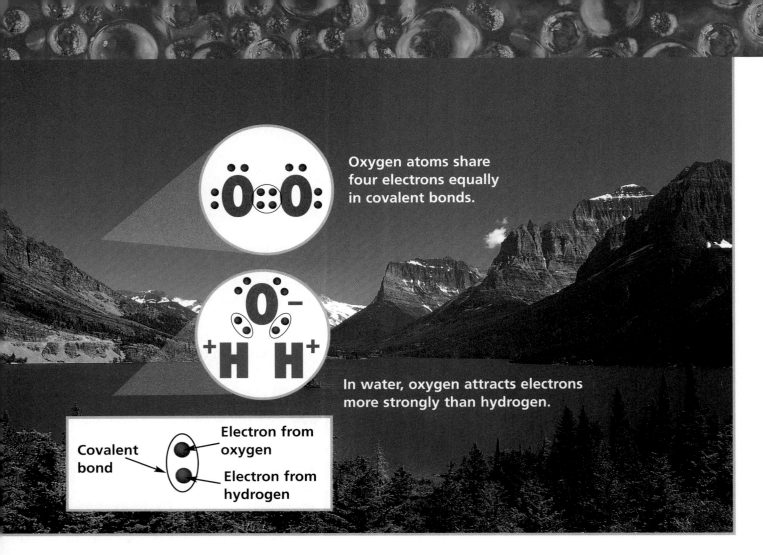

Oxygen atoms share four electrons equally in covalent bonds.

In water, oxygen attracts electrons more strongly than hydrogen.

Covalent bond

Electron from oxygen

Electron from hydrogen

How Do Covalent Bonds Form?

As you read before, every atom contains a nucleus that is positively charged. Surrounding the nucleus are electrons, which are negatively charged. The atom stays together because opposite charges attract.

Sometimes the nucleus of one atom attracts some of the outer electrons of another atom. When two nuclei attract the same electrons, they form a type of chemical bond called a *covalent bond*. In a covalent bond, two atoms share electrons. The diagram above shows electrons represented as dots. Circled dots represent a covalent bond.

Usually the elements that form covalent bonds are nonmetals, such as hydrogen, oxygen, carbon, and nitrogen. For example, every hydrogen atom has one proton and one electron. When two hydrogen atoms meet, they share their electrons in a covalent bond. Covalent bonds may form between atoms of the same element or different elements.

When the atoms are identical, they share electrons equally. When the atoms are different, one atom attracts the electrons more strongly than the other.

READING Summarize

Why do covalent bonds form?

How Do Ionic Bonds Form?

Atoms of nonmetals often have a strong ability to attract extra electrons. However, atoms of most metals have little attraction for extra electrons and may even hold some of their own electrons weakly. When these two types of atoms come into contact, the non-metallic atoms may be able to "take" electrons from the metallic atoms.

The diagram shows how an atom of the nonmetal chlorine can take an electron from an atom of the metal sodium. Note how both the sodium atom and the chlorine atom become a particle with unequal numbers of protons and electrons, called an **ion** (IGH·uhn). An ion has an electric charge. Negative ions are named by adding an -ide ending, so *chlorine* becomes *chloride* as a –1 ion.

The sodium ion in the diagram has an electric charge of +1 because it has one more proton than electron. Similarly, the chloride ion has an electric charge of –1 because it has one extra electron. Since opposite charges attract, sodium ions and chloride ions are attracted to one another. This attraction creates a type of chemical bond called an *ionic bond*.

When sodium and chlorine bond ionically, they form a compound known as sodium chloride. Sodium chloride is made up of equal numbers of sodium and chloride ions, so its chemical formula is NaCl.

▶ **Why do ionic bonds form?**

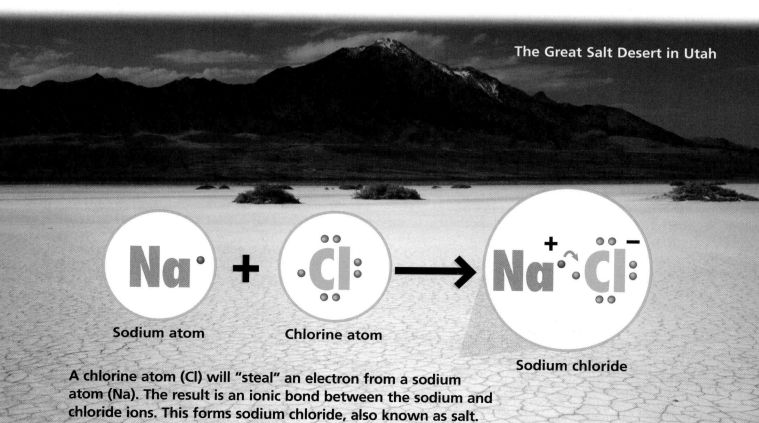

The Great Salt Desert in Utah

Sodium atom + Chlorine atom → Sodium chloride

A chlorine atom (Cl) will "steal" an electron from a sodium atom (Na). The result is an ionic bond between the sodium and chloride ions. This forms sodium chloride, also known as salt.

What Are Chemical Reactions?

Chemical changes are often called *chemical reactions*. In a chemical reaction, the original substances are called the *reactants*. The new substances are the *products*. In every chemical reaction, the reactants' atoms and bonds are rearranged to form the new products.

Many chemical reactions fall into one of several main types. Three key types of chemical reactions are a synthesis reaction, a replacement reaction, and a decomposition reaction. Synthesis reactions are so named because they involve two separate things joining together to form one compound. A decomposition is the opposite. It is the breaking down of a more complex substance into two simpler substances. A replacement reaction takes place when elements switch, or replace each other.

Synthesis Reaction

Reactants

A + B

Product

AB

$$4Fe + 3O_2 \longrightarrow 2Fe_2O_3$$

Iron   Oxygen   Iron oxide

Two elements or compounds join together to make a new compound. The rusting of steel wool is one example of a synthesis reaction.

Decomposition Reaction

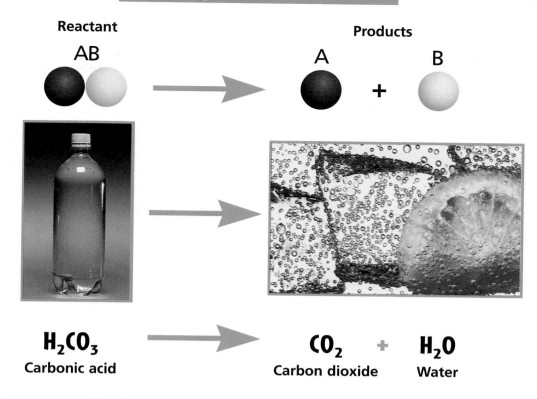

Reactant

AB

Products

A + B

$$H_2CO_3 \longrightarrow CO_2 + H_2O$$

Carbonic acid — Carbon dioxide — Water

A compound breaks apart into simpler substances. The bubbles in your favorite carbonated beverage come from a decomposition reaction.

Replacement Reaction

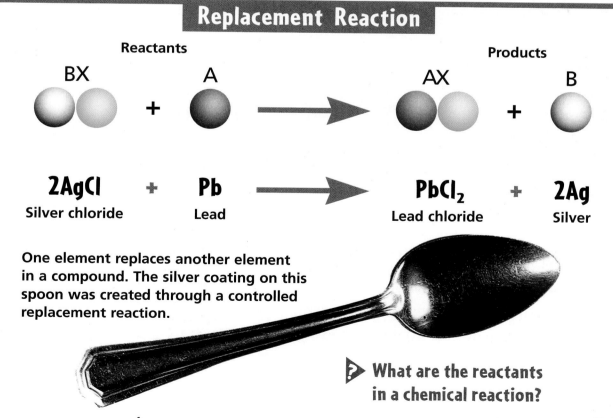

Reactants

BX + A

Products

AX + B

$$2AgCl + Pb \longrightarrow PbCl_2 + 2Ag$$

Silver chloride — Lead — Lead chloride — Silver

One element replaces another element in a compound. The silver coating on this spoon was created through a controlled replacement reaction.

▷ **What are the reactants in a chemical reaction?**

What Are an Element's Chemical Properties?

When sodium metal is dropped into water, it reacts strongly, producing hydrogen gas, sodium hydroxide, and lots of heat. The heat often causes the hydrogen to burn. Sodium's reaction to water is an example of a **chemical property**—a way of describing a substance by how it reacts to other substances.

You may recall that the elements in columns of the periodic table have similar chemical properties. The other metals in sodium's column, for example, are also quite reactive with water. An ability of a substance to undergo a chemical change is its *reactivity*. How the substance actually reacts is determined by the substance itself, and where it lies on the periodic table. The first column of the periodic table contains very reactive metals. Just exposing some of these metals to air can result in an explosion.

The last column of the periodic table contains the most *stable* elements—the noble gases. These gases rarely react with other substances.

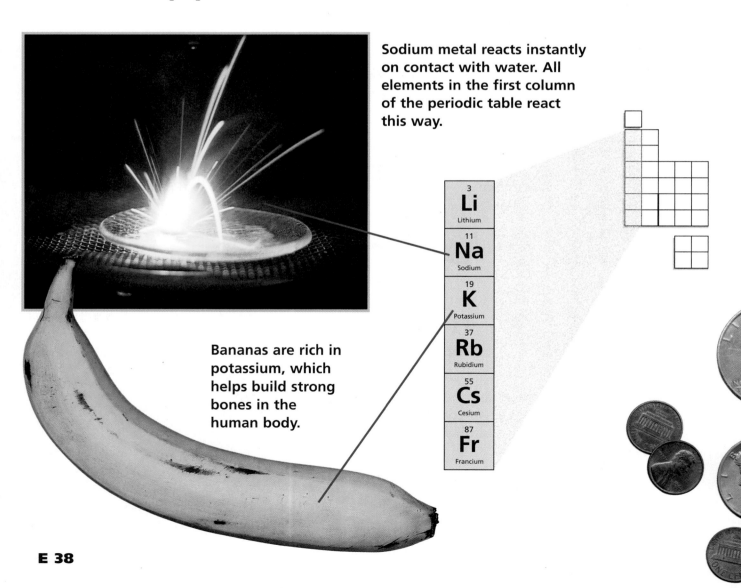

Sodium metal reacts instantly on contact with water. All elements in the first column of the periodic table react this way.

Bananas are rich in potassium, which helps build strong bones in the human body.

3
Li
Lithium

11
Na
Sodium

19
K
Potassium

37
Rb
Rubidium

55
Cs
Cesium

87
Fr
Francium

We can see why elements in columns of the periodic table share similar chemical properties if we look at the arrangements of their electrons. Electrons are organized in "layers" around atomic nuclei. If two elements have the same number of electrons in the outer layer of their atoms, they will tend to react with other substances in a similar way.

? **How does an element's placement on the periodic table determine its chemical properties?**

READING
Diagrams

1. Which elements are noble gases?

2. Name two elements that have properties similar to gold.

Because helium is less dense than air, it is used to inflate balloons.

Neon and argon can be made to glow inside signs like this one. The elements in the last column of the periodic table are called the noble gases. They rarely form compounds with other elements.

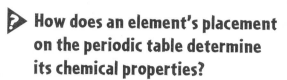

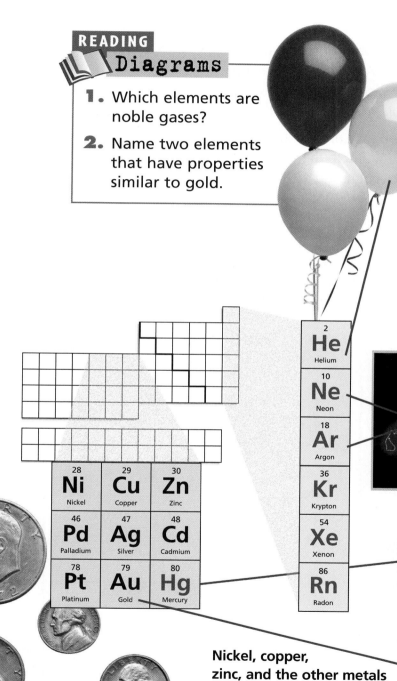

| 2 **He** Helium |
| 10 **Ne** Neon |
| 18 **Ar** Argon |
| 36 **Kr** Krypton |
| 54 **Xe** Xenon |
| 86 **Rn** Radon |

28 **Ni** Nickel	29 **Cu** Copper	30 **Zn** Zinc
46 **Pd** Palladium	47 **Ag** Silver	48 **Cd** Cadmium
78 **Pt** Platinum	79 **Au** Gold	80 **Hg** Mercury

Mercury, the only metal that is a liquid at room temperature, is used in thermometers.

Nickel, copper, zinc, and the other metals in the middle of the periodic table are much more stable than sodium. This is why they can be used to make coins.

Gold is the most valuable of all the coinage metals.

Inquiry Skill
BUILDER

SKILL Communicate

How Can You Represent Chemical Formulas?

You can represent almost any substance with a chemical formula. Here are some simple rules for writing formulas. A chemical formula is a simple way to communicate what a compound is made of. Written correctly, it can be understood around the world.

- The elements with the strongest attraction for extra electrons are written last. Elements that are higher up and farther to the right in the periodic table tend to attract electrons more strongly.

- For molecules, subscripts indicate the actual number of atoms in each molecule. For example, the formula H_2O indicates a molecule with two hydrogen atoms and one oxygen atom.

- For ionic compounds, subscripts indicate the simplest ratio of ions present.

Procedure

1 **Make a Model** The diagram shows models of several substances. Use clay balls to represent these substances. Use a different color for each element. Draw your results.

2 **Use Numbers** Write out the name of each substance. Then write a correct chemical formula below each name.

Drawing Conclusions

Communicate For each formula, write a description of how you used numbers to arrive at your answer.

Materials

clay of different colors

periodic table

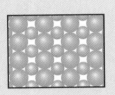

Cadmium chloride
◔ = Cadmium (Cd)
◔ = Chlorine (Cl)

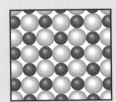

Potassium fluoride
○ = Potassium (K)
◔ = Fluorine (F)

Carbon monoxide
● = Carbon (C)
○ = Oxygen (O)

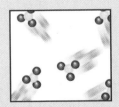

Sulfur trioxide
○ = Sulfur (S)
○ = Oxygen (O)

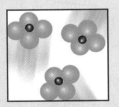

Carbon tetrachloride
● = Carbon (C)
○ = Chlorine (Cl)

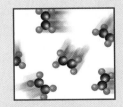

Tetrafluoroethylene
● = Carbon (C)
◔ = Fluorine (F)

What Is a Molecule?

When atoms bond covalently with one another, they can form a group of atoms called a **molecule**. The atoms of a molecule are so tightly bonded that they act like a single particle. Both elements and compounds can be made of molecules. The molecules of any given substance are always alike.

Ionic compounds are not made up of molecules. Instead, they are just collections of ions that are held together by their opposite charges. Sodium and chloride ions cluster together in the ionic compound sodium chloride, NaCl.

The ions in NaCl line up in an orderly fashion. However, there is no clear way to pair off the ions. Even though there are equal numbers of sodium and chloride ions, each ion is surrounded by many oppositely charged ions.

▷ **What compounds are made of molecules?**

The sting of an ant bite comes from a compound called formic acid. The molecule contains one carbon atom, two oxygen atoms, and two hydrogen atoms.

Ammonia in water is used to clean windows. An ammonia molecule contains three hydrogen atoms bonded to a nitrogen atom.

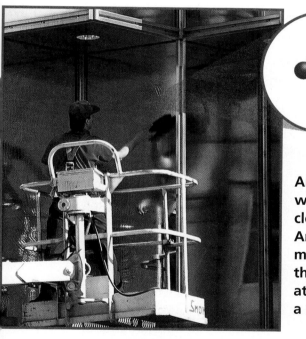

Salt does not exist as molecules. Instead blocks of sodium and chloride ions pack together in a crystal.

The tart taste of lemons, grapefruit, oranges, and many other fruits comes from an acid called citric acid.

What Is an Acid?

How are lemon juice, vinegar, and buttermilk alike? They all taste tart. They all contain compounds known as *acids*. The word *acid* refers to a wide variety of compounds with different properties and uses. However, different as they are, these compounds share some chemical and physical properties when they are dissolved in water. The properties are used to help define what acids are.

Sour taste is one common property of acids dissolved in water. However, it is not safe to taste a solution for the presence of an acid. Some acids are corrosive. They can wear away metal as well as burn skin. A safe way to test for acids is to use an *indicator* (IN·di·kay·tuhr). An indicator is a substance that changes color in the presence of a test substance. The color results from a chemical change.

For example, litmus (LIT·muhs) paper is an indicator for acids. Litmus comes in red and blue paper strips. Acids cause blue litmus paper to turn red. What if you dip litmus paper into an unknown solution? If you see a change from blue to red, you know the solution contains an acid.

A better indicator is pH paper. It measures the exact strength of acids. The pH scale is often used to determine the acidity of soil. Many plants will not grow in acidic soil.

In a car battery, metal atoms react with an acid and form a scaly crust as a product. A second product is hydrogen gas.

You may have seen the result of a similar reaction in buildings and statues made of stone. The metallic compounds in the stone react with small amounts of acid in the air. Substances from factory and car exhausts dissolve in rainwater, forming acids. When this rainwater soaks into stone, acids can react with metallic compounds and gradually wear the stone away.

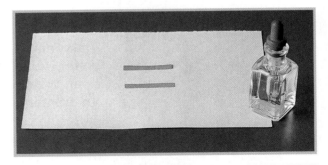

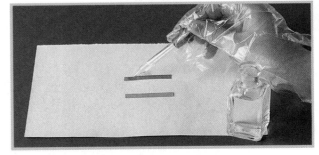

▶ **What color is blue litmus in the presence of acid?**

What Is a Base?

Luckily, milk of magnesia comes flavored. However, if your parents or a doctor ever gave you the unflavored kind, you might remember the unpleasant taste. Milk of magnesia contains a *base* mixed with water. Bases are a group of compounds that share some special properties.

Bitter taste is one common property of bases. So is a slippery feel when touched. However, you should never taste or touch a solution to see if it contains a base. Many bases are poisonous. Many can burn your skin.

Strong bases react chemically with animal substances. They dissolve hair, wool, grease, and fingernails. This property makes them useful for cleaning clogged drains. Many drain cleaners contain sodium hydroxide, a strong base that is also called lye. Lye is dangerous, however. Read the warning label on any can of drain cleaner.

Other bases are used for cleaning. You use mild bases every day when you wash with soap or shampoo your hair. More powerful bases, such as ammonium hydroxide, are used to clean floors, bathtubs, and windows.

In fact, bases serve all sorts of purposes. Inside your body bases help digest food and move oxygen in and out of your blood. A very strong base called lime is used in mortar, which holds bricks together. Another base, aluminum hydroxide, is used in deodorants.

Indicators can be used to identify bases as well as acids. Blue litmus is red in the presence of an acid. In the presence of bases, red litmus turns blue.

▷ **What color is red litmus in the presence of a base?**

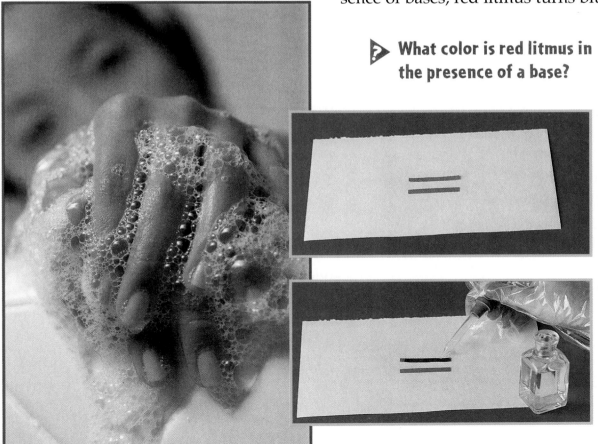

What Are Exothermic and Endothermic Reactions?

What are some signs that a chemical reaction is going on? Giving off heat and light are signs. The torch shown here produces enough heat to cut through metal. The heat is given off by oxygen gas from the green tank reacting with acetylene gas from the black tank as the gases flow out of the torch. Chemical reactions that give off heat are said to be **exothermic**.

However, not all exothermic reactions produce a flame—some release energy in smaller amounts or more slowly. For example, the temperature rises as zinc metal dissolves in a solution called sulfuric acid, but no flame is produced.

Chemical reactions can also absorb energy. Such reactions are said to be **endothermic**. While exothermic reactions can keep themselves going once started, endothermic reactions require a constant supply of energy. A constant supply of electric energy converts water into hydrogen gas and oxygen gas. As soon as the energy is turned off, the reaction stops. Why do you think hydrogen and oxygen are produced? Hint: The formula for water is H_2O.

The exothermic reaction that produces the flame is acetylene gas + oxygen → carbon dioxide + water + energy.

This exothermic reaction produces heat but no flame. The reaction is zinc + sulfuric acid → zinc sulfate + hydrogen + energy.

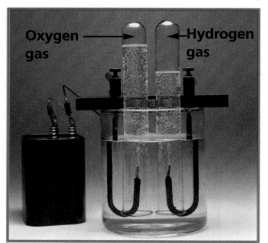

Oxygen gas

Hydrogen gas

The endothermic reaction occurring here is water + energy → hydrogen gas + oxygen gas.

▷ **What is the difference between exothermic and endothermic reactions?**

Why It Matters

A chemical change provides the energy you need to live. Food is a storehouse of chemical energy. When food is digested, your cells combine it with oxygen. This reaction is *exothermic,* because it releases the stored energy as heat. When you inhale the oxygen and exhale the two waste products, carbon dioxide and water, the reaction is called *respiration.*

e-Journal Visit our Web site www.science.mmhschool.com to do a research project on chemical changes.

Think and Write

1. What are some examples of chemical changes that you might observe? Explain your answer.

2. Are the bonds in water (H_2O) ionic or covalent? How do you know?

3. What are some kinds of chemical changes that release energy?

4. **INQUIRY SKILL** **Communicate** Pure hydrogen and oxygen are both gases. However, when they combine, they make liquid water. How can you represent this reaction using chemical formulas?

5. **Critical Thinking** Why would bromine atoms and chlorine atoms tend to have similar chemical properties?

L·I·N·K·S

LITERATURE LINK

Read *Building the Hoover Dam* to learn about what it would be like to be part of the crew building the dam. Try the activities at the end of the book.

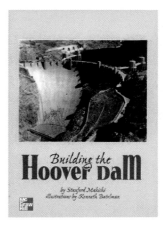

WRITING LINK

Writing That Compares How are lemon juice, vinegar, and buttermilk alike? Make a list of properties common to all three. Then make a list of differences. Use your lists to write an essay that compares and contrasts two of these acids.

MATH LINK

Find ratios. Look at different compounds, such as HF, KCl, $MgCl_2$, CCl_4, and H_2S. Find the ratio of elements in each.

TECHNOLOGY LINK

 LOG ON Visit www.science.mmhschool.com for more links.

History of Science

Atoms Through Time

Aristotle, another Greek, teaches that the world is made not of atoms but of four elements—earth, air, water, and fire. He's a very influential thinker, so his theory holds for nearly 2,000 years!

French chemist Antoine Lavoisier discovers the Law of Conservation of Mass. He proves that elements combine to form compounds confirming English scientist Robert Boyle's hypothesis made over 100 years earlier. He shows that burning fuels rapidly combine with oxygen. Today, Lavoisier is called the father of modern day chemistry.

| 430 B.C | 335 B.C. | 1788 | 1803 |

Democritus, a philosopher in ancient Greece, suggests that matter is made of atoms, but he can't prove it. *Atom* is Greek for "unbreakable."

Ancient Greece

Aegean Sea

Turkey

Athens

Rhodes

Crete

The English chemist John Dalton proves that atoms exist. He determines a compound's elements, then calculates the weight of each element's atom in that compound. He discovers that atoms of different elements have different weights. However, he thinks a compound has only one atom of an element, so water is HO. Italian scientist Amadeo Avogadro discovers that a compound can have more than one atom of an element, as in H_2O.

J. J. Thomson, an English scientist, finds electrons. He decides that an atom is a positively charged sphere in which there are also tiny negatively charged particles called electrons.

Niels Bohr, a Danish scientist, discovers that the number of electrons in the outside orbit, or "shell," of an atom, determines its chemical properties.

1897   **1911**   **1913**

English scientist Ernest Rutherford discovers that atoms consist of a positively charged nucleus that has electrons rotating around it at great speeds.

Write
ABOUT IT

1. Compare Rutherford's model with Dalton's.

2. Why is it important to know how many electrons are in the outside orbit of an atom?

LOG ON Visit **www.science.mmhschool.com** to learn more about atoms.

E 47

Vocabulary

Fill each blank with the best word or words from the list.

chemical change, E32
density, E7
electron, E20
endothermic, E44
exothermic, E44
matter, E6
neutron, E20
physical change, E10
proton, E20
volume, E6

1. The amount of space an object takes up is called its _____.

2. A positively charged particle in the nucleus of an atom is called a(n) _____.

3. A reaction that releases heat is _____.

4. A neutral particle in the nucleus of an atom is called a(n) _____.

5. Boiling and freezing are examples of a(n) _____.

6. All things are made up of _____.

7. A substance with new and different properties is produced by a(n) _____.

8. An object with less _____ than water will float on water.

9. A particle with a negative charge that moves around the nucleus of an atom is a(n) _____.

10. A reaction that takes in heat is _____.

Test Prep

11. Which object has the greatest mass?
   A a table tennis ball
   B a volleyball
   C a bowling ball
   D a baseball

12. A penny is an example of a(n) _____.
   F solution
   G alloy
   H colloid
   J emulsion

13. All of the following are examples of chemical changes EXCEPT _____.
   A toast browning
   B milk souring
   C ice melting
   D candles burning

14. Which of the following are properties of metals?

- **F** They conduct heat and electricity.
- **G** They are shiny when polished.
- **H** They bend rather than break.
- **J** All of the above

15. A particle with uneven numbers of protons and electrons is a(n) _____.

- **A** ion
- **B** compound
- **C** molecule
- **D** atom

Concepts and Skills

16. Reading in Science A friend doesn't believe atoms exist. What evidence might convince your friend atoms do exist?

17. Critical Thinking If you seal an empty glass pickle jar and drop it in water, it floats. How can it float if the glass is denser than water?

18. INQUIRY SKILL **Communicate** Keep a diary of all the chemical changes and physical changes you come across during one day. How do these changes affect you?

19. Scientific Methods You shaped a lump of clay into a tiny dog. Describe a method you could use to find the volume of the clay.

20. Decision Making Why would it be inaccurate to speak of an NaCl molecule?

Did You Ever Wonder?

INQUIRY SKILL **Experiment** Take two slices of bread. Toast one piece well done. Place both pieces on separate paper plates. What differences do you observe? What kind of change has taken place in the toasted slice?

LOG ON Visit www.science.mmhschool.com to boost your test scores.

Heat Energy

Did You Ever Wonder?

How hot is the Sun? Actually, the temperature changes from about 6,000°C (10,800°F) at the Sun's surface to 15,000,000°C (27,000,000°F) deep inside the Sun. Is temperature the same as heat? How can we use heat energy from the Sun?

INQUIRY SKILL Infer In cold climates, why do people wear two to three layers of clothing?

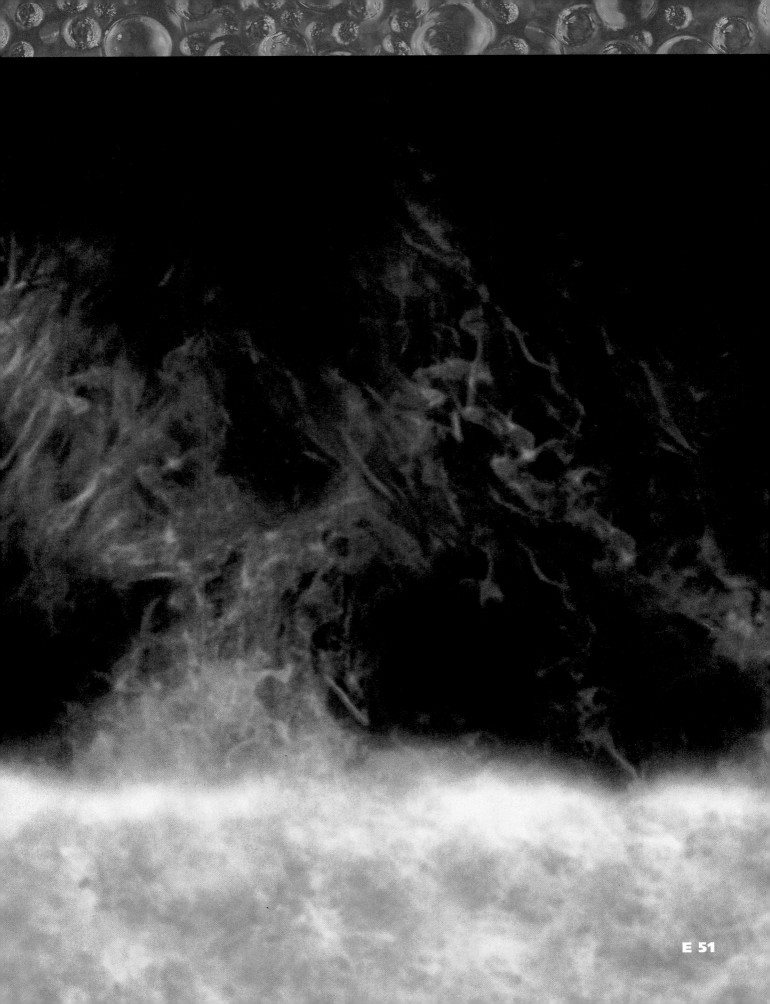

LESSON 4

Temperature and Heat

Vocabulary

kinetic energy, E55

potential energy, E55

temperature, E56

heat, E57

radiation, E58

conduction, E59

convection, E59

insulation, E62

Get Ready

Your skin is filled with nerve endings. They are sensitive to touch, to pressure, to pain, and to hot and cold.

How good is your skin at telling hot from cold? Usually it is good enough to trigger you to pull your hand away from extreme heat or cold—even before you get a chance to think about it. Can your skin recognize smaller differences in temperature?

Inquiry Skill

You experiment when you perform a test to support or disprove a hypothesis.

Explore Activity

How Can You Tell Warm from Cold?

Procedure

1 **Investigate** How reliable are your fingers as temperature sensors? Fill glass 1 with warm water, not hot water. Fill glass 2 with room-temperature water. Fill glass 3 with cold water from a refrigerator.

2 **Observe** Hold the three middle fingers of your left hand in the warm water. Hold the three middle fingers of your right hand in the cold water. Record the difference in what you feel.

3 **Experiment** Hold your fingers in the same glasses again, as in step 2. Then quickly put both the left- and right-hand fingers in room-temperature water. Record what you feel.

Drawing Conclusions

1 **Hypothesize** When you put both hands in the room-temperature water, did they feel the same? Explain why you felt what you did.

2 **Evaluate** Based on your observations, do you think your skin is a reliable way to tell how hot or cold something is?

3 FURTHER INQUIRY **Experiment** Determine how small a difference in temperature you can detect. 5°C? 2°C? 1°C? Is the 2-degree difference more detectable in cool water or warm water?

Main Idea Heat energy can flow from one material to another, changing the temperature of the material.

How Is Energy Related to Motion?

The words *hot*, *warm*, *cool*, and *cold* are words used to describe the *temperature* of something. For example, the heating coils of a toaster oven are red hot. They have an extremely high temperature. You must not touch them because you would severely burn yourself. Why do they have a high temperature? The answer to this important question has to do with the movement of molecules or atoms.

Although we can easily see the motion of large objects—trees swaying in the wind, cars speeding down the highway, or rocks tumbling down a mountainside—we cannot see the tiny molecules that make up all of these things. What kind of motion do the molecules themselves have?

Through many experiments scientists have learned about molecular motion. For example, molecules in solids vibrate back and forth. Molecules

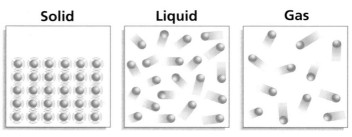

Solid	Liquid	Gas

Motion of molecules in solids, liquids, and gases

in gases move in straight lines between collisions. Molecules in liquids show a mix of these types of motion.

Any moving object—from a molecule to a car—has energy due to its motion. This energy is not a fluid that can flow from the moving object, nor is it any kind of matter we could pluck from the moving object. Energy is more like an ability than a material "thing"—it is the ability to move other matter around. A swung bat, for example, shows that it has energy by knocking a baseball into the outfield.

▷ **What is energy?**

The heating coils in a toaster oven are extremely hot. Some of the coils' energy warms and toasts the bread.

The energy of a roller coaster changes between kinetic energy (motion) and potential energy (height).

	Form of Energy	Source
Kinds of potential energy	atomic	radioactive materials
	chemical	batteries
	gravitational	any two masses in the universe
Kinds of kinetic energy	heat	the Sun
	mechanical	machines
	sound	vibrations

What Are Two Main Kinds of Energy?

The energy of any moving object is called **kinetic** (ki·NET·ik) **energy**. A speeding roller coaster has a great deal of kinetic energy as it reaches the bottom of the first hill. What happens to this energy when the roller coaster slows as it climbs the next hill?

Since about 1840, scientists have known that energy cannot be destroyed or created. It can only be changed from one form to another. The kinetic energy of the roller coaster cannot disappear. In fact, the kinetic energy turns into a new form, called **potential** (puh·TEN·shuhl) **energy**, as the roller coaster climbs a hill.

Potential energy is energy stored in an object or material. Moving an object upward against gravity is one way to give it potential energy. Chemical bonds can also be a source of potential energy.

Regardless of the type or source of energy, we measure it with the same units. The amount of kinetic energy gained by a 1-kilogram object falling from a height of 10.2 centimeters is known as a *joule* (JEWL). A joule is also equal to 0.24 calorie. One calorie is the amount of energy that will raise the temperature of 1 gram of water by 1°C.

> **How are kinetic energy and potential energy different?**

This mass will gain 1 joule of kinetic energy if the student lets it fall to the tabletop.

If these cars were molecules, the temperature would be related to the average speed of the cars.

A thermometer works because a liquid inside expands as it gets hotter.

What Is Temperature?

When you watch cars go by, they are traveling at a number of different speeds. However, if you think of them as a group, you can understand what the average speed of the cars is. Many of the cars will move at speeds near the average speed, while only a few will drive at extra-high or extra-low speeds.

Like the cars, the molecules in a material move about at different speeds. Taken together they have an average speed. Most of the molecules have speeds near the average, while only a few molecules travel at speeds far above or below the average.

The average speed of the molecules in a material determines the molecules' average kinetic energy. In turn, the average kinetic energy of the molecules determines how hot or cold the material is—its **temperature**.

A temperature reading tells you something about the average kinetic energy of a material's molecules.

Thermometers can be used to measure temperature. They often have a liquid that expands when the thermometer is placed in warmer materials. The expansion pushes the liquid along a scale that has degree marks. Scientists prefer to use instruments like thermometers to avoid having to depend directly on human senses for measurements.

▷ **How can temperature be measured?**

What Is Heat?

Two containers of water are connected by a metal bar. The containers are made of a material that heat cannot move through—from outside in or from inside out. Metals, you recall, conduct heat. The metal bar is wrapped with thick rubber, which will not let the heat escape. The water in the two containers is at different temperatures.

What will happen to the temperature readings as time goes by?

The diagram below shows what happens when a hot object is placed in contact with a cooler one—energy always flows from the hotter object to the cooler one, never the reverse. Energy will continue to flow until the two objects reach the same temperature. When the objects are both at the same temperature, their molecules will have the same average kinetic energy, as in the diagram.

When energy flows between two objects because they have different temperatures, we call the energy **heat**. Heat is a form of energy. We measure it in energy units—such as joules or calories.

READING **Sequence of Events**
What happens when you put a hot object in contact with a cooler one?

Measuring Heat Flow

At Start

Temperature = 80°C   Temperature = 60°C

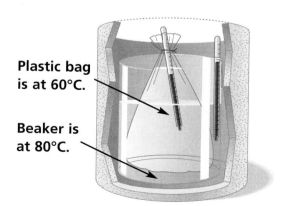

Plastic bag is at 60°C.

Beaker is at 80°C.

One Hour Later

Temperature = 70°C   Temperature = 70°C

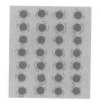 

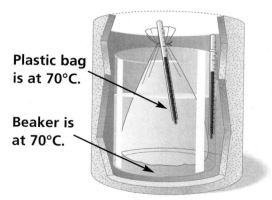

Plastic bag is at 70°C.

Beaker is at 70°C.

What Are Radiation, Conduction, and Convection?

Radiation is the transfer of energy by electromagnetic waves. The Sun producing light is one example of radiation. All objects give off a wide range of electromagnetic waves. Electromagnetic radiation can travel from the Sun to Earth through space. However, radiation also can be produced by objects on Earth. It comes in the forms of infrared, visible, and ultraviolet waves. The strength of each type of radiation depends on the temperature of the object.

Objects with temperatures near or below room temperature give off mainly infrared radiation, which our eyes cannot see. However, when

When a stove burner is hot enough, some of its electromagnetic waves are visible as red light.

objects are heated to about 600°C (1,112°F), they begin to give off a lot of visible light. We can see them "glowing" dull red, like the stove burner in the photograph. As the temperature rises to thousands of degrees, the color becomes yellowish and then blue-white.

Electromagnetic waves carry energy, so objects that absorb electromagnetic radiation receive energy. Energy is transferred from one object to another by the electromagnetic waves.

When a material absorbs electro-magnetic energy, many things can happen. The material's temperature may rise, as in the solar collectors shown in the photograph.

The material may change from one state of matter to another, such as snow melting in warm sunshine. The energy in the Sun's rays, especially the ultraviolet waves, can even cause chemical changes in the molecules of materials. This is how sunlight causes the color of outdoor paint to fade or a sunbather's skin to burn.

Radiation from the Sun contains a lot of energy. Solar panels can absorb that radiation. The energy can be used to heat homes or make electricity.

What happens to the sauce in a pan when the heater is on? It gets warmer. Why? The answer has to do with the movement of atoms and molecules in the burner, pan, and sauce.

The burner on a stove is very hot, which means its atoms are moving very, very fast. When these fast-moving atoms hit the pan, the pan's atoms move faster. When the pan's atoms hit the molecules in the sauce, the sauce molecules speed up, making the sauce hotter.

The movement of energy through direct contact is called **conduction**. Conduction is the only way heat can travel through solids.

Another type of heat transfer, called **convection**, can occur in liquids and gases. Convection is the transfer of energy by the flow of a liquid or gas. In the atmosphere, for example, warmer air carries heat upward. The warm air rises because of its lower density. Cooler air is more dense and sinks.

> ▶ **What is the difference between conduction and convection?**

Conduction and Convection

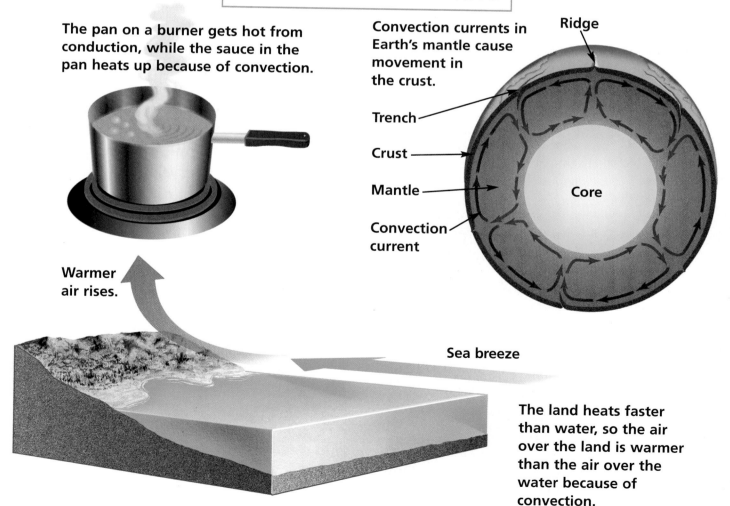

The pan on a burner gets hot from conduction, while the sauce in the pan heats up because of convection.

Warmer air rises.

Convection currents in Earth's mantle cause movement in the crust.

Ridge

Trench

Crust

Mantle

Core

Convection current

Sea breeze

The land heats faster than water, so the air over the land is warmer than the air over the water because of convection.

Do Some Materials Warm Faster than Others?

The photograph shows an experiment: identical beakers, one containing 1 kilogram of water and the other containing 1 kilogram of copper pellets, are placed on a hot plate. The graph shows how the temperatures of the water and copper change. As you can see, the copper wins the temperature race—it warms up faster than the water.

The copper and the water show us that equal masses of different materials have a different temperature change for the same amount of heat absorbed. The particular rate at which a material warms up upon absorbing heat is a physical property. We can use this property to tell one material or substance from another. Examine the

Which warms up faster— liquid water or solid water?

Materials		Temperature Rise for 1 Gram Absorbing 1 Calorie of Heat
Water	(liquid)	1.0°C
Water	(solid)	1.7°C
Aluminum	(solid)	4.7°C
Rock	(solid)	4.8–5.6°C
Copper	(solid)	10.8°C
Mercury	(liquid)	30.3°C

table to see how the temperature of 1 gram of various materials will rise for each calorie of heat absorbed.

You can see from the table that 1 gram of liquid water rises less in temperature than 1 gram of many other substances per calorie of heat absorbed. This makes water a good coolant. When cool water is pumped through a hot car engine, for example, the water can absorb a relatively large amount of heat as it warms toward the temperature of the engine.

▶ **Which material warms up faster–copper or water?**

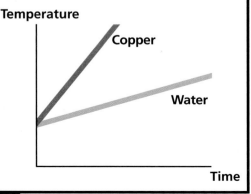

Inquiry Skill
BUILDER

Which Warms Faster—Water or Sand?

Perhaps you have visited a sandy beach on a sunny day and noticed that the sand is too hot to walk on, while the water feels comfortable. Does sand warm up faster than water from the same amount of heat? Design an experiment to answer this question.

In an experiment a variable is something that can affect the outcome. For example, in testing how rapidly water and sand warm up, the length of time the materials are heated would affect their temperature. To make the test "fair," you would have to heat both materials for the same length of time. Making sure that a variable is the same for all samples being tested is called *controlling* the variable.

Materials
desk lamp

thermometers

sand

water

2 containers

Procedure

1 **Hypothesize** Which warms up faster—water or sand? Write a hypothesis.

2 **Use Variables** Make a list of the variables that could affect how rapidly sand and water would warm up when heated.

3 Write a procedure to compare how fast water and sand warm up for the same amount of heat. Have your teacher check your plan.

4 If possible, carry out your procedure. Write a report that describes your results.

Drawing Conclusions

Interpret Data Summarize your results. Use graphs to show temperature changes of the two substances over time. Explain your results.

The Trans-Alaska Pipeline carries hot crude oil about 1,287 kilometers (800 miles) across Alaska. The oil must be kept hot to keep it flowing well. To keep the oil hot, the pipeline is insulated with fiberglass. The insulation also prevents heat from damaging the frozen land where the pipe is buried.

This worker is blowing loose-fill fiberglass insulation into the attic of a home.

What Is Insulation?

There are many instances in our everyday lives where it is important to keep heat from entering or leaving something.

Preventing heat from flowing in or out of a material is called **insulation**. You *insulate* something by wrapping it securely with a material that is not a good conductor of heat.

In cold months much of the heat lost from a home tends to escape through the roof, so it is important to insulate the attic well. The glass fibers in the insulation are poor conductors of heat. More importantly, there is a great deal of air trapped in the fluffy material. Air is a very poor conductor of heat, and the air adds greatly to the insulating ability of the fiberglass.

Foam, made by mixing air into plastic, makes a good insulator.

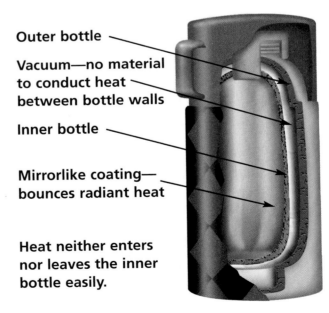

Outer bottle

Vacuum—no material to conduct heat between bottle walls

Inner bottle

Mirrorlike coating— bounces radiant heat

Heat neither enters nor leaves the inner bottle easily.

▷ **What are some examples of insulation?**

Why It Matters

Does your family cook meals in a microwave oven? If so, you may have noticed that the food gets hot but the dish does not. Microwave ovens take advantage of the transfer of heat by radiation. They produce microwaves, which only water molecules tend to absorb. Anything containing water, such as food, gets hot, but materials without water do not.

e-Journal Visit our Web site **www.science.mmhschool.com** to do a research project on temperature and heat.

Think and Write

1. How does energy change as a bicycle rider coasts down a hill?

2. How do molecules in an ice cube at 0°C compare with molecules at 20°C?

3. If you stand near a hot toaster, why can you feel the heat?

4. **INQUIRY SKILL** **Use Variables** To see which warms faster, Ralph heats a liter of water and a liter of oil on his stove. Which variables should he control in this experiment?

5. **Critical Thinking** Will wrapping a warm sandwich in aluminum foil keep it warm longer than a foam box? Make a hypothesis. How would you test it?

MATH LINK

Solve a problem. Liquid water rises 1°C for every calorie it absorbs; however, solid water rises 1.7°C for every calorie it absorbs. How many more calories will it take to increase the temperature of one gram of liquid water 10°C than it will take to increase the temperature of one gram of solid water 10°C?

Materials	Temperature Rise for 1 Gram Absorbing 1 Calorie of Heat
Water (liquid)	1.0°C
Water (solid)	1.7°C

WRITING LINK

Expository Writing What is insulation? How is it important in conserving energy? Research this topic and write a report. Summarize information from more than one source. Draw a conclusion based on the information you find.

TECHNOLOGY LINK

Science Newsroom CD-ROM Choose *Heat Flow* to learn more about how heat moves through matter.

LOG ON Visit **www.science.mmhschool.com** for more links.

GLOBAL WARMING

The average temperature on Earth's surface is 14°C (57°F). The coldest temperature, –89°C (–128.6°F), was recorded in Antarctica in 1983. The highest temperature, 58°C (136°F), was recorded in northern Africa in 1922. In comparison the temperature of Earth's core is thought to be about 5,000°C (9,032°F) or more!

Record highs and lows like these are exceptions. Looking at the average temperatures in the five climate zones gives a clearer picture of how hot or cold Earth's air is.

°F | °C

Record high

140 · 60
120 · 50
100 · 40
80 · 30
· 20
60
40 · 10
· 0
20
· –10
0 · –20
–20 · –30
–40 · –40
–60 · –50
–80 · –60
–100 · –70
· –80
–120 · –90

Record low

The Sun warms Earth by radiation, and Earth heats the air above it by convection. The farther air is from Earth's surface, the less heat it gets by convection.

Some scientists believe that a buildup of gases, such as carbon dioxide, nitric oxide, and methane trap heat that normally would escape from Earth. Called the "greenhouse effect," this raises temperatures and leads to global warming.

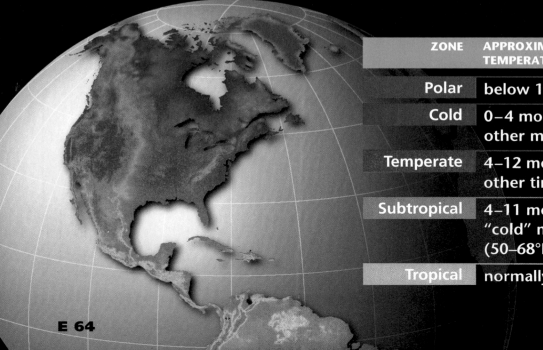

ZONE	APPROXIMATE AVERAGE TEMPERATURES
Polar	below 10°C (50°F) all year
Cold	0–4 months at 10–20°C, other months colder
Temperate	4–12 months at 10–20°C, other times colder
Subtropical	4–11 months above 20°C, "cold" months 10–20°C (50–68°F)
Tropical	normally above 20°C (68°F)

Since 1850 the average temperature on Earth has risen about 1°C (1.8°F). Some scientists predict it will rise 2°C (3.5°F) more by the year 2100. They believe this will lead to many problems, including the melting of polar ice caps that would cause sea levels to rise and flood coastal areas.

At the troposphere's outer edge, temperatures are –51°C to –79°C (–60°F to –110°F). The ozone layer, located at the outermost part of the troposphere, filters the Sun's radiation, so temperatures rise. In the thermosphere temperatures can reach 1,000°C (1,830°F) or more.

Exosphere

Thermosphere

Mesosphere

Stratosphere

Troposphere

Write ABOUT IT

1. What is global warming?

2. How have people contributed to an increase in Earth's temperatures?

 LOG ON Visit www.science.mmhschool.com to learn more about global warming.

How Heat Affects Matter

Inquiry Skill

You **hypothesize** when you make a statement that can be tested to answer a question.

Get Ready

What effect does heating have on the air? These balloonists use burners to heat the air in each of the balloon's bags. Why does a balloon filled with heated air rise?

Explore Activity

What Can Heat Do to Matter?

Materials
balloon
2 deep pans
warm water
ice-cold water
tape measure

Procedure

1. **Predict** What do you think will happen to the size of an inflated balloon if it is heated? Cooled? Record your predictions.

2. Blow up a balloon to the point where it is filled with just enough air to keep its shape and be slightly firm to the touch. Measure it around its greatest circumference with the tape measure. Record your data.

3. **Experiment** Hold the balloon under the warm water for five minutes.

4. **Observe** Remove the balloon and measure it again. Record your data. How did it change from step 2?

5. **Experiment** Repeat steps 3 and 4 with the ice water. Record your data.

Drawing Conclusions

1. **Communicate** What happened when you put the balloon in the warm water? The ice water?

2. **Infer** How does heat affect a gas?

3. FURTHER INQUIRY
   Hypothesize What do you think will happen if you use larger or smaller balloons? How important is the amount of time that you leave the balloon submerged? Try an experiment to find out.

Main Idea Adding or removing heat energy can cause matter to change between solid, liquid, or gas states.

What Is Thermal Expansion?

What happens to a gas that is heated? A gas expands when it is heated. In general, any kind of matter expands when its temperature is raised. We call this effect **thermal expansion**.

For example, as the coolant in a car becomes hotter, it expands. The plastic container shown in the photograph provides extra space for hot coolant to expand into. When the engine is cool, the fluid contracts and no longer overflows into the container.

A bimetallic strip is made of two different metals fused together. When heated, one metal expands more than the other. This causes the strip to bend. Bimetallic strips are used in thermostat switches that turn devices on or off depending on temperature.

If it were not for separations placed between sections of a roadway, like those shown in the photograph, the roadway might buckle and bend on the hottest days. Similar separations are placed in concrete sidewalks to prevent damage due to thermal expansion.

The steel in this roadway expands on hot days and contracts on cold days.

Cars have a liquid coolant that flows through the engine to remove excess heat.

An unheated bimetallic strip

A heated bimetallic strip

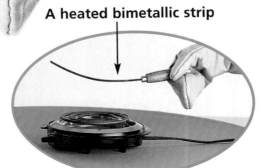

How Heat Affects Volume

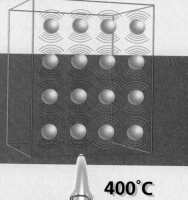

25°C   400°C

The molecules move farther apart in the hot solid as they vibrate back and forth. This causes the hot solid to take up more space.

READING
Diagrams

What happens to the volume of a heated solid? Why?

What happens inside a solid, liquid, or gas as its temperature goes up? As the temperature of a solid, liquid, or gas is raised, its particles move around faster. Each particle moves over a larger region and tends to keep neighboring molecules out of its space. As a result, the material that is made up of the particles increases in volume.

Different materials expand or contract with changing temperature at their own particular rate. An aluminum rod, for example, expands about three times more than a glass rod from the same change in temperature.

A glass that is very hot shatters when it is placed in cold water. Why do you think this happens? Upon touching the cold water, the glass begins to contract. However, glass does not conduct heat well, so parts of the glass that are not yet in contact with the water remain expanded. The uneven contraction can cause enough stress to break the glass.

Laboratory glassware is made of a special glass that expands much less with temperature changes than ordinary glass. The smaller amount of thermal expansion makes laboratory glassware less likely to break when heated or cooled rapidly.

▷ **What causes thermal expansion?**

This beaker is made of a special heat-resistant glass.

What Is Pressure?

What are tires on motor vehicles and bicycles filled with? How can gases support the weight of a motor vehicle or a bike and rider? Gases are made of particles that fly around in rapid motion. The molecules hit each other and the walls of their container—a tire in this case.

The countless hits of tiny particles against the tire walls each second add up to create a push called the **pressure** of the gas. Pressure is the force on each unit of area of a surface, such as the inside surface of the tire. If enough air is pumped into a tire, the pressure can easily support a heavy vehicle.

Perhaps you have pumped air into a tire yourself with a hand pump. If so, you know that the pressure of the gas gets greater as you move the handle down. Why does this happen? Air enters the pump when you pull up on the handle. The particles in the air under these conditions are fairly spread out. When you press down on the handle, the particles are forced into a smaller volume. They crowd together and hit the walls of the pump more often. More hits each second causes the pressure to be greater, and the higher-pressure air is forced into the tire.

The pressure in the tire results from colliding gas molecules inside it.

Charles' Law

The atmosphere pushes the mercury down.

The air in the bottle pushes the mercury up.

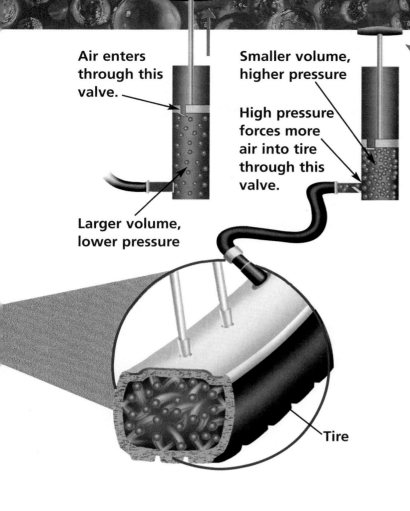

Air enters through this valve.

Larger volume, lower pressure

Smaller volume, higher pressure

High pressure forces more air into tire through this valve.

Tire

You have just seen how the pressure of a gas gets greater when its volume becomes smaller, a relationship known as Boyle's law. This is completely true only when the temperature of the gas does not change. A change in temperature can also affect the pressure of a gas. Therefore, we have to be careful to take into account both the volume and the temperature of a gas when predicting its pressure.

Exactly how does the pressure of a gas depend on its temperature? You know that particles travel faster at higher temperatures. In a heated gas, the increased speed of the particles makes them hit the walls of the container with more force. As long as the container's volume does not change, the particles also hit the walls more often. The increased force and greater number of collisions cause the pressure to go up as the temperature of the gas rises.

We also find that the volume of a gas increases when we raise its temperature while keeping its pressure constant. This relationship is known as Charles' law. The diagram shows an experiment that would demonstrate how a gas sample obeys Charles' law.

The drop of mercury in the tube indicates the volume of the gas in the bottle.

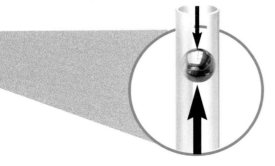

As the temperature rises, the air in the bottle expands. This pushes the mercury drop higher.

 **What causes pressure?**

What Causes Changes of State?

Matter commonly exists in one of three states—solid, liquid, or gas. Adding or removing energy causes matter to change from one state to another.

In a solid the particles are "locked" into organized positions. The particles move but can only vibrate back and forth from their individual positions. You can think of the particles as "jogging" in place.

When heat is supplied to a solid, the particles begin to vibrate faster and faster as their temperature rises. Eventually, a point is reached where the particles move fast enough to break free of the forces holding them in place. The particles begin sliding past one another. This process is called **melting**. Melting is the changing of a solid to a liquid.

The particles in the liquid still vibrate but move freely past one another. However, the particles do remain close together because of forces of attraction. If heat is steadily supplied to a liquid, the particles will once again move faster and faster as the temperature rises. At some point they will move with enough speed to escape the liquid and form a gas. The change of a liquid to a gas is called **vaporization**. In the gaseous state, the particles have great freedom of motion and are very spread out.

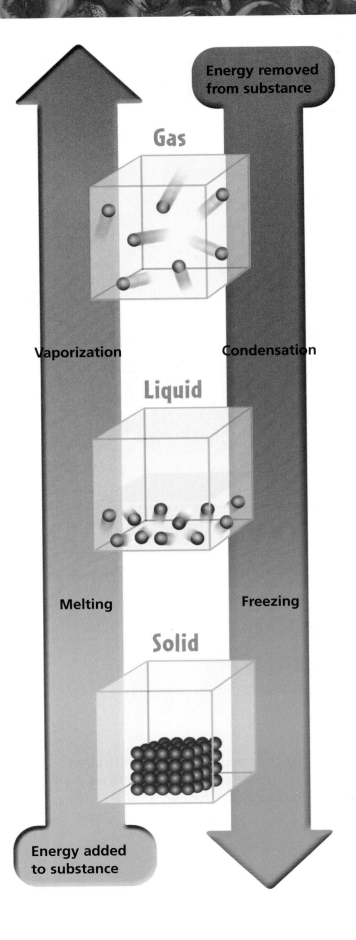

If energy is steadily removed from a gas, the particles slow down as the temperature falls. Eventually, the attractive forces cause **condensation**—the gas turns back into a liquid. If energy is steadily removed from the liquid, the particles will eventually be locked back into fixed positions by attractive forces. This change of the liquid to a solid is called **freezing**.

The temperature of a substance does not change while a change of state occurs. During melting or vaporization, the energy flowing into the substance breaks the attraction between particles. The temperature does not rise until all of the substance has changed state.

In a similar way, the energy it took to break attraction in melting or vaporization must be removed when particles come back together during condensation or freezing. The surroundings are so busy removing this energy that they cannot slow the particles down and cause their temperature to fall.

The temperature of a vaporizing liquid stays unchanged while a liquid is **boiling**, even though the liquid is being heated. Boiling occurs when bubbles of vapor escape from a liquid as a result of heating. Liquids may also turn to gas at lower temperatures when particles vaporize at the surface. This process is called **evaporation**.

▷ **How can matter be changed from a solid to a liquid?**

READING

Graphs

How does the amount of energy in a substance change as the substance changes from solid to liquid? From liquid to gas?

Temperature and Change of State

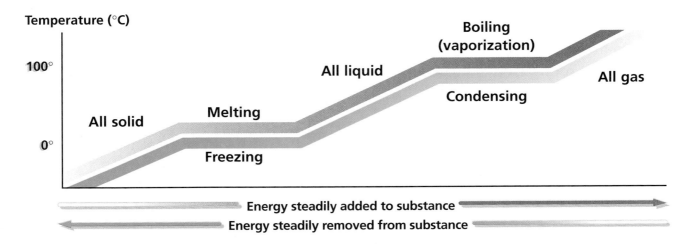

Temperature (°C)

100°

All solid

Melting

Freezing

All liquid

0°

Boiling (vaporization)

Condensing

All gas

Energy steadily added to substance →
← Energy steadily removed from substance

What Are Two Ways to Heat a Room?

Many homes and other buildings are heated by steam. In this type of heating system, changes of state in water are used to transfer energy from a fire in a furnace to air in a room. Follow what is happening in the diagram on this page.

Air in the room itself is heated by conduction and radiation. Conduction means that the air in the room comes into contact with the hot pipes of the radiator. Molecular collisions spread from the metal of the pipes to the molecules of gases in the air touching the pipes. Radiation means that waves of energy—infrared energy in this case—spread through the room.

Convection helps circulate the air in the room. That means that air circulates because heated air is less dense than cooler air and rises in the room. As it cools, it sinks back down.

Rooms in homes and buildings can also be heated with air alone. Such systems are often called forced-air heating. Note that forced-air heating does not involve changes of state, like steam heating.

Air in the room itself is heated largely by hot air forced up from the furnace. As with steam heating, convection helps to circulate air.

Steam Heat

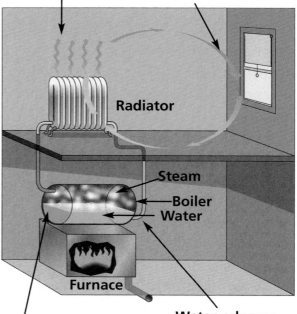

Hot pipes give off heat to the room by conduction and radiation.

Air heated by conduction circulates through the room by convection.

Radiator

Steam

Boiler

Water

Furnace

Water stores heat from the flame by vaporizing into steam.

Water releases stored heat by condensing from steam into liquid.

READING Diagrams

1. What happens at the radiator?
2. In which ways is heat transferred to the air in the room?

Forced-Air Heat

Hot air is blown out of vents into the room, where it cools as it transfers energy to the living space.

Convection helps to circulate air in the room.

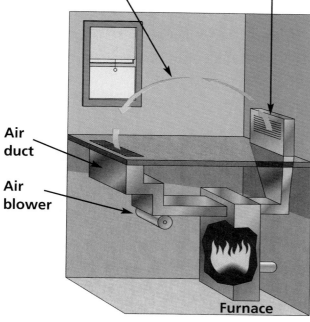

Air duct

Air blower

Furnace

Air blowers: The air blower forces air through the furnace, where it is heated by a flame.

Air duct: Cooler air is led back to the blower by the air duct.

READING Diagrams

1. How is the furnace in this system used differently from the furnace in a steam-heating system?

2. How is air in the room heated from the air vents?

▷ How is a forced-air heating system different from a steam-heating system?

QUICK LAB

Color Swirl

FOLDABLES Make a Half-Book with three tabs cut to look like a beaker. (See page R 41.) Label as shown.

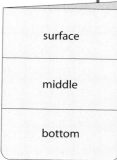

surface

middle

bottom

1. Fill a 250-mL beaker three-fourths full of warm water. Use a tablespoon to gently lower a food-colored ice cube into the water until it floats off. Keep the water as still as possible. Slide the spoon out of the water.

2. **Observe** Watch the beaker for several minutes. Sketch on your Half-Book what happens. Record the data in the Half-Book.

3. Measure the water temperature at the bottom, the middle, and just below the surface. Record the data.

4. Repeat step 3 after several minutes.

5. **Infer** What do you see in the beaker? Why is it happening? Be sure your idea is supported by all your data.

How Can Gases Drive a Car?

In the engine of a motor vehicle, gasoline is burned. The heat from the burning gasoline warms gases produced by the burning to high temperatures. The high temperatures, in turn, cause the gases to push on pistons, which are forced downward. A mechanical linkage then allows the motion of the pistons to propel the vehicle.

Most gasoline engines have a four-stroke cycle. Examine the diagram to learn what happens in each stroke and how the key parts of the engine do their jobs.

READING Sequence of Events
What is the sequence of strokes in a four-stroke engine?

Four-Stroke Engine Cycle

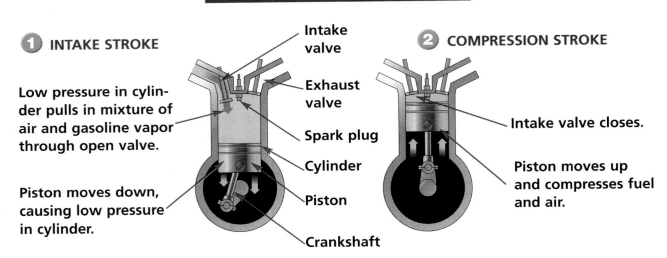

1 INTAKE STROKE

Low pressure in cylinder pulls in mixture of air and gasoline vapor through open valve.

Piston moves down, causing low pressure in cylinder.

Intake valve

Exhaust valve

Spark plug

Cylinder

Piston

Crankshaft

2 COMPRESSION STROKE

Intake valve closes.

Piston moves up and compresses fuel and air.

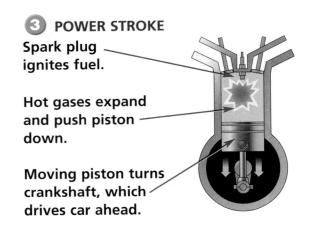

3 POWER STROKE

Spark plug ignites fuel.

Hot gases expand and push piston down.

Moving piston turns crankshaft, which drives car ahead.

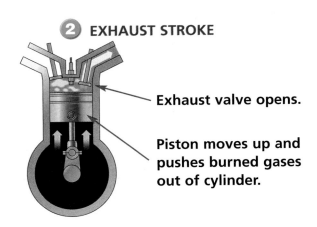

2 EXHAUST STROKE

Exhaust valve opens.

Piston moves up and pushes burned gases out of cylinder.

Why It Matters

Melting ice and evaporating liquids absorb heat, cooling their surroundings. As long as the ice in a drink or cooler is melting, the contents remain at 0°C, just right for keeping foods fresh or pleasantly cold.

A refrigerator uses a chilled coolant pumped through tubing to absorb the heat inside. An engine then compresses the warm coolant into a hot liquid that is air-cooled by coils outside the refrigerator. The liquid coolant is further chilled by evaporating it. This is why it's warm behind the refrigerator.

e-Journal Visit our Web site **www.science.mmhschool.com** to do a research project on how heat affects matter.

Think and Write

1. What happens to matter when its temperature is raised?

2. What can cause the pressure of a gas to change?

3. Does a substance get "hotter" while it is melting? Explain.

4. What do room heating systems, gasoline engines, and refrigerators have in common?

5. Critical Thinking When you step out of a pool on a breezy day, your skin feels cold. Why?

L·I·N·K·S

SOCIAL STUDIES LINK

Research steam engines. How was using steam for energy first discovered? What historical event came about due to this discovery? What sources of energy has steam been replaced by? Use the Internet or encyclopedias for your research. Write a report.

WRITING LINK

Explanatory Writing The properties of expansion and compression are used in tools, machines, and construction. Choose a structure, invention, or tool that uses these properties. Explain how expansion and contraction are used.

MATH LINK

Make a graph. As the temperature of a gas increases, the pressure also increases. Construct a graph that demonstrates this relationship. Use one axis for temperature and the other axis for pressure.

TECHNOLOGY LINK

 LOG ON Visit **www.science.mmhschool.com** for more links.

Sources of Energy

Get Ready

How many kinds of energy do you use each day? How much energy do you use? How might you tell?

Where does all the energy you use each day come from? One way or another, most of our energy supplies come from sunlight. How do the solar panels in the photo use sunlight directly as a source of heat?

Inquiry Skill

You infer when you form an idea from facts or observations.

Explore Activity

How Can Energy from the Sun Be Used?

Materials

construction paper

aluminum foil

clear plastic wrap

tape

shoebox or similar

thermometer

scissors

sunny shelf or heat lamp

Procedure

1 **Make a model** You are going to design a model solar heated house using a small cardboard box, such as a shoebox. Your objective is to design a house that warms up as much as possible in sunlight.

2 Construct your house so that the temperature can be read through a window. CAUTION: INSERT THE THERMOMETER GENTLY!

3 **Experiment** Place your house under the lamp or on the sunny shelf for 10 minutes. Record starting and ending temperatures.

4 **Observe** What happens to your house when the lamp is turned off?

Drawing Conclusions

1 **Communicate** Share your data with the class. Compare what happened to the temperature of your house when it was under the lamp? What design had the highest temperature?

2 What design stayed warm the longest?

3 FURTHER INQUIRY **Experiment** Do a test to see which is a better collector of heat— one large window or several smaller ones with the same total area. Does it matter how you position the shoebox? What if you make a tall house by putting the box on its end? Which is easier to heat, a larger or a smaller house?

Read to Learn

Main Idea Different kinds of energy can be used for various applications.

How Can the Sun's Energy Be Used?

Most of the living things on Earth obtain their energy directly or indirectly from the Sun. Plants convert the Sun's energy into chemical energy stored in compounds called carbohydrates. Animals then feed on the plants or eat other animals that feed on plants.

Humans, too, consume "solar energy" by eating plants and animals. Humans also build devices to capture energy from the Sun and put it to practical use. There are two basic types of solar heating systems—active and passive.

Active Solar Heating

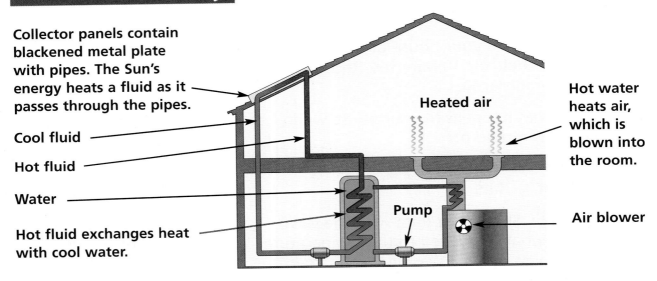

Collector panels contain blackened metal plate with pipes. The Sun's energy heats a fluid as it passes through the pipes.

Cool fluid

Hot fluid

Water

Hot fluid exchanges heat with cool water.

Heated air

Hot water heats air, which is blown into the room.

Pump

Air blower

Passive Solar Heating

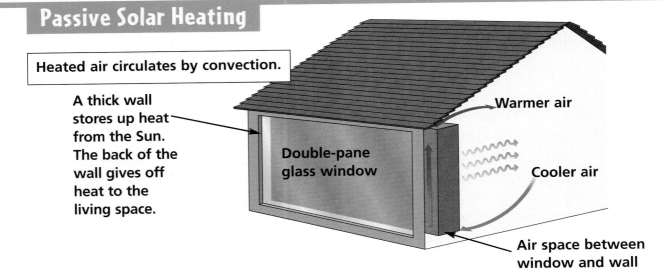

Heated air circulates by convection.

A thick wall stores up heat from the Sun. The back of the wall gives off heat to the living space.

Double-pane glass window

Warmer air

Cooler air

Air space between window and wall

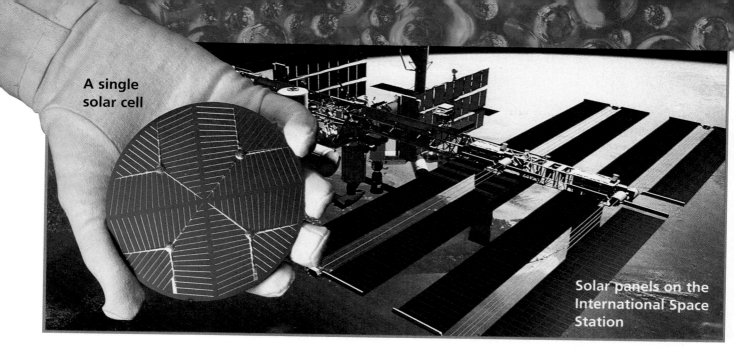

A single
solar cell

Solar panels on the
International Space
Station

Scientists have developed materials made mainly of silicon that can produce electrons when struck by light. When layered properly, these materials can be made into **solar cells**. Solar cells generate an electric current from sunlight. The electricity can be used to charge batteries or run motors. Solar cells can power an electric vehicle. Solar cells can also be positioned on rooftops to provide electricity for buildings.

In some locations engineers have built large power plants that use many mirrors to focus the Sun's rays onto a central collector. The focused rays heat water to boiling or melt salt at high temperatures in the collector. The heat energy is used to make steam, which in turn spins a turbine and generates electricity.

One such power plant is located at Daggett, California. Called Solar Two, this facility began operating in 1996.

It has nearly 2,000 mirrors and can provide 10,000 homes with electricity.

Scientists predict that billions of years from now, the Sun will burn out. Until then, however, it will produce a steady supply of energy. You might describe the Sun's energy as inexhaustible, meaning it will always be there for us to use.

▷ **How can sunlight be turned into electricity?**

An experimental electric car powered by many solar cells connected together

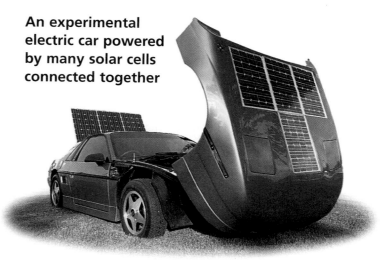

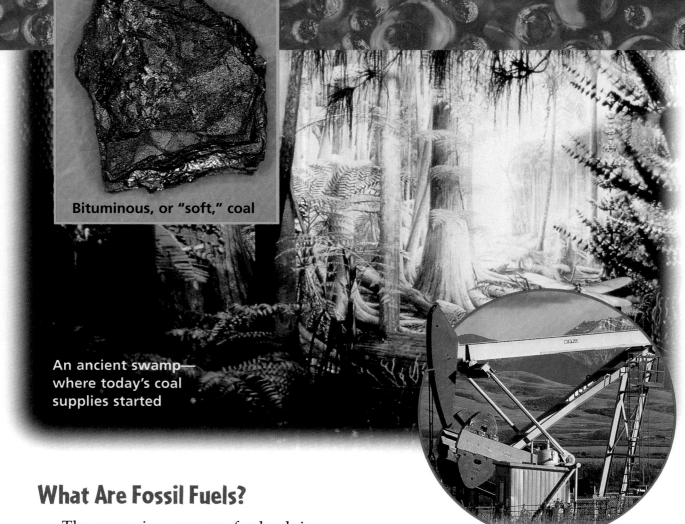

Bituminous, or "soft," coal

An ancient swamp— where today's coal supplies started

What Are Fossil Fuels?

The scene is a swamp far back in Earth's history. Scientists believe that the plants in such swamps became buried as they died. Over time the plants' remains were covered by sand or other mineral matter. Eventually heat and pressure converted the plant remains into a mineral called coal.

In a similar manner, the remains of tiny ocean-dwelling plants and animals became buried under mud and sand on the ocean bottom millions of years ago. As time passed, the organisms' remains were squeezed by the weight of the mineral layers over them into a thick liquid called crude oil. In many cases part of the remains was also changed into a gas called natural gas.

Coal, oil, and natural gas all give off large amounts of heat when burned, so they are very good fuels. Because these materials all formed from ancient plants and animals, we call them fossil fuels. *Fossils* are the remains of ancient plants and animals.

Because fossil fuels take millions of years to form, they are examples of *nonrenewable* resources. *Nonrenewable* means that once we use the resources, we cannot get them back.

READING **Sequence of Events**
How do fossil fuels form?

Kelp, a kind of seaweed, grows rapidly in the ocean. It can be used as biomass for bacteria that produce methane.

WARNING: Do not use in standard gasoline engine. Use only in methanol designated vehicle.

THIS SALE

GALLONS

Methanol

102

California Energy Commission

M

The sugar in an ear of corn can be turned into ethanol, a fuel that mixes well with gasoline.

How Can Modern Plant and Animal Matter Give Us Energy?

Fossil fuels were once living plants and animals. Can matter from plants and animals living today produce energy and help to conserve fossil fuels?

Farmers have used animal wastes as a fuel for centuries. When dried in sunlight, cow and horse manure burn readily. However, new methods allow us to change both plant and animal materials into high-quality fuels. We refer to this kind of change as **biomass conversion** (BIGH·oh·mas kuhn·VUR·zhuhn).

In one method, grains are mixed in a large container with yeast cells. The yeast cells change the sugar in the grains into ethyl alcohol (ethanol) and carbon dioxide. The ethyl alcohol is a good fuel and can be mixed with gasoline.

In another method, bacteria are used to digest the biomass in conditions where air is lacking. Garbage buried deep in landfills or plant matter placed in airtight tanks provide the proper conditions. The bacteria produce methane gas, which is the main ingredient of natural gas.

The fuels from biomass conversion are examples of *renewable* resources. *Renewable* means that we can make more of the resources and use them again and again.

▷ **How is grain turned into energy?**

What Is Nuclear Fission?

In a nuclear reaction, the number of protons in the nuclei of atoms often changes. Since the identity of any atom is determined by the number of protons it has, a change in the number of protons produces a different atom.

One type of nuclear reaction is called **nuclear fission** (NEW·klee·uhr FISH·uhn). Nuclear fission is the splitting of a nucleus into two pieces. The nucleus can be split when struck with a slow-moving neutron. Neutrons and energy are also produced by nuclear fission.

If enough large nuclei are present, the neutrons released by one splitting atom can strike additional nuclei and make them split. These nuclei then release several more neutrons, which can split even more nuclei. Much as a single match can start a large fire, a single neutron can start a large nuclear reaction. We say that the first neutron starts a **chain reaction** of splitting nuclei. In a chain reaction, products of the reaction keep the reaction going.

Because the forces in an atomic nucleus are very strong, the energy released is much greater than the energy produced by chemical reactions. Allowing the atoms in about 0.25 gram of uranium to split, for example, yields as much energy as burning half a ton of coal!

▷ **How can atomic nuclei produce energy by splitting?**

Nuclear Fission

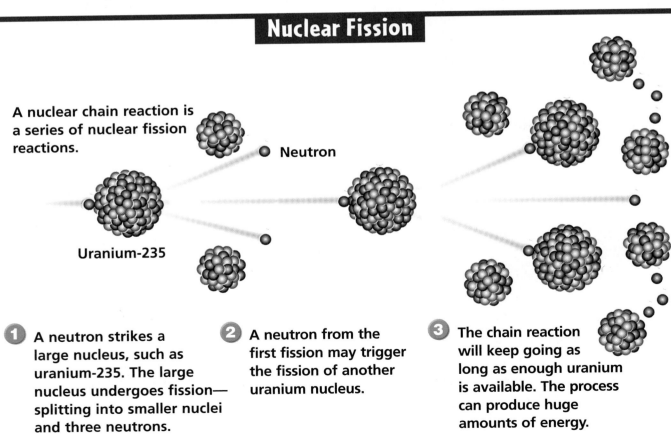

A nuclear chain reaction is a series of nuclear fission reactions.

Neutron

Uranium-235

1 A neutron strikes a large nucleus, such as uranium-235. The large nucleus undergoes fission— splitting into smaller nuclei and three neutrons.

2 A neutron from the first fission may trigger the fission of another uranium nucleus.

3 The chain reaction will keep going as long as enough uranium is available. The process can produce huge amounts of energy.

1 If two nuclei are traveling extremely fast, they may have enough energy to collide and combine.

2 When the nuclei combine, a tiny amount of their mass is changed into energy.

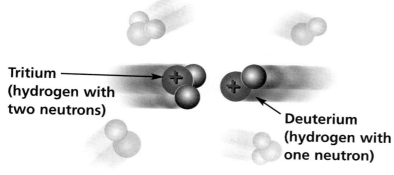

Tritium (hydrogen with two neutrons)

Deuterium (hydrogen with one neutron)

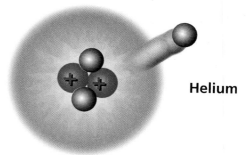

Helium

What Is Nuclear Fusion?

You've seen how nuclei of heavy atoms can split into medium-sized nuclei and release energy. Energy can also be released when nuclei with smaller masses merge to make a nucleus with a larger mass. This process is called **nuclear fusion** (NEW·klee·uhr FYEW·zhuhn).

During the fusion reactions in the diagram, some of the mass of the particles seems to disappear—the helium nucleus at the end has less mass than the particles from which it was made. Scientists have learned that the missing mass gets turned into a large amount of energy. It may seem odd that matter can change into energy. It was not until 1905 that Albert Einstein predicted that this could happen.

Nuclear fusion reactions occur only at very high temperatures. The nuclei that must merge have a positive charge and repel one another. The nuclei must be traveling at high speeds to be able to get close enough to fuse. In nature, temperatures great enough for nuclear fusion to happen are found in the cores of stars. There nuclear fusion reactions produce vast amounts of energy and allow stars to shine brightly for billions of years.

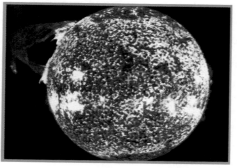

The huge amount of energy that the Sun produces comes from nuclear fusion reactions. The temperature in the center of the Sun is about 15,000,000°C.

▷ **How can atomic nuclei produce energy by merging?**

E 85

A Chain Reaction

FOLDABLES™ Make a Two-Tab Book. (See p. R 41.) Label as shown.

```
A CHAIN REACTION


Successful  Unsuccessful
```

1. Design a model of a nuclear chain reaction. Use materials, such as foam balls, dried beans, or colored paper to represent nuclei and neutrons. You could present your model on a poster, in a diorama, or as a class activity. Describe your model inside the book.

2. **Make a Model** With your teacher's approval, build your model. Your teacher may ask you to write an explanation of the model or to discuss the model with the class.

3. How successful was your model? How could it be improved? Record your answers on the book's tabs.

Which Is Better—Fission or Fusion?

Today, nuclear fission reactors produce electricity across the United States, in Europe, and in many other places on Earth. The reactors are quiet, do not pollute the atmosphere, and help conserve fossil fuels.

Nuclear reactors produce energy through a controlled chain reaction. To control the amount of energy released by the chain reaction, two things can be done. First, the nuclear fuel used must not contain too many nuclei that can split. Second, pieces of neutron-absorbing material can be put around the nuclear fuel. These pieces "soak up" some of the neutrons from splitting nuclei and prevent the neutrons from causing too much fission.

The core of a nuclear power plant

A large number of power plants have been built around the world that use a fission chain reaction to produce electricity. Most of these plants use uranium as a nuclear fuel. Uranium ore from mines naturally contains a very small amount of a form of uranium that can undergo fission. Special processing increases the amount of the fissionable uranium to the point that there are enough nuclei to support a safe chain reaction.

However, these reactors cause problems. Their most serious problem is the waste products of nuclear fission, which stay highly radioactive for thousands of years. These wastes must be stored safely for a very long time. They are dangerous to living things. One way scientists have dealt with this problem has been to store the wastes underground in shielded containers. These containers are a temporary solution. For now they protect living organisms from being exposed to these wastes. Unfortunately, these containers may not hold up indefinitely.

A nuclear fusion reactor would not have these problems. Nuclear fusion produces far less radioactive waste than nuclear fission. Also the fuels for nuclear fusion are special forms of hydrogen called deuterium and tritium. Both of these forms are safe and easily obtained from nature.

Unfortunately, researchers have not yet succeeded in developing a working

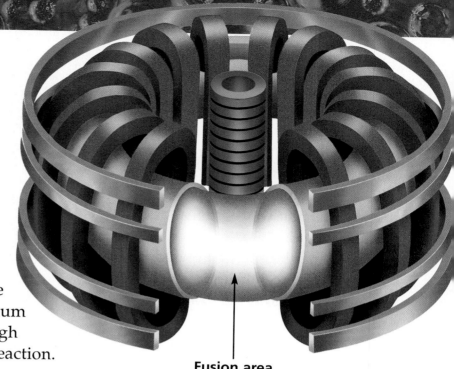

Fusion area

This diagram shows how a tokamak reactor would confine a white-hot mixture of fusing deuterium and tritium.

fusion reactor. The problem is that temperatures greater than 100 million degrees are needed to keep the fusion going. Ordinary materials cannot withstand such high temperatures.

Researchers are trying to use magnetic fields to confine the reaction. The tokamak design, shown above, uses a donut-shaped magnetic field to hold the heated deuterium and tritium fuel. Scientists are hopeful that nuclear fusion reactors like the tokamak may become practical by the middle of the 21st century.

▷ **What is the difference between fusion and fission reactors?**

How Can We Capture Energy from Wind?

It may surprise you to know that wind is a form of solar energy. Wind is caused by uneven heating of Earth's surface by the Sun—air moves from colder areas into warmer areas and produces wind.

Capturing the energy in wind is not a new idea. For centuries farmers have used windmills to grind grain. In America windmills have been used for over 100 years to pump water on farms, as shown. Also many small wind-driven electric generators were put in service between 1930 and 1960, especially in remote areas. By 1960 electric companies had strung wires to most parts of the United States, and the need for wind-driven generators lessened greatly.

However, the growing demand for energy in America has recently led to a renewed interest in wind energy. Manufacturers have developed large wind turbines that can convert wind into electricity.

California has most of the wind turbines in the United States. About one percent of this state's electricity comes from wind turbines, many of them on wind farms. While wind power is clean and will never be used up, some people object to the noise and appearance of the large turbines.

These wind turbines are 50 meters tall. In a 28-mile-per-hour wind, they produce about one-thousandth the electricity of a medium-sized fossil-fuel electric power plant.

A windmill on a farm

Thousands of wind turbines can be assembled to make wind farms like this one in California.

▶ **How can we use the wind to make energy?**

How Can Falling Water Give Us Energy?

The kinetic energy of falling water can be captured and used to turn a wheel. This principle can be used to generate electricity. Water from the lake behind a dam can be made to flow through turbines, causing them to spin and drive electric generators. When electricity is produced by flowing water in this fashion, it is called **hydroelectricity**.

Like wind power, hydroelectricity is really a form of solar energy. The Sun warms water in oceans and lakes, causing it to evaporate. The water vapor rises high in the atmosphere and can fall as precipitation at high elevations. As the water from the precipitation runs downhill due to gravity, it gains kinetic energy. This is the energy that can be tapped for hydroelectricity.

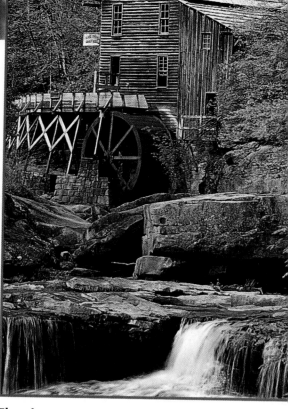

Flowing water causes this wheel to turn.

Hoover Dam creates Lake Mead. Lake water rushing through the turbines below the dam structure makes electricity.

Presently the United States gets about 15 percent of its electricity from hydroelectricity. Hydroelectricity causes little pollution and it will always be available as long as it rains or snows. However, hydroelectricity does present problems. There are few sites where more large dams can be built. Building such dams can harm the environment. It takes very careful planning to make sure animal and plant species are not harmed in some way by dams.

Dams in the Pacific Northwest could stop salmon from migrating upstream. Fish ladders, shown above, allow fish to get past dams.

▶ How is water turned into energy?

How Can Fossil Fuels Be Used to Make Electricity?

Fossil fuels are really a form of solar energy. They contain chemical energy that was originally light from the Sun used by ancient plants for growth. Fossil fuels are composed mainly of carbon and hydrogen. When they are burned, they combine with oxygen in the air to make water, carbon dioxide, and heat. Study the diagram to see how this heat is used to make electricity that is sent to homes, offices, and factories.

READING

Diagrams

How does fossil fuel energy become electricity?

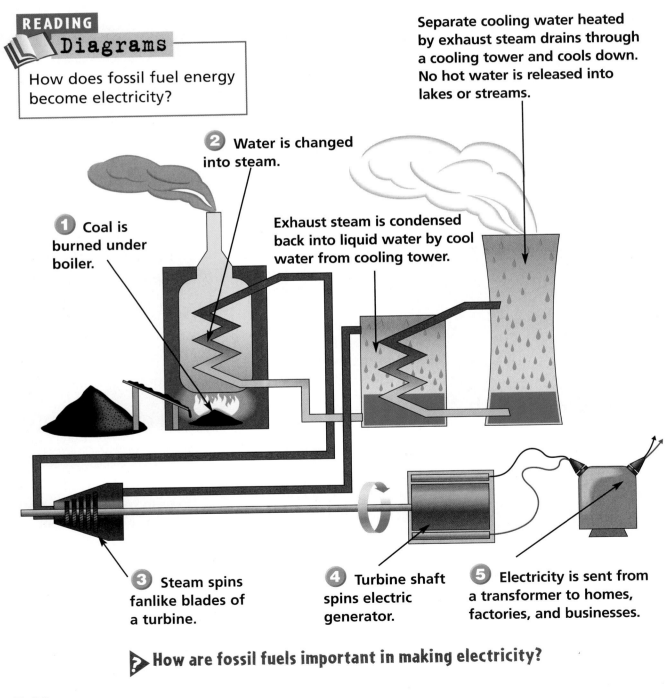

Separate cooling water heated by exhaust steam drains through a cooling tower and cools down. No hot water is released into lakes or streams.

2 Water is changed into steam.

1 Coal is burned under boiler.

Exhaust steam is condensed back into liquid water by cool water from cooling tower.

3 Steam spins fanlike blades of a turbine.

4 Turbine shaft spins electric generator.

5 Electricity is sent from a transformer to homes, factories, and businesses.

▶ **How are fossil fuels important in making electricity?**

Why It Matters

Studies show that our demand for energy is steadily increasing. However, the supplies of oil and other fossil fuels will not last forever. Alternative energy sources such as the Sun, wind, and water can help to conserve fossil fuels. However, it is important that each of us conserve as much energy as possible in our daily activities.

 -Journal Visit our Web site **www.science.mmhschool.com** to do a research project on energy conservation.

Think and Write

1. How can energy from the Sun be captured directly and used?

2. Why are coal, oil, and natural gas called fossil fuels?

3. What is the difference between nuclear fission and nuclear fusion?

4. Why can hydroelectricity be thought of as a form of solar energy?

5. **Critical Thinking** How does energy from a power plant reach your home?

L·I·N·K·S

WRITING LINK

Explanatory Writing How can turning off the lights in an empty room help to save fossil fuels? Write a step-by-step explanation of what you can do in your daily activities to save fossil fuels.

MATH LINK

Research fuel usage. Compare the gallons of fuel consumed by an economy car or van and a luxury vehicle if driven 10,000 miles per year. Do research to find the answer.

SOCIAL STUDIES LINK

Investigate global warming. What is the greenhouse effect? What is its relationship to global warming? Research this issue.

LITERATURE LINK

Read *Marie Curie* to learn about her work with radioactivity. Try the activities at the end of the book.

TECHNOLOGY LINK

LOG ON Visit **www.science.mmhschool.com** for more links.

Chapter 10 Review

Vocabulary

Fill each blank with the best word or words from the list.

chain reaction, E84
convection, E59
evaporation, E73
freezing, E73
hydroelectricity, E89
kinetic energy, E55
potential energy, E55
pressure, E70
solar cell, E81
thermal expansion, E68

1. You can capture sunlight to make electricity with a _____.

2. Electricity from falling water is called _____.

3. The process of changing from liquid to solid is called _____.

4. Molecules colliding against a container create _____.

5. The energy of motion is called _____.

6. A process that continues by itself is called a(n) _____.

7. If you mix hot and cold water, all of the water becomes the same temperature due to _____.

8. The extreme sag of a power line on a hot, sunny day is an example of _____.

9. The process in which a liquid becomes a gas is _____.

10. Stored energy is called _____.

Test Prep

11. What causes thermal expansion?
    A chemical change
    B increased motion of molecules
    C change in gas pressure
    D reduction of volume

12. Solar cells generate electricity from _____.
    F light
    G water
    H chemical change
    J pressure

13. Convection usually occurs in _____.
    A liquids
    B solids
    C gases
    D both A and C

14. A solid may change from a liquid to a gas by _____.

   F freezing

   G melting

   H condensing

   J evaporating

15. What does temperature measure?

   A heat

   B motion of molecules

   C radiation

   D hydroelectricity

Concepts and Skills

16. Reading in Science Describe the changes a sample of steam (gaseous water) would undergo as heat is steadily removed from it.

17. [INQUIRY SKILL] **Use Variables** What if you have samples of six different fabrics? Design an experiment to show which fabric best keeps an object warm. In your experiment identify the variable you are testing and the variables you are controlling.

18. Critical Thinking Imagine that you want to build a solar-heated home. Describe all the characteristics the ideal location for a solar home would have.

19. Scientific Methods Consider a piece of nuclear fuel that contains nuclei that can be split by neutrons. As the size of the piece becomes smaller, it is less likely that a chain reaction can be maintained. Suggest a reason why.

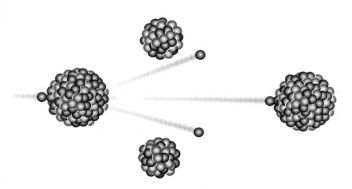

20. Product Ads Describe the types of housing insulation used in your part of the country. Is it more important to keep heat in or out? Why is that so? What resources can insulation save?

Did You Ever Wonder?

[INQUIRY SKILL] **Classify** Name three ways of cooking an egg. Classify how the heat energy is transferred to the egg.

LOG ON Visit www.science.mmhschool.com to boost your test scores.

Electricity and Magnetism

Did You Ever Wonder?

Where does electricity come from? Electricity is generated in power plants and sent through wires to homes, schools, and office buildings all over the country. How do we use electricity once it reaches our homes?

INQUIRY SKILL **Observe** List all of the appliances in your home that are powered by electricity. Compare the list to the appliances in your home that are powered by other forms of energy. Why do you think electrical energy is used so much?

Static Electricity

Vocabulary

electricity, E98

static electricity, E98

induced charge, E100

conductor, E102

insulator, E102

grounding, E103

Get Ready

When you shuffle your feet across the carpet and reach for a doorknob, a spark may jump and give you a small shock. What is the spark made of? Where did it come from? You may have seen lightning charge from the sky and reach all the way to the ground. What causes lightning? How does it reach from the sky to Earth?

Inquiry Skill

You **hypothesize** when you make a statement that can be tested to answer a question.

Explore Activity

Materials

cellophane tape

What Happens to Charged Objects That Are Brought Together?

Procedure

1 Press two pieces of cellophane tape tightly to your desk, folding one side over to make a tab.

2 **Predict** What will happen when you pull the strips of tape off the desk and hold them near each other? Test your prediction.

3 **Experiment** Tightly tape two strips of tape to your desk, one on top of the other. Pull both strips off the desk and then apart from each other. Hold the ends close together and observe. Record your observations.

Drawing Conclusions

1 **Communicate** What happened in step 2 when you brought the ends of the tape near each other? What happened in step 3?

2 What did pulling the strips of tape off the desk do to them?

3 What might have caused the difference in steps 2 and 3?

4 **FURTHER INQUIRY** **Hypothesize** How could you prevent the charge from building up on the tape strips? Test your hypothesis.

Main Idea Static electricity results from the buildup of positive and negative charges.

What Is Electricity?

All matter is made of atoms, which in turn are made of protons, neutrons, and electrons. The protons have a positive charge, and the electrons have a negative charge. Under the proper conditions, these charges can transmit energy in the form of **electricity**.

When two different materials are brought into close contact, some of the electrons move from one material onto the other. This causes the materials to become electrically charged. The material that gains extra electrons becomes negatively charged because it has more electrons than protons. The

material that loses some of its electrons becomes positively charged because it has fewer electrons than protons. The diagram shows how strips of cellophane gain a charge when rubbed against glass. Where the glass and cellophane touch, electrons move into the cellophane from the glass. This gives the cellophane a negative charge and the glass a positive charge.

When electrons move from one place to another and cause a buildup of separated positive and negative charges, the charges are called **static electricity**. Static electricity can develop on two different materials that have touched. It can also develop in different parts of a single material. Strips of tape gain static electricity when they are pressed against the top of a desk because the tape is a different material from the desk.

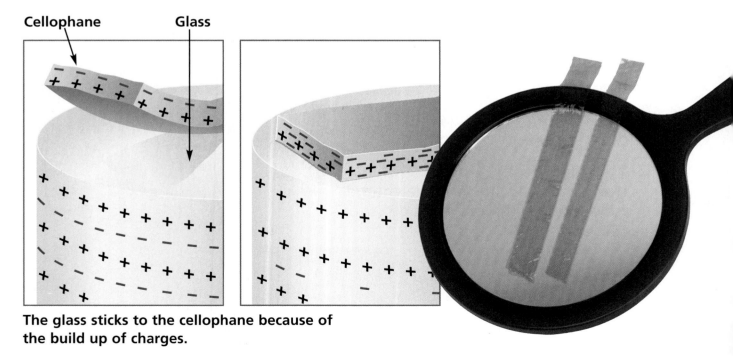

Cellophane   **Glass**

The glass sticks to the cellophane because of the build up of charges.

The glass and cellophane examples describe how static electric charges can push or pull on one another. A very important principle of electricity is that a positive charge and a negative charge will pull each other together, while two positive charges or two negative charges will push each other apart. Put another way, *opposite charges attract, and like charges repel.*

The forces between electric charges cause many interesting effects in our world. You've probably experienced static electricity while seated in a car. Look at the photographs to see other examples of what static electricity can do.

▷ **How is static electricity produced?**

The student in the photo is touching a metal ball that has a very large static charge. Some of this charge has moved onto her hair. The hairs all have the same charge, so they repel each other and stand on end. If you are outside and your hair does this when a rainstorm is coming, go inside immediately. Lightning may be about to strike!

Lightning strikes buildings or lightning rods.

What Is Induced Charge?

The student in the photograph rubbed the balloon on her hair. The contact between her hair and the rubber of the balloon caused a negative static electric charge to build up on the balloon. When she moved the balloon near the wall, it was pulled onto the wall and held there. Since the balloon was attracted to the wall, the balloon and the wall must have had opposite static electric charges. However, the wall was not first placed in contact with a different material. How did the wall gain a static charge?

With the balloon far away, the positive and negative charges in the wall are evenly spread out. When the balloon is brought near, however, its extra negative charges repel the negative charges in the wall. Some of the wall's negative charges are pushed away from the surface, leaving the surface positively charged. The attraction between the extra negative charge on the balloon and the positive charge at the wall's surface holds the balloon to the wall.

The balloon and the wall show how a charged object can cause negative and positive charges in a nearby object to move apart. The static charge that results in the second object is called an **induced charge** .

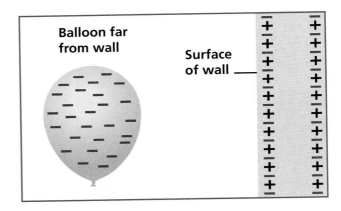

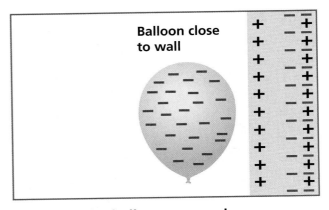

READING Cause and Effect
How can a balloon induce a charge on a wall?

When the balloon approaches the wall, the surface of the wall becomes positively charged.

This balloon induced a charge on the wall.

Drum

1 The copier has a charged, rolling drum with a light-sensitive coating.

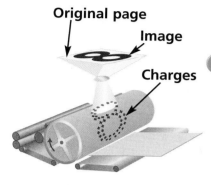

Original page

Image

Charges

2 The machine casts an image onto the drum. When light strikes the drum, charges are removed except where an image is present.

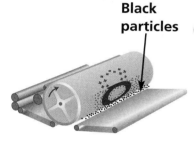

Black particles

3 Tiny black particles are attracted to charges on the drum. The induced charges on the particles make them stick to the parts of the drum where an image is present.

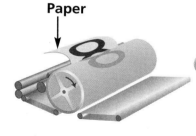

Paper

4 The black particles are transferred to a piece of paper.

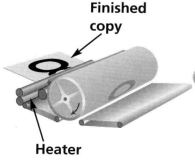

Finished copy

5 A heater melts the particles into a permanent image.

Heater

QUICK LAB

Static Charge

FOLDABLES Make a Folded Table. (See page R 44.) Label as shown.

STATIC CHARGE STRENGTH	
TEST	NUMBER OF PIECES
1	
2	
3	

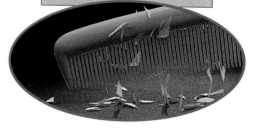

1. Place a static charge on a comb by rubbing it with a piece of cloth.

2. **Observe** Hold the comb over a pile of confetti, and note about how much paper the comb picks up.

3. **Hypothesize** What could you do to increase the charge on the comb so that more confetti sticks to it?

4. **Use Variables** Test your ideas, but be careful to change only how you charge the comb.

5. **Communicate** Present your results using a graph or a table.

6. Why would it be important to hold the comb at the same distance from the confetti for each test?

What Are Conductors and Insulators?

Static electricity can build up so much that it jumps to lessen the charge. Have you ever shuffled your feet across a carpet? If you bring your finger close to a doorknob, a spark will probably jump and cause a small shock.

The diagram shows how static electricity could discharge with a spark between you and the doorknob. The contact between your feet and the carpet causes electrons to move from the carpet onto your feet. Human tissue is a fairly good **conductor** of electricity, meaning electrons move through the body fairly easily. As a result, electrons from your feet move all over your body, making even your hands negatively charged.

It is easier to discharge negative static electricity from your finger by reaching for a doorknob than by reaching for a plaster wall. Plaster is an **insulator**—it does not allow electrons to move through it easily. When you bring your finger near a wall, the electrons in the plaster cannot move far. Only a small induced positive charge can build up. The attraction between the charge on your finger and the weak induced charge is generally not great enough to produce a spark.

▶ **What is the difference between a conductor and an insulator?**

1 The hand moving toward the doorknob has many more negative charges than positive charges, so it has a static electric charge. The doorknob, though, has no net charge.

2 When the hand gets close enough to the doorknob, negative charges jump as a sudden spark. The spark moves some of the extra negative charge on the hand to the doorknob.

3 After the spark has jumped, both the doorknob and the hand have about the same excess of negative charges. The spark has shared the negative charges between the hand and doorknob.

How Is Electricity Grounded?

A computer on a school desk operates on electricity that it receives from the wall outlet. Two conducting wires carry the electricity to the computer. However, if the bare wires were exposed, anyone who touched them would get a dangerous shock. To keep the computer safe, the manufacturer uses wires that are coated with an insulator, usually plastic.

Sometimes the insulation on the wiring inside appliances like a computer can become worn, exposing the bare wires. If the bare wires touch the metal case of the appliance, it can become electrified with a dangerous static charge. For this reason, a third **grounding** wire is connected to the metal case.

The grounding wire of an appliance connects the metal case to the ground through the household wiring. The ground, especially moist soil, is a good conductor of electricity. If a dangerous charge builds up on an appliance's metal case, the grounding wire allows the case to share the charge with the ground. When the charge is shared this way, it is made much smaller, as in the diagram.

This prong connects the metal case of the computer to the ground.

These two prongs carry electrical energy to the computer.

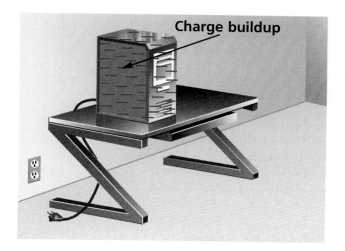

Charge buildup

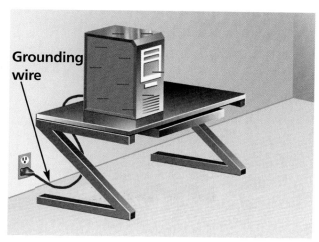

Grounding wire

▷ Why is grounding electricity important?

How Is Lightning Produced?

You are sitting in your living room, and it's raining outside. You see a very bright flash and get ready for a loud crash—lightning has struck nearby! You hope that no one was hurt and no damage resulted.

Lightning is much like a spark jumping from your finger to a doorknob, but with much, much more electrical energy—so much energy, in fact, that it is deadly. In the United States, about 20,000,000 lightning bolts strike the ground each year. What causes these dangerous strikes?

Lightning is produced by static electricity. In a thunderstorm cloud, water droplets are carried up to cooler regions in the air, and they begin freezing. The combination of water,

ice, and motion gives the lower part of the cloud a negative charge. At the same time, the ground below acquires a positive charge.

When the attraction between the negative and positive charges grows great enough, a conductive path allows negative charges to surge from the cloud to the ground. The surge of high-energy electricity heats the air to glowing, and we see the flash. In the same instant, the heat makes the air expand rapidly. The expansion creates the clap of thunder that we hear.

How Can You Protect Yourself from Lightning?
DO plan ahead in case of a storm—where will you go if lightning threatens?
DO stay away from water.
DO seek shelter in a substantial building with wiring and plumbing. A car with a metal body is also fairly safe as long as you don't touch anything metal inside.
DO grow cautious the minute a storm begins brewing nearby.
DON'T be the tallest object or stand near a tall object.
DON'T seek shelter under a tree or picnic canopy.
DON'T use electrical appliances or run water if you're in a building.
DON'T assume there is no danger if it isn't raining—lightning often strikes before and after the rain.

 What causes lightning?

L·I·N·K·S

Why It Matters

Static electricity can be very important. Without static charges, for example, electricity would not flow to our homes. Transistors in computer chips would not be possible. These electronic devices enable computers to perform a wide range of functions. Other devices, such as calculators, microwave ovens, and videocassette recorders, also rely on transistors.

e-Journal Visit our Web site **www.science.mmhschool.com** to do a research project on static electricity.

Think and Write

1. What is static electricity?

2. If you press two pieces of cellophane tape together, sticky side to sticky side, will they have a static charge when you pull them apart? Why?

3. What is the difference between a conductor and an insulator?

4. How can you stay safe from lightning?

5. **Critical Thinking** Friction is not needed for static electricity to develop. However, rubbing a balloon against your hair seems to increase the charge. Why?

WRITING LINK

Personal Narrative What if you lived in a world in which everything was statically charged? How would you get dressed? How would you eat? Write about a day in your life in this statically charged world. Include what you do to make your life manageable. Use your own voice and the *I* point of view.

MATH LINK

Solve. The odds of being struck by lightning are about 1 in 700,000 per year. There are 280 million people in the United States. How many are likely to get struck each year?

SOCIAL STUDIES LINK

Research the history of the light bulb. How do modern light bulbs compare with the earliest types? Explain the dangers that inventors faced in inventing and improving them. Write a report.

TECHNOLOGY LINK

 LOG ON Visit **www.science.mmhschool.com** for more links.

Circuits

Get Ready

Wires provide a path for electricity to follow in order to light these strings of lights. How do you think the electricity travels to every bulb in a string?

Some strings of lights go out when you unscrew just one bulb. Other strings stay lit. Do the paths for the electricity differ in each kind of string? Can an electrical path affect lights in other ways?

Inquiry Skill

You **infer** when you form an idea from facts or observations.

Explore Activity

How Does an Electrical Path Affect the Brightness of a Light?

Materials

2 D batteries

2 battery holders

6 wire leads

2 small light bulbs

2 light bulb holders

Procedure

1 **Predict** Look at each of the combinations of batteries and bulbs. Which setup will give the brightest light? Which will give the dimmest light?

2 **Predict** What will happen to the other light bulb when you unscrew one of them in each setup?

3 Test your predictions by constructing each setup and connecting all the wires as shown. Record your observations.

Drawing Conclusions

1 **Observe** Rank the setups in order from brightest bulbs to dimmest bulbs.

2 **Observe** What happened in each case when you unscrewed one of the bulbs?

3 How were the setups alike? How were they different?

4 **FURTHER INQUIRY** **Infer** Which type of wiring pattern is used in your school for providing electricity? Use your setups to explain your answer.

1

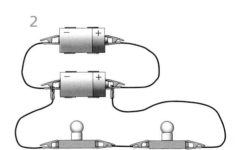

2

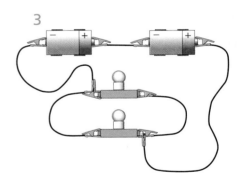

3

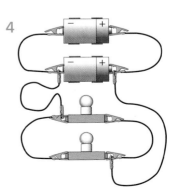

4

Main Idea Circuits provide a path for charged particles, which results in a flow of electricity.

What Is a Circuit?

Light bulbs can be found in just about any room in any building. Electricity can flow through wires and light bulbs in different ways. Each path for the electricity is an example of a **circuit**—a path along which charged particles can travel. In circuits electrons are the charged particles that move through the wires and bulbs.

Simple circuits have a source of electricity, devices such as lamps, and connecting wires. When the wires are connected, the source of electricity starts pushing and pulling on the electrons in all parts of the wires and devices. Electrons everywhere begin flowing towards the source's positive end. Electrons that leave the wires at the positive end of the electricity source are balanced by others that move onto the wires at the negative end.

A flow of charged particles, such as electrons moving through a circuit, is called a **current**. Light bulbs light up because batteries push a current of electrons through them. The crowded electrons at the negative end of the battery repel electrons

in the wire, while the positive end of the battery pulls on the electrons. The result is that electrons begin moving from negative to positive through the wire and device.

To help you understand how a current is produced, imagine a crowd of students waiting behind the school doors. Opening the doors is like connecting the parts of a circuit. When the doors are opened, the students in the crowd start moving through them. At the same instant, people standing in the hallway see the students coming and also move forward, forming a "current."

Surprisingly, the electrons in a current move slowly—perhaps 1 cm each second. The bulb lights up the instant the battery is connected because the battery immediately sets electrons in motion throughout the entire circuit.

A Simple Circuit

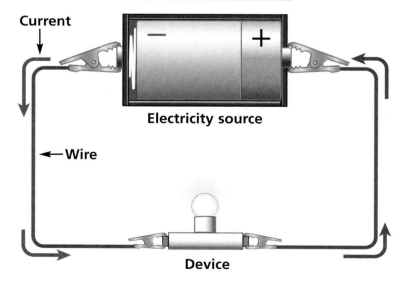

Current

Electricity source

← Wire

Device

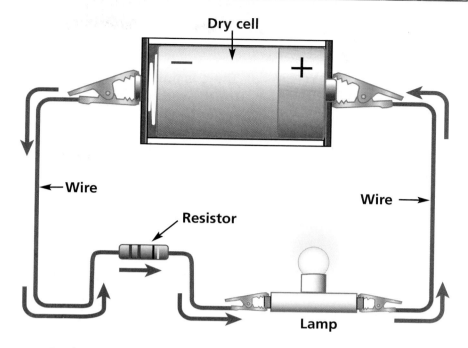

Dry cell

← Wire

Wire →

Resistor

Lamp

Resistors are added to a circuit to reduce the current, or flow of electrons. The resistor opposes the flow of electrons in this circuit.

Resistors

Sources of electricity are rated by voltage. As the voltage becomes greater, a given source is able to crowd more negative charges at one end and more positive charges at the other. When the charges at the ends are more crowded, electrons in the attached wires move faster. This causes current to increase in the circuit to which the electricity source is attached.

Current in a circuit is made smaller when a **resistor** is added to the path. A resistor opposes a flow of electrons. Frequent collisions between electrons and atoms slow the electrons down and also transfer energy to the atoms. This causes the resistor to grow warmer at the same time that the current is reduced. Resistors are added to circuits to control current. The circuit in the

diagram, for example, would burn up the small lamp if it were not for the resistor. Since the resistor opposes current, its presence reduces the number of electrons flowing through the lamp to a safe level.

If the current is not reduced by a resistor, a **short circuit** could occur. A short circuit is a very conductive path that bypasses less conductive parts of a circuit. It is dangerous because wire offers very little opposition to current. The current, in turn, heats the wire greatly. In many cases the heat can actually start fires.

READING Cause and Effect
How does a resistor affect the current in a circuit?

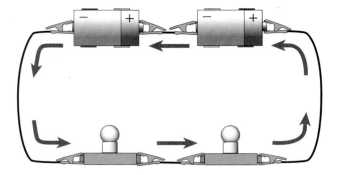

There is only one path for the current in a series circuit.

What Are Series and Parallel Circuits?

Examine the circuit above. The arrows show you that there is only one path for the electric current. This is how a **series circuit** is connected.

When batteries are connected in series, their voltages add together. As a result, there is increased crowding of electrons at the negative end of one battery and increased removal of electrons at the positive end of the other. This, in turn, puts more force on electrons in the wires and bulbs, tending to produce more current.

Like resistors, light bulbs and other electrical devices oppose current. In a series circuit, the resistances of the devices to current add together. For example, two identical light bulbs in series oppose current twice as much as either bulb would alone.

All series circuits share an important property—the flow of charges is the same at any point. The diagram below shows how the push on the electrons in each part of the circuit keeps the current equal everywhere.

For a short time after the battery is connected, electrons move faster in the wires than in the resistors. Some of the electrons begin "piling up" in front of the resistors. Soon these electrons push back on approaching electrons, slowing them down. They also push forward on electrons in the resistors, causing them to move at the same rate as the electrons in the wires. From then on, for each electron that enters one part of the circuit, another leaves.

Soon after the battery is connected in a series circuit, the electrons begin to move at the same rate throughout the circuit.

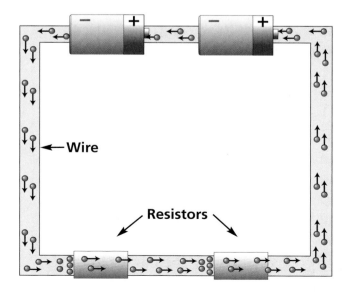

Wire

Resistors

The diagram below shows a **parallel circuit**. This is a circuit with more than one path for current. Electrons are set into motion in each path, causing current. The electricity source can make each path feel the same crowding of charges.

When another path is added to a parallel circuit, the total current increases even though another resistor is now present.

The current in each path of a parallel circuit depends on the strength of its resistor. Paths with a stronger resistor carry less current. The currents are added together to find the total current of the circuit. Even though the current in any path might not be the same as in another, the total current is the same at any point before and after it is shared among the different paths.

▷ **How is a parallel circuit different from a series circuit?**

Parallel Circuit

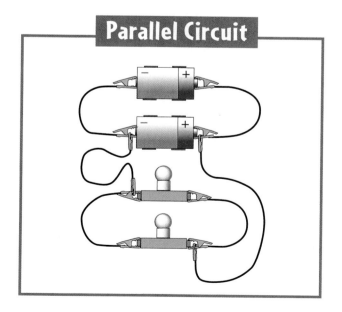

QUICK LAB

Parallel Circuits

FOLDABLES Make a Two-Tab Book. (See page R 41.) Label as shown.

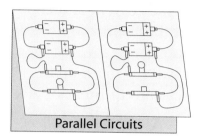

Parallel Circuits

1. **Make a Model** Using two batteries, two cell holders, six wires, two small light bulbs, and two light bulb holders, make a parallel circuit like the one shown on this page.

2. Unscrew one of the bulbs. Draw a diagram of this circuit on the front of one tab of your book. Use arrows to show the direction the electrons are moving.

3. Rescrew the first bulb, and unscrew the other one. Draw a diagram with arrows of the new circuit on the front of the second tab.

4. **Interpret Data** What happens to the flow of current when one of the bulbs is unscrewed. Explain under the tabs.

What Are Open and Closed Circuits?

Look at the two series circuits below. Notice that the bulb in Circuit 2 is lit, but the bulb in Circuit 1 is not. Can you tell why? In Circuit 1 the path for the current is incomplete. A circuit that is incomplete is called an **open circuit**.

The battery in an open circuit can push a certain number of electrons onto the wire attached to its negative end. It can also remove electrons from the wire attached to its positive end. This gives both wires a small static charge. However, once the static charge builds up, electrons will no longer move in the wires, and there will be no current.

Since there is no current in an open circuit, electrical devices such as light bulbs do not receive any energy from the circuit. Without this energy, they cannot operate. That is why the bulb in Circuit 1 is not lit.

Circuit 2, unlike Circuit 1, has an unbroken path from the battery's negative end to its positive end. When a circuit has a complete path for current, it is a **closed circuit**. The instant a battery is connected to this type of circuit, current flows in the wires and the devices. The current transfers energy to the devices, such as the bulb in Circuit 2.

It is often important to be able to open and close a circuit easily. The device we use for this task is a **switch**.

In the *on* position, the switch closes a circuit; in the *off* position, it opens the circuit.

Switches come in many varieties, such as the on/off button on a simple flashlight or the circuit breakers that open or close main circuits in a home. In all cases the parts of a switch act to create a gap in a circuit when the switch is in the *off* position.

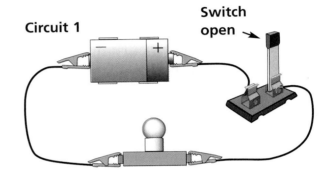

Circuit 1 — Switch open

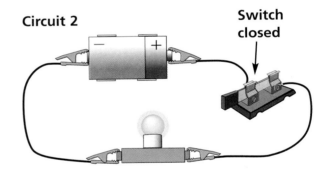

Circuit 2 — Switch closed

READING Diagrams

Why is the light bulb lit in Circuit 2 but not in Circuit 1?

▷ **How do switches control whether a circuit is open or closed?**

Why It Matters

Every electrical appliance—from a computer to an electric toothbrush—uses circuits to get electricity to perform a useful task. Most circuits in your home are parallel circuits. Each wall outlet plugs into a separate branch of a main circuit. When you turn off an appliance in one branch, electrons can still flow through the other branches. Appliances plugged into those other branches will still work. If your home were wired only in series, every appliance would go off as soon as you turned one off.

e-Journal Visit our Web site **www.science.mmhschool.com** to do a research project on electric circuits.

Think and Write

1. What is a circuit?
2. If everything else is the same, will two bulbs be brighter wired in series or wired in parallel? Why?
3. What is the difference between an open circuit and a closed circuit?
4. How do switches control circuits?
5. **Critical Thinking** If you were to add a resistor to a series circuit that includes a light bulb, would the brightness of the bulb change? Why?

L·I·N·K·S

MATH LINK

Do a math problem. What will happen to the amount of current in a series circuit if you double the number of bulbs—will it double, stay the same, or be cut in half? Use a circuit diagram to explain your answer.

WRITING LINK

Expository Writing Research different jobs in which people use or fix electrical circuits. What kind of educational background do these people need? What are important things to know to do these jobs safely? Use the library or the Internet. Write a report of your findings. You may use your report to make a careers kit of jobs that involve using or fixing electrical circuits.

TECHNOLOGY LINK

 LOG ON Visit **www.science.mmhschool.com** for more links.

Current Jobs

Do you like to take things apart and then put them back together again? There are many jobs for people who are interested in knowing how something works and understanding how they can fix it. Auto mechanics, electricians, and even doctors use electricity in their jobs.

All these colorful wires are parts of circuits carrying electricity.

Why are these jobs important? While you may not think about how a car moves when it is working properly, once it breaks, you are eager to find out what's wrong. Auto mechanics understand the circuits in a car. These circuits carry electricity to the spark plugs, the lights, the radio, and the windshield wiper motors. Circuits in the computer chips linked to the motor even control how fuel is fed to the engine. Auto mechanics use complicated equipment to analyze and fix any electrical problems that can go wrong in these circuits.

Electricians are responsible for the electrical wiring in entire buildings! They must know all about electrical parts and be able to find and fix electrical problems. It is very important for them to follow safety rules when working around electricity. Their job is difficult because they have to make sure they make safe connections and do not overload the systems. Too much electricity, as well as loose or broken wires, can cause fires or shocks to both the electrician and the people in the building.

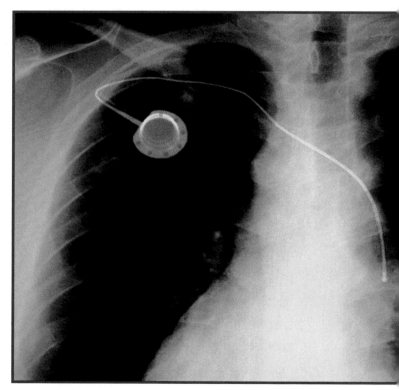

This x-ray photograph shows an implanted pacemaker.

Doctors who work on heart patients may need to place a pacemaker in a patient's body if the patient has a problem with his heartbeat. A pacemaker uses electricity to ensure a weak heart beats properly.

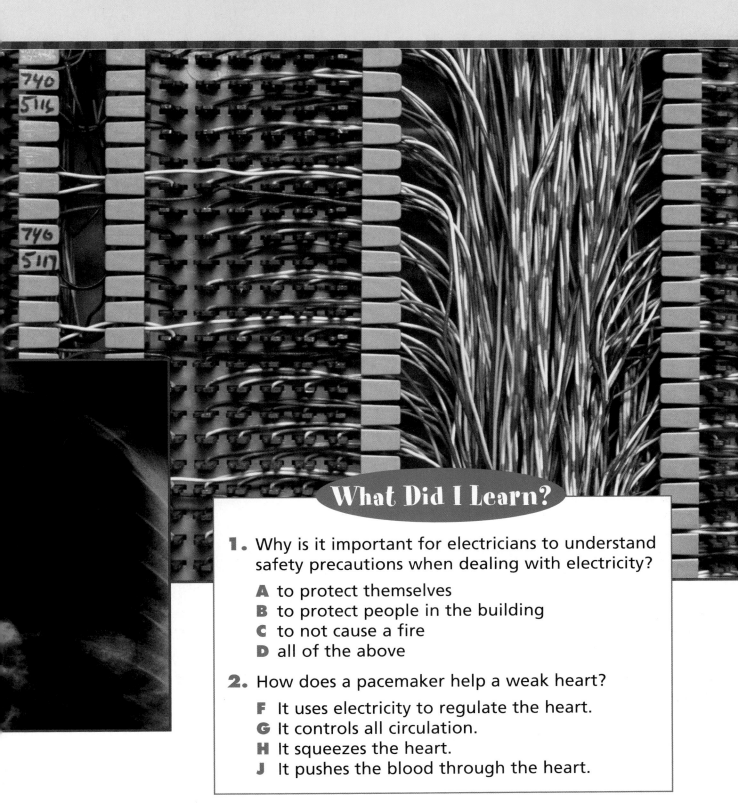

What Did I Learn?

1. Why is it important for electricians to understand safety precautions when dealing with electricity?

   A to protect themselves
   B to protect people in the building
   C to not cause a fire
   D all of the above

2. How does a pacemaker help a weak heart?

   F It uses electricity to regulate the heart.
   G It controls all circulation.
   H It squeezes the heart.
   J It pushes the blood through the heart.

LOG ON Visit www.science.mmhschool.com to learn more about current jobs.

Electromagnets

Vocabulary

magnet, E118

pole, E118

electromagnet, E119

magnetic field, E120

Get Ready

The crane operator in the photograph is lifting scrap metal with an electromagnet. You, too, have probably used electromagnets many times without even knowing it. If you have ever watched television or listened to music played by speakers, you've used an electromagnet! How are electromagnets made? What makes them stronger or weaker?

Inquiry Skill

You **predict** when you state possible results of an event or experiment.

Explore Activity

How Can You Make an Electromagnet Stronger?

Materials
1.5-V battery
large steel nail
insulated wire
steel paper clips
various small objects

Procedure

1. Tightly wrap 20 turns of wire around a large steel nail, as shown in the photograph. Leave a long, free piece of wire at each end.

2. **Experiment** Connect the bare ends of the wire to the battery. See if your electromagnet can pick up steel paper clips and other small objects.

3. **Predict** How long a chain of paper clips can your electromagnet pick up? Test your prediction.

4. **Communicate** Record your observations using a data table like the one shown.

5. **Predict** What do you think will happen to the strength of your electromagnet if you use twice as many turns of wire or two batteries instead of one? Test your predictions.

Sample Data Table		
	Number of Clips Picked Up	
Number of Turns	1 Battery	2 Batteries
20		
40		
60		

Drawing Conclusions

1. **Communicate** Describe how you would construct the strongest possible magnet with the materials used in this investigation.

2. **Hypothesize** Why did the electromagnet pick up some materials but not others?

3. FURTHER INQUIRY **Predict** What other things could you change in your electromagnet to make it stronger? Carry out tests, and record your observations.

Main Idea Electromagnets made by a current in a wire are used in many common devices.

What Is a Magnet?

A current-carrying wire coil can pick up certain metal objects. The moving electric charges in the current turn the wire coil into a **magnet**. You probably use magnets often at home and at school. Common magnets attract metal objects made of iron, cobalt, or nickel. Magnets also attract or repel other magnets.

All magnets have two **poles**—a north-seeking pole (N) and a south-seeking pole (S). If a magnet is suspended by a string so it can spin freely, its north-seeking pole will point toward the North Pole of Earth, and its south-seeking pole will point in the opposite direction. Even if a magnet is cut in half, each half will have a north-seeking pole and a south-seeking pole.

The south pole of one magnet repels the south pole of another magnet. The same thing happens for two north poles. A north magnetic pole, however, attracts a south magnetic pole. The attraction or repulsion is strongest at the poles but is observed all around a magnet.

Objects made of iron, cobalt, or nickel can become permanent magnets. The magnetism comes from the motions of electrons in atoms. The moving electrons cause each individual atom to act as a tiny magnet. All the atoms in the entire object line up in the same direction, as shown in the diagram on page E119. The atoms in permanent magnets remain lined up this way for long periods of time.

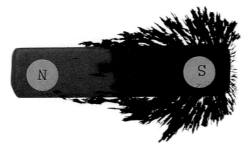 

The south poles of the magnets above are repelling each other.

Below, a north magnetic pole is attracting a south magnetic pole.

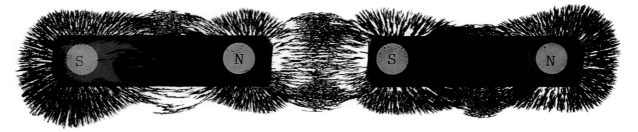

A single iron atom

N ← ● — S

Nonmagnetic object

N

S

Magnetic object

READING

Diagrams

Compare the positions of atoms in a magnetic object and a nonmagnetic object.

Moving electrons in an electric current also produce magnetism. The magnetism around a current-carrying wire becomes much stronger when the wire is wrapped into a coil. Each turn of the coil adds to the magnetism of all the other turns. If an iron, cobalt, or nickel core is placed in the coil, the magnet becomes even stronger. Devices that are made magnetic by an electric current are called **electromagnets**. Electromagnets are convenient because the magnetism disappears when the current is turned off.

When an electromagnet or a permanent magnet is brought near an object made of iron, cobalt, or nickel, the atoms in the metal object temporarily line up as shown in the diagram above. The magnet then attracts the object and can pick it up.

Actually, the magnetism of iron, cobalt, or nickel is unusual. In most other materials, the magnetism from the motions of the electrons in the atoms cancels out, and the atoms do not act as tiny magnets. When an electromagnet or permanent magnet is brought near an object made of nonmagnetic material, there is no attraction, and the magnet cannot pick the object up.

▷ **How do permanent magnets and electromagnets differ?**

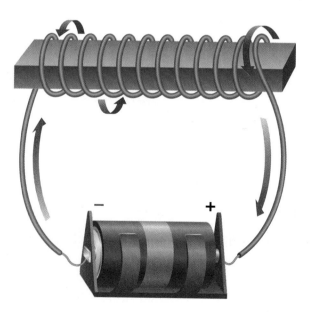

The greater the number of turns of the coil, the stronger the magnetism of this electromagnet.

How Is a Magnetic Field Produced?

Imagine a piece of thin, clear plastic is placed over a strong bar magnet. Then tiny whiskers of iron, called iron filings, are sprinkled onto the plastic. When the plastic is tapped to allow the iron filings to move, they line up in a special pattern like the one in the photo. What causes this pattern?

The magnetism of the bar magnet makes each tiny iron filing become a temporary bar magnet itself. As you can see, the poles of the iron filings point in specific directions. The push or pull that causes the iron filings to line up this way comes from the bar's **magnetic field**. A magnetic field is the area around a magnet in which other magnets can feel attraction or repulsion.

Scientists draw arrows to represent magnetic fields around magnets. The diagram shows such a representation for a bar magnet. Note how the arrows outside the magnet move from the north pole to the south pole and always form closed loops.

The push or pull felt by one magnet when placed in the magnetic field of another is strongest where the arrows are most crowded. The direction of the push or pull is given by the direction of the arrows.

The magnetic lines of force, as shown by the arrows, are in the same pattern as the iron filings in the photo below.

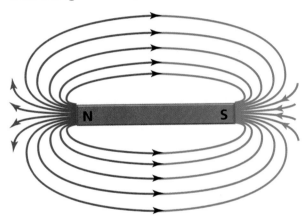

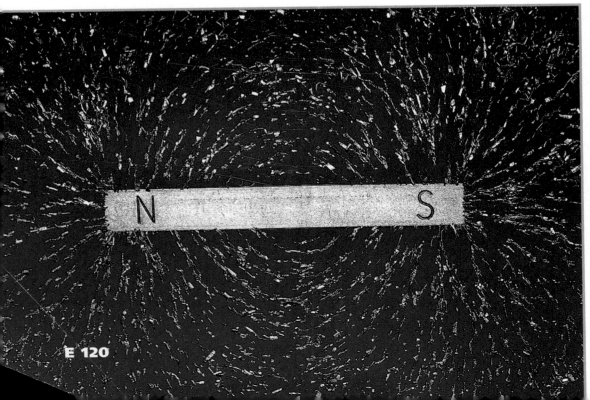

This magnet's magnetic field caused the iron filings to line up in a special pattern.

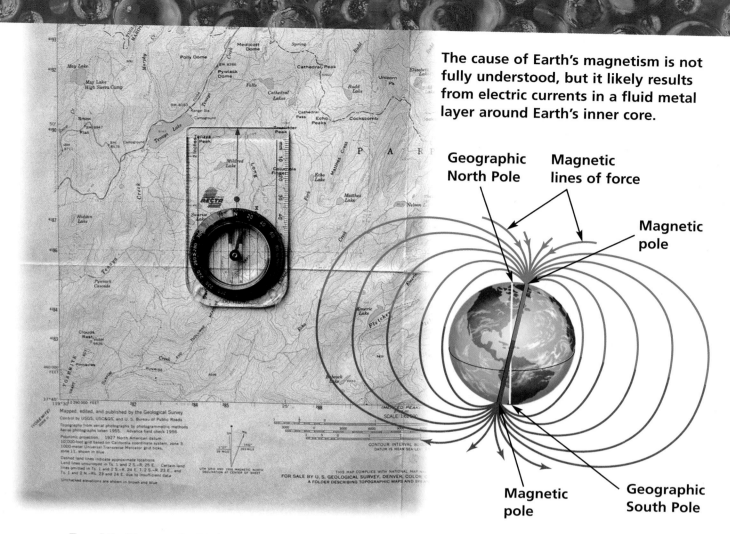

The cause of Earth's magnetism is not fully understood, but it likely results from electric currents in a fluid metal layer around Earth's inner core.

Geographic North Pole

Magnetic lines of force

Magnetic pole

Magnetic pole

Geographic South Pole

Earth's Magnetic Field

Compass needles pointing north show us that Earth has a magnetic field. As the diagram shows, Earth's magnetic field is similar to the field of a stubby bar magnet.

A compass is simply a thin bar magnet—the compass needle—placed on a post. The needle is free to spin with little friction. As long as the compass is not held near a metal object, the north-seeking pole of the needle swings around to point to the north.

The locations of Earth's magnetic poles are about 11° off the true geographic North and South poles. The effect of Earth's rotation on its molten interior may cause this. It also may cause the positions of the magnetic poles to change over time.

A compass needle always points to magnetic north. A map of any given location shows the local difference between true north and magnetic north for people who want to plot a course using a compass. The map gives the number of degrees to add or subtract to the compass reading to find the direction of true north.

READING Cause and Effect

How does Earth's magnetic field affect a compass needle?

This toy car is powered by an electric motor.

What Is an Electric Motor?

Electric motors are used in many different kinds of important devices. Among other things they power toys, elevators, fans, air compressors, cranes, and even certain cars and bicycles. Did you know that the spinning force in an electric motor comes from an electromagnet?

The diagram below gives you an idea about how an electric motor works. A wire is placed between the north and south poles of two permanent magnets (A). When the ends of the wire are connected to a battery (B), the wire jumps up.

The wire jumps because the current it carries makes it an electromagnet. The wire's magnetic field is pushed on by the field between the two permanent magnets, causing the wire to move up. The push depends on the direction of the flow of electrons in the wire as well as the direction of the magnetic field.

In an electric motor, a loop of wire is placed in the field between two permanent magnets. When current passes through the wire, the loop becomes an electromagnet and rotates between the permanent magnets.

▷ **What causes the spinning force in an electric motor?**

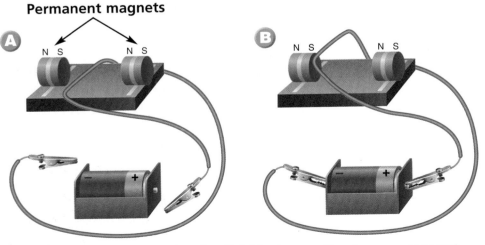

The wire is pushed up by the field between the two permanent magnets when the battery connection is made.

How Are Electromagnets Used in Medicine?

Under the right conditions, a doctor can turn a patient's body into a radio transmitter. The technique is called magnetic resonance imaging, or MRI.

The patient in the photograph is undergoing MRI. His body is about to go inside the tube surrounded by a very strong magnetic field produced by electromagnets. In his body the nuclei of certain atoms, especially hydrogen atoms, act like little magnets. These nuclei tend to line up with the magnetic field, much like a compass needle lines up with Earth's magnetic field.

When radio waves are beamed at the patient's body, the magnetic nuclei absorb them and return radio waves of their own. These radio waves are analyzed by a computer to produce striking images of tissues inside the body.

▷ **How does MRI use electromagnets?**

The images provided by MRI help diagnose health problems.

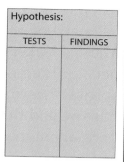

QUICK LAB

Electric Motor

FOLDABLES™

Make a Folded Chart. (See page R 44.) Label as shown.

Hypothesis:	
TESTS	FINDINGS

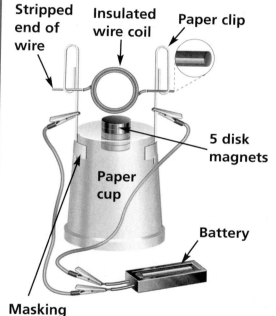

Stripped end of wire

Insulated wire coil

Paper clip

5 disk magnets

Paper cup

Battery

Masking tape

1. Make an electric motor as shown.

2. Connect the battery, and flick the coil to give it a start.

3. Why was it necessary to paint the top half of one of the exposed ends of the wires with a marker?

4. **Hypothesize** What could make the motor go faster? Carry out tests. Report your findings on the chart.

How Can Electromagnets Make Sound?

Stereo speakers that allow us to listen to music or voices are used in CD players, radios, and televisions. These speakers depend on electromagnets for their operation. The cone in a speaker has an electromagnet at its narrow end that sits in the field of a permanent magnet. The sound to be reproduced is fed to the electromagnet as bursts of current.

The spacing between the bursts of current matches the spacing between the sound waves in the recording. As each burst of current passes through the electromagnet, the electromagnet is moved by the permanent magnet's field. The back-and-forth motion of the electromagnet makes the speaker cone diaphragm vibrate to produce sound waves that we hear as music or voices.

▷ **What is the purpose of an electromagnet in a speaker?**

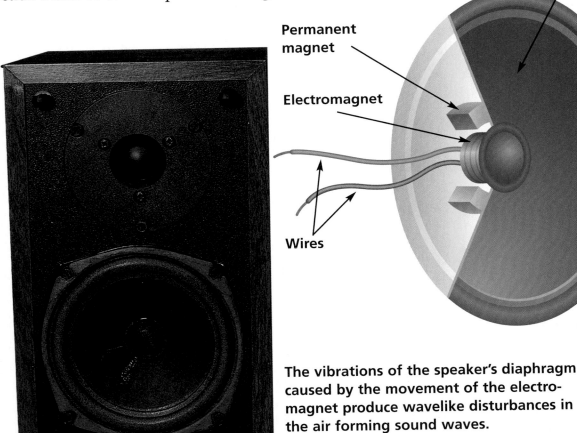

Permanent magnet

Electromagnet

Wires

Vibrating diaphragm

The vibrations of the speaker's diaphragm caused by the movement of the electromagnet produce wavelike disturbances in the air forming sound waves.

Why It Matters

Television screens, like stereo speakers, rely on electromagnets. The image on a TV screen is produced by narrow beams of electrons that sweep across the screen many times per second. Electromagnets varying in strength deflect the electron beams, making them rapidly trace out a path that covers the entire screen.

e-Journal Visit our Web site www.science.mmhschool.com to do a research project on electromagnets.

Think and Write

1. What is a magnet?

2. What is an electromagnet?

3. How are permanent magnets and electromagnets alike? How are they different?

4. Why is Earth's magnetic north pole not true north?

5. **Critical Thinking** Is the magnetic pole near Earth's true North Pole a magnetic south pole or a magnetic north pole? Why?

LINKS

MATH LINK

Solve a problem. The greater the number of turns of the wire coil, the stronger the magnetism of the electromagnet. How many turns of the wire coil would you have to make to produce an electromagnet that is four times as strong as an electromagnet with 250 turns?

WRITING LINK

Explanatory Writing A pen pal writes to you, saying that he just got a compass and a map of the woods behind his new home. The map shows that a pond can be found 3 kilometers due north of his house. He wants to visit the pond by walking due north until he finds it. Write a letter telling your pen pal how to use his compass to find true north. Give him clear step-by-step directions. Use the correct form for writing a friendly letter.

HEALTH LINK

Learn more about MRI. How has this technology affected the work of doctors? How has it helped patients? What diseases can it help doctors diagnose?

TECHNOLOGY LINK

LOG ON Visit www.science.mmhschool.com for more links.

Using Electricity

Get Ready

Can you think of examples in your life where you have used electricity to do something around your home or school? How did the device change the electrical energy into heat, light, or sound? What was the heat, light, or sound used for?

The electricity in this toy train set came from a wall outlet. How did the electricity get to the wall outlet? How was it produced in the first place?

Inquiry Skill

You experiment when you perform a test to support or disprove a hypothesis.

Explore Activity

How Can an Electric Current Be Produced?

Materials
goggles
3 cups
lemon juice
compass
enameled wire
3 copper strips
3 zinc strips
tape

Procedure

BE CAREFUL! Wear goggles.

1. Assemble one, two, or three wet cells as shown. Connect a copper strip in one cell to a zinc strip in another cell. Make as many wire loops around the compass as possible while leaving two long free ends. Connect each to an unattached zinc or copper strip.

2. Watch the needle on the compass, and record what happens. How does it vary when more cells are used?

3. Did your wet cells produce current? How do you know?

4. **Infer** Why was the lemon juice important in your experiment?

Drawing Conclusions

1. **Predict** Do you think your wet cells will produce current when you change them by
   - using two strips of the same metal in each cell?
   - using different metals but pure water instead of lemon juice?

2. **Experiment** Test your predictions. Write a description of what happens.

3. **FURTHER INQUIRY** **Experiment** Can you use your wet cells to run an electrical device? Remove the battery from a simple liquid crystal display watch. Touch the wires from your wet cells to the battery terminals instead of the compass (the wire from the zinc attaches to the negative terminal). Does the watch run?

Main Idea Electricity gives us energy that we can change into useful forms.

What Are Wet Cells and Dry Cells?

A device that produces a current in a solution is a **wet cell**. All wet cells use chemical reactions to produce electric current. When we connect a wet cell to a circuit, the current it produces consists of charged particles that always continue to move in the same direction. As a result, the current from a wet cell is called a **direct current**.

A wet cell generally consists of plates made of two different materials that are placed in a conducting solution. When the plates are linked by a wire, chemical reactions between them and the solution cause electrons to move onto one plate and off the other.

The crowding of electrons on one plate and the lack of electrons on the other produce a *voltage* that can produce current in a circuit. Voltage is the difference in the amount of potential, or stored, energy between the plates, or the ends of a cell. That is, the negative plate, or end, has more potential energy than the positive end. Voltage describes the amount of energy the cell provides to move charged particles from the negative end, through a circuit, to the positive end. The amount of voltage of a cell is measured in *volts*. You can think of the

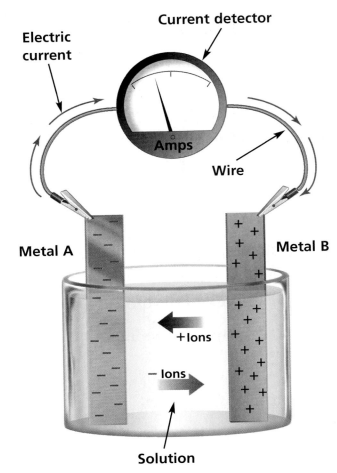

Wet Cell

Electric current

Current detector

Amps

Wire

Metal A

Metal B

+ Ions

− Ions

Solution

voltage as the amount of "push" the cell provides for the charged particles.

The amount of current can be measured by a device called an *ammeter*. The unit for measuring current is the *ampere* (AM·peer)—or *amp*, for short. One ampere of current is a flow of about 6 billion billion charged particles per second through any point in a circuit.

Electric current can also be produced by cells containing a moist conducting paste instead of a solution. Such cells are said to be **dry cells**, because the paste is not a liquid like the solution of a wet cell. Still, a dry cell works very much like a wet cell—chemical reactions between the paste and the plates crowd electrons on one plate and remove electrons from the other. The "plates," however, may be in the form of rods, powders, or cans.

The voltage of a particular type of cell is always the same (unless it is run-down). For example, an alkaline dry cell produces 1.5 volts. If we need a 9-volt source of electricity, how can we assemble it from 1.5-volt cells? Simply connect six 1.5-volt cells together in series. Cells connected in this fashion are called a *battery*.

Common carbon-zinc dry cells produce 1.5 volts. However, differences in some of the chemicals allow alkaline dry cells to last up to ten times longer than carbon-zinc dry cells.

Carbon-zinc and alkaline dry cells are just two of many different chemical systems upon which dry cells are based. Small camera batteries, for example, often use lithium-containing chemicals because these substances are readily able to supply electricity in surges.

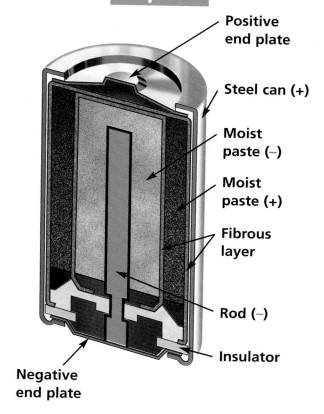

Positive end plate

Steel can (+)

Moist paste (–)

Moist paste (+)

Fibrous layer

Rod (–)

Insulator

Negative end plate

READING **Cause and Effect**

How does a wet cell produce current?

The 9-volt alkaline battery and the six 1.5-volt dry cells connected in series produce the same amount of electricity.

9-volt alkaline battery

Dry cells

1.5 volts
1.5 volts
1.5 volts
1.5 volts
1.5 volts
1.5 volts

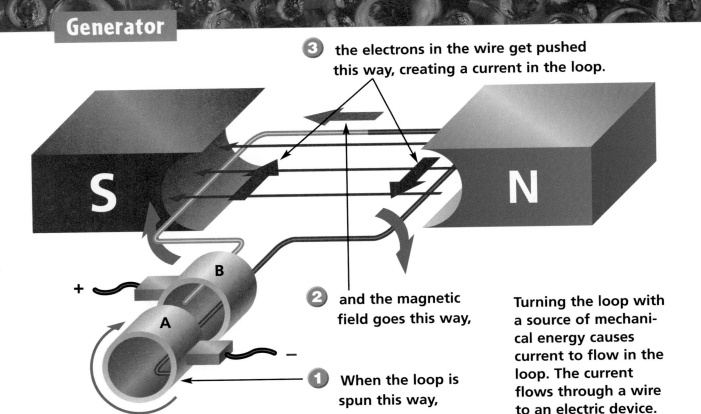

3 the electrons in the wire get pushed this way, creating a current in the loop.

S N

+

B

A

−

2 and the magnetic field goes this way,

1 When the loop is spun this way,

Turning the loop with a source of mechanical energy causes current to flow in the loop. The current flows through a wire to an electric device.

What Is a Generator?

A **generator** uses mechanical energy from machines such as a hand crank, a steam-driven wheel, or a gasoline motor to make electricity. The top diagram shows how mechanical energy spinning a wire loop in a magnetic field can produce electric current.

With the loop in the position shown, ring A gets extra electrons, while ring B has a lack of electrons. Imagine that the orange section of the loop in the diagram has spun to the brown section's original position. The electrons in the orange section will be pushed toward you, the reverse of their original direction. This makes ring B negative and ring A positive. However, the current will reverse itself again as the orange section returns to

its starting position. The changes in the direction of the current that occur during each turn of the loop produce an **alternating current**.

Electric power plants use more complicated generators to produce electricity for homes and businesses. The electricity is sent in the form of alternating current that completes 60 back-and-forth cycles each second. Devices known as **transformers** are used to increase or decrease the voltage of the current for various applications. *Step-up* transformers increase the voltage. *Step-down* transformers decrease the voltage.

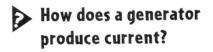

How does a generator produce current?

How Do Transformers Change Volts?

When scientists use numbers and make measurements, they can often report observations and find patterns in data more exactly. In this activity you will be looking for a pattern in the number of volts going into and out of five different transformers. Transformer A is a step-down transformer. The left side of transformer A has 10 times as many loops as the right side. Ten times as many volts go into the transformer as out. The 110 volts going in are reduced 10 times to 11 volts. Transformer B is a step-up transformer. The right side of transformer B has 10 times as many loops as the left side. Ten times fewer volts go into the transformer as go out. The 15 volts going in are increased 10 times to 150 volts.

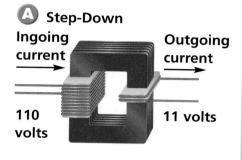

A Step-Down
Ingoing current
Outgoing current
110 volts
11 volts

Procedure

Interpret Data Do you notice a pattern in the transformers? How can you use a ratio to express the pattern? Write the number of volts for diagrams C–E.

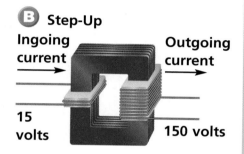

B Step-Up
Ingoing current
Outgoing current
15 volts
150 volts

Drawing Conclusions

1. **Interpret Data** What is the pattern that you noticed in the transformers?

2. **Measure** In which transformers is the voltage increased? Decreased? Make a table of your results.

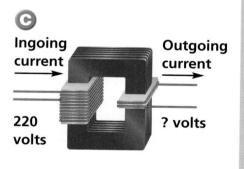

C
Ingoing current
Outgoing current
220 volts
? volts

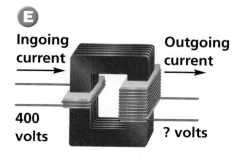

E
Ingoing current
Outgoing current
400 volts
? volts

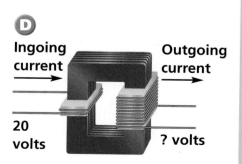

D
Ingoing current
Outgoing current
20 volts
? volts

How Does Electric Current Reach Your Home?

Electric current is produced by huge generators at power plants. Power lines span great distances from power plants to cities and towns. Some of the electric energy traveling in the lines is changed into heat. The heat is wasted energy. One way to prevent such waste is to send low currents through the lines. However, to send useful amounts of electric power using low currents, thousands of volts are needed.

Electric current from a generator is first conducted to a transformer that increases the voltage. The voltage can be increased to anywhere from 120,000 to 500,000 volts. Such high voltages are extremely dangerous. Before reaching your home, the current reaches transformers that decrease the voltage. Household circuits often use 120 volts.

From Generator to Home

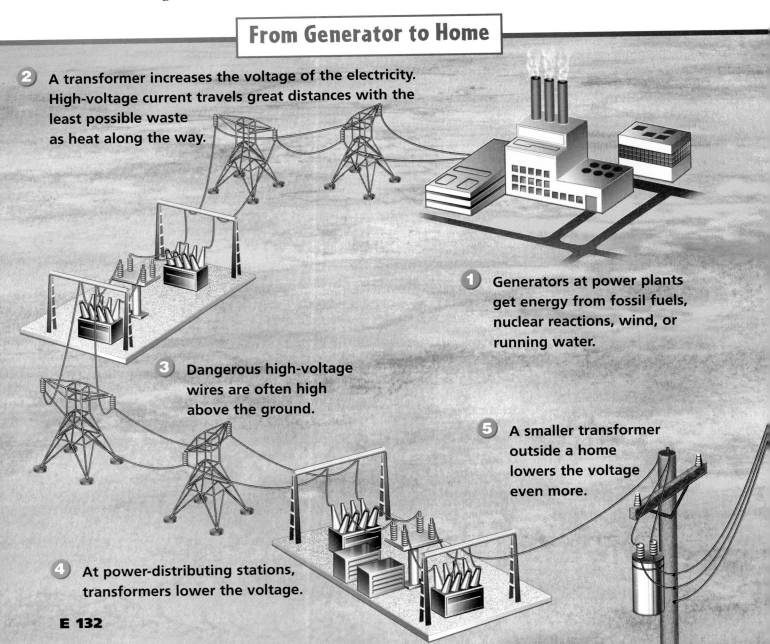

2 A transformer increases the voltage of the electricity. High-voltage current travels great distances with the least possible waste as heat along the way.

1 Generators at power plants get energy from fossil fuels, nuclear reactions, wind, or running water.

3 Dangerous high-voltage wires are often high above the ground.

5 A smaller transformer outside a home lowers the voltage even more.

4 At power-distributing stations, transformers lower the voltage.

The total current supplied to an entire house or apartment is usually no more than 100 or 200 amps. Each circuit within a house or apartment carries a portion of the total current. A kitchen circuit, for example, may have only 20 amps. That means you could run appliances in that circuit at the same time if they do not use more than 20 amps altogether.

A short circuit can occur when too much current flows through a wire. This can happen, for example, when uninsulated wires in the wall touch. Overloading a circuit with more appliances than the circuit can handle also causes this problem. Wires heat up. Wall materials can catch on fire. *Fuses* and *circuit breakers* protect against this problem.

▷ **What is the path of electricity from a generator to your home?**

READING
Diagrams

How do the transformers differ in this diagram?

Circuit breaker panel

6 Current enters a home.

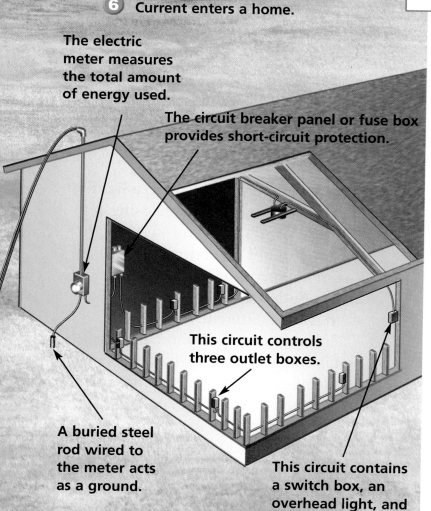

The electric meter measures the total amount of energy used.

The circuit breaker panel or fuse box provides short-circuit protection.

This circuit controls three outlet boxes.

A buried steel rod wired to the meter acts as a ground.

This circuit contains a switch box, an overhead light, and two outlet boxes.

This overloaded circuit could lead to a fire.

How Do You Use Electrical Energy at Home?

Any form of energy can be changed, or transformed, into other forms. Electrical energy can be put to use in many ways because it can be changed into almost any other form of energy.

Mechanical Energy

Electrical energy can be changed into mechanical energy in any device that uses a motor. Food blenders, electric fans, and power tools are examples that run on current from a household circuit. Cars and many mechanical toys are examples that run on batteries.

Heat

The coils in a toaster oven get hot enough to chemically change the bread's taste and color because of an electric current. Electrons in the current collide with atoms in the coil and transfer energy to the atoms, making them move faster. The temperature of the coil rises.

Portable heaters, electric blankets, and hair dryers all contain a heating element. The heating element is a resistor. The strength of the resistor is carefully chosen so that it produces the proper heat.

Sound

A loudspeaker turns electrical energy into sound. Changes in current cause an electromagnet to move a diaphragm back and forth, producing sound waves. That is how sound is produced in radios, televisions, and stereo and tape players.

Have you ever heard a watch alarm beep? Tiny speakers in such watches use crystals attached to a diaphragm. Varying the voltage varies the crystal shapes and drives the diaphragm back and forth. Sound waves are produced.

Light

Every time you "turn on" a light by flicking a switch, you are closing a circuit. Current flows through a light bulb, and light is produced. There are two main forms of lighting in homes today. Both use electrical energy, but each uses it differently.

Incandescent (in·kuhn·DES·uhnt) bulbs contain a thin metal wire, or filament, that acts as a resistor. Current heats it to about 2,500°F. At this temperature, atoms in the filament give off heat and visible light. Only about 12 percent of the energy is light. The rest is wasted as heat.

The heating element in this electric hair dryer functions as a resistor.

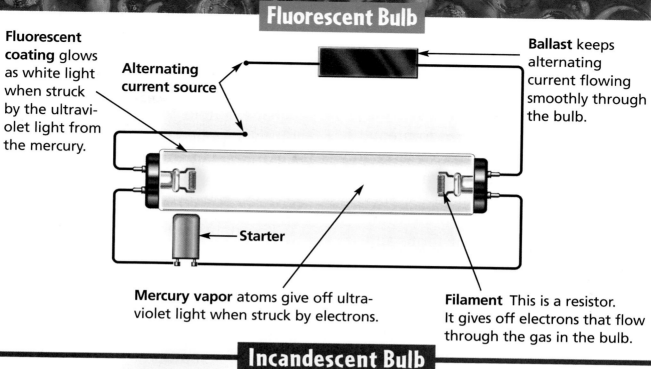

Fluorescent coating glows as white light when struck by the ultraviolet light from the mercury.

Alternating current source

Ballast keeps alternating current flowing smoothly through the bulb.

Starter

Mercury vapor atoms give off ultraviolet light when struck by electrons.

Filament This is a resistor. It gives off electrons that flow through the gas in the bulb.

Incandescent Bulb

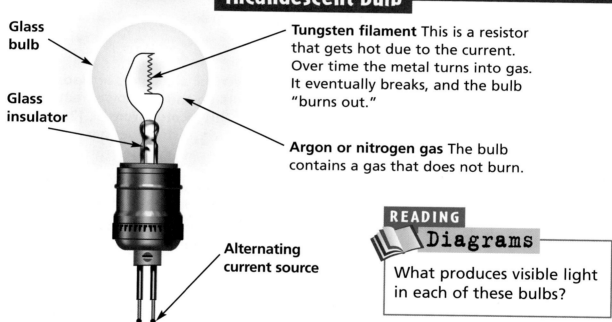

Glass bulb

Glass insulator

Tungsten filament This is a resistor that gets hot due to the current. Over time the metal turns into gas. It eventually breaks, and the bulb "burns out."

Argon or nitrogen gas The bulb contains a gas that does not burn.

Alternating current source

READING
Diagrams

What produces visible light in each of these bulbs?

Fluorescent (floo·RES·uhnt) bulbs, on the other hand, produce much more light than heat. A series of collisions causes gas inside the glass to produce invisible light. The fluorescent coating on the inside of the glass, in turn, glows white.

The coating on any bulb determines how much light you see. If a bulb were *opaque*, it would absorb and block off all light from the inside. Therefore many bulbs are *transparent*, that is, clear. These allow all light through. *Translucent* bulbs let only some light through. They produce a softer glow.

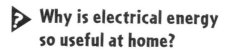 **Why is electrical energy so useful at home?**

How Much Electricity Do You Use?

An adult at home can show you where the electric meter is located. It measures the amount of electric energy your household uses. Electrical energy is measured in units called *kilowatt-hours*. To understand what this unit means, first review some terms and learn some others.

Volts and Amps

The voltage in a circuit, recall, depends on the transformers directly outside the house. Most homes operate at 120 volts. The voltage "pushes" the current through the circuits. The amount of current a device uses is measured in units called amperes, or amps.

Electric Power

The suppliers who provide electricity for homes and buildings are called power companies. They provide *electric power*. To you, the word *power* may mean "strength" or "force." However, electric power is a rate. It is the rate at which electric energy changes into another form when it is used. That is, it changes into mechanical energy, heat, light, or sound.

The unit of electric power is the *watt*. You may have seen the word *watt* on package labels, such as for a 60-watt bulb. These labels indicate the power a device uses per hour. You can calculate electric power by using the following formula.

$$power = voltage \times current$$
$$or$$
$$watts = volts \times amps$$

For example, the voltage of the current supplied to a home is 120 volts. A light bulb might use about 0.5 amp.

$$power = 120 \text{ volts} \times 0.5 \text{ amp}$$
$$= 60 \text{ watts}$$

The more power a bulb uses, the brighter it is. Household bulbs use about 100 watts or 150 watts. Motors and appliances use much more power. *Kilowatts* are units that measure large amounts of power. The prefix *kilo-* means "one thousand." A kilowatt is 1,000 watts.

All electrical appliances are labeled with the voltage and the power required to run them. This recorder runs at 120 volts and uses 17 watts of power per hour.

Amounts of Current	
Item	Current (amps)
60-watt bulb	0.500
Table radio	0.200
Electric clock	0.025
Microwave oven	10.000
Electric clothes dryer	16.000
Lightning bolt	20,000.000

Electric Energy

The amount of electric energy used in a household depends on two things. First, it depends on the total power used by all the electric appliances. Second, it depends on the total time they are used. The formula to find electric power is:

$$\text{energy} = \text{power} \times \text{time}$$
or
$$\text{kilowatt-hours} = \text{kilowatts} \times \text{hours}$$

How much energy is used to run a 600-watt refrigerator for 24 hours?

$$\text{energy} = 0.6 \text{ kW} \times 24 \text{ hours}$$
$$= 14.4 \text{ kilowatt-hours}$$

The Cost of Electricity

An electric meter measures energy in kilowatt-hours. During any day the dials turn quickly or slowly. The speed depends on how many kilowatt-hours you use. Take a reading one day. Then take a reading at the same time a day later. The difference between the two readings is the amount of kilowatt-hours you used in a day.

To find out how much that amount of power costs, multiply the amount by the power company cost. A company may charge 10 cents per kilowatt-hour. To find out how much the 600-watt refrigerator costs to run for 24 hours:

$$\text{total cost} = \text{energy} \times \text{cost per kilowatt-hour}$$
$$= 14.4 \text{ kilowatt-hours} \times \$0.10/\text{kilowatt-hour}$$
$$= \$1.44$$

Each dial is like a place value in a place-value chart. The dial at the right reads in ones. The next dial to the left reads in tens, the next in hundreds, and so on.

Power Used by Common Appliances

Appliance	Watts	Kilowatts (kW)
Refrigerator	600	0.6
Toaster	700	0.7
Microwave oven	1,450	1.450
Table radio	100	0.1
Electric clock	3	0.003
Electric clothes dryer	4,000	4.0

▷ **How much does it cost for a 100-watt bulb to stay lighted for 24 hours at 10 cents per kilowatt-hour?**

What Must You Remember About Electricity?

There are two basic ideas to keep in mind whenever you use electricity. They are: "Be Safe" and "Save Energy."

Be Safe

Electric devices are helpful—but only if you use them properly. Here are some rules to follow when using electricity:

- Never touch a wall socket with anything but a plug.
- Never touch the metal part of a plug when you plug it in.
- Never use a plug that is torn. It can cause a short circuit.
- Do not use the cord to pull out a plug.
- Do not overload an outlet with many plugs. They use too much current.
- Keep away from high-voltage wires.
- Never use electric devices when you are wet or standing in water.

Save Energy

Electric energy costs money. What's more, it uses up fuels and may pollute the environment. Many generators are run by steam. The steam is produced by burning fossil fuels, such as coal and oil. By turning off appliances, you are saving money—and you are saving our supply of fossil fuels.

Many power plants release heat into the environment. They release hot water left over from the process of making steam. This hot water released into rivers or lakes produces **thermal pollution** . This pollution can kill living things in those water ecosystems. Power companies deal with this problem by cooling the water in cooling towers. The cool water is reusable. However, the burning of fuels to run generators pollutes air and land. Power companies are searching for cleaner methods of producing energy, methods that do not use up valuable fossil fuels.

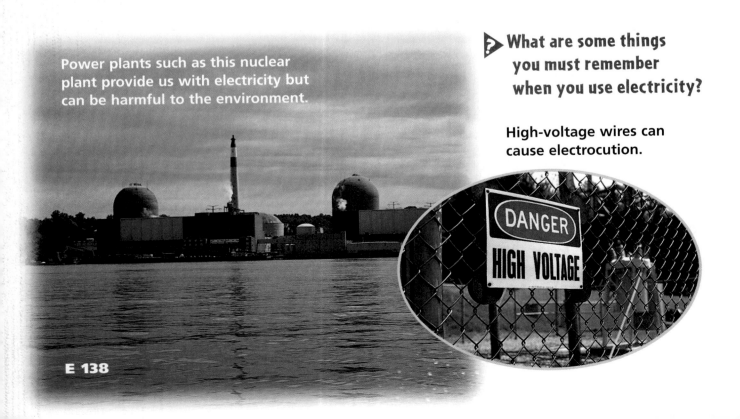

Power plants such as this nuclear plant provide us with electricity but can be harmful to the environment.

▶ **What are some things you must remember when you use electricity?**

High-voltage wires can cause electrocution.

DANGER
HIGH VOLTAGE

LINKS

Why It Matters

Cooling towers control thermal pollution from power plants. The warm water that has been used to condense exhaust steam is allowed to trickle down over several decks in the tower. The water cools as it comes into contact with the air. By the time it reaches the bottom of the tower, it is cool enough to once again condense exhaust steam.

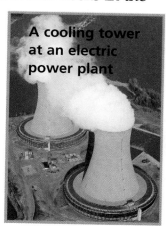

A cooling tower at an electric power plant

e-Journal Visit our Web site **www.science.mmhschool.com** to do a research project on using electricity.

Think and Write

1. Compare wet and dry cells.

2. Compare direct current and alternating current.

3. How do coils on a transformer control voltage?

4. **INQUIRY SKILL** Measure A 100-watt bulb operates on a 120-volt circuit. How many amperes of current does it use?

5. **Critical Thinking** The chemical reactions in a car battery produce about 2 volts in a wet cell. The battery has 12 volts. How is this possible?

WRITING LINK

Writing a Story George Westinghouse and Thomas Edison argued forcefully at the turn of the 20th century about direct versus alternating current. Research this argument, and write a story about it. Use dialogue, and test it on a partner to see if it sounds like real speech. You could turn your story into a radio play to record for the class.

LITERATURE LINK

Read *Capture the Wind* to learn about how wind can be used to produce electricity. Try the activities at the end of the book.

MATH LINK

Solve a problem. How much energy in kilowatt-hours is used to run a 4000-watt electric clothes dryer for three-quarters of an hour?

TECHNOLOGY LINK

LOG ON Visit **www.science.mmhschool.com** for more links.

Vocabulary

Fill each blank with the best word or words from the list.

circuit, E108
conductor, E102
generator, E130
magnet, E118
open circuit, E112
parallel circuit, E111
pole, E118
static electricity, E98
thermal pollution, E138
transformer, E130

1. Hot water released from a power plant into the environment can contribute to _____.

2. Any path along which charged particles can travel is a(n) _____.

3. A magnet has both a north and a south _____.

4. When the light switch in the room is in the *off* position, it causes a(n) _____.

5. A material that allows electrons to move through it easily is a(n) _____.

6. You can change the voltage of the current from a generator with a(n) _____.

7. A circuit with more than one path for current is a(n) _____.

8. An object that attracts other objects made of iron, cobalt, or nickel is a(n) _____.

9. Attraction between pieces of clothing in a dryer is usually due to _____.

10. Mechanical energy is changed into electrical energy by a(n) _____.

Test Prep

11. A(n) _____ occurs when a path in a circuit bypasses a less conductive path.
  A open circuit
  B closed circuit
  C short circuit
  D current

12. A device that is made magnetic by an electric current is a(n)

  _____.
  F electromagnet
  G magnet
  H generator
  J transformer

13. All of the following are a type of circuit EXCEPT _____.
  A open
  B closed
  C short
  D long

14. What type of cell containing a moist conducting paste produces electric current?

F wet cell

G circuit cell

H dry cell

J moist cell

15. Electricity that is safely connected to or released to Earth is _____.

A current

B grounded

C insulated

D conducted

Concepts and Skills

16. Reading in Science How is electricity produced in a power plant?

17. Critical Thinking How does a compass used by someone in Egypt compare with a compass you would use?

18. INQUIRY SKILL **Measure** Using the data table on page E137, measure your energy usage for one day in kilowatt-hours. Consider only the appliances listed in the table.

19. Scientific Methods How do electricians determine how to set up the electricity in a building? Can they predict the placement of switches and the brightness of lights?

20. Decision Making What can you do to conserve electricity?

Did You Ever Wonder?

INQUIRY SKILL **Measure** A 23-watt fluorescent bulb lasts 10,000 hours and provides as much light as a 100-watt incandescent bulb that lasts 750 hours. How much energy could you save in your home if the bulbs are used for 7500 hours? How many bulbs would you have to buy?

 LOG ON Visit www.science.mmhschool.com to boost your test scores.

Meet a Scientist

Steven Chu

Physicist

When Steven Chu was a boy in Garden City, New York, he says, "I approached schoolwork like a chore." Thanks to a great high school physics teacher, Chu's attitude toward learning began to change. He went to college, studied physics, and went into research.

"One of the skills you need as a research scientist is to ask, 'Why is this happening?'" he says. "You ask why does something work and not just accept that it does."

Chu's questions paid off. In 1997 he won the Nobel Prize for physics, one of the most important scientific prizes in the world.

Chu shared the prize with two other physicists, William D. Phillips and Claude Cohen-Tannoudji. Although thousands of miles apart, the three scientists had been working on the same problem. Chu was in California,

Phillips was in Maryland, and Cohen-Tannoudji was in France. Each contributed to a new technique that uses laser beams to slow down and cool atoms held in a magnetic trap. Their work has led to miniature devices used to guide airplanes and to explore for oil and other natural resources.

It's not unusual for scientists to share a prize. Scientists in different labs around the world often work on the same problem. "What was particularly nice about this," Chu explains, "was that although we were working very hard on our own, we also shared information with each other." Sharing information and cooperating brought important answers to all three scientists—not to mention the Nobel Prize!

LOG ON Visit www.science.mmhschool.com to learn more about the work of physicists.

TOP 5 Common Uses for Lasers

Steven Chu uses lasers in his work on slowing down atoms. Here are some other uses for lasers. How many are you familiar with?

1. CD players
2. Supermarket checkout barcode readers
3. Eye surgery
4. Diamond-cutting
5. Telephone transmission by optic fiber

Write About It

1. Why is working together on a problem useful?
2. What kind of science project would you like to collaborate on? Why?

Comparing Change

Your goal is to compare changes to matter.

What to Do

1. Label two jars, one "cold" and one "hot." Half fill the jars with cold or hot water. Add two spoonfuls of vinegar to each.

2. Put a spoonful of baking soda in two plastic bags. Don't get baking soda in the jars. Fasten the bags over the jars with rubber bands.

3. Record the time. Drop the baking soda into the jars at the same time. Record any changes and when they stop.

Analyze Your Results

What type of change did you observe in each jar? How were the changes in each jar different? Why? How was energy involved?

SAND SHAKE

Your goal is to measure and graph the temperature of sand.

What to Do

Put sand in a jar. Cover with a lid. Shake the jar about 100 times. Repeat this step 6 more times. After each step measure and record the temperature of the sand.

Analyze Your Results

Make a line graph. Put temperature on the vertical axis, and number of shakes on the horizontal axis. Interpret your graph.

MAKE A CIRCUIT

Your goal is to make series and parallel circuits and draw diagrams of them.

What to Do

1. Make a series circuit. Draw it.

2. Make a parallel circuit. Draw it.

Analyze Your Results

Label each diagram series or parallel. Show the direction of current through each circuit.

UNIT F

Motion, Work, and Machines

Motion, Work, and Machines

LOOK!

Cars are put together by huge robots in an automated production line. How do robots and other machines help us do work?

CHAPTER 12

Objects in Motion

Did You Ever Wonder?

How is a locomotive able to pull a long line of train cars?
This old-fashioned steam engine on the Durango-Silverton
Railroad in Colorado, produces enough of a pull, or force, to
set the train in motion. How does the train's motion change
when it goes around a curve?

INQUIRY SKILL **Use Numbers** What's the fastest you have traveled on
land? A roller coaster built in 2003 reaches a top speed of 193.1 kilometers
per hour (120 miles per hour). How does this speed compare with your
fastest speed?

F 2

Speed and Distance

Get Ready

Gazelles are among the fastest animals on Earth. Do you think you could catch a herd of running gazelles if you were following them in a car?

How do you know when the car or bus you are in is moving? How can you tell this if your eyes are closed?

Inquiry Skill

You **experiment when you** perform a test to support or disprove a hypothesis.

Explore Activity

How Can You Tell Who Moves Faster?

Materials

meterstick

stopwatch (or watch with a second hand)

masking tape

calculator

Procedure

1 **Measure** Use a meterstick to measure a distance of 20 m on the school playground or in the gymnasium. Mark the start and finish lines with masking tape.

2 **Predict** With a partner, predict how long it will take each of you to walk 20 m. Record your prediction.

3 **Measure** Keep the time as your partner walks along the 20-m course. Record the time.

4 Repeat steps 1–3, but this time predict and measure your jogging time.

5 **Use Numbers** For both walking and jogging, use a calculator to determine how fast you moved:
speed = distance/time = 20 m/time (seconds).

Drawing Conclusions

1 **Interpret Data** What measurements do you need to tell how fast you walk or jog?

2 Were your predictions close to your actual times? Why might one prediction have been closer than another?

3 Which partner walked faster? Who jogged faster? Compare your finish times and the speeds you calculated.

4 **FURTHER INQUIRY** **Experiment** How long would it take you to walk 100 m? Jog 100 m? Test your predictions.

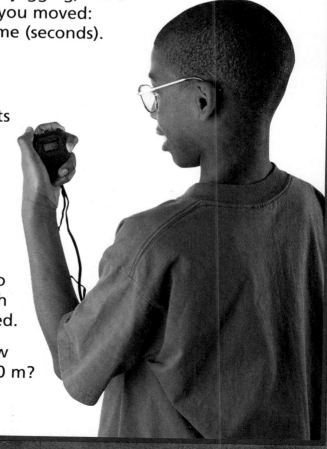

Main Idea Speed, velocity, and acceleration are characteristics of motion that help determine the position of an object at any given time.

How Are Position and Motion Related?

Billy has just come out of a movie, and he has missed the city bus. He is calling his father for a ride home. Billy must describe his location to his father so his father can pick him up.

Billy might say that he is standing on the corner of Spruce Street and 1st Avenue. To give his father a more complete description of his location, Billy might add that he is on the northeast corner, 2 feet west of the mailbox.

Look at the map of a city park. If you are telling a friend how to find the soccer field you might say, "The soccer field is at the corner of 47th Street and 7th Avenue." The two streets clearly tell your friend where the soccer field is located. You might also want to tell someone where the playground area is located. You could say, "The playground is 40 feet south of the boathouse." In this case you have used a distance and a direction to describe where an object is located.

Using streets or a distance and a direction are ways of giving the **position** of something. An object's position is its location compared with things around it.

A runner also uses position to tell where she is during a race. Start and finish lines are reference marks. These marks show her position as she runs the course. She can describe her position by saying something like "I am 5 meters from the start."

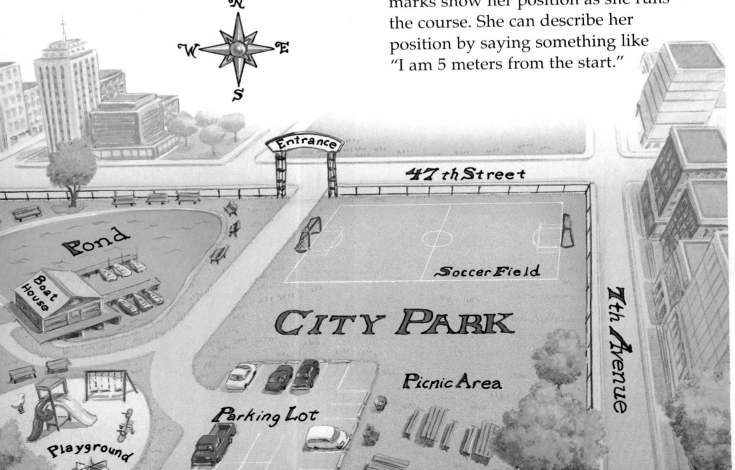

In a race runners move from the start line to the finish line. They can tell they are moving because they leave the starting line farther and farther behind. The runners can also see a change in their position from objects that remain still while they are in motion.

Motion is a change in an object's position compared with fixed objects around it. When you are driving in a car, you can tell the car is moving because trees, lampposts, and other objects sweep past your view. Within the car you are motionless compared with the dashboard or the seat because your position in relation to these objects is not changing. Have you ever been sitting in a train when another train next to you started rolling slowly backward?

READING

Graphs

1. How far did runner 1 travel in 7 seconds? How far did runner 2 travel in 7 seconds?

2. How many seconds did it take runner 1 to finish the 100-meter race? Runner 2? Which runner was faster?

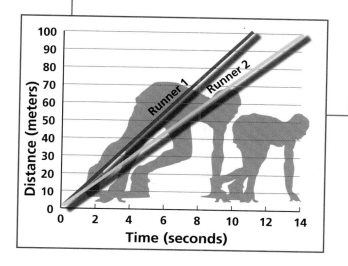

Without other objects as references, it was probably hard to tell if the other train was moving backward or if you were moving ahead.

Motion can be described by giving an object's position at different times. The table shows the positions of two runners in a 100-meter dash every second. The position is measured as the **distance** from the starting line.

We can also describe the motion of the two runners with a graph. The graph shows at a glance which runner is faster.

 **What are two ways to describe motion?**

Distance from Start

Time in Seconds	Distance from Start in Meters (feet)	
	Runner 1	Runner 2
0.0	0.0 (0.0)	0.0 (0.0)
1.0	9.1 (30)	7.1 (23)
2.0	18.2 (60)	14.3 (47)
3.0	27.3 (104)	21.4 (70)
4.0	36.4 (119)	28.6 (94)
5.0	45.5 (149)	35.7 (117)
6.0	54.5 (179)	42.9 (141)
7.0	63.6 (209)	50.0 (164)
8.0	72.7 (238)	57.1 (187)
9.0	81.8 (268)	64.3 (211)
10.0	90.9 (298)	71.4 (234)
11.0	100.0 (328)	78.6 (252)
12.0		85.7 (281)
13.0		92.9 (305)
14.0		100.0 (328)

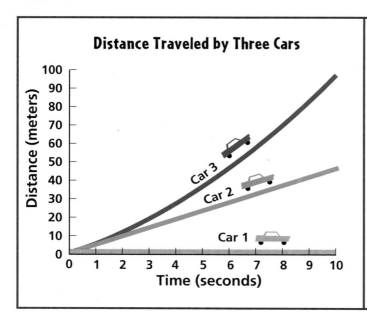

Distance Traveled by Three Cars

Car 3
Car 2
Car 1

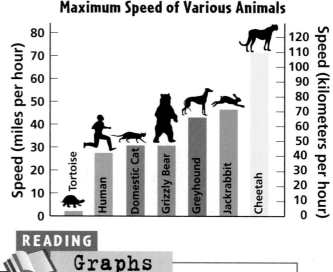

Maximum Speed of Various Animals

Tortoise · Human · Domestic Cat · Grizzly Bear · Greyhound · Jackrabbit · Cheetah

READING

Graphs

1. Compare the lines of the three cars. What do they tell you about their speed?

2. Which can run 20 meters in less time—a domestic cat or a jackrabbit?

How Fast Are You Moving?

When you describe "how fast" something is moving, you are describing its **speed**. Speed is how fast an object's position changes with time at any given moment.

For example, a car with a speed of 97 kilometers per hour (60 miles per hour) is traveling faster than a car with a speed of 72 kilometers per hour (45 miles per hour). The first car travels 97 kilometers (60 miles) in 1 hour, while the second car travels only 72 kilometers (45 miles). The first car's change in position is greater over the same amount of time, so its speed is greater.

Speed can change from moment to moment. If you are at rest, you have zero speed. If you walk, then jog, then run, your speed increases. The distance-time graph on this page shows the distance traveled by three cars over time. Car 1 is at rest, car 2 is traveling with a constant speed, and car 3 is steadily speeding up. Car 1's distance remains zero, car 2's distance builds up steadily, and car 3's distance builds up more rapidly.

Look at the chart of the maximum speeds of various animals. The fastest animal is the cheetah. Over short distances a cheetah can keep pace with a car traveling at the speed limit on an interstate highway. In a 100-meter (328-foot) race, a cheetah could finish in less than 4 seconds, a human in about 8 seconds, and a tortoise in about 1,000 seconds.

▶ **How can you describe how fast you are moving?**

How Do You Find Average Speed?

Speed is how fast an object moves at a certain moment. In walking to a friend's house, you might stand on a street corner, walk along the sidewalk, or jog across a street. Your speed is how fast your position is changing at any given moment. Depending on what you are doing, your speed could be fast, slow, or even zero.

Instead of looking at your speed from moment to moment, you might be interested only in the total distance you walked and the time it took you to arrive at your friend's house. If you divide the total distance traveled by the amount of time, you get the **average speed**. For example, what if you walked 5 km in 1 h to get to your friend's house? Your average speed would be:

$$\text{average speed} = \text{distance} \div \text{time}$$
$$= 5 \text{ km} \div 1 \text{ h}$$
$$= 5 \text{ km/h}$$

Remember that traveling with an average speed of 5 km/h does not mean than you actually moved at 5 km/h for the whole trip. You might have traveled at 3 km/h at some

Quarayaq Glacier

moments and 7 km/h at others. On average your speed was 5 km/h. The bar graph below shows how two cars could have the same average speed for a trip even though they often had different speeds at any moment. Speed has units of distance over time.

Speeding objects can also be found in nature. Glaciers creep down mountainsides at different speeds. Most glaciers advance about 3–60 cm (1–24 in.) per day. However, the Quarayaq glacier in Greenland is a speedster. It can flow at up to 20 meters (66 feet) a day!

▷ **How can you find the average speed of the Quarayaq glacier?**

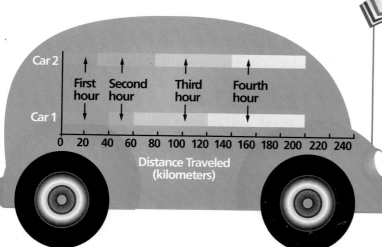

Car 2

First hour | Second hour | Third hour | Fourth hour

Car 1

0 20 40 60 80 100 120 140 160 180 200 220 240

Distance Traveled (kilometers)

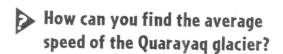

READING

Graphs

1. What was the average speed of both cars?

2. If car 1 travels for another hour at the same speed it had in the fourth hour, how far would it travel during the additional hour? How would you show that on the graph?

What Is Velocity?

What if you need to predict where an airplane will be in 1 hour? You would need to know its starting position and speed. However, you would also need to know the direction in which the plane is flying. The description of both the speed and the direction of the airplane is called the plane's **velocity**. If the velocity of the plane is 160 km/h going north, you can predict that the plane will be 160 kilometers north of its starting position 1 hour into its flight.

Two objects can have the same speed but have different velocities. Imagine two buses, one going north at 50 km/h and another going south at 50 km/h. Even though both buses have a speed of 50 km/h, they have different velocities because they are traveling in different

A car's velocity changes as its direction changes.

directions. To describe the velocity of each bus, we have to give both its speed and its direction of travel.

Just as the speed of an object can change with time, so can the direction of an object's motion. If either the speed or direction of motion of an object changes, its velocity changes. What if the car in the photograph is rounding a curve in the road at a constant speed? The direction of the car changes. As a result the velocity of the car steadily changes as it travels around the curve. The velocity is constant when the car travels in a straight line at a steady speed.

READING Main Idea
What determines the velocity of a moving object?

The velocities of six buses

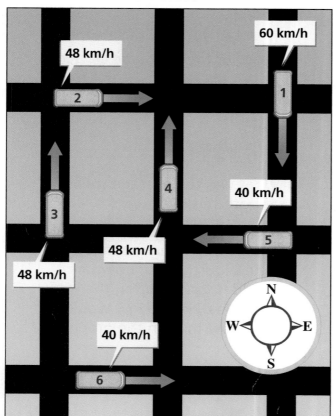

Inquiry Skill
BUILDER

SKILL Predict

How Can You Find Speed?

Table 1 lists the distance traveled by a car over time. The graph shows how the data can be plotted. If the car continues to move in the same manner, the graph or the data table can easily be used to predict how far the car will travel. For example, blue is used to show how to extend the line until a time of 10 seconds is reached.

Materials

graph paper

Procedure

1. **Communicate** Using graph paper, plot a distance-time graph for the data in Table 2. Follow the graph shown here as a model.

2. **Predict** Predict how far the car will travel in 10 seconds. Try to find a pattern in the numbers to make each prediction.

3. **Use Numbers** Check your answers by extending the line on the graph.

Drawing Conclusions

1. **Interpret Data** What pattern in the data in Table 2 helped you predict the distance at 10 seconds?

2. **Analyze** Construct a data table for a partner. Think of a pattern in time and distance. Exchange data tables and repeat the activity.

Table 1		
Time (seconds)	Distance (meters)	Distance (feet)
0	0	0
1	10	33
2	20	66
3	30	99
4	40	132
5	50	165
6	60	198
7	70	231
8	80	264

Table 2		
Time (seconds)	Distance (meters)	Distance (feet)
0	0	0
1	1	3
2	4	13
3	9	30
4	16	53
5	25	83
6	36	119
7	49	162
8	64	211

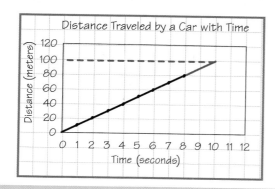

Distance Traveled by a Car with Time

How Can Velocity Change?

Imagine you are in a car when the driver steps on the gas pedal on a straight road. You can feel yourself being pressed back into the seat. If you watch the speedometer, you see the needle climb toward higher speeds. Since the car's speed is increasing, its velocity must be changing. The change of an object's velocity with time is the object's **acceleration**. When a car's speedometer shows an increase in speed with time, the car is *accelerating*.

If the driver of the car steps off the gas pedal and applies the brakes, the speedometer needle falls to slower speeds. This change in velocity is a special case of acceleration called *deceleration*. The speed of a decelerating object decreases with time.

The ball dropped by the student speeds up as it falls to the ground.

A car can also accelerate without a change in speed. Remember that velocity changes when the direction of travel alone changes. A car can drive around a corner with the speedometer reading a steady speed. The car's direction of travel steadily changes throughout the curve, so its velocity also steadily changes with time. This means that the car is accelerating.

The pictures on this page give additional examples of acceleration. The acceleration of the falling ball is due to a change in speed alone. The accelerations of the horses and riders are due to a change in direction alone.

▷ **What affects the velocity of an object?**

The horses and riders are traveling in a circle at a steady speed, but their velocity is constantly changing.

What Affects Acceleration?

When a merry-go-round ride first starts, the speed of the riders increases for several moments at the same time that the riders undergo a steady change in direction of travel. In such a case, the riders are accelerating for two reasons, a change in speed and a change in direction. In a similar manner, the motorcycle racer on this page is accelerating because he is applying the brakes at the same time that he is guiding his motorcycle around the first part of a turn. The brakes cause his speed to slow with time (a deceleration), and the curved path causes his direction of travel to change steadily. Both the change in speed and the change in direction contribute to the motorcycle racer's acceleration during the turn.

▶ **What affects the motorcycle racer's acceleration?**

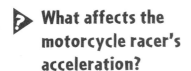

Acceleration

FOLDABLES™ Make an Eight-Row Folded Table (See p. R44.) Label as shown.

Interval	Distance Traveled
0-1 s	
1-2 s	
2-3 s	
3-4 s	
4-5 s	
5-6 s	
Explain	

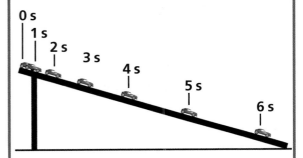

1. **Measure** Use a metric ruler to measure the distance the car in the diagram rolls between 0s and 1s. Record the distance in the table.

2. Repeat by measuring the distance the car travels from 1s to 2s, 2s to 3s, and so on, to 5s to 6s.

3. Based on the data you collected, what is happening to the speed of the car from second to second?

4. How does the change in distance between 1-second intervals compare from interval to interval?

Where Can You See Things Accelerate?

The jet taking off in the photograph first starts at rest. When the pilot releases the brakes with the engines throttled up, the plane begins accelerating. It moves faster and faster down the runway until the air passing over its wings lifts it aloft. When the plane has reached the desired speed, the pilot may reduce the strength of the push from the engines to keep the plane flying at a constant speed. If the pilot reduces the power of the engines enough, air resistance may cause the plane to decelerate. When the plane lands, the pilot applies the brakes and decelerates the plane to a stop.

When any object begins moving from rest, such as a plane taking off, a car starting out at a green light, or an arrow flying from a bow, the object must first accelerate. It may reach a constant speed for a period of time and may even reach a constant velocity if it travels in a straight line. It may also accelerate or decelerate in between periods of constant speed or velocity. The accelerations could be a change in speed, a change in direction, or both. As you can see, motion in the real world can be quite complex. The next time you ride somewhere in a car, pay attention to whether or not the car is accelerating or traveling with constant velocity. You'll see that the car's motion changes frequently!

Athletes like the runners in the photograph are very aware of the need to accelerate. At the start of the race, they must accelerate up to their desired speed. In a sprint race, they may accelerate to the fastest speed they can reach. However, if they tire during the race, they may decelerate and lose ground to their competitors. In longer races the runners accelerate as they round turns, simply because they are changing direction. At the finish of a long race, it is common to see runners accelerate to a sprint for the last 50 meters or so.

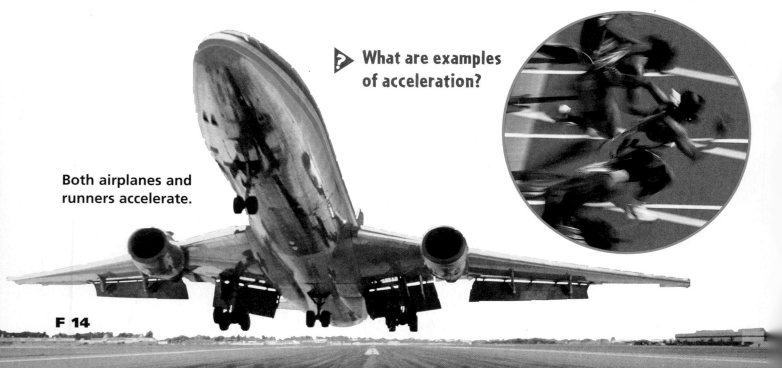

▶ What are examples of acceleration?

Both airplanes and runners accelerate.

LINKS

Why It Matters

Knowing how to use velocity and acceleration is very important. Air bags that keep passengers in cars from striking the dashboard are activated by an accelerometer. When the accelerometer detects too great a deceleration, such as a sudden stop during a crash, it triggers the air bag's release.

e-Journal Visit our Web site **www.science.mmhschool.com** to do a research project on speed and distance.

Think and Write

1. How do you find average speed?

2. Why is velocity more useful than speed in predicting the location of a moving object?

3. A car goes around a corner at a steady 30 km/h. Did the car accelerate? Why or why not?

4. INQUIRY SKILL **Predict** A car moving with constant speed travels 24 m in 3 seconds. How far will it travel in 2 seconds?

5. **Critical Thinking** Make a sketch of a chessboard. Describe a system that could locate any square on the board.

LITERATURE LINK

Read *Skates, Bikes, and Rockets* to learn about how motion plays a part in your life. Try the activities at the end of the book.

WRITING LINK

Writing a Story Imagine that you are a pilot who is flying a plane to a city 100 miles north of you. What would you need to know about the wind? How could you alter your plane's velocity to stay on course to the city? Introduce this problem in the plot of your story. Be sure to solve it at the end.

MATH LINK

Solve a problem. You walk to school each day of the week. Last week your elapsed times were 18 min, 14 min, 14 min, 18 min, and 16 min. The distance to school is 1.6 km (1 mi). What is your average speed?

TECHNOLOGY LINK

LOG ON Visit **www.science.mmhschool.com** for more links.

Forces and Motion

Get Ready

How do you stop if you are riding a bike or in-line skating? One way is to let yourself coast to a stop. You just stop pedaling or stop skating forward. How long might it take to stop?

The quicker way to stop a bike is to use the brakes. If you are skating, how do you stop quickly? Even with brakes, do you stop right away?

What if you are coasting to a stop on a bicycle? How far will you go before you stop?

Inquiry Skill

You predict when you state possible results of an event or experiment.

Explore Activity
Why Do Moving Objects Stop?

Materials

ball

2 flat surfaces
to use as ramps

protractor
(optional)

Procedure

1 Arrange the two ramps so that the ball rolls down the fixed ramp and up the adjustable ramp, as shown in the photo. Set the adjustable ramp to 45°.

2 **Measure** Roll the ball down the fixed ramp— let the ball roll from rest at the same height throughout the experiment. Measure the distance the ball travels along the adjustable ramp. Record your observations.

3 Vary the angle of the adjustable ramp. Repeat step 2. Start steep, and each time decrease the slope of the ramp. Finally, the ramp will be horizontal, and you can simply let the ball roll onto the table.

4 **Observe** As you decrease the slope, note how long it takes the ball to slow down.

Slope (degrees)	Distance (centimeters)
45	
35	
25	
15	
0	

Drawing Conclusions

1 **Interpret Data** What slope made the ball go the farthest?

2 What is the relationship between slope and distance?

3 Did the ball stop? If so, why?

4 FURTHER INQUIRY Predict How would the slope of the ramp affect the ball's collision with an object standing still? Test your prediction using different ramp angles and objects.

Read to Learn

Main Idea Force affects all objects by changing the direction and magnitude of their motion.

How Do Forces Affect Objects?

How many ways do you push things and make them move? Pull things and make them move? Have you ever pulled back a moving object and made it stop moving? Pushing a shopping cart and making it move is an example of a **force**. In general a force is a push or a pull that one object exerts on another. The objects could be

- a magnet pulling an iron nail,
- a person pulling a luggage cart,
- a tugboat pushing a barge upriver,
- the Sun and Earth pulling each other in a way that keeps Earth in orbit.

Forces can change the motion of objects. For example, a rocket's engine provides a strong push that makes the rocket accelerate upward and away from the launch pad. In this case, the force operates continuously for as long as the rocket engine burns fuel.

The arrow shows the direction of the force produced by the rocket's engine.

Another example of a force changing the motion of an object is a batter who has just struck a ball with a bat. The bat exerted a force on the ball and has sent it flying toward the outfield. Even though the bat pushed on the ball for only a brief instant, the ball may have gained enough velocity to clear the fence for a home run!

Forces can also change the shape of objects. For example, you have probably worked with clay. You know that the force your muscles can apply to the clay through your hands can squeeze the clay into different forms. You may also have squeezed an empty aluminum soda can tightly with your hands. If so, you know that the force your hands applied to the can crumpled it into a new, squashed shape.

Did the bat exert enough force on the ball for a home run?

▷ **What are two ways a force can affect an object?**

How Do You Measure Forces?

How can you measure the force of a push or a pull? If you attach a spring to a box and pull on the spring to move the box, the amount that the spring stretches gives you an idea of how much force you are using.

To measure force we use a spring scale. The spring scale shown here is marked off in units called *newtons*. A newton is a unit for measuring force. One newton is a push or pull with the same strength as the weight of a 0.225-pound object, such as a D cell. The abbreviation for the newton is N.

If you pull a wooden block across a tabletop with a spring scale, as shown in the picture, you can feel a drag along the surface. The block resists sliding due to a force called **friction**. Friction is a force that opposes the motion of one object sliding over another. To get the block moving, the student in the picture must pull with enough newtons of force to overcome friction and set the block in motion. The pointer on the spring scale shows that 2.0 N of force is needed to keep the block moving.

How does the spring scale work? As its name suggests, it has a spring inside. When the spring is connected to the wooden block, pulling on the spring scale's handle causes the spring inside to stretch. As the spring stretches, it applies more and more force to the block. The student in the picture has stretched the spring so that it exerts enough force on the wooden block to set it in motion. A pointer is attached to the spring, and its position gives the amount of force in newtons.

When we describe a force, we have to state both an amount and a direction to describe it completely, just as we do for velocity. The amount of force is the strength of the push or pull. The direction tells which way the push or pull operates on an object. For example, we might describe the force of a jet airplane as "100,000 N in the northerly direction." Here the amount of force is 100,000 N, and the direction of the force is to the north.

▷ How can a force be measured?

Spring scale

The student is pulling the wooden block across the tabletop by applying a force to it through the spring scale.

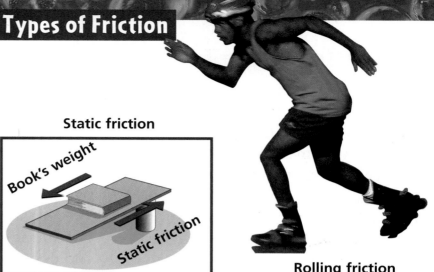

Types of Friction

Worker's push

Friction

Sliding friction

Static friction

Book's weight

Static friction

Rolling friction

What Are Types of Friction?

Have your hands ever gotten so cold that you rubbed them back and forth against one another to warm them up? Your hands seem to stick together, especially when you press them tightly, and you must use force from your muscles to make your hands slide back and forth. The force is needed to overcome the friction between your hands. The friction is actually a force that opposes the motion of your hands as they slide over one another.

Friction acts anytime the surfaces of objects are in contact. There are three kinds of friction:

1. *Sliding friction* Look at the picture of the worker pushing the box. The blue arrow shows the force applied to the box by the worker. The red arrow shows the force of friction that opposes the motion of the box. Notice how the force applied by the worker and the friction act in opposite directions. Since the strength of the force applied by the

worker is greater than the strength of the friction, the box accelerates.

2. *Static friction* Look at the diagram of a book on a slanted wooden board. Static friction prevents the start of any movement between surfaces in contact. If the surface was smoother or the board was steeper, the static friction might not be enough to hold the book in place, and it might slide down the wooden board. Static friction enables you to walk about. Your feet push rearward against the ground, and static friction pushes your feet forward, allowing you to walk ahead.

3. *Rolling friction* Wheels and rollers are used to reduce friction. However, this friction also allows wheels to move us forward. Friction between skate wheels and the ground pushes a skater ahead.

READING Main Idea
When does each type of friction act?

How Do Drag Forces Act?

Hold a book in one hand and a piece of paper in the other at the same height as the book. Let them both drop at the same time. The book lands first. Now place the paper on top of the book and let them drop. They fall together. What made the difference? When an object moves through a gas, such as air, or any liquid, there is a force that opposes the motion. This force is called the **drag force**. As an object moves through air, the air molecules bump into it (a drag force), which causes the object to slow down. When the paper is on top of the book, the book blocks the air so that there is no drag force.

The drag force is similar to the force of sliding friction because both oppose motion. The drag force slows down a falling piece of paper, just as sliding friction slows down a sliding object. However, there are differences. Sliding friction does not depend on the speed of the sliding object or its shape. The drag force does depend on speed. The faster the speed, the greater the drag force. The drag force also depends on the size and shape of the object. For example, a crumpled piece of paper falls faster than the same piece of paper when not crumpled.

Drag forces affect anything that moves through a gas or liquid. For example, drag forces act on cars and airplanes. This must be taken into account by engineers who design them. Air drag increases the amount of fuel needed.

▷ **How does a drag force affect an object?**

Book and paper were dropped next to each other at the same time from the same height.

Book and paper were dropped with paper on top at the same time from the same height.

What Makes Objects Attract?

When you throw a ball into the air, why does it fall down? The answer is that all objects attract each other with a force called **gravity**. Gravity helps keep the Moon going around Earth and Earth going around the Sun.

Pick any two objects, such as Earth and a ball you have thrown into the air. Earth pulls on the ball, and the ball pulls on Earth. These forces of gravity are equal and opposite. The pull of Earth makes the ball fall to Earth. The pull of the ball on Earth also makes Earth move, but not by much, because Earth is hard to budge. There is also a force of gravity between you and a ball you have just thrown. However, this force is so small that you do not notice it. Why is the gravity between the ball and Earth strong, yet the gravity between you and the same ball weak?

The answer is that the mass of Earth is much greater than your mass. Mass is a property of every object. Mass is what produces gravity. Mass is measured in kilograms (kg). An adult might have a mass of 60 kg, whereas Earth has a mass in kilograms of 6 with 24 zeros after it! That is why Earth's gravity is so much stronger than the gravity of a person.

▷ **What makes two objects attract each other?**

Equal and opposite forces

Equal and opposite forces

What Affects Gravity?

If all objects attract each other, then how is it you don't notice the gravity between all objects? For example, there is a force of gravity between the desks in your classroom. However, you never see two desks move toward each other! Why not? Because the masses of the desks are relatively small.

The force of gravity between two objects depends on both the masses of the two objects and the distance between the objects. The closer the objects are to each other, the stronger the force of gravity that they exert on each other. Also, the more mass the objects have, the greater the pull they will have on each other. For example, the force of gravity between the Sun and a spacecraft near Earth is greater than the force of gravity between the Sun and the same spacecraft when it is near Pluto, the farthest planet from the Sun.

The force of gravity did not change because of a change in mass. Mass is measured using a balance. The mass of the spacecraft is the same whether it is on Earth or on Pluto. The force of gravity changed because the distance between the Sun and Pluto is greater than the distance between the Sun and Earth. The mass of the spacecraft is the same in both places.

Weight

Although the mass of the spacecraft has not changed, its *weight* has. The weight of an object is the force of gravity between Earth (or any planet, asteroid, or star) and the object. Weight is measured on a scale, such as the bathroom scale shown in the photo. The reading on the scale, whether in newtons or pounds, measures the force with which the object is being pulled toward the center of Earth.

The spacecraft's weight is different near Pluto than near Earth because the force of gravity on each planet is different. Each planet is pulling on the spacecraft's mass differently.

> **How is gravity related to mass and distance?**

Gravity pulls a person toward Earth.

What Are Balanced Forces?

How many forces are there in a game of tug-of-war? As the arrows in the diagram show, both teams pull with a great deal of force on the rope. The center of the rope, though, does not move in either direction because the forces exerted by the students offset one another. Since the forces have the same strength but are acting in opposite directions, the center of the rope behaves as though no force was acting on it. Scientists say that the **net force** is zero. The net force is the combined effect of all the forces acting on an object.

Think of what happens when you weigh something using a spring scale. You hook the object to the scale and lift the scale and object up. Gravity pulls the object down. The object pulls on the spring, making it stretch. When the pull of the spring offsets the pull of gravity, the spring stops stretching, and the object stops moving downward.

It is also possible for three or more forces to offset one another. For example, a stoplight may be supported by two cables. The weight of the stoplight pulls it downward. This pull causes the stoplight to tug on the cables. The cables, in turn, resist being stretched

Both this stoplight and the calculator are hanging motionless.

and pull up on the stoplight. Altogether there are three forces acting on the stoplight. Since the stoplight moves neither up nor down, it is behaving as if there was no force on it at all. This tells us that the three forces on the stoplight must completely offset one another.

Anytime two or more forces acting on an object completely offset one another, we say that they are **balanced forces**. You can tell when forces are balanced because the motion of the object is unchanged. It is as if no force was acting on the object. When the forces on an object are balanced, the net force on the object is zero.

▷ **When is the net force on an object equal to zero?**

1,000 N   1,000 N

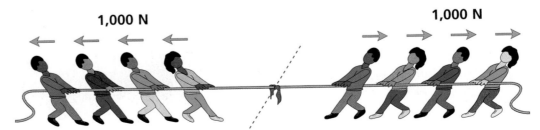

Neither team can move the flag closer to its side because each team pulls with the same force.

What Are Unbalanced Forces?

Look at the teams here. The team on the right has two new students. This team exerts a greater force to the right than the other team does to the left. The team on the right pulls with 1,500 N of force, while the team on the left pulls with 1,000 N of force. The 1,000-N pull to the left offsets 1,000 N of the pull to the right. This leaves 500 N (1,500 N – 1,000 N = 500 N) of force still acting to the right. Due to the leftover pull to the right, the team on the right is winning the tug-of-war by moving the flag on the rope toward its side.

When the force or forces acting on an object do not completely offset one another, they are said to be **unbalanced forces**. The leftover force can be represented as a single push or pull of a certain strength and direction. When a force is unbalanced, it means the net force is not zero.

The other diagram shows unbalanced forces. Every object will undergo a change of motion when there is a net force. The push of the rocket thruster on the left is greater than the push of the thruster on the right. This causes the rocket to move to the right. The yellow arrow shows the net force that produces this motion.

> **When is the net force on an object not equal to zero?**

READING

Diagrams

In the diagram of the rocket thrusters, what is the strength of the force represented by the orange arrow?

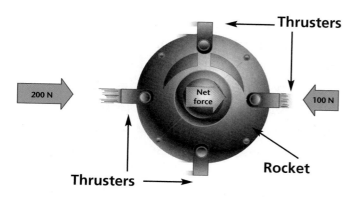

200 N · Net force · 100 N · Thrusters · Rocket · Thrusters

The forces from the thrusters do not offset completely, so the rocket moves.

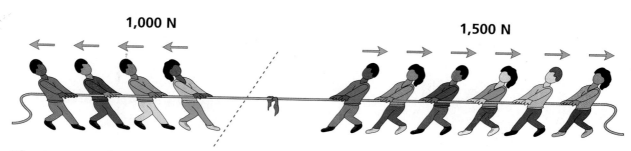

1,000 N   1,500 N

The team on the right exerts more force than the team on the left, so the right-hand team moves the flag toward its side.

What Is Newton's First Law?

Sir Isaac Newton said that the velocity of an object tends to remain unchanged. In other words

- an object at rest (velocity = 0) tends to stay at rest,
- an object moving in a straight line at constant speed tends to keep moving that way.

An object's velocity can only be changed by applying a force to it. This is known as Newton's *first law of motion*.

For example: A bus is traveling along with constant velocity. It is moving at 30 km/h on a straight road. A ball is sitting in the aisle, at rest beside one of the passengers. The driver steps on the brakes, and the bus slows down for an upcoming stop sign. The ball begins rolling toward the front of the bus. No one kicked or pushed the ball. Why did it start moving?

The bus is traveling at constant velocity.

The bus is slowing down.

Before the driver started applying the brakes, the bus, the passengers and the ball were all moving forward at 30 km/h. Newton's first law says this motion can only be changed by applying a force. The brakes provide this force for the bus and anything attached to it.

When the brakes are applied by the driver, the velocity of the bus decreases. However, the ball is not attached firmly to the bus. As a result the ball continues to move ahead at 30 km/h. The ball will go forward until it does encounter a force that changes its velocity. It might hit into a seat or the front of the bus.

The ball in this case gives you an example of **inertia**. Inertia is the tendency of an object to oppose any change in its motion. That is, the ball tends to keep moving even as the bus is slowing to a stop. Only when a force is applied to an object does its velocity change.

When the driver steps on the brakes, the passengers in the bus continue moving forward because of their inertia. If the bus stops gradually, the friction between the seat cushions and the passengers can reduce the velocity of the passengers to match the slowing of the vehicle. In a quick stop, however, the inertia of the passengers can make them slip or even jolt forward.

▷ **How is the ball's motion affected by Newton's first law?**

How Does Inertia Affect You?

Jolting forward when a bus stops quickly is only one way you tend to keep moving because of inertia.

Have you ever gone around a curve in a car and felt like you had to lean into the turn? If you didn't, you would tip in the other direction. Your inertia makes you feel this way. The friction between the tires and the road is the force that changes the velocity of the car. The car in the picture changes its direction of travel to the left because of this force. The passengers in the car, though, tend to continue moving straight ahead. This makes them feel like they are tipping to the right. Actually, the car is turning out from underneath them. It takes a force from a seat belt, chair cushion, or door to make the passengers' velocity change along with the car's.

Inertia is why seat belts are so important. You might be able to control yourself in a car when you know it is

The seat belt and the air bag both help to decelerate the driver less rapidly during a crash.

going to make a turn. It is almost impossible to control your movement in a car that suddenly stops or changes direction. Seat belts keep you moving with the car or, in this case, stop you from moving when the driver brakes.

Front-end car crashes put passengers at great risk of being injured by flying forward into the dashboard or windshield. Seat belts are the most important system for keeping car passengers from being injured in this manner.

Newer car models are equipped with an additional safety device called an air bag. Although these safety devices have caused some injuries, major injuries or even deaths have been prevented because of them. When safety belts and air bags are used together, deaths in front-end car crashes are reduced by about 50 percent!

You may feel like you are tipping to the outside of the turn as a car turns.

The inertia of the passengers makes them tend to follow this path.

Friction between tires and road makes the car turn along this path.

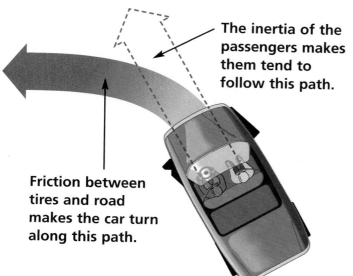

▷ **How can inertia affect you in a front-end car crash?**

Investigating Inertia

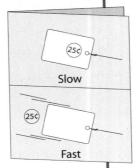

FOLDABLES™ Make a Two-Tab Book. (See p. R41.) Label as shown. Record your observations under the tabs.

1. Attach a thread to a playing card, and place a quarter on it.

2. **Observe** Pull slowly on the thread. How does the quarter move?

3. Now pull on the thread very rapidly. What does the quarter do now?

4. At the start the quarter and the card are at rest. Why would they naturally tend to stay at rest?

5. What does the thread do when you pull it?

6. Explain why the quarter moved differently in your tests.

What Makes Objects Travel in a Circle?

You know from Lesson 1 that an object that is traveling in a circle is accelerating even if it moves at a steady speed. It accelerates because its direction of travel is constantly changing.

The student in the picture is swinging a beanbag tied to a string in a circle over her head. The pull of the string is the force that changes the velocity of the beanbag and keeps it on a circular path. This is similar to the way the force of Earth's gravity pulls on the Moon.

What if the string breaks at point A? The lines labeled 1, 2, and 3 show several guesses students might make for the path the beanbag follows when the string breaks. Which path do you think is correct? The answer is given by Newton's first law of motion. Once the string breaks, there will no longer be any unbalanced force on the beanbag. Its inertia will carry it straight ahead at a constant speed. As you can see, this is path 2.

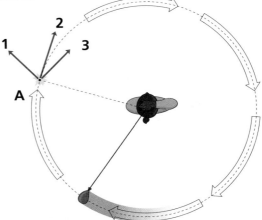

▷ **Why does the beanbag follow a circular path?**

Why It Matters

The more we learn about the forces acting on the universe, the better we can understand and use these forces.

Scientists on the space shuttle *Endeavour* performed tests to better understand how the body reacts to little or no gravity. Information from this and further experiments may one day prove helpful when humans try to inhabit other planets.

e-Journal Visit our Web site **www.science.mmhschool.com** to do a research project on forces and motion.

Think and Write

1. What forces make a ball slow down and come to a stop?

2. A child pushes a wagon forward with 100 N of force. Another pushes it back with 120 N. Which way will the wagon move? Why?

3. Why is Earth's gravity so strong?

4. A truck stops suddenly. A box in the truck slides forward. Why?

5. Critical Thinking You are traveling in an airliner at 500 mi/h in a straight line. Drop a ball! Will it fall to the back of the plane or straight down? Why?

L·I·N·K·S

MATH LINK

Calculate mass. A ball with a mass of 1 kg weighs about 10 N on Earth. If the weight of the ball is less than 2 N on the Moon, what is its mass?

WRITING LINK

Writing That Compares Imagine a trip to the Moon. How do the changing forces of inertia and gravity affect you? Compare how you feel on the Moon with how you feel on Earth. Focus on the differences.

LITERATURE LINK

Read *Einstein, Newton, and Gravity* to learn about what you would do to prove the existence of gravity. Try the activities at the end of the book.

Einstein, Newton, and Gravity

by Dan Greenberg
illustrated by Tim Robinson

TECHNOLOGY LINK

Science Newsroom CD-ROM Choose *Notions on Motion* to learn how forces make things move.

LOG ON Visit **www.science.mmhschool.com** for more links.

INERTIA: An Idea in Motion

If you throw a ball, it falls. However, the Sun, Moon, and stars keep moving without falling. Why? It's simple, they're following the laws of motion!

Motion seems like a simple idea, but early scientists had trouble explaining it. Aristotle noted that inanimate objects move only when a force moves them. To explain why an object moves a bit even after a force stops, he said that as air pushes the object, it leaves behind a vacuum. More air rushes in to fill the vacuum, pushing the object a bit. However, Aristotle said heavenly bodies move because something unknown provides a constant force.

By the 1300s scientists knew that an opposing force, like friction, was needed to stop motion. They said that heavenly bodies keep moving because there's no opposing force to stop them. The scientists believed that a driving force, or impetus,

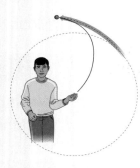

Would a ball's path be curved or straight? The majority of American college students said it would be curved, but physics students knew it would be straight.

moved an object. For example, they thought that a cannonball moved in a straight line, ran out of impetus, and fell to Earth. Later they noted that as the ball ran low on impetus, its path curved before falling straight down. In 1546 mathematician Nicoló Tartaglia suggested that the ball really began to curve as soon as it left the cannon.

Galileo came up with a new theory of motion: If an object in motion has no resistance, the impetus is constant and the object remains in motion. This idea of inertia changed scientists' view of impetus, because all objects have inertia, whether in motion or at rest!

Isaac Newton simplified the rule of inertia: An object at rest tends to stay at rest and an object in motion moves at a constant speed unless a force changes it. Newton's laws reverse Aristotle's, because air slows a moving ball instead of keeping it in motion!

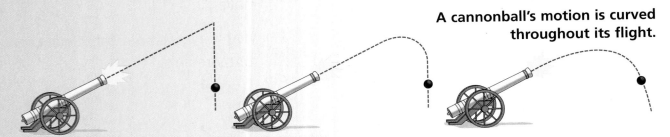

A cannonball's motion is curved throughout its flight.

LOG ON Visit www.science.mmhschool.com to learn more about the laws of motion.

What Did I Learn?

1. How does Aristotle's idea of how a thrown object moves through space compare to Newton's views?

  A air moves an object versus air slows an object

  B air slows an object versus air moves an object

  C both agreed air has no effect on an object

  D none of the above

2. How did scientists in the 1300s explain a cannonball's motion?

  F constantly straight

  G straight line until it dropped

  H curving path until it dropped

  J curved throughout the flight

Acceleration and Momentum

Vocabulary

momentum, F38

What do you think it takes to get a house to move? What if you had to move a house to another city? Would it be easier if you took the furniture out? Why or why not? What else could you do to make the move easier?

Think about what it takes to get any object moving from rest—a crate, a car, a desk. How can you make the task easier?

Inquiry Skill

You infer when you form an idea from facts or observations.

Explore Activity

What Affects Acceleration?

Materials

balloon-powered toy car

4 nickels

meterstick

tape

lightweight cardboard

scissors

Procedure

BE CAREFUL! Handle scissors carefully.

1 Make three balloon-inflation gauges of different sizes (12 cm, 8 cm, and 4 cm in diameter) by cutting the cardboard into U shapes. Mark a starting line by sticking the tape on a smooth, level floor.

2 **Measure** Blow up the balloon to 12 cm using the 12-cm gauge. Attach the balloon to a toy car, set it at the tape, and let it go. Measure how far the car travels. What factors affect how far it goes? How will mass affect the distance traveled? Record your results.

3 **Predict** How will mass affect the distance traveled? Use a piece of tape to attach a nickel to the car. Repeat step 2 for one nickel, two nickels, three nickels, and four nickels.

4 Repeat steps 2 and 3 using the 8-cm gauge and the 4-cm gauge.

Drawing Conclusions

1 What happened to the acceleration of the car as more mass was added?

2 What happened to the acceleration of the car as more force was used?

3 **FURTHER INQUIRY** **Infer** Why do race car drivers try to reduce the weight of their cars as much as possible? Can you make a car carrying four nickels accelerate as fast as one with none? Test your answer.

Main Idea Forces make objects move and change direction and speed.

What Is the Second Law of Motion?

The diagram on this page shows a simple experiment using rubber bands stretched by the same amount, for the same amount of time, and a small cart loaded with books. By using two rubber bands, you can double the force, and by using twice as many books, you can increase the mass of the cart.

After studying the picture, can you see that the cart travels farthest when the force is greatest and the number of books is smallest? A large force on an object with small mass results in a large acceleration. In contrast the distance traveled by the cart is least when the weakest force is applied and

READING Diagrams

1. What happens to the distance traveled by the cart when two rubber bands are used instead of one for the same number of books?

2. What happens to the distance traveled by the cart when two books are put on the cart instead of four?

Acceleration

0 m   1 m

Trial 1
One rubber band
two books

0 m

Trial 2
Two rubber bands
two books

2 m

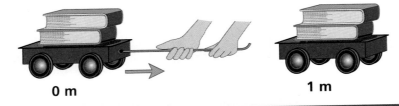

0 m   1 m

Trial 3
Two rubber bands
four books

the most books are placed on the cart. As a result, we know that a small force applied to an object with large mass causes a small acceleration.

If you are moving a house or pushing a bookcase, how can you make the job easier? Take the furniture out of the house. Take the books out of the bookcase. When a force is applied, objects with less mass accelerate more quickly. An empty bookcase has less mass than a filled bookcase. Less force is needed to get an empty bookcase to move.

The experiment with the cart, books, and rubber bands shows how acceleration, mass, and force are related. Isaac Newton summarized the relationship in his *second law of motion*. This law says that the acceleration of an object is related to the object's mass and to the amount of force applied to the object. The law is written as

$$a = F/m$$

or an object's acceleration equals the net force of an object divided by the object's mass.

The net force is the combined effect of all the forces together. When you learned about the first law, you saw that a net force is needed to make an object accelerate. The second law says exactly how much a certain net force will make an object accelerate. Two results of Newton's second law are:

1. For a given net force, objects with a greater mass have less acceleration.

2. For objects of a given mass, a greater force results in a greater acceleration.

▷ **How does the second law of motion relate force and mass?**

What Is the Third Law of Motion?

Boy and girl getting ready for a game of tug-of-war.

An ice skater pushes against the wall of a skating rink and ends up accelerating in the other direction. The yellow arrow represents the force that must have caused this acceleration. Where did this force come from?

The force the ice skater exerts on the wall is an *action* force. The wall pushes back on the skater. This push is called a *reaction* force. The reaction force accelerates the skater away from the wall.

Anytime one object exerts a force on another object, a pair of forces acts—an action-reaction pair of forces. The two forces have the same strength but act in opposite directions. Newton described

Both students move, and the girl goes faster.

Reaction **Action**

Skater pushing against the wall of a rink

Velocity **Skater in motion**

this in his *third law of motion:* If object A exerts a force on object B, then object B exerts a force on object A that is equal in strength and opposite in direction.

Look at the two pictures of the boy and girl sitting in identical wagons. The boy has more mass than the girl. In the first picture, the boy and girl are getting ready for a tug-of-war. In the second picture, both students end up moving, and the girl accelerates more than the boy. How do Newton's laws of motion explain what has happened?

Both students must grip the rope tightly. Newton's third law says when the boy pulls on the girl, she must pull back on the boy with the same force. The girl cannot avoid exerting a force back on the boy. Since they both experience a force, they both move. The boy has a greater mass than the girl, so his acceleration is less, as Newton's second law predicts.

Action-reaction pair

The rocket shown in the photo uses Newton's third law to fly. Hot gases from burned fuel are pushed downward out of the engine by the walls of the combustion chamber. The reaction force is the push of the hot gases upward on the walls of the combustion chamber. This upward force propels the rocket aloft.

You might think that a rocket engine works by pushing on the surrounding air, like an ice skater pushing off a wall. However, this is not what happens. The force that moves the rocket ahead does not depend on the surrounding air. In fact rockets are able to accelerate in space, where there is no air at all.

Newton's third and second laws also explain how you are able to walk. When you take a step, static friction momentarily "connects" your foot to the floor, which is attached to Earth. You use your muscles to apply a rearward push on the floor. The floor exerts a reaction force back on you, which pushes you forward.

When things fall to Earth, action and reaction forces are also at work. Imagine dropping a pencil. The force of gravity causes Earth to pull the pencil downward. The third law of motion, though, tells us that the pencil pulls back on Earth. In fact the pencil pulls just as hard on Earth as Earth pulls on it. Nonetheless, we don't see Earth rushing up to meet the falling pencil halfway. The mass of Earth is so large compared with the pencil that Earth's acceleration cannot be seen, whereas the pencil's acceleration is quite rapid.

▷ **What makes a rocket move?**

Rocket engine pushes on hot gases, forcing them downward.

Hot gases push back on rocket engine, forcing the rocket upward.

What Is Momentum?

What if a baseball pitcher throws his best fastball to you? Imagine the amount of force you need to stop the baseball when you catch it in your glove. Now imagine the pitcher throwing you a tennis ball at the same speed. Which is easier to catch—the tennis ball or the baseball? If you think the tennis ball, you are right, because the tennis ball has less mass than the baseball.

Now imagine the pitcher throwing a baseball to you as slowly as he can. Compared with the fastball, how hard would it be to stop the baseball this time? That's right, it's easier to stop the slowball than the fastball. This shows you how an object is easier to stop

The massive truck has a lot of momentum.

when it is moving slowly compared with when it is moving rapidly.

The quantity that measures both the mass of an object and how fast the object is moving is **momentum**. A baseball has more momentum than a tennis ball when the two are traveling at the same speed because the baseball has more mass. However, a tennis ball can have more momentum than a baseball if its speed is great enough.

Momentum is simply mass times velocity. Since velocity has both speed and direction, momentum also has a direction. When an object's mass is measured in kilograms and its velocity is measured in meters/second, its momentum has units of kilograms-meters/second. The greater an object's momentum, the more force and time it takes to bring it to a stop.

The baseball has little momentum.

▷ **How does momentum explain why a baseball is harder to stop than a tennis ball moving at the same speed?**

Two skaters at rest

Velocity   Velocity

Same two skaters moving
away from each other

How Is Momentum Conserved?

Momentum is a very helpful quantity in studying motion. The total momentum does not change if there are no outside forces acting on the system. Scientists call this principle the *conservation of momentum*.

The diagrams of the skaters illustrate the conservation of momentum. The first picture shows two skaters who are not moving. The girl is about to push on the boy in front of her. Since neither skater is moving, the momentum of each is zero. The total momentum of both skaters combined is also zero.

What happens when the girl pushes the boy? He travels off to the right. Due to his velocity to the right, the boy has momentum to the right. Before the girl pushed him, the total momentum of the two skaters was zero. The total momentum cannot change, since there is no outside force. The only force is

between the boy and the girl. The total momentum must still be zero after the girl pushes the boy. This means the girl must have enough momentum to the left to cancel the boy's momentum to the right.

The girl's force on the boy is the action force. However, by Newton's third law, there is a reaction force that pushes back on the girl and sets her in motion.

Conservation of momentum neatly explains why rockets fly. Before launch the total momentum of the rocket and its fuel is zero because they are at rest. After launch the total momentum must still be zero. To cancel the momentum of the burned fuel shooting out of the engine in one direction, the rocket must be moving in the opposite direction.

READING **Main Idea**
How does conservation of momentum explain a rocket's motion?

A satellite moves in a circular path, or orbit, around Earth.

This astronaut weighs about six times less on the Moon than on Earth.

How Do Weight and Mass Compare?

What is mass? You've seen that the greater the mass of an object, the more force it takes to accelerate the object. This is true anywhere in the universe. If you apply a known force to an object and then measure the acceleration, you can calculate its mass.

Weight is not the same thing as mass. Weight is the force of gravity pulling down on objects located at the surface of Earth. If you are standing on top of a mountain, your weight will be slightly less than your weight at sea level!

The weight of an object depends on its location in the universe. However, the mass of the object does not change. For example, if your mass is 30 kg, you

weigh about 294 N. If you were standing on the Moon, would you still weigh 294 N? No, because on the Moon the force of gravity would be much smaller. You would be attracted to the Moon with a force of about 50 N, so your weight would now be 50 N. Still, your mass would remain 30 kg on the Moon. Why is your weight 294 N on Earth but only 50 N on the Moon? It's because the Moon has much less mass than Earth.

As you move around on Earth, it is normal for your weight to change very slightly. Other things being equal, weight decreases very slightly as you move to higher elevations. If you bravely venture into space and orbit Earth in a spacecraft, your weight is reduced even further. Note, though, that you have to travel very far from Earth before your weight decreases by a significant amount.

The satellite shown on this page travels in a circular path around Earth. It takes a force to make an object travel in a circle. In the case of the satellite, its weight provides this force.

Did you ever hear or read that astronauts in orbiting spacecraft are "weightless"? Does weight disappear in space? Look at the photograph on this page.

The gravitational pull of Earth is quite large even several hundred kilometers from the surface. Spacecraft and the astronauts in them have weight as they orbit Earth. Why then do objects in the photograph float around as if they have no weight?

A weightless astronaut

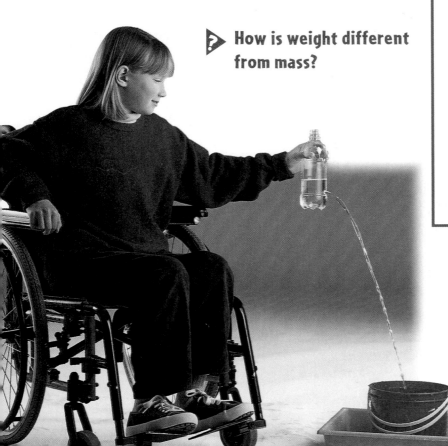

▷ **How is weight different from mass?**

QUICK LAB

Free Fall

FOLDABLES Make a Shutter Fold. (See p. R42.) Label as shown.

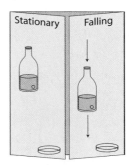

Stationary   Falling

1. Put a hole in the side of a plastic bottle near the bottom. Fill the bottle with water, keeping your finger over the hole. Go outside or in a marked safe area.

2. Remove your finger from the hole. Observe if water comes out.

3. **Observe** Now hold the bottle high and drop it, watching the hole. Draw your observations of when water comes out of the hole on the tabs.

4. **Infer** When does the water appear to have weight and when does it appear to be weightless? Explain your answers under the tabs.

F 41

What Is Weightlessness?

Imagine a parachutist standing in a plane on a weight scale. The scale would read the parachutist's normal weight. What if a trapdoor then opened, allowing the parachutist and the scale to begin falling freely? There would be nothing to keep the parachutist pressed onto the scale—the scale would no longer read any weight.

In fact anything else that fell through the trapdoor of the plane would fall alongside the parachutist and the scale, because all things fall at the same rate. The parachutist, the scale, and any other falling objects would appear to be floating with respect to one another. They would all have weight, but this weight could not be detected.

Like the parachutist and the scale, astronauts in an orbiting spacecraft are falling freely to Earth. Since everything in the spacecraft is falling together, the weight of any object cannot be detected.

Astronauts often train underwater.

To prepare for performing tasks in space, astronauts must practice in simulated weightless conditions. As the photograph above shows, one method is to work underwater, because water reduces the weight of submerged objects. The photograph below shows astronauts flying in a jet that travels on a curved path. The result is a number of seconds of free fall, which feels just like the conditions in an orbiting spacecraft.

Satellites

Why does a satellite stay in orbit? Why doesn't it simply plunge to Earth like a bullet fired from a gun? Gravity and inertia keep a satellite in orbit. Both motions happen continuously, and they combine to keep the satellite on a curved path. Placing a satellite in orbit requires accelerating it to a sideways velocity great enough to keep its path of motion from colliding with the surface of Earth.

Astronauts in free fall feel weightless.

▷ **Why do astronauts in space seem weightless?**

L·I·N·K·S

Why It Matters

Newton's laws help us to understand motion and forces. This helps engineers design and build everything from cars to aircraft to satellites. For example, a rocket must reach a velocity of about 11 km/s to escape the gravity of Earth. Knowing this, engineers can determine just how much force a rocket engine must develop to carry a rocket of a given mass into deep space.

e-Journal Visit our Web site www.science.mmhschool.com to do a research project on space exploration.

Think and Write

1. A heavy truck and a light car have exactly the same motor. Which can accelerate faster?

2. You are standing on skates and toss a heavy ball forward. What will happen to you?

3. One train car is at rest. An identical car moves into it, going to the right at 2 m/s. The two couple together and move to the right at 1 m/s. Why do they move to the right? Why do they move at 1 m/s instead of 2 m/s?

4. What would happen to your mass if you went to Mars? Why?

5. **Critical Thinking** How could you compare the mass of objects in deep space?

WRITING LINK

Personal Narrative
Suppose your home was in free fall and everything in it acted as if it were weightless? How would your daily activities change?

Share events in a diary entry or in a letter to a friend. Tell how you felt about the experience.

MATH LINK

Solve a problem. The strength of gravity on the surface of the Moon is one-sixth that of the Earth. If a person weighs 50 newtons on the Moon, how much will they weigh on Earth?

HEALTH LINK

Research bone loss. Astronauts and cosmonauts who experienced long periods of weightlessness were noticed to have lost some bone matter and muscle strength. Find out how these effects are overcome. How can this information help you take better care of yourself?

TECHNOLOGY LINK

LOG ON Visit www.science.mmhschool.com for more links.

Soap Box Derby

The Gravity Grand Prix

For 70 years, boys and girls have built race cars to compete in "soap box derbies." Racers start at the top of a hill and coast downhill, picking up speed all the way to the finish line.

What does it take to build a racer? You can build one from a kit, but let's say you're going to design your own. You'll want a complete design on paper before you start putting the pieces together. What if the steering cables interfere with the brakes? It's better to find out on paper than on your first test ride!

Your goal is to design a car that will accelerate as much as possible as it rolls down the hill. Your biggest enemies are air resistance and car vibrations. Design the car to reduce them.

You'll want your racer to be aerodynamic to reduce drag—and the right shape and size for you to fit inside. What material will you choose for the body? How about fiberglass?

To build your racer, you'll create full-size paper patterns from drawings. Cut the patterns out and glue flexible wooden slats to them. Cover the slats with fiberglass and let it set. It will be stiff but light. Remove the guides, and you have a fiberglass shell!

Now cut a floorboard from a stiff piece of wood. Attach the axles to hold the wheels. Connect the steering cables and the brakes, and then glue the fiberglass shell to the floorboard. Sand it, paint it, and hop in!

Show up on race day with a helmet and full protective gear. Some cars blow past the finish line at over 30 mph!

Today's derby racers are high-tech. Early cars were built from wooden crates and junk from the trash heap.

What Did I Learn?

1. You want your car to be:

    A as light as possible.
    B as flexible as possible.
    C as aerodynamic as possible.
    D as noisy as possible.

2. To build your car you will probably use all of these except:

    F fiberglass
    G metal
    H wood
    J soap

LOG ON Visit www.science.mmhschool.com to learn more about building models.

Vocabulary

Fill each blank with the best word or words from the list.

> **acceleration,** F12
> **average speed,** F9
> **drag force,** F21
> **friction,** F19
> **gravity,** F22
> **inertia,** F26
> **momentum,** F38
> **position,** F6
> **unbalanced forces,** F25
> **velocity,** F10

1. Dividing the total distance traveled by the amount of time allows you to find your _____.

2. The tendency of an object to oppose a change in motion is due to _____.

3. The losing team in a tug-of-war contest is a victim of _____.

4. The location of an object is its _____.

5. The speed and direction of a moving object determine its _____.

6. All objects with mass experience a force of attraction between them called _____.

7. The _____ of a system must be conserved if there are no outside forces acting on it.

8. A falling object feels a(n) _____, causing it to slow down.

9. A car's speedometer shows an increase of speed with time; therefore the car is undergoing a(n) _____.

10. A force that always opposes motion is _____.

Test Prep

11. A rock is tied to a string and swung in a circle. The string breaks and the rock _____.
  A drops to the floor
  B continues in a circle
  C flies straight ahead
  D follows the string

12. A girl is pulling on a wagon to the right, while her friend pulls to the left. The wagon does not move. The forces acting on the object are _____.
  F unbalanced
  G weak
  H strong
  J balanced

13. You need to move a box of books across the room. How can you get it to the other side faster?

    A use less force

    B take out some books

    C put in more books

    D pull it with a string

14. What is used to measure a force needed to pull a block across a tabletop?

    F a balance

    G a bathroom scale

    H a ruler

    J a spring scale

15. Anytime one object exerts a force on another object, a pair of forces acts. This is known as a(n) _____ pair of forces.

    A action-reaction

    B balanced-unbalanced

    C friction-drag

    D action-friction

Concepts and Skills

16. Reading in Science Why do objects float around inside a spacecraft that is orbiting Earth even though they are not weightless?

17. Safety Why would it be very difficult to walk on a tile floor if someone has just mopped the floor?

18. Critical Thinking Why is it wrong to show a spacecraft traveling at constant velocity with its main engines blazing?

19. INQUIRY SKILL **Predict** A train travels 24 m in 1 s, 48 m in 2 s, and 72 m in 3 s. What will its distance be at 4 s if it moves at a constant speed?

20. Scientific Methods Why do car engineers carry out test crashes with model passengers? Why do they need to carry out many tests?

Did You Ever Wonder?

INQUIRY SKILL **Make a Model** Using a piece of plastic tubing and a marble, make a model of a roller coaster. Describe your design using vocabulary words as position, motion, speed, velocity, acceleration, friction, and force.

LOG ON Visit www.science.mmhschool.com to better your test scores.

Work and Machines

Did You Ever Wonder?

How do machines help us do work? This giant front-end loader can dig and move more dirt than construction workers using only shovels. You have probably used ordinary machines, such as screwdrivers. How did they make your job easier?

INQUIRY SKILL **Predict** You have two screwdrivers with shafts of equal length and thickness. One has a large-diameter handle. The other has a small-diameter handle. Which screwdriver will require less effort?

Energy and Work

Vocabulary

potential energy, F52

gravitational potential energy, F52

kinetic energy, F53

work, F56

Get Ready

One difference in roller coasters is the very first hill, the one you climb up s-l-o-w-l-y. Some of those first hills are much higher than others. How does this difference change what happens on the way down? Does the speed of a roller coaster depend on how tall the hills are? If so, which would give the faster ride—tall hills or lower hills?

Inquiry Skill

You use variables when you identify and separate things in an experiment that can be changed or controlled.

Explore Activity

How Are Height and Speed Related?

Materials
marble
ruler with
a groove
spool

Procedure: Design Your Own

1 Roll a marble from rest down the groove in a ruler (or something similar). Let the marble hit a spool, which then rolls. Vary the slope and thus the height of the top of the ruler. The distance the spool rolls is a measure of how fast the marble was moving at the bottom of the ruler. Plan an experiment in which you can test how the starting height of the marble is related to the speed at the bottom of the ruler.

2 **Communicate** Prepare a table that summarizes the results of your experiment.

Drawing Conclusions

1 **Interpret Data** What is the relationship between starting height and the speed at the bottom of the ruler?

2 Explain your results. If speed depends on starting height, why do you think that is? If not, then why not?

3 **FURTHER INQUIRY** **Use Variables** How would your results change if, instead of starting the marble from rest, you started it in motion? Test your prediction.

Main Idea Energy can be changed into various forms as it is used to do work.

How Are Height and Speed Related?

You know that if you drop a rock, gravity will accelerate it toward Earth. The higher you hold the rock, the greater the time it accelerates before hitting the ground. Therefore, it will reach a higher speed. An object rolling down a hill behaves in the same way.

The road sign above is important for this reason. Roads that are built by the side of a mountain are often threatened by falling rocks. This is a hazard to drivers, because rocks that are high on the mountain can cause serious damage to cars and their passengers if they fall. The rock has stored energy because of its position, or height above the ground. This type of energy is called **potential energy**.

If the student releases the rubber band she is holding, it will snap back to its original shape. This shows that energy is stored in the stretched band.

Anytime an object is raised above the ground, the potential energy it gains is **gravitational potential energy**. The greater the object's height and weight, the more gravitational potential energy it gains. You can calculate the amount of gravitational potential energy in an object by multiplying its weight by its height. If the weight is measured in newtons and the height is measured in meters, the gravitational potential energy has units of *joules* (JEWLZ).

Potential energy can also be stored in an elastic (springy) object that is stretched or squashed and held that way. When you release the object, its stored energy turns into motion as it springs back to its old shape. Energy stored in stretched or squashed elastic objects is *elastic potential energy*.

READING **Draw Conclusions**
Why does height affect an object's gravitational potential energy?

How Does Energy Change?

A moving object has energy due to its motion. This energy is called **kinetic energy** . The kinetic energy of a moving object depends on both its speed and its mass—the greater the mass or the higher the speed, the greater the kinetic energy.

The bowling ball has kinetic energy because of its motion.

A bowling ball, for example, has much more kinetic energy than a table tennis ball if the two are traveling at the same speed. The table tennis ball, though, could have as much kinetic energy as the bowling ball if it traveled fast enough.

As a marble begins rolling down a ramp from its starting position, its potential energy begins changing to kinetic energy. At the bottom of the ramp, the marble reaches its highest speed because all of its potential energy has become kinetic energy.

A roller coaster shows how potential energy and kinetic energy can be changed back and forth. When the roller coaster is just coming over the top of a hill, it travels very slowly. Most of its energy is potential energy. When the roller coaster starts down an incline, its potential energy begins changing to kinetic energy, and it speeds up. By the time the roller coaster reaches the bottom of the hill, it reaches its highest speed because its potential energy has now completely changed to kinetic energy. Then, as the roller coaster travels up the next hill, it slows down as its kinetic energy changes back into potential energy.

Friction between a roller coaster's wheels and the track changes some of the kinetic energy into heat energy. As a result there isn't enough kinetic energy to allow the roller coaster to reach the potential energy it had on the preceding hill. That is why each successive hill must be lower in height to allow the roller coaster to complete its ride.

The food we eat provides another example of energy changes. We eat food because it contains potential energy stored in various kinds of chemicals. Our bodies change the food energy into other forms, such as kinetic energy for moving about, electrical energy for our nerves to carry signals, or thermal (heat) energy for our bodies to keep warm.

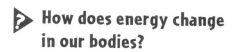 **How does energy change in our bodies?**

What Are Some Forms of Energy?

Energy can take many forms. A number of them are summarized in the table. Under the proper conditions, any of the forms of energy in the table can be changed from one into the other. Here are some examples.

Forms of Energy

Form of Energy	Example of Source
Atomic	radioactive material
Chemical	food
Electrical	household outlet
Light	the Sun
Mechanical	moving parts in a machine
Sound	vibrations of a stereo speaker
Thermal (heat)	hot water in a radiator

READING

Diagrams

1. What kind of energy change takes place in the solar cell?

2. What kind of energy change takes place in the battery?

▷ **What are some forms of energy that make your life easier?**

Energy Transformations

Sunlight to electricity

Electrical energy to light energy and heat energy

Electricity to mechanical energy

Chemical energy to electrical energy

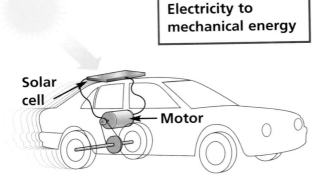

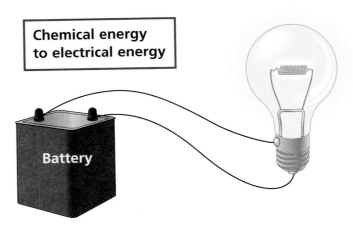

This model car is powered by a solar cell. Electricity from the solar cell runs an electric motor that propels the car ahead. Solar cells are used aboard space shuttles and other spacecraft.

A battery converts chemical energy into electricity that can power a light bulb.

How Do Batteries Work?

Batteries change chemical energy into electricity. Typically, chemical reactions that produce electrons occur in one part of the battery. The electrons are made to flow through a circuit attached to the battery. When the electrons return to the battery, they cause further chemical reactions to take place.

The first diagram shows a common dry-cell battery. This type of battery is called a primary cell because it can be used only once and then must be discarded. Dead dry-cell batteries should be removed from equipment immediately. Over time a chemical inside may eat its way through the sealed zinc can, allowing harmful chemicals to spill out.

The next diagram shows a different type of battery, a lead-acid, secondary battery. Secondary batteries are designed so that they can be recharged. Recharging consists of using an outside source of electricity that forces electrons through the battery. The electrons are made to flow "backward" through the battery. This reverses the chemical reactions that normally make the battery produce electricity. Once the chemicals are changed back to their original form, the battery is ready to be used again.

You may be familiar with a popular secondary battery, the nickel-cadmium battery. This battery is used in laptop computers, camcorders, portable tools, and space satellites.

▷ **How do batteries produce electricity?**

Dry-Cell Battery

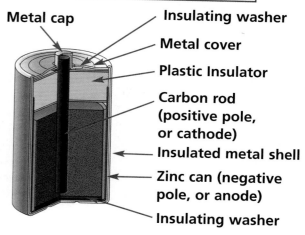

Metal cap
Insulating washer
Metal cover
Plastic Insulator
Carbon rod (positive pole, or cathode)
Insulated metal shell
Zinc can (negative pole, or anode)
Insulating washer

In this carbon-zinc dry cell, chemical reactions change chemical energy into electrical energy.

Storage Battery

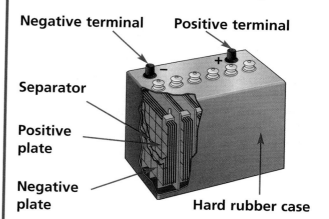

Negative terminal   Positive terminal
Separator
Positive plate
Negative plate   Hard rubber case

Lead-acid storage batteries like this one are used in cars. They discharge to start car engines, lights, or radios. They recharge when the car is running.

READING
Diagrams

1. What elements are used in the dry-cell battery?

2. What does the "separator" separate in the storage battery?

When Is Work Really Work?

What if you had to hold a heavy box up for a minute or two while your friend made a place for it on a basement shelf? Your arms might get tired, and you might start sweating a little.

The boy pushes very hard, but the box doesn't move.

It certainly would be tempting to say that you worked very hard while you held the box up. However, you actually did no work in the scientific sense. How can this be?

Scientists define **work** in a special way: Work is applying a force to an object to move it through a distance. The amount of work is calculated by multiplying the distance by the force. If the force is expressed in newtons and the distance is expressed in meters, the resulting units for the work are joules.

This definition of work explains why simply holding up a heavy box results in no work being done. You are applying a force to the box. However, you are not moving the box through a distance. Since the distance is zero, the force times the distance is zero, and no work is done.

When you lift the box up to the height where you hold it, you are doing work. In this case, the box is moved through a distance by the force you apply. The force times the distance gives you the amount of work done.

When work is done on an object, energy is added to it. If you lift a box off the ground to a certain height, for example, you increase the gravitational potential energy of the box. The work you do equals the increase in the potential energy of the box. You might also do work on a ball by throwing it. In this case, your hand exerts a force on the ball and accelerates it to a certain speed. The work you do is equal to the kinetic energy gained by the ball.

▶ **How do you do work on an object?**

The boy does work on the box as he lifts it up. He does no work on it when he holds it still.

How Can Work Turn into Heat?

The student in the picture is sliding books across a tabletop. The velocity of the books is constant, so the kinetic energy is not increasing. However, the student is applying a force that keeps the books moving through a distance. This force is necessary to offset friction between the tabletop and the books. If the force exactly offsets the friction, the books will travel with a constant velocity because the forces are balanced.

The student must be doing work on the books because she is applying a force and moving the books through a distance. Thus, she must be adding energy to them. Where is the energy going?

The friction between the books and the tabletop turns the energy into heat energy. The amount of heat energy produced is equal to the work done by the student.

▷ **How is work changed to heat in the photo?**

This girl is doing work on the books.

QUICK LAB

A Swinging Pendulum

FOLDABLES™ Make a Two-Tab Book. (See p. R 41.) Label as shown.

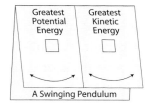

Greatest Potential Energy	Greatest Kinetic Energy
☐	☐

A Swinging Pendulum

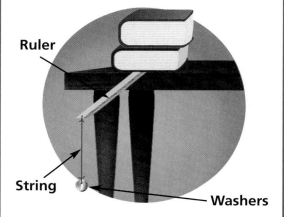

Ruler

String

Washers

1. Construct a pendulum as shown.

2. **Observe** Pull the washers to one side keeping the string taut. Release it. Draw on the tabs how it swings.

3. **Infer** Where does the pendulum's energy come from? Explain under the tabs.

4. Draw the washers and string on each tab where the potential energy and the kinetic energy are greatest.

5. **Interpret Data** How does the pendulum show it loses energy? Explain under the tabs.

How Is Work Calculated?

As you know, work is equal to the force multiplied by the distance the object moves. The force must act in the same direction as the motion. Look at the diagram showing a student who uses a rope to lift a bucket filled with tools up to a tree house. The weight of the bucket is 36 newtons. How do we calculate the work done on the bucket by the student?

When an object is lifted, the force is equal to the weight of the object. Since the bucket has a weight of 36 newtons, the student must have applied an upward force of 36 newtons to the bucket.

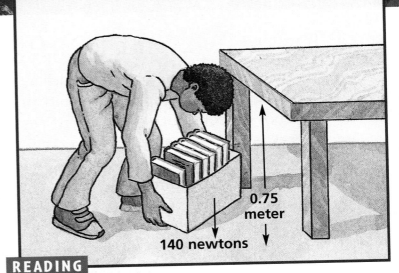

0.75 meter

140 newtons

READING

Diagrams

Calculate the work done by the student.

8 meters

36 newtons

Now that we know the applied force, we must look for the distance the object moved. The diagram tells us that the bucket was lifted 8 meters. Knowing both the applied force and the distance, we can now find the work done:

work = force × distance
work = 36 newtons × 8 meters
work = 288 joules

This means the energy added to the bucket was 288 joules. To give you an idea of how much energy this is, imagine an amount of water that would fill a soda can. The 288 joules of energy would raise the temperature of this amount of water by about 0.2°C. As you can see, the water does not warm up very much. The next time you boil a kettle of water on a stove, you can appreciate how many joules of energy the stove burner is producing!

The people in the diagram are pushing a stalled car into a parking space. How much work is done if they push the car 8 meters? To calculate the work, we must know the applied force and the distance the car moves. The distance is 8 meters. As the diagram shows, each person applies a force of 300 newtons. Since there are two people, the total applied force must be 600 newtons. Now we can find the work:

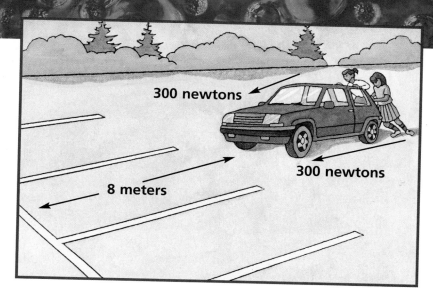

300 newtons

300 newtons

8 meters

work = force × distance
work = 600 newtons × 8 meters
work = 4,800 joules

In the photograph the girl pulls a wagon a distance of 10 meters. Notice that the force she applies through the handle is 25 newtons. However, this is not the force that is acting in the direction that the wagon moves. As the photograph shows, only 20 newtons of the force acts in the direction that the wagon moves. The other 5 newtons of force pull up on the wagon and lighten its weight, but they do not act to move it forward.

To find the work the girl does, we must multiply the distance by the force that acts in the same direction as the

motion. The distance is 10 meters and the force is 20 newtons. Now we can find the work:

work = force × distance
work = 20 newtons × 10 meters
work = 200 joules

▷ **What is the equation used to calculate work?**

25 newtons

20 newtons

What kind of energy changes can you see in this photograph?

Can Energy Be Created or Destroyed?

The bicycle rider in the photograph stores energy from food in her body. Then she changes this energy into kinetic energy by pedaling her bike to move it forward. As she rides across the countryside, she gains potential energy as she climbs hills. As she coasts down hills, her potential energy is changed back into kinetic energy, and she speeds up. When she stops, friction between the brake pads and the wheels slows the bike. The pads and the wheels get slightly warmer, releasing heat into the air.

The bicycle rider illustrates many changes of energy. Despite all of these changes, scientists believe that the total amount of energy in the universe remains constant. Energy may change in form, but it cannot be created or destroyed. The bicyclist cannot create energy—she must change some type of energy into the mechanical energy of the bike's turning pedals. She must use food energy stored in her body to turn the pedals.

The requirement that the total energy of the universe remain constant is called the *law of conservation of energy*. This law also applies to systems smaller than the universe as long as no energy is allowed to enter or leave the system.

For example, we might define a system to be a roller coaster and the surrounding air. At the top of the first hill, all of the roller coaster's energy is potential energy. As it accelerates down the first hill, its potential energy changes to kinetic energy. At the same time, though, it loses some energy to air friction and friction between the wheels and the tracks. Friction always lowers the amount of useful energy by turning it into heat and sound. The energy of heat and sound is wasted in the air instead of increasing roller coaster motion.

The total energy of the roller coaster and surrounding air remains constant at all points during the ride. The total amount of each form of energy at any instant is equal to the potential energy the roller coaster had at the top of the first hill.

▷ **What is the law of conservation of energy?**

We eat food to provide our bodies with energy. Energy is used to do work and to keep our body at 98.6°F. In a proper diet, the amount of food a person consumes must match the work done. If too much food is consumed, the person might gain unnecessary weight. If too little food is consumed, the person might lose weight and become weak.

ⓔ-Journal Visit our Web site **www.science.mmhschool.com** to do a research project on energy and work.

Think and Write

1. Do books have more potential energy on the top shelf or bottom shelf of a bookcase?

2. Describe the energy changes that occur when a rubber ball falls to the floor and bounces.

3. A steel beam weighing 4,000 N is lifted 12 m. How much work is done?

4. A worker applies a 200-N force to a crate that he pushes 10 m across a floor. How much work does he do?

5. Critical Thinking What if you lift a box from the floor to a height of 0.75 m? Then you carry it 4 m over to a 0.75-m-high table and place it there. Did carrying the box over to the table add to the amount of work done? Why?

L·I·N·K·S

LITERATURE LINK

Read *Perpetual Motion Machines.* Read about attempts to build machines that never stop. Try the activities at the end of the book.

WRITING LINK

Writing a Poem Suppose you invented a perpetual motion machine. How would it work? What would it do? Write a humorous poem about your machine. Use words, such as *thud*, to imitate the sound your machine would make. Use rhyme and repeated sounds at the beginning of words to convey perpetual motion.

MATH LINK

Calculate work. Student A lifts a 10-N mass 1 m. Student B lifts a 5-N mass 2 m. Who does more work?

TECHNOLOGY LINK

Science Newsroom CD-ROM Choose *You Have Potential* to learn about energy changes.

 LOG ON Visit **www.science.mmhschool.com** for more links.

Can Car Crashes Be Safer?

Crash tests determine how much damage will be done to a car and its occupants.

Why are so many people injured in car crashes? One reason is that an impact can crush anyone in the car.

A moving car has kinetic energy. When it stops after hitting another car or a wall, its kinetic energy is converted into other forms of energy. Some kinetic energy is converted to sound energy, so you hear a crash. Some kinetic energy becomes thermal energy, raising the temperature of the objects involved. Some of the energy is used to crush or break the colliding objects.

How much will be crushed? It depends on the number of objects involved, what they're made of, and how fast they were moving when they hit. If two identical cars, moving at the same speed, hit head on, the kinetic energy is divided equally between them. They'll be equally damaged. However, if a car hits a solid concrete wall that doesn't crush easily, most of the kinetic energy goes into damaging the car. It's impossible to make cars that don't crush or break in collisions.

However, auto makers can reduce the damage to the passenger area. For example, a car's hood, fenders, and bumpers are designed to absorb a lot of energy that could otherwise injure the car's occupants. Auto engineers also try to design the car's frame so that if it collapses, it will push the engine and other parts away from people inside the car.

As long as people drive cars, there'll be crashes. However, auto engineers are using their knowledge of physics to help make cars as safe as possible.

Engineers use computer models to design safer cars.

What Did I Learn?

1. What type of energy conversion happens during a car crash?

  A kinetic to sound
  B kinetic to thermal
  C kinetic to mechanical
  D all of the above

2. Engineers are working to make sure that

  F cars do not crumble in crashes.
  G car parts absorb most of the energy in a crash.
  H the engine moves toward the passengers in a crash.
  J all of the above

 LOG ON Visit **www.science.mmhschool.com** to learn more about the physics of car crashes.

How Levers Work

Get Ready

What does it take to win a rowing race? Lots of practice and teamwork are two answers. Each rower must pull on the oars with as much force as possible.

Why are oars used instead of paddles? Why is more of the oar over the side of the boat than on the inside? Do you think it matters where you hold the oar?

Inquiry Skill

You use numbers when you order, count, add, subtract, multiply, and divide to explain data.

Explore Activity

How Do Machines Affect Force?

Materials

spring scale

meterstick

short piece of string

large washers

large paper clip

Procedure

1 Investigate how a lever affects the amount of force it takes to lift the washers. Use the spring scale to measure the force it takes to lift the washers directly. Record your data.

2 Have your partner tie and hold the string to the meterstick at its midpoint as shown.

3 Use the large paper clip to hang the washers from the meterstick 20 cm away from the string. At the other end of the meterstick, attach the spring scale 20 cm away from the balance point. Measure how much force it takes to raise the weights. Record your results.

4 **Predict** What will happen to the force if the scale is 30 cm from the balance point? Try it.

5 **Experiment** Repeat with the scale 40 cm away.

Drawing Conclusions

1 **Observe** Which direction did you pull on the stick? Which direction did the weights move?

2 Was the force you exerted ever equal to the force exerted by the weight of the washers?

3 What happened as you moved the spring scale farther and farther away from the balance point?

4 FURTHER INQUIRY **Use Numbers** In order to lift the weights 15 cm, how far do you have to pull down on the spring scale? Does it matter if the spring scale is 20, 30, or 40 cm away from the balance point? Experiment to find out.

Main Idea Levers and pulleys help decrease the amount of force necessary to do work.

What Are Simple Machines?

A machine is simply a device that makes it easier for us to do work. You should recall that in order to do work, you must apply a force to something and move it through a distance.

Machines can range from very basic, such as the hammer in the photograph, to very complex. The most basic kinds are **simple machines**. These machines have few, if any, moving parts. The hammer is an example of a simple machine. When many simple machines are combined, a compound machine results.

Sometimes a simple machine merely changes the direction of a force we apply to something. This is an important way that a simple machine can make it more convenient to apply a force. Look at the hammer being used in the photograph. The force being applied to the handle by the person's hand is sideways. The force being applied to the nail by the hammer, though, is upward.

Machines can also increase the strength of an applied force. Imagine pulling the nail out of the board with your bare hands! The hammer makes the job much easier. Measurements show that the upward force applied by the hammer to the nail is greater than the sideways force applied by the person's hand to the hammer handle.

The force that you apply to a simple machine is called the **effort force**. The force against which the machine acts, for example the resistance of the nail to being pulled in the photograph, is the **resistance force**. The force the machine applies to an object in response to our effort force is called the *output force*.

A hammer used to pull a nail increases the force that is applied to it.

Your arm acts as a machine to lift an object.

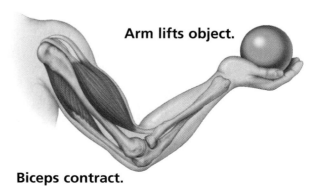

Arm lifts object.

Biceps contract.

There are six kinds of simple machines—the lever, the pulley, the wheel and axle, the inclined plane, the screw, and the wedge. Examples are shown in the diagram; look them over carefully.

Levers are very important simple machines. All levers have a rigid bar that rests on a pivot point of some kind. The pivot point is called the **fulcrum**. In addition, the side of the bar on which a person applies an effort force is called the *effort arm*. The side of the bar on which the lever produces an output force is called the *resistance arm*. The first diagram on this page shows the fulcrum, effort arm, and resistance arm for a lever.

For levers, the positions of the fulcrum, effort force, and output force can be different. As a result, there are three classes of levers. The lever shown here is an example of a *first-class lever*. In such a lever, the fulcrum lies between the effort force and the output force. A hammer being used to pull a nail or one child lifting another on a seesaw are additional examples of first-class levers. Note how first-class levers reverse the direction of the effort force.

▷ **What are the six different kinds of simple machines?**

Simple Machines

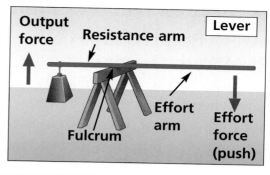

Lever — Output force, Resistance arm, Fulcrum, Effort arm, Effort force (push)

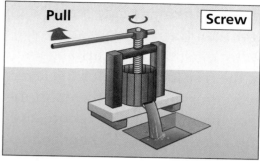

Screw — Pull

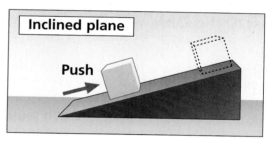

Inclined plane — Push

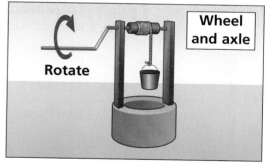

Wheel and axle — Rotate

Wedge

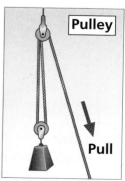

Pulley — Pull

How Do Levers Multiply Effort?

A first-class lever can produce an output force that is greater than the effort force. As the diagram shows, this occurs when the fulcrum is placed closer to the output force than to the effort force. The output force becomes increasingly greater than the effort force as the effort arm is made increasingly longer than the resistance arm.

Why must the effort arm be longer than the resistance arm for the lever to increase the strength of the effort force?

For the moment let's ignore any friction in machines. If there is no friction, the work put into a machine must be the same as the work done by the machine. Look at the diagram. The work input for a lever equals the effort force times the distance the effort arm is moved. In addition, the work output equals the output force times the distance the resistance arm is moved.

See how the distance moved by the effort arm is greater than the distance moved by the resistance arm. In order for the work input to equal the work output, the output force must be greater than the effort force. The output force has to be greater to make up for the smaller distance moved by the resistance arm.

READING **Draw Conclusions**
How can a lever's output force be greater than the effort force?

The diagram shows that the lever's work input (280 N x 1.5 m = 420 joules) equals the work output (560 N x 0.75 m = 420 joules).

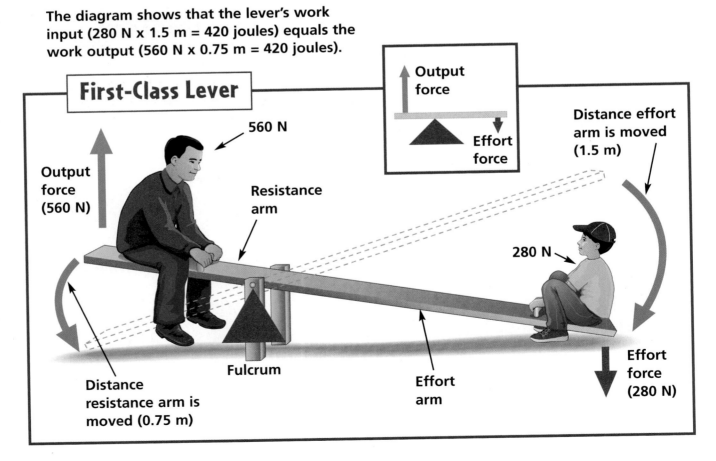

First-Class Lever

560 N

Output force (560 N)

Resistance arm

Output force

Effort force

Distance effort arm is moved (1.5 m)

280 N

Fulcrum

Effort arm

Effort force (280 N)

Distance resistance arm is moved (0.75 m)

What Are Other Classes of Levers?

You have learned that the fulcrum lies between the effort force and the output force in a first-class lever. The diagram shows the position of the fulcrum in relation to the effort and output forces for *second-* and *third-class levers*. Study the diagram carefully.

Note in the diagram that second-class levers have the output force between the effort force and the fulcrum. Second-class levers do not change the direction of the effort force. However, they do produce an output force that is greater than the effort force. You can see why by looking at the lengths of the effort arm and the resistance arm. The effort arm is longer in second-class levers.

The diagram also shows that third-class levers have the effort force between the output force and the fulcrum. Like second-class levers, third-class levers do not change the direction of the effort force. Unlike second-class levers, however, third-class levers produce an output force that is less than the effort force. Why would anyone find this useful? As a fishing rod shows, a third-class lever multiplies the distance of your effort. You only need to move your hands a small distance to move the tip of the rod through a large distance. This allows you to cast a lure a long distance.

▷ **What is the operation of second- and third-class levers?**

Second-Class Lever

A wheelbarrow is a second-class lever. Other examples are a nutcracker (two connected levers), a bottle opener, and a paper cutter.

Third-Class Lever

A fishing rod is a third-class lever. Other examples are tweezers (two connected levers), a human forearm and a broom.

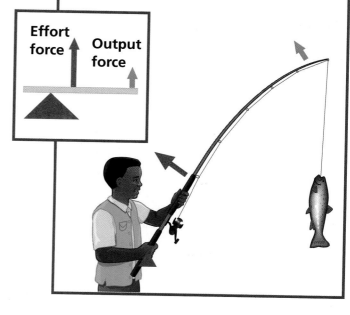

What Is a Machine's Advantage?

For any simple machine, there is a number that tells us how much the machine should multiply our effort. This number is called the **mechanical advantage** of the machine. A lever's mechanical advantage is found by dividing the distance the effort arm moves by the distance the resistance arm moves as the lever does work.

If we ignore friction, a machine's mechanical advantage can also be given by dividing the output force by the effort force. The diagram above shows how the mechanical advantage can be found for a pair of scissors.

When the output force is greater than the input force, the mechanical

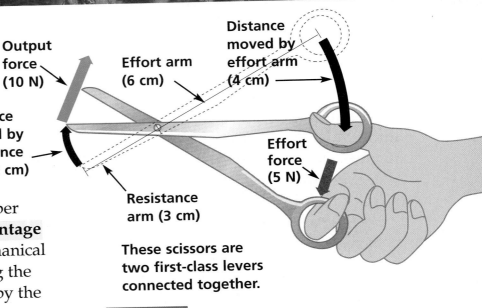

Output force (10 N)

Distance moved by resistance arm (2 cm)

Effort arm (6 cm)

Distance moved by effort arm (4 cm)

Effort force (5 N)

Resistance arm (3 cm)

These scissors are two first-class levers connected together.

READING

Diagrams

Which changes the direction of the effort force, the scissors or the broom?

advantage is greater than one. It is also possible for the mechanical advantage to be less than one. The diagram to the left shows how a third-class lever has a mechanical advantage of less than one. The effort force applied to a broom is greater than the output force because the resistance arm is moved through a greater distance than the effort arm.

For levers it turns out that the mechanical advantage can be found by dividing the length of the effort arm by the length of the resistance arm. You can check this formula with values from the diagrams. The formula works because the lengths of the effort and resistance arms are directly related to how far each arm moves.

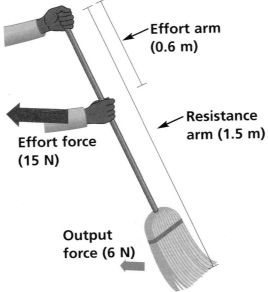

A small motion of the sweeper's bottom hand becomes a large motion of the head of the broom.

Effort arm (0.6 m)

Resistance arm (1.5 m)

Effort force (15 N)

Output force (6 N)

▷ **What is mechanical advantage?**

What Are Double Levers?

A student has assembled models of several double levers using wooden sticks. The levers are shown in the diagrams. Each stick has a hole in one end where string can be inserted and tied to make a fulcrum. The red arrows show where you would place your fingers to apply an effort force. The effort force would allow you to use the lever to hold a pencil as shown. The output force is located at the point where the lever contacts the pencil.

Procedure

1. **Observe** Look at each lever carefully. Try to find things that the levers have in common and things that are different.

2. **Define** Write a definition of a lever that would include all three levers. Base your definition on what the levers do and how they work.

3. **Define** Now write a definition for each lever that tells it apart from the other levers.

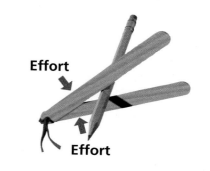

4. **Define** Levers are examples of simple machines. Write a definition of simple machines based on what they do and how they work. Revise your definition as you study other machines in this lesson.

Drawing Conclusions

1. How did your definitions compare with those of others? Were there any differences? Why?

2. Using the diagrams on pages F68 and F69, state the class of each lever. What information in the definition you wrote would allow you to find the class of each lever?

Each of these devices is actually two levers connected together. They are called double levers.

How Do Pulleys Work?

The photograph shows a system of wheels and ropes. The ropes fit in grooves in the wheels. When the ropes move, they turn the wheels. Each wheel and the rope passing over it is called a **pulley**. Pulleys are a type of simple machine.

A pulley system is made up of several pulleys acting together. Single pulleys acting alone may either be fixed or movable. The diagram shows each type. For the fixed pulley, the wheel itself is attached to a fixed support. The fixed pulley does not multiply the effort force. It only changes the direction of the effort force. Pulling down on a rope can be easier than lifting an object straight up by hand, especially if the footing is slippery.

The diagram also shows a movable pulley. Here the pulley is attached to the object and moves with it. A movable pulley multiplies the effort force by two. This means that a movable pulley

This device is a system of pulleys that makes lifting objects easier.

has a mechanical advantage of 2. However, a movable pulley does not change the direction of the effort.

Although it may not seem obvious, pulleys are a type of lever. The wheel can be thought of as a large number of levers that continuously roll into place. The

READING
Diagrams

How are fixed and movable pulleys the same? How are they different?

FIXED PULLEY

400 N

400 N

400 N weight

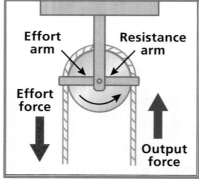

Effort arm

Resistance arm

Effort force

Output force

The fixed pulley has a mechanical advantage of 1, since the effort force equals the output force.

MOVABLE PULLEY

200 N

200 N

200 N

400 N weight

middle part of the diagram shows how a fixed pulley is really a first-class lever.

Fixed and movable pulleys can be combined to make pulley systems like the one in the photograph on page F72. Such a system is sometimes called a *block and tackle*.

The motion of all of the ropes in a pulley system can be complicated. To get a better idea of how fixed and movable pulleys can work together in a pulley system, look at the diagram of two pulleys below. This pulley system has the same mechanical advantage as a single movable pulley. However, the addition of the fixed pulley changes the direction of the effort, which is something a movable pulley alone would not do.

▷ How does a pulley system work?

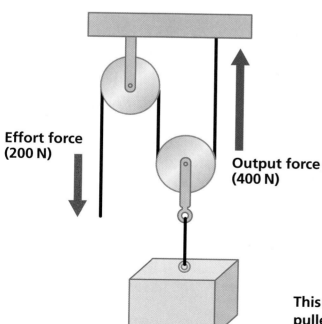

Effort force (200 N)

Output force (400 N)

Weight = 400 N

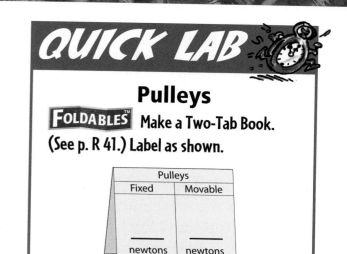

QUICK LAB

Pulleys

FOLDABLES Make a Two-Tab Book. (See p. R 41.) Label as shown.

Pulleys	
Fixed	Movable
———	———
newtons	newtons

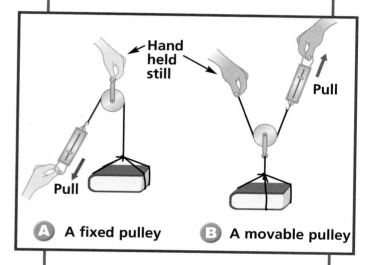

A A fixed pulley   **B** A movable pulley

1. **Observe** Assemble a pulley like the one in diagram A. Read the force shown on the scale. Record it on the Foldables tab.

2. **Experiment** Repeat step 1 using the set-up in diagram B.

3. **Interpret Data** Which pulley needed less force? Explain under the tabs.

This pulley system is made of one fixed pulley and one movable pulley. The system multiplies the effort by two and also changes the direction of the effort.

What Is a Pulley's Mechanical Advantage?

Pulley systems can be very helpful in lifting heavy loads with a small effort force. By increasing the number of wheels and ropes, we can increase the mechanical advantage of a pulley system. As the mechanical advantage increases, the effort force required to lift a given load decreases. The diagram illustrates this idea. Look to see how the mechanical advantage of each pulley compares with the others. Then look at the number of wheels and ropes in each pulley system.

In real pulley systems, friction occurs. The amount of friction increases as more wheels are added because the ropes rub in more places and more wheels have to turn on axles. This causes you to exert a little more force to offset the rubbing and turning friction. As a result the mechanical advantage of the pulley system is reduced.

The mechanical advantage of a pulley system depends on how far it moves an object compared with how far its rope must be pulled when the effort is applied. The mechanical advantage is the distance moved by the effort rope

Mechanical Advantage of Pulley Systems

Three different pulley systems. Notice how the mechanical advantage increases as the number of wheels and ropes increases.

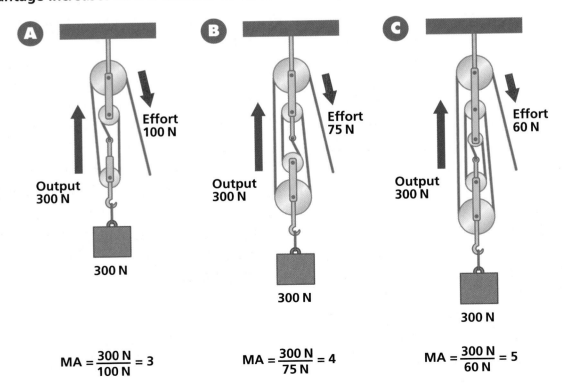

A

Effort
100 N

Output
300 N

300 N

$$MA = \frac{300\ N}{100\ N} = 3$$

B

Effort
75 N

Output
300 N

300 N

$$MA = \frac{300\ N}{75\ N} = 4$$

C

Effort
60 N

Output
300 N

300 N

$$MA = \frac{300\ N}{60\ N} = 5$$

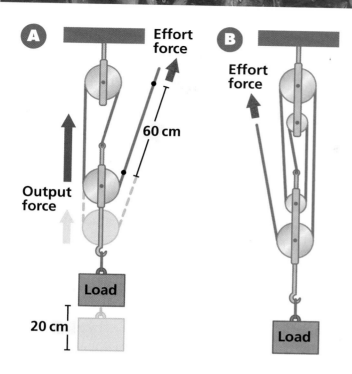

A Effort force

60 cm

Output force

Load

20 cm

B Effort force

Load

READING
Diagrams

What is the mechanical advantage
of each pulley system? Explain.

divided by the distance moved by the object. The simple pulley in diagram A shows how the effort rope and the object move in a certain pulley system. The mechanical advantage for this pulley system is 60 cm ÷ 20 cm = 3.

In complicated pulley systems, it can be difficult to predict the distance the effort rope and the object will move. This in turn makes it hard to predict the mechanical advantage of the pulley system by dividing these distances. However, there is a simple way to predict the mechanical advantage of a pulley system. Just count the number of rope strands that feel a downward pull from the object being lifted.

Look again at the diagram on page F74. Pulley A has three strands of rope that feel a downward pull from the 300-newton block. The rope that passes over the top pulley and is pulled downward by the effort force does not feel a downward pull from the block. As a result this rope does not count. Since three strands of rope feel a downward pull from the block, we predict a mechanical advantage of 3 for pulley system A. As you can see, this is correct.

In a similar manner, you can see that pulley B has four strands of rope that feel a downward pull from the 300-newton block, so we correctly predict that it would have a mechanical advantage of 4. Pulley C has five strands of rope that we should count, so we correctly predict a mechanical advantage of 5.

▶ **What are two ways to find a pulley's mechanical advantage?**

How Does a Wheel and Axle Work?

Look at the simple machine below. Although it may not look like it, this machine is actually a type of first-class lever. You know that pulleys are levers that rotate continuously. This machine works in a similar way. The fulcrum, effort arm, and resistance arm are all shown in the diagram. Look to see how the fulcrum lies between the effort arm and the resistance arm as in any first-class lever.

This machine consists of a wheel that applies the effort force and a smaller axle that produces the output force. We call this type of machine a **wheel and axle**. The mechanical advantage of a wheel and axle is the length of the effort arm divided by the length of the resistance arm, as it would be for any lever.

As the following diagram shows, the effort arm is the radius (half the distance across the circle through its center) of the wheel, while the resistance arm is the radius of the axle.

The radius of the axle in a wheel and axle can be quite small in comparison to the radius of the wheel. For that reason a wheel and axle often has a large mechanical advantage. It can also carry your effort to places that are hard to reach. The axle can be quite long and can transmit your effort force some distance away from where you apply it.

Below is an example of a wheel and axle. A crank can be used to raise water safely and easily out of a well. Imagine trying to stand over the center of a well to lift a water-filled bucket with your hands alone. Not only would this be very dangerous, it would be much harder to lift the bucket!

▷ **What is a wheel and axle?**

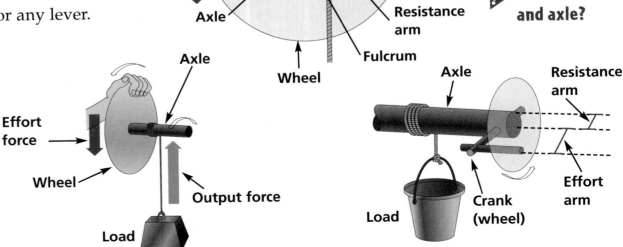

L·I·N·K·S

Why It Matters

Did you know that the human body is a machine? The muscles and bones work together to make tasks easier. Picking up an object or nodding your head would be almost impossible if the different parts of your body didn't work together.

e-Journal Visit our Web site www.science.mmhschool.com to do a research project on levers.

Think and Write

1. What if you want a first-class lever with a mechanical advantage that is less than 1? Where do you place the fulcrum? Why?

2. Your aunt wants to put a pulley in her garage to lift the top of her jeep upward from the side. Which is better—a single movable pulley or a single fixed pulley? Why?

3. What pries the lid off a paint can more easily—a long screwdriver or a short one? Why?

4. FURTHER INQUIRY Define What is a wheel and axle? Is a doorknob an example? What are other examples?

5. Critical Thinking Design a pulley system that has a mechanical advantage of 6. Sketch your system.

MATH LINK

Calculate mechanical advantage. Make a list of the different kitchen utensils that are levers. Measure the effort arm and the resistance arm. Use these measurements to find the mechanical advantage of each item.

WRITING LINK

Expository Writing Simple machines have been important throughout history, from catapults used in warfare to tractions used in healthcare. Research the history of several different simple machines. Write a report about how these machines have improved with new technology.

HEALTH LINK

Examine exercise machines. Many cardiovascular and strength training machines use pulley systems to manage the resistance weights. Find a photograph of such an apparatus, and label the pulleys. Describe how they are used to change the direction of force.

TECHNOLOGY LINK

 LOG ON Visit www.science.mmhschool.com for more links.

How Inclined Planes Work

Get Ready

Why are mountain roads long and winding? If you have ever ridden a bicycle up a steep hill, you know that it can be hard to pedal.

What if the hill were broken up into several less steep hills? Would it be easier to reach the top?

Inquiry Skill

You experiment when you perform a test to support or disprove a hypothesis.

Explore Activity

How Is a Ramp a Machine?

Materials

flat cardboard or board

spring scale

book with string tied around it

meterstick

several books

wax paper

tape

Procedure

1 **Measure** Measure how much force it takes to lift the book straight up to a height of 20 cm. Will using a ramp affect how much force is needed to lift the book?

2 Stack several books to a height of 20 cm. Set up a ramp so that the top of the ramp reaches the top.

3 **Predict** Predict how much force it will take to use the spring scale to pull the book up the ramp. Then pull the book up at a slow, steady speed. Record the results.

4 **Experiment** Adjust the board so that it makes a steeper ramp. That is, the halfway mark of the ramp reaches the top of the stack. Predict the force you need to pull the book. Try it. Record your results.

Drawing Conclusions

1 **Interpret Data** Which took more force, lifting the book or pulling it up the ramp? Explain your answer.

2 Which used less force? Why do you think this is so?

3 With which method did the book move the least distance? The most? Explain.

4 FURTHER INQUIRY **Experiment** Tape wax paper to the surface of the ramp. Repeat the activity. Explain any differences in the results.

Main Idea Inclined planes are simple machines that decrease the amount of force needed to do work.

What Is an Inclined Plane?

In the diagram two workers are moving barrels from the ground onto a loading dock. One worker lifts the barrels straight up. The other worker rolls the barrels up a ramp. The ramp makes it easier to move the barrels to a greater height.

The ramp is an example of a simple machine called an **inclined plane**. An inclined plane is a straight, slanted surface. Without any moving parts, inclined planes can make it easier to do work because they multiply the effort force.

Each barrel weighs 500 N. This weight is the output force the inclined plane must produce to raise a barrel to a greater height. A worker only has to apply an effort force of 150 N to roll a barrel up the inclined plane. The mechanical advantage of the inclined plane is

$$MA = \text{output force/input force}$$
$$= 500 \text{ N} \div 150 \text{ N}$$
$$= 3.3$$

This particular inclined plane multiplies the effort force 3.3 times.

You might wonder why the output force is taken to be 500 N. However, you have learned that sideways motion at constant speed does not affect the work done when something is lifted—all that matters is the weight of the object and the vertical distance it is lifted.

The other worker, on the other hand, pushes in the same direction as the slant of the inclined plane. Since she is not pushing straight up on the barrel, she does not have to offset its entire weight. The surface of the inclined plane also pushes on the barrel and adds to the worker's effort. The combined pushes act to lift the barrel against its weight.

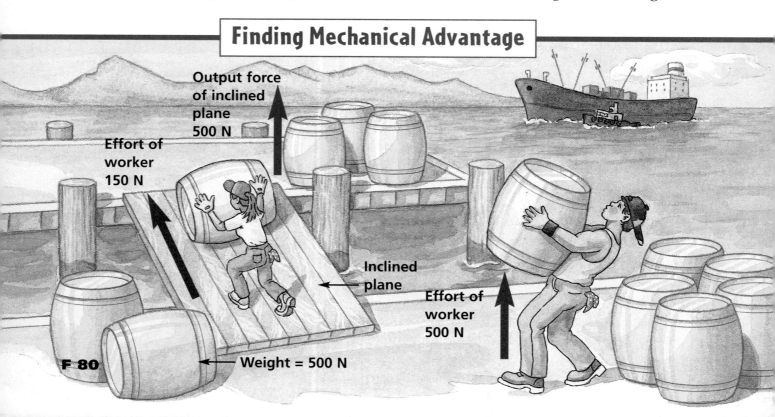

Finding Mechanical Advantage

Output force of inclined plane 500 N

Effort of worker 150 N

Inclined plane

Weight = 500 N

Effort of worker 500 N

The Amount of Work Done

You might think that the worker lifting the barrel straight up ends up doing more work. After all, the worker must exert 500 N of force as he lifts a barrel straight up. The other worker has to apply only 150 N of force because she uses the inclined plane. Let's see if either worker performs more work.

To offset the weight of a barrel, the worker lifting the barrel straight up must apply 500 N of force upward. The height of the dock is 1.8 m. Since work is force times distance, the work is

$$\text{work} = \text{force} \times \text{distance}$$
$$= 500 \text{ N} \times 1.8 \text{ m}$$
$$= 900 \text{ joules}$$

The other worker applies a force of 150 N over a distance of 6 m (the length of the inclined plane). The work done by this person is

$$\text{work} = \text{force} \times \text{distance}$$
$$= 150 \text{ N} \times 6 \text{ m}$$
$$= 900 \text{ joules}$$

Both workers do the same amount of work in moving a barrel up onto the dock—900 joules!

How is it that both workers could do the same amount of work when one has to apply only 150 N of force compared with the other's 500 N of force? The answer is that the 150 N of force must be applied over a longer distance. The worker using the ramp must push each barrel 6 m, while the other worker lifts his barrels only 1.8 m.

This example is typical of simple machines that multiply effort. The effort force must act over a greater distance than the output force. Remember that the work put into a machine must equal the work produced by the machine (assuming no friction). Otherwise the law of conservation of energy would not be obeyed.

▷ **How do inclined planes make a job easier?**

Finding Work Done

Effort of worker 150 N

Length of inclined plane 6 m

Height of dock 1.8 m

Effort of worker 500 N

What Is a Ramp's Mechanical Advantage?

The diagram below shows two students sliding identical boxes up boards onto the school stage. The boards are acting as inclined planes. By using simple machines, the students are able to move the boxes to a greater height with a force that is less than the weight of each box.

Notice, though, that the students are not applying the same force to move the boxes. What is the difference that requires one to apply more force than the other? You probably recognized that the inclined planes they are using are not equally steep. When the inclined plane is steeper, more force is required to move an object up the incline.

For both inclined planes, the work done on each box is the same—the boxes weigh the same, and they are lifted to the same height. However, you can see that the steeper incline is also shorter. The student using the steeper inclined plane applies her effort force over a shorter distance to lift a box to the stage. To do the same amount of work in a shorter distance, she must exert a greater force.

It makes sense that a steeper inclined plane requires a greater effort force for a given job. Think about an inclined plane so steep that it is almost straight up. If you slid an object up such a ramp, you would be pushing nearly straight up. In fact you would almost be lifting the object without any help from the ramp at all. If the ramp is not helping you very much, your effort would have to be nearly as great as the object's actual weight.

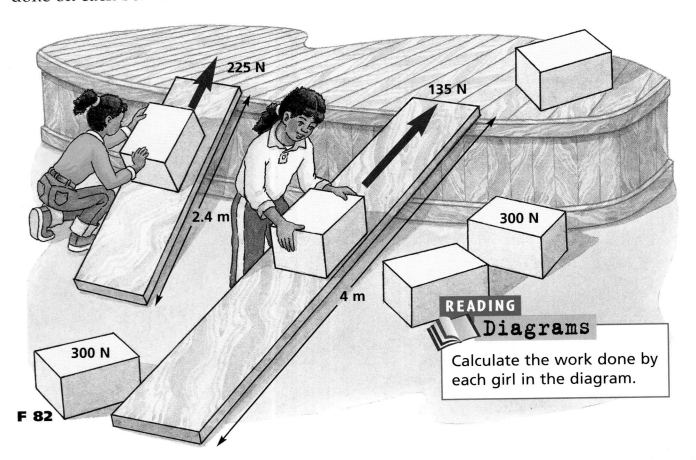

225 N

2.4 m

135 N

300 N

4 m

300 N

READING Diagrams

Calculate the work done by each girl in the diagram.

The two inclined planes from page F82 are shown here from the side. Look at the angle, height, and length of each incline. When the angle is greater, the length of an inclined plane is shorter in comparison to its height.

A machine's mechanical advantage is given by the output force divided by the effort force. For inclined planes dividing the length of the incline by its height also gives you the mechanical advantage (assuming no friction).

To illustrate these ideas, let's calculate the mechanical advantage of the inclined planes in the diagram. If we look at the forces, we see that the output force of either incline is the weight of a box, 300 N. For the steeper ramp, the effort force is 225 N, so its mechanical advantage is

MA = output force/effort force
= 300 N ÷ 225 N
= 1.33

We can also find the mechanical advantage for the steeper ramp from its length and height:

MA = length/height
= 2.4 m ÷ 1.8 m
= 1.33

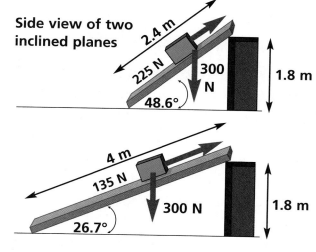

Side view of two inclined planes

2.4 m
225 N
300 N
48.6°
1.8 m

4 m
135 N
300 N
26.7°
1.8 m

For the less steep ramp, the calculations are

MA = output force/input force
= 300 N ÷ 135 N
= 2.22

or

MA = length/height
= 4 m ÷ 1.8 m
= 2.22

The longer ramp has the greater mechanical advantage. Moving the effort through a longer distance allows the effort to be smaller for a given amount of work.

▷ **How can you find a ramp's mechanical advantage?**

READING
Diagrams

1. Calculate the mechanical advantage of the ramp.

2. How would the result change if the ramp were made steeper?

8m

2m

Modeling Screws

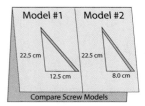 **FOLDABLES™** Make a Two-Tab Book. (See p. R 41.) Label as shown.

1. **Measure** Make a right triangle out of paper. The sides that form the right angle should be 22.5 cm and 12.5 cm long. Color the diagonal side with a marker.

2. **Make a Model** Lay a pencil over the 12.5-cm side of the triangle. Roll the triangle tightly around the pencil so that the colored edge makes a model of the threads on a screw. Tape the paper in place.

3. **Repeat** steps 1 and 2 using a triangle whose sides are 22.5 cm and 8.0 cm.

4. Which inclined plane (triangle) was steepest? Which screw had more "threads" for a given distance? Record answers under the tabs.

How Does a Screw Work?

The diagram shows a **screw**. A screw is actually a type of simple machine that multiplies effort. The mechanical advantage of screws can be very high.

A screw is created by wrapping an inclined plane around a central bar. The spiral ridges are the threads of the screw. The distance from thread to thread is called the pitch. The diagram shows how the revolution of the head of a screw can cause a screw to move into an object. The distance around the head of the screw is the distance the effort moves. The distance through which the output moves is equal to the pitch of the screw.

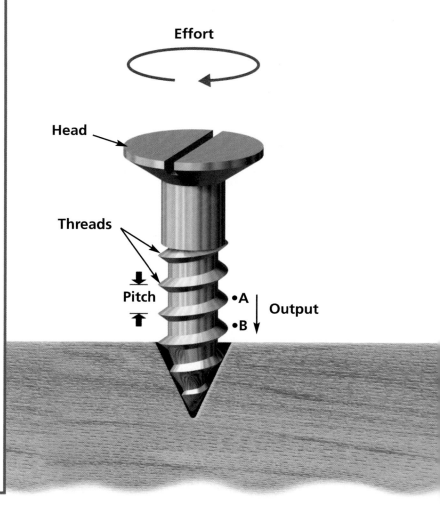

You know that one way to find the mechanical advantage of a simple machine is to divide the effort distance by the output distance. As a result the mechanical advantage of a screw is the distance around the head of the screw divided by the pitch of the screw.

For example, what if a screw has threads that are 0.1 cm apart, meaning the pitch is 0.1 cm? If the distance around the head of this screw is 1.5 cm, its mechanical advantage would be

MA = distance around head ÷ pitch
= 1.5 cm ÷ 0.1 cm
= 15

As this example shows, screws with a larger pitch (the threads are farther apart) tend to have lower mechanical advantages. The threads are farther apart when the inclined plane of the screw is steeper. This is what we would expect, since steeper inclined planes have a lower mechanical advantage.

Screws can be made with large heads and very close, fine threads. Such screws have large mechanical advantages, perhaps as high as 35 to 40. This allows screws to join parts of objects together very tightly.

Friction helps screws that hold objects together to do their job. If there were no friction in such cases, a screw could unscrew itself and the object would fall apart!

Friction, however, keeps screws in place once they are driven in with a tool.

Screws come in all shapes and sizes. You are probably familiar with screws that hold metal and wood pieces together. Other less obvious versions of screws are shown in the photographs.

Screws are used in, from top to bottom, the car jack, the ship propeller, and the wrench.

▷ How is a screw a kind of inclined plane?

**Dull blade—
thicker wedge**

**Sharp blade—
thinner wedge**

A wedge is a kind of inclined plane that moves when an effort force is applied.

What Is a Wedge?

The first photograph shows how a simple machine called a **wedge** can change the direction of an effort and increase its strength. A wedge may have one or two slanted surfaces. It is basically a single inclined plane or two inclined planes joined back-to-back. However, while an inclined plane remains stationary, a wedge must be moved by an effort force.

You know that inclined planes that are long in comparison to their height have higher mechanical advantages. In a similar way, wedges that are thin have higher mechanical advantages. Knife blades, ax heads, chisels, and other cutting tools are actually wedges. They work best when they are sharpened.

As the diagrams show, sharpening keeps the wedge of the blade thin so that it has the greatest possible mechanical advantage.

Wedges, like screws, may need friction to work effectively. The worker in the second photograph, for example, is driving a wedge under a heavy object to lift it to a higher position. Friction keeps the wedge in place between hammer blows. If there were no friction, the resistance force of the object's weight would squeeze the wedge back out between blows. The worker would never make progress in lifting the object.

READING **Draw Conclusions**
How is a wedge an inclined plane?

How Can Simple Machines Work Together?

Scissors are a relatively basic device. However, scissors are made of more than one simple machine. When we make a device that is a combination of two or more simple machines, a **compound machine** results.

What are the simple machines in scissors? Scissors contain two first-class levers. The pivot point for the blades and handles is the fulcrum for the levers. Scissors also contain wedges—the sharpened blades that actually do the cutting. The wedges and the levers act together when scissors are used, so scissors are a compound machine.

A screwdriver being used to turn a screw is another example of a compound machine. The screwdriver

itself is a wheel and axle. A screw, itself, is an inclined plane. The screwdriver and the screw combine to make a compound machine.

Can you tell how the worker in the diagram below is using a compound machine? The wheelbarrow is a second-class lever. It multiplies the effort of the worker in lifting the sand. The worker is also using an inclined plane by pushing the wheelbarrow up the ramp. The inclined plane further multiplies the effort of the worker. The wheelbarrow and the inclined plane act together as a compound machine.

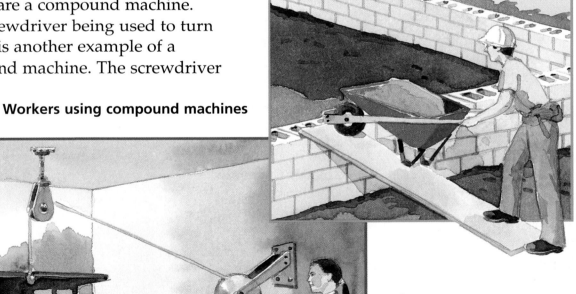

Workers using compound machines

> **What is a compound machine?**

What Is Efficiency?

A machine changes work done by an effort force into work done by the machine's output force. In a machine with no friction, the work input equals the work output. However, no machine truly runs without friction.

When there is friction, some of the work input is changed into heat energy. This means not all of the work input becomes work output. It does not become work done by the machine. As a result friction makes the work put into a machine greater than the work done by the machine.

We can measure the amount of useful work a machine can do with a quantity called **efficiency**. To calculate the efficiency, you write a ratio.

$$\text{efficiency} = \frac{\text{work done by machine}}{\text{work put into machine}}$$

If you want to express the result as a percent, you multiply this ratio by 100 percent. The closer the efficiency of a machine is to 100 percent, the less energy the machine wastes.

For example, what if a machine does 1,200 joules of work when 1,800 joules of work are put into it? The machine's percent efficiency would be

$$\text{efficiency} = \frac{\text{work out}}{\text{work in}} \times 100\%$$

$$= \frac{1,200 \text{ joules}}{1,800 \text{ joules}} \times 100\%$$

$$= 66.6\%$$

In pulley systems, adding pulleys can increase the mechanical advantage of the machine. However, there is more friction with more pulleys. There may be enough added friction to significantly reduce the gain in mechanical advantage.

▷ **How does friction affect efficiency?**

Where Friction Occurs

The arrows in each case show where friction occurs.

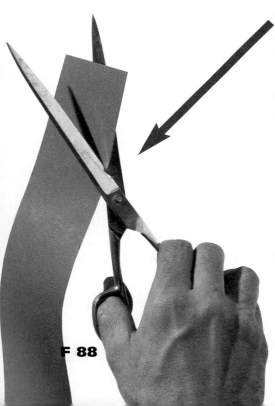

Friction occurs where the blades rub on the pivot and where they cut the paper.

The box rubs on the surface of the inclined plane, causing friction.

Friction is caused by the axle rubbing on its supports and the rope rubbing on the axle.

How Do Machines Help Us?

It would be very difficult to live in a world without machines. If your bare hands were the only tools you had, think how hard life would be! Thankfully, we have simple machines like ramps, screwdrivers, and pulleys to make tasks easier. In addition, we use many kinds of compound machines. For example, pliers are just two levers attached at their fulcrums. So are scissors. Gears are compound machines that have connected wheels with teeth to keep them from slipping. Almost any machine that has circular motion, from a bicycle to a food processor, uses gears to increase its speed or force.

On a bicycle, the pedals and front sprocket form a large wheel. A chain transfers the force to the rear sprockets which act as axles. Smaller sprockets provide high speeds, but require greater effort. Larger sprockets allow less effort, but at slower speeds.

Pedals and sprockets on a bike

Complex machines like cars, which we depend on heavily, are made from a combination of many simple machines. Understanding simple machines helps us to design even better complex machines.

▷ **How do machines help make our lives easier?**

Plumbers often use wrenches with very long handles to remove stuck pipe fittings. Why can wrenches turn the fitting easily, whereas the plumbers cannot do it using their bare hands? The long handle acts as a long lever.

How Is Your Body a Complex Machine?

You use machines every day of your life. Your body is the most important machine you will ever use. The bones and the muscles of your body work together to help you perform tasks. When you swim, your arms act like levers to help you push the water behind you. Your legs are levers that propel you forward through the water. Remember, all of these simple machines working together make up an amazingly complex machine—the human body.

Writing requires you to use your body as a machine. Your hand becomes two levers when you hold a pen. The pointer finger applies force from the top, while your thumb applies force from below. This allows you to hold the pen and write.

▷ **What simple machines make up the human body?**

When a ballerina turns on her toes, her body acts as a wheel and axle, and her foot acts as a lever. They work together to help her turn gracefully.

A softball pitcher gets her speed by using her body as a machine. Her arm acts as a third-class lever. A small motion of her upper arm results in a larger and faster motion of her hand. This causes the ball to be released at a high speed.

Why It Matters

Fighting friction is an important job for engineers. In automobiles, for example, friction wastes energy that could go into the energy of motion. Car designers are always looking for better materials to use in making the moving parts of car motors and the wheels and axles of cars.

The body is a machine, too. It needs to protect its parts from wear and tear caused by friction. Special fluid protects your bones as you move.

e-Journal Visit our Web site **www.science.mmhschool.com** to do a research project on inclined planes.

Think and Write

1. A 10-m ramp leads to a 2-m high platform. What is the ramp's mechanical advantage?

2. One screw is made with a steep inclined plane. Another has a shallow inclined plane. Which screw has threads that are closer together? Which has the greater mechanical advantage?

3. What is the difference between a wedge and an inclined plane?

4. A mountain road winds back and forth so that it can have a gradual slope. What kind of simple machine is the road?

5. **Critical Thinking** How can you minimize friction on a bicycle?

L·I·N·K·S

MATH LINK

Solve this problem. Student A is capable of exerting a force of 100 N while pushing a wagon up an incline with a distance of 10 meters. If student B is to do the same amount of work, but can only exert 80 N, how long must the inclined plane be?

WRITING LINK

Expository Writing Your body is an important machine. Research the Americans with Disabilities Act of 1990. In an essay, explain how it changed our society and its laws, as well as life for disabled people. You could present your essay as part of a multimedia display.

ART LINK

Draw a diagram. Design a method that will show how two or more simple machines might be used to move a heavy safe onto a truck.

TECHNOLOGY LINK

 LOG ON Visit **www.science.mmhschool.com** for more links.

Vocabulary

Fill each blank with the best word or words from the list.

> **compound machines,** F87
> **inclined plane,** F80
> **kinetic energy,** F53
> **lever,** F67
> **potential energy,** F52
> **pulley,** F72
> **screw,** F84
> **wedge,** F86
> **wheel and axle,** F76
> **work,** F56

1. A simple machine that uses a rope passing over a grooved wheel is a _____.

2. When an object is lifted, it gains _____.

3. When you use force to move an object through a distance, you are doing _____.

4. All moving objects possess _____.

5. The slanted sides of a(n) _____ multiply effort when it is moved.

6. A simple machine that can multiply effort without itself moving is a(n) _____.

7. The pedal of a bicycle and its sprocket are an example of a(n) _____.

8. A simple machine made in the form of a spiral inclined plane is a _____.

9. Scissors and bicycles are two kinds of _____.

10. A rigid bar that rotates around a fixed point is a _____.

Test Prep

11. A moving object's energy that is due to its motion is called

  A kinetic energy.

  B potential energy.

  C gravitational potential energy.

  D heat energy.

12. A car going down a hill speeds up because of

  F kinetic energy.

  G potential energy.

  H gravitational potential energy.

  J heat energy.

13. All of the following are simple machines EXCEPT _____.

  A scissors

  B a screw

  C an ax

  D a ramp

14. The energy used to overcome friction becomes

    F speed.

    G sound.

    H work.

    J heat.

15. All of the following are forms of energy EXCEPT _____.

    A light

    B electrical

    C friction

    D chemical

Concepts and Skills

16. Reading in Science In reality, work output is always less than the work input. Why?

17. Critical Thinking One worker lifts a large crate up to a truck. Another worker applies less force by using a pulley to put the same kind of crate in the truck. How can both workers do the same amount of work?

18. Product Ads Advertisements for many products claim to make work easier. Choose a product advertised in your local newspaper. How can you determine whether or not these claims are true?

19. **INQUIRY SKILL** **Define Based on Observations** Define the terms *dry-cell* and *lead-acid*. This definition should include both terms. Then define these terms separately.

20. Scientific Methods How could you make a job you have to do around your house easier? Use the scientific method to design and test a machine to make your chores easier. What was your result?

Did You Ever Wonder?

INQUIRY SKILL **Make a Model** A person using a wheelchair requires a ramp built from the ground to a high front door. A short ramp is too steep. There is not enough space on the property to build a long, straight ramp. Draw a ramp design to solve this problem.

 LOG ON Visit www.science.mmhschool.com to better your test scores.

Cherrill Spencer
Experimental Physicist

When Cherrill Spencer was growing up in England in the 1950s and 1960s, girls weren't encouraged to become scientists. "But science was exciting to me," she explains, "because it was about the future."

Spencer's interest in science has led her to design very powerful magnets. The magnets are part of a large machine called a particle accelerator. Spencer works with other scientists to try to answer one important question: What is everything made of?

Of course, all matter is made up of atoms. But what are atoms made of? Inside atoms are smaller particles called protons, neutrons, and electrons. Protons and neutrons are made up of even smaller particles called quarks. Spencer and her team study quarks. In order to do this, they have to shake the smaller particles loose from the bigger ones.

At one end of the accelerator at the Stanford Linear Accelerator Center, there is a machine called an electron gun. It shoots electrons down a narrow pipe that's two miles long. At the far end of the pipe, the electrons smash into protons, releasing a shower of smaller particles.

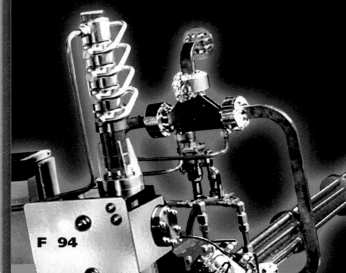

TOP 5 Common Uses for Magnets

Cherrill Spencer works with very special magnets, but magnets are found in many household items. Here are some:

1. Videotape recorder
2. Microwave oven
3. Stereo speakers
4. Television set
5. Telephone

"It's like a fireworks explosion," Spencer explains. "Except you can't see it, even with the most powerful microscope. Instead we study the tracks these tiny particles make as they travel through different materials." Spencer's magnets are designed to guide the electrons as they travel through the accelerator pipe. "Magnetic fields can bend and focus the electron beam," she says. "Sort of the way a glass lens can bend and focus light."

Write About It

1. What are quarks?
2. What qualities do you think Spencer had in order for her to go into physics when there were few women in the field?

LOG ON Visit **www.science.mmhschool.com** to learn more about the work at the Stanford Linear Accelerator Center.

ROLL THE BALL

Your goal is to compare the motions of different masses.

What to Do

1. Create a chart to include balls in pairs. Compare the motions of various balls.

2. Compare the motions of Ball 1 and Ball 2. Which ball is harder to move?

3. Repeat step 2 for Balls 3 and 4; for Balls 5 and 6.

Analyze Your Results

If you gave all of the balls you tested a push of equal force, which ball would accelerate most? What is the reason for your answer?

Objects	Harder to Move	Greater Mass	Greater Size
Ball 1			
Ball 2			

How hard do you work ?

Your goal is to measure force and distance in order to calculate work.

What to Do

1. Make a table like the one shown here.

2. Perform the following activities. Measure the force you use with a spring scale or force meter. Also measure the distance you move each one of the objects. Record the data in the table.

   a. Open a door. b. Pull out a drawer. c. Lift this book from the floor over your head.
   d. Pull a 1-kg mass a distance of 2 m across the floor.

Analyze Your Results

Use your data to calculate the work done for each activity. Record the results in your table.

Object	Force (N)	Distance (m)	Work (J)
door			
drawer			
book			
1-kg mass			

For Your Reference

Science Handbook

Health Handbook

Units of Measurement

The temperature is 77 degrees Fahrenheit.

That is the same as 25 degrees Celsius.

Water boils at 212 degrees Fahrenheit.

Water freezes at 0 degrees Celsius.

I weigh 85 pounds.

That baseball bat weighs 32 ounces.

32 ounces is the same as 2 pounds.

The mass of the bat is 907 grams.

This classroom is 10 meters wide and 20 meters long.

That means the area is 200 square meters.

Units of Measurement

This bottle of juice has a volume of 1 liter.

That is a little more than 1 quart.

She can walk 20 meters in 5 seconds.

That means her speed is 4 meters per second.

Table of Measurements

International System of Units (SI)	English System of Units
Temperature	**Temperature**
Water freezes at 0°C and boils at 100°C.	Water freezes at 32°F and boils at 212°F.
Length and Distance	**Length and Distance**
1,000 meters (m) = 1 kilometer (km)	5,280 feet = 1 mile
100 centimeters (cm) = 1 meter	3 feet = 1 yard
10 millimeters (mm) = 1 centimeter	12 inches = 1 foot
Volume	**Volume of Fluids**
1,000 milliliters (mL) = 1 liter (L)	4 quarts = 1 gallon
1 cubic centimeter (cm³) = 1 milliliter	2 pints = 1 quart
Mass	2 cups = 1 pint
1,000 grams (g) = 1 kilogram (kg)	8 fluid ounces = 1 cup
	Weight
	2,000 pounds = 1 ton
	16 ounces = 1 pound

Use a Hand Lens

You use a hand lens to magnify an object, or make the object look larger. With a hand lens, you can see details that would be hard to see without the hand lens.

Magnify a Piece of Cereal

1. Place a piece of your favorite cereal on a flat surface. Look at the cereal carefully. Draw a picture of it.
2. Look at the cereal through the large lens of a hand lens. Move the lens toward or away from the cereal until it looks larger and in focus. Draw a picture of the cereal as you see it through the hand lens. Fill in details that you did not see before.
3. Look at the cereal through the smaller lens, which will magnify the cereal even more. If you notice more details, add them to your drawing.
4. Repeat this activity using objects you are studying in science. It might be a rock, some soil, or a seed.

Observe Seeds in a Petri Dish

Can you observe a seed as it sprouts? You can if it's in a petri dish. A petri dish is a shallow, clear, round dish with a cover.

1. Line the sides and bottom of a petri dish with a double layer of filter paper or paper towel. You may have to cut the paper to make it fit.
2. Sprinkle water on the paper to wet it.
3. Place three or four radish seeds on the wet paper in different areas of the dish. Put the lid on the dish, and keep it in a warm place.
4. Observe the seeds every day for a week. Use a hand lens to look for a tiny root pushing through the seed. Record how long it takes each seed to sprout.

Use a Microscope

Hand lenses make objects look several times larger. A microscope, however, can magnify an object to look hundreds of times larger.

Examine Salt Grains

1. Look at the photograph to learn the different parts of your microscope.
2. Place the microscope on a flat surface. Always carry a microscope with both hands. Hold the arm with one hand, and put your other hand beneath the base.
3. Move the mirror so that it reflects light up toward the stage. Never point the mirror directly at the Sun or a bright light. Bright light can cause permanent eye damage.
4. Place a few grains of salt on the slide. Put the slide under the stage clips. Be sure that the salt grains you are going to examine are over the hole in the stage.
5. Look through the eyepiece. Turn the focusing knob slowly until the salt grains come into focus.
6. Draw what the grains look like through the microscope.
7. Look at other objects through the microscope. Try a piece of leaf, a human hair, or a pencil mark.

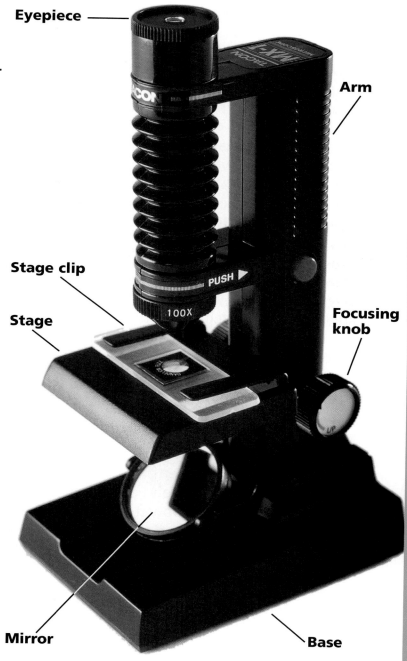

Eyepiece

Arm

Stage clip

Stage

Focusing knob

Mirror

Base

Measure Time

You use timing devices to measure how long something takes to happen. Some timing devices you use in science are a clock with a second hand and a stopwatch. Which one is more accurate?

Comparing a Clock and Stopwatch

1. Look at a clock with a second hand. The second hand is the hand that you can see moving. It measures seconds.
2. Get an egg timer with falling sand or some device like a wind-up toy that runs down after a certain length of time. When the second hand of the clock points to 12, tell your partner to start the egg timer. Watch the clock while the sand in the egg timer is falling.
3. When the sand stops falling, count how many seconds it took. Record this measurement. Repeat the activity, and compare the two measurements.
4. Switch roles with your partner.
5. Look at a stopwatch. Click the button on the top right. This starts the time. Click the button again. This stops the time. Click the button on the top left. This sets the stopwatch back to zero. Notice that the stopwatch tells time in minutes, seconds, and hundredths of a second.
6. Repeat the activity in steps 1–3, using the stopwatch instead of a clock. Make sure the stopwatch is set to zero. Click the top right button to start timing the reading. Click it again when the sand stops falling. Make sure you and your partner time each other twice.

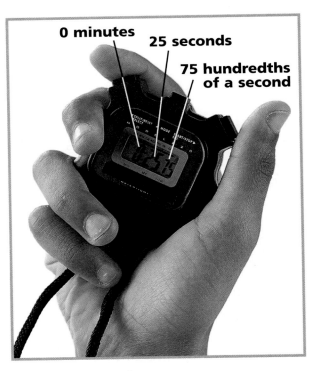

0 minutes
25 seconds
75 hundredths of a second

More About Time

1. Use the stopwatch to time how long it takes an ice cube to melt under cold running water. How long does an ice cube take to melt under warm running water?
2. Match each of these times with the action you think took that amount of time.

   a. 00:14:55
   b. 44:39:45
   c. 10:23:00

   1. Taking a shower
   2. Saying the Pledge of Allegiance
   3. Recess

Measure Length

Find Length with a Ruler

1. Look at this section of a ruler. Each centimeter is divided into 10 millimeters. How long is the paper clip?
2. The length of the paper clip is 3 centimeters plus 2 millimeters. You can write this length as 3.2 centimeters.
3. Place the ruler on your desk. Lay a pencil against the ruler so that one end of the pencil lines up with the left edge of the ruler. Record the length of the pencil.
4. Trade your pencil with a classmate. Measure and record the length of each other's pencil. Compare your answers.

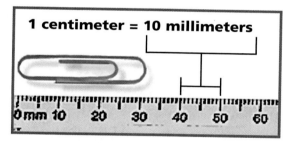

1 centimeter = 10 millimeters

0 mm 10   20   30   40   50   60

Measuring Area

Area is the amount of surface something covers. To find the area of a rectangle, multiply the rectangle's length by its width. For example, the rectangle here is 3 centimeters long and 2 centimeters wide. Its area is 3 cm x 2 cm = 6 square centimeters. You write the area as 6 cm^2.

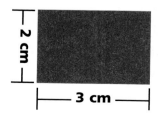

2 cm

3 cm

Opposite sides of a rectangle are parallel. The adjacent sides are perpendicular to each other (at right angles). Rectangles have symmetry. When folded in half, both halves are identical in size and shape. This is known as congruence. The two halves fit over each other exactly.

Find Length with a Meterstick

1. Line up the meterstick with the left edge of the chalkboard. Make a chalk mark on the board at the right end of the meterstick.
2. Move the meterstick so that the left edge lines up with the chalk mark. Keep the stick level. Make another mark on the board at the right end of the meterstick.
3. Continue to move the meterstick and make chalk marks until the meterstick meets or overlaps the right edge of the board.
4. Record the length of the chalkboard in centimeters by adding all the measurements you've made. Remember, a meterstick has 100 centimeters.

Estimating Length

Try estimating the length of objects in the room. Then measure the length, and compare the estimation with the measurement.

Measure Mass

Mass is the amount of matter an object has. You use a balance to measure mass. To find the mass of an object, you balance it with objects whose masses you know. Let's find the mass of a box of crayons.

Measure the Mass of a Box of Crayons

1. Place the balance on a flat, level surface. Check that the two pans are empty and clean.
2. Make sure the empty pans are balanced with each other. The pointer should point to the middle mark. If it does not, move the slider a little to the right or left to balance the pans.
3. Gently place a box of crayons on the left pan. This pan will drop lower.
4. Add masses to the right pan until the pans are balanced.
5. Add the numbers on the masses that are in the right pan. The total is the mass of the box of crayons, in grams. Record this number. After the number write a g for "grams."

Estimating Mass

Once you become familiar with the mass of objects, you can try estimating the masses of objects. Then you can compare the estimation with the actual mass.

More About Mass

The mass of your crayons was probably less than 100 grams. You may not have enough masses to balance a pineapple. It has a mass of about 1,000 grams. That's the same as 1 kilogram, because *kilo* means "1,000."

50 500 100 100 20 20 5 2 2 1

1. How many kilograms do all these masses add up to?
2. Which of these objects have a mass greater than 1 kilogram?

Measure Volume

Volume is the amount of space something takes up. In science you usually measure the volume of liquids by using beakers and graduated cylinders. These containers are marked in milliliters (mL).

Measure the Volume of a Liquid

1. Look at the beaker and at the graduated cylinder. The beaker has marks for each 25 mL up to 200 mL. The graduated cylinder has marks for each 1 mL up to 100 mL.
2. The surface of the water in the graduated cylinder curves up at the sides. You measure the volume by reading the height of the water at the flat part. What is the volume of water in the graduated cylinder? How much water is in the beaker? They both contain 75 mL of water.
3. Pour 50 mL of water from a pitcher into a beaker.
4. Now pour the 50 mL of water into a graduated cylinder.

Find the Volume of a Solid

Here's a way to find the volume of a solid, such as a rock.

1. Start with 50 mL of water in a graduated cylinder.
2. Place a small rock in the water. The water level rises.
3. Measure the new water level. Subtract 50 mL from the new reading. The difference is the volume of the rock. Record the volume in cm^3.

Estimating Volume

Once you become familiar with the volumes of liquids and solids, you can estimate volumes. Estimate the amount of liquid in a glass or can. Estimate the volume of an eraser.

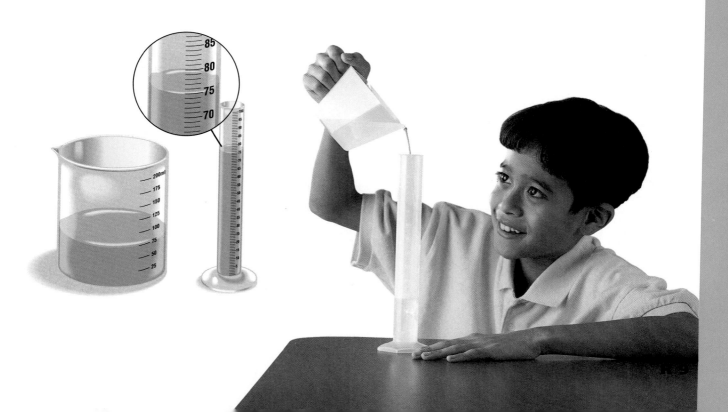

Measure Weight/Force

You use a spring scale to measure weight. An object has weight because the force of gravity pulls down on the object. Therefore, weight is a force. Weight is measured in newtons (N) like all forces.

Measure the Weight of an Object

1. Look at your spring scale to see how many newtons it measures. See how the measurements are divided. The spring scale shown here measures up to 5 N. It has a mark for every 0.1 N.
2. Hold the spring scale by the top loop. Put the object to be measured on the bottom hook. If the object will not stay on the hook, place it in a net bag. Then hang the bag from the hook.
3. Let go of the object slowly. It will pull down on a spring inside the scale. The spring is connected to a pointer. The pointer on the spring scale shown here is a small bar.
4. Wait for the pointer to stop moving. Read the number of newtons next to the pointer. This is the object's weight. The mug in the picture weighs 4 N.

More About Spring Scales

You probably weigh yourself by standing on a bathroom scale. This is a spring scale. The force of your body stretches a spring inside the scale. The dial on the scale is probably marked in pounds—the English unit of weight. One pound is equal to about 4.5 newtons.

A bathroom scale, a grocery scale, and a kitchen scale are some other spring scales you may have seen.

Measure Temperature

You use a thermometer to measure temperature—how hot or cold something is. A thermometer is made of a thin tube with colored liquid inside. When the liquid gets warmer, it expands and moves up the tube. When the liquid gets cooler, it contracts and moves down the tube. You may have seen most temperatures measured in degrees Fahrenheit (°F). Scientists measure temperature in degrees Celsius (°C).

°F   °C

Water boils

Water freezes

Room temperature

Read a Thermometer

1. Look at the thermometer shown here. It has two scales—a Fahrenheit scale and a Celsius scale.
2. What is the temperature shown on the thermometer? At what temperature does water freeze?

What Is Convection?

1. Fill a large beaker about two-thirds full of cool water. Find the temperature of the water by holding a thermometer in the water. Do not let the bulb at the bottom of the thermometer touch the sides or bottom of the beaker.
2. Keep the thermometer in the water until the liquid in the tube stops moving—about 1 minute. Read and record the temperature in °C.
3. Sprinkle a little fish food on the surface of the water in the beaker. Do not knock the beaker, and most of the food will stay on top.
4. Carefully place the beaker on a hot plate. A hot plate is a small electric stove. Plug in the hot plate, and turn the control knob to a middle setting.
5. After 1 minute measure the temperature of water near the bottom of the beaker. At the same time, a classmate should measure the temperature of water near the top of the beaker. Record these temperatures. Is water near the bottom of the beaker heating up faster than near the top?
6. As the water heats up, notice what happens to the fish food. How do you know that warmer water at the bottom of the beaker rises and cooler water at the top sinks?

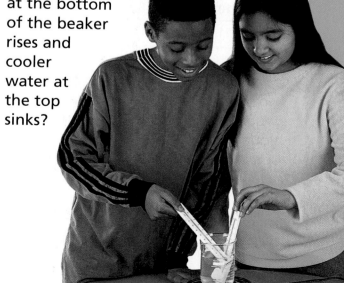

Use Calculators

Sometimes after you make measurements, you have to analyze your data to see what it means. This might involve doing calculations with your data. A calculator helps you do time-consuming calculations.

Find an Average

After you collect a set of measurements, you may want to get an idea of a typical measurement in that set. What if, for example, you are doing a weather project? As part of the project, you are studying rainfall data of a nearby town. The table shows how much rain fell in that town each week during the summer.

Week	Rain (cm)
1	2.0
2	1.4
3	0.0
4	0.5
5	1.2
6	2.5
7	1.8
8	1.4
9	2.4
10	8.6
11	7.5

What if you want to get an idea of how much rain fell during a typical week in the summer? In other words, you want to find the average for the set of data. There are three kinds of averages—mean, median, and mode. Does it matter which one you use?

Find the Mean

The mean is what most people think of when they hear the word *average*. You can use a calculator to find the mean.

1. Make sure the calculator is on.
2. Add the numbers. To add a series of numbers, enter the first number and press ⊞. Repeat until you enter the last number. See the hints below. After your last number, press ⊜. Your total should be 29.3.
3. While entering so many numbers, it's easy to make a mistake and hit the wrong key. If you make a mistake, correct it by pressing the clear entry key, CE. Then continue entering the rest of the numbers.
4. Find the mean by dividing your total by the number of weeks. If 29.3 is displayed, press ÷ 1 1 ⊜. Rounded up to one decimal point, your mean should be 2.7.

Hints:

- If the only number to the right of the decimal point is 0, you don't have to enter it into the calculator. To enter 2.0, just press 2.
- If the only number to the left of the decimal point is 0, you don't have to enter it into the calculator. To enter 0.5, just press . 5.

Use Technology

Find the Median

The median is the middle number when the numbers are arranged in order of size. When the rainfall measurements are arranged in order of size, they look like this.

0.0
0.5
1.2
1.4
1.4
1.8 ——— The median is 1.8. This number is in the middle; there are five numbers above it and five numbers below it.
2.0
2.4
2.5
7.5
8.6

Find the Mode

The mode is the number that occurs most frequently. From the ranked set of data above, you can see that the most frequent number is 1.4. It occurs twice. Here are your three different averages from the same set of data.

Average Weekly Rainfall (cm)

Mean	2.7
Median	1.8
Mode	1.4

Why is the mean so much higher than the median or mode? The mean is affected greatly by the last two weeks when it rained a lot. A typical week for that summer was much drier than either of those last two weeks. The median or mode gives a better idea of rainfall for a typical week.

Find the Percent

Sometimes numbers are given as percents (%). *Percent* literally means "per hundred." For example, 28% means 28 out of 100. What if there are about 14,000 trees in the forest and 28% are over 50 years old? How many of them are over 50 years old? Use your calculator. You want to find 28% of 14,000. Press $\boxed{1}\boxed{4}\boxed{0}\boxed{0}\boxed{0}$ $\boxed{\times}$ $\boxed{2}\boxed{8}\boxed{\%}$. The answer should be 3,920.

Mathematical Operations

Addition and subtraction are reverse operations, or inverses of each other. For example:

$2 + 3 = 5;$
$5 - 3 = 2;$
$5 - 2 = 3.$

Similarly, multiplication and division are also inverses of each other. For example:

$6 \times 3 = 18;$
$18 \div 6 = 3;$
$18 \div 3 = 6.$

Mathematical Statements

Mathematical statements using symbols may be true only when the symbols are replaced by certain numbers. For example:

$A < B$

If $A = 2$ and $B = 3$, the statement is true.
If $A = 3$ and $B = 2$, the statement is false.

Use Computers

A computer has many uses. The Internet connects your computer to many other computers around the world, so you can collect all kinds of information. You can use a computer to show this information and write reports. Best of all you can use a computer to explore, discover, and learn.

You can also get information from CD-ROMs. They are computer disks that can hold large amounts of information. You can fit a whole encyclopedia on one CD-ROM.

Use Computers for a Project

Here is how one group of students uses computers as they work on a weather project.

1. The students use instruments to measure temperature, wind speed, wind direction, and other parts of the weather. They input this information, or data, into the computer. The students keep the data in a table. This helps them compare the data from one day to the next.

Use Technology

2. The teacher finds out that another group of students in a town 200 kilometers to the west is also doing a weather project. The two groups use the Internet to talk to each other and share data. When a storm happens in the town to the west, that group tells the other group that it's coming their way.

3. The students want to find out more. They decide to stay on the Internet and send questions to a local TV weather forecaster. She has a Web site and answers questions from students every day.

4. Meanwhile some students go to the library to gather more information from a CD-ROM. The CD-ROM has an encyclopedia that includes movie clips. The clips give examples of different kinds of storms.

5. The students have kept all their information in a folder called Weather Project. Now they use that information to write a report about the weather. On the computer they can move around paragraphs, add words, take out words, put in diagrams, and draw weather maps. Then they print the report in color.

Make Graphs to Organize Data

When you do an experiment in science, you collect information. To find out what your information means, you can organize it into graphs. There are many kinds of graphs.

Bar Graphs

A bar graph uses bars to show information. For example, what if you do an experiment by wrapping wire around a nail and connecting the ends of the wire to a battery? The nail then becomes a magnet that can pick up paper clips. The graph shows that the more you wrap the wire around the nail, the more paper clips it picks up. How many paper clips did the nail with 20 coils pick up? With 50 coils?

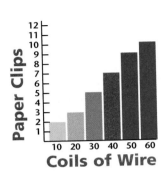

Pictographs

A pictograph uses symbols, or pictures, to show information. What if you collect information about how much water your family uses each day? The table shows what you find.

You can organize this information into the pictograph shown here. The pictograph has to explain what the symbol on the graph means. In this case each bottle means 20 liters of water. A half bottle means half of 20, or 10 liters of water.

1. Which activity uses the most water?
2. Which activity uses the least water?

Activity	Water Used Each Day (L)
Drinking	10
Showering	180
Bathing	240
Brushing teeth	80
Washing dishes	140
Washing hands	30
Washing clothes	280
Flushing toilet	90

A Family's Daily Use of Water

= 20 liters of water

Drinking	
Showering	
Bathing	
Brushing teeth	
Washing dishes	
Washing hands	
Washing clothes	
Flushing toilet	

Represent Data

Circle Graphs

A circle graph is helpful to show how a complete set of data is divided into parts. The circle graph here shows how water is used in the United States. What is the single largest use of water?

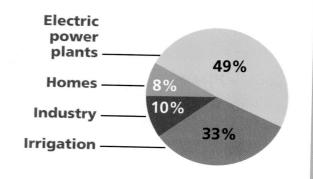

Line Graphs

A line graph shows information by connecting dots plotted on the graph. It shows change over time. For example, what if you measure the temperature out of doors every hour starting at 6 A.M.? The table shows what you find.

You can organize this information into a line graph. Follow these steps.

1. Make a scale along the bottom and side of the graph. The scales should include all the numbers in the chart. Label the scales.

2. Plot points on the graph. For example, place your finger at the "6 A.M." on the bottom line. Place a finger from your other hand on the "10" on the left line. Move your "6 A.M." finger up and your "10" finger to the right until they meet, and make a pencil point. Plot the other points in this way.

3. Connect the points with a line.

Time	Temperature (°C)
6 A.M.	10
7 A.M.	12
8 A.M.	14
9 A.M.	16
10 A.M.	18
11 A.M.	20

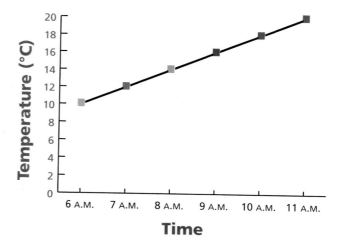

The line graph to the right organizes measurements you collected so that you can easily compare them.

1. Between which two weeks did the plant grow most?

2. When did plant growth begin to level off?

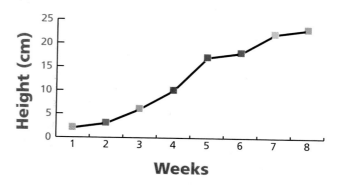

Represent Data
Make Maps to Show Information

Locate Places

A map is a drawing that shows an area from above. Most maps have coordinates—numbers and letters along the top and side. Coordinates help you find places easily. For example, what if you wanted to find the library on the map? It is located at B4. Place a finger on the letter B along the side of the map, and another finger on the number 4 at the top. Then move your fingers straight across and down the map until they meet. The library is located where the coordinates B and 4 meet, or very nearby.

1. What color building is located at F6?
2. The hospital is located three blocks north and two blocks east of the library. What are its coordinates?
3. Make a map of an area in your community. It might be a park or the area between your home and school. Include coordinates. Use a compass to find north, and mark north on your map. Exchange maps with classmates, and answer each other's questions.

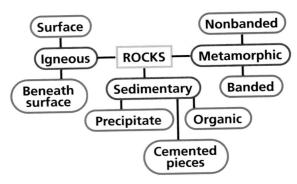

Idea Maps

The map below shows how places are connected to each other. Idea maps, on the other hand, show how ideas are connected to each other. Idea maps help you organize information about a topic.

The idea map above connects ideas about rocks. This map shows that there are three major types of rock—igneous, sedimentary, and metamorphic. Connections to each rock type provide further information. For example, this map reminds you that igneous rocks are classified into those that form at Earth's surface and far beneath it.

Make an idea map about a topic you are learning in science. Your map can include words, phrases, or even sentences. Arrange your map in a way that makes sense to you and helps you understand the ideas.

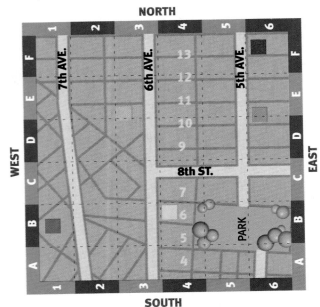

Make Tables and Charts to Organize Information

Tables help you organize data during experiments. Most tables have columns that run up and down, and rows that run across. The columns and rows have headings that tell you what kind of data goes in each part of the table.

A Sample Table

What if you are going to do an experiment to find out how long different kinds of seeds take to sprout? Before you begin the experiment, you should set up your table. Follow these steps.

1. In this experiment you will plant 20 radish seeds, 20 bean seeds, and 20 corn seeds. Your table must show how many radish seeds, bean seeds, and corn seeds sprouted on days 1, 2, 3, 4, and 5.

2. Make your table with columns, rows, and headings. You might use a computer to make a table. Some computer programs let you build a table with just the click of a mouse. You can delete or add columns and rows if you need to.
3. Give your table a title. Your table could look like the one here.

Make a Table

Now what if you are going to do an experiment to find out how temperature affects the sprouting of seeds? You will plant 20 bean seeds in each of two trays. You will keep each tray at a different temperature, as shown below, and observe the trays for seven days. Make a table you can use for this experiment.

Make a Chart

A chart is simply a table with pictures as well as words to label the rows or columns.

R 19

The Human Body

Like all organisms, humans are made up of cells. In fact, the human body is made of trillions of cells. These cells are organized into tissues, a group of similar cells that perform a specific function. Tissues, in turn, form organs. Your heart and lungs are examples of organs. Finally, organs work together as part of organ systems. Your heart, for example, is part of the circulatory system.

Levels of Organization

- Cells
- Tissues
- Organs
- Organ Systems
- Organism

Including the skin, or integumentary system, the human body has 11 major organ systems. These body systems each have specific functions, and they also work together as parts of the human body as a whole.

Human Body Systems	
System	**Function**
Nervous System	control
Skeletal System	support
Integumentary System	protection
Muscular System	movement
Circulatory System	transport
Respiratory System	oxygen/ carbon dioxide exchange
Digestive System	food absorption
Excretory System	waste removal
Endocrine System	regulation and control
Reproductive System	reproduction
Immune System	protection

The Nervous System

The nervous system has two parts. The brain and the spinal cord are the central nervous system. All other nerves are the outer, or peripheral, nervous system.

The largest part of the brain is the cerebrum. A deep groove separates the right half, or hemisphere, of the cerebrum from the left half. Both the right and left hemispheres of the cerebrum contain control centers for the senses.

The cerebellum lies below the cerebrum. It coordinates the skeletal muscles so they work smoothly together. It also helps in keeping balance.

The brain stem connects to the spinal cord. The lowest part of the brain stem is the medulla. It controls heartbeat, breathing, blood pressure, and the muscles in the digestive system.

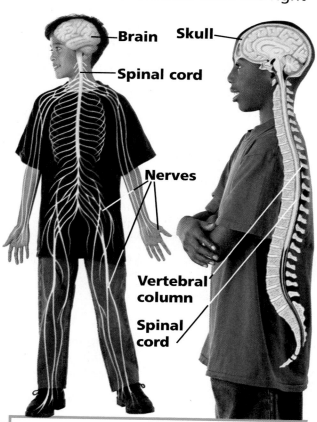

Brain
Skull
Spinal cord
Nerves
Vertebral column
Spinal cord

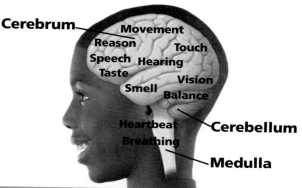

Cerebrum
Movement
Reason
Touch
Speech
Hearing
Taste
Vision
Smell
Balance
Heartbeat
Breathing
Cerebellum
Medulla

Parts of a Neuron

The nerves in the nervous system are made up of nerve cells called *neurons.* Each neuron has three main parts—a cell body, dendrites, and an axon. Dendrites are branching nerve fibers that carry impulses, or electrical signals, toward the cell body. An axon is a nerve fiber that carries impulses away from the cell body.

When an impulse reaches the tip of an axon, it must cross a tiny gap to reach the next neuron. This gap between neurons is called a *synapse.*

CARE!

- Wear protective headgear when you play sports or exercise.

- Stay away from drugs, such as stimulants, which can speed up the nervous system.

- Stay away from alcohol, which is a depressant and slows down the nervous system.

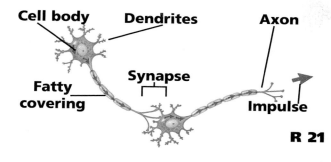

Cell body
Dendrites
Axon
Synapse
Fatty covering
Impulse

The Senses

Seeing

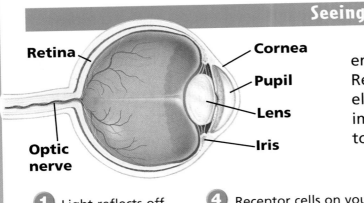

Retina
Cornea
Pupil
Lens
Iris
Optic nerve

Light reflected from an object enters the eye and falls on the retina. Receptor cells change the light into electrical signals, or impulses. These impulses travel along the optic nerve to the vision center of the brain.

1 Light reflects off the tree and into your eyes.

4 Receptor cells on your retina change the light into electrical signals.

2 The light passes through your cornea and the pupil in your iris.

3 Your eye bends the light so it hits your retina.

5 The impulses travel along neurons in your optic nerve to the seeing center of your brain.

Hearing

Sound waves enter the ear and cause the eardrum to vibrate. Receptor cells in the ear change the sound waves into impulses that travel along the auditory nerve to the hearing center of the brain.

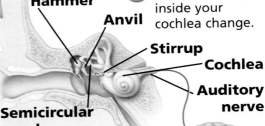

1 Your outer ear collects sound waves.

6 Receptor cells inside your cochlea change.

Hammer
Anvil
Stirrup
Cochlea
Auditory nerve
Semicircular canals

2 They are funneled down your ear canal.

3 The eardrum vibrates.

4 Three tiny ear bones vibrate.

5 The cochlea vibrates.

Hearing center

7 The impulses travel along your auditory nerve to the brain's hearing center.

CARE!

- To avoid straining your eye muscles, don't sit too close to the TV screen or computer monitor.

- Avoid loud music. Turn down the volume when wearing headphones.

The Senses

Smelling

The sense of smell is really the ability to detect chemicals in the air. When a person breathes, chemicals dissolve in mucus in the upper part of the nose. When the chemicals come in contact with receptor cells, the cells send impulses along the olfactory nerve to the smelling center of the brain.

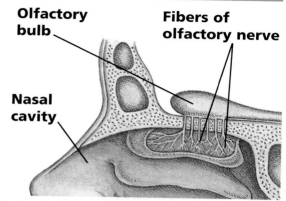

Olfactory bulb

Fibers of olfactory nerve

Nasal cavity

Tasting

When a person eats, chemicals in food dissolve in saliva. Saliva carries the chemicals to taste buds on the tongue. Inside each taste bud are receptors that can sense the four main tastes—sweet, sour, salty, and bitter. The receptors send impulses along a nerve to the taste center of the brain. The brain identifies the taste of the food, which is usually a combination of the four main tastes.

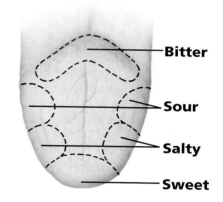

Bitter

Sour

Salty

Sweet

Touching

Receptor cells in the skin help a person tell hot from cold, wet from dry, and the light touch of a feather from the pressure of stepping on a stone. Each receptor cell sends impulses along sensory nerves to the spinal cord. The spinal cord then sends the impulses to the touch center of the brain.

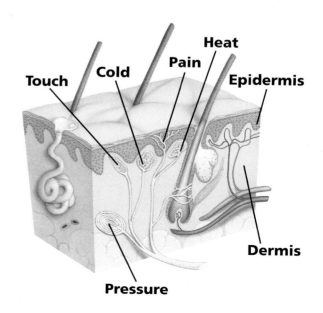

Touch   Cold   Pain   Heat

Epidermis

Dermis

Pressure

CARE!

- To prevent the spread of germs, always cover your mouth and nose when you cough or sneeze.

The Skeletal System

The body has a supporting frame, called a skeleton, which is made up of bones. The skeleton has several jobs.

- It gives the body its shape.
- It protects organs in the body.
- It works with muscles to move the body.

Each of the 206 bones of the skeleton is the size and shape best fitted to do its job. For example, long and strong leg bones support the body's weight.

CARE!

- Exercise to keep your skeletal system in good shape.
- Don't overextend your joints.
- Eat foods rich in vitamins and minerals. Your bones need the minerals, calcium, and phosphorus to grow strong.

The Integumentary System

The skeleton and the organ systems are covered by an outer layer of skin. The skin is the largest organ of the human body. It is part of the integumentary system. Other parts of the integumentary system are your hair, nails, and glands in the skin. The skin has several functions.

- It protects your internal organs.
- It protects your body from injury and infection.
- It helps regulate body temperature.
- It helps remove wastes.

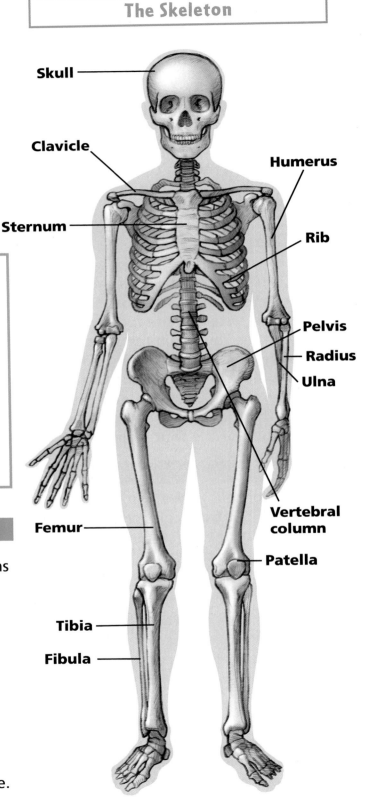

The Skeleton

- Skull
- Clavicle
- Humerus
- Sternum
- Rib
- Pelvis
- Radius
- Ulna
- Vertebral column
- Femur
- Patella
- Tibia
- Fibula

Joints

The skeleton has different types of joints. A joint is a place where two or more bones meet. Joints can be classified into three major groups—immovable joints, partly movable joints, and movable joints.

Types of Joints

Immovable Joints

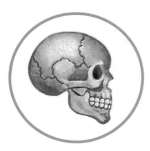

Head

Immovable joints are places where bones fit together too tightly to move. Nearly all the 29 bones in the skull meet at immovable joints. Only the lower jaw can move.

Partly Movable Joints

Partly movable joints are places where bones can move only a little. Ribs are connected to the sternum, or breastbone, with these joints.

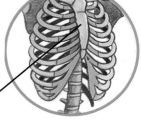

Ribs

Sternum

Movable Joints

Movable joints are places where bones can move easily.

Gliding joint

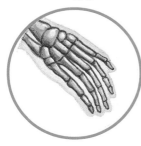

Hand and wrist

Small bones in the wrists and ankles meet at gliding joints. The bones can slide against one another. These joints allow some movement in all directions.

The hips are examples of ball-and-socket joints. The ball of one bone fits into the socket, or cup, of another bone. These joints allow bones to move back and forth, in a circle, and side to side.

Ball-and-socket joint

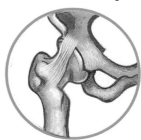

Hip

Hinge joint

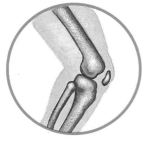

Knee

The knees are hinge joints. A hinge joint is similar to a door hinge. It allows bones to move back and forth in one direction.

The joint between the skull and neck is a pivot joint. It allows the head to move up and down, and side to side.

Pivot joint

Neck

R 25

The Muscular System

Three types of muscles make up the body—skeletal muscle, cardiac muscle, and smooth muscle.

The muscles that are attached to and move bones are called *skeletal muscles.* These muscles are attached to bones by a tough cord called a *tendon.* Skeletal muscles pull bones to move them. Muscles do not push bones.

Cardiac muscles are found in only one place in the body—the heart. The walls of the heart are made of strong cardiac muscles. When cardiac muscles contract, they squeeze blood out of the heart. When cardiac muscles relax, the heart fills with more blood.

Smooth muscles make up internal organs and blood vessels. Smooth muscles in the lungs help a person breathe. Those in the blood vessels help control blood flow around the body.

CARE!

- **Exercise to strengthen your muscles.**
- **Eat the right foods.**
- **Get plenty of rest.**
- **Never take steroids unless your doctor tells you to.**

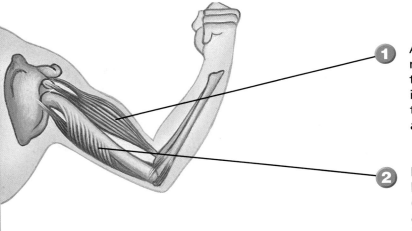

1. A message from your brain causes this muscle, called the biceps (BIGH·seps), to contract. When a muscle contracts, it becomes shorter and thicker. As the biceps contracts, it pulls on the arm bone it is attached to.

2. Most muscles work in pairs to move bones. This muscle, called the triceps (TRIGH·seps), relaxes when the biceps contracts. When a muscle relaxes, it becomes longer and thinner.

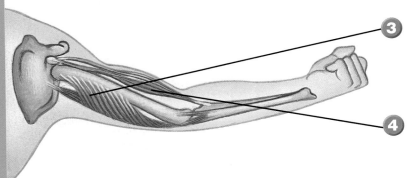

3. To straighten your arm, a message from your brain causes the triceps to contract. When the triceps contracts, it pulls on the bone it is attached to.

4. As the triceps contracts, the biceps relaxes. Your arm straightens.

Stimulus and Response

The nervous system, the skeletal system, and the muscular system work together to help you adjust to your surroundings. Anything in the environment that requires your body to adjust is called a *stimulus* (plural: stimuli). A reaction to a stimulus is called a *response*.

As you learned, nerve cells are called *neurons.* There are three kinds of neurons: sensory, associative, and motor. Each kind does a different job to help your body respond to stimuli.

- The job of your sensory neurons is to collect information from stimuli and send it to your brain and spinal cord. When you touch a sharp tack, sensory neurons alert your brain. The sensory neurons carry the message that your finger has touched a tack (stimulus) to the associative neurons in the brain and spinal cord.

- Associative neurons pass impulses from sensory to motor neurons. The message is interpreted and sent to the motor neurons.

- Motor neurons carry impulses from your brain and spinal cord to your muscles. The motor neurons cause your finger to move away from the tack (response).

In addition to responding to external stimuli, your body also responds to internal changes. Your body regulates its internal environment to maintain a stable condition for survival. This is called a *steady-state* condition.

Nerve Response

Nerves respond to a sharp object.

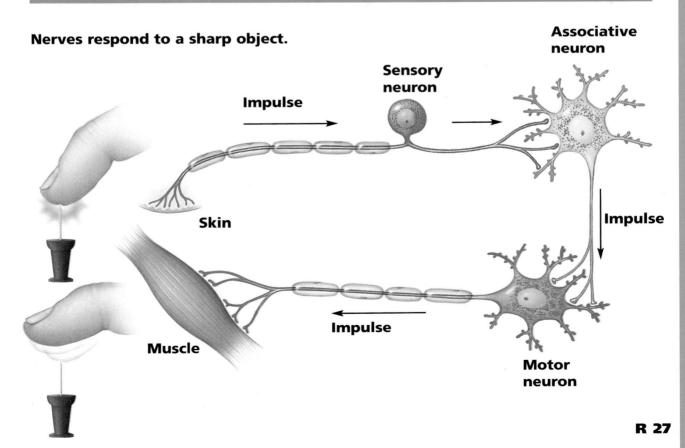

Impulse

Sensory neuron

Associative neuron

Skin

Impulse

Muscle

Impulse

Motor neuron

The Circulatory System

The circulatory system consists of the heart, blood vessels, and blood. Circulation is the flow of blood through the body. Blood is a liquid that contains red blood cells, white blood cells, and platelets. Red blood cells carry oxygen and nutrients to cells. White blood cells work to fight germs that enter the body. Platelets are cell fragments that make the blood clot.

The heart is a muscular organ about the size of a fist. It beats about 70 to 90 times a minute, pumping blood through the blood vessels. Arteries carry blood away from the heart. Some arteries carry blood to the lungs, where the cells pick up oxygen. Other arteries carry oxygen-rich blood from the lungs to all other parts of the body. Veins carry blood from other parts of the body back to the heart. Blood in most veins carries the wastes released by cells and has little oxygen. Blood flows from arteries to veins through narrow vessels called capillaries.

Pulse Rate and Pulse Points

You can tell how fast your heart is beating by checking your *pulse rate*. Take your pulse by putting the first and second fingers of one hand on the inside of the wrist of the other hand, just below the thumb. What you feel is the blood being pumped by your heart through arteries that lie close to the surface of the skin. Count the number of times you feel your heart pump in one minute. This is your pulse rate.

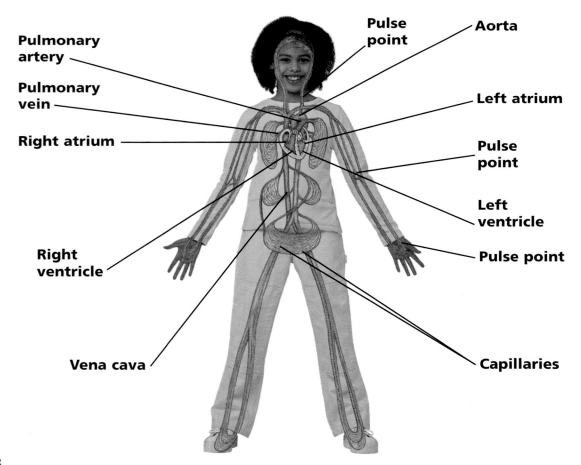

Pulmonary artery
Pulmonary vein
Right atrium
Right ventricle
Vena cava
Pulse point
Aorta
Left atrium
Pulse point
Left ventricle
Pulse point
Capillaries

The Heart

The heart has two sides, right and left, separated by a thick muscular wall. Each side has two chambers for blood. The upper chamber is the atrium. The lower chamber is the ventricle. Blood enters the heart through the vena cava. It leaves the heart through the aorta.

The pulmonary artery carries blood from the body into the lungs. Here carbon dioxide leaves the blood to be exhaled by the lungs. Fresh oxygen enters the blood to be carried to every cell in the body. Blood returns from the lungs to the heart through the pulmonary veins.

CARE!

● Don't smoke. The nicotine in tobacco makes the heart beat faster and work harder to pump blood.

● Never take illegal drugs, such as cocaine or heroin. They can damage the heart and cause heart failure.

How the Heart Works

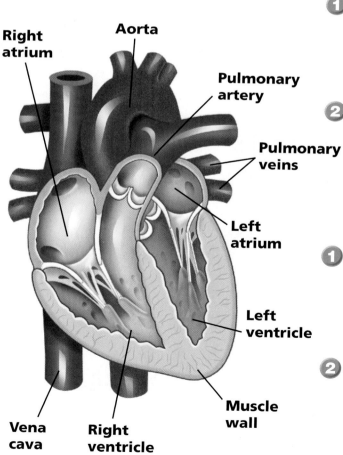

Right atrium

Aorta

Pulmonary artery

Pulmonary veins

Left atrium

Left ventricle

Muscle wall

Vena cava

Right ventricle

To the Lungs

1 The right atrium fills.

Right atrium

2 Right atrium squeezes blood into right ventricle.

3 Right ventricle squeezes blood into pulmonary artery.

One-way valve

Right ventricle

From the Lungs

1 The left atrium fills.

2 Left atrium squeezes blood into left ventricle.

3 Left ventricle squeezes blood into aorta.

Left atrium

One-way valve

Left ventricle

The Respiratory System

The process of getting and using oxygen in the body is called respiration. When a person inhales, air is pulled into the nose or mouth. The air travels down into the trachea. In the chest the trachea divides into two bronchial tubes. One bronchial tube enters each lung. Each bronchial tube branches into smaller tubes called bronchioles.

At the end of each bronchiole are tiny air sacs called alveoli. The alveoli exchange carbon dioxide for oxygen.

Oxygen comes from the air a person breathes. Two main muscles control breathing. One is located between the ribs. The other is a dome-shaped sheet of muscle called the diaphragm.

To inhale, the diaphragm contracts and pulls down. Other muscles pull the ribs up and out. This makes more room in the chest. Air rushes into the lungs and fills the space.

To exhale, the diaphragm relaxes and returns to its dome shape. The lungs get smaller and force the air out.

CARE!

- **Don't smoke. Smoking damages your respiratory system.**

- **Exercise to strengthen your breathing muscles.**

- **If you ever have trouble breathing, tell an adult at once.**

1. Carbon dioxide diffuses into the alveoli. From there it is exhaled.

2. Fresh oxygen diffuses from the alveoli to the blood.

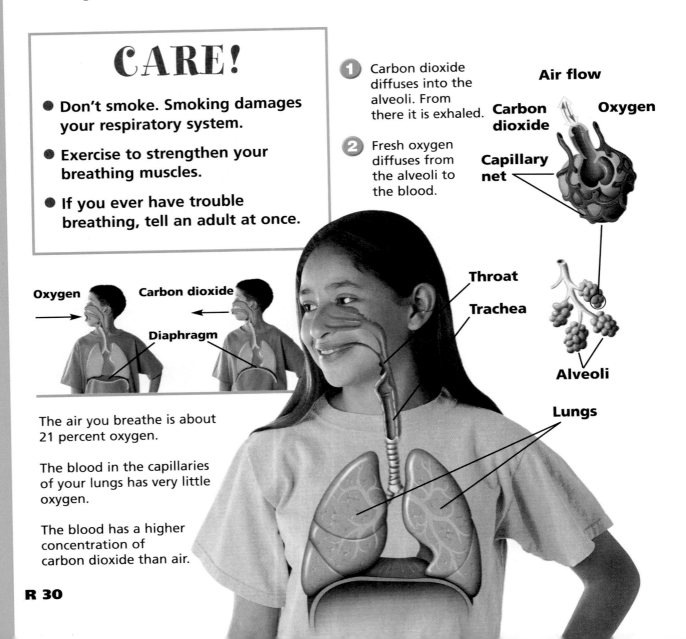

Air flow

Carbon dioxide

Oxygen

Capillary net

Throat

Trachea

Alveoli

Lungs

Oxygen

Carbon dioxide

Diaphragm

The air you breathe is about 21 percent oxygen.

The blood in the capillaries of your lungs has very little oxygen.

The blood has a higher concentration of carbon dioxide than air.

Effects of Exercise

Any type of exercise uses your muscles. When you exercise, your muscles need three things:

- They need oxygen.
- They need to remove wastes.
- They need to get rid of heat.

When you exercise, several things happen to your body. Your heart beats faster, you breathe heavier and faster, and you sweat.

If you are going to be exercising for more than a couple of minutes, your body needs to get oxygen to the muscles or the muscles will stop working. Your body increases the flow of oxygen-rich blood to working muscle as follows:

- Your rate and depth of breathing increase to take in more oxygen.
- Your heart beats faster so that it can pump more oxygen-rich blood to the muscles.

Sweating helps remove both wastes and heat that result from exercise.

The Digestive System

Digestion is the process of breaking down food into simple substances the body can use. Digestion begins when a person chews food. Chewing breaks the food down into smaller pieces and moistens it with saliva. Saliva is produced by the salivary glands.

Digested food is absorbed in the small intestine. The walls of the small intestine are lined with villi. Villi are tiny fingerlike projections that absorb digested food. From the villi the blood transports nutrients to every part of the body.

CARE!

- Chew your food well.
- Drink plenty of water to help move food through your digestive system.

The shape of the small intestine's villi increases the amount of nutrients that can be absorbed from the food.

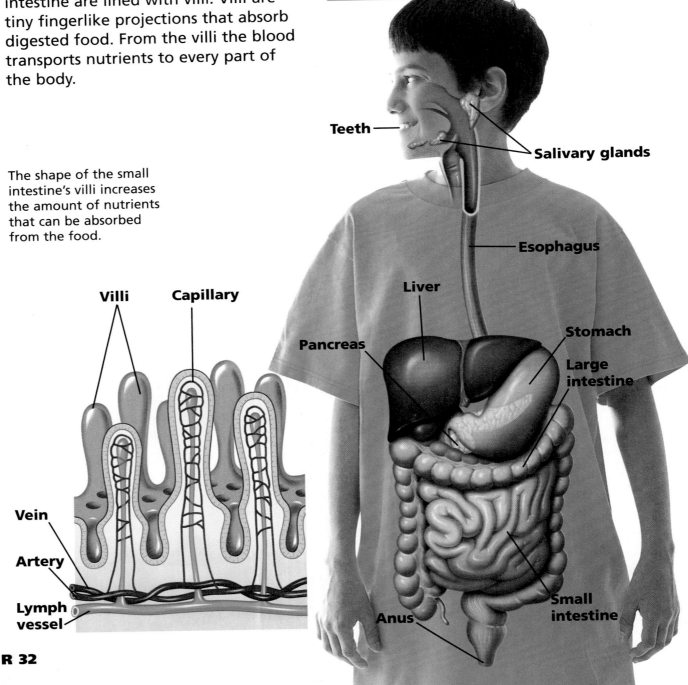

Villi

Capillary

Vein

Artery

Lymph vessel

Teeth

Salivary glands

Esophagus

Liver

Pancreas

Stomach

Large intestine

Small intestine

Anus

The Digestive System

Mechanical and Chemical Digestion

Digestion is both mechanical and chemical. Chewing is the first step in digestion. Chewing is *mechanical digestion*, the physical process of breaking food down into smaller pieces. As you chew, saliva begins to break the food into simpler molecules. This is *chemical digestion*.

After you swallow your food, both mechanical and chemical digestion continue in the stomach. Stomach muscles churn food particles into smaller pieces. Glands lining the stomach produce strong digestive juices.

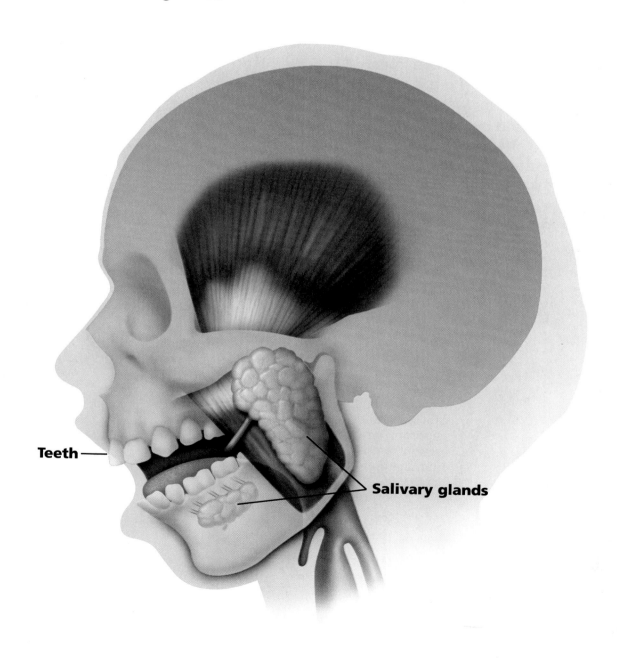

Teeth

Salivary glands

The Excretory System

Excretion is the process of removing waste products from the body. The liver filters wastes from the blood and converts them into urea. Urea is then carried to the kidneys for excretion. Each kidney contains more than a million nephrons. Nephrons are structures in the kidneys that filter blood.

The skin takes part in excretion when a person sweats. Glands in the inner layer of the skin produce sweat. Sweat is mostly water. Sweat tastes salty because it contains mineral salts the body doesn't need. There is also a tiny amount of urea in sweat.

Sweat is excreted by the sweat glands onto the outer layer of the skin. There it evaporates into the air. Evaporation takes place in part because of body heat. When sweat evaporates, a person feels cooler. On hot days or when exercising, a person sweats more to keep the body from overheating.

How You Sweat

Glands under your skin push sweat up to the surface, where it collects.

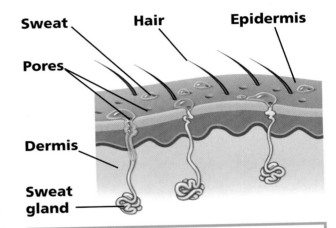

Sweat   Hair   Epidermis
Pores
Dermis
Sweat gland

How Your Kidneys Work

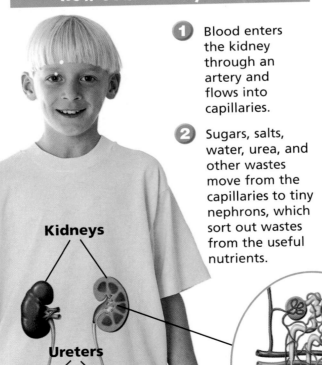

Kidneys
Ureters
Bladder
Urethra

R 34

1. Blood enters the kidney through an artery and flows into capillaries.

2. Sugars, salts, water, urea, and other wastes move from the capillaries to tiny nephrons, which sort out wastes from the useful nutrients.

3. The nutrients return to the blood and flow back out through veins.

4. Urea and other wastes become urine, which flows down the ureters.

5. Urine is stored in the bladder and excreted through the urethra.

CARE!

- Drink plenty of water to help the kidneys do their job and to replace water loss from sweating.
- Wash regularly to avoid body odor, clogged pores, and skin irritation.

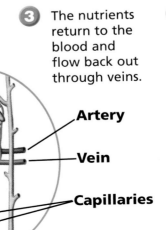

Artery
Vein
Capillaries

The Excretory System

Removing Excess Heat

In addition to waste removal, one of the skin's most important jobs is to maintain internal body temperature. The skin does this by removing excess heat. Two things happen when you exercise: your face gets red and you sweat. Both are ways of getting rid of excess heat.

The nervous system, the circulatory system, and the skin all work together to regulate body temperature. The diagram below shows what happens when your body heats up as a result of exercise.

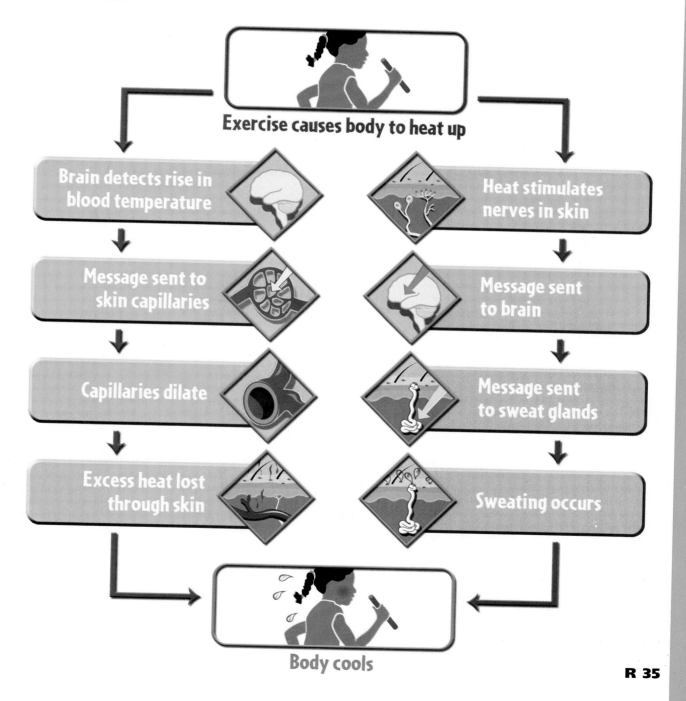

Exercise causes body to heat up

Brain detects rise in blood temperature

Heat stimulates nerves in skin

Message sent to skin capillaries

Message sent to brain

Capillaries dilate

Message sent to sweat glands

Excess heat lost through skin

Sweating occurs

Body cools

The Endocrine System

Hormones are chemicals that control body functions. A gland that produces hormones is called an endocrine gland. Sweat from sweat glands flows out of tubes called ducts. Endocrine glands have no ducts.

The endocrine glands are scattered around the body. Each gland makes one or more hormones. Every hormone seeks out a target organ, the place in the body where the hormone acts.

The endocrine glands help to maintain a *steady-state* condition in your body. They can turn the production of hormones on or off when they sense that too little or too much is being produced.

CARE!

- Doctors can treat many diseases, such as diabetes, caused by endocrine glands that produce too little or too much of a hormone.

Some Glands in the Endocrine System

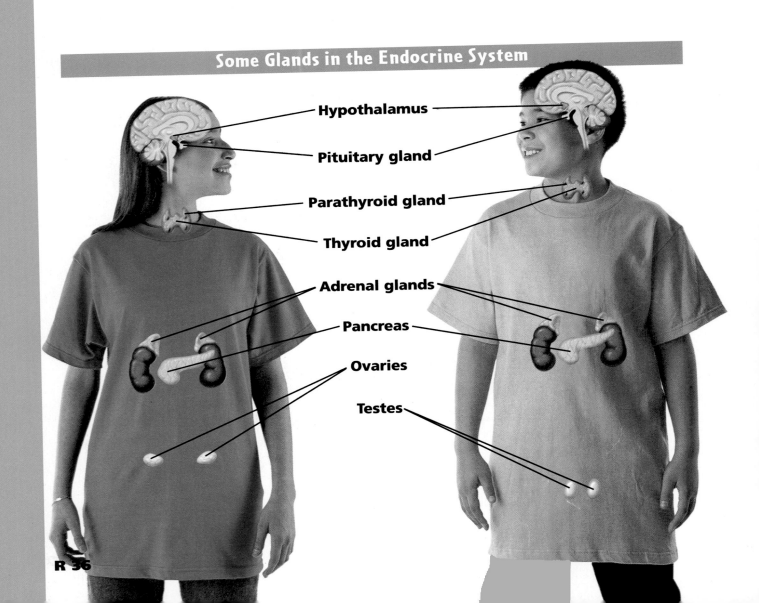

Hypothalamus

Pituitary gland

Parathyroid gland

Thyroid gland

Adrenal glands

Pancreas

Ovaries

Testes

The Reproductive System

The testes are the male reproductive organs. At puberty the testes begin to produce sperm. Sperm move through sperm ducts, where they mix with fluid from endocrine glands.

The ovaries are the female reproductive organs, which contain eggs. After puberty one mature egg is released about once every 28 days. The egg moves to the oviduct, a narrow tube leading from the ovary.

The Male Reproductive System

Sperm move from the testes through sperm ducts, where they mix with fluid from the glands. The sperm and fluid move through the urethra.

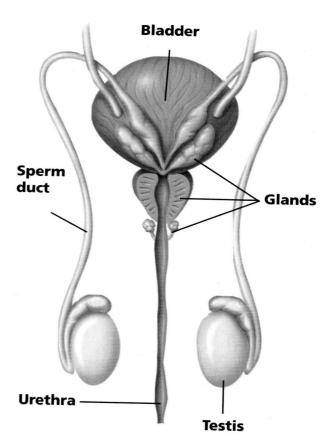

Bladder

Sperm duct

Glands

Urethra

Testis

CARE!

- **Abstinence is the only sure way to avoid sexually transmitted diseases.**

The Female Reproductive System

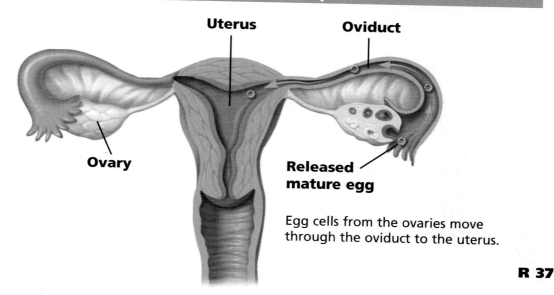

Uterus

Oviduct

Ovary

Released mature egg

Egg cells from the ovaries move through the oviduct to the uterus.

The Immune System

The immune system helps the body fight disease. Inside some bones is a soft tissue known as red marrow that fills the spaces in spongy bone. Red marrow makes new red blood cells, platelets that stop a cut from bleeding, and germ-fighting white blood cells.

There are white blood cells in the blood vessels and in the lymph vessels. Lymph vessels are similar to blood vessels. Instead of blood, they carry lymph. Lymph is a straw-colored fluid surrounding body cells.

Lymph nodes filter out harmful materials in lymph. Like red marrow, they also produce white blood cells to fight infections. Swollen lymph nodes in the neck are a clue that the body is fighting germs.

CARE!

- Be sure to get immunized against common diseases.
- Keep cuts clean to prevent infection.

1 A bone is covered with a tough but thin membrane that has many small blood vessels. The blood vessels bring nutrients and oxygen to the living parts of the bone and remove wastes.

2 Inside some bones is a soft tissue known as marrow. Yellow marrow is made mostly of fat cells and is one of the body's energy reserves. It is usually found in the long, hollow spaces of long bones.

3 Part of the bone is compact, or solid. It is made up of living bone cells and nonliving materials. The nonliving part is made up of layers of hardened minerals such as calcium and phosphorus. In between the mineral layers are living bone cells.

4 Red marrow fills the spaces in spongy bone. Red marrow makes new red blood cells, germ-fighting white blood cells, and platelets that stop a cut from bleeding.

5 Part of the bone is made of bone tissue that looks like a dry sponge. It is made of strong, hard tubes. It is also found in the middle of short, flat bones.

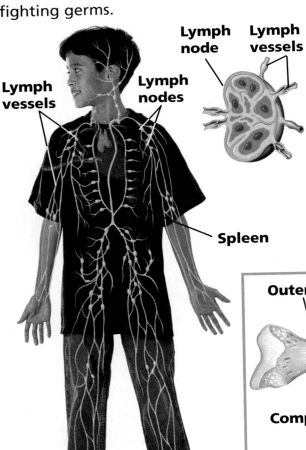

Lymph node

Lymph vessels

Lymph vessels

Lymph nodes

Spleen

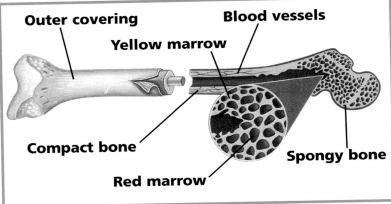

Outer covering

Blood vessels

Yellow marrow

Compact bone

Spongy bone

Red marrow

Infectious Diseases

A disease is anything that breaks down the normal functions of the body. Some diseases are inherited. Others are caused by harmful materials in the environment. Many diseases, however, are caused by organisms.

Disease-causing organisms include bacteria and viruses. Diseases caused by these organisms are called *infectious diseases* because the organisms enter, or infect, the body.

Human Infectious Diseases		
Disease	**Caused by**	**Organ System Affected**
Chicken pox	Virus	Skin
Smallpox	Virus	Skin
Polio	Virus	Nervous system
Rabies	Virus	Nervous system
Influenza	Virus	Respiratory system
Measles	Virus	Skin
Mumps	Virus	Salivary glands
Tuberculosis	Bacteria	Respiratory system
Tetanus	Bacteria	Nervous system
Food poisoning	Bacteria	Digestive system

White blood cells are your body's main protection against infectious disease. The white blood cells leave the blood vessels or lymph vessels to fight disease organisms in your tissues.

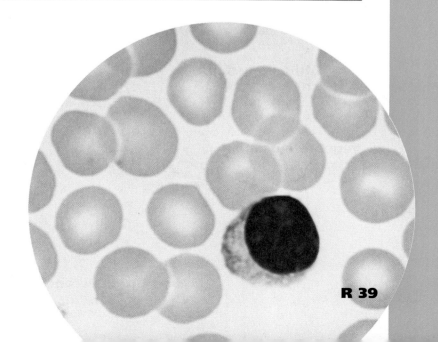

Staying Healthy

Physical fitness is the condition in which the body is healthy and works the best it can. It involves working the skeletal muscles, bones, joints, heart, and respiratory system.

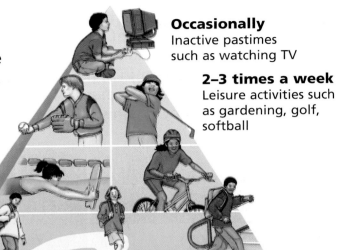

Occasionally
Inactive pastimes such as watching TV

2–3 times a week
Leisure activities such as gardening, golf, softball

3–5 times a week Aerobic activities such as swimming; sports activities such as basketball, handball

Daily Substitute activity for inactivity—take the stairs, walk instead of riding

Activity Pyramid

CARE!

- Stay active every day.
- Eat a balanced diet.
- Drink plenty of water—6 to 8 large glasses a day.

There is more to fitness than exercise. To make sure your body gets all the nutrients you need, you should eat a balanced diet. *A balanced diet* includes all the major food groups.

A balanced diet provides the calories, or energy from food, that you need to stay healthy. The number of calories needed varies from person to person, depending on their metabolism. *Metabolism* is the rate at which you burn energy. It is determined by weight, age, sex, and level of activity.

Fats, oils, and sweets
Use sparingly

Milk, yogurt, and cheese group
2–3 servings

Meat, poultry, fish, dry beans, eggs, and nuts group
2–3 servings

Vegetable group
3–5 servings

Fruit group
2–4 servings

Bread, cereal, rice, and pasta group
6–11 servings

Food Guide Pyramid

FOLDABLES™

by Dinah Zike

Folding Instructions

So how do you make a Foldables data organizer? The following pages offer step-by-step instructions—where and when to fold, where to cut—for making 11 basic Foldables data organizers. The instructions begin with the basic shapes, such as the hot dog fold, that were introduced on page xv.

Half-Book

Fold a sheet of paper (8½" x 11") in half.

1. This book can be folded vertically like a hot dog or …

2. … it can be folded horizontally like a hamburger.

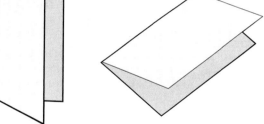

Folded Book

1. Make a Half-Book.

2. Fold in half again like a hamburger.

This makes a ready-made cover and two small pages inside for recording information.

Two-Tab Book

Take a Folded Book and cut up the valley of the inside fold toward the mountain top.

This cut forms two large tabs that can be used front and back for writing and illustrations.

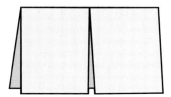

Pocket Book

1. Fold a sheet of paper ($8\frac{1}{2}$ " x 11") in half like a hamburger.

2. Open the folded paper and fold one of the long sides up two inches to form a pocket. Refold along the hamburger fold so that the newly formed pockets are on the inside.

3. Glue the outer edges of the two-inch fold with a small amount of glue.

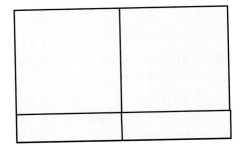

Shutter Fold

1. Begin as if you were going to make a hamburger, but instead of creasing the paper, pinch it to show the midpoint.

2. Fold the outer edges of the paper to meet at the pinch, or midpoint, forming a Shutter Fold.

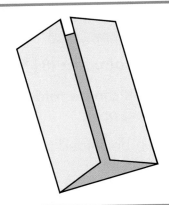

Trifold Book

1. Fold a sheet of paper ($8\frac{1}{2}$ " x 11") into thirds.

2. Use this book as is, or cut into shapes.

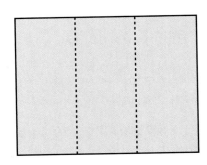

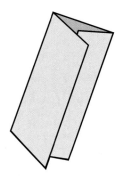

Three-Tab Book

1. Fold a sheet of paper like a hot dog.

2. With the paper horizontal and the fold of the hot dog up, fold the right side toward the center, trying to cover one half of the paper.

3. Fold the left side over the right side to make a book with three folds.

4. Open the folded book. Place one hand between the two thicknesses of paper and cut up the two valleys on one side only. This will create three tabs.

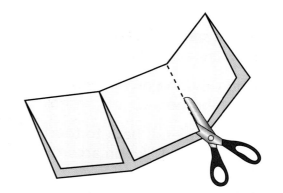

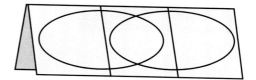

Layered-Look Book

1. Stack two sheets of paper ($8\frac{1}{2}$" x 11") so that the back sheet is one inch higher than the front sheet.

2. Bring the bottoms of both sheets upward and align the edges so that all of the layers or tabs are the same distance apart.

3. When all the tabs are an equal distance apart, fold the papers and crease well.

4. Open the papers and glue them together along the valley, or inner center fold, or staple them along the mountain.

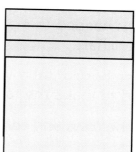

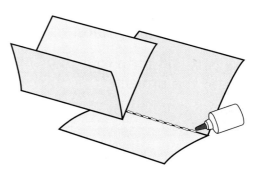

Four-Tab Book

1. Fold a sheet of paper ($8\frac{1}{2}$" x 11") in half like a hot dog.

2. Fold this long rectangle in half like a hamburger.

3. Fold both ends back to touch the mountain top or fold it like an accordion.

4. On the side with two valleys and one mountain top, make vertical cuts through one thickness of paper, forming four tabs.

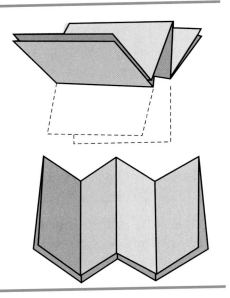

Four-Door Book

1. Make a Shutter Fold using 11" x 17" or 12" x 18" paper.

2. Fold the Shutter Fold in half like a hamburger. Crease well.

3. Open the project and cut along the two inside valley folds.

These cuts will form four doors on the inside of the project.

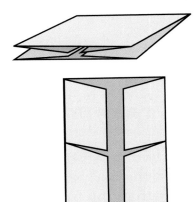

Folded Table or Chart

1. Fold the number of vertical columns needed to make the table or chart.

2. Fold the horizontal rows needed to make the table or chart.

3. Label the rows and columns.

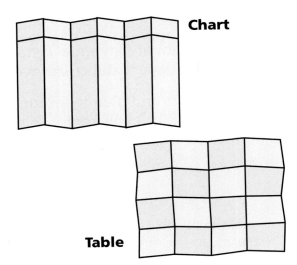

Chart

Table

Glossary

This Glossary will help you to pronounce and understand the meanings of the Science Words introduced in this book. The page number at the end of the definition tells where the word appears.

A

abiotic factor (ā′bī ot′ik fak′tər) Any nonliving part of an ecosystem, such as water, minerals, sunlight, air, and soil. (p. A68)

absolute age (ab′sə lüt′ āj) The age of a rock in years, as determined by measuring the decay rate of its radioactive elements. (p. D86)

absolute magnitude (ab′sə lüt′ mag′ni tüd′) The actual brightness of a star. (p. C72)

acceleration (ak sel′ə rā′shən) The change in velocity of a moving object with time. (p. F12)

action and reaction forces (ak′shən and rē ak′shən fôrs′əz) Two forces acting on different objects, having equal strength but opposite direction. (p. F36)

active transport (ak′tiv trans′pôrt′) The movement of molecules through a cell membrane, requiring energy. (p. B31)

adaptation (a′ dəp tā′shən) A feature that helps the survival of a species in its ecosystem. (p. A56)

aftershock (af′tər shok′) Shaking of Earth's crust after the initial shaking of an earthquake. (p. D22)

agriculture (ag′ri kul′chər) The science and art of cultivating soil and raising livestock. (p. A74)

alloy (al′oi) A mixture of two or more metals. (p. F13)

alternating current (ôl′tər nā ting kūr′ənt) Current that flows in a circuit first in one direction, then in the opposite direction. (p. E130)

amplitude (am′ pli tüd′) The height of a wave from trough to crest is a measure of its power. (p. E23)

angiosperm (an′jē ə spûrm′) A seed plant that produces flowers. *See* **gymnosperm**. (p. A28)

apparent magnitude (ə par′ənt mag′ni tüd′) The brightness of a star as seen in the night sky on Earth. (p. C73)

arachnid (ə rak′nid) Any eight-legged arthropod of the class Arachnida, such as the spider, mite, tick, or scorpion. (p. A42)

arthropod (är′thrə pod′) Any invertebrate of the phylum Arthropoda, with jointed legs and a body divided into sections. (p. A37)

artificial satellite (är′tə fish′əl sat′ə līt′) A device sent into orbit around Earth. (p. C12)

PRONUNCIATION KEY

The following symbols are used throughout the Macmillan/McGraw-Hill Science Glossaries.

a	at	e	end	o	hot	u	up	hw	white	ə	about
ā	ape	ē	me	ō	old	ū	use	ng	song		taken
ä	far	i	it	ôr	fork	ü	rule	th	thin		pencil
âr	care	ī	ice	oi	oil	u̇	pull	th	this		lemon
ô	law	îr	pierce	ou	out	ûr	turn	zh	measure		circus

′ = primary accent; shows which syllable takes the main stress, such as **kil** in **kilogram** (kil′ə gram′).

′ = secondary accent; shows which syllables take lighter stresses, such as **gram** in **kilogram.**

asexual reproduction (ā sek'shü əl rē'prə duk'shən) The production of a new organism from one parent. (p. A25)

asteroid (as'tə roid') A rocky, metallic object that orbits the Sun. (p. C54)

atom (at'əm) The smallest particle of an element that has the same chemical properties of the element. *See* **molecule**. (pp. B21, E18)

atomic number (ə tom'ik num'bər) The number of protons in an atom. (p. E21)

average speed (av'rij spēd) The total distance traveled by the amount of time. (p. F9)

B

background radiation (bak'ground' rā'dē ā'shən) Electromagnetic radiation left over from the big-bang beginning of the universe. (p. C88)

balanced forces (bal'ənst fôrs'əz) Forces that cancel each other out when acting together on a single object. (p. F24)

batholith (bath'ə lith) An irregularly shaped structure that is among the largest and deepest of all underground magma formations. (p. D35)

benthos (ben'thos) Organisms that live on the bottom in aquatic ecosystems. (p. A88)

big bang (big bang) The beginning moment of the universe when the density and temperature of the universe were very high. (p. C87)

biodiversity (bī'ō di vûr'si tē) The wide variety of life on Earth. (p. A84)

biomass conversion (bī'ō mas' kən vûr'zhən) A method for changing both plant and animal material into high-quality fuels. (p. E83)

biome (bī'ōm) A large land region of Earth with a given climate based on amount of sunlight, precipitation, and temperature. Each biome has its own kind of plant life and contains a number of ecosystems supported by those plants. (p. A69)

biotic factor (bī ot'ik fak'tər) Any plant, animal, or other living thing that is part of a biome. (p. A68)

black hole (blak hōl) An object whose gravity is so strong that light cannot escape it. (p. C77)

boiling (boil'ing) The formation of bubbles of vapor that escape from a liquid that is being heated. (p. E73)

boiling point (boil'ing point) The temperature at which a substance turns from a liquid to a gas. (p. E11)

buoyant force (boi'ənt fôrs) The force in a fluid that pushes an object toward the surface. (p. F14)

C

caldera (kal dâr'ə) A very wide crater formed by the collapse of a volcano. (p. D30)

carbohydrate (kär'bō hī'drāt) One of the carbon compounds, such as sugars and starches, that supply energy for cell activities. (p. B23)

carrier (kar'ē ər) An individual who has inherited a factor for a trait but does not show the trait. (p. B72)

cartilage (kär'tə lij') A body tissue that is not as hard as bone or as soft as flesh, such as the tip of the nose or the flaps of the ears (p. A57)

cell (sel) The basic unit of life. (p. B7)

cell cycle (sel sī'kəl) Growth and division cycle of the cell. (p. B41)

cell membrane (sel mem'brān) A cell's outer covering, which gives the cell shape and helps control materials that move in and out of the cell. (p. B18)

cell wall (sel wôl) A stiff covering outside the cell membrane of a plant cell. (p. B19)

chain reaction (chān rē ak'shən) A reaction that is kept going by products of the reaction. (p. E84)

chemical bond (kem'i kəl bond) A link that atoms or atomic-sized particles can form with each other. (p. E33)

chemical change (kem'i kəl chānj)) A change in matter that produces a new substance with different properties from the original. *See* **physical change.** (p. E32)

chemical formula (kem'i kəl fôr'myə lə) A way of using letters and numbers to show how much of each element is in a substance. (p. E33)

chemical property (kem'i kəl prop'ər tē) A way of describing a substance by how it reacts chemically to other substances. (p. E38)

chemical reaction (kəm'i kəl rē ak'shən) Another name for chemical change. The three key types are synthesis, replacement, and decomposition reactions. (p. E36)

chemical weathering (kem'i kəl weth'ər ing) The breaking down of rocks by oxidation or the dissolving action of acids. (p. D49)

chlorophyll (klôr'ə fil') A green chemical in plant cells that allows plants to use the Sun's energy for making food. (p. B19)

chloroplast (klôr'ə plast') A green structure in a plant cell where food is produced. Chloroplasts contain the green pigment chlorophyll and are also found in some protist cells. (p. B19)

chordate (kôr'dāt) Any animal that sometime in its life has a nerve cord running down its back. (p. A48)

chromosome (krō'mə sōm') A long strand in the nucleus that stores directions for cell activities. Chromsomes act like blueprints for transferring information to the next generation of cells. (p. B19)

chromosphere (krō'mə sfîr') The pinkish layer of the Sun just below the corona that can be seen only during a total eclipse. (p. C80)

cinder-cone volcano (sin'dər kōn vol kā'nō) A steep-sided cone that forms from explosive eruptions of hot rocks, ranging from particles to boulders. (p. D32)

circuit (sûr'kit) A path along which charged particles can flow to produce electricity. (p. E108)

class (klas) One of the groupings of similar members within a phylum. (p. A9)

classify (klas'ə fī) To place things that share properties together in groups. (p. S3)

climate (klī'mit) The average weather pattern of a region. (p. A68)

clone (klōn) A living thing that receives all of its DNA from just one parent. (p. B103)

closed circuit (klōzd sûr'kit) A circuit that has no gap in the path for current. (p. E112)

cold-blooded (kōld blud'əd) Said of animals, such as reptiles, that cannot automatically keep their body temperatures steady. (p. A53)

colloid (kol'oid) A special type of mixture in which the particles of one material are scattered through another and block the passage of light without settling out. (p. E12)

comet (kom'it) A ball of ice and rock that orbits the Sun. Comets come from the outer fringes of the solar system and circle the Sun in long elliptical orbits. (p. C64)

communicate (kə mū'ni kāt') To share information. (p. S11)

community (kə mū'ni tē) All the populations living together in the same place. (p. A82)

composite volcano (kəm poz'it vol kā'nō) A cone formed from explosive eruptions of hot rocks followed by a flow of lava, over and over. (p. D33)

PRONUNCIATION KEY

a at; ā ape; ä far; âr care; ô law; e end; ē me; i it; ī ice; îr pierce; o hot; ō old; ôr fork; oi oil; ou out; u up; ū use; ü rule; u̇ pull; ûr turn; hw white; ng song; th thin; <u>th</u> this; zh measure; ə about, taken, pencil, lemon, circus

compound (*n.*, kom'pound) A chemical combination of two or more elements. (pp. B22, E32)

compound machine (kom'pound mə shēn') A combination of two or more machines. (p. F87)

compression (kəm pre'shən) A movement of plates in Earth's crust that causes layers of the crust to be pressed or squeezed together. (D6)

condensation (kon'den sā'shən) The changing of a gas into a liquid as heat is removed from it. (p. E73)

conduction (kən duk'shən) The movement of energy through direct contact. (p. E59)

conductor (kən duk'tər) A material through which electricity flows easily. (p. E102)

conservation of momentum (kon'sər vā'shən uv mō men'təm) The total momentum of a group that does not change unless the group is acted upon by outside forces. (p. F39)

constellation (kon'stə lā'shən) A number of stars that appears to form a pattern. (p. C72)

consumer (kən sü'mər) Any animal that eats plants or eats other plant-eating animals. (p. A85)

continental drift (kon'tə nen'təl drift) The idea that a supercontinent split apart into pieces, the continents, which drifted in time to their present locations. *See* **Pangaea**. (p. D7)

convection (kən vek'shən) The transfer of energy by the flow of a liquid or gas. (p. E59)

convergent boundary (kən vûr'jənt boun'də rē) Places where tectonic plates are colliding. (p. D12)

corona (kə rō'nə) The outermost part of the Sun that can be seen only in a total eclipse. (p. C80)

crater (krā'tər) **1.** A depression in the Moon's surface formed by the impact of objects from space. (p. C38) **2.** A cuplike hollow that forms at the top of a volcano around the vent. (p. D30)

cross-pollination (krôs'po'lə nā'shən)) The pollination of a flower's female parts by pollen transported from a different flower. (p. B61)

crust (krust) Earth's solid, rocky surface containing the continents and ocean floor. (p. D6)

current (kûr'ənt) A flow of charged particles, such as electrons, moving through a circuit. (p. E108)

cytoplasm (sī'tə plaz'əm) A gel-like substance that surrounds a cell's nucleus and is the place where most cell activities occur. (p. B19)

D

deceleration (dē sel'ə rā'shən) The decrease of speed in a moving object over time. (p. F12)

decomposer (dē'kəm pōz'ər) Any of the fungi and bacteria that break down dead plants and animals into useful materials that enrich soil. (p. A84)

decomposition reaction (dē'kom pə zish'ən rē ak'shən) A chemical change in which a compound breaks apart into simpler substances. (p. E37)

define based on observations (di fīn' bāst ôn ob'zər vā'shənz) To put together a description that relies on examination and experience. (p. S5)

density (den'si tē) The amount of mass in a certain volume of material; found by dividing the mass of an object by its volume. (p. E7)

deposition (dep'ə zish'ən) The dropping off of sediment. (p. D58)

diffusion (di fū'zhən) The movement of molecules from areas of higher to lower concentration. (p. B28)

dike (dīk) An underground structure that forms when magma hardens in vertical cracks. (p. D35)

direct current (di rekt′ kûr′ənt) Current that flows in one direction through a circuit. (p. E128)

distance (dis′təns) The length between any two points on the path of an object. (p. F7)

divergent boundary (di vûr′jənt boun′də rē) A place where tectonic plates are moving apart. (p. D12)

DNA (dē en ā) A long, complex molecule containing the codes that control your cells' activites, your chemical makeup, and your heredity (p. B98)

dome mountain (dōm moun′tən) A broad, circular mountain formed from uplifted rock layers. (p. D35)

dominant factor (dom′ə nənt fak′tər) The trait expressed in offspring when the factors in a pair are different. (p. B65)

dominant trait (dom′ə nənt trāt) The form of a trait that appears in the hybrid generation. (p. B63)

dormant volcano (dôr′mənt vol kā′nō) A volcano that has not been active for a long time but has erupted before. (p. D34)

drag force (drag fôrs) A force that opposes the motion of an object through a liquid or gas. (p. F21)

dry cell (drī sel) A battery that changes chemical energy into electrical energy by using a moist conducting paste instead of the liquid in a wet cell. (p. E129)

E

echinoderm (i kī′nə dûrm′) A spiny-skinned invertebrate of the phylum Echinodermata with a water-pumping system and radial symmertry, such as the starfish. (pp. A37, A41)

ecosystem (ek′ō sis′təm) The living and nonliving things in an area interacting with each other. (p. A82)

efficiency (i fish′ən sē) A ratio of the work done by a machine compared with the work put into the machine. (p. F88)

effort force (ef′ərt fôrs) The force applied to a machine. (p. F66)

egg (eg) A female sex cell. (p. B44)

electricity (i lek tris′i tē) The energy caused by the flow of particles with negative electrical charges. (p. E98)

electromagnet (i lek′trō mag′nit) A temporary magnet created when current flows through wire wrapped in coils around an iron bar. (p. E119)

electromagnetic spectrum (i lek′trō mag net′ik spek′trəm) Waves of light in order by wavelength. (p. C9)

electron (i lek′tron) A negatively charged particle that moves around an atom's nucleus. (p. E20)

element (el′ə mənt) A substance that cannot be broken down any further into anything simpler. (p. E18)

elliptical galaxy (i lip′ti kəl gal′ək sē) A galaxy shaped like a football with no spiral arms and very little or no galactic dust. (p. C84)

PRONUNCIATION KEY

a **at**; ā **ape**; ä **far**; âr **care**; ô **law**; e **end**; ē **me**; i **it**; ī **ice**; îr **pierce**; o **hot**; ō **old**; ôr **fork**; oi **oil**; ou **out**; u **up**; ū **use**; ü **rule**; u̇ **pull**; ûr **turn**; hw **white**; ng **song**; th **thin**; <u>th</u> **this**; zh **measure**; ə **about, taken, pencil, lemon, circus**

emulsion (i mul'shən) A mixture of very small droplets suspended, rather than dissolved, in another liquid. (p. E12)

endoskeleton (en'dō skel'i tən) An internal supporting structure of bone. (p. A48)

endothermic (en'dō thûr'mik) A reaction that absorbs heat. (p. E44)

epicenter (ep'i sen'tər) The point on Earth's surface directly above the focus of an earthquake. (p. D22)

equilibrium (ē'kwə lib'rē əm) Balance, such as an equal concentration of water molecules on both sides of a cell membrane. (p. B30)

era (îr'ə) One of the four long stretches of time in Earth's history: from the earliest Precambrian era, through the Paleozoic and Mesozoic eras, to the current Cenozoic era. (p. D86)

erosion (i rō'zhən) The picking up and removal of rock particles. (p. D47)

evaporation (i vap'ə rā'shən) The changing of a liquid to a gas when particles vaporize at the surface. (p. E73)

exoskeleton (ek'sō skel'i tən) A hard outer body covering that protects an invertebrate. (p. A42)

exothermic (ek'sō thûr'mik) A reaction that gives off heat. (p. E44)

expansion redshift (ek span'shən red'shift') The spectrum shift of a galaxy toward longer (redder) wavelengths because of the expansion of space. (p. C86)

experiment (ek sper'ə ment') To perform a test to support or disprove a hypothesis. (p. S6)

external fertilization (ek stûr'nəl fûr'tə lə zā'shən) The coming together of egg and sperm cells outside the female's body. (p. B44)

extinct (ek stingkt') **1.** Said of a volcano that has not erupted in recorded history. (p. D34) **2.** Said of a life form that has died out completely. (p. D85)

family (fam'ə lē) One of the groupings of similar members within an order. (p. A9)

fault (fôlt) A huge crack in Earth's crust at or below the surface, the sides of which may show evidence of motions. (p. D21)

fault-block mountain (fôlt blok moun'tən) A mountain made by huge tilted blocks of rocks separated from surrounding rocks by faults. (p. D46)

fermentation (fûr'men tā'shən) Respiration in a cell that is carried on without oxygen. (p. B33)

fertilization (fûr'tə lə zā'shən) The joining of the male sex cell and female sex cell. (pp. B45, B60)

first law of motion, Newton's (fûrst lô uv mō'shən, nü'tənz) An object's velocity can only be changed by applying an unbalanced force to it. (p. F26)

first quarter (fûrst kwôr'tər) A phase of the waxing Moon in which the right half is visible and growing larger. (p. C32)

focus (fō'kəs) The point where an earthquake starts as rocks begin to slide past each other. (p. D22)

fold mountain (fōld moun'tən) A mountain made up mostly of rock layers folded by being squeezed together. (p. D46)

food chain (füd chān) A model of how the energy in food is passed from organism to organism in an ecosystem. (p. A85)

food web (füd web) A model of overlapping food chains in an ecosystem. (p. A85)

force (fôrs) A push or pull exerted by one object on another, causing a change in motion. (p. F18)

form a hypothesis (fôrm ə hī poth'ə sis) To make a statement that can be tested to answer to a question. (p. S4)

fossil (fos'əl) Any trace, imprint, or remains of a living thing preserved in Earth's crust. (pp. D84, E82)

freezing (frēz′ing) The changing of a liquid into a solid as heat is removed from it. (p. E73)

frequency (frē′kwən sē) The number of waves that pass through a point in a second. (pp. C9, F23)

friction (frik′shən) A force that opposes motion of an object in contact with a surface. (p. F19)

fulcrum (fül′krəm) The pivot point of a lever. (p. F67)

full Moon (fül mün) or **second quarter** The phase of the Moon in which all of its sunlit half is visible from Earth. (p. C32)

G

galaxy (gal′ək sē) A large group of stars that are held together by gravity. The three main types of galaxies are: spiral, elliptical, and irregular. (p. C84)

Galilean satellite (gal′ə lē′ən sat′ə līt′) The four largest moons of Jupiter, first seen by Galileo in 1610. Their names are Ganymede, Io, Europa, and Callisto. (p. C66)

gene (jēn) A portion of a chromosome that controls a particular inherited trait. (p. B98)

generation (jen′ə rā′shen) Parents and offspring; parents are one *generation*, their offspring another. (p. B58)

generator (jen′ə rā′tər) A device that uses the mehanical energy in such machines as a hand crank, a steam-driven wheel, or a gasoline motor to make electricity. (p. E130)

gene-splicing (jēn splī′sing) Attaching the genes from one organism to the genes in another organism. (p. B102)

genetic engineering (jə net′ik en′jə nir′ing) A way of changing the DNA sequence in a gene so that the gene will produce a particular trait. (p. B101)

geneticist (jə net′ə sist) A scientist who studies how heredity works. (p. B65)

genetics (jə net′iks) The study of how heredity works. (p. B59)

genus (jēn′əs) A grouping of the most similar family members. (p. A9)

geologic column (jē′ə loj′ik kol′əm) A listing of Earth's rock layers in order from oldest to youngest. (p. D83)

geothermal energy (jē′ō thûr′məl en′ər jē) Heat from below Earth's surface. (p. D36)

geyser (gī′zər) An opening in the ground through which hot water and steam erupt periodically. (p. D36)

glacier (glā′shər) A huge sheet of ice and snow that moves slowly over the land. (p. D62)

glassy (glas′ē) Said of a mineral that has the properties of glass; smooth to the touch. (p. D71)

gravitational potential energy (grav′i tā′shən əl pə ten′shəl en′ər jē) The gain in potential energy when an object is lifted up against gravity. (p. F52)

gravity (grav′i tē) A force of attraction that exists between any objects with mass. (p. F22)

grounding wire (ground′ing wīr) The wire of an appliance that connects its metal case to the earth through the household wiring. (p. E102)

groundwater (ground wô′tər) Water that soaks into soil and rock by collecting in spaces between rock particles. (p. D52)

PRONUNCIATION KEY

a at; ā ape; ä far; âr care; ô law; e end; ē me; i it; ī ice; îr pierce; o hot; ō old; ôr fork; oi oil; ou out; u up; ū use; ü rule; ù pull; ûr turn; hw white; ng song; th thin; th̲ this; zh measure; ə about, taken, pencil, lemon, circus

gymnosperm (jim nə spûrm′) A seed plant that does not produce flowers. *See* **angiosperm**. (p. A28)

H

half-life (haf′līf′) The time it takes for half the mass of a radioactive element in a rock to break apart, or decay, into other elements. (p. D86)

hardness (härd′ness) How a mineral resists scratching. (p. D70)

heat (hēt) Energy that flows between objects that have different temperatures. (p. E57)

heredity (hə red′i tē) The passing of inherited traits from parents to offspring. (p. B58)

Hertzsprung-Russell (H-R) diagram (hert′sprúng rus′əl dī′ə gram′) A table comparing the temperatures of stars to their absolute magnitudes. (p. C74)

highland (hī′lənd) Any light-colored, heavily cratered region on the Moon at an elevation higher than a mare. (p. C38)

hot spot (hot spot) A very hot part of the Sun's mantle, where magma can melt through a plate moving above it. (p. D31)

hot spring (hot spring) An opening in the ground where hot water and gases escape from magma heated deep underground. (p. D36)

humus (hū′məs) Material in soil formed by the breakdown of plant and animal material. (p. D50)

hybrid (hī′brid) An organism produced by the crossing of parents that have two different forms of the same trait. (p. B62)

hydroelectricity (hī′drō i lek tris′i tē) The use of flowing water to generate electricity. (p. E89)

I

igneous rock (ig′nē əs rok) A rock that forms when hot, liquid lava cools and hardens into a solid. (p. D72)

impermeable (im pûr′mē ə bəl) Said of soil with few or no connecting pores, preventing water from passing through easily. (p. D52)

inclined plane (in klīnd′ plān) A straight, slanted surface that is not moved when it is used. (p. F80)

incomplete dominance (in′kəm plēt′ dom′ə nəns) A genetic pattern in which neither of the two forms of a trait completely masks the other. (p. B71)

index fossil (in′deks fos′əl) The remains of a living thing that was widespread but lived for only a short part of Earth's history. (p. D85)

indicator (in′di kā′tər) A substance, such as litmus paper, that changes color in the presence of a test substance. Acids turn blue litmus paper red. Bases turn red litmus paper blue. (p. E42)

induced charge (in düst′ chärj) The static charge in one object that is caused by the presence of an already charged object. (p. E100)

inertia (i nûr′shə) The tendency of an object to oppose a change in motion. (p. F26)

infer (in fûr′) To form an idea from facts or observations. (p. S5)

inherited trait (in her′i təd trāt) A characteristic that is passed from parent to offspring. (p. B58)

inner planet (in′ər plan′it) One of the four planets closer to the Sun—Mercury, Venus, Earth, or Mars. (p. C60)

insulation (in′sə lā′shən) The prevention of heat or electricity from flowing into or out of a material. (p. E62)

insulator (in′sə lā′tər) A material through which heat or electricity does not flow easily. (p. E102)

internal fertilization (in tûr′nəl fûr′tə lə zā′shən) The coming together of egg and sperm cells inside a female's body. (p. B44)

International Date Line (in′tər nash′ə nəl dāt līn) The 180° line of longitude. Going west across this line adds one day to the date; going east subtracts a day. (p. C23)

interpret data (in tûr′prit dā′tə) To use the information that has been gathered to answer questions or solve a problem. (p. S9)

invertebrate (in vûr′tə brāt′) An animal that does not have a backbone. Invertebrates are one of the two major groupings of animals. *See* **vertebrate.** (p. A36)

ion (ī′ən) An electrically charged particle with unequal numbers of protons and electrons. (p. E35)

ionic bond (ī on′ik bond) A type of chemical bond created by the attraction between oppositely charged ions. (p. E35)

irregular galaxy (i reg′yə lər gal′ək sē) A galaxy that has no recognizable shape, possibly as the result of a galactic collision. (p. C84)

island arc (ī′lənd ark) A string of volcanic islands made when melted rock rises up from beneath the sea floor. (p. D14)

isotope (ī′sə tōp′) Any of two or more atoms of the same element that have different numbers of neutrons. (p. E21)

joule (jül) a measurement of the work done by a force of 1 newton acting through a distance of 1 meter. (p. F52)

kinetic energy (ki net′ik en′ər jē) The energy of a moving object. *See* **potential energy.** (pp. E55, F53)

kingdom (king′dəm) One of the largest groups used to classify living things. (p. A8)

Kuiper Belt (kī′pər belt) A region of the solar system that stretches 45 billion kilometers beyond Pluto's orbit and contains tens of thousands of comets. (p. C64)

laccolith (lak′ə lith) A dome formed by thick magma that pushes upward rather than horizontally. (p. D35)

larva (lar′və), *pl.* **larvae** (-vē) The second of four stages in the life cycle of some insects, which are: egg, larva, pupa, adult. (p. B39)

lava (lä′və) Magma that reaches Earth's surface and flows out of a vent. (p. D30)

lever (lev′ər) A simple machine made of a rigid bar on a pivot point. (p. F67)

life cycle (līf sī′kəl) The life stages of a living organism, including birth, reproduction, and death, that go on generation after generation (p. B38)

life expectancy (līf ek spek′tən sē) The average amount of time an individual animal might live, based on such environmental conditions as access to food, water, and shelter. (p. B48)

PRONUNCIATION KEY

a at; ā ape; ä far; âr care; ô law; e end; ē me; i it; ī ice; îr pierce; o hot; ō old; ôr fork; oi oil; ou out; u up; ū use; ü rule; ù pull; ûr turn; hw white; ng song; th thin; <u>th</u> this; zh measure; ə about, taken, pencil, lemon, circus

life span (līf span) The characteristic length of time an animal can live under the best conditions. (p. B48)

light-year (līt′yîr′) The distance light travels in a year. (p. C73)

lipid (lip′id) Fat; one of the carbon compounds that release even more energy than carbohydrates. (p. B23)

lunar eclipse (lü′nər i klips′) A blocking of a view of the full Moon when the Moon passes into Earth's shadow. (p. C34)

luster (lus′tər) Said of a mineral that reflects light. (p. D70)

magma (mag′mə) Hot, molten rock below Earth's surface. (p. D8)

magnet (mag′nit) Any object that attracts or repels other magnets and also attracts metal objects made of iron, cobalt, or nickel. (p. E118)

magnetic field (mag net′ik fēld) The area around the magnet in which other magents can feel attraction or repulsion. (p. E120)

magnitude (mag′ni tüd′) **1.** The brightness of a star. (p. C73) **2.** The amount of energy released by an earthquake. (pp. C72, D25)

main-sequence star (mān sē′kwəns stär) A star that fuses hydrogen into helium. (p. C76)

make a model (māk ə mod′əl) To make something to represent an object or event. (p. S7)

mammary gland (mam′ə rē gland) An organ in female mammals that makes milk for feeding their young. (p. A55)

mantle (man′təl) The layer beneath Earth's crust. (p. D11)

mare (mär′ā), *pl.* **maria** (mär′ē ə) A large, flat, dark area on the Moon formed by huge lava flows billions of years ago. (p. C38)

mass (mas) The amount of matter in an object. (p. E6)

mass wasting (mas wās′ting) The downhill movement of Earth material caused by gravity. (p. D58)

matter (mat′ər) Everything that makes up the world around you; anything that has mass and volume. (p. E6)

mature (mə chùr′) The final or fully developed stage in a process. *Mature* sex cells are those that are capable of reproduction. (p. B46)

measure (mezh′ər) To find the size, volume, area, mass, weight, or temperature of an object, or how long an event occurs. (p. S9)

mechanical advantage (mə kan′i kəl ad van′tij) The number of times a machine multiplies the force applied. (p. F70)

mechanical weathering (mə kan′i kəl weth′ər ing) The breaking down of rock by physical changes. (p. D48)

meiosis (mī ō′sis) The division of the nucleus resulting in cells with half as many chromosomes as in other cells. (pp. B46, B47)

melting (melt′ing) The changing of a solid into a liquid. (p. E72)

melting point (melt′ing point) The temperature at which a substance changes from a solid to a liquid. (p. E11)

metal (met′əl) Any of a group of elements that conducts heat and electricity, and is shiny and bendable. *See* **metalloid** and **nonmetal**. (p. E23)

metalloid (met′ə loid) Any of the elements that have properties of both metals and nonmetals and are often used as conductors of electricity. *See* **metal** and **nonmetal**. (p. E23)

metamorphic (met′ə môr′fik) Changed, as when one kind of rock is turned into rock with different properties. (p. D76)

metamorphic rock (met′ə môr′fik rok) A rock that forms from another kind of rock that is changed by heat, pressure, or a chemical reaction. (p. D76)

metamorphosis (met′ə môr′fə sis) The changes of body form that some animals go through in their life cycle. Complete metamorphosis includes four different stages—egg, larva, pupa, adult; incomplete metamorphosis includes three—egg, nymph, adult. (p. B39)

meteor (mē′tē ər) A meteoroid that enters Earth's atmosphere and burns with a streak of light. (p. C65)

meteorite (mē′tē ə rīt′) Any part of a meteoroid that reaches Earth's surface. (p. C65)

meteoroid (mē′tē ə roid′) Small, rocky objects that orbit the Sun in both the outer and inner regions of the solar system. (p. C65)

microbe (mī′krōb) A living thing so small that it can be seen only with a microscope. (p. A14)

Milky Way (mil′kē wā), The medium-sized spiral galaxy that is our home galaxy. (p. C85)

mineral (min′ər əl) A naturally occurring solid in Earth's crust with a definite structure and composition. (p. D70)

mitochondrion (mī′tə kon′drē ən), *pl.* **mitochondria** (-drē ə) One of the rod-shaped structures in the cytoplasm that supplies the cell with energy. (p. B19)

mitosis (mī tō′sis) The division of the nucleus while a cell is dividing into two identical cells. (pp. B41, B42)

mixture (miks′chər) A physical combination of two or more substances that are blended together without forming new substances. (p. E12)

molecule (mol′ə kūl′) A group of tightly bonded atoms that acts like a single particle. (pp. B28, E41)

mollusk (mol′əsk) Any invertebrate in the phylum Mollusca. Most mullusks live in the sea and many have shells, such as the clam, oyster, and snail. (p. A40)

momentum (mō men′təm) The mass of an object multiplied by its velocity. (p. F38)

moraine (mə rān′) A deposit of many sizes of sediment in front of or along the sides of a glacier. (p. D64)

motion (mō′shən) A change in an object's position compared to fixed objects around it. (p. F7)

mountain (moun′tən) An elevated land mass on Earth or a similar feature on the Moon. *Mountains* on the Moon are often crater-shaped, indicating their formation by the impact of objects from space (pp. C38, D35, D46)

N

neap tide (nēp tīd) The slightest change from high to low tide that occurs when the Sun, the Moon, and Earth form a right angle or are perpendicular to each other. (p. C36)

nebula (neb′yə lə) *n., pl.,* **nebulae** (-ē) An enormous cloud of gas and dust in space that is the first stage of star formation. (p. C76)

nekton (nek′ton) Organisms that swim through the water in aquatic ecosystems. (p. A88)

net force (net fôrs) The combined effect of all the forces acting on an object. (p. F24)

PRONUNCIATION KEY

a at; ā ape; ä far; âr care; ô law; e end; ē me; i it; ī ice; îr pierce; o hot; ō old; ôr fork; oi oil; ou out; u up; ū use; ū rule; ù pull; ûr turn; hw white; ng song; th thin; <u>th</u> this; zh measure; ə about, taken, pencil, lemon, circus

neutron (nü′tron) A particle with no charge inside an atom's nucleus. (p. E20)

neutron star (nü′tron stär) The remnant of a supernova that has become an extremely dense star made up entirely of tightly packed neutrons. (p. C77)

new Moon (nü mün) A phase of the Moon in which none of its sunlit half is visible from Earth. (p. C32)

niche (nich) The role a kind of living thing, or species, plays in a food web. (p. A82)

nonmetal (non met′əl) Any of the elements with properties that are basically the opposite of metals. At room temperature, *nonmetals* are mostly gases or brittle solids that are poor conductors of heat and electricity. *See* **metal** and **metalloid**. (p. E23)

nonrenewable resource (non′ri nü′ə bəl rē′sôrs′) A resource that cannot be replaced when it is used up. (p. E82)

nonvascular (non vas′kyə lər) Containing no plant tissue through which water and food move. (p. A24)

nuclear fission (nü′klē ər fish′ən) The process of splitting a nucleus with a large mass into two nuclei with smaller masses. The energy released can then be used to produce electricity. (p. E84)

nuclear fusion (nü′klē ər fü′zhən) The process of merging nuclei with smaller masses into a nucleus with a larger mass. The energy released by this reaction may someday be used to produce electricity. (p. E85)

nucleic acid (nü klē′ik as′id) One of the carbon compounds that contains codes that allow cells to build proteins. (p. B23)

nucleus (nü′klē əs), *pl.* **nuclei** (-klē ī′) **1.** The largest, most visible part of a cell, which has its own membrane and is the control center of a cell's activities. (p. B18) **2.** An atom's dense center, where most of its mass is. (p. E20)

observe (əb sûrv′) To use one or more of the senses to identify or learn about an object or event. (p. S3)

one-celled organism (wun seld ôr′gə niz′əm) A living thing that is made up of only one cell. (p. B24)

Oort Cloud (ôrt cloud) A region beyond the Kuiper Belt where long-period comets originate. (p. C64)

opaque (ō pāk′) Completely blocking light from passing through it. (p. F23)

open circuit (ō′pən sûr′kit) A current containing a gap. (p. E112)

order (ôr′dər) One of the groupings of similar members within a class. (p. A9)

organ (ôr′gən) A group of different tissues working together to do certain jobs. (p. B11)

organ system (ôr′gən sis′təm) Different organs working together to do certain jobs. (p. B12)

organism (ôr′gə niz′əm) Any living thing that can carry out its life activities on its own. (p. B12)

original horizontality (ə rij′ə nəl hôr′ə zän′ta′lə tē) The idea that many kinds of rocks form flat, horizontal layers. (p. D6)

osmosis (oz mō′sis) The diffusion of water through a cell membrane. (p. B30)

outer planet (out′ər plan′it) One of the five planets farther from the Sun—Jupiter, Saturn, Uranus, Neptune, or Pluto. (p. C60)

output force (out′pùt′ fôrs) The force the machine applies to an object in response to our effort force. (p. F66)

Pangaea (pan jē′ə) According to theory, the supercontinent that once contained all the present continents before they split apart and drifted in time to their present locations. *See* **continental drift.** (p. D7)

parallax (par′ə laks′) The apparent shift in an object's location when viewed from two positions. (p. C73)

parallel circuit (pār′ə lel′ sûr′kit) A circuit with more than one path for current. (p. E111)

passive transport (pas′iv trans′pôrt′) The movement of molecules through a cell membrane without the use of energy. (p. B29)

pedigree (ped′i grē) A chart used to trace the history of traits in a family. (p. B72)

permeable (pûr′mē ə bəl) Said of soil with connected pores through which water can pass easily. (p. D52)

phase of the Moon (fāz uv thə mün) One of the shapes of the lighted part of the Moon seen from Earth at any time. (p. C32)

photosphere (fō′tə sfîr′) The visible yellow surface of the Sun beneath the chromosphere. (p. C80)

photosynthesis (fō′tə sin′thə sis) A process in producers that makes food by using sunlight. (p. B32)

phylum (fī′ləm), *pl.* **phyla** (fī′lə) A main group within a kingdom, whose members share a main characteristic. (p. A8)

physical change (fiz′i kəl chānj) A change in size, shape, or state, without forming a new substance. *See* **chemical change.** (p. E10)

physical property (fiz′i kəl prop′ər tē) A property that can be observed without changing the identity of a substance. (p. E8)

planet (plan′it) A large body orbiting the Sun or other star. (p. C48)

plankton (plank′tən) Organisms that float on the water in aquatic ecosystems. (p. A88)

plate tectonics (plāt tek ton′iks) The idea that Earth's surface is broken into plates that slide slowly across the mantle. (p. D11)

plateau (pla tō′) A large area of flat land of high elevation that was created by crustal movement. (p. D47)

pole (pōl) One of two ends of a magnet, where a magnet's pull is strongest. (p. E118)

pollination (pol′ə nā′shən) The transfer of pollen from the male part to the female part of a flower. (p. B60)

pollinator (pol′ə nā′tər) Animals such as bees and butterflies that fertilize plants by moving pollen from one flower to another. (p. A30)

population (pop′yə lā′shən) All the organisms of the same kind living in the same place. (p. A82)

position (pə zish′ən) The location of an object compared with things around it. (p. F6)

potential energy (pə ten′shəl en′ər jē) The energy stored in an object or material. *See* **kinetic energy.** (pp. E55, F52)

predict (pri dikt′) To state possible results of an event or experiment. (p. S7)

pressure (presh′ər) **1.** The weight that presses down on a layer of sediment. (p. D74) **2.** The force on each unit of area of a surface. (p. E70)

primary wave (prī′mer ē wāv) One of the back-and-forth vibrations of rocks in an earthquake, called *P waves* for short. They travel faster than secondary waves. (p. D22)

PRONUNCIATION KEY

a **at**; ā **ape**; ä **far**; âr **care**; ô **law**; e **end**; ē **me**; i **it**; ī **ice**; îr **pierce**; o **hot**; ō **old**; ôr **fork**; oi **oil**; ou **out**; u **up**; ū **use**; ü **rule**; u̇ **pull**; ûr **turn**; hw **white**; ng **song**; th **thin**; th **this**; zh **measure**; ə **about, taken, pencil, lemon, circus**

probability (prob′ə bil′i tē) A measure of how likely it is for something to happen. (p. B66)

producer (prə dü′sər) Any green plant or one-celled organism that can make its own food. (pp. A85, B32)

product (prod′ukt) A new substance produced by a chemical change. (p. E36)

protein (prō′tēn) One of the carbon compounds that are needed for cell growth and repair. (p. B23)

proton (prō′ton) A positively charged particle inside an atom's nucleus. (p. E20)

protostar (prō′tə stär′) A young star that glows as gravity makes it collapse. (p. C76)

pulley (pùl′ē) A grooved wheel that turns by the action of a rope in the groove. (p. F72)

pulsar (pul′sär) A neutron star that blinks on and off like the light from a lighthouse. (p. C77)

Punnett square (pun′ət skwâr) A table for predicting the outcome of crossing different forms of a trait. (p. B68)

purebred (pyùr′bred′) Said of a self-pollinated organism that shows the same form of a trait in all of its offspring for several generations of self-pollination. (p. B62)

Q

quasar (kwā′zär) An extremely bright, extremely distant high-energy source, shining with the light of a trillion suns. (p. C90)

R

radiation (rā′dē ā′shən) The transfer of energy by electromagnetic waves. (p. E58)

ratio (rā′shē ō′) A mathematical term that describes the relationship between two quantities. (p. B63)

reactant (rē ak′tənt) An original substance at the beginning of a chemical reaction. (p. E36)

recessive factor (ri ses′iv fak′tər) The trait masked in offspring when the factors in a pair are different. (p. B65)

recessive trait (ri ses′iv trāt) The form of a trait that is hidden, or masked, in the hybrid generation. (p. B63)

reflection (ri flek′shən) The bouncing of waves off a surface. (p. C8)

refraction (ri frak′shən) The bending of waves as they go from one substance to another. (p. C8)

regeneration (rē jen′ə rā′shən) A form of asexual reproduction in simple animals where a whole animal develops from just a part of the original animal. (p. B44)

relative age (rel′ə tiv āj) The age of a rock as compared with another rock. (p. D82)

renewable resource (ri nü′ə bəl rē′sôrs′) A resource that can be readily replaced and so can be used again and again. (p. E83)

replacement reaction (ri plās′mənt rē ak′shən) A chemical change in which one element replaces another element in a compound. (p. E37)

reproduction (rē′prə duk′shən) The process that a living thing uses to produce more of its own kind. (p. B38)

resistance force (ri zis′təns fôrs) The force that a machine acts against. (p. F66)

resistor (ri zis′tər) A material which opposes a flow of electrons. (p. E109)

respiration (res′pə rā′shən) The process of "unlocking" energy in sugar that takes place in the mitochondria of a cell. (p. B33)

revolution (rev′ə lü′shən) One complete trip around the Sun. Earth completes one revolution in 365 days. (p. C24)

rift volcano (rift vol kā′nō) Volcanoes that form along the gaps at the edges of tectonic plates that are moving apart. (p. D31)

rock cycle (rok sī′kəl) Rocks continually changing from one kind into another in a never-ending process. (p. D78)

rolling friction, (rō′ling frik′shən) The friction between wheels or rollers and a moving object that allows the object to move forward. (p. F20)

rotation (rō tā′shən) A complete spin on an axis. Earth makes a rotation every 24 hours. (p. C20)

S

scientific name (sī′ən tif′ik nām) A two-word term for a living thing, based on its classification. (p. A9)

screw (skrü) An inclined plane wrapped around a central bar. (p. F84)

sea-floor spreading (sē flôr spred′ing) The idea that new crust is forming at ridges in the sea floor, spreading apart the crust on either side of the ridges. (p. D8)

second law of motion, Newton's (sek′ənd lô uv mō′shən, nü′tənz) Force = mass x acceleration. (p. F35)

secondary wave (sek′ən der′ē wāv) One of the up-and-down vibrations of rocks in an earthquake, called *S waves* for short. They travel more slowly than primary waves. (p. D22)

sedimentary rock (sed′ə men′tə rē rok) A rock that forms from pieces of other rocks that are squeezed or cemented together. (p. D74)

seed dispersal (sēd di spûr′səl) The spreading out of seeds in all directions. (p. A29)

seismic-safe (sīz′mik sāf) The design of buildings and highways to keep them from collapsing in an earthquake. (p. D26)

seismic wave (sīz′mik wāv) A vibration that spreads out away from a focus when an earthquake happens. (p. D22)

seismograph (sīz′mə graf′) A sensitive device that detects the shaking of Earth's crust during an earthquake. (p. D22)

selective breeding (si lek′tiv brēd′ing) The process of crossing plants or animals to produce offspring with certain desirable traits. (p. B100)

self-pollination (self′pol′ə nā′shən) The pollination of a flower's female parts by pollen from the male parts of the same flower. (p. B61)

series circuit (sîr′ēz sûr′kit) A circuit in which there is only one path for the electric current. (p. E110)

sex-linked gene (seks′lingkt′ jēn) A gene carried on an X chromosome but not a Y chromosome. (p. B90)

sexual reproduction (sek′shü əl rē′prə duk′shən) The production of a new organism from two parents. (p. A25)

shield volcano (shēld vol kā′nō) A wide, gently sloped cone that forms from flows of lava. (p. D32)

short circuit (shôrt sûr′kit) A very conductive path that bypasses less conductive parts of a circuit and can cause a fire. (pp. E109, E133)

sill (sil) An underground structure that forms when magma hardens between horizontal layers of rock. (p. D35)

simple machine (sim′pəl mə shēn′) A machine with few moving parts, making it easier to do work. (p. F66)

sliding friction (slī′ding frik′shən) Friction that resists the force of something being pushed or pulled. (p. F20)

soil (soil) A mixture of weathered rock, decayed plant and animal matter, living things, air, and water. (p. D50)

PRONUNCIATION KEY

a at; ā ape; ä far; âr care; ô law; e end; ē me; i it; ī ice; îr pierce; o hot; ō old; ôr fork; oi oil; ou out; u up; ū use; ü rule; ù pull; ûr turn; hw white; ng song; th thin; <u>th</u> this; zh measure; ə about, taken, pencil, lemon, circus

soil horizon (soil hə rī′zən) Any of the layers of soil from the surface to the bedrock below. (p. D51)

solar cell (sō′lər sel) A device that generates an electric current from sunlight. (p. E81)

solar eclipse (sō′lər i klips′) A blocking out of a view of the Sun when Earth passes through the Moon's shadow. (p. C35)

solar system (sō′lər sis′təm) A star, such as the Sun, and all the objects orbiting it. (p. C48)

soluble (sol′yə bəl) Capable of being dissolved. (p. E13)

solute (sol′ūt) The substance in a solution that is dissolved by a solvent. *See* **solvent.** (p. E13)

solution (sə lü′shən) A mixture of one substance dissolved in another so that the properties are the same throughout. (p. E12)

solvent (sol′vənt) The part of a solution that dissolves the solute. *See* **solute.** (p. E13)

space probe (spās prōb) A vehicle sent beyond Earth to study planets and other objects within our solar system. (p. C10)

species (spē′shēz) A group of similar organisms in a genus that can reproduce more of their own kind. (p. A9)

spectrum (spek′trəm) A band of colors made when white light is broken up. (p. C86)

speed (spēd) How fast an object's position changes with time at any given moment. (p. F8)

sperm (spûrm) A male sex cell. (p. B44)

spiral galaxy (spī′rəl gal′ək sē) A galaxy that is like a whirlpool in shape. (p. C84)

spring tide (spring tīd) The greatest changes from high to low tide that occur when the Sun, the Moon, and Earth are lined up. (p. C36)

standard time zone (stan′dərd tīm zōn) A belt 15° wide in longitude in which all places have the same time. (p. C22)

star (stär) A large, hot ball of gases, which is held together by gravity and gives off its own light. (p. C72)

static electricity (stat′ik i lek tris′i tē) A buildup of an electric charge. (p. E98)

static friction (stat′ik frik′shən) Friction that prevents the start of any movement between surfaces in contact. (p. F20)

structure (struk′chər) The way the pieces of materials in a mineral fit together. (p. D71)

subduction (səb duk′shən) The sliding of a denser ocean plate under another plate when they collide. (p. D14)

supernova (sü′pər nō′və) A star that explodes, often a supergiant that has become unstable. (p. C77)

superposition (sü′pər pə zish′ən) The idea that in a series of rock layers, the bottom layer is the oldest and the top layer is the youngest. (p. D82)

surface wave (sûr′fis wāv) One of the wavelike vibrations of an earthquake that cause much of the damage to structures on Earth's surface. (p. D23)

suspension (sə spen′shən) A mixture of small particles or droplets dispersed throughout a liquid. (p. E12)

switch (swich) A device that can open or close an electric circuit. (p. E112)

synthesis reaction (sin′thə sis rē ak′shən) A chemical change in which two elements or compounds join together to make a new compound. (p. E36)

telescope (tel'ə skōp') A device that collects light and makes distant objects appear closer and larger. (p. C7)

temperature (tem'pər ə chər) The average kinetic energy of the molecules in a material. (p. E56)

tetrapod (tet'rə pod') Any vertebrate with four legs or limbs, such as the turtle, salamander, eagle, or horse. (p. A55)

texture (teks'chər) How the surface of a mineral feels to the touch. (p. D71)

thermal expansion (thûr'məl ek span'shən) The expansion of matter when its temperature is raised. (p. E68)

thermal pollution (thûr'məl pə lü'shən) The excess heating of the environment. (p. E138)

third law of motion, Newton's (thûrd lô uv mō'shən, nü'tənz) For every action force, there is a reaction force that is equal in strength and opposite in direction. (p. F36)

third quarter (thûrd kwôr'tər) or **last quarter** The phase of the waning Moon in which the left half is visible but growing smaller. (p. C33)

tide (tīd) The regular rise and fall of the water level along a shoreline. This twice-daily rise and fall of ocean-water levels is caused by the gravity of the Moon and Sun. (p. C36)

till (til) A jumble of many sizes of sediment deposited by a glacier. (p. D64)

timberline (tim'bər līn') A natural boundary on mountains above which the atmosphere is too thin to allow trees to grow. (p. A73)

tissue (tish'ü) A group of similar cells working together at the same job. (p. B10)

transform fault (trans'fôrm fôlt) A boundary where tectonic plates slide past each other. (p. D13)

transformer (trans fôr'mər) A device that can be used to increase or decrease the voltage of current. (p. E130)

translucent (trans lü'sənt) Letting only some light through, so that objects on the other side appear blurry. (p. F23)

transparent (trans pâr'ənt) Letting all light through, so that objects on the other side can be seen clearly. (p. F23)

transport system (trans pôrt sis'təm) A system that aids transport between the nucleus and other parts of the cell. (p. B18)

trench (trench) A deep valley in the sea floor. (p. D8)

tsunami (tsü nä'mē) A huge ocean wave caused by the seismic waves of an undersea earthquake. (p. D23)

unbalanced forces (un bal'ənst fôrs'əz) Forces that do not cancel each other out when acting together on a single object. (p. F25)

universe (ū'nə vûrs') Everything that exists. (p. C6)

use numbers (ūz num'bərz) To order, count, add, subtract, multiply, and divide to explain data. (p. S9)

use variables (ūz vâr'ē ə bəlz) To identify and separate things in an experiment that can be changed or controlled. (p. S7)

PRONUNCIATION KEY

a **at**; ā **ape**; ä **far**; âr **care**; ô **law**; e **end**; ē **me**; i **it**; ī **ice**; îr **pierce**; o **hot**; ō **old**; ôr **fork**; oi **oil**; ou **out**; u **up**; ū **use**; ü **rule**; ú **pull**; ûr **turn**; hw **white**; ng **song**; th **thin**; <u>th</u> **this**; zh **measure**; ə **about, taken, pencil, lemon, circus**

vacuole (vak′ū ōl) A sac-like space in a cell's cytoplasm for storing materials such as food or waste. Plant vacuoles are larger than those in animals. (p. B19)

valley (val′ē) A cigar-shaped depression on the Moon's surface. (p. C38)

vaporization (vā′pər ə zā′shən) The changing of a liquid into a gas as heat is applied to it. (p. E72)

variation (vâr′ē ā′shən) A species has variation when organisms have different traits. (p. B47)

vascular (vas′kyə lər) Containing plant tissue through which water moves up and food moves down. (p. A24)

velocity (və los′i tē) The speed and direction of a moving object. (p. F10)

vent (vent) The central opening in a volcanic area through which magma may escape. (p. D30)

vertebrate (vûr′tə brāt′) An animal of the phylum Chordata that has a backbone and two sets of paired appendages. Vertebrates are one of the two major groupings of animals. *See* **invertebrate**. (p. A36)

volume (vol′ūm) The amount of space an object takes up. (p. E6)

waning crescent (wān′ing kres′ənt) A phase of the Moon between the third quarter and the new Moon in which the visible part is growing smaller. (p. C33)

waning gibbous (wān′ing gib′əs) A phase of the Moon between the full Moon and the third quarter in which the visible part is growing smaller. (p. C33)

warm-blooded (wôrm blud′əd) Said of animals, such as birds or mammals, that can automatically keep their body temperatures constant and warm. (p. A54)

water table (wô′tər tā′bəl) A layer of soil and rocks that are filled with water. (p. D52)

watershed (wô′tər shed′) Land that contributes water to a river or groundwater system. (p. D52)

wavelength (wāv′lengkth′) The distance from one peak to the next on a wave. (pp. C9, F23)

waxing crescent (waks′ing kres′ənt) A phase between the new Moon and the first quarter in which the visible part is growing larger. (p. C32)

waxing gibbous (waks′ing gib′əs) A phase of the Moon between the first quarter and the full Moon in which the visible part is growing larger. (p. C32)

weathering (weth′ər ing) The breaking down of rocks into smaller pieces by natural processes. (p. D47)

wedge (wej) One or a combination of two inclined planes that is moved when used. (p. F86)

weight (wāt) The force of gravity between Earth (or any planet, asteroid, or star) and an object being weighed. (p. F23)

wet cell (wet sel) A device that produces direct current using chemical reactions. (p. E128)

wheel and axle (hwēl and ak′səl) A simple machine made of a handle or axis attached to the center of a wheel. (p. F76)

wind turbine (wind tûr′bin) An engine that can convert wind energy into electricity. (p. E88)

work (wûrk) Force applied to an object times the distance the object moves in the direction of the force. (p. F56)

X and Y chromosomes (eks and wī krō′mə sōmz) Chromosomes that determine a person's sex. (p. B90)

Index

*Indicates an activity related to this topic.

*Indicates an activity related to this topic.

*Indicates an activity related to this topic.

Excretion of wastes, B6, B34
Exoskeleton, A42
Exosphere, E65
Exothermic reactions, E44
Exotic species, A57
Expansion redshift, C86, C87
Explorer 1, C51
External fertilization, B44
Extinct species, A57
Extinct volcanoes, D34
Extrusive rocks, D73

Family, A8
Fault-block mountain, D46
Faults, D13, D21, D46
Fens, A89
Fermentation, B33, B35
Ferns, A13, A22
Fertilization, A25, B44, B45, B51, B60
Fig tree, A26
First-class lever, F67, F68
First law of motion, F26, F28
First quarter Moon, C32, C33
Fish, types of, A49–52
Fission, nuclear, E84, E86–87
Fixed pulley, F72, F73
Flatworms, A36, A39
Fleming, Alexander, A14
Fleming, Walther, B42
Flowering plants, A12, A28, A30, A32–33, B60–61
Fluorescent bulbs, E135
Focus of earthquake, D22
Fold mountains, D46
Food
    energy stored in, B32, E45, F53, F61
    genetic engineering of, B94
    in space missions, C14
Food chain, A85, A85–86, A89*
Food web, A86, A87, A88
Forced-air heating, E74–75
Force(s), F16–31
    action-reaction pair of, F36–37
    affecting acceleration, F33*, F34–37

balanced, F24
drag, F21
effect of machines on, F65*, F66
effort, F66, F67, F68, F69, F70, F74, F81, F83
friction, F19–20
gravity, F22–23, F29
inertia and, F26–27, F28*, F30–31
measuring, F19
motion and, F17*, F18
net, F24, F25, F35
Newton's first law of motion, F26, F28
output, F66, F67, F68, F69, F70, F81, F83
resistance, F66
shape and, F18
steepness of inclined plane and, F82
unbalanced, F25, F28
work and, F56
Forests, A20, A70, A74
    food chain in, A85
Formic acid, E41
Fossil fuels, C26, D91, E82–83, E90
Fossils, D84–85, D88, D89, D90, E82
Foucault, C20
Four-stroke engine cycle, E76
Free fall, F41*, F42
Freezing, D48*, E73
Frequency, C9, E23
Freshwater ecosystem, A88–89
Friction, F19–20, F53, F57
    efficiency and, F88
    force of, F19–20
    mechanical advantage and, F74
    screws and, F85
    types of, F20, F37
    in wedge, F86
Frogs, A52, B39
Frost action, D48
Fruits, A28
Fuel cell, F54
Fuels, C26, D91, E82–83, E90. *See also* Energy sources
Fulcrum, F67, F68, F69, F76
Full Moon, C32, C33
Fungi, A14
Fungus kingdom, A14
Fuses, E133

Fusion, nuclear, E85, E86–87

Galaxies, C82–95
    classification of, C83*
    formation of, C88, C89
    grouping of stars in, C84
    movement away from each other, C86–87
    quasars and, C90
    size and structure of, C84
Galileo, C66
Galileo, F30
Ganymede, C66
Gases, B28, E9, E11, E70, E71, E72, E73, E76
Gaspra asteroid, C54
Generation, B59
Generator, electric, E130, E132
Genes, B78–79, B84, B90
Gene-splicing, B94, B102–103
Genetic code, B78–79, B85. *See also* DNA
Genetic counseling, B94
Genetic engineering, B94, B95, B101, B104–105
Geneticists, B65
Genetics, B56–75, B86–109
    characteristics studied in, B57*
    DNA and, B76–85, B101
    gene-splicing, B94, B102–103
    genetic engineering, B94, B95, B101, B104–105
    history of, B59–65
    inherited disorders, B89, B92–93, B94, B95, B96–97
    inherited traits, B58, B60–65, B86, B87*, B88–93
    probability and predicting outcome of, B67–69, B70*
    selective breeding and, B99*, B100
    sex-linked traits, B90–91, B92
    sex of child, determination of, B90
    uses of, B94
Genus, A9
Geographic Information Systems

*Indicates an activity related to this topic.

*Indicates an activity related to this topic.

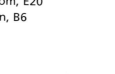

*Indicates an activity related to this topic.

*Indicates an activity related to this topic.

*Indicates an activity related to this topic.

Credits

Hutchings/Richard Hutchings Photography. F12: (bl) Paul Hurd/Tony Stone Images. F13: (b) Liaison Agency Inc/E.B. Graphics. F14: (b) David Lawrence/The Stock Market. F14: (br) Thomas Zimmermann/Tony Stone Images. F16-F17: (bkgd) Spencer Grant/PhotoEdit. F17: (br) Richard Hutchings/Richard Hutchings Photography. F18: (bl) Lewis Portnoy/The Stock Market. F18: (tr) Telegraph Colour Library/FPG International. F19: (b) Richard Hutchings/Richard Hutchings Photography. F20: (tr) Michael Kevin Daly/The Stock Market. F21: (br) Richard Hutchings/Richard Hutchings Photography. F21: (bl) Richard Hutchings/Richard Hutchings Photography. F22: (b) Richard Hutchings/Richard Hutchings Photography. F23: (br) Richard Hutchings/Richard Hutchings Photography. F24: (tr) Richard Hutchings/Richard Hutchings Photography. F24: (tc) Max & Bea Hunn/Visuals Unlimited. F27: (tr) Donald Johnston/Tony Stone Images. F28: (tcl) Function Thru Form/Function Thru Form. F29: (tcr) VCG/FPG. F32-F33: (bkgd) Joseph Sohm/Stock Boston. F33: (br) Richard Hutchings/Richard Hutchings Photography. F35: (r) Science Visuals Unlimited. F37: (tl) NASA/Peter Arnold Inc. F38: (bl) Andy Levin/Photo Researchers Inc. F38: (tr) Calvin Larsen/Photo Researchers Inc. F40: (tr) PhotoTake/NASA. F40: (tl) Dr. Seth Shostak/Photo Researchers Inc. F41: (cl) NASA/NASA. F41: (bl) Richard Hutchings/Richard Hutchings Photography. F42: (tr) NASA/NASA. F42: (bl) NASA/NASA. F44-5: AP/Wide World Photos. F47: (cr) Donald Johnston/Tony Stone Images. F48-F49: (bkgd) Wendell Metzen/Bruce Coleman Inc. F50-F51: (bkgd) Bill Aron/Photo Researchers Inc. F51: (b) Richard Hutchings/Richard Hutchings Photography. F52: (tr) Myrleen Cate/PhotoEdit. F53: (tr) Zigy Kaluznuy/Tony Stone Images. F56: (br) Richard Hutchings/Richard Hutchings Photography. F56: (t) Richard Hutchings/Richard Hutchings Photography. F57: (bl) Richard Hutchings/Richard Hutchings Photography. F59: (br) Richard Hutchings/Richard Hutchings Photography. F60: (t) Gary Brettnacher/Tony Stone Images. F62: (t) Gamma-Liaison/Liaison Agency Inc. F63: (bl) Ford Motor Company/(c)Courtesy Ford Motor Company. F64-F65: (bkgd) (c)Addison Geary/Stock Boston. F66: (bl) Richard Megna/Fundamental Photographs. F72: (tr) Elena Rooraid/PhotoEdit. F77: (tr) Dave Ryan/Index Stock Imagery. F78-F79: (bkgd) FPG/(c)Telegraph Colour Library/FPG International. F79: (br) Richard Hutchings/Richard Hutchings Photography. F84: (tl) Tom McCarthy/PhotoEdit. F85: (cr) Raymond Gendreau/Tony Stone Images. F85: (bcl) Yoav Levy/PhotoTake. F85: (tcr) Chris Sorenson/The Stock Market. F86: (tl) Novastock/PhotoEdit. F86: (tr) Yoav Levy/PhotoTake. F88: (bl) Fundamental Photographs. F88: (cr) Chris Jones/The Stock Market. F88: (br) K. Rehm/Camerique/H. Armstrong Roberts Inc. F89: (tr) Richard Megna/Fundamental Photographs. F90: (tr) Rob Lewine/The Stock Market. F90: (bl) Bob Daemmrich/Stock Boston. F90: (br) Lawrence Migdale/Photo Researchers Inc. F91: (cr) Amy C. Etra/PhotoEdit. F94-F95: Diana Rogers/Stanford Linear Accelerator Center. F94-F95: David Young/Wolff/Photo Edit. F94-F95: Norman Graf/Stanford Linear Accelerator Center. F94-F95: Stanford Linear Accelerator Center.

Resources: R1: (bkgd)Robert Glusic/PhotoDisc. R1: (1) PhotoSpin 2000. R2: (tcl) Richard Hutchings/Richard Hutchings Photography. R2: (tr) Richard Hutchings/Richard Hutchings Photography. R2: (bl) Richard Hutchings/Richard Hutchings Photography. R2: (br) Richard Hutchings/Richard Hutchings Photography. R3: (tl) Richard Hutchings/Richard Hutchings Photography. R3: (tr) Richard Hutchings/Richard Hutchings Photography. R4: (bc) Richard Hutchings/Richard Hutchings Photography. R5: (r) Richard Hutchings/Richard Hutchings Photography. R6: (tr) Richard Hutchings/Richard Hutchings Photography. R7: (cl) Richard Hutchings/Richard Hutchings Photography. R7: (br) Richard Hutchings/Richard Hutchings Photography. R8: (b) Richard Hutchings/Richard Hutchings Photography. R9: (br) Richard Hutchings/Richard Hutchings Photography. R10: (tl) Richard Hutchings/Richard Hutchings Photography. R10: (bl) Richard Hutchings/Richard Hutchings Photography. R10: (br) Richard Hutchings/Richard Hutchings Photography. R10: (cr) Jim Harrison/Stock Boston/PNI. R11: (br) Richard Hutchings/Richard Hutchings Photography. R14: (bcl) G.R. Roberts/Photo Researchers Inc. R14: (bcl) PhotoDisc. R14: (bl) Richard Hutchings/Richard Hutchings Photography. R14: (cr) Richard Hutchings/Richard Hutchings Photography. R15: (bc) Accuweather/NASA. R15: (tr) Richard Hutchings/Richard Hutchings Photography. R15: (bl) Richard Hutchings/Richard Hutchings Photography. R19: (cl) Richard Hutchings/Richard Hutchings Photography. R19: (br) Richard Hutchings/Richard Hutchings Photography. R20: David Madison/Getty Images. R23: (c) Richard Hutchings/Richard Hutchings Photography. R25: (bl) Richard Hutchings/Richard Hutchings Photography. R25: (bcl) Richard Hutchings/Richard Hutchings Photography. R25: (bcr) Richard Hutchings/Richard Hutchings Photography. R27: (r) Richard Hutchings/Richard Hutchings Photography. R28: (bl) Richard Hutchings/Richard Hutchings Photography. R29: (l) Richard Hutchings/Richard Hutchings Photography. R29: (c) Richard Hutchings/Richard Hutchings Photography. R29: (cr) Richard Hutchings/Richard Hutchings Photography. R31: Ingram/PictureQuest. R32: (bl) Richard Hutchings/Richard Hutchings Photography. R33: (bl) Richard Hutchings/Richard Hutchings Photography. R33: (br) Richard Hutchings/Richard Hutchings Photography. R39: Lester V. Bergman/CORBIS. S001: stocktrek/CORBIS. S001: EPA/AP/WideWorld. S002-S003: Photo by NASA/Jet Propulsion Laboratory/Cornell University via Getty Images. S004-S005: ESA/AFP/Getty Images. S005: Yann-Arthus-Bertra/CORBIS. S006-S007: NASA. S007: Gabe Palmer/CORBIS. S008-S009: REUTERS. S008-S009: Kevin Anthony Horgan/Getty Images. S010-S011: Gene Blevins/LA Daily News/CORBIS. xvi: Taxi / Getty Images. xvi: NASA / CORBIS.